CONTINUATIONS:
ADULT
DEVELOPMENT
AND AGING

CONTINUATIONS: ADULT DEVELOPMENT AND AGING

LILLIAN E. TROLL

Rutgers University

Brooks/Cole Publishing Company

Monterey, California

Brooks/Cole Publishing Company
A Division of Wadsworth, Inc.

Printed in the United States of America

10 9 8 7 6 5 4 3 2 1

Library of Congress Cataloging in Publication Data

Troll, Lillian E.
    Continuations : adult development and aging.

    Bibliography: p.
    Includes index.
    1. Adulthood—Psychological aspects.
2. Aging—Psychological aspects.   3. Developmental psychology.   I. Title.
BF724.5.T75   155.6   81–10272
ISBN 0-8185-0484-6   AACR2

Subject Editor: *C. Deborah Laughton*
Manuscript Editor: *Linda Purrington*
Production Editor: *Fiorella Ljunggren*
Interior and Cover Design: *Stan Rice*
Illustrations: *Renaissance Studios*
Typesetting: *TriStar Graphics, Minneapolis, Minnesota*

Preface

The psychology of adult development and aging has come of age. When this book is published, it will join a shelf full of comparable texts available to the student. At the time this book was requested by Todd Lueders of Brooks/Cole, who had been the editor for my earlier volume *Early and Middle Adulthood*, many of my friends in the field of gerontology had also been approached by publishers who wanted a basic textbook for the courses being added in almost every college across the country. We found ourselves competitors for what seemed to be a limited market, and our feelings of cooperation, which had been promoted by the pioneer feeling of exploring a new field, were upset.

Because I felt that several of us shared a basic orientation and were thus likely to write books that would be somewhat redundant, I decided to adopt a more personal approach than I would otherwise have done. My own reading of the state of the literature, both theoretical and empirical, is undoubtedly different from that of others, even others with whom I share basic orientations. In some cases, in fact, I am not sure what the state of the art really is. On the issue of transitions and critical life events, for example, I am of two minds and can only present the evidence as it exists, with all its conflicts and contradictions. In other cases, my own preexisting biases color my interpretation of research findings and my attitudes toward theoretical positions. Again, I can only try to announce my bias where I am aware of it and let the reader decide how much it may have indeed colored my interpretations. I try to present all sides of the evidence, even where I seem to accept one line more than others.

One of my personal biases is for a multidisciplinary approach to the study of human development. Therefore I provide information about biological processes as well as cognitive and personality processes and about interactional and situational developments in family and job areas as well as intrapersonal events. Because this is primarily a basic psychology text, however, I try to give the most detailed reviews and coverage in psychological areas, with biological and sociological information treated as a background against which these psychological processes must be understood.

Because the different chapters deal with topics that vary in familiarity to students, some will seem more difficult than others. Chapters 1 and 2 are probably the most difficult, dealing as they do with more abstract concepts. Although I considered placing these chapters at the end, I decided that serious students would want to read them first, before going on to more specific information. Teachers can readily accommodate to this arrangement by either assigning the beginning chapters last or skipping them altogether for elementary courses.

I have tried to cover the most recent frontiers of research as much as length and ease of reading would allow. At the same time, I have tried to flavor my material with my personal experiences as a teacher, both graduate and undergraduate, as a counseling psychologist of adults in the throes of difficult times and decisions, and, most of all, as a member of a long-lived family. My mother, who is now very old, has shown me many of the perils and joys of growing old in a modified extended family. I am experiencing my own aging, as I watch that of friends and colleagues. But I also see the adult development of my children, nieces, and nephews, as they partly replicate and partly transform the early-adult experiences I had a generation or two ago. Like Heraclitus' river, all is change, yet all remains the same. Physiology looms important at all ages, but so do interactions, jobs, love, hate, efforts to emulate, and efforts to do just the opposite of those who serve as models.

My first entry into the field of adult development and aging was under the aegis of my long-time friend and mentor Bernice Neugarten. Because her orientation fitted mine, it was a pleasure to learn from her the vast amount of knowledge and wisdom she brings to the field. Most of my closest colleagues have also been her students, and Bernice's image accompanies our growth, sometimes in parallel paths, sometimes separate.

Annual meetings of the few scientific societies devoted to life-span development issues have consistently been occasions for mind stretching and for validation of new hunches. The Gerontological Society, the American Psychological Association, the Society for Research in Child Development, and the National Council for Family Relations are arenas in which I have shared new and old interests, learned about ongoing research, and enjoyed the company of old and new friends. I hesitate to name any of these colleague friends because I would have to leave out some who are equally important. In the forefront, however, of those who have shaped my perspective are Mildred Selt-

zer, Robert Atchley, Vern Bengtson, Gisela Labouvie-Vief, Gunhild Hagestad, Bert Cohler, Nancy Datan, Sheldon Tobin, Margaret Huyck, Beth Hess, Vivian Wood, and Flo Livson.

Just as important in my scientific development have been my students at the Merrill-Palmer Institute, at Wayne State University, and now at Rutgers University. In the final analysis, it is with them that I confront contradictions, try to explain obscurities, introduce new ideas, and enjoy week-by-week interaction. A few of those whose launching has made me proud include Carol Nowak, Sandra Candy, Eugenia Parron, and Cherlyn Granrose.

Finally, I must acknowledge the debt to those who helped move this manuscript along, from Todd Lueders at its inception, to Julie Wald, who was a student assistant, to C. Deborah Laughton, who took Todd's place as editor at Brooks/Cole, to Jacqueline McGinnis, who typed the whole manuscript and brought many errors to my attention, to Fiorella Ljunggren, the coordinating production editor, to Linda Purrington, the manuscript editor, and the colleagues who reviewed early drafts and showed me how to improve them: Vern Bengtson of the University of Southern California, Pat Blumenthal, Nancy Datan of West Virginia University, Irene Hulicka of the State University of New York at Buffalo, Donald H. Kausler of the University of Missouri, and Ronald Tikofsky of the University of Wisconsin.

Lillian E. Troll

CREDITS

Pages 10 and 11, scattered quotations. From "Sociological Perspectives on the Life Cycle," by B. L. Neugarten and N. Datan. In P. B. Baltes and K. W. Schaie (Eds.), *Life-Span Developmental Psychology: Personality and Socialization.* Copyright © 1973 by Academic Press. Reprinted by permission.

Page 16, Table 2.1. From "Continuities in Childhood and Adult Moral Development Revisited," by L. Kohlberg. In P. B. Baltes and K. W. Schaie (Eds.), *Life-Span Developmental Psychology: Personality and Socialization.* Copyright © 1973 by Academic Press. Reprinted by permission.

Page 17, Table 2.2. Adapted from *Developmental Tasks and Education,* by R. Havighurst. (New York: David McKay, © 1952.) Reprinted by permission.

Page 17, Table 2.3. Adapted from "Periods in the Adult Development of Men: Ages 18 to 45," by D. Levinson, C. Darrow, E. Klein, M. Levinson, and B. McKee. In Ricks, David F., Alexander Thomas, and Merrill Roff (Eds.), *Life History Research in Psychopathology,* University of Minnesota, Minneapolis. Copyright © 1974 by the University of Minnesota. (Also published in N. Schlossberg and A. Entine (Eds.), *Counseling Adults,* 1977, by Brooks/Cole Publishing Company.)

Page 22, Figures 2.1 and 2.2. From "The Sensory and Perceptual Responses in Aging," by R. A. McFarland. In K. W. Schaie (Ed.), *Theory and Methods of Research on Aging.* Copyright 1968 by West Virginia University. Reprinted by permission.

Page 23, Figure 2.3. From "A Reinterpretation of Age-Related Changes in Cognitive Structure and Functioning," by K. W. Schaie. In L. R. Goulet and P. B. Baltes (Eds.), *Life-Span Developmental Psychology: Research and Theory.* Copyright © 1970 by Academic Press. Reprinted by permission.

Page 25, Table 2.9. From "Generations and Inter-Generational Relations: Perspectives on Age Groups and Social Change," by V. L. Bengtson and N. Cutler. In R. H. Binstock and E. Shanas (Eds.), *Handbook of Aging and the Social Sciences.* © 1976 by Litton Educational Publishing, Inc. Reprinted by permission.

Page 26, Table 2.10. From "External Validity in the Study of Human Development: Theoretical and Methodological Issues," by D. F. Hultsch and T. Hickey. In *Human Development,* 1978, *21,* 76–91. Reprinted by permission.

Page 35, quotation. From "The Sociologic Meaning of Aging," by R. Havighurst. In *Geriatrics,* 1958, *13*(1), 43–50. Reprinted by permission.

Page 36, Figure 3.1 and Tables 3.1, 3.2, 3.3, and 3.4. From "Ageism Compared to Racism and Sexism," by E. Palmore and K. Manton. Reprinted by permission of the *Journal of Gerontology,* 1973, *38*(3), 353–369.

Page 42, Table 4.4; page 43, Figures 4.1 and 4.2. From "The Impact of Social Structure on Aging Individuals," by V. L. Bengtson, P. Kasschau, and P. K. Ragan. In J. E. Birren and K. W. Schaie (Eds.), *Handbook of the Psychology of Aging.* © 1977 by Litton Educational Publishing, Inc. Reprinted by permission.

Page 45, Figure 4.4. From "Demography of the Aged," by N. E. Cutler and R. Harootyan. In D. Woodruff and J. E. Birren (Eds.), *Aging: Scientific Perspectives and Social Issues.* Copyright © 1975 by Van Nostrand-Reinhold Company. Reprinted by permission.

Pages 52–55, From *The Process of Aging* by Dr. Alex Comfort. Copyright © 1964 by Alex Comfort. Reprinted by arrangement with The New American Library, Inc., New York, New York.

Page 58, Table 5.1. From "Percentage of the Elderly in the Populations of Selected Nations." In *Demographic Yearbook,* 1971. Copyright, United Nations, 1972. Reprinted by permission.

Page 59, Table 5.2. From "Individual Differences in Constitution and Genetic Background," by F. Kallman and L. Jarvik. In J. E. Birren (Ed.), *Handbook of Aging and the Individual: Psychological and Biological Aspects.* Reprinted by permission of The University of Chicago Press, copyright © 1959.

Page 63, Table 5.3; page 97, Table 7.2; page 191, Figure 13.1. From *The Social Forces in Later Life,* 2nd Edition, by R. Atchley. Copyright © 1977 by Wadsworth Publishing Company, Inc. Belmont, California. Reprinted by permission.

Page 64, quotation. From "The Ponce de Leon Trail Today," by G. Moment. Reprinted with permission from the 1975, *25*(10), 627, *Bio-*

science, published by the American Institute of Biological Sciences.

Page 68, Figure 6.1. Reprinted from "A Longitudinal Study of the Decline of Adult Height with Age in Two Welsh Communities," by W. E. Miall, M. Ashcroft, H. Lovell, and F. A. Moore. In *Human Biology,* 1967, *39,* 445–454, by permission of the Wayne State University Press.

Page 69, Figure 6.2. Adapted from "Aging, Total Body Potassium, Fat-Free Mass, and Cell Mass in Males and Females between Ages 18 and 85 Years," by L. Novak. Reprinted by permission of the *Journal of Gerontology,* 1972, *27*(4), 438–443.

Page 71, Figure 6.3. From "Longitudinal and Cross-Sectional Assessments of Age Changes in Physical Strength as Related to Sex, Social Class, and Mental Ability," by F. J. Clement. Reprinted by permission of the *Journal of Gerontology,* 1974, *29*(4), 423–429.

Page 72, Figure 6.4. From "Heart and Cardiovascular System," by R. R. Kohn. In C. Finch and L. Hayflick (Eds.), *Handbook of the Physiology of Aging.* Copyright © 1977 by Van Nostrand-Reinhold Company. Reprinted by permission.

Page 72, Figure 6.5. From "Relation between Change of Blood Pressure and Age," by W. E. Miall and H. G. Lovell. In *British Medical Journal,* 1967, *2,* 660–664. Reprinted by permission.

Page 73, Figure 6.6. From *The Research News,* Division of Research and Development, University of Michigan, by Donald Thackrey (Ed.), November-December, 1975, *27*(5–6), 5. Copyright 1975 by *The Research News* and Leon Pastalan of the Institute of Gerontology. Reprinted by permission.

Page 78, Figure 6.7. From *Handbook of Obstetrics and Gynecology,* 6th Edition, by R. C. Benson. Copyright © 1977 by Lange Medical Publications. Reprinted by permission. (Also published in *Toward Understanding Women,* by V. O'Leary, © 1977 by Brooks/Cole Publishing Company.)

Page 82, Table 6.1; page 83, Table 6.2. From "Quantitative Morphological Investigations of the Follicular System in Women: Variations at Different Ages," by E. Block. In *Acta Anatomica,* 1952, *14,* 108–123. Reprinted by permission.

Page 83, Figure 6.8. From "Reproduction at Menarche and Menopause in Women," by W. J. A. Francis. In *Journal of Reproduction and Fertility,* 1970, Suppl. 12, 89–98. Reprinted by permission.

Page 85, quotations. From *Sex after Sixty: A Guide for Men and Women for Their Later Years,* by R. N. Butler and M. Lewis. Copyright © 1976 by Harper & Row Publishers. Reprinted by permission.

Page 92, Figure 7.1; page 93, Figure 7.2. From *The Ills of Man: Life and Death and Medicine,* by J. Dingle. Copyright © 1973 by Scientific American, Inc. All rights reserved. Reprinted by permission.

Page 94, Figure 7.3; page 95, Figure 7.4. From R. W. McCammon, *Human Growth and Development,* 1970. Courtesy of Charles C Thomas, Publisher, Springfield, Illinois.

Page 96, Table 7.5. From "Cancer and Aging: The Epidemiological Evidence," by R. Doll. In *Tenth International Cancer Congress,* pp. 133–160. Copyright 1970 by Year Book Medical Publishers. Reprinted by permission.

Page 96, Table 7.1. Adapted from "Health Status of People over 65," by W. F. Laurie. In *Center Reports on Advances in Research,* Summer 1977, *1*(2) B-1. Reprinted by permission of Duke University Center for the Study of Aging and Human Development.

Page 98, Table 7.3. Reprinted by permission of the publisher from "Psychological Reactions of Hospitalized Male Patients to a Heart Attack: Age and Social Class Differences," by J. Rosen and G. Bibring, *Psychosomatic Medicine,* *28*(6), 62–67. Copyright 1966 by The American Psychosomatic Society, Inc.

Page 102, Table 7.5. From "Final Report on Forced Relocation: Setting, Staff, and Patient Effects," by N. Bourestom and L. Pastalan, *The Research News,* 1975, Institute of Gerontology at The University of Michigan. Reprinted by permission.

Page 103, Figures 7.6 and 7.7. From "A Collection of Cartoons: A Way of Examining Practices in a Treatment Setting," compiled by Lena Metzelaar (Ann Arbor: Institute of Gerontology at The University of Michigan, 1975). Reprinted by permission.

Pages 109–110, scattered quotations. From *Death, Society, and Human Experience,* by R. Kastenbaum. Copyright © 1977 by The C. V. Mosby Company. Reprinted by permission.

Page 110, Figures 8.1 and 8.2. From "Age and Awareness of Finitude in Developmental Gerontology," by V. Marshall. In *Omega,* 1975, *6*(2), 113–127. Reprinted by permission of Baywood Publishing Company, Inc.

Page 111, Table 8.3. From "Death Anxiety: Age, Sex, and Parental Resemblance in Diverse Populations," by D. Templer, C. Ruff, and

C. Franks. In *Developmental Psychology,* 1971, *4*(1), 108. Copyright 1971 by the American Psychological Association. Adapted by permission of the publisher and the author.

Page 117, Table 8.4. Adapted from "The Demographic Epidemiology of Suicide," by L. L. Linden and W. Breed. In E. Shneidman (Ed.), *Suicidology: Contemporary Developments.* Copyright © 1976 by Grune & Stratton, Inc. Reprinted by permission.

Page 120, Table 8.6. From "Multiple Perspectives on a Geriatric 'Death Valley,'" by R. Kastenbaum. In *Community Mental Health Journal,* 1967, *3*(1), 21–29. Reprinted by permission of Human Sciences Press, New York.

Page 129, Figure 9.3. Reprinted from Larry W. Thompson and John B. Nowlin, "Relation of Increased Attention to Central and Autonomic Nervous System States," p. 144. In Lissy F. Jervik, Carl Eisdorfer, and June E. Blum (Eds.), *Intellectual Functioning in Adults.* Copyright © 1973 by Springer Publishing Company, Inc., New York. Used by permission.

Page 131, Figure 9.4. Adapted from "Maze Learning of Mature Young and Aged Rats as a Function of Distribution of Practice," by C. L. Goodrick. In *Journal of Experimental Psychology,* 1973, *98*(2), 344–349. Copyright 1973 by the American Psychological Association. Reprinted by permission.

Page 132, Figure 9.5. From "A Program of Research in Adult Differences in Cognitive Performance and Learning: Backgrounds for Adult Education and Vocational Retraining," by R. Monge and E. Gardner. (Final Report, Department of Psychology, Syracuse University, 1972. Project No. 6-1963.) Reprinted by permission.

Page 133, Figure 9.6; page 134, Figure 9.8. From "Perception of Part-Whole Relationships in Middle and Old Age," by S. Wapner, H. Werner, and P. E. Comalli, Jr. Reprinted by permission of the *Journal of Gerontology,* 1960, *15*(4), 412–415.

Page 133, Figure 9.7; page 134, Figure 9.9; page 135, Figure 9.10; page 137, Figure 9.12. From "Life-Span Changes in Visual Perception," by P. E. Comalli, Jr. In L. R. Goulet and P. B. Baltes (Eds.), *Life-Span Developmental Psychology: Research and Theory.* Copyright © 1970 by Academic Press. Reprinted by permission.

Page 136, Figure 9.11. From "Age and Sex Differences in the Processing of Verbal and Non-Verbal Stimuli," by M. Elias and M. Kinsbourne. Reprinted by permission of the *Journal of Gerontology,* 1974, *29*(2), 162.

Page 140, Figure 9.1. From "Paced and Self-Paced Learning in Young and Elderly Adults," by R. E. Canestrari, Jr. Reprinted by permission of the *Journal of Gerontology,* 1963, *18*(2), 165–168.

Page 142, Table 9.2. From "Age-Group Comparisons for the Use of Mediators in Paired-Associate Learning," by I. Hulicka and J. Grossman. Reprinted by permission of the *Journal of Gerontology,* 1967, *22*(1), 46–51.

Page 148, Figure 10.1. From "Recent Developments in Short-Term Memory," by B. Murdock, Jr. In *British Journal of Psychology,* 1967, *58*(3/4), 421–433. Reprinted by permission

Page 149, Figure 10.2. From "Memory Storage and Aging," by D. Schonfield and B. Robertson. In *Canadian Journal of Psychology,* 1966, *20*(2), 228–236. Reprinted by permission.

Page 150, Figure 10.3. From "The Baltimore Longitudinal Study," by D. Arenberg. Paper presented at the meeting of the American Psychological Association, New York, 1979.

Page 151, Figure 10.4. From "Fifty Years of Memory for Names and Faces: A Cross-Sectional Approach," by H. P. Bahrick, P. O. Bahrick, and R. Wittlinger. In *Journal of Experimental Psychology: General,* 1975, *104*(1), 54–75. Copyright 1975 by the American Psychological Association. Reprinted by permission.

Page 151, Table 10.1. From "A Questionnaire Technique for Investigating Very Long-Term Memory," by E. Warrington and M. Silberstein. In *Quarterly Journal of Experimental Psychology,* 1970, *22*(3), 508–512. Reprinted by permission.

Page 156, Table 10.2. From "Age and Creative Productivity," by W. Dennis. Reprinted by permission of the *Journal of Gerontology,* 1966, *21*(1), 1–8.

Page 163, Figure 11.1. From "Generational and Cohort-Specific Differences in Adult Cognitive Functioning: A Fourteen-Year Study of Independent Samples," by K. W. Schaie, J. P. Labouvie, and B. Buech. In *Developmental Psychology,* 1973, *9*(2), 18. Copyright 1973 by the American Psychological Association. Reprinted by permission.

Page 166, Figure 11.2. From "Organization of Data on Life-Span Development of Human Abilities," by J. Horn. In L. R. Goulet and P. B. Baltes (Eds.), *Life-Span Developmental Psychology: Research and Theory.* Copyright © 1970 by Academic Press. Reprinted by permission.

Page 173, scattered quotations. From *Working,* by S. Terkel. Copyright © 1972 by Random House, Inc. Reprinted by permission of Pantheon Books, a Division of Random House, Inc.

Page 174, Table 12.1; page 185, Figure 12.3; page 197, Figure 13.4; page 222, Figure 14.5; page 271, Table 16.13; page 297, Table 18.2; page 298, Figure 18.1. Reprinted from *Children of the Great Depression,* by G. Elder, by permission of The University of Chicago Press, copyright 1974.

Page 176, Table 12.2. From "Career Success and Life Satisfactions of Middle-Aged Managers," by D. Bray and A. Howard. Paper presented at the Fourth Vermont Conference on the Primary Prevention of Psychopathology, June 1978.

Page 177, Figure 12.1. Adapted from "Career Stability and Redirection in Adulthood," by R. Gottfredson. In *Journal of Applied Psychology,* 1977, *62*(1), 436–445. Copyright 1977 by the American Psychological Association. Reprinted by permission.

Page 178, Figure 12.2. Adapted from "The New Psychological Contracts at Work," by D. Yankelovich. In *Psychology Today,* May 1978. Reprinted by permission.

Page 179, Figure 12.2. From *The 1977 Quality of Employment Survey,* by R. P. Quinn and G. L. Staines. Copyright © 1979 by the Survey Research Center, Institute for Social Research, University of Michigan, Ann Arbor. Reprinted by permission.

Page 180, Table 12.4. From "Spillover versus Compensation: A Review of the Literature on the Relationship between Work and Nonwork." by G. L. Staines. In *Human Relations,* 1980, *33*(2), 111–129. Reprinted by permission.

Page 181, Table 12.5. From "Mid-Life Career Change," by S. Arbeiter. In *AAHE Bulletin,* 1979, *32*(2), 11–12. Reprinted by permission of the American Association of Higher Education.

Page 190, Table 13.2. From "Life-Cycle Career Patterns: A Typological Approach to Female Status Attainment," by J. S. Fischer, S. C. Carlton-Ford, and B. J. Briles. In *Technical Bulletin No. 8,* Center for the Study of Aging, University of Alabama, 1979.

Page 200, Table 13.3. From "The Motivation to Be Promoted among Non-Exempt Employees: An Expectancy Theory Approach," by G. Homall. Unpublished Master's Thesis, Cornell University, 1974. Reprinted by permission.

Page 210, Table 14.1. From "Growing Old in a Garment Factory: The Effects of Occupational Segregation and Runaway Shops on Working-Class Women," by C. Goodman. Unpublished Master's Thesis, Rutgers University, 1978. Reprinted by permission.

Page 215, Figure 14.1; page 218, Figure 14.2; page 219, Figure 14.3; page 220, Figure 14.4. From "Leisure and Lives: Personal Expressivity across the Life Span," by C. Gordon, C. Gaitz, and J. Scott, Jr. In R. H. Binstock and E. Shanas (Eds.), *Handbook of Aging and the Social Sciences.* © 1976 by Litton Educational Publishing, Inc. Reprinted by permission.

Page 216, Table 14.2. From *Leisure: A Suburban Study,* by G. A. Lundberg, M. Komarovsky, and M. A. McInerny. Copyright © 1934 by Columbia University Press. Reprinted by permission.

Page 217, Table 14.3. From "Use of Leisure Time in Middle Life," by E. Pfeiffer and G. Davis. Reprinted by permission of *The Gerontologist,* 1971, *11,* 187–195.

Page 217, Table 14.4. Reprinted/excerpted from *The Myth and Reality of Aging in America,* a study prepared by Louis Harris and Associates, Inc. for the National Council on Aging, Inc., Washington, D.C. © 1975.

Page 224, Table 14.5. From "Recreation Participation Patterns and Successful Aging," by T. De Carlo. Reprinted by permission of the *Journal of Gerontology,* 1974, *29*(4), 416–422.

Page 232, Table 15.1. From "Age Differences in the Quality of Subjective Experience," by M. Csikszentmihalyi, R. Graef, and R. Larson. Paper presented at the meeting of the American Psychological Association, San Francisco, 1979.

Page 234, Figures 15.2 and 15.3; page 235, Figure 15.4. From "Generations and Aging: A Longitudinal Study," by J. Meddin. In *International Journal of Aging and Human Development,* 1975, *6*(2), 85–101. Reprinted by permission of Baywood Publishing Company, Inc.

Page 236, Table 15.2. From "Moral Judgment in Adults: Effects of Education," by J. Dortzbach. Paper presented at the meeting of the American Psychological Association, San Francisco, 1979.

Page 243, Figure 15.6. Reprinted by permission of the author and editors of *Experimental Aging Research.* From "Structure of the Self-Concept from Adolescence through Old Age," by R. Monge. In *Experimental Aging Research,* 1975, *1*(2), 281–291.

Page 248, Table 15.3. From "The Importance of Age to Conservative Options: A Multivariate Analysis," by F. Glamser. Reprinted by permission of the *Journal of Gerontology,* 1974, *29,* 549–554.

Page 255, Table 16.1. From "Age, Occupation, and Life Satisfaction," by J. P. Alston and C. J. Dudley. Reprinted by permission of *The Gerontologist*, 1973, *13*, 58–61.

Page 257, Table 16.2. Adapted from "Proposed Model of Ego Functioning: Coping and Defense Mechanisms in Relationship to I.Q. Change," by N. Haan. In *Psychological Monographs*, 1963, *77*, 1–23. Reprinted by permission.

Page 257, Figure 16.1; page 258, Table 16.3 and Figures 16.2 and 16.3. From *Adaptation to Life*, by G. E. Vaillant. Copyright © 1977 by George E. Vaillant. By permission of Little, Brown and Company.

Page 261, Table 16.4. Reprinted with permission from *Journal of Psychosomatic Research*, 1967, *11*(3), 213–218, T. Holmes and R. Rahe, "The Social Readjustment Rating Scale," Copyright 1967, Pergamon Press, Ltd.

Page 263, Table 16.5. From *Four Stage of Life*, by M. Lowenthal, M. Thurnher, and D. Chiriboga. Copyright © 1975 by Jossey-Bass, San Francisco, California. Reprinted by permission.

Page 263, Table 16.6. Adapted from "The Nature of Stress in Middle Age," by M. Parent. Paper presented at the meeting of the Gerontological Society, Dallas, 1978.

Page 265, Table 16.7. From "Career Success and Life Satisfactions of Middle-Aged Managers," by D. Bray and A. Howard. Paper presented at the Fourth Vermont Conference on the Primary Prevention of Psychopathology, June 1978.

Page 266, Table 16.8; page 267, Figure 16.4. From "Patterns of Use of Psychiatric Facilities by the Aged: Past, Present, and Future," by M. Kramer, C. Taube, and R. Redick. In C. Eisdorfer and P. Lawton (Eds.), *The Psychology of Adult Development and Aging*. Copyright 1973 by the American Psychological Association. Reprinted by permission.

Page 269, Table 16.10; page 278, Table 17.2. From Joseph H. Britton and Jean O. Britton, *Personality Changes in Aging: A Longitudinal Study of Community Residents*. Copyright © 1972 by Springer Publishing Co., New York. Used by permission.

Page 270, Tables 16.11 and 16.12. From "The Midtown Manhattan Study: Longitudinal Focus on Aging Genders and Life Transitions," by L. Srole and A. Fischer. Paper presented at the meeting of the Gerontological Society, Dallas, 1978.

Page 276, Figure 17.1. From "Social Networks and Older Women," by A. Stueve and C. Fischer. Presented at the Workshop on Older Women, Washington, D.C., September 1978.

Page 277, Table 17.1. From: *Growing Old: The Process of Disengagement*, by Elaine Cumming and William E. Henry. © 1961 by Basic Books Publishing Company, Inc. Used by permission.

Page 285, Tables 17.3 and 17.4. Reprinted with permission of Macmillan Publishing Co., Inc., from *Social Integration of the Aged*, by I. Rosow. Copyright © 1967 by The Free Press, a division of The Macmillan Company.

Page 286, Table 17.5. From "Changes in Informal Social Support Networks," by T. Antonucci and J. Bornstein. Paper presented at the meeting of the American Psychological Association, Toronto, 1978.

Page 294, Table 18.1. From "How Do Lovers Grow Older Together? Types of Lovers and Age," by M. Reedy and J. E. Birren. Paper presented at the meeting of the Gerontological Society, Dallas, 1978.

Page 307, Figure 19.1. From *Early and Middle Adulthood*, by L. E. Troll. Copyright © 1975 by Wadsworth, Inc. Reprinted by permission of the publisher, Brooks/Cole Publishing Company, Monterey, California.

Page 309, Table 19.1. From "Sex and Stage Differences in Perceptions of Marital and Family Relationships," by E. Lurie. In *Journal of Marriage and the Family*, 1974 *36*(2), 260–269. Copyrighted 1974 by the National Council on Family Relations. Reprinted by permission.

Page 312, Table 19.2. From "Primary Ties of Aged Men," by N. Babchuk. Paper presented at the meeting of the Gerontological Society, Washington, D.C., 1979.

Page 317, Figure 19.2. From "Measuring Marital Satisfaction in Three Generations: Positive and Negative Dimensions," by R. Gilford and V. L. Bengtson. In *Journal of Marriage and the Family*, 1979, *41*(2), 15–50. Copyrighted 1979 by the National Council on Family Relations. Reprinted by permission.

Page 318, Figure 19.3. From *Sexual Behavior in the Human Female*, by A. C. Kinsey, W. B. Pomeroy, C. E. Martin, and P. H. Gebhard. Copyright © 1953 by the Institute for Sex Research, Inc. (Philadelphia: W. B. Saunders, 1953.) Reprinted by permission of the Institute for Sex Research, Inc.

Page 325, Figure 20.2. From *Adulthood and Aging*, 2nd Edition, by D. Kimmel. Copyright © 1980, 1974 by John Wiley & Sons, Inc. Reprinted by permission.

Page 327, Figure 20.3; page 330, Figure 20.4. From *Marriage and Divorce: A Social and Economic Study*, by H. Carter and P. C. Glick. Copyright © 1970 by Harvard University Press. Reprinted by permission.

Page 340, Figure 21.1; page 354, Table 21.4; page 368, Table 22.3. From *Family Development in Three Generations*, by R. Hill, N. Foote, J. Aldous, R. Carlson, and R. Macdonald. Copyright © 1970 by Schenkman Publishing Company. Reprinted by permission.

Page 342, Figure 21.2. From "Updating the Life Cycle of the Family," by P. C. Glick. In *Journal of Marriage and the Family*, 1977, *39*(1), 6. Copyrighted 1977 by the National Council on Family Relations. Reprinted by permission.

Page 344, quotation. From "The Value of Children to Parents," by L. W. Hoffman and M. L. Hoffman. In J. T. Fawcett (Ed.), *Psychological Perspectives on Population*. Copyright © 1973 by Basic Books Publishing Company, Inc. Reprinted by permission.

Page 366, Tables 22.1 and 22.2. From "Grandparenthood from the Perspective of the Developing Grandchild," by B. Kahana and E. Kahana. In *Developmental Psychology*, 1970, *3*(1), 98–105. Copyright 1970 by the American Psychological Association. Reprinted by permission.

Page 368, Table 22.4. From "The Changing American Grandparent," by B. L. Neugarten and K. Weinstein. In *Journal of Marriage and the Family*, 1964, *26*(2), 201. Copyrighted 1964 by the National Council on Family Relations. Reprinted by permission.

Page 370, Table 22.5. From "The Significance of Grandparenthood," by V. Wood and J. Robertson. In J. Gubrium (Ed.), *Time, Roles and Self in Old Age*. Copyright © 1976 by Human Sciences Press, New York. Reprinted by permission.

Photo credits: page xvi © Sepp Seitz/Woodfin Camp & Associates; page 13 © Hella Hammid, Rapho/Photo Researchers; page 14 © Erika Stone; page 28 and page 170 © F. B. Grunzweig/Photo Researchers; page 38 © Rafael Macia/Photo Researchers; page 50 © Yoichi R. Okamoto/Photo Researchers; page 65 © H. Armstrong Roberts; page 66 © John Blaustein/Woodfin Camp & Associates; page 90 © Ira Berger/Black Star; page 105 and page 146 © Irene Bayer/Monkmeyer; page 106 © Jacques-Henri Lartigue/Photo Researchers; page 124 © David S. Strickler/Monkmeyer; page 145 © Jim Anderson/Woodfin Camp & Associates; page 159 © Alfred Eris/Monkmeyer; page 160 © Irving Fitzig/Monkmeyer; page 188 © Erika Stone/Photo Researchers; page 206 © Susanne Anderson/Monkmeyer; page 226 © Joanne Leonard/Woodfin Camp & Associates; page 252 © Bruce Roberts/Photo Researchers; page 274 © Robert M. Mottar/Photo Researchers; page 287 © Kira Godbe; page 288 © Chester Higgins, Rapho/Photo Researchers; page 303 © Alice Kandell/Photo Researchers; page 304 © Hanna Schreiber, Rapho/Photo Researchers; page 320 © Christa Armstrong/Photo Researchers; page 337 © Ron Engh/Photo Researchers; page 338 © Jean-Marie Simon/Taurus Photos; page 362 © Jay Lurie/Black Star; page 378 © Elinor S. Beckwith/Taurus Photos.

Contents

CONTINUATIONS:
ADULT
DEVELOPMENT
AND AGING

1

Life-Span Views and Issues

"What will you be when you grow up?" This familiar question implicitly sets off childhood from adulthood and implies that development ends with the end of childhood. It says that, although life can go on for many more years, postchildhood life is of a different order. Adults are no longer expected to change or grow. An adult is there, has arrived. Or, to say it another way, an adult has no place left to go but down.

Until very recently, this viewpoint was common among developmental psychologists as well as the general public. Most textbooks on developmental psychology ended at adolescence. In fact, even adolescence was relegated to a final short chapter. In the last few years, though, a group of "life-span developmental psychologists" has adopted a different perspective. Now every developmental-psychology textbook has at least a final short chapter on adulthood and old age.

Lengthening our life view

Why are developmental psychologists lengthening the life view *now*? Perhaps one of the most important reasons is illustrated in Figure 1.1. Life expectancy has increased enormously over the past century, at least in industrialized countries of the world. Many more people live to be old—live out their full life span—and that means there are more and more older people

around. When only a few people lived beyond age 30 (as in prehistoric times) or 40 (as is true in undeveloped countries today and was true even in industrialized countries a century ago), there was no occasion to distinguish among different epochs of adulthood. It was triumph enough to live beyond childhood. But now, when a majority of the population realizes that its members will probably outlast child rearing and work, and when they have several living generations ahead of them instead of being the oldest generation alive, they enlarge their vision of their present and their future. The question asked at the beginning of this chapter, "What will you be when you grow up?" changes slowly to "What will you be doing next? And then? And after that?"

Social complexity

Not only has the life view been lengthening because of the greater possibilities for living longer, but also our lives have been becoming more complex. People do many different kinds of things; learn to think in many different kinds of ways; have many different kinds of models to shape their lives. They may have many different options to choose from along the way. Differences can be seen between one part of life and another, between one part of childhood and another, between adolescence and adult-

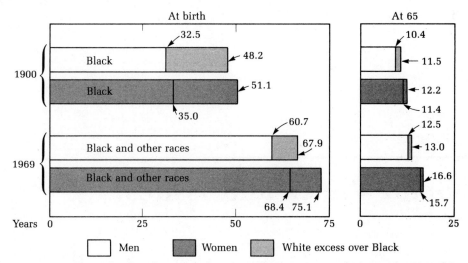

Figure 1.1. Life expectancy at birth and at age 65 by race and sex in 1900 and 1969 in the United States. Most of the increase is the result of reduced childhood mortality; the increases for older people are less dramatic. *(Source: U.S. Department of Commerce, Bureau of the Census, 1973.)*

hood, between early adulthood and middle adulthood and later adulthood, between adulthood and old age, and even between different parts of old age.

Separating out different parts of the life span is a relatively new phenomenon (Aries, 1962). A century ago, most people did not make large distinctions between children and adults, for example. A child was just a small person and, in fact, wore the same kinds of clothes and did many of the same kinds of tasks as adults. It was only after World War II that the children's clothing industry standardized children's sizes. Before then, children's clothes were styled after those of their parents—smaller, but still sufficiently large "to grow on." Styling to show different proportions to equal advantage came only when people of one age were distinguished from those of other ages. Adolescence—the teens—was separated out when the children of the post-World War II baby boom turned 13. Not only were there many of them, but economic affluence kept them out of the job market and separated them from adults. At the same time, it gave them money to spend. Businesses knew a good market when they saw one.

Now it is the turn of the later years. There are many older people out of the job market, and Social Security has given them more money to spend. Television commercials are just beginning to make appeals to older consumers, even

though the advertisers still see the aged as poor, dumb, and ugly. Cosmetics, playroomlike condominiums, fur coats, and tax tips are now offered to older as well as younger consumers.

Some times of life are characterized by conspicuous change, while other times seem to show relatively no change. Three human periods of rapid change are infancy, adolescence, and terminal old age. Two periods of slower change are "latency," or school-age children, and the long years of adulthood. What can we learn about susceptibility to change, or consequences of change, from comparing different periods of life? What can we learn about humans' reactions to change? How can we explain change altogether?

Most readers will want to know not only whether people change during adulthood and why they change but also whether changing is hard or painful. Do people fall apart when they reach middle age? Do they get heart attacks when they retire? Do they become senile when their hair turns gray? This book considers many of these popular notions and fears as well as some of the more theoretical questions asked by scientists. Unfortunately, the present state of our information does not allow us to give complete answers to most of these questions.

Life-span developmental psychologists do not all see their field from the same point of view. Their different perspectives about people and about life affect what they consider important in behavior as well as in behavioral development. The next section outlines some questions and issues that are in the forefront of research and thinking at this time and some different viewpoints on each of them.

Issues in the study of life-span development

Ten major issues are considered in these next pages: biological versus social determination of change; mechanistic versus organismic perspectives; openness of the human system; change versus development; positive or negative development; state versus process; turning points or crises; time; adaptation; and universality versus diversity.

1. IS BIOLOGY DESTINY?

In a sense, the issue of biological versus social dynamics for development is but a slight transformation of the earlier frustrating issue of heredity versus environment. The earlier issue was concerned with the relative influence of genes and experience on behavior. The more recent version concerns the relative importance of biological and social determinants in inducing change or development at different times of life.

Many developmental psychologists who are primarily interested in the early years of life have resolved this problem by an interactionist solution (Freedman, 1965). These psychologists say that neither heredity (biology) nor environment (experience) can be thought of apart from the other; both are intertwined from the first moment of conception. As soon as the newly formed unicellular embryo changes to a two-cell organism, these two cells are no longer identical. Each one is influenced by its surrounding environment—just as this surrounding environment is reciprocally changed by the presence of the developing embryo.

At every point of development from then on, the genetic "program" can only be spelled out on the material provided for it. It is impossible to separate the effects of the DNA genetic message from the combination of cells and systems and chemical and structural uterine surround-

ings existing while the message is being carried out. A cell at one end of a four-cell organism, which has the genetic capacity to become any part of the body, starts on the path of becoming the cardiovascular system, for instance, because of its placement among the other three cells.

At a later point, identical twins will assume nonidentical personalities because of their differing roles in their family constellation. Both may be programmed to be relatively aggressive, let us say, but one will become more aggressive than the other because it happened to win more skirmishes at an early point in time and thereafter was deferred to by other family members and implicitly encouraged along an aggressive path. Unfortunately, many psychologists who are comfortable with this point of view tend to be uninterested in development beyond adolescence because they see adulthood as free of the kind of biological changes that would induce modifications in personality.

Some of the early life-span psychologists, such as Buhler (1968) and Kuhlen (1964), described the adult years as a period of stability. Recently, however, the revised *Handbook of the Psychology of Aging*, edited by James Birren and K. Warner Schaie (1977), devotes three separate chapters to the issue of change during the adult years. Chapter 5 is entitled "Biological Theories of Aging" (by Shock), Chapter 6 is "Toward a Sociological Theory of Change in Adulthood and Old Age" (by Lowenthal), and Chapter 7 is "Toward Psychological Theories of Aging and Development" (by Baltes and Willis). Biological change is not absent from the years of adulthood, and certainly social change is everpresent. Both biological and social dynamics probably interact in intricate fashion throughout life.

2. MECHANISTIC VERSUS ORGANISMIC PERSPECTIVE

Does development occur because of changes within the organism or because of changes external to it? Looft (1973, p. 29) felt that "this issue could very well be the most fundamental premise underlying any psychological model" of development. The use of the term *locus of control*, which derives from Rotter's (1966) theory of perception of personal power, is a related idea, connected with the way people feel about themselves and the world. Looft implies that viewing development as coming from "inside" individuals instead of from powers "outside" them represents a more "active" mode and that we can have more control over "internal," organismic factors than we could over "external," mechanistic ones. By "internal," he means "determined by the person's maneuvers"; he does not mean biological determinism.

Baltes and his colleagues (for example, Baltes, Reese, & Nesselroade, 1977; Hultsch & Plemons, 1979) classify views of humans—as well as of the universe—as (1) mechanistic, (2) organismic, or (3) dialectic. At one extreme, the mechanistic world view conceives of life and the world as a machine, which has no internal motive power. Change occurs by the application of force from outside. Such machinelike systems cannot grow, although they can deteriorate; they can function more poorly over time. Parts do not change, and no new parts can be added, either, although poorly functioning parts can be fixed or replaced. System change—or development—can thus be only quantitative: parts wear out or are replaced. Responses equal the sum of forces applied from outside. The goal of research from this perspective is to find out what forces can be applied in order to cause the changes we want or what kinds of changes can be predicted from particular kinds of outside forces. Life-span developmental models that come from this perspective make much of biological determinism, with biological events seen as outside the person system. Similarly, major life events themselves, such as family and job crises, are also conceived of as external forces.

According to the opposite world view, the organismic, the human is an integrated process, neither a static machine waiting to be maneuvered nor a structure made up of independent parts. Because the essence of the process here is change, the goal of research is to identify the principles of organization and the rules by which change comes about. Such a world view has often been associated with a final end point that directs the successive steps of the process from the beginning, and it is, therefore, teleological, or goal organized. Thus, many stage theories derive from an organismic perspective. Change, according to this world view, is qualitative rather than, or in addition to, quantitative. People can become truly different from the way they were before.

Klaus Riegel (1975) adapted Hegelian dialectic theory to the study of development. This third,

and in some ways intermediate, perspective sees development as the result of opposition or contradictions. The conflict or challenge is solved by creating a new condition that incorporates both initial opposites. The Piagetian opposites of assimilation and accommodation are an example of such basic conflict. Both quantitative and qualitative change are possible. A small amount of change would not alter the underlying structure, but a larger change could lead to transformation of the object being changed.

According to Piaget, development begins with the taking in of new information or experiences from the environment—whether in an active or passive mode does not matter in this context. In the process of assimilating this new material, people must change their total structure of thinking—or feeling—to accommodate it. Because he was trained as a biologist, Piaget perceives the process of psychological assimilation to be analogous to the body's assimilation of food through digestion. To use Sigel and Cocking's words (1977, p. 15), "As the body can only accept appropriate nutrients and reject others, so too the human organism can only take in or assimilate that class of information which the cognitive system is capable of dealing with at that point in time."

After accommodation has occurred, the revised system is prepared to assimilate more-complex or higher-order material, or at least new kinds of information or experiences, which in turn makes it go on to accommodate again and become transformed again. In this way, we can think of development as spiraling upward in an alternation of these two processes. Most Piagetian theorists have confined their thinking and research to the childhood years. They believe that this kind of developmental process must end with maturity—usually biological maturity—when presumably the system is set and can no longer undergo the radical qualitative changes in cognitive structure implied by this model.

Labouvie-Vief (1979), who classifies Piaget's theory as organismic—contextual—derives from it an adaptational or contextual model of development past adolescence. The logic or formal operations that reach their presumably highest level in the adolescent years can be seen as a merely preparatory stage for adult thought, which is characterized by adaptation to the environment and thus by continued, high-level assimilation and accommodation.

3. OPEN VERSUS CLOSED SYSTEM

The organismic view sees humans as either open or closed to outside influence. For example, it is possible to be more open at certain times of life than at others, or under certain conditions more than under others. It is also possible to be either too open or too closed. People can shut off all outside influence and live in the closed world of autism or schizophrenia. They can, alternatively, be so open that they are overwhelmed. (See the following section for a discussion of the developmental consequences of openness.)

A quarter century ago, the Minnesota psychologist John Anderson described the aging person as a progressively more closed system. If adolescence is the time of greatest openness, old age is the time, perhaps, of greatest closedness. Many adults restrict the variety of their experiences, become less open, and probably develop "backward" instead of "forward." More adults, perhaps, regulate the input of new experience in a way that enables them to remain essentially stable over most of the rest of their lives. They may regulate new experiences in some areas while they remain relatively more open in others. It is also possible that some people are always more open to new experiences than others are and that some people are more open at some parts of their lives than at others. The combination of physiologically rapid change, combined with the alterations of social expectations that occur at adolescence, for example, can make that life period one of extremes of openness. Disengagement theory illustrates progressive "closing in" in old age.

Developmental consequences of openness. There are four alternative situations for development that are based on the degree to which people—at any age—are open to environmental changes:

a. If people close in and exclude new information or experience, denying the existence of ongoing changes, no assimilation and therefore no accommodation to these changes are possible. People who "dig in" in this way are in danger of warped or retrogressive development. Only if they live in a relatively static environment and are not changing internally can they even remain stable. For example, some people refuse to recognize changes in their husbands or wives and continue to interact with their spouses as they had when they first got married—an attitude that can result in one-sided, nonmutual, and therefore nonfunctional relationships. Some middle-aged people fail to perceive changes in their appearance and continue to believe they look the same as they did years ago. They are likely to be caught short by the changed behavior of others toward them or to act inappropriately. Shutting out new experiences or new information can thus result in aborted development, at least in areas affected.

b. The opposite approach can also be dangerous. If people "open up" beyond their capacity to control, or, to put it in our theoretical framework, beyond the capacity of preexisting structures to assimilate and then accommodate, they may end up becoming "swamped" by the flood of new information and experiences, to the point of "fracturing" their ego structure or control. An example is the kind of behavior of converts to such movements as encounter groups or charismatic religions. It may be no accident that adolescents, for whom options and new experiences are at a maximum, are most prone to the fracturing of ego control defined as *schizophrenia*.

c. Most adults probably try to absorb just enough new information and experience to maintain a status quo. Adulthood is the most stable period of the life course, and such stability is achieved by maintaining just that minimum of assimilation and accommodation required for homeostatic adjustment. An example is those people who, following widowhood or divorce, marry new spouses who replicate most of the previous spouses' characteristics. Another example is the attempt to find a new job that duplicates the one just lost.

d. The fourth possibility is the one we would call "true positive development." It refers to people who open up more than those described in the third possibility but less than those described in the second possibility. That is, they continue to seek new information and new experiences, pursuing a process of assimilation and accommodation sufficient for structural or qualitative change and self-transformation without feeling overwhelmed by the new experience. An example is the return to school or college of people in the adult or later years. This possibility is probably the least frequent.

Disengagement theory: Becoming more closed. The first major theory to evolve from the early work in gerontology in this country was disengagement theory. It attempted to integrate social behavior with psychological and even, in a way, with biological variables. In the book that presented this theory, Elaine Cumming and William Henry (1961, p. 14), of the University of Chicago Committee on Human Development, stated that with increasing age there is "an inevitable mutual withdrawal or disengagement resulting in decreased interaction between an aging person and others in the social system he belongs to." Cumming and Henry believed at that time that this was the final life stage. Earlier, the same group of scholars had proposed what has been called the *activity theory*, which stated that the organism's continuing demands for activity, complexity, novelty, and conflict are the essence of life itself and remain important to the end, although toward the end of life active exploring might give way to a more-receiving mode of absorbing stimulation (Anderson, 1959). At any rate, according to the activity theory, inactivity and passivity at any time of life have negative consequences—boredom, dullness, and a lessened sense of well-being.

Disengagement theory took the opposite view. Because of approaching death and the desirability of loosening ties with one's life and the people and things one has loved, older people are better off if they do not remain active. The more they disengage, the better they should feel. People who are getting old—and presumably begin to realize they will die—should reduce the number of social roles they play, lessen the variety of these roles, and weaken the intensity of their involvement. On its side, society allows aging individuals freedom from most social rules and obligations and thereby gives them permission to withdraw.

Since the late 1950s, when these ideas were first discussed, these theoretical questions have led to much controversy, much research, and, more recently, more-sophisticated analyses and revisions of thinking. In general, while much subsequent research of the 1960s did replicate the progressively lower social involvement of older people, it found no evidence for the other part of the theory that claims older people who disengage most have the highest morale. If anything, the opposite seems true: those who remain most engaged are happier.

4. CHANGE VERSUS DEVELOPMENT

Although logically it is impossible to develop without changing, it may be possible to change without developing. Defining development, however, is a problem. In fact, the simplest definition is one that makes no sharp distinction between development and change. Neugarten and Datan (1973, pp. 312–313), for example, say that developmental processes are those "in which the organism is irreversibly changed or transformed . . . and which vary in an orderly way with age regardless of the direction of change." By including both "changed" and "transformed," they keep clear of the problem of quantitative versus qualitative change. However, they do insist that development must be limited to irreversible changes and must occur in an orderly manner, with time as the central index.

An opposite kind of definition is derived from the theories of Werner (1948) and Piaget. It involves a progression from simple to complex behavior, from global to differentiated to integrated. The metaphor for change is the chameleon; the metaphor for development is the frog. Development, in this view, implies transformation, and it is a view of development that is implicit in most discussions in this book.

5. POSITIVE VERSUS NEGATIVE DEVELOPMENT

Neugarten and Datan's definition of development includes the requirement of irreversibility. Although it is important to distinguish between transitory and more permanent kinds of changes, this requirement leads to a different kind of dilemma. What about regression or retrogressive changes? We are less likely to notice such changes in childhood and adolescence—although they are undoubtedly more common even in these early parts of the life course than we care to acknowledge—than to recognize them in old age and, to a lesser extent, during the adult years. If our concepts of life-span development are to be truly appropriate for the full span of life, they must encompass changes that lead to decreasing complexity and integration as well as those that lead to increasing complexity and integration.

Labouvie-Vief (1979) points out that adult adaptation involves tradeoffs. To become more "developed" or complex in one sphere, we may have to become less complex in another. Toddlers who turn to exploration of their physical environment may regress in their language development, at least for a time. Adults who progress in their careers may regress in their intimate relationships. Terminal changes at the end of life, even though they may be rapid and occur over a couple of years at most, must be described and explained in any life-span schemata. So also must the slow decrements in certain characteristics during the adult years.

6. STATE VERSUS PROCESS

One way to look at a progression such as the life course is to separate out the "rungs of the ladder"—periods that are distinguishable from those before and after—and pretty much ignore transitions between them, or the ongoing nature of the life progression itself. We can try to learn all we can about each stage or state we have separated out and describe it as accurately as possible, viewing each stage as qualitatively different from other stages. The "terrible 2s" can be treated as different beings from the "adorable toddlers" and "sensible 3s." Wild adolescents are different from industrious schoolagers and committed young adults. Men and women exploring a midlife crisis are as different from responsible adults as from settled retirees. Parents of a 20-month-old who grabs all the cans off the supermarket shelf can beam at her cuteness but look forward with dread to not being able to control her six months later. Although this may result in a "self-fulfilling prophecy," at least they can anticipate an end to that stage, too. Forty-year-old men may abandon themselves to narcissistic irresponsibility because they feel that it is expected of them, and their families and colleagues can endure them by assigning them the label of *midlife crisis*—which implies "they'll get over it."

Another approach is to focus on the transitions from one state to the next. This can be either descriptive or explanatory. If descriptive, we look at what it is like to go from infancy to childhood, from childhood to adolescence, from adolescence to adulthood, from adulthood to old age. We ask whether transitions have characteristics in common or whether each transition is unique. Do different people go through the same transition the same way?

Some scholars compare the course of a person's life to a career or to a combination of careers, such as family and job. Spence and Lonner (1971), for example, suggest that some careers of life start early and others start much later. Some last only a few years, while others last throughout life. Neugarten and Datan (1973) stress the importance of timing and synchronizing our various life careers.

Finally, we can focus on the process of development as such, on life change itself. By comparing periods of rapid change with periods of slow change, we can try to understand the basic nature of development—what starts it and what stops it; what speeds it up or slows it down. Are there universal sequences through which all humans progress, or is it possible to follow different roads? To what extent is development biologically determined; to what extent, socially? To what extent is it fixed? Will future generations go through their adult and older years the same way present generations have, or are present generations developing differently from past and future generations? If so, why?

7. CONTINUITY VERSUS TURNING POINTS

As can be deduced from the discussion so far, it is not easy to put together a theory or model of life-span development. Human behavior is complex, and it appears even more complex when we try to trace it over time. One of the big unanswered questions in the field deals with the problem of life crisis or critical periods. Scholars are caught between two opposing points of view on this question. At one end are those who see "development as a progression by qualitative leaps and structural reorganizations" (Riegel, 1975, p. 123). At the other end are those who see "development as a continuous accumulation of bits of experience or information and deemphasize structural reorganizations" (p. 123).

Some theorists emphasize crises (Erikson, for example) or critical periods (Jung or Piaget, for example). Others think of new behavior and structures as the outcome of past behavior and experience (the social-learning theorists, for example). Also, some believe that all humans go through pretty much the same type of crises or drastic changes at pretty much the same times of their lives. Others feel that some people do and others don't, depending on the kind of people they are—that there are no universal crisis points.

Ethologists, who study nonhuman species' development and natural behavior, point out that there may be particular points in the course of development when certain kinds of experiences have greater effect than at other times. They call these *critical periods*. For example, the events of early childhood may have more profound consequences in shaping personality and future behavior than those of adulthood or later life. Certain experiences, such as falling in love or having sexual intercourse, may have very different effects during adolescence than during the 40s or 60s. Becoming a parent can be a very different kind of event in the 20s than in the 30s or 40s. Widowhood in the 30s or 40s can be very different from widowhood in the 60s.

At some points of life, when biological events come to turning points, or beginnings or endings, it is easier to take the side of the crisis theorists. A child's first walking, or talking, or mastery of sphincter control, for example, can seem to happen overnight and can have momentous consequences for that child's subsequent actions. The onset of puberty, although more drawn out than most of the events just listed, is a later example, as is, for some people, the first sexual experience.

Later in life, there is the climacterium and, of course, death. Aside from these universals, biological events come about idiosyncratically—not "normally." For the woman, childbirth may be an exception, as may menopause. Otherwise, it is only illness or disability that can have the impact we are thinking about. In a broad sense, however, there is no illness or disability that is universal, not even at the end of life, although the approach of death in old age may have a significant psychological component (Lieberman, 1965), as we note in a later chapter.

Some turning points are given social significance by rituals that anthropologists call *rites of passage*. These turning points are important to the society in which the people live. Most societies celebrate the onset of puberty (although again, with our changing views on premarital sex, we have dropped many of the sex-related rituals once associated with the wedding). In our society, the turning points we celebrate are much more likely to be social changes than biological ones. It is graduation from school—elementary school, high school, or college—that is celebrated, not the onset of puberty. It is the social wedding, not the first sexual encounter. It is the birth of a child as a social, not a biological, event. It is a new job, or a promotion, or retirement. However, it is still the funeral.

Midlife crisis.   A number of life-span theories focus on what we might call a "midlife mystique." Although each theory looks at it in a different way, they all maintain that "middle age" is a time of reversal. One of the earliest theorists to point to a major change of life direction and character in middle age was Carl Jung. Following from his view of personality polarity, the concept of reversal is logical. He sees the adult as having a conscious or—to use a Freudian term—"ego-dominant" stance of either extroversion or introversion that is balanced by an opposite unconscious stance. If we are extroverted in most overt or conscious behavior, we are likely to be introverted in that part of ourselves that is "buried"—of which we are unaware. Essentially, according to Jung's view, we make a choice early in adult life between these two postures: we choose one and suppress the other. Similarly, according to Jung, we acquire our sex-appropriate identity—*animus* for male or *anima* for female—by suppressing our opposite-sex characteristics.

In middle age, however, we recover these previously buried or suppressed modes of behavior. If we have been highly extroverted, we become aware of our introverted tendencies. If we have been highly "masculine," we rediscover our "feminine" characteristics. This emergence of suppressed parts of the personality is assumed to lead to confusion and anxiety. We may, in middle age, need help in incorporating these opposites into our conscious personalities in order to be whole. It should be noted that such a model concentrates essentially on only one major life "peak"—or nadir—or turning point. Thus, we would expect no profound changes or development during the years between adolescence and whenever middle age "strikes." Furthermore, once this midlife crisis is resolved, or once the reversal or reincorporation of opposite characteristics is accomplished, change would again be minimal.

8. TIME

Neugarten and Datan (1973, p. 54) review three time perspectives on the human life cycle:

"life time, or chronological age; social time, or age grading and age expectations that shape the life cycle; and historical time, or the succession of political, economic, and social events which shape the setting into which the individual is born and make up the dynamic, constantly changing background against which his life is lived." Let us consider these separately.

Life time. How old you are is measured most simply by counting the months and years since you were born. Chronological age, however, although useful in a statistical way to predict the incidence of particular diseases or the number of people born a certain year who are expected to be alive at some later date, is at best a crude measure. People born at the same time can differ widely in how long they may be "programmed" to live and in the rate at which different parts of their bodies may mature and age and die. Anyone looking at a group of newborn infants in a nursery cannot help but be impressed by the differences in "maturity," alertness, and vigor. These differences increase with every passing moment, not only as a result of variations in biological characteristics but also as a result of variations in their life circumstances. A seventh-grade classroom, populated primarily by 12-year-olds, can be a striking example of variation in rate of maturation. Some look physically like adults, while others could "pass" in a third-grade room. Some girls have been menstruating for more than a year, while others have not even begun to exhibit any of the body changes of puberty. Most—but not all—of the boys are still several years away from the beginning of puberty.

What is true for physical appearance is also true for psychological characteristics—for both intellect and personality. Although some of the adolescent physical and sexual variation evens out by the 20s, other characteristics can spread out and combine with personality residues of earlier variations. By the adult years, whatever predictive power chronological age had earlier becomes markedly lessened. Variance on almost any characteristic increases with every decade of life.

After adolescence, in fact, prospective age of death would be a more meaningful index than age since birth. Consider a group of 40-year-olds. Some will reach the end of their natural lives in a year or two, while others will not die for another 60 or 70 years. The difference is

almost as long as an average life span! Because of these problems with using chronological age as a measure, efforts have long been made to derive a *developmental age* that would provide a more accurate estimate of how far an individual is toward maturity or death. These efforts date back to the work of Halstead and his colleagues at the University of Chicago, starting in the 1930s. Halstead's team searched for years to find some body change that could be used as an index of aging. So far such efforts have been relatively unrewarding.

Most recently, a multidisciplinary team at the Boston Veterans Administration Hospital has been involved in a massive attempt to derive a measure of *functional age* (Fozard, Nuttall, & Waugh, 1972). By analyzing a large number of measurements of 600 healthy men between 20 and 80 years of age, these researchers derived six preliminary aspects of functional age. These aspects are blood serum and urine; auditory functioning; anthropometric descriptions; verbal, perceptual, and motor abilities; personality; and sociological assessments. Unfortunately, these aspects of functional age were calibrated against chronological age and so are not independent of it. They are based on those measurements that change most directly with chronological age. It is hoped that eventually a functional age can be found that will measure how far along in his or her life span any person is, so that a person with an old functional age would, in fact, die before one with a young functional age, regardless of when they were born.

So far, the Veterans Administration study measure that correlates highest with chronological age is grayness of hair. Although some people gray early and others never, looking at their (undyed) hair color seems to be the best way known to estimate how long they have lived. It will probably not tell us much about how young or old they feel or at what level they are functioning or even how old they think they look. It certainly will not tell us how long they have left to live.

Kastenbaum, Derbin, Sabatini, and Artt (1972) have been exploring functional age from a psychological perspective by asking people how old they look, feel, think, and act. They find that old respondents (around 60 years of age) deviate more from chronological age in their reported "personal ages" than do younger respondents (around 20). The older subjects say they look, feel, think, and act much younger than their chronological ages. Of the four personal ages, "looks age" is closest to chronological age. People generally believe that they "look their age."

Aside from individual differences in potential life time, which would make developmental age a useful measure if we could find it, age is also less than a useful predictor of many forms of social and psychological behavior. For example, "In the United States the typical 14-year-old girl is a schoolgirl, while in a rural village in the Near East she may be the mother of two children" (Neugarten & Datan, 1973, p. 57).

A number of writers have pointed out the importance to the person of confronting his or her own mortality. Neugarten (1968) has defined middle age as the time of life when we no longer count back to how long we have lived but shift our time perspective from "time lived" to "time left to live." This shift includes not only a reversal in directionality but also an awareness that time is finite. In middle age, the death of someone close has a different impact from the impact such a death would have in youth. A middle-aged man whom Neugarten interviewed said "There is now the realization that death is very real. Those things don't quite penetrate when you're in your twenties and you think that life is all ahead of you. Now you know that death will come to you, too" (p. 97). Erikson (1950) might consider his last stage, integrity versus despair, most descriptive of people nearing death, whether they are as young as 40 or as old as 90.

Social time.   All societies divide time into socially relevant units, transforming calendar time into social time. For example, a man in a simple society may pass from infancy to childhood to warrior-apprentice to warrior (and simultaneously to husband and father) and finally to elder. Age-strata and age-status systems are found in all societies, not only simple ones, and are associated with particular duties, rights, and rewards. When the division of labor is simple and social change is slow, a single age-grade system can become formalized, attached to family, work, religious, and political roles. In a complex society, on the other hand, more than one system of age status becomes differentiated. Even in American society, however, certain events are tied to chronological age: starting school, becoming eligible to vote, assuming legal responsibility.

Every society has a system of social expectations for age-appropriate behavior, and all members of that society learn these rules as they grow up. There is a time when people are expected to go to work, to marry, to have children, to retire. There is even a time to grow sick and to die. The extent to which people attach importance to age norms increases significantly with age. Middle-aged and older people see greater constraints in the age-norm system than do the young: they have learned that there can be negative consequences of being "off time."

> These studies illustrate the point that the age-status structure of a society, age-group identifications, the internalization of age norms, and age norms as a network of social controls are important dimensions of the social and cultural context in which the life course must be viewed. Many of the major punctuation marks of the life cycle are not only orderly and sequential, but many are social rather than biological in nature, and their timing is socially regulated. These concepts point to one way of structuring the passage of time in the life span of the individual; and in delineating a social time clock that can be superimposed upon the biological clock, these concepts are helpful in comprehending the life cycle [Neugarten & Datan, 1973, p. 58].

Not all life-time clocks are synchronous. Individual developmental expectations can conflict with family developmental expectations as well as with biological development. (See Chapter 3 for more about age expectations.)

Historical time.   In Neugarten and Datan's (1973, p. 58) definition,

> Historical time refers not only to long-term processes, such as industrialization and urbanization which create the social-cultural context and changing definitions of the phases of the life cycle. History is also a series of economic, political, and social events that directly influence the life course of the individuals who experience those events. The life cycle of an individual is shaped, then, by the long-term historical processes of change that gradually alter social institutions; but the life cycle is also affected by discrete historical events. Some sense of the interplay between historical time and life time emerges if, for example, one considers World War II as it impinged on a young man, a child, or a young mother.
> In the first case, a young man who becomes a soldier may achieve some resolution of masculine identity by taking on a highly stereotyped male role. In the second case, the child may go fatherless for the first few years of his life.

Going fatherless may have profound effects on future development. And the mother who has to bring up her child alone has less money, strength, and moral support than she might have had if her husband were around.

The timing of major historical events in the life of an individual is important. Neugarten and Datan (1973, p. 58) say:

> Cain (1967) has presented sets of data to show that a historical "hinge" or "watershed" developed in America at the end of World War I with regard to levels of education, fertility patterns, sexual mores, reduction of hours in the work week, labor force participation patterns, and so on. This watershed produced a sharp contrast in lifestyles between the cohort of persons born before the turn of the century (persons who are presently over 70) and the cohort born after 1900 (persons who are now entering old age), with the results indicating that the needs of the new cohort of the aged will be very different from the needs of cohorts that preceded it.

Time as an explanation. Although all these aspects of time are highly relevant to the study of human development, using time to explain development is tautological. Baltes and Schaie (1973) stress that time per se does not cause anything. Furthermore, these authors suggest that it is not always necessary to look back at distant events to explain current behavior; sometimes concurrent behavior is as good an explanatory variable as earlier (childhood) events. Social-learning theory, in particular, claims that explanations of ongoing behavior in terms of age or time are essentially wasteful. It would be much more worthwhile to examine that behavior carefully and determine what conditions seem to initiate it than to trace it over the person's past life (Ahammer, 1973).

Baltes feels that developmental psychology should be concerned with three things: describing a particular behavior, finding out what caused it, and then finding out how to modify it—if we thought it undesirable. If the third goal is the one we really want, it is unparsimonious to do anything but find out how to modify the behavior. The best way to change a certain behavior, in fact, may not be to change its antecedent at all, particularly if what we want to do is prevent something from occurring or to optimize or ensure its occurrence.

However, not all scholars in the field feel that age or time is irrelevant to developmental re-

search. Birren and Renner (1977, p. 6) argue that "to be a cause of something, the cause must occur before the consequence, and the ordering of events in time is crucial to understanding the development of mankind." Thus the issue of time is far from settled.

9. ADAPTATION

The structuralist/functionalist issue has been prominent in all search for knowledge from the beginning of philosophical inquiry. On the one hand, structuralists are concerned with the nature of things, no matter whether they see these forms as primarily biological, organismic, open, or changing. Structuralists are less interested in whether these forms are better at surviving or more successful in any other way. Functionalists, on the other hand, are primarily concerned with success or outcome. Clinicians, whether they treat the body or the psyche, see structure only as information relevant to function. From Havighurst's theory of developmental tasks to Labouvie-Vief's theory of adult development as adaptation to changing contexts, there has been a recurrent theme of functionalism.

10. UNIVERSALITY

We seem to find it easier to think in terms of commonality and universality of characteristics and events than we do to think in terms of variability. Most theories speak of *the* human life course, *the* midlife crisis, *the* effects of retirement, or *the* concomitants of menopause. Most research findings are reported in terms of means and averages and interpreted as if the average were the *true* nature of the event and the dispersion around the mean were merely an indication of error—presumably error of measurement. Yet, as discussed already, variety is at least as true as universality. Some humans round out their lives in 40 years; others in 100 years. Some humans experience a crisis at some point during their adult years; others do not. Some people find retirement to have little significance in their lives, and others are devastated by it. Some women have to stop to think whether they are in the menopause, and others find their lives completely altered by it. The issue of universality and commonality is last in this list, but not least important.

Summary

I have sketched out ten primary themes or issues prevalent in current thinking about life-span development, particularly that portion of developmental theory related to changes after adolescence. Readers might keep these issues in mind as they review the research findings that come from these questions or perspectives. It is particularly useful for students to ask themselves how someone with an opposite viewpoint might go about trying to find out the same kind of information—or how someone of an opposite viewpoint might interpret findings.

The ten issues deal with

1. The separation of biological from environmental effects
2. The interpretation of development as a process either outside the individual's control or organized by the individual—or something in between
3. The effect of the degree of openness or closedness to outside influence on development
4. The relation between change and development
5. The consideration of retrogressive as well as progressive changes
6. The focus on "rungs of the ladder"—states or stages—or on the process of development, the careers of life, transitions as well as states
7. The continuity of the life process or the possible existence of prominent turning points and crises
8. The different meanings of time that are central to the study of life-span development—life time, social time, and historical time—and the problem of whether time itself can cause development
9. The focus on structural changes or on those changes that help people adapt to their environment
10. The focus on the commonality or universality of various events and experiences of life or on their variability

Comparative Guide to
AMERICAN
Comparative Guide to
AMERICAN COLLEGES
CASS and BIRNBAUM
Admission requirements
Special programs

2

Models and Methods

Most models of development focus on childhood, but recently a few consider the later years. Those that can be considered life-span theories are reviewed here in terms of the ten issues discussed in Chapter 1. The first broad group consists of stage theories and is relevant to Issues 4 through 10.

Stage theories

Although current stage theories differ widely, almost all assume that:

1. Everybody goes through life in the same way (*universality*).
2. Everybody goes through the stages in the same order (*sequentiality*).
3. There is a predetermining end point to the sequence (*teleology*).
4. There is a good way, as well as a bad way, to go through the sequence (*adaptation*).

Many of these theories also make a fifth assumption:

5. The good way is in tune with current middle-class values (*class bias*).

Although many life-span developmental psychologists find one or more of these assumptions untenable and therefore any stage theory unsatisfactory, it is stage models of development that are most familiar to the general public.

These models also appeal to the applied branches of the behavioral sciences because they are easy to understand and provide clear guidelines for both anticipating and evaluating behavior. People can label their ongoing experience, estimate how well they are doing, and anticipate their future behavior. Medical or psychological practitioners also find the labels useful for categorizing the behavior they are witnessing in their clients, for judging whether to consider this behavior "normal" or "abnormal," and for planning their treatment in order to adjust these clients to the norm or to cure them of their deviations from the norm.

Current stage theories can be divided into three categories according to their basis: structure, life situation, and issue.

STAGE THEORIES BASED ON STRUCTURE

Most structurally determined theories that have evolved from child development are biologically oriented. Those that consider later development are more cognitively oriented, deriving from the thinking of Jean Piaget. Note, however, that Piaget has stated that most true development ends with adolescence and that only wisdom (a quantitative change instead of a transformation) continues to grow in adulthood. Kohlberg (1973) and Loevinger (1976), although they are Piagetians, see the possibility of further development beyond adolescence. In a way, Kohlberg's adult stages are elaborations of growth in wisdom. He deviates from Piaget in saying that there can be true qualitative change in later life, not just what Piaget calls "horizontal decalage"—generalization of earlier ways of thinking to new areas. It is moral judgment that Kohlberg sees as significant: moral development based on cognitive development. That is, a particular cognitive level must have been achieved before the equivalent moral-judgment level; the inverse is not true. One could master formal operations, the highest cognitive-development stage, and yet never reach the highest level of moral judgment. Thus, cognitive level is a necessary but not sufficient prerequisite for moral-judgment level. Table 2.1 shows the parallel cognitive (Piaget) and moral-judgment (Kohlberg) stages. More recently, Kohlberg (1973) has proposed an additional (seventh) stage, occurring late in adulthood. He describes it as a "cosmic perspective," when "we begin to see our lives as finite from some infinite perspective and value life from this standpoint" (p. 203).

Loevinger's model also derives from Piaget but focuses on ego development. Her stages progress from "impulse ridden" to autonomous.

TABLE 2.1 Relations between Piaget's logical stages and Kohlberg's moral stages

Moral stage	Logical stage
Stage 0. The good is what I want and like	Symbolic, intuitive thought
Stage 1. Punishment-obedience orientation	Concrete operations, Substage 1: categorical classification
Stage 2. Instrumental hedonism and concrete reciprocity	Concrete operations, Substage 2: reversible concrete thought
Stage 3. Orientation to interpersonal relations of mutuality	Formal operations, Substage 1: relations involving the inverse of the reciprocal
Stage 4. Maintenance of social order, fixed rules and authority	Formal operations, Substage 2
Stage 5A. Social contract, utilitarian law-making perspective	Formal operations, Substage 3
Stage 5B. Higher law and conscience orientation	
Stage 6. Universal ethical principle orientation	

Source: Kohlberg, 1973.

One characteristic of Piagetian-derived theories is that they stress the transformation of earlier structures into later ones. Rather than the image of a ladder, in which the person climbs from one state to the next, such models evoke that of metamorphosis, of drastic changes in form that result in essentially new individuals, even though the new individual is composed of parts of the former self.

It is not precisely true that there are no biologically determined stage theories for later life. A number of gerontologists speak of the difference between "young old" and "old old," for example, which is based primarily on biological competence. Such differentiations are reserved for the end of adulthood, when biological causes are once more thought to be prominent. Probably major reasons for the absence of generalized life-span biological theories are (1) the long plateau of little biological change during the adult years and (2) the wide variation of biological changes at any chronological age.

STAGE THEORIES BASED ON LIFE SITUATIONS

Stage theories based on life situations generally present a sequence of developmental tasks. One of the simplest of these is Havighurst's (1952). Table 2.2 lists the tasks for his adult and old-age stages.

An adaptation of Havighurst's model that focuses primarily on the last years of life is Clark and Anderson's (1967). It lists five necessary adaptive tasks for late adulthood and old age:

1. Recognition of aging and definition of instrumental limitations
2. Redefinition of physical and social life space
3. Substitution of alternate sources of need satisfaction
4. Reassessment of criteria for evaluation of the self
5. Reintegration of values and life goals

Clark and Anderson's tasks are different from Havighurst's in that they are more general, related to the changes experienced by most older people. Like Havighurst's, they are normative or necessary prescriptions.

A variation of stage theory is proposed by Daniel Levinson on the basis of clinical studies

TABLE 2.2 Havighurst's developmental tasks for adulthood and old age

Early adulthood

Selecting a mate
Learning to live with a marriage partner
Starting a family
Rearing children
Managing a home
Getting started in an occupation
Taking on civic responsibility
Finding a congenial social group

Middle age

Achieving adult civic and social responsibility
Establishing and maintaining an economic standard of living
Assisting teenage children to become responsible and happy adults
Developing adult leisure-time activities
Relating to one's spouse as a person
Accepting and adjusting to the physiological changes of middle age
Adjusting to aging parents

Old age

Adjusting to decreasing strength and health
Adjusting to retirement and reduced income
Adjusting to death of spouse
Establishing an explicit affiliation with members of one's own age group
Meeting social and civic obligations
Establishing satisfactory physical living arrangements

Source: Havighurst, 1952a.

TABLE 2.3 Levinson's stages

Leaving the family (20–24): A transitional period from adolescence to early adulthood that involves moving out of the family home and establishing psychological distance from the family, analogous to Erikson's stage of identity versus role diffusion

Getting into the adult world (early 20s to 27–29): A time of exploration and provisional commitment to adult roles in occupational and interpersonal areas and of fashioning an initial "life structure"

Settling down (early 30s to early 40s): A period of deeper commitment, sometimes involving the expansion motif of Jung and Kuhlen

Becoming one's own man (35–39): The high point of early adulthood

The midlife transition (early 40s): A developmental transition involving a sense of bodily decline and a vivid recognition of one's mortality, as well as an integration of the feminine aspects of the self as postulated by Jung

Restabilization and the beginning of middle adulthood (middle 40s): A period in which some men make new creative strides but others lose their vitality

Source: Levinson, Darrow, Klein, Levinson, and McKee, 1977. (Originally published, 1974.)

of men. He and his colleagues (Levinson, Darrow, Klein, Levinson, & McKee, 1977) differentiate three "gross" chronological periods in the adult life course—early, middle, and late adulthood—which are connected by intervening transitions. The resulting sequence of stages is listed in Table 2.3.

It must be remembered that Levinson's model is derived from data on men only and that it focuses primarily on early and middle adulthood. The facts that it is closely linked to chronological age and that the stages are described in detailed form make it appealing for lay readers. A number of journalists (such as Sheehy, 1976) have written articles and books based on this theory, and it is currently perhaps the most widely known adult-development model of all those mentioned here. A similar model by Gould (1972), also derived from experiences with psychotherapy patients, is less tied to chronological age (see Table 2.4).

STAGE THEORIES BASED ON ISSUES

A different kind of life-span stage theory is that of Erikson (1950), who based his model on Freud's developmental views. He incorporated social experiences more than Freud had and also extended development to the whole of life

TABLE 2.4 Gould's stages

16–18 years: People feel a strong desire to get away from parents, but autonomy is precarious

18–22 years: Feel halfway out of family and worry about being reclaimed; peer group important ally in cutting family ties

22–28 years: Feel established, autonomous, and separate from family; feel "now" is the time for living, growing, and building; peers still important, but self-reliance paramount

29–34 years: Begin to question what they are doing; feel weary of being what they are supposed to be, but continue

35–43 years: Feel that time seems to constrict for shaping the behavior of their adolescent children or "making it"; their own parents turn to them with muffled renewal of old conflicts

43–53 years: Feel "die is cast" and view life with bitterness; blame parents and find fault with children but seek sympathy from spouse

53–60 years: Feel less negative feelings than in the 40s; relationships with selves, parents, children, and friends become warmer and more mellow; marital happiness and contentment increase

Source: Gould, 1972.

instead of ending with early adulthood. The emphasis of both Freud and Erikson is not so much on description of states as on the crises or prominent issues that introduce or precipitate new states. Each of Erikson's eight stages starts with a new *issue* that involves a choice between two opposites—one good, the other bad. This choice influences all future life. In this way, his model has a good/bad component like those of Havighurst and of Clark and Anderson. It is also essentially based on a homeostatic assumption. Freud, in particular, explained the drive to resolve tensions created by new issues as an effort to return to homeostasis or equilibrium.

TABLE 2.5 Adaptation of Erikson's stages

Stage	Positive resolution	Negative resolution
1. Basic trust versus basic mistrust	Person likes or trusts work associates, friends, relatives; feels essentially optimistic about people and their motives; has confidence in self and the world in general.	Person distrusts people; prefers to be alone because friends "get you into trouble"; dislikes confiding in anyone; distrusts self and the world in general.
2. Autonomy versus shame and doubt	Has own attitudes and ways of doing things, not because others expect them; is not afraid to hold own opinions or do what he or she wants.	Is self-conscious about own ideas and ways of doing things and prefers to stay with tried and trusted ways; avoids asserting self in group; emphasizes how much like others he or she acts and feels.
3. Initiative versus guilt	Takes pleasure in planning and initiating action; plans ahead and designs own schedule.	Lets others initiate action; plays down success or accomplishment.
4. Industry versus inferiority	Likes to make things and carry them to completion; strives for skill mastery; has pride in production.	Is passive; leaves things undone; feels inadequate about ability to do things or produce work.
5. Ego identity versus role diffusion	Has strongly defined social roles; feels at home in work, family, affiliations, sex role; enjoys carrying out role behavior; has sense of belonging; takes comfort in style of life and daily activities; is definite about self and who he or she is; feels continuity with past and present.	Is ill at ease in roles, lost in groups and affiliations; does not enter into required role behavior with much conviction; may make radical switches in work or residence without meaning or purpose.
6. Intimacy versus isolation	Has close, intimate relationship with spouse, children, and friends, sharing thoughts, spending time with them, expressing warm feelings for them.	Lives relatively isolated from friends, spouse, children; avoids contact with others on an intimate basis; is either absorbed in self or indiscriminately sociable; relations with people are stereotyped or formal.
7. Generativity versus stagnation	Has plans for future that require sustained application and utilization of skills and abilities; invests energy and ideas into something new; has sense of continuity with future generations.	Seems to be vegetating; does nothing more than routines of work and necessary daily activities; is preoccupied with self.
8. Integrity versus despair	Feels satisfied and happy with life, work, accomplishments; accepts responsibility for life; maximizes successes.	Feels depressed and unhappy about life, emphasizing failures; would change life or career if had another chance; does not accept present age and mode of life, emphasizing past; fears getting older; fears death.

span developmental theorists. For example, Erikson (1950, p. 268) says of the individual in Stage 8: "He knows that an individual life is the accidental coincidence of but one life cycle with but one segment of history; and that for him all human integrity stands or falls with the one style of integrity of which he partakes. . . . In such final consolidation, death loses its sting." Kohlberg also incorporates such a transcendent view into his final, seventh stage. This theme echoes the beliefs of many Eastern religions that the approach of personal death is the approach to the supernatural. Sometimes this approach is seen, as in primitive religions (Swanson, 1966), as an enhancement of personal power; at other times, as in Peck's model, it is seen as a threat that must be coped with.

In the last few years, a number of personality theorists have turned to another psychoanalytic thinker for inspiration. Carl Jung's (1930/1971) stage theory is based primarily on consciousness and offers a progression in content of awareness. Jung's theory has appealed particularly to psychologists interested in a midlife crisis or transition. Jung saw midlife as a critical turning point of life, a time of reversals in behavior and reversals in consciousness. His stages are listed in Table 2.7. One image associated with his theory is the waxing and waning of life, the early

vided each of these periods again into stages and said that these stages may occur in a different time sequence for different individuals and thus do not imply sequentiality. Peck's stages of later life are presented in Table 2.6.

The theme of transcendence iterated by Peck appears in the thinking of several other life-

TABLE 2.6 Peck's stages

Middle age
1. Appreciation of wisdom versus appreciation of physical powers.
2. Socializing versus sexualizing in human relationships.
3. Cathectic flexibility versus cathectic impoverishment. Here Peck felt that it was valuable to be able to shift emotional investments from one person to another and from one activity to another.
4. Mental flexibility versus mental rigidity.

Old age
1. Ego differentiation versus work-role preoccupation. Here Peck states the desirability of shifting the value system of the retiring person so as to provide a basis for reappraising and redefining worth in terms of something other than the work role.
2. Body transcendence versus body preoccupation.
3. Ego transcendence versus ego preoccupation. As Peck (1968, p. 91) puts it, "The constructive way of living the late years might be defined in this way: To live so generously and unselfishly that the prospect of personal death—the night of the ego, it might be called—looks and feels less important than the secure knowledge that one has built for a broader, longer future than any one ego ever could encompass."

Source: Peck, 1968.

TABLE 2.7 Jung's stages

1. *Anarchic or chaotic state:* There is a simple connection between two or more psychic contents, but no continuous memory; there are islands of consciousness.
2. *Monarchic or monistic state:* Although there is continuity in ego memories, the individual is still dependent on parents, still governed by impulse.
3. *Dualistic:* At puberty, there is a conscious distinction between ego and parents; a state of inner tension when what was earlier external limitation to impulses becomes internalized, when one impulse opposes itself to another. This can estrange one from oneself.
4. *Youth (puberty to midlife, 35–40):* One develops roots in the world. Achievement, not personality, is rewarded. One limits oneself to the attainable and renounces other potentialities.
5. *Middle life:* This is a time of gradual change in character, with old traits reappearing and with new interests and inclinations. There is also a hardening of hitherto-accepted moral principles (fanaticism). This change does not come about until one's parents have died. If they die later, an almost catastrophic ripening occurs. Values, even body, tend to undergo reversal into the opposite; there are a sex reversal and a shift from unfolding of potential and actualization to contracting; one necessarily is occupied with oneself.
6. *Old age:* Probably no more consciousness develops.

years being ones of expansion, and the later years of constriction.

Buhler (1968), a pioneer in life-span psychology, divided the life span into phases of goal setting. She saw the first 20 years of life as a period for establishing goals and the next period (adulthood) as a time for fulfilling them. In middle age, some people reexamine and set new goals, but others opt for stability and retirement. Although Buhler does not stress the reversibility theme of Jung and others, she does stress the turning-point aspect of middle age.

An expansion/contraction model leads to some interesting implications. For example, to apply Piaget's (1970) assimilation/accommodation process, one could postulate that the more open people are to new experiences, the more new experiences they are likely to assimilate, and consequently the more they are likely to change or develop as a result of accommodating to the conflicting elements between old and new information. If people have an outward thrust and orientation in young adulthood and then become constricted and turn inward in middle age, they should change and develop more in young adulthood and less after middle age. Even if environmental changes are relatively minor in early life, they might have more impact on the personality than do major changes later in life. This is related to the "critical-period" issue discussed in Chapter 1.

Nonstage theories

Some of the stage models of development just described, like Havighurst's and Levinson's, are specific about the demands and behaviors for particular ages. Other stage models are much more general, and some even indicate alternate pathways at each stage. Some psychologists who are trying to develop theories of adult development feel that any commonalities we find at particular ages or in particular sequences are accidental; at least, they are the result of common experiences within a common culture rather than being predetermined by inner maturational processes (Bandura, 1969). Similarly, social-learning theories stress the social determinants of adult behavior (Ahammer, 1973; Baltes, 1979; Brim, 1977; and Neugarten & Datan, 1973), and the influence of important life events.

According to most social-learning theorists, behavior change should be looked at from a "molecular" instead of a "molar" level. They hold that if we look at units of behavior—a molecular approach—we can often understand their sequence by ascertaining what came just before or at the same time; we do not have to look far back, at what Baltes (1973) calls "distal" antecedents. Furthermore, we do not have to use different mechanisms of behavior change for organisms of different ages. If we are concerned with modifying present behavior, the social-learning approach can be particularly useful and has, indeed, been adopted by many psychologists who try to alter behavior.

A wider view

Brim (1977, p. 7) provides a cautionary note:

It may be that the field of adult development is similar to child development some fifty years ago in its exploration of age-linked developmental sequences. And, like child development then, it is in real danger from pop culture renderings of "life stages," from the public seizing on the idea of age-linked stages of development, such as the "male mid-life crisis," just as it seizes on astrology and tea-leaf reading. Certainly, the evidence does not justify linkage of crises either to stages, or to specific ages, during the mid-life period.

Baltes and Willis (1977, p. 128) make a similar point: "The *Zeitgeist* in psychology is not one of comprehensive, unitary, monistic theory building but one of pluralism dealing with the formulation of diverse and domain-specific miniature theories."

Neugarten and Datan (1973) and Lowenthal (1977), struggling to understand research data on age differences, are less anxious about theory and model building as such than they are about the issues that must be addressed or the questions that must be answered by any model of life-span development. In some respects, Lowenthal (1977) reflects G. H. Mead's (1934) perspective when she says that

A truly sociopsychological approach requires two simultaneous, juxtaposed perspectives: (1) close examination . . . of how individuals at various stages of the life course perceive and effectively respond to individuals, networks, and institutions within their cognitive range; and (2) study of the networks themselves as they encompass, respond to, or reject individuals at various stages of the life course.

Neugarten and her colleagues at the University of Chicago Committee on Human Development tend to be even more open-ended as they assess, in a variety of studies, many different concomitants of age.

Schaie (1965, 1973) looked for three principal causes of age differences: ontogenetic or age change, intergenerational or cohort differences, and time of measurement differences.

Riegel (1971) proposed a dialectic approach. He pointed out that development can be seen as involving either qualitative changes—a progression in leaps and jumps—or quantitative changes—a continuous progression toward an abstract goal. Qualitative development is more characteristic of closed systems, those that have ceilings or limits to the amount of continuous growth that can occur. Development in such closed systems thus must happen through restructuring of old ways, using the old to form the new; it is not possible to keep adding on. Open systems lend themselves to more quantitative change; it is possible to keep adding on new information or abilities or ways of doing things and still keep the old as it was. Because human beings are semiopen—or semiclosed (Anderson, 1957)—we can expect to find some of both kinds of development occurring. Examples of qualitative developmental models are

Erikson's, Levinson's, and Kohlberg's. Examples of quantitative models are the social-learning theories.

Not only do developmental models have to consider such issues as the openness of the developing organism and whether or not development is qualitative or quantitative, but they must also consider how passive or active an individual is and, according to Riegel (1971), how passive or active the environment is in which the individual develops. Riegel sees four major viewpoints of human beings and their environment. In the first, both people and their environment are essentially passive. The individual starts out as a *tabula rasa*—a "blank page"—and development is the result of stimuli or experiences surrounding him or her. Behaviorists and social-learning theories tend toward this first orientation.

The second viewpoint assumes an active individual in a passive environment. Piaget's theory and those derived from it (Kohlberg's and Loevinger's) generally fit this model. The third viewpoint assumes a passive individual in an active environment. Theories in this category attribute age differences primarily to cohort or generational or historical changes. Finally, the

TABLE 2.8 Comparison of developmental theories

Issues	Kohlberg and Loevinger	Havighurst	Levinson	Erikson	Jung	Social learning
Biology	Cognitive, on biological base	Social	Not relevant	Partly biological	Mostly biological	Social
Mechanistic versus organismic perspective	Organismic	Organismic	Organismic	Organismic	Organismic	Mechanistic
Open versus closed system	Not relevant	Open to normative demands	Relatively closed	Selectively open	More open at some periods than at others	Open
Change versus development	Development	Change	Development	Development	Development	Change
Positive versus negative evaluation	Positive	Not relevant	Some positive, some negative	Positive or negative	Generally positive	Not relevant
State versus process	State	State	State, but some process	State and process	Mostly state	Process
Turning points	No	Implicit	Universal and prominent	Universal and prominent	Universal and prominent	No
Time	Not relevant	Implicit chronological age	Explicit chronological age	Social time	Biological time	Not relevant
Adaptation	Yes	Yes	Yes	Yes	No	Incidental
Universality	Yes	Yes	Yes	Yes	Yes	No

fourth viewpoint is Riegel's favorite, the dialectic, in which both individual and environment are active participants in two-way interaction.

A comparison of six of the models presented is found in Table 2.8 (p. 21). These models are compared on the ten issues discussed in Chapter 1.

Methodological issues

Baltes, Reese, and Nesselroade (1977, p. 1) start out their book on research methods in developmental psychology by stating that "developmental psychology deals with behavioral changes within persons across the life span, and with differences between and similarities among persons in the nature of these changes. Its aim, however, is not only to *describe* these intraindividual changes and interindividual differences, but also to *explain* how they come about and to find ways to *modify* them in an optimum way." So far, most research on adult development and aging has been descriptive, and beyond that most has been cross-sectional, comparing different groups of people of different ages measured at the same time. Figure 2.1 illustrates some findings about hearing loss with age obtained by McFarland (1968) from measurements of Americans of different ages. These data show a clear age-related pattern of hearing differences in the higher frequencies. They would lead us to believe that older age groups hear high notes less well than younger age groups—or at least that they did in 1968.

We might further conclude that hearing loss comes about inevitably as people get older. But why? What happens, as we age, to produce hearing loss? We have a description, but we

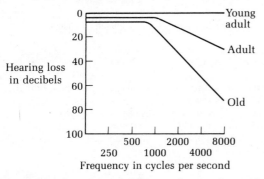

Figure 2.1. Cross-sectional data on hearing loss with age. *(Source: McFarland, 1968.)*

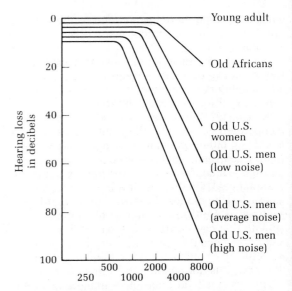

Figure 2.2. Cross-cultural, cross-sectional data on hearing loss with age. *(Source: McFarland, 1968.)*

have no explanation, and so we have no clue to preventing such a disability. Now look at Figure 2.2. By adding several strategic groups to his investigation of hearing abilities, McFarland (1968) showed that hearing loss with age depended on sex (male or female) and on how much one had been exposed to noise. Young-adult Americans still show uniform acuity over all sound frequencies; they can hear higher tones as well as lower tones. However, old Africans, who have lived their lives in an environment of little noise, are almost as good, and older American men show more or less deficit depending on the amount of noise they have been exposed to—but all old Americans show more deficit than do old Africans. Presumably even what we consider a low noise level in America is more noise than what these Africans had experienced.

Now we can begin to explain. One possible explanation is that living in a noisy environment gradually destroys hearing. If so, we should try to reduce noise levels and protect the ears of people who have to work in very noisy places. Of course, this extra information—comparisons across cultures and between sexes—provides us with the possibilities of alternate explanations. There could be some genetic differences between Africans and Americans that make Americans more vulnerable to noise than Africans and make men more vulnerable than women. It is possible that American women, however, are not as likely to be exposed to noise levels as high as American men are exposed to. It would have helped if McFarland had presented data for African women, too, to see whether African women similarly show less differential loss than do African men.

We would need another kind of information to see whether the age differences are due to biological losses, to cumulative exposure to noise over life, or to a combination of both. At any rate, we have taken a big step toward explanation and prevention. We should protect young men's hearing more than women's on the growing assumption that there may be sex differences.

AGE DIFFERENCE VERSUS AGE CHANGE

One major question in life-span research is whether the age differences seen are the result of particular conditions that affected the particular age groups of people studied or whether they are going to happen to all people as they get older. A leading psychological researcher, K. Warner Schaie (1970), warns us that we can make serious mistakes by concluding that cross-sectional research findings give us age *changes*, when all they really show is age *differences*. For example, a group of 20-year-olds may be compared with a group of 40-year-olds and a group of 60-year-olds, as illustrated in the third column of Figure 2.3, the 1960 round of comparisons.

The differences found between 20-year-olds and 40-year-olds, unfortunately, are too often reported as changes from age 20 to age 40. It is assumed that the 20-year-olds will become like the 40-year-olds in 20 years, then like the 60-year-olds in another 20 years. This kind of assumption has led to serious errors. In any society that changes—and ours changes very rapidly—the three age groups are going to be different from one another for many reasons besides age. Their differences are as likely to be due to different amounts of schooling, to differences in lifelong health care and nutrition, to differences in density of population when they were growing up, or to the impact of different critical historical events. They might also have been raised by different standards of child care and socialization. The chances for the 20-year-olds in 1960 to be like the 40-year-olds of 1960

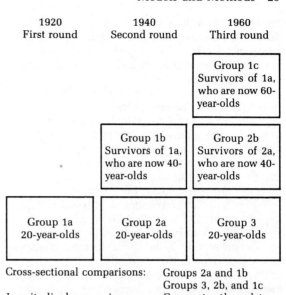

Cross-sectional comparisons: Groups 2a and 1b
                              Groups 3, 2b, and 1c
Longitudinal comparisons: Groups 1a, 1b, and 1c
                              Groups 2a and 2b
Cultural change comparisons: Groups 1a, 2a, and 3
                              Groups 1b and 2b

Figure 2.3. Hypothetical cross-sequential research model. *(Source: Schaie, 1970.)*

when they get to be 40 in 20 years are thus sufficiently low to make the "age difference equals age change" assumption treacherous.

One of the most dramatic examples of this error is seen in the interpretation of intelligence-test results, to be discussed in Chapter 11. Comparisons of older with younger Americans show higher intelligence-test scores for the younger ones. But, when years of schooling are taken into account, these differences virtually disappear. And, when we follow the same people along over time, we see no age change.

Longitudinal research is an improvement over cross-sectional studies. It compares the performance of a particular group of subjects with that group's own performance at another period in time. For example, researchers measure a group of 20-year-olds, as in the 1920 round of Figure 2.3, and then wait 20 years to measure them again when they are 40 in 1940. Then in 1960—if the researchers are still alive—they round them up again (or those of them who have survived) to remeasure them another time when they are 60 years old. This kind of comparison is shown in the diagonals of Figure 2.3. This group is called 1a in 1920 when it is 20, 1b in

1940 when it is 40, and 1c in 1960. This procedure will yield age *changes* for *that particular* group of people, or rather for those of them who are still available for measuring at the time of the third round.

Because of the rapidity of social change, unfortunately, the changes in the group that was first studied 40 years ago may not be helpful for predicting age changes in groups born at other times. The 2a group changes over 20 years into the 2b group in a different way from the way that the 1a group changes to the 1b group. Maybe they "grow up" faster, for instance.

Schaie has, therefore, suggested three further improvements in research strategy: cross-sequential research, time-sequential research, and cohort-sequential research. In cross-sequential research, as in the longitudinal method, a group of 20-year-olds is measured and then re-measured 20 years later. At the time of the second measurement, a new group of 20-year-olds is also measured. And on the third round of measurement, when the original group is 60 years old and the second group 40 years old, a third group of 20-year-olds is added. It is thus possible to assess the effects of historical as well as developmental changes by combining information about the three groups of 20-year-olds as each grows older. Age changes can be corrected for historical changes and a more accurate estimate of actual development obtained. Only in this way can we begin to make predictions about how adults in general are likely to change over 20 or 40 years of living. And only then can we plan how to prevent those changes we do not want.

Other serious problems of longitudinal research will not be so easy to overcome, however. One is the problem of survivor bias. In general, more-advantaged and more-vigorous individuals tend to survive longer than those who are less advantaged and healthy. So the group of subjects in later rounds of testing or observation is not really the same group as the one that started out. The people at the low end of the distribution—on almost any measurement, in fact—are probably no longer alive. Therefore, the group average seems better than it would have been if the complete original group had survived (Riegel, Riegel, & Meyer, 1967). Because of this effect, it is important to underinterpret curves of change from long-term

studies. Abilities may seem to improve over time, but they may not have really changed at all, or they may seem stable and yet may really have deteriorated.

Repeating measurements is another serious problem. Part of the assumption made in retesting is that the measurement is the same each time. Yet more and more research shows this assumption to be wrong. Each time a test is given, it is a different experience and therefore it is not getting at the same underlying ability (for example, see Labouvie, 1980). If the measuring stick changes along with the person being measured, and at a different rate as well, how can we tell whether the person is changing? The seriousness of this problem has been shown in recent evaluations of research intended to reverse some of the cognitive losses in old age. It now seems that what originally looked like effective improvements of functioning with behavior-modification therapies is instead the result of repeating the tests. Just retaking a test improves performance.

Time-sequential research focuses on the effects of time on different groups of people. In Figure 2.3, for example, the differences among the three groups of 20-year-olds (1a, 2a, and 3) or the differences between the two groups of 40-year-olds (1b and 2b) may be due to the effect of time. A variation of time-sequential research focuses on what is called the *period effect,* or the influence of being alive in a particular historical period, or of taking the measurement at a particular moment in time. Thus, all ages measured at one point in time (for example, the first round in Figure 2.3) are compared with all ages measured at another point in time (second round in Figure 2.3).

An illustration of such research is given in Table 2.9, which shows attitudes of people of different ages toward medical-aid programs over the years from 1956 to 1972. Both period and cohort differences appear. More of both young and old respondents approved of government medical aid in 1960 than either earlier, in 1956, or later, in 1972, even though the pattern of approval fluctuated differently for younger than for older people.

Cohort-sequential research focuses on the variation in change patterns for different cohorts of people. Woodruff and Birren (1972) studied personality-test performance of people

TABLE 2.9 Attitudes toward federal governmental medical-aid programs (percentage in favor)

Age group	1956[a]	1960	1964	1968	1972
21–24	70	77	67	67	
25–28		69	62	56	56
Change:		**−1**	**−15**	**−12**	**−11**
61–64	69	84	64	72	
65–68		85	73	76	69
Change:		**+16**	**−11**	**+12**	**−4**
Total sample	70	77	65	67	61
Change:		**+7**	**−12**	**+2**	**−6**

[a]The questions read, for 1956 and 1960, "The government ought to help people get doctors and hospital care at low cost"; for 1964 and 1968, "Some people say the government in Washington ought to help people get doctors and hospital care at low cost; others say the government should not get into this. Have you been interested enough in this to favor one side or the other?"; and for 1972, "There is much concern about the rapid rise in medical and hospital costs. Some feel there should be a government insurance plan which would cover all medical expenses. Others feel that medical expenses should be paid by individuals through private insurance like the Blue Cross. Which side do you favor?"

Source: Bengtson and Cutler, 1976. (Data were made available by the Interuniversity Consortium for Political and Social Research, through the USC Political and Social Data Laboratory.)

who were in college in 1950 compared to those who were in college in 1970. Those who had been in college in 1950 were significantly less "neurotic" both in youth and middle age than the cohort who were in college in 1970. The latter cohort presumably would continue to be a more "neurotic" group of people throughout their lives than those who were in college earlier—and perhaps also than those who were in college later.

In a recent paper on the usefulness and complexities of cohort analysis, Cutler (1977) points to the three kinds of differences mentioned by Schaie (1965, 1973) that enter into cohort comparisons: (1) aging effects—differences due to the sociological, psychological, and biological effects of growing older; (2) cohort effects—differences due to variations in socialization and historical experiences; and (3) period effects—differences attributable to the particular historical period in which the measurement or observation was made. Cutler points out that each of the three effects he mentions is a statistical function of the other two, and thus there are design problems in trying to separate them. As he puts it, "Most of the cohort analysis based

upon successive cross-sectional samples has used what might be called the 'ocular centroid' approach—visual examination of the cohort matrix until something hits the analyst between the eyes" (Cutler, 1977, p. 10).

Cutler suggests, for example, that we should standardize responses so that they would be equivalent in weight. This approach would enable us to use uniform statistical techniques such as regression analysis or successive analyses of variance to estimate the relative importance of aging, cohort, or period effects. Such procedures would not, unfortunately, be without their own problems. Standardizing responses often means distorting their meaning to some extent. Ignoring interaction effects produces another kind of distortion. Glenn (1975) offers an approach that objectifies Cutler's "ocular centroid" one: the use of "side information," or information known to the person analyzing the data that is outside the cohort analysis itself.

THEORETICAL PERSPECTIVE

The kind of research preferred will differ with the kind of theoretical "world view." Baltes, Reese, and Nesselroade (1977) state that the criteria for determining what is true are not the same for different world views. For example, one basic dichotomy that would lead to differential analysis is mechanistic versus organismic systems, discussed in Chapter 1. The basic "facts" for mechanistic systems are observations, and a basic technique for determining whether these observations show significant differences in reactive change would be to apply some form of analysis of variance. The major criterion of validity in mechanistic research would be generalizability of inferences across people, settings, and time. Most of our present methodology has this aim.

The basic facts for organismic systems, on the other hand, are inferences. Because from this position, cognitive processes, for example, would be "emergent"—not predictable from past experience—traditional statistical techniques would be irrelevant. To show that, under given circumstances, change is transformational or qualitative (developmental), one might be more interested in explaining the process by determining the changing dimensions of the system along the way than in explaining what outside causes would induce change in supposedly passive subjects. Organismic researchers would prefer the techniques of logic, focusing on "dynamic interaction, simultaneous mutual causation, joint concern for ontogenetic and historical change, and a lack of complete determinacy" (Baltes et al., 1977, p. 27).

EXTERNAL VALIDITY

Different world views would lead to differences in the kinds of validation procedures necessary. According to the dialectic perspective, for example, the whole is not just the sum of its parts but an organized totality in which the interactions among the parts are strategic to un-

derstanding the whole. The validation process becomes the inverse of the traditional one now used. Table 2.10 contrasts the two procedures. It is evident not only that the steps are in different order but that they involve different kinds of processes and are aimed at different goals.

One basic difference between the two approaches is the use of empirical, experimental research versus naturalistic observation. Another is the interpretation of interaction effects. In traditional (mechanistic) analysis, interactions are seen as errors. In dialectic (organismic) analysis, they are the important foci of behavior. The implications of these two approaches are fundamental and affect our interpretations of most of our research information.

TABLE 2.10 Validation procedures for traditional and dialectic world views

	Traditional	Dialectic
Step 1.	*Statistical conclusion-validity*. Demonstrate that a potential cause and its potential effect do indeed covary or show a significant statistical relationship. Approach is empirical, external manipulation of artificially controlled situations.	*External validity*. Determine the adequacy with which the organized complexity and its reciprocal interactions are "dimensionalized"—the extent to which they fit the theoretical assumptions. Approach is rational rather than empirical, derived by cognitive analysis of naturally occurring behavior.
Step 2.	*Internal validity*. Eliminate alternatively possible explanations so that only one potential cause stands out.	*Construct validity*. Determine the principles of organization that link the various dimensions—the formal and final cause—using logic.
Step 3.	*Construct validity*. Refine constructs used to eliminate possible confounding variables.	*Internal validity*. Specify sequence of formal causes that lead to final cause, using logic.
Step 4.	*External validity*. Ensure that the cause/effect relationship demonstrated is generalizable across different people, settings, and times of measurement.	*Statistical conclusion validity*. Develop statistical statements about the linkages among the principles of organization.

Source: Hultsch and Hickey, 1978.

DIFFERENTIAL RELIABILITY AND VALIDITY

As noted earlier, another basic problem in comparing performance at different ages is the probability that the same measures may not measure the same things at different ages. Most of our present cognitive measures, for example, were devised for children and youth. Expecting older people to react to them the same way—even if the subjects have the same underlying (genotypic) ability—leads to serious errors (Labouvie, 1980). For example, older people have accumulated a large store of information over the years. Can we assume that a set amount of irrelevant information included as conflicting stimuli in a reaction-time experiment is equally irrelevant for youth, who have little stored information, as for older subjects, whose accumulation of information is enormous?

The life-span contribution to developmental research has shown that changes occur in different patterns over different characteristics (*multidimensionality*), that changes occur along different trajectories for different people and behaviors (*multidirectionality*), and that there is increasing *variability* in all characteristics with age (Baltes & Baltes, 1980). Any kind of change can start at different times, move along at different rates, and show different forms for different people and different characteristics (Nesselroade & Harkins, 1980). Some characteristics may first increase and then decrease. Others may do the opposite: first decrease and then increase. People may be increasing in one way as they decrease in another. The discussion earlier in this chapter on models of development concluded with the suggestion that the picture is very complicated and that any simple model or theory is inaccurate. Because of this complexity, the problems of research are multiple, and the conclusions to be drawn should be arrived at cautiously.

Summary

A variety of theories and models for development have been proposed for changes past adolescence. The simplest and most appealing to the public are stage theories that make assumptions of universality, sequentiality, teleology, and adaptive purpose that render them suspect to scientific psychologists. Some stage theories are based on structural change, such as Kohlberg's moral-judgment model derived from Piaget's cognitive-development theory. Some, such as Havighurst's "developmental tasks," are based on life situations. Some, such as Erikson's, are based on sequences of critical issues faced at different points of life.

Critics of these neat models say that similar behavior can occur at the same age because of common experiences within a common culture and prefer a model that makes fewer assumptions, like social-learning theory, which stresses the social determinants of adult behavior and urges a "molecular" instead of a "molar" approach, restricting the search for causes of present behavior to recent instead of past events. An even wider view is suggested by Brim, by Neugarten and Datan, and by Lowenthal, who in different ways say that we are not yet ready for a final word on life-span developmental models and should pursue a broad spectrum of research strategies. Riegel's dialectic model, in fact, attempts to incorporate all factors, with both individual and environment as active participants in a two-way interaction throughout life.

Given the diversity of life views and models, and the problems inherent in measuring change and development, current methodological theories stress the multiplicity of design problems involved in life-span research. Age differences are not necessarily age changes, and cross-sectional research is being supplanted by longitudinal and even more sophisticated cross-sequential designs proposed by Schaie. Even so, problems such as survivor bias and the reliability and validity of measurement over time alert us to the need for new techniques if we are to be able to answer basic questions about ontogenetic development over the life span.

3

Ageism, Age Expectations, and Age Bias

Even though chronological age has minimal relevance to development during adulthood and old age, it does have a profound effect on our interpretation of that development. Age expectations influence our judgments of our own progress as well as that of others. They also underlie our positive or negative attitudes about different ages and our preconceived notions about what people of different ages are like.

From early childhood on, our first question when we meet new people is "How old are you?" Children are more likely to ask this question directly and explicitly; the rest of us make our estimates so automatically that we are not aware we are doing so. Whether we ask the question overtly or implicitly, however, the answer is certain to determine our assumptions about what attitudes those other people have toward the world, what life experiences they have had, and what they want out of life. Furthermore, we share these assumptions with most others who belong to our culture (Neugarten & Datan, 1973). In fact, such stereotypes are group expectations of how people should be and how they should act. They come from our early socialization and prove remarkably resistant to change in the face of contradictory evidence.

Parts of this chapter are adapted from "'How old are you?'— The question of age bias in the counseling of adults," by Lillian Troll and Carol Nowak, *Counseling Psychologist*, 1976, 6(1), 41-44, and from other earlier writings.

When they keep us from seeing individualized characteristics, they could be called *biases* or *prejudices*. They can distort judgments and decisions and can warp all interactions.

Kinds of age bias

In general, three kinds of age bias or age prejudice can be noted:

1. Age restrictiveness: setting of age limits for any behavior
2. Age distortion: misperceiving the behavior or characteristics to fit age stereotypes
3. "Ageism": negative attitudes toward any age group

All three kinds of bias are applied to people of all ages. For example, the norm of dignity can be just as restrictive for middle adults as the norm of disengagement from social roles can be for older people. Misperceptions about children and adolescents are probably as common as misperceptions about older generations. And many people have more-negative attitudes toward adolescents than they do toward the old. However, studies to date point to different kinds of bias for different times of life—restrictiveness as the primary mode for youth and negative attitudes for the older years.

AGE RESTRICTIVENESS

Restrictions can be expressed in a variety of ways. Limits can be set for entry into or exit from particular roles or activities. One can be considered either too young or too old to go to school, to hold certain jobs, to get married, to make political decisions, or to engage in specific kinds of recreation. Limits can be set on what is appropriate behavior for a given age group and what is inappropriate for that age. It may be considered proper to be impulsive or romantic in youth but not later on. It may be considered desirable to be sober and restrained in middle age but not earlier. Many studies (for example, Neugarten, Moore, & Lowe, 1965) found remarkable consistency among Americans—young and old, middle-class and working-class—with regard to their ideas about age-appropriate behavior.

AGE EXPECTATIONS

Our general age expectations are summarized as follows, by age period.

Youth.   Primarily, men and women in their 20s are supposed to be entering into adult roles. They are supposed to be establishing themselves in life, job, and family and to be turning to each other and away from their parents and other kin. The 20s are supposed to be a time of goal orientation, of job and family establishment, and of movement and activity. Men and women are expected to do things at different ages—most age limits are usually earlier for women. In fact, Atchley and George (1973) found that standards for women are generally tied more closely to chronological age altogether. For example, women are expected to marry between 19 and 24, men between 20 and 25. Although it is considered important for young men to be getting started in the job world, getting married and having children is most important for women. For women, also, youth is the prime time for "good looks"; for men, it is for strength and virility.

Middle age.   In general, competence, maturity, responsibility, and stability are the normative personality characteristics for middle-aged adults, although there are foreshadowings of unpleasant things to come. Middle age is a time of control and restraint. It is supposed to be a time of arrival—a time to reap the harvest of earlier labors in the form of vicarious enjoyment of the successes of children and grandchildren, status due to job success, and an active social life with friends and acquaintances. Both men and women are supposed to stop parenting and to begin grandparenting. Wood's (1971) respondents in Wisconsin saw middle-aged people as "too old to adopt a baby" but right for grandparenting.

Sex differences persist in the stereotypes for middle age. Middle-aged men are supposed to be at the "prime of life," to accomplish most, hold their top jobs, and have the most responsibilities. Middle-aged women, however, are considered to be at the "tail end" of responsibilities and accomplishments, because their principal duties are seen as child rearing and then child launching. They are supposed to "let go" of their children and remove themselves from this central role that has so far regulated their lives. Men are supposed to reap the harvest of their own labors, but women are supposed to get their status from the job success of their husbands or, to some extent, of their sons.

Two major areas of stereotyping about middle age for women are the menopause and the "empty nest." The menopause is supposed to be accompanied not only by distressing physical symptoms but by a wide variety of psychological discomforts as well. The departure of children is supposed to leave women desolate and deserted. Finally, middle-aged women are expected to show dramatic declines in physical attractiveness, particularly from "the neck up." In some cases, it is as though a quick "haglike" transformation into old age were expected to take place, a move from youthful beauty to a wrinkled, gray, and pallid decline.

But women are not the only ones to be stereotyped. Older men are supposed to lose health, strength, power, and sexual potency. The very attributes that enhance the attractiveness of women and men in their prime are those that are seen to be lost at older ages.

Old age.   The overall expectation for old age is gloomy. Typically, old people are portrayed as socially, psychologically, and physically isolated, restricted, and deteriorated. According to a recent Harris poll (Harris and Associates, 1975), the image of old people in America is that of "senile, lonely, used-up bodies, rotting away and waiting to die."

The expectation is that old people should be leaving former roles and not thinking about entering new, age-inappropriate ones. It is time to retire from work and assume the leisurely, more aimless role of retiree. It is not the time to run for public office. Neugarten, Moore, and Lowe's (1965) respondents thought people should be ready to retire between the ages of 60 and 65. In fact, 65 was seen as a cutoff age for almost all activities. Subjects in another study, that of Whittington, Wilkie, and Eisdorfer (1972), did not differentiate between 65- and 75-year-old men—when you're old, you're old!

Some specific examples of behavior not approved of for old people (Wood & O'Brien, 1971) were (1) a widower of 70 remarrying against the objection of his children; (2) a retired couple wearing shorts to go shopping downtown; (3) a recently widowed woman of 65 buying a red convertible; (4) a retired couple attending nightclubs frequently; and (5) a 68-year-old widow inviting a widower to her home for dinner.

Sex differences in stereotyping appear for old age as well as for younger ages, but here they tend toward less differentiated rather than more differentiated roles. Neugarten and Gutmann (1968) report that the old man in the Thematic Apperception Test picture they used was seen as losing his familial authority and becoming a passive figure, while the old woman was perceived as relatively demanding and aggressive. Both were seen as moving toward the behavior characteristic of the opposite sex.

There is another aspect to age restrictiveness: there is greater pressure to act one's age during the entry phase than during the exit phase of adulthood. Another way to look at this aspect is that it is worse to be an "age deviant" in youth than in the later years of life. Pincus, Wood, and Kondrat (1974, p. 3) state

In comparing the entry and exit scores within each sample group, both the young and old respondents have higher restrictiveness for entry items than for exit items. . . . This also confirms our earlier finding that there is a greater acceptance of age as a criterion for entry into roles and for engaging in behavior than as a criterion for relinquishing roles and behaviors.

Similarly, Troll and Schlossberg (1970) found that counselors felt there should be less leeway allowed for the timing of the onset of adult activities, such as beginning career and marriage, than for the timing of the events of later life, such as job success or retirement. This aspect of age restrictiveness may be seen as a paradox because youth is also allowed greater experimentation and vacillation in roles (Wood, 1971).

Social time, age grading, age status, and age norms refer to present-day social realities, as demonstrated in a series of empirical studies by Neugarten and her colleagues. One of the first studies in this series found that middle-aged people perceive adulthood as composed of four different life periods, each with its characteristic pattern of personal and social behavior: young adulthood, maturity, middle age, and old age (Neugarten & Peterson, 1957). Progression from one period to the next was described along one or more of five pathways: career line (such as major promotion and retirement), health and physical vigor, the family cycle (children entering school and leaving the family home), psychological attributes ("Middle age is when you become mellow"), and social responsibilities ("Old age is when you can take things easy and let others do the worrying").

There appears to be a set of social-age definitions that provide a frame of reference by which the experiences of adult life are perceived as orderly and rhythmical. Although perceptions vary somewhat by age and sex, and especially by social class (for example, middle age and old age are seen as beginning earlier by working-class than by middle-class people), the high degree of consensus was striking.

Expectations regarding the timing of major life events can also be charted. Interviewees respond easily to questions such as "What is the best age for a man to marry?" or "What is the best age to become a grandmother?" and they readily give chronological ages for phrases such as "a mature woman" or "when a man should hold his top job." Most middle-class men and women agree that a man is young between 18 and 22, middle-aged between 40 and 50, and old between 65 and 75 and that men have the most responsibilities between 35 and 50. There is greater consensus regarding age-appropriate behavior for women than for men and greater consensus regarding age expectations for the period of young adulthood than for moving on to successive phases of maturity and old age. Once people are locked into appropriate adult tracks, it seems, they can be allowed some leeway in adapting them to fit their personality.

SOCIAL CLOCKS AND AGE DEVIANCY

When people are expected to behave in particular ways, they feel they have failed if they don't. Even if Western culture does not have elaborate initiation ceremonies to mark the moment of leaving one age period and entering another, we do have what Neugarten (1968) calls "built-in social clocks" by which to judge whether we are on time in particular behaviors. There is a time to go to school and a time to marry, a time to have one's first child and a time to start a career. To be "off time" is to be an "age deviant." It feels good to be on time, and it feels bad to be off time—either early or late. A woman who was not married by 25 used to (and maybe still does) feel shame. It is as "bad" to have a baby at 15 as at 45. A man who is still in school at 30 feels shame. Huyck (1970) found, for instance, that with advancing age army officers who were age deviants in their careers—either early or late—were more and more sensitive to age in their attitudes about career competence.

Thus, the system of age expectations is normative. Everybody feels some degree of social pressure to conform to them. People know whether they are "on time" or "off time" and, Neugarten believes, try to be more "on time." They tell you "I married early" or "I was late getting started because of the Depression." Furthermore, they feel good about themselves when they are "on time," but they feel bad if they have been either early or late. People seem to take age norms so much for granted that they can't tell you how they learned these rules.

DISTORTION

Stereotypes or biases are frequently accompanied by distortion. Strong expectations for certain kinds of behavior do not so much cloud our vision as warp it. We tend to fit the perception to the expectation. If we expect adolescents to be extravagant and reckless, irresponsible and radical, we interpret their actions as extravagant and reckless, irresponsible and radical. If we expect old people to be rigid and conservative and short on intelligence, we interpret their behavior as rigid and conservative and short on intelligence.

Two separate investigations, Ahammer and Baltes (1972) and Bengtson (1971), compared the values and personality characteristics expressed by people of particular age groups with the values and personality characteristics attributed to them by people of other age groups. In general, the greatest distortions tended to be for the two extreme age groups: adolescence and old age. Judgments of the beliefs and reactions of young and middle adults tended to agree more with the beliefs and attitudes they reported for themselves.

NEGATIVE ATTITUDES

Robert Butler (1969) has written about the "ageism" prevalent in our society. Old age has a decidedly negative valence. People classified as "old"—and this may encompass anybody over 35, or even 20—are seen as intellectually unfit, narrow-minded, ineffective, and ready to die at any moment.

In a communication experiment, college students "talked down" to presumed children and old people but gave more complex instructions to those targets they believed were adults of their own age or older (Rubin & Brown, 1975). They demonstrated their expectations that "older people" would have deficient cognitive and personality structures and would need to be treated like children instead of adults.

The older one gets, the less exciting, full, and worthwhile one is expected to find life. It is no wonder, then, that people tend to consider themselves relatively younger as they get chronologically older (Streib, 1968). In fact, "felt" age or subjective age is more closely related to psychological adjustment than is actual chronological age (Peters, 1971). Those who think of themselves as younger tend to be better adjusted, to have higher morale, and to react more favorably to role changes than do their age mates who have older age identifications.

Two large-scale surveys of Americans during the last few years have documented the sweeping negative attitudes toward older citizens. One by Harris and Associates (1975), which was sponsored by the National Council of Retired Citizens, found that younger Americans see older Americans as dull, narrow-minded, ineffective, sexually finished, and rotting away in poor health, too poor to pay for proper medical care. Another, by the University of Southern California Andrus Gerontology Center, found almost all the same kinds of negative images (Bengtson, Kasschau, & Ragan, 1977).

Age of respondent.   Age concepts seem to be learned early in life and modified only partially thereafter. Even before they start school, children assign ages to figures in drawings (Britton & Britton, 1969a). By ages 5 and 6, they associate "old" with physical decline and death (Treybig, 1974). However, they do not attribute particular personality characteristics to particular ages until the school years. This differentiation seems to be a part of general cognitive development (Britton & Britton, 1969b; Hickey, Hickey, & Kalish, 1968; Hickey & Kalish, 1968).

One study conducted with Southwestern schoolchildren in grades 6, 8, 10, and 12 found that stories written about pictures of young, middle-aged, and old men were, like those in previous investigations, stereotyped and superficial. However, unlike other groups studied, these subjects depicted old men as good and wise, not lonely, bored, and inactive (Thomas & Yamamoto, 1975). Because the girls were even more likely to see old men as nice than were the boys, there may be more of a sex effect than has generally been found.

Studies of children's literature (for example, Robin, 1973; Seltzer & Atchley, 1971a) that examined the way older people were presented did not find a direct relationship between the number of old people pictured and the negative attitudes or stereotypes about them (Seltzer & Atchley). There *was* evidence, though, that age of the characters presented in school readers varied by grade levels (Robin). For example, infants and young children were more likely to be found in first- and second-grade readers, while teenagers and adults of all ages were found in higher-grade readers.

Adolescents on the whole tend to be lowest of all age groups in restrictiveness (Sabatini & Nowak, 1975). Their descriptions of adult characteristics are more valid than adults' descriptions of them (Ahammer & Baltes, 1972). However, they still tend to exaggerate older people's needs for dependency and nurturance.

College students who have close contact with their grandparents or other older people are less likely to have negative attitudes toward the old.

Conversely, those who had experience with institutionalized older people hold more-negative attitudes. It is certainly not surprising that contact with more "normal" living old people produces more-positive attitudes than does contact with more "abnormal" socially isolated old people.

Among adults, there is an essentially linear relationship between age and restrictiveness. Middle-aged people are more age restrictive than young adults, and the old are the most age restrictive of all (for example, see Kogan & Wallach, 1961; Wood & O'Brien, 1971). Age distortion seems to follow a different pattern. Ahammer and Baltes (1972) report, for instance, that their middle-aged subjects were the most likely to misperceive the characteristics of other age groups and to see old age in a negative light. These subjects had a dim view of their own future. On the other hand, middle-aged mothers surveyed by Traxler (1973) were slightly more tolerant of "old people" than their college-student daughters. They might not want to get old themselves but they can put up with people who are old, who perhaps help them feel younger.

Older people are not exempt from age bias. Although they see middle age more positively than do college students (Whittington, Wilkie, & Eisdorfer, 1972) and old age less negatively than do most younger people (Colette-Pratt, 1975), they are notably age restrictive. Older people are particularly intolerant of disabled people (Gozali, 1970), at least if they are not disabled themselves. This attitude is opposite to the tolerance of the middle-aged for the old and needs more study.

When Colette-Pratt (1975) tried to find the strongest predictors of ageism, she found negative attitudes toward death and poor health the strongest. All age groups, from college students to old people themselves, devalued old age. The prevalence of ageism is evident not only in self-reported attitudes in children's literature but also in the mass media. In a brief review of television programming between 1969 and 1971, Aranoff (1974) found that only 4.9% of the characters were old and that aging was associated with evil, failure, and unhappiness. Old age became a popular subject of movies and television drama during the 1970s. The pervasive theme of these shows is that of heroism in accepting an abused and outcast status. Resolutions are commonly a mixture of defiance, deviance, and pathos. A theme of death underlies all action. In a study of magazine fiction, Martel (1968) described the situation of older people as one of "psychological abandonment"; that is, they were excluded from the mainstream of life. There is similarly a pervasive negativism about old age in jokes and cartoons (Palmore, 1971)—a negativism that is especially evident with regard to old women.

Social class.   Middle-class Americans tend to assign older ages to life events and to labels such as "middle age" than do working-class Americans (Neugarten & Moore, 1968). For example, working-class respondents are likely to set the beginning of middle age around 35 and middle-class respondents around 55, even though their descriptions of what middle age is like are essentially similar. Middle-class people may also have fewer negative attitudes about old age and tend to be less age restrictive (Hickey, Hickey, & Kalish, 1968).

Education.   So far as amount of education is concerned, more schooling is generally associated with more positive feelings toward the aged (for example, see Campbell, 1971; Thorson, Hancock, & Whatley, 1974). Troll and Schlossberg (1971) found that counselors who had taken counseling courses were more likely to be age restrictive than those who had not. The effect of such courses seems to have been to lead the counselors to believe that they knew the "facts" about age decrements in abilities that would justify restrictive counseling.

What is more, all studies to date show that professional people who work with older clients or patients view them as rigid and slow to respond to treatment. Thus, treatment prescriptions for anyone defined as "old" would be more likely limited to custodial, impersonal care. This is as true of physicians and dentists as of physical therapists, nurses, and social workers (for example, see Coe, 1967).

Urban versus rural environment.   The perceptions of rural dwellers as compared with urban dwellers are more like those of working class compared with middle class (Youmans, 1971). That is, old age is seen to occur earlier in the rural than in the urban environment. Also, both young and old respondents in rural areas see early-middle-aged people (22 to 45) as the most respected and most influential.

State of the field

Unfortunately, almost all the studies reviewed here are cross-sectional. People of different ages were examined at the same point in time. What we are guessing to be age changes in attitudes may in fact be only age differences, and we may be seeing historical rather than developmental effects. The finding that older adults are more age restrictive or more age biased than younger adults or adolescents, for example, may be due to a general societal shift away from age restrictiveness. The present group of adolescents and young adults may continue to be more flexible and less biased than their parents throughout their lives.

In addition, most studies in the field are preliminary. They tend to be deficient—or at least casual—in sampling, in methodology, and in interpretation. Most samples are small in size and seem to be obtained on a "catch as catch can" basis. Age categories are particularly arbitrary. Definitions of "youth" range from 10 to 30, and of "old" from 40 to 90. It is often difficult to judge whether a behavior is characteristic of "old" or of "older" individuals. This difficulty can be awkward if "older" is just "older than college students."

One psychologist in the forefront of age-stereotyping research is Nathan Kogan, who has been studying this subject for over 20 years. In a recent review of the research to date (Kogan, 1979), he concludes that we need much better data before we can assume that negative attitudes reflect age bias. We have long noticed that rich old people are never labeled old and that media presentations of "old people" seek out the "poor, dumb, and ugly"—the derelicts of society. Kogan criticizes most of the research as poor methodologically in a number of ways. The fact that little relation has been found between expressed attitude and behavior and that specific evaluations of people are based more on their occupations than on their ages, leads us to suspect that many negative attitudes reflect actual economic and educational discrepancies.

Age consciousness

To what extent do people feel identified with their own age group? Obviously, the extent of age bias, or anyway of negative attitudes toward a particular age group, is going to affect the willingness of people that age to feel identified with others that age. This is certainly true of old people who generally call themselves middle-aged rather than old. On the other hand, according to Rosow (1967, p. 14), "one of the most insidious" consequences of ageism is that older people view their own future selves negatively. They "may not be unfriendly, complaining, closed-minded, lonely, poor, or sick now, but how long can they hang in there, with 'most' older people having lost out to these perils?"

In 1970, Neugarten wrote that antagonisms between the young and old were beginning to appear and that anger toward the old might be on the increase (Neugarten, 1970). However, she did not see any convincing evidence for what Rose (1965) was calling the "subculture of the aged." A definition of a subculture would include shared values, a group identity, using each other as a reference group, shared norms, similar behavior, assigned behavior or roles, specialized institutions, maybe even a special language. This pattern seemed much more true of youths in the 1960s than of other age groups. Recently, though, several formalized groups of older people have emerged, which suggests that Rose's prediction may be valid. Witness the power in Washington of the National Council of Older Americans and the American Association of Retired Persons, as well as the even more visible and visionary Gray Panthers.

The courses of life

To speak of *the* life course ignores the fact that there is usually more than one. As Havighurst (1958, pp. 43–44) pointed out,

> The word *aging* is extraordinarily fluid in its meaning. The term is used by the biologist, psychologist, and sociologist, each against his own frame of reference....
>
> In the biologic sense, aging is a concept that can be applied to some organs and systems of the body while it is still quite young. The red corpuscles and the skin cells age and die from the earliest days of life. By the time a man or woman is in the 40s, a good part of the body is showing phenomena of senescence.... In the psychologic sense, aging is both objective and subjective. There are objective changes in the abilities which psychologists measure—cognitive and perceptive. There are also changes in the way a person feels about himself.... The experience of growing older is inescapable to people after 40. Increasingly, during the next two decades, the person suffers insults to his ego which he interprets as the cost of growing older.... Looking at aging from the sociologic point of view means looking at the way a social group defines old age and middle age.... Social groups make what may be called a functional definition and a legal definition of aging. According to the functional definition, a person is old when he is too old to carry on some important social function. For instance, people are judged to be old in relation to their capacity to work.... Society gives a legal definition of old age if it writes laws for social security, and this legal definition may carry over into the attitudes of people and thus contribute to a social definition of old age.

We can talk about people's physical age, their psychological age, and their social age, and there may be great differences in the three in any one individual. It is possible for a man to be physically middle-aged, psychologically young, and socially old, for instance. Consider a 30-year-old college professor, an expert in his field. From lack of exercise, his body has weakened. From constant thinking, his mind is keen and young. From lack of social participation except as an authority to others, his social interactions resemble those of an oldish man. Similarly, a 30-year-old laborer or lower-class housewife who has been out of school and has not functioned intellectually for 10 years might be physically young, psychologically old, and socially middle-aged.

Kastenbaum introduced the term "personal age" to mean how old a person seems to him- or herself; he counterbalances this with "interpersonal age," to describe how old that person seems to others. In one article written with several of his students, he reported on an "Ages of Me" test he devised to measure the various personal ages: look age, feel age, and so on (Kastenbaum, Derbin, Sabatini, & Artt, 1972). People estimate how old they feel, look, have interests and activities, look to people who know them casually, and look to people who know them well. Because there is no typical behavior for any age, let alone older ages, this multiple approach should have value for future research.

Consequences

So far, the discussion has been focused on perceptions, expectations, and stereotypes. That these are translated into actual inequalities has been demonstrated by Palmore and Manton (1973). They look at differences in income, education, and occupation for people of different race, sex, and age. As shown in Figure 3.1, the greatest handicap in income is age. The existence of double jeopardy or triple jeopardy is demonstrated in Tables 3.1 through 3.4. Black old women are much the worst off, particularly in income. (The lowest numbers in the tables show the least equality or the most inequality.) Or, to put it another way, men and older people are more affected by race inequality than women and younger people; age has more effect on men than on women and on non-Whites than on Whites. In talking about income, the authors say "As for whether non-White women suffer more from race than sex inequality, the relevant comparison shows that they are much less equal to non-White men than to White women" (p. 367). There seem to be trends from 1950 to 1970 toward greater equality in all three areas between the races, but little or no change by sex. As for age inequality, that seems to be getting worse!

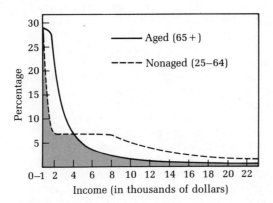

Figure 3.1. Percentage distribution of aged and nonaged by per capita income for 1969. *(Source: Palmore and Manton, 1973.)*

TABLE 3.1 Equality indexes (EI) showing joint effects of race, sex, and age (1970)

Groups	Income EI	Occupation EI	Education EI
Non-White 65+/ White 25–64	50	47[a]	36
Females 65+/males 25–64	25	52[a]	67
Non-White females/ White males	40	39[a]	77
Non-White females 65+/White males	13	26[a]	40

[a] Estimate for 1970.
Source: Palmore and Manton, 1973.

TABLE 3.2 Non-White/White income equality index for sex and age subgroups (1970)

	Males	Females	Total
25–64	65	96	81
65+	67	82	76
Total	68	97	83

Source: Palmore and Manton, 1973.

TABLE 3.3 Female/male income equality index for race and age subgroups (1970)

	White	Non-White	Total
25–64	36	58	39
65+	57	70	59
Total	43	61	45

Source: Palmore and Manton, 1973.

TABLE 3.4 65+/25–64 income equality index for race and sex subgroups (1970)

	White	Non-White	Total
Males	44	45	45
Females	82	62	82
Total	65	57	65

Source: Palmore and Manton, 1973.

Summary

Age is one of the basic categories into which people classify themselves and everybody else. Specific kinds of behavior are expected from people of different ages, and these expectations can have important consequences, particularly if age restrictions are involved—if certain behavior is only appropriate at certain ages or if everybody of a certain age must behave in a specific way. There is a tendency to distort others' behavior to fit age expectations. It is considered good to be on time and bad to be an age deviant, in accord with "built-in social clocks." Finally, some ages are viewed negatively, particularly old age. Age concepts are learned very early in life and are remarkably persistent. Sex differences pervade all age expectations. Adolescents tend to be less restrictive in their age expectations than people of other ages. Middle-class people tend to be less restrictive than working-class people, and more educated people are less restrictive than less educated people.

4

Variability

People differ as widely in timing and pattern of development as they do in everything else. Men and women follow different life paths. Middle-class men and women age differently from working-class men and women. The timing of events is often different for Blacks and Whites, for Italians, Irish, Poles, and Jews. Each generation starts out differently from any other and moves along in its own unique way. Moreover, between-group differences are superimposed on fundamental individual differences. And these variations themselves can intertwine. For example, a difference between middle-class and working-class women may be a function not only of class differences but also of historical time. A century ago, the "empty nest" experience might have been more alike for all women than it is today, because there were probably fewer differences, by social class, in childbearing patterns. All women—except spinsters and the infertile—would have continued to bear and raise children until almost the end of their lives. In general, though, it is safe to say that people are not alike at any time of life, from the moment after conception to the moment of dying. This chapter considers some prominent separating influences on adult development: gender, social class, ethnicity, and generation.

Gender differences

From early adolescence on, gender is one of the most important factors in development. Women move through their adult years and their old age in a notably different fashion from the way men do. Perhaps only the variable of health has as great an effect. In part, this difference is due to such biological factors as differential longevity and, now, differential life expectancy, which lead to differential health and vigor. Tables 4.1, 4.2, and 4.3 show sex differences in death rates and the resultant sex ratios by age, at least in 1971.

Table 4.1 shows that more males die at every age, from premature infants to men over 85. Table 4.2 shows that, from adulthood on, more

TABLE 4.1 Death rates in
males and females, by age, in 1972
(United States)

Age	Deaths per 1000 population	
	Male	Female
Under 1	17.8	13.7
1–4	0.8	0.0
5–14	0.5	0.3
15–24	1.7	0.6
25–34	1.8	0.8
35–44	3.2	1.8
45–54	8.7	4.4
55–59	17.0	8.0
60–64	26.3	12.0
65–69	40.3	19.5
70–74	59.0	30.3
75–79	86.9	51.2
80–84	128.0	87.6
85 and over	184.2	157.9
Stillbirths	16.3	14.7

Source: U.S. Department of Health, Education, and Welfare, 1973.

women are living than men of the same age. After the age of 75, there are 156 women to every 100 men. Under 25 years of age, in 1971, there were slightly fewer women than men—98 women to 100 men—which may be explained by higher birthrates for boys. Even boys' higher death rates don't counter initial male oversupply until the adult years.

TABLE 4.2 Sex ratio in the U.S. population by age

Age	Women per 100 men
Under 25	98.4
25–44	104.7
45–64	109.1
65+	138.5
65–74	128.8
75 and over	156.2

Source: Brotman, 1971.

Table 4.3 shows that the longevity advantage of women went up between 1950 and 1960 and again between 1960 and 1970. In addition to biological and numerical gender differences,

TABLE 4.3 Sex-ratio trend in population

Year	Older women per 100 older men (65+)
1950	111.5
1960	120.7
1970	138.5

Source: Brotman, 1971.

differences in sex-role expectations affect how life events are interpreted, encouraged, or discouraged. In her discussion of age roles, Neugarten (1968) states that one should really speak of "age/sex roles," because men and women differ on every age expectation and age norm. Both men and women are generally expected to marry in their 20s, but women are expected to—and do—marry about two years earlier than men. Also, the implications of getting married or not getting married are different for men and women.

In the beginning, the human embryo is differentiated only genetically. Although genetic sex is established at the time of fertilization, the influence of these sex genes is not activated until the seventh week of fetal life, when gonadal and consequent hormonal differences develop. Even eight months later, at birth, however, sex differences in behavior or capacity are hard to find. But, although research has trouble finding differences, mothers, fathers, uncles, aunts, and grandparents do not. Infants are treated differently according to their gender from the very beginning (Moss, 1967). Girls are talked to and cuddled more; they are jostled less than boys. Boys initially are handled more often and more roughly than girls, but the amount of handling diminishes with age. Boys are also discouraged from clinging (Lewis, 1972). As children grow older, these differences in treatment are enhanced. In addition, boys are shown that they are considered to be of higher value. Over the next few months and years, boys gradually become more like what boys are expected to be, and girls become more like what girls are expected to be (Kagan & Moss, 1962).

Puberty brings wide physical divergence in appearance, size, strength, educational and intellectual performance, and conformity to prevailing sex-role stereotypes. Although most traits continue to vary more within each sex than between sexes, by early adulthood it is generally easy to distinguish between men and women, not only in appearance, but also in behavior and pattern of daily life. Societies often differ widely in what they consider proper feminine and masculine behavior, but all societies seem to differentiate between proper masculine and feminine behavior. The social clock and the developmental rhythm of a woman's life have very different timings from those of a man's life. And so far, in spite of the determination of many young—and older—adults of today to achieve a more uniform status and lifestyle, shifts in most sex-linked characteristics have been slow in coming.

The women's movement and the influx of women into the labor market have changed the character of family and job, but women's place in the family, at least after the birth of the first child, remains clearly different from men's place in the family. And women's status, earnings, and career progress in the job world are different from those of men. Men are much better off, as far as property and prestige are concerned, in more settled and more complex societies (Simmons, 1945). Women have the advantage in more primitive hunting and fishing groups. Culturally determined gender differences in patterns of sexuality, fertility, climacteric, and dealing with the losses of the later years stand out, too.

All this does not necessarily mean that one sex is better off than the other. When all differences are balanced out by the end of life, the score may be more equal than might be judged at some earlier time of life. For example, early in life men seem to have more power than do women, and, later, women seem to have better health than do men.

Social-class differences

Almost as pervasive as sex differences are those of social class. The lives and life spans of middle-class men and women differ in many ways from those of working-class men and women. Although many people would argue that there is a biological component to these differences (as they would argue for sex), class-linked variations in what people eat, where they live, what kinds of health care they experience, and how strenuous their work is also can affect physical characteristics and life expectancy. Class differences in education and associated lifestyle characteristics, such as time spent in reading and other intellectual endeavors, can affect cognitive performance, both initial levels as well as stability and decline over time. Greater conventionalism and traditionalism in values can affect personality, family, and career patterns. Such values are class linked.

Unfortunately, most research on the adult years has used middle-class, primarily White, samples, and most research on older people has used lower-class, primarily institutionalized or handicapped, samples. To eliminate the confounding effects of social class—or even to describe the dimensions of class differences that exist—we need much more balanced studies than we have so far had available.

Socioeconomic status can be measured in terms of income, education, or occupation, along a continuum of four broad categories: the very poor; the lower-middle class or blue-collar; the middle-income, or white-collar; and the upper-class or wealthy or highly educated. Variations

Tell me something about yourself.

Grandfather, age 76
Well, my dad was a superintendent of schools while I was going to school. We moved around some. I graduated from the university, specializing in dairy production. I joined the army and served overseas as a road engineer during the war.

Father, age 50
Born in North Dakota. I lived on the grounds of a hospital institution where my father was dairy herdsman. I lived there until I went into the service. I returned home and finished my education. Worked in the automobile industry for 20 years. Currently working on my master's degree.

Son, age 20
Looking back, it was probably the way I was raised in comparison to other kids, and then the position in the family—the oldest of four. I had to fight for what I'd get. You know, how late I could stay out at night and things my sister could do that I couldn't do that young.

Tell me something about yourself.

Grandmother, age 59
We were kept strict. My mother always worked. My father drank. They were born on the other side. It was church—everything in the Russian prayers.

Mother, age 39
My parents were very strict. You did what you were supposed to, and you didn't think about it. I changed my religion when I was about 10, from Greek Orthodox to Roman Catholic. We were very sheltered.

Daughter, age 12
It's pretty much just going to school. I went to catechism all last year. My father is good to me. He gets me almost everything I want, even if he can't afford it.

in these categories affect all phases of the life span. For example, the decrements associated with aging come later in life for people with higher socioeconomic status than for those with lower status. Health, longevity, and living arrangements are all affected by socioeconomic status. Even age perceptions are affected: people in the upper classes hold less-negative attitudes about older people, perhaps in part because they tend to be happier themselves (Bengtson, Kasschau, & Ragan, 1977). People who have higher incomes, education, and occupational levels, furthermore, tend to take a more active role in planning their lives, from early occupational and marriage choices to later job and family moves and retirement. Interactions with family, friends, and neighbors appear to be more frequent and to include more people among upper socioeconomic levels, at all ages.

Ethnic and cross-cultural differences

If we want to understand how growing up or growing older differs in different ecological and social settings, we can consider any distinct human subgroup as an ethnic or cultural entity. Thus, we can compare subgroups within a country, such as Blacks and Whites or Jews and Spanish-Americans in the United States, or we can compare the United States with Asia or Africa. Such comparisons have been more commonly undertaken by anthropologists and demographers than by psychologists, particularly by developmental psychologists interested in the years after childhood. Therefore, for our purposes we can't do much more than point out issues and problems.

One major problem in making such comparisons is getting truly equivalent data. As Gutmann (1977, p. 302) points out, "Overtly similar behaviors noted in different cultures can have markedly different functions relative to their setting, just as seemingly different behaviors can have similar functions." Clark (1967) believes that the general bias among most developmental psychologists toward the almost exclusive importance of development in childhood has blinded us to the orderly changes in personality that occur later in life, too. Cross-cultural, cross-national, cross-ethnic, and rural/urban comparisons could, however, shed light on such important issues as persistence versus change in adult personality and the psychological effects of longevity (Gutmann, 1977). To study most of these questions, we particularly need a combination of cross-sequential and cross-cultural design.

In this country, or in any country with more and less advantaged subgroups, we must remember that the less advantaged incur what the National Urban League (1964) has called "double jeopardy." In many cases, this can be more

accurately described as quadruple jeopardy; for example, in this country, one can be poor and Black and a woman *and* old. When Blacks, Mexican-Americans, and Anglos were compared in a recent Southern California study (Bengtson et al., 1977), multiple effects were obvious in self-perceived health, self-identification as old, and self-predicted length of future life (see Table 4.4 and Figures 4.1 and 4.2).

TABLE 4.4 Perceived health status by ethnicity

	Percent who consider their health to be poor or very poor		
	Black (N=413)	Mexican-American (N=449)	Anglo (N=407)
45–54	13.8	16.9	1.7
55–64	15.2	20.8	9.1
65–75	27.0	23.2	4.0

Source: Bengtson, Kasschau, and Ragan, 1977.

Anglos consistently tended to say they were in good health. Only 4% said their health was poor even when they were "old" (65–75). At the same age, 25% of the other two groups said they were in poor health. In fact, there were more reports of poor health by Blacks and Mexican-Americans between 45 and 54 than by Whites 20 years older. As for identification as old, the percentage of Whites who did so was consistently lower than that in the other two groups (see Figure 4.1). Only 30% of the Whites called themselves old at age 72–75. This was the percentage of the other two groups who called themselves old in their 50s. It is as if disadvantaged ethnic membership pushes one into old age 20 years ahead of one's time. However, more Blacks expected to live over 10 more years (Figure 4.2). Of those Blacks who reached their 70s, 70% expected to live to their 80s, but only 30% of the Anglos did and even fewer of the Mexican-Americans.

It is not hard to explain health and economic differences in terms of differential advantages. If one group has better access to health-yielding resources such as food, housing, or medical care, that group tends to profit from the relative advantage. Simmons (1945), an anthropologist, says that older people have better survival chances when there is group sharing of food.

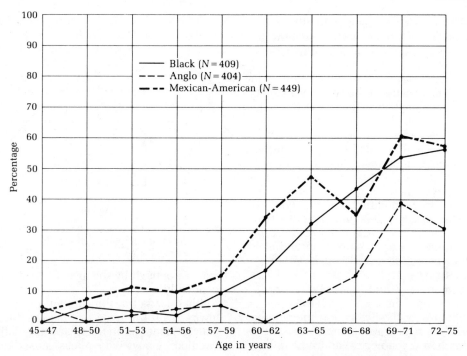

Figure 4.1. Percentage considering themselves "old" or "elderly." *(Source: Bengtson, Kasschau, and Ragan, 1977.)*

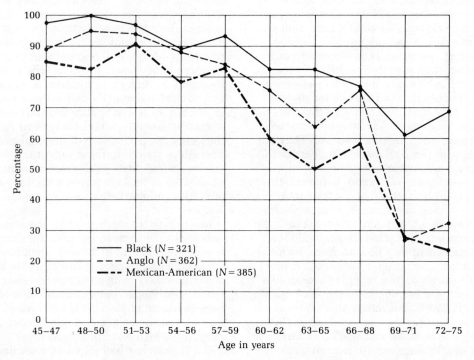

Figure 4.2. Percentage expecting to live over 10 more years. *(Source: Bengtson, Kasschau, and Ragan, 1977.)*

Such sharing is more common in hunting and fishing societies, or in more severe climates, he believes, than in more equitable and more settled agricultural groups.

Property rights have also tended to help older people survive, because if they have managed to accumulate enough over their lives they can reward younger people who help them. A linear relationship between advantages and survival seems reasonable. This relationship has not always been found in cross-cultural data, though. Both U-shaped and J-shaped curves of survival advantage or goodness of life are reported. Life can be easier in the middle range of advantage than in either extreme. It is possible to be too rich as well as too poor. Affluent societies can be as discriminatory or harsh on their old members as very poor societies, although probably in different ways.

Datan, Antonovsky, and Maoz (1981) found that it was not only the most "modern" or advantaged groups (in the five Israeli subcultures they studied) in which menopausal women showed the best psychological adjustment, but also the most "traditional." Women in the middle or "transitional" groups had the worst time with menopause, perhaps precisely because of their transitional status. They had lost the psychological advantages—freedom from restrictions in movement, in work, and in decision making—that would have come to them on reclassification from sexual to postsexual women. Postmenopausal Arab women who were unaffected by modernization fared better psychologically and socially, even though they had not gained the "liberation" advantages of the western European and American women. They had been worse off during their fertile years but reaped some advantage from aging.

Some writers (see, for example, Marotz-Baden & Tallman, 1977) suggest that the important factors in explaining differences among societies are the ways in which people think about themselves and about the options available to them—options that may be associated with the complexity of their society. This effect is illustrated in Figure 4.3. In a "simple" society—we are not talking about degree of mechanization or industrialization but rather about how much one has to learn before one can function independently—individuals can reach "maturity" at an early age. Perhaps they may even have

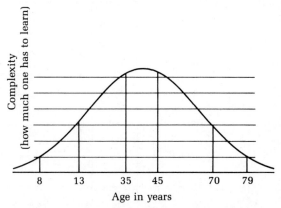

Figure 4.3. Level of development needed to "make it," by level of complexity of society.

learned enough by the age of 8 to survive independently.

When I was traveling around rural Mexican towns in 1974, I noted that most of the hotel management and marketplace negotiations were handled by boys who at least *looked* not much older than 8. They knew as much as was needed to assume responsibility for such jobs because the jobs were simpler than they would be in a more complex society. Of course, being a guest in their hotels or shopping in their markets was not as comfortable and well-oiled a procedure as it is in this country or in more "modern" hotels or markets in urban Mexican locations. In such rural societies, it would also be possible to remain "adult" almost to the end of life. Those few who survived illness or accidents, for example, could manage all right until they were 80, particularly if they did not need strength or speed. In these same rural towns, I also noted that very old-looking men and women seemed to be as involved with daily affairs of family and marketplace as younger men and women.

In a somewhat more complex society, individuals might not achieve the necessary competence before age 12 or 13 and might have to move out of the center of life by 70. In a very complex society such as ours, one might not reach "adulthood" before 35 and then might have to retreat at 45. This is true today at least for medical specialties and other occupations requiring a high level of competence.

If a culture has had a long-enough time to

survive in its ecological niche, it is likely to achieve a successful system of interrelationships, attitudes, and expectations for behavior. When this system is upset in any way, the members of the culture must adapt. During the period of transition, many people in that culture probably experience acute distress, like that of the "transitional" Israeli women, because they have grown up expecting one kind of future and now must face a different kind. This may be true even if, in the long run, they—or other people in the same category—may end up "better off."

Mass migrations into industrialized centers over the past couple of centuries have put previously rural groups into positions of profound transition and change. Rural people tend to maintain traditional, familistic, and intergenerational patterns of deference (Aldrich, 1974), while urban residents are more individuated and are not categorically deferential to elders. Adult development and aging would be very different under these two conditions. For example, Jackson (1970) found that Blacks in the rural U.S. South turn first to their families for help, while those in Southern cities turn to hospitals or churches. We cannot say how much of this kind of difference can be explained by transitionality and will resolve into other patterns later on.

Cohort, generation, and historical differences

We must separate developmental events from historical events. Bengtson and his associates (1977, p. 343) point out that "At the same time men and women progress through patterned sequences of roles, institutionalized within a particular social system, the very social system itself is undergoing change." This social change is happening in practically every society today, and the pace of this change has been accelerating. If we compare performance or behavior between two age groups at any one time, therefore, we cannot be sure whether any difference we find is attributable to age differences or to historical differences in the times the two groups were born and socialized. Most 70-year-olds today grew up in a very different world from the world of most 20-year-olds today. The

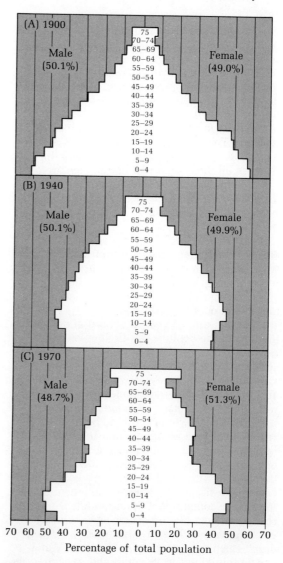

Figure 4.4. Age/sex population pyramids for the United States: 1900, 1940, 1970. (*Source: Cutler and Harootyan, 1975.*)

radio hadn't been invented; electricity was a luxury and cars a curiosity. There were large open spaces, couples had many children, and death was as common among infants and children as among older people. In fact, there weren't many older people around. Figure 4.4 shows population changes over the past century.

The relative proportions for both age and sex have changed dramatically between 1900 and

1970. From a neat age pyramid in 1900, somewhat skewed toward more men, we shifted to a distorted pattern in 1970, containing more older people than there used to be, particularly women, fewer children than there used to be, and a markedly pinched proportion of those between 20 and 40. Neugarten (1975) believes that those 65 and over will comprise between 10 and 12% of the American population for the next few decades. They will not increase to 30% by the year 2000, as the mass media are predicting, because all those who will be that age are already born. Moreover, in spite of some recent drops in birthrate, there is no reason to believe babies will not continue to be born during the next 25 years.

Period differences in technology, population, and living circumstances are translated into what have been called *cohort* or *generation effects*. These are illustrated in the following generalized descriptions of seven age cohorts living today—not counting children.

1. The 80- and 90-year-olds born at or before the turn of the century can be lumped together, because time moved less rapidly then. Their childhood was likely to have been in rural surroundings. Even if they grew up in cities, fields and vacant lots abounded, and most streets were unpaved. Horses were everywhere. The world had narrower geographic boundaries, but one tended to know more about the space within. It was important who one's next-door neighbor was, and a 10-mile separation between relatives was significant. The country's economy was on the rise, and a spirit of optimism made for greater commitment to one's endeavors. It really was possible to become successful by working hard and saving your money—if you didn't catch your death of cold. World War I caught this cohort in its youth and expanded its horizons.

2. The 70-year-olds, born a decade later, witnessed the enormous immigration of Eastern Europeans. In fact, most older people in America today were either immigrants or the children of recent immigrants. The Depression hit them in what would have been the full stride of their maturity and colored the rest of their lives, making them more pessimistic, more future oriented, and eventually perhaps more narcissistic. These are today's retirees, who are avid for the pleasure life and unwilling to be a burden on their children.

Tell me something about yourself.

Grandfather, age 89
I was born on a fruit farm. I had a high school education and wanted to go to college, but I had little money. Going to college in those days was a big thing. I started to work for General Motors in Detroit. I worked there for 39 years and 8 months. When I retired, I was a supervisor.

Father, age 62
I was born in Detroit. I had a happy childhood and wonderful parents. My family consisted of one younger brother and one older sister. My sister now lives in Indiana, and my brother is a dean of a college out East. I was married when I was 25 and my lovely wife was 20. Both my wife and I are graduates from Wayne State University. My mother died when I was 10 years old, but my father is still living; he's 89.

Son, age 23
I was born January 2nd, 1946, in Detroit at the Woman's General Hospital. I moved to Northern Michigan at the age of 2, and I moved again at the age of about 7 or 8. I then entered kindergarten and graduated from Kingsford High School. And then I went to college.

---

3. The 60-year-olds, born about 1915, were preschool children during World War I. They entered their teens during the late 1920s, when for most Americans a high school education seemed a lofty goal. Relatives were still arriving from foreign countries or the farms, and the urban way of life was mitigated in ethnic neighborhoods. They looked forward to a work career (if they were men, but also often if they were middle-class women) in the ambiance of the Protestant ethic. They were bewildered and embittered by the Depression, which hit them in their adolescence, and many postponed getting married or having children because of poverty. Many were directly involved in World War II, which occurred when they were in their 20s. Others, both men and women, were involved in the war industry rather than the armed forces. After the war, when they were in their 30s, they moved to the suburbs with the expectation of increasing social mobility for their children (and themselves). Many tended to be more concerned about material comfort for their families than about a more romantic interpretation of "love." This move to "bedroom communities" was an unexpected isolation for

those women who had previously been highly involved with jobs and extended-kinship relationships. When their children grew up, half of them went back to work. They are now grandparents of young grandchildren, still giving a great deal of help to their children as well as to their aged and dying parents. Many of this age cohort are themselves concerned with their own and their spouses' failing health and with widowhood. They are facing retirement and social isolation, which will soon launch them from middle age into old age.

4. The 50-year-olds, born about 1925, were young children in the 1920s and the Depression, when they were surrounded by needy relatives flocking together from rural areas. They were highly involved in World War II: the men in the armed forces; the women, left without men, employed in the jobs formerly held by men. After the war, many men went to college on GI loans and on to middle-class bureaucratic "organization-man" positions. Their wives returned as soon as possible, with enthusiasm, to the traditional roles of mother and housewife and to the conspicuous consumption associated with suburban affluence and many children. Their indulgence in the "feminine mystique" thus complemented their husbands' occupational conformity. Their children, born in the late 1940s and 1950s, were ripe fodder for the drug-imbued counterculture, and these children have frightened and depressed them. If their parents are still living—and many are, particularly their mothers—they may still be living independently, but they are starting to fail in health. The people in this cohort, therefore, may be burdened with prolonged responsibilities to both parents and children. Nevertheless, many have been enjoying the comforts and even luxuries of economic affluence not previously available to them.

5. The 40-year-olds, born about 1935, were children during World War II and were teenagers in the postwar period of affluence. A few of them were involved in the Korean conflict. They were expected to go to college, supported either by their parents or by readily found employment or stipends. They married early, had children early, and went in for even larger families than did the cohort ahead of them. They take suburban affluence as a matter of course, and it is easy for them to have confidence in themselves, their future, and their world. They

---

Tell me something about yourself.

Grandmother, age 85
I'm a very old lady now—about 85 years old, I think. I had a very bad childhood in Russia. My mother died when I was only 8, and my father remarried right away. Then not only did I have a mean stepmother but she brought her mother into the house, and she was even meaner and stingier than her daughter. They begrudged me even the food I ate, and I had to be the maid of all the work. I was always hungry and had to steal food when they were not around. My father was a good man but weak. Then I got married and had five children. I always prayed that the Lord would allow me to live to take care of them. My mother died in childbirth. She was told by the doctor that she would die if she got pregnant again, but it happened anyway. Nobody knew anything like they do now about birth control or abortion.

Mother, age 60
I was born in Europe and came to America when I was 5. I had a nice childhood even though we were poor. I was the eldest of five children. My parents did as much for us as they could. I graduated from high school and then went to business college. I worked as a bookkeeper, getting what was considered a high salary for those days. I married and had two children, a girl and a boy. My husband is a fine man and quite successful. We had a men's clothing store.

Daughter, age 30
I was born in Flint, Michigan. I graduated from the University of Michigan as a school teacher, but I never had the chance to teach. I married a doctor, and have three children. I had a nice life as a child. My father, mother, brother, and I did a lot of things together. We had good times together.

---

may not be as involved with their children as the previous two decade groups were, and, because most of their parents are still working and in good health, they are not beset by as many anxieties as are the 50-year-olds.

6. The 30-year-olds, born about 1945, were part of the postwar baby boom. They were scared by the atom bomb, became blasé about space travel, and heard about corruption in high places on television. They were young children during the postwar period of affluence, and they expected M.A.'s, Ph.D.'s, or high-level jobs to come naturally—so naturally that many disdained them and "dropped out." They went in

for early marriage and early childbearing, but few children. Self-actualization is their goal, and the worthwhile life their value. They can welcome changes in marriage or in lifestyle because they grew up in security.

7. The 20-year-olds, born about 1955, were also part of the postwar baby boom and grew up in a denser, more highly populated world than that experienced by any previous generation. Their world has been one of constant minor anxieties—Vietnam, the atom bomb, rising prices, crimes, violence, drugs, and hard rock—rather than major crises such as war and depression. Where they are going it is too soon to know. During their adult years, they may have to deal with crises or tragedies greater than those faced by any of the earlier cohorts described.

KINDS OF GENERATIONS

An individual's development is interwoven with development of the social systems in which the individual exists. All these developmental processes, furthermore, are associated with generational processes (see Figure 4.5). One such process can be said to take place over the individual life span from one life stage (or generation) to the next. For example, a person can move from the generation of young adulthood, into the generation of middle adulthood, then to the generation of middle age, and finally into the generation of the old. This movement is shown in the first column of Figure 4.5. The second developmental process is the family lineage, from grandparent to parent to grandchild. The third is from one age cohort or generation within the larger social group to the next: from the youth-movement members of the late 1960s to the next cohort of youth, that of the 1970s, or alternatively, from youth to members of the "establishment."

As people move ontologically from early to middle adulthood, their parents are simultaneously moving from middle adulthood to middle age, their children are moving from childhood to adolescence, and their grandparents from middle to old age. As a societal age cohort moves from youth to "established" adulthood, its parents' age cohort may still be in the social position of established adulthood, even if, perhaps, with another set of values. Meanwhile a new age cohort is already replacing the youth in

their earlier social niche. Simultaneously, the society as a whole is changing. Any attempt to understand development, particularly in adulthood, must recognize the complex effects of the intertwining of these different kinds of generations and generational processes (see Baltes, Reese, & Nesselroade, 1977; Bengtson, 1975; Troll & Bengtson, 1979).

Mannheim (1952), a German sociologist whose thinking about generations has influenced most of us today, said that generation was something like social class—a location in society. He even suggested that people could become "generation conscious," in the way that people can be class conscious. Indeed, this happened in America in the late 1960s. In addition to his idea about "generation units" to describe subgroups of age cohorts who share the same experiences, he pointed out that there are generation "forerunners." For example, an individual who is "romantically inclined"—presumably by personality makeup—would, if he or she lived in an era that was essentially romantic, become even more romantic than he or she would otherwise be. Such a person would be a "leading type" of his or her generation. A rationalist—Mannheim was talking about such characteristics as taste in art when he used the terms *romantic* and *rationalist*—who lived in a romantic age would either be stultified and become, at least overtly, faintly romantic in behavior, or be isolated in his or her own time.

Troll and Bengtson (1979) adopted Mannheim's propositions to apply particularly to generations in the family. By incorporating the concepts of Hess and Handel (1959) on "family themes," they proposed that a romantic person would have come from a romantically inclined family. Moreover, forerunners would be recruited from families that had prepared them by inculcating or heightening themes that, when the time was ripe, brought the lucky youth of that family forward as leaders of societal movements.

The young old.   In her predictions for the older population in the year 2000, Neugarten (1975) stresses the importance of what she calls the "young old." These will be the generation now in middle age who will retire in good health, with better income, more education, and more complex life experiences than many of those who are now over 65. She believes that

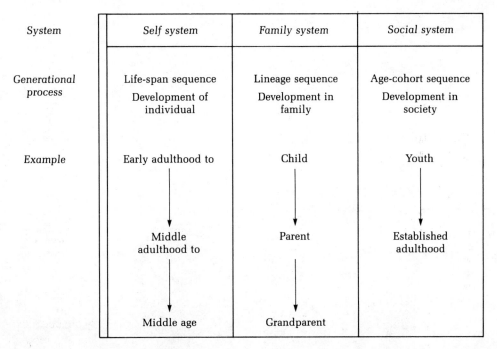

System	Self system	Family system	Social system
Generational process	Life-span sequence Development of individual	Lineage sequence Development in family	Age-cohort sequence Development in society
Example	Early adulthood to ↓ Middle adulthood to ↓ Middle age	Child ↓ Parent ↓ Grandparent	Youth ↓ Established adulthood

Figure 4.5. Generational processes.

they will constitute a significantly different cohort of older people.

Centenarians. There are 4451 people over 100 years old on the rolls of the U.S. Social Security Administration (Stark, 1972, p. 22), and the American Medical Association estimates there may be 2500 more who are not listed by Social Security. Some investigators claim that centenarians are more vigorous than most people of 80—that they come from more vigorous stock, have more vigor-making genes. Most of them seem to be the tail end of the longevity distribution, differing in many ways, such as intellectual alertness, warmth, interest in life, and general health. They do not seem to have any uniform recipe for a long life—not even yogurt. The possibility that they are more prevalent in isolated, mountainous regions of the world, such as the Andes, the Urals, or the Himalayas, is appealing to the imagination. However, the impossibility of verifying birthdates or life histories in such remote and generally nonliterate regions leaves most of their astonishing stories open to doubt.

Summary

Issue 10, mentioned in Chapter 1, is that of universality versus variation. The theme of this chapter is variation. Whether one is a man or a woman, middle-class or working-class, Black, White, or Hispanic can make an enormous difference in development throughout life, and these factors for difference can multiply. A Black, working-class woman experiences the disadvantages of all three of her categories, and a White, middle-class man reaps the advantages of his. One's cohort or generational placement in society at a given moment in history is also an important determinant of development, making for different life experiences from members of other generations and of other times in history. Beyond all this, each individual is unlike any other individual. Generalizations are helpful and averages highlight a condition or trend, but both are treacherous if they imply universality.

5

Length of Life

Are we becoming a gerontocracy—a country ruled by old people? Are old people soon going to outnumber all other age groups? Is a small number of younger adults going to have to support an overwhelming number of older people? Will we soon be able to live 200 years? If we eat yogurt or avoid meat, can we at least live to 120? Are there really people in those far-off mountains who are 160 and still vigorous and virile?

These questions are asked daily in newspapers, on television, and by audiences at lectures on aging. The answers, in brief, are as follows. First, all the people who will be old in 30 years are now alive, and thus there is no way they will outnumber other age groups or rule over other age groups unless generations yet unborn diminish beyond all reason. Second, the human life span, genetically, seems to be 120, and this hasn't changed since *Homo sapiens* first evolved. Third, those ancients in the mountains have no records or other evidence for their age claims. Fourth, short of extreme nutritional deprivation, good nutrition makes for health but does not affect length of life. The rest of this chapter considers these points in more detail.

Terminology

To begin with terminology, discussions about length of life often confuse six terms: *longevity, life span, life expectancy, life cycle, aging,* and *senescence.* These terms are defined in the following paragraphs.

LONGEVITY

The word *longevity* usually refers to the *average* length of life for a species. It can be calculated by averaging the ages of death for all members of that species. Thus, for male houseflies longevity is 16.88 days; for humans, about 70 years (Rockstein, Chesky, & Sussman, 1977). Because the life circumstances of humans are not as easily controlled as those of houseflies in the laboratory, figures for humans can only be approximate. Furthermore, scientists can manipulate living conditions for houseflies in the laboratory to develop estimates of factors that affect longevity. Their study of humans can only compare living conditions and survival rates of people in their "natural settings." Thus we can only hint at the conditions associated with longer or shorter life, whether these be foods eaten, physical activity, climate, or "pollution."

LIFE SPAN

Some houseflies live considerably longer than 16.88 days—in fact, some as long as 58 or 59 days (Rockstein et al., 1977)—and some humans live to 115 or 120 years. Some houseflies and some humans also live considerably less. Many individuals of all species, in fact, don't even make it to birth. Life span is the maximum longevity. It shows the survival *potential* of a species, the upper limit. Figure 5.1 shows the comparative life spans for a wide variety of familiar species. As Alex Comfort (1964) notes, there is no one factor that correlates with life span, not

Herring gull 40–50

Dove 42

Gull, crow family, pigeon 30–45

Pelican, crane, goose 40–55

Zebra 38+

Ostrich 30–40

Horse 40+

Chimpanzee 39+
Larger apes 30–40

Hippopotamus 49

Toad 36

Giant salamander 50+

Carp 50+

Lobster 50

Figure 5.1.   Maximum well-attested ages for representative animal species and groups cover a remarkable range for which there is no simple explanation. Broadly speaking, large size is correlated with a long life span, but there are many exceptions, even within families. It might appear that incentive is lacking for evolution to provide small animals with a long potential life, because predators will not let them live to enjoy it. Yet many small birds have lived for decades when protected from harm. The longest-lived animals are probably tortoises, with fishes and human beings not far behind. *(Source: Comfort, 1964.)*

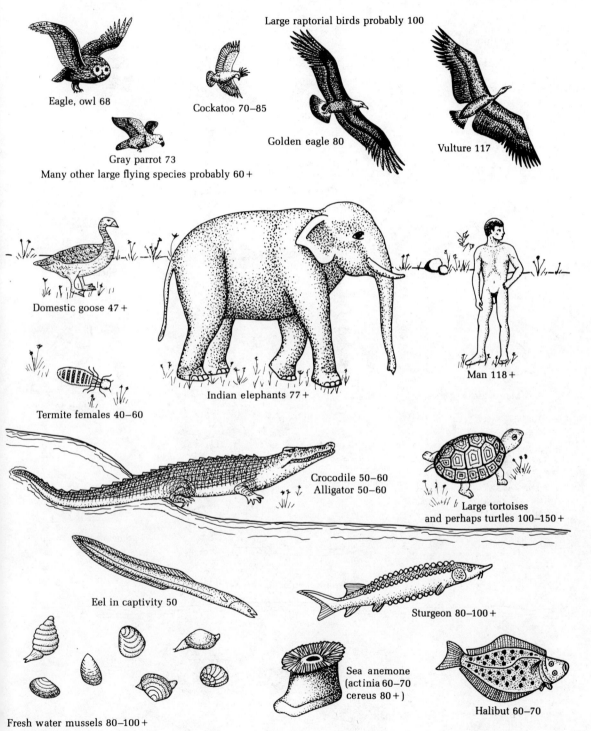

Large raptorial birds probably 100

Eagle, owl 68

Cockatoo 70–85

Gray parrot 73

Golden eagle 80

Vulture 117

Many other large flying species probably 60+

Domestic goose 47+

Indian elephants 77+

Man 118+

Termite females 40–60

Crocodile 50–60
Alligator 50–60

Large tortoises
and perhaps turtles 100–150+

Eel in captivity 50

Sturgeon 80–100+

Fresh water mussels 80–100+

Sea anemone
(actinia 60–70
cereus 80+)

Halibut 60–70

(Figure 5.1 continues)

Figure 5.1 (continued)

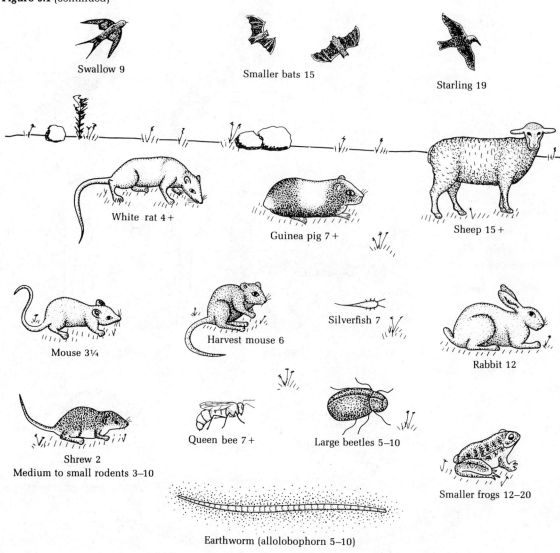

Swallow 9

Smaller bats 15

Starling 19

White rat 4 +

Guinea pig 7 +

Sheep 15 +

Mouse 3¼

Harvest mouse 6

Silverfish 7

Rabbit 12

Shrew 2
Medium to small rodents 3–10

Queen bee 7 +

Large beetles 5–10

Smaller frogs 12–20

Earthworm (allolobophorn 5–10)

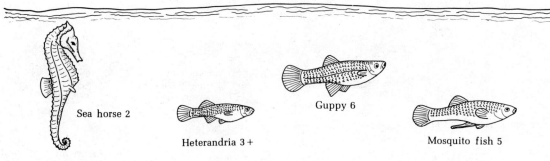

Sea horse 2

Heterandria 3 +

Guppy 6

Mosquito fish 5

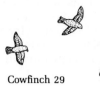

Cowfinch 29

Smaller finches, waders, parakeet 10–30

Arctic tern 27

Domestic pigeon 35

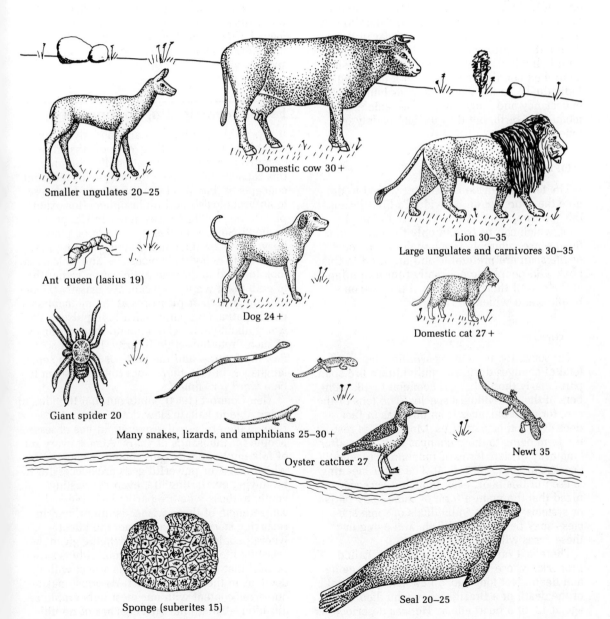

Domestic cow 30+

Smaller ungulates 20–25

Lion 30–35
Large ungulates and carnivores 30–35

Ant queen (lasius 19)

Dog 24+

Domestic cat 27+

Giant spider 20

Many snakes, lizards, and amphibians 25–30+

Oyster catcher 27

Newt 35

Sponge (suberites 15)

Seal 20–25

even size. Although large size is associated with longer life, there are many exceptions to this rule. Because we are humans, we may take comfort (an unintended pun) from the fact that our life span is one of the longest.

LIFE EXPECTANCY

The average number of years (or days) that any individual born at a given time can expect to stay alive is actually calculated from the rate of dying for everybody born that year or day. Again, this figure is more exact when it deals with individuals brought up under laboratory, controlled conditions than when it deals with individuals "in the wild"—such as humans. Life expectancy and longevity are the same at the moment of birth, but they deviate widely over time.

LIFE CYCLE

The term *life cycle* is frequently used to denote the course of an individual's life. Because this term implies a cyclical nature to the process, which can be true in only the most superficial sense, alternate terms such as *life course* or *life span* are preferable and are used in this book. Old people do not really return to infancy at the end of their lives, even if they become helpless and witless.

AGING

For some, the term *aging* signifies the sum total of changes during an individual's life span, particularly those changes common to all members of that individual's species. The lens of the eye, for example, ages from birth, as in fact does every other part of us. Most writers restrict the term *aging* to those changes that occur after "maturity of size, form, or function is reached" (Rockstein et al., 1977, p. 4). The latter meaning is used in this book, even though it is recognized that the mature form of some body parts or systems—or even individuals of some species—may be present at birth, and aging in these cases will begin at birth.

There is a rare and curious disease, called *progeria*, whose victims show premature aging and death. Not long ago, a newspaper item told of the death of a Brazilian boy who died of old age at 12, of a heart attack. He was described as

"physically 90" at the time of his death. At 6 months, his teeth were crooked and yellow. His hair started to turn white and fall out before he was 2 years old. At 10, his skin was wrinkled and dry, and his blood vessels began to harden.

SENESCENCE

The term *senescence* connotes deteriorative changes occurring in the terminal phase of the life course. As with the term *aging*, the chronological ages for decline may vary widely, not only between species but also within any given species.

Factors contributing to longevity

It is possible that humans are the only animals capable of foreseeing their own deaths, at least cognitively even if not emotionally. Whether this capacity has something to do with different concepts of time has been a subject of interest to anthropologists and philosophers (for example, Cottle, 1967) and was noted in Chapter 1 (Issue 8). Some societies, such as ours, place heavy stress on time and timing. We train our children to delay their pleasures and to learn to look forward to them in anticipation rather than to grab them while they can. We classify people who do grab their pleasures at the moment as psychopathic and pathologically impulsive. We worry about youth who demand the overthrow of such Protestant-ethic futurity. In other societies, the future—and the past—is *now*. In some languages, in fact, there does not even seem to be a word for "time."

Alex Comfort (1964) points out that the idea of being able to halt, to slow down, or even to reverse the process of growing old has obsessed people for thousands of years. Almost every set of folk myths and legends includes some in which magic or powerful gods are successful in bestowing everlasting life, even everlasting youth, to those who are particularly blessed. The strength of those wishes is underlined in recurring stories with a boomerang effect—where people are punished by being given everlasting life. The wish for immortality is so painful that it has been seen as a pact with the devil, as in the story of Faust. We must make ourselves content with our most unbearable realization—that all our strivings are of no ultimate use. Rich and poor, successful and unsuccessful, weak and powerful, all end in a common grave. Comfort reminds us of Gulliver's meeting with the Struldbrugs, who can't die but just keep on getting older, weaker, and crazier. He notes the disaster that befell the Greek goddess Aurora when her wishes for eternal life for her husband resulted in his continuing to get more and more decrepit. And he mentions the Wandering Jew, who was cursed with being unable to grow old and die. The ultimate in human power is that of being able to control the life or death of others. The powers of the priest, the magician, and the physician (whose functions are sometimes interchangeable) come from assumptions that these people have such control.

The futility of the search for eternal youth and life is documented in stories as old as those that tell of its success. Humans, because of their intrinsically searching nature, are punished by being thrown out of the Garden of Eden, a place with no time. Immortal gods are almost always distinguished from mortal humans. In some tales, humans can become immortal only after they die. In Tibetan and other Far Eastern religions, the closer one gets to death, the more sacred one gets—the closer to immortality.

One of the most popular legends concerns the fountain of youth. If you bathe in it, you never grow old. It seems to have appeared first in the writings of Pausanias in the second century A.D., to have recurred in medieval European literature, and then during the Renaissance to have influenced the explorations of Ponce de Leon in America, in the course of which he discovered Florida—but no fountain.

Along with the wish stories of eternal youth and life went the professional rejuvenators. In a 4000-year-old Egyptian papyrus manuscript, there is a recipe for an oil that removed baldness and unsightly spots. The introduction advertises the book in Madison Avenue fashion as "the beginning of the book for making an old man into a youth" (Comfort, 1964, p. 9). The search for an "imperishable medicine" that would prolong youth and life has gone on for many centuries. Chinese sages long ago said that one could stay young by eating from gold plates, and the association between gold as a "pure" metal and long life persisted. It evolved into a search for the "philosopher's stone" that would convert baser metals into precious gold

and, in parallel fashion, ennoble life by making it last forever. Many alchemists who engaged in this effort were charlatans, but others truly believed that if they persisted their search would be rewarded. In 1737, Abram Kaau von Boerhaave wrote:

O hope of the Stone, how you charm our minds: with what promise you soothe us! To maintain an unfailing bodily health, a constant vigor and tranquillity of mind, and to preserve them into a green and rugged old age until, without sickness or struggle, body and soul part company! The old grandam regains her buxomness, gray hairs drop out, she straightens and she shines; even old, molted fowls feather and lay eggs again [in Comfort, 1964, pp. 14–15].

These wishes have not disappeared in modern times. Witness the rush for transplantation of monkey glands (literally, chimpanzee testicles) in the first quarter of this century, and journeys to partake of the cure of Dr. Aslan in Rumania—she used a novocaine derivative called "Gerovital"—not to mention the commercial success of Geritol. Moment (1975) points out that if young primate glands were efficacious, eunuchs should die younger—but they don't. Their maximum life span is the same as noncastrates'. Yogurt, another early and persistent remedy, may be good for health, but it won't prolong life. The traveling medicine men have been replaced by the stationary television sets, but what they sell is the same false promise. In fact, Comfort believes that most research gerontologists themselves are motivated in their research by the wish to avert and reverse aging.

Like the association between gold and immortality there is one between rejuvenation and sexuality, perhaps evolving from an association between women and life giving. In the Old Testament, old men bedded with young girls. This was considered more a health measure than a recreational one. King David apparently used Abishag this way (Comfort, 1964). Elaborate erotic carvings in the Indian medieval temples at Khajuraho depict kinds of rejuvenating sexual rites performed by young girls. The power of women was seen as related to their age; Indian lore writes that "the young girl gives life, the young woman consumes it; the grown woman brings old age, the old woman brings death" (Comfort, 1964, p. 12). One of the early-Renaissance stories by Rabelais is a variation of this theme (Comfort, 1964, p. 11). In this story, old women are melted down and converted into pretty girls of 15 or 16. "The only difference was a curious effect on their feet, which remained much shorter than in their first youth—and as a result of this, they much more readily fall on their backs if one gives them a push." When Rabelais's character Pantagruel asked the wizard if he could be rejuvenated too, he was told the process only worked for women, but that all that men had to do was to cohabit with a woman in order to become reconditioned too.

In 1964, Comfort concluded from research at that time that in general longevity in mammals was "roughly correlated with size, more closely with the relative size of the brain, and most closely with the speed at which they reproduce." Thirteen years later, Rockstein and his colleagues (1977) decided that, although maximum length of life is genetically determined, an individual's actual life span depends on physical and biological factors in its environment. Some of these factors are as follows.

ACCIDENTS AND ILLNESSES

The difference in longevity and life expectancy between laboratory and wild animals mentioned at the beginning of this chapter indicates the hazardous effect of "natural" environments. Attacks by predators have always been a prominent cause of death. Lions and tigers are not very important for modern Americans, but bacteria and viruses are still with us. In recent centuries, humans have also been killed off by other humans, sometimes in wars, sometimes in street violence, sometimes in violence engendered by close personal living, and sometimes in the random hazards of our lives, such as automobile misuse and malfunction. We might also include emotional interactions that lead people to kill themselves instead of others. There does not seem to be any way to raise and maintain humans in an accident- or illness-free environment such as we can provide for houseflies or even for rats and dogs.

GENETIC FACTORS

Longevity may be correlated with a number of genetic factors. Sex is one: in most species, the female outlives the male. There are exceptions, however: stallions live longer than mares, and male Syrian hamsters live longer than female Syrian hamsters (Rockstein et al., 1977, p. 7). One of the best predictors of anyone's chances for a long life is the length of life of that individual's ancestors. Although this is generally true, recent calculations show that having long-lived grandparents may add four years to life expectancy, but environmental factors such as living in rural instead of urban areas could add six years. The elimination of cancer and heart disease might add only two years. Before all of us move to the country, though, we might consider Birren and Renner's (1977) suggestion that environmental conditions experienced in later childhood or adulthood—including nutrition or pollution—are nowhere near as influential in determining length of life as are conditions during infancy and early childhood. In fact, one's grandmother's nutritional and life situation at the time she was pregnant with one's mother may be more important to length of life than the food one eats oneself or the way one lives one's life. We can shorten our years more easily than lengthen them. Of course, if we prevent premature death by not smoking, by "living right," and by not going to war we are in fact lengthening our lives.

When environmental conditions improve, women's life expectancy and longevity increase more than men's. Table 5.1 shows the percentage of men and women in 13 countries who were over 65 around 1971. These data suggest that the countries differed widely in their treatment of

TABLE 5.1 Percentage of the elderly in the populations of selected nations

	Percentage of entire population over age 65	Percentage of people over age 65	
		Males	*Females*
Hong Kong (1970)	1.4	81	19
Colombia (1964)	2.9	46	54
Iran (1966)	3.4	59	41
Mexico (1970)	3.7	48	52
Kenya (1969)	3.9	57	43
Turkey (1965)	3.9	43	57
Japan (1970)	7.0	44	56
Canada (1971)	7.9	45	55
New Zealand (1969)	8.1	40	60
Malta (1970)	9.0	44	56
United States (1970)	9.9	42	58
Sweden (1970)	13.7	45	55
Austria (1970)	14.1	38	62

Source: U.N. Department of Economic and Social Affairs, 1972.

girls and women a century ago. In Hong Kong, for instance, where only 19% of the old population was female (81% male), we could suspect vast discrimination in favor of males to offset the natural female advantage in longevity. There must also have been hard living conditions for everybody, because only about one of every 100 people living in Hong Kong in 1971 was over 65. However, a low percentage of old people could also be due to an enormous increase in the birthrate at a later time.

The opposite situation is seen in Austria, where there appears to have been a cutting off of men. Of the 14% of older people in the population, almost two-thirds are women. There must also be a low birthrate, because to produce such a large proportion of people over 65 later cohorts would be very small. In Hong Kong, poverty and negative attitudes toward females could be important. In Austria, war and positive attitudes toward women seem to be combined.

Although monks and nuns live longer than the general population—perhaps because of a more regulated or controlled environment and less stress—nuns live longer than monks. Age of death of twins and siblings is compared to the age at death of their parents in Table 5.2. This table shows, first, a relationship between parental longevity and child longevity. The highest ages for death were for people whose parents lived to over 70. This is true when both fathers and mothers are considered. It is equally true for sons and daughters. The sex of the parent seems to make little difference in this case, although daughters lived longer than sons in al-most every comparison (there were just two exceptions to this trend).

The table also shows a "regression to the mean." Children of parents who die young—before 55—are likely to live somewhat longer than did their parents, and children of parents who live the longest—over 70—tend to die at a younger age than did their parents. Data from a study of nonagenarians (Pearl & Pearl, 1934) do not completely support the hypothesis that parental longevity is the best predictor of child longevity, however. When Abbott, Murphy, Bolling, and Abbey (1974) investigated the life span of the descendants of the Pearls' nonagenarians, they found only a slight correlation between the life span of the long-lived parents and that of their offspring.

BODY SIZE

In general, larger animals live longer than smaller ones, as Figure 5.1 shows. However, there are exceptions here, too. Dogs, for example, although larger than cats, do not live as long as cats. And humans, although considerably smaller than many other mammals, are one of the longest-lived species (Rockstein et al., 1977).

DIET

Although the food that people—or other animals—eat may not extend their maximum potential length of life, it does influence their chances for reaching this potential. Research with rats (McCay, Maynard, Sperling, & Barnes,

TABLE 5.2 Effect of parental age on mean life spans of 1429 senescent twin index pairs and their siblings

	Mother died			Father died			Either parent died			Both parents died		
	Under 55	55–69	70 and over	Under 55	55–69	70 and over	Under 55	55–69	70 and over	Under 55	55–69	70 and over
Twins and sibs:												
Sons	55.8	58.8	59.6	56.3	57.2	60.2	55.9	57.4	59.6	51.8	59.6	61.4
Daughters	64.8	60.0	66.4	63.0	64.3	65.3	64.1	62.0	65.7	62.1	59.3	66.8
Total	58.5	57.8	62.1	58.5	60.0	61.5	58.5	59.0	61.8	55.9	59.4	62.9
Sibs only:												
Sons	48.6	51.6	52.9	48.5	50.4	53.1	48.5	50.9	53.1	45.8	55.1	55.2
Daughters	55.7	50.8	60.0	51.6	51.5	58.3	53.7	54.3	59.1	54.3	55.8	60.7
Total	51.7	51.2	56.4	49.9	54.0	55.8	50.9	52.7	56.1	49.5	55.4	57.9

Source: Kallmann and Jarvik, 1959.

1939; Ross, 1959, 1961) shows that nutrition can modify the life span of male rats, either directly or by modifying the incidence of disease. Restricted diets have been found to double the life span of newly weaned male rats (McCay, Crowell, & Maynard, 1935; Berg & Simms, 1960, 1961) and to increase the life span of guppies (Comfort, 1964).

These findings were initially greeted with great joy by gerontologists who felt that they had found the path to the long-sought fountain of youth. However, the starving of baby animals may increase length of life in some species, or at least one sex of some species, but these starved animals do not seem to be able to attain sexual maturity. As Rockstein and his colleagues (1977, pp. 7–8) conclude, "There appear to be many interacting factors contributing to life span in relation to diet and dietary restriction and, at this time, it is unlikely that a restricted diet can be considered as the most important deterrent to early death or, conversely, uniquely important in prolongation of life."

In general, nutrition may make a lot of difference, both in the level of peaks reached in physical development (for example, how tall people will grow) and in the decline thereafter (how long they will stay at their maximum height). Yet, for every group of people who follow a particular kind of diet with particular apparent consequences, it is possible to find another group who follow the same diet without these consequences. For example, Timiras (1972) reports that men of the Masai tribe in Africa, who eat only milk, meat, or blood after the age of 14, appear to maintain good cardiovascular functioning into old age and to be less likely to die "prematurely" from cardiovascular ailments than other people around the world. Yet people in neighboring tribes who eat essentially the same diet have higher cholesterol levels, and people of the Masai tribe in other regions with different diets function as well as their "meat, milk, and blood" relatives. At the extreme end of diet restriction, of course, is starvation, which is uncommon in our society or in others of moderate affluence but which can kill enfeebled old people who have to hunt their own food. In this respect, Simmons (1945) points out that living in groups, as most humans do, is beneficial for older people. The younger and stronger members of the group can share food with them.

TEMPERATURE

Although some gerontologists have proposed that lowering the body temperature of mammals will extend their life span, there is little evidence to support this hypothesis. Some cold-blooded vertebrates living in warm climates have shorter life spans than those living in colder climates, but others, such as alligators, live longer at higher temperatures. Mammals are capable of maintaining a constant internal body temperature; there is little relationship between the temperature of their environment and their longevity. As a matter of fact, several studies have found that rats reared in colder environments have lower life expectancies (see Rockstein et al., 1977, p. 8).

Among humans, while climate seems to be an important influence, different climates are better for different human groups. In general, Caucasoids grow the tallest in places where winters are mildly cold and wet, and Mongoloids in still colder but drier areas, North American Indians in climates between these two, and Australoids where monsoons prevail (Timiras, 1972).

EXERCISE

Like diet and climate, exercise can be important in influencing health and, at least indirectly, length of life. For example, it can improve the strength and circulation of cardiac muscles and can reduce the severity of arteriosclerotic lesions. Exercise of the leg muscles seems particularly effective in facilitating the flow of blood to the heart and thus indirectly maintaining body functioning in all areas, including the brain. Timiras (1972) quotes the saying "If you want to know how flabby your brain is, feel your leg muscles." It may very well be true that the optimum diet, climate, and exercise vary for different groups of humans, different species of animals, and different individuals within these groups. What is ideal or at least good for one kind of individual could be bad for another. Because of this variation, it would be very dangerous to prescribe standard regimens of diet or exercise.

PARENTAL AGE

In lower animals such as rotifers (Lansing, 1954) and houseflies (Rockstein & Miquel, 1973), longer-lived children are produced after several generations of selecting young mothers instead of older mothers. The evidence for higher animals, including humans, is less clear and points more to extrachromosomal factors than to genetic factors. Younger mothers seem to provide a prenatal (or perhaps even postnatal) environment that leads to longer-lived children (Rockstein et al., 1977).

REPRODUCTION

There is some evidence that the long human life span, compared to other species of animals, is related partly to a delay in puberty and a longer growth period. This relationship is far from universal, however, because some squirrels and rabbits that have late maturity and much longer growth periods also have short lives (Rockstein et al., 1977). A curious relationship has been found in some species between reproduction and terminal body changes. Salmon, for instance, undergo testicular degeneration and other degenerative changes in the process of spawning, and if they are kept from spawning these changes do not occur (Robertson, 1957, 1961). Castrated mice have a longer maximum life span than noncastrates (Muhlbock, 1959). Similar results have been found for cats, but the evidence for humans is mixed (Hamilton, Hamilton, & Mestler, 1969; Moment, 1975)—not sufficient, however, to justify the use of castration as a rejuvenation or immortality technique.

IMMUNITY

One school of biologists (for example, Burnet, 1974) has tried to connect aging and death with the immune system, which ordinarily serves to fight foreign organisms such as bacteria or viruses. Some biologists believe that the immune system itself deteriorates with age, so that we can no longer ward off infections. Others see the problem as being in the autoimmune system, which keeps the immune system from fighting its own body. With aging, they say, this control or autoimmune system deteriorates, leading to self-destruction.

INFORMATION THEORY

Sacher (1968) suggested that deterioration of the organism over time can be ascribed to (1) disorganization of information and (2) disruption of transmitting or decoding mechanisms. Increased "noise" or irrelevant information creeps in as the organism ages. At a cellular level, there may be either changes in DNA, which gives "orders" or messages, or changes in RNA, which delivers these messages to the cells—or changes in both. This model assumes an underlying systematic process of deterioration overriding random unsystematic changes. Signs of this process are losses of central-nervous-system cells or losses in ego energy.

PATHOLOGY

An early theory was that senility is a pathological condition, an illness, and that if we could find its cure we would not age. A variation of this idea is that the cumulative effects of illnesses or diseases eventually reach the "breaking point."

"UNNECESSARY" MODEL

A century ago, Weismann (1889) proposed that when the human species first evolved it was "programmed" genetically to live 120 years, but because it wasn't necessary for the survival of the species to live so long, this maximum figure decreased over time. Present findings about long-lived individuals and groups suggest, however, that 120 may still be the maximum human life span. A few rare individuals reached this maximum age in early human history, and there are still a few rare individuals who do so in modern times.

COUNTERPART THEORY

Birren (for example, see Birren & Renner, 1977) has suggested that longevity is the counterpart of other human characteristics that do have survival value, such as the enlarged frontal lobe, which makes for superior control over self and environment. Although it is hard to see why living past the reproductive age has survival value for the species, it might be argued that, because humans are preeminently group-living animals, there is a survival benefit to the group—and therefore to all individuals in the group—in having wise old people around whose memories stretch back to encompass a variety of possible solutions to intermittent catastrophic conditions. For example, older members would be able to warn the rest of the group when they saw the early signs of a typhoon or tidal wave, earthquake, or other kind of disaster that hadn't happened during the lifetime of the younger people. Strehler and Mildvan (1960), however, point out that eliminating the old may contribute to the success of the species if the old are burdens to the survival of the young.

VULNERABILITY AND STRESS

The deterioration of homeostatic or control mechanisms over time may not be apparent under steady environmental conditions but may only show up under stress. Selye (1970), among others, believes that the exhaustion that follows the alarm reaction is cumulative. People who experience an unusual amount of stress, therefore, would show gradual weakening of their adaptive systems.

PSYCHOLOGICAL VARIABLES

A number of theories hypothesize that characteristics such as hope (looking forward to the future) or narcissism (being engrossed with oneself) can help people live longer. The relation between emotions and illness, and even emotions and death, has been observed informally by many investigators over many years, yet few systematic studies have been done. A related concept is "locus of control." Chapter 16, dealing with personality and mental health, discusses the relation between such psychological variables and health.

AGING HORMONE

Some believe that an active malign hormone or similar destructive substance, manufactured by the aging body, produces deterioration. Welford (1977) found, for example, that skin grafts from an older person onto a younger one would not "take."

RADIATION

Szilard (1959) stated that exposure to radiation, which is lethal in large doses, is cumulative as are stress and illnesses. Over a lifetime, these accumulated traumas shorten life, although the individuals affected might die of a number of other causes because of their generally weakened condition. Birren and Renner (1977) suggest that such effects may be specific to parts of the body—affecting DNA in the cells, for instance, more than other parts.

CONCLUSION

Over sixty-five years ago, Child, in *Senescence and Rejuvenescence* (1915), described two general types of life-ending theories: "wear and tear" and genetic. Examples of the "wear and tear" view that we have mentioned are the immune, information-theory, vulnerability and stress, and radiation models. Examples of the genetic view are the pathology and the aging-hormone view. Everett (1973) spoke of an "aging clock," and Finch (1971) spoke of "pacemakers of aging." Moment (1975) points out that so far evidence is lacking for any conclusion. Aging and length of life may be multidetermined, a combination of all the preceding hypothetical antecedents or, anyway, several of them.

Predictors of longevity

The Duke Center for the Study of Aging and Human Development, in Durham, North Carolina, has been conducting a longitudinal study of older men and women since 1958. The team of investigators there (Palmore, 1969) has developed a "longevity quotient" that consists of the number of years survived (chronological age, or CA), divided by the number of years left to live. The life expectancy is based on age, sex, and race data. This quotient has been used to find some of the predictors of living longer than expected. A quotient over 1.00 indicates prediction of longer than the average expected life for that person, considering his or her age, sex, and race. The four significant predictors of longevity are physical mobility, education, occupation, and employment. Unimpaired mobility by itself was the single best predictor; active people lived longer. However, when education and occupation were added in to the equation, the predictions were even better. The longevity quotients for education were Ph.D., 1.23; M.A. or equivalent, 1.13; B.A., 1.10; some college, 1.04; high school or business school, 1.00; three to eight years of elementary school, 0.98; and less than three years of elementary school, 0.82. The average education for the people who are now old is high school; this *is* the average. The quotients for occupation were professors, 1.22; other white-collar, 1.06; blue-collar, 0.95; housewife, 0.87; farmer, 0.77; employed, 1.11; retired, 0.94. In a second followup of the original sample of 864 people (in 1958), education was most important, and performance IQ was second most important. Another psychological measure, work satisfaction, was also important. Marital status, incidentally, was not a significant factor. In general, the Duke Center results are not inconsistent with others: healthier, more-advantaged people who are enjoying their lives are probably going to have a better chance of living out their potential life spans.

A different longitudinal study was done of 47 carefully selected healthy older men and a control group of healthy young men (Libow, 1974), measured first in 1956. Libow was able to separate out those factors that, in the followups, differentiated those older men who survived from those who died. Factors associated with survival over 11 years were: lower systolic blood pressure, higher weight; lower serum cholesterol or no cigarette smoking or both, low serum albumin; high intelligence-test scores; good adaptation to aging (composite score); good mental status; speed of copying digits and words; complexity and variability of daily behavior; and fewer environmental losses. Some of these are biomedical parameters, some intellectual, and some sociological or psychological. These variables are, of course, not necessarily directly causal. Although some of the findings are not

unexpected, others are. For example, it is not low weight, as hypothesized in the theories reported earlier in this chapter, but higher weight that goes together with longer life. Also, those who discontinued smoking, even late in life and even within the last three years, had a lower mortality rate—even if they had been smoking most of their lives. Serum cholesterol was connected with those who died from apparent coronary heart disease, and serum albumin with those who died from intestinal cancer.

Morbidity by age

Chances of dying are different at different ages, as shown in Table 5.3. This table, based on 1970 census data, shows first that chances of dying are higher during the first year of life than they are between ages 1 and 65. They are higher for males than for females, and for non-Whites than for Whites in our country. Atchley (1977, p. 180) points out that the leading causes of death among older people are exactly the same now as they were in 1900: "The main difference now is that more people live to reach the ages at which these diseases become prevalent." He also points out that death rates for people over 85 have fallen rapidly since 1960—from a rate of 198.6 in 1960 to 163.4 in 1970, meaning that there is an increasing rate of survival not only *to* very old ages but also *at* very old ages.

The causes of death vary by age. Between 25 and 44, most people die (in this order) from accidents, heart and circulatory disorders, cancer, suicide, and cirrhosis of the liver. Older

TABLE 5.3 Death rates by age, color, and sex (United States, 1970)

	Under 1	1–4	5–14	15–24	25–34	35–44	45–54	55–64	65–74	75–84	85 and over
Total	21.4	0.8	0.4	1.3	1.6	3.1	7.3	16.6	35.8	80.0	163.4
Male											
Total	24.1	0.9	0.5	1.9	2.2	4.0	9.6	22.8	48.7	100.1	178.2
White	21.1	0.8	0.5	1.7	1.8	3.4	8.8	22.0	48.1	101.0	185.5
Other	40.2	1.4	0.7	3.0	5.0	8.7	16.5	30.5	54.7	89.8	114.1
Female											
Total	18.6	0.8	0.3	0.7	1,0	2.3	5.2	11.0	25.8	66.8	155.2
White	16.1	0.7	0.3	0.6	0.8	1.9	4.6	10.1	24.7	67.0	159.8
Other	31.7	1.2	0.4	1.1	2.2	4.9	9.8	18.9	36.8	63.9	102.9

Source: Atchley, 1977, after U.S. Department of Health, Education, and Welfare, National Center for Health Statistics, 1974a.

people die most from heart disease, then from cancer, strokes, influenza, and pneumonia. Infectious diseases such as colds or bacterial infections, more common among younger people, have declined in the population as it has aged. Older people are more likely to have chronic diseases such as arthritis and diabetes (Atchley, 1977). This topic is discussed further in Chapters 6 and 7.

Clonal aging: Are cells immortal?

About 15 years ago, Hayflick (1977) found that cells that were removed from the body and kept alive in a chemical solution (*in vitro* instead of *in vivo*) did *not* survive indefinitely. (Earlier researchers such as Alexis Carrel had concluded from research with cells from more primitive animals, such as chicks, that such cells *did* survive indefinitely.) Rather, these *in vitro* cells underwent a finite number of doublings and then died. Human embryonic cells died after about 50 doublings, and this death was an inherent property of the cells themselves. Since Hayflick's early work, other investigators have also found that there is a direct correlation between age and the number of doublings of cultured cells. It may be, says Hayflick, that "acquisition of the potential for unlimited cell division or escape from senescent changes by mammalian cells *in vitro* or *in vivo* can only be achieved by cells that have acquired some or all of the properties of cancer cells or germ (sex) cells" (Hayflick, 1977, p. 30). Very few normal cells in the body survive to their full potential doublings, though, because a host of other kinds of losses produce cell aging and death before that happens. We must conclude, therefore, that cells do not seem to be immortal, even when removed from an optimum location in the body.

So far none of the heralded breakthroughs to prolonging life have been unequivocal. However, some biologists, such as Moment (1975), are not ready to close the books for good. As Moment (p. 627) says:

> There is no reason to doubt a continuing flow of beneficent discoveries. The goal of making it possible to age well will be achieved so that a satisfying old age both physically and mentally will be the good fortune of people everywhere. What is the possibility of a radical discovery, extending not just life expectancy so that more people will live out the proverbial three-score years and ten, but a discovery extending the maximum lifespan to 200, 500, or even 10,000 years? Such a discovery seems highly improbable, but science in the past has been full of surprises. . . . Some thinking has already begun about the problems that would arise in the event of such a discovery (Segerberg, 1974; Strehler, 1975). The population problem would immediately assume a new degree of urgency. . . . To begin with, at what age would you choose to stop the clock? Would an age of 9 or 10 seem the really best years, or the late teens, or perhaps young adulthood, or would you prefer a comfortable middle age? . . . In some very fundamental ways, life might not seem very different. . . . In comparison to the immense stretches of astronomical time open to our investigation, 10,000 times 10,000 is but an instant . . . we can still take courage from the words of Cicero . . . "The short period of life is yet long enough for living well and honorably."

Summary

The maximum human life span is probably 120 years, but average longevity is much less—about 70 or 75 years under good conditions. Women live longer than men, probably because of genetic factors. Many factors have been cited as contributing to greater length of life, including lifestyle, genetic programming, body size, diet and exercise appropriate to climatic conditions, parental age, integrity of the autoimmune system, general health, and maintenance of central control mechanisms. At the present time, none of these theories is convincingly supported; longevity may be multidetermined. Data on prediction of mortality show that physical activity, higher education, higher-status occupation, and continued employment are all related to longer life. It is likely, however, that at least some of these variables are *indicators* rather than *causes*. There is no guarantee that any prescription offered now will bring more years to a person's life, although certain ways of life are more likely to bring an earlier death than would otherwise have occurred.

6

Physical Development

Because ours is a more physically oriented culture than some, we are concerned with our bodies. From adulthood on, Americans hope to look years younger than they actually are. They want to be physically fit and strong. Women probably care more about appearance and men more about strength and vigor—and sexual prowess. Both fear the body's deterioration. It is easy to sell cosmetics and fashions that promise youthful appearance. Drugstore shelves are filled with nostrums for diminishing strength or virility. A new diet book can make its author rich. A new and simple prescription for vigor, from running to pushups, can make its author famous. Most people hesitate to speak the word *menopause* aloud, or the word *impotence*.

This chapter describes changes in body parts, functions, and systems during the years past adolescence. A comprehensive review of all physiological changes is not intended, but rather a selection relevant to psychological development. Unfortunately, most information available is not only cross-sectional, but is also limited in many other ways.

Primary and secondary aging

Throughout this chapter, it will be seen that certain changes seem to be inevitable and universal—that everybody who lives long enough will show them. Other changes—probably most

that are to be described—while more frequent in the later years of life than in earlier years, are not inevitable. The first kind of change could be considered *primary aging*. It can be assumed that such aging is the concomitant of living long. Such would be the climacteric, chemical changes in cells, or gradual loss of adaptive reserve capacity. The second kind of change could be considered *secondary aging*. It can occur at any time of life, but is found in greater frequency among older people. It may be the result of reduced reserve capacity and thus greater vulnerability or perhaps the result of idiosyncratic reactions to other conditions. This kind of aging includes sensory loss, chronic diseases such as arteriosclerosis or diabetes, and chronic brain syndrome. In this case, we are dealing with the tenth issue noted in Chapter 1—universality. Few physical changes are primary, or inevitable and universal, in the human species.

General body dimensions

HEIGHT

Most people have reached their full heights by their middle 20s; the average age at which all the skeleton has been converted to bone is 18 (Timiras, 1972). Longitudinal studies show considerable variability, however, with regard to both the time when full height is reached and the time when there is a decline from that point. Büchi (1950), for example, found increases in height into the 40s among men, mostly in sitting height. Gsell (1967) similarly reported that some people grow as much as 1 centimeter (cm) after their 25th birthdays.

Cross-sectional studies have consistently shown decreases in height starting about the age of 50, but these decreases are largely due to secular trends. Successive generations are taller than earlier generations, at least over the few centuries since measurements have been recorded. Succeeding generations have not only been getting taller, they have also been getting heavier and maturing earlier. For example, puberty has occurred four months earlier each decade since 1840. Explanations for secular trends include better nutrition, improved environmental conditions, or evolutionary changes in the gene pool. The mingling and interbreeding of previously isolated populations resulting from widely increased mobility can lead to "hybrid vigor." Whatever the reason, older people

who are shorter than their grandchildren may be thought to have shrunk with age, although they really never reached the taller heights of their descendants.

Although most of the cross-sectional evidence for shrinking in later life can be attributed to secular trends, longitudinal data do show a gradual decrease in height, on the average, starting about the age of 55 (Kent, 1976). This longitudinal study of healthy men, originally measured between the ages of 20 and 96 by a team of researchers at the Gerontology Research Center in Baltimore and now under the auspices of the National Institute of Aging, is providing us with significant developmental data on many variables. The decrease in height noticed among these men has been attributed to "settling" of the spinal column because of decline in density of the long bones and vertebrae (Timiras, 1972). The lifetime loss in height of women is on the order of 4.9 cm and of men 2.0 cm (Rossman, 1977).

As can be seen in Figure 6.1, there seem to be both sex and environmental differences in

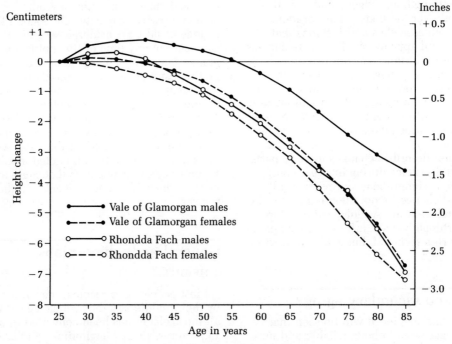

Figure 6.1. Decrements in height for two groups in Wales, based on remeasurements. The decline appears somewhat earlier and is more marked in the Rhondda Fach (mining area) group, presumably reflecting poorer environmental circumstances. *(Source: Miall, Ashcroft, Lovell, and Moore, 1967.)*

height decrements with age (Miall et al., 1967). The curves shown in this figure are derived from a longitudinal study of two communities in Wales, one (Vale of Glamorgan) more economically advantaged than the other (Rhondda Fach). Although all four groups decreased in height after middle age, the more advantaged men decreased the least. In fact, these Glamorgan men continued to grow to the age of 40. It is interesting that the Glamorgan women showed about the same growth pattern as both men and women of the mining community. These sex differences are hard to explain, because they apparently run counter to sex differences in many other physical measurements, in which women deteriorate later than men. However, women reach their maximum height about two years earlier than men. Perhaps women's bones are more fragile than men's. Osteoporosis, the loss of bone tissue in old age, is a more common problem for women than for men.

Before we make too much of shrinking of height in the later years of life, however, we should remember that we are talking about less than 1 inch total loss in men and less than 2 inches in women. If people kept clothes for a lifetime, pants and skirts could be shortened to compensate. A 5-foot 10-inch man whose son is 6 feet tall, however, would now feel even shorter, and this could contribute to shifts in family status and power differentials.

WEIGHT

Men in a Philadelphia Gerontology Research Center study continued to gain weight during their adult years until about the age of 55 and then began to lose (Kent, 1976). This agrees with the findings of cross-sectional studies, which have generally reported weight loss beginning in the 50s to the 70s. It is true that there have been secular trends toward increased weight corresponding to those toward increased stature. Furthermore, declines may seem exaggerated because fatter people may have less chances of surviving, leaving the leaner ones to skew the distribution in later years. Figure 6.2 shows age changes in the percentage of body weight that is fat. Even though women have more fat than men at all ages, the percentage of fat increases

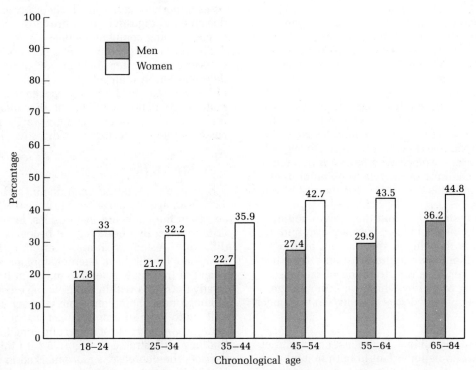

Figure 6.2.   Percentage of body weight that is fat, for men and women. *(Source: Novak, 1972.)*

for both. After 65, the difference between men and women noticeably decreases. A different sample of Midwestern men, measured by Novak (1972), reached their peak of weight about ten years earlier than those studied in Baltimore, although the shape of the curves may not be essentially different. In a U.S. Health Examination survey (Stoudt, Damon, McFarland, & Roberts, 1965), men were heaviest (average 172 pounds) between the ages of 34 and 54 years. Those men who were between 55 and 64 years old were 6 pounds lighter (166 pounds), and those ten years older 20 pounds lighter yet (140 pounds). Remember that these are cross-sectional data. Women in the same survey reached their maximum of 152 pounds between 55 and 65 years. Those between 65 and 74 were 6 pounds lighter (146 pounds), and those between 75 and 85 weighed only 138 pounds. Thus, women's weight continued to climb for two decades longer than men's, although their decline was proportionally less. If you recall, Libow's (1974) finding that heavier men lived longer than lighter men was cited in the last chapter. Those results may be explainable in part by selective factors: those who lived longer had not yet begun to lose weight.

In general, the problem of obesity seems to be greater for women than for men (Weg, 1977). The number of obese women does not drop until the late 60s and 70s; even among women over 80, 20% are overweight. The average body fat in men increases from 18% at age 20 to 36% at age 65; in women, from 33% at age 20 to 45% at age 65. Apparently more women become fat earlier. The fact that fewer people seem to be added to the obesity category with age suggests that American women who have not become fat in youth continue to struggle to maintain their weight (and thus their looks) for the rest of their lives.

Not only do people find themselves getting heavier as they get older, but they also find themselves changing in shape. Arms and legs become thinner, while the waist and trunk become thicker. This redistribution of fat causes the shifting profile by which we estimate age. Thin older people do not look like thin younger people.

Diet and digestion.   In the last chapter, diet was shown to be important to both mental and physical health, possibly even to living out a full life span. A good diet for one group, however, is not necessarily a good diet for another. Many dietitians feel that it would help older people if they ate a better selection of foods, and nutritional researchers have looked for general rules of good diet for older Americans. Weg (1977) concludes that the "Westernized diet" of most Americans today, which is high in cholesterol and other fats, sugar, and refined grains, leads to tooth decay, atherosclerosis, obesity, diabetes, and heart disease. Because it lacks bulk, it may also contribute to cancer (Burkitt, 1973). Furthermore, the refining, processing, canning, and overcooking of most of our foods destroy from 20 to 90% of micronutrients: vitamins and minerals that are essential to a wide range of body functions. In a general way, it seems safe to say that eating more whole grains, more vegetables, and less fat is better than eating prepared foods and sweets.

We must remember, though, that older people are survivors and that what has kept them alive is what they have eaten. To change their diets radically can lead to depression and a greater feeling of deprivation than before. The social surroundings of meals, furthermore, may also be as important as the meals themselves. Stress does not aid digestion. Pleasure in the company of good dining companions does.

There is a noticeable decline in the secretion of gastric juices after about age 30, as well as deterioration in their effective chemical components (Timiras, 1972). As a consequence, by middle age, people who do not alter their diets find themselves not only gaining weight more easily but also suffering more digestive upsets.

STRENGTH

Maximum strength in men declines about 42% from age 30 to age 80. Most weakening occurs in the back and leg muscles, less in the arm muscles. By middle age, it becomes more difficult to sustain great muscular effort. However, people who have been champions at the height of their power tend to maintain their relative prowess within their own age cohort, although new champions from younger cohorts will outdo them in time. The consistency of decline between cross-sectional and longitudinal findings is illustrated in Figure 6.3. In this comparison, the decrease is more marked in the longitudinal data than in the cross-sectional.

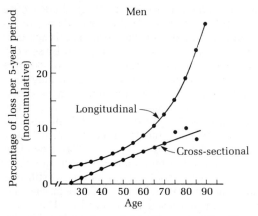 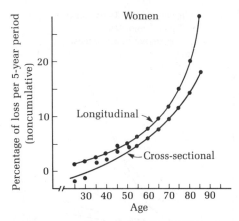

Figure 6.3. Relative loss of muscular strength with age in men and women. *(Source: Clement, 1974.)*

Perhaps younger cohorts are not much stronger than their parents; with regard to strength, there does not seem to have been a major secular trend. Figure 6.3 also shows that maximum strength follows maximum height, with a peak usually between the ages of 25 and 30. After this peak, there is a slight but steady loss of strength through the adult years, reaching a 10% loss by the age of 60.

Explanations for loss in strength tie it to progressive decline in energy production. Because the thyroid hormone, which regulates the rate of cellular metabolism, does not seem to decrease during the adult years, the decrease in metabolism may be caused by loss of metabolizing tissue rather than by deficiencies in thyroid function (Kent, 1976).

Exercise can help maintain power and sometimes even restore strength to muscles that have not been used much for a while. And one can maximize one's strength in later years by such strategies as reserving top capacity for special occasions, interspersing effort with rest periods, generally working at a slower pace, and exercising regularly (Timiras, 1972). When men between 42 and 83 were given training with strength exercises (Liemohn, 1975), all showed significant improvement.

Endocrine system

Because the primary function of the hormonal system is adaptation to environmental changes, the major effect of degeneration in this system is a generalized decrement in adaptation. It is therefore more meaningful to look at general adaptive functioning rather than changes in any particular glands. In a healthy person, defects in any one gland are quickly balanced by input from other glands. Even under disturbed conditions, repair of either the gland or the system is possible, and only with serious disease is there permanent disability. During the years of adulthood, although there may be progressive decrements in secretion of some glands, these defects are almost always compensated for. Only in the later years of old age do endocrine problems require serious consideration (Timiras, 1972). And even in old age, the findings are far from conclusive; it is much too early to say that there are consistent age decrements in endocrine functioning as a whole.

Cardiovascular system

Deaths from arteriosclerotic heart disease are noticeable from about the age of 35 in White men, 45 in White women. Black men and women are even more vulnerable. Kohn (1977) states bluntly that the cardiovascular system was not designed to last indefinitely, because it is composed of postmitotic cells, which do not renew themselves during life. These cells inevitably age, therefore, losing elasticity and undergoing other degenerative changes. As Figure 6.4 shows, cardiovascular failures account for an overwhelming majority of deaths after about the age of 50. Blood pressure begins to rise in childhood, and in Western countries elevates sharply in men during adolescence and again after age

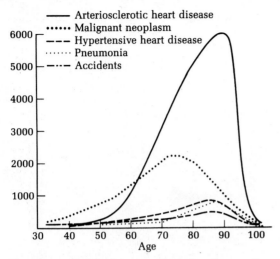

Figure 6.4. Deaths from specific major diseases in a U.S. female cohort of 100,000 at the 1966 rate. *(Source: Kohn, 1977.)*

50. In women, there is a more gradual rise during childhood, but a higher level than that for men is reached after 60. Perhaps this sex difference in later life can be explained by selective survival, because men with higher blood pressure will not have survived; women may be able to compensate better than men. Systolic blood pressure was significantly higher at the beginning of the study for those National Institute of Health subjects who died during the 11 years of the research (Libow, 1974). Age changes are explainable by (1) a decrease in the ability of the heart to contract; (2) increased stiffness of large arteries, which is partially compensated for by an increased volume of blood in the aorta; and (3) an increase in peripheral resistance.

Hypertension, or elevated blood pressure, seems to be highly influenced by environmental conditions. It is also rather easily reversed. In Figure 6.5, the two Welsh populations are

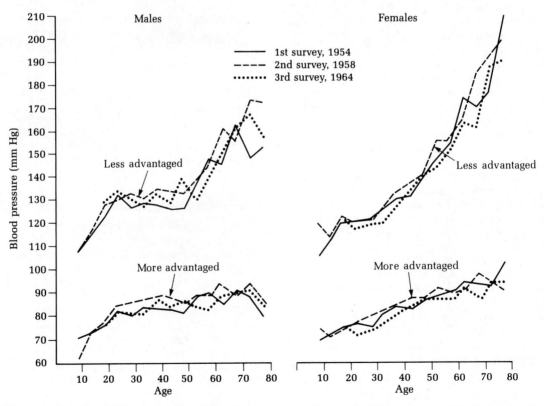

Figure 6.5. Relationship between age and blood pressure in a Welsh population. *(Source: Miall and Lovell, 1967.)*

shown. The less advantaged (coal miners) have significantly higher blood pressure all through life than the more advantaged. Their life is harder in many ways, and they are consequently under greater stress. Stress, smoking, and diet all affect the level of blood pressure and thus reducing stress, stopping smoking, and changing diet can all improve it. Libow (1974) reports that stopping smoking in late life, after many years of smoking, can still increase life expectancy.

Nervous system

The brain gets progressively smaller after about 30, and there is an increase in moisture in the cerebral cortex at the expense of solids. However, what effects these changes have on behavior is hard to say. Both cross-sectional and longitudinal studies have found age changes in electroencephalographic (EEG) records (Obrist, Henry, & Justiss, 1961; Wang & Busse, 1969). These changes are particularly noticeable in alpha rhythms, which seem to be related to attentiveness. These rhythms decrease steadily with age during the adult years. However, this effect may be due less to aging than to diseases that increase with age—such as vascular pathology, which reduces the flow of blood to the brain (Thompson & Marsh, 1973). Treatment of such diseases might minimize deterioration in this function and therefore in its behavioral consequences.

Other EEG findings are even harder to interpret. For example, fast EEG activity is higher in the middle-aged, in psychiatric patients, and in women than it is in younger and older subjects, "normal" people, and men. Perhaps such findings reflect a complicated self-regulatory system in which changes in one part of the system set off compensatory changes in other parts.

In addition to such EEG results, Timiras (1972) cites evidence for the slowing of conductivity in the peripheral nerves and across synapses. In general, the chief behavioral effect of most nervous-system changes during adulthood may be a generalized slowing down of almost all functions and processes. If so, this could be the most significant behavioral change of the second half of life, and may be a major example of *primary aging.* If one reads more slowly and writes more slowly, walks more slowly and jumps away from danger more slowly, talks

more slowly, and follows what others are saying more slowly, one is literally "on another wavelength."

SENSES

We communicate with the outer world through our senses. Blunting or losses in any sense can have profound psychological conse-

Figure 6.6. The upper picture shows a street scene as a young person with normal vision would see it. The lower picture was taken through a coated lens, scientifically developed to record the image as it might be seen by an elderly person (late 70s) with normal age-related diminishment of visual acuity. Pairs of pictures such as these are a part of an audio-slide presentation prepared at the Institute of Gerontology. *(Source: Thackrey and Pastalan, 1975.)*

es, amounting in some cases to "sensory deprivation." Leon Pastalan, at the University of Michigan, developed several techniques for the use of students and young people in general to simulate the blunting of visual, auditory, and tactile stimulation. It is often hard for people who have good sensory acuity to realize the feelings of despair that can result from such blunting. See Figure 6.6 for an illustration of how different the world looks to people whose vision is less acute.

Vision. The lens of the eye starts aging from infancy; it becomes more opaque and less elastic each year, because it continues to grow without shedding its older cells (which undergo chemical changes). Thus its shape changes. These lens changes affect the visual processes of accommodation and convergence, or distance of focus. More and more people, as they get older, need corrective glasses, until by age 50 almost everybody has at least one pair of reading glasses. The tendency to farsightedness increases about tenfold between 10 and 60. Watch, for example, how embarrassed older people are when they have to hold a letter as far away from them as their hands can reach or grope frantically for their reading glasses to look at a photograph. Also, because the diameter of the pupil tends to decrease around 50, less light comes into the eye and brighter lighting is needed. Dimmed lights of darkened theaters and restaurants can make middle-aged people functionally blind even though they may be able to read without glasses on a sunlit park bench.

Recovery from glare and adaptation to the dark take longer in middle age, so that driving at night becomes more difficult. However, color vision seems to hold up through late middle age, even though more light may be needed to appreciate the colors (art galleries should be brightly lighted).

Because retinal changes are rare before age 60, most adults have no trouble seeing, at least with glasses. Visual acuity is best at about 20, remains relatively constant to 40, and only then begins a slow decline (Timiras, 1972). Like almost all degenerative changes in later life, a wide variety of visual changes increase in frequency with each year lived. On the other hand, none of them are universal, or *primary aging*. It is possible to live to a ripe old age without ever needing glasses, or having any other eye problem. Nevertheless, many older people are prone not only to lens deterioration but also to changes in the eyelids that make them hang down in folds; to subconjunctival hemorrhages that cause red "veins" in the white of the eye, which turns more yellow; to tendencies to shed tears more easily in wind, dust, or cold; and to cataracts (Timiras, 1972). Timiras states that, although the age of onset varies widely, "practically every person will acquire cataracts if he lives long enough" (p. 517). Many of these changes are more of a nuisance or of cosmetic importance than they are disastrous. Few lead to blindness. However, as illustrated in Figure 6.6, blunting of vision can markedly alter the quality of life. Studies by Palmer (1968) do, in fact, show that older adult men with high visual acuity tend to look for more stimulation in their experiences than those with poor vision. Poor vision, like other kinds of sensory deprivation, dulls many other aspects of life.

Hearing. Hearing seems to be best at about age 20. From then on there is a gradual loss, more for high tones than for low, and, after 55, more for men than for women. Most hearing loss is not noticed, however, because it involves sounds that are not relevant to behavior (Timiras, 1972). We noted in Chapter 2 that environmental differences, particularly exposure to loud noise, have marked influence on hearing acuity. Timiras (1972) feels that, until we know a lot more about differential noise effects, we cannot determine hearing losses attributable to degenerative processes as such, whether in the sense organs, the conducting nerves, or the organizing cortex. So far, none of these locations seem to show unequivocal aging effects, or *primary aging*.

Other senses. There is no obvious change in taste sensitivity until about 50. After this age, although there may be no problem in discriminating the four basic tastes of sweet, sour, salt, and bitter, there may be less ability to distinguish finer nuances of taste. The number of taste buds diminishes after childhood, and those that remain tend to become less sensitive. A food that may seem too bland to the dulled taste sense of adults may be highly flavorful to children. The piquant spicing enjoyed by the gourmet is often unpleasant to the more sensitive child.

After about 40, sensitivity to smell decreases slightly. This loss may also influence sensitivity to taste—although it might have some advantages in polluted atmospheres.

Sensitivity to touch appears to increase from birth to about 45 and then to decrease sharply. There is no evidence of a drop in sensitivity to heat or cold. Sensitivity to pain tends to remain steady to 50 and then to decline differentially for different parts of the body. To complicate matters, pain tolerance may decrease, so that the person reacts to less pain with greater distress, although evidence here is contradictory and may be related to ethnic, cohort, and even sex-role differences in expressing pain. The sense of balance is at its best between 40 and 50—later than for most other senses (Timiras, 1972).

An interesting psychophysical cross-sectional study of sensitivity to smell (Rovee, Cohen, & Shlapek, 1975) found remarkable similarity across ages. The authors conclude that smell, which like touch is one of the earliest sensitivities, may be one of the last to decline under stress or in aging. Overall, sensory losses are *secondary aging* effects.

SLEEP

Although some aspects of sleep remain fairly stable during the adult years, others show clear age changes. Thompson and Marsh (1973), on reviewing the research in this area, feel that these changes are the result of central-nervous-system changes. Specifically, the total number of hours people sleep per night remains about the same, as does the amount of rapid-eye-movement (REM) sleep. However, as people get older—particularly after about age 40—they wake up more during the night and get progressively less of the deepest kind of sleep. By late middle age, therefore, they may spend more hours in bed—more and more of these in lying awake—and end up feeling less rested in the morning.

Appearance

Change in health and appearance are prominent triggers for change in how old one feels, at least in modern American society. There is relatively little change in the way people look dur-

ing early adulthood, but middle age is characterized by massive alterations in appearance. For one thing, there is an increased tendency to gain weight, a redistribution of fat in the body, and a conversion of muscle to fat. As Bischof (1969) points out, the middle-aged stop growing at both ends and grow in the middle. Whereas body fat is only 10% of body weight in adolescence, it is at least 20% by middle age, and most of it settles around the waist. The bust or chest becomes smaller, and the abdomen and hips larger.

Perhaps the next most obvious change is in the hair. During the 40s, the hairline recedes—particularly in men—and the hair thins out. Again, mostly in men, baldness increases. Grayness increases at about the same time, so that by the 50s most men and women in our country are gray-haired, and some are even white-haired. There are other, less noticeable hair changes. Stiff hair appears in the nose, ears, and eyelashes of men, and on the upper lip and chin of women. Men need to shave less often and women more often.

The skin covers approximately 18 square feet, constitutes about 6% of total body weight, and contains a yard of blood vessels, four yards of nerves, 25 nerve ends, and more than a hundred sweat and oil glands. It may show signs of aging as early as 25 years, or as late as 50. These signs include changes in color to sallowness, mottled with "liver spots," and loss of elasticity with wrinkling, "crows' feet," and sagging. Benign and malignant growths develop, and freckles become more prominent. The bags and dark circles appearing under the eyes are more noticeable because the rest of the surface pales.

The critical area of the face is the lowest third. The distance between the bottom of the nose and the chin gets smaller as a result of changes in the teeth, bone, muscles, and connective tissue.

Posture and movements become less graceful because of such factors as stiffening of joints and loss of resiliency in muscles.

The voice slowly loses timbre and quality and becomes more highpitched. By late middle age, most singers decide to retire.

The total effect of all these changes may make middle-aged people reluctant to look in the mirror. The reunion of old friends after several years' separation can be painful, for each is shocked at the changed appearance of the other, and each realizes that what is true for the other must also be true for the self.

Berscheid and Walster (1978), in a review of studies relating to social stereotypes associated with physical attractiveness, found a general tendency for people considered attractive to be assigned socially desirable attributes. Women are judged even more strongly than men on the basis of their appearance (Adams & Huston, 1977), and older people tend to focus on appearance more strongly than younger ones. Campbell, Converse, and Rodgers (1976) found, furthermore, that interviewer ratings of attractiveness were related to scores on internal locus of control more for women than for men and especially for women under 35 and over 65—not the middle-aged in this case. Attractive young and old women feel more in control of their lives—but not attractive middle-aged women.

Both sex and social-class differences exist with respect to changes in appearance, just as they do with respect to health in our society. Because counteractive measures take time, money, and effort, middle-class people can continue to look more attractive and youthful many years longer than lower-class people. Similarly, because it is considered more important for women than for men to look youthful and attractive (see Sontag, 1972, for a discussion of the "double standard of aging"), women usually succeed in doing so, or at least they try harder. Diet, exercise, clothing, and cosmetics preoccupy many middle-class middle-aged American women. In an exploratory comparison of men and women's concerns with attractiveness and youthfulness, Nowak (1975) found the greatest concern with attractiveness was among middle-aged women. Concern with youthfulness was progressively greater with each older group. Altogether, women of all ages tend to be more concerned with youthfulness than with attractiveness; middle-aged women cannot even separate the two concepts. They feel that if one is attractive, one is youthful, and if one looks young one therefore looks attractive. Incidentally, in the Nowak (1975) study young women gave higher attractiveness ratings to older men, and vice versa: older men exaggerated the attractiveness of young women.

As a rule, those people who derive their feelings of worth from their bodies (for example, strong men, athletes, or beautiful women) are likely to be more sensitive to decreases in physical attributes than are people who have other ways of assessing their own value. Buhler (1959), who collected diverse biographical material about people's lives over centuries, found that what she calls the "biographical curve of life" is closest in timing to the biological curve for subjects whose self-image is most centered on their body. People who value themselves for their strength or physical prowess show psychological patterns of aging as soon as their bodies start aging, whereas those who value themselves for such nonphysical attributes as intelligence or interpersonal competence may continue to function and feel young for many years after their hair turns gray and their leg muscles weaken. For this reason, too great an emphasis on physical development in childhood and adolescence may boomerang later in life, although some may be lucky enough to continue athletics as a way of life. Senior Olympics have become accepted events. Will we see Senior Beauty Contests next?

Sex

Because of the enormous importance of sexual behavior to the survival of species or cultures, it is impossible to separate physiological from social factors in this area or to tell which age differences might be inevitable age changes. Most of our developmental information has come from three cross-sectional studies (Kinsey, Pomeroy, & Martin, 1948; Kinsey, Pomeroy, Martin, & Gebhard, 1953; Masters & Johnson, 1966) and one longitudinal study of older people at Duke University (Pfeiffer & Davis, 1972). Because every society overlays sexual activity with a gridwork of regulations and legends, and because there has been rapid social change (period effects) in attitudes toward sex in recent years (Troll & Bengtson, 1979), our present information may not apply to future generations. The widespread notion that men are more "sexual" than women—that men have stronger sex drives while women are by nature passive receptacles—is prevalent among older cohorts but not among younger ones. So is the belief that sex is exclusively for procreation (held by older cohorts) instead of for recreation (held by younger cohorts). Such beliefs inevitably influence practices.

It is important to distinguish among several sex-related variables that are frequently confused. Sexual *morphology* refers to physical sex differences, external as well as internal. Sex or gender *identity* refers to whether one *feels* like a man or woman—whether or not one *is* a man or a woman. Sexual *activity* refers to the manner of sexual behavior. This can vary from masturbation to coitus, from coitus with a same-sex partner to coitus with an opposite-sex partner. *Hormone* production is independent of both sexual identity and manner of sexual activity. Finally, *fertility* refers to ability to produce children. Each variable shows its own developmental pattern, and, to complicate matters further, there are differences between men and women in each. A related topic, *sex-role* behavior, which refers to societal expectations for femininity and masculinity, is discussed later in Chapters 15, 16, and 20.

Fertility and sexual activity can be separated logically, but their lack of separation in the minds of most older people today leads many of them to think that, because sexual activity is primarily for the purpose of reproduction, it should end with the end of fertility. Hence, the "dirty old man" idea, or the notion of the nonsexual old woman.

GENDER

Whether one becomes a man or a woman is determined partly by one's genes, partly by one's hormones, and partly by the way one was raised. Practically every new embryo has either an XX genetic combination, if female, or an XY, if male. For the first six or seven weeks of prenatal existence, both genetic females and genetic males are alike, however. Only when the male hormones—the androgens—come into play are the genetic programs set in motion to make the potential males different from potential females. At that time, their basic female gonads are changed to male gonads and other male structures appear. At the same time, females start acquiring female gonads. Females thus have a more continuous gender development than males, who go through a sharp transformation from female morphology to male. By the time the baby is born, it is easy for all curious relatives to find out whether it is a boy or a girl. After birth, the hormones that played such an important part during the embryonic period "lie low" until puberty. There is a growing body of evidence, however, that prenatal hormone activity can have delayed effects—not seen before puberty (Doering, 1980) but "set" before birth.

During these early years, the attitudes of parents and other humans around become the important determiners of appropriate gender classification. A child may be genetically male and hormonally male (in utero) but may be raised female and, to all intents and purposes, may feel and act and even look female—or vice versa.

Hormones play a more important role again from puberty onward. These sex hormones are chemically steroids and are produced in the adrenal glands and gonads: the ovaries of women and the testes of men. The predominantly female sex hormones are estrogen and progesterone; the predominantly male sex hormones are androgens, including testosterone. All these hormones are influenced by the pituitary gland in the brain. Female adolescence begins with a sharp growth spurt and the gradual appearance of secondary sex characteristics such as axillary (underarm) and pubic hair and breasts, starting about age 10 and ending about age 18 or later, when maximum growth is reached (Timiras, 1972).

MENSTRUAL CYCLE AND HORMONES

The beginning of reproductive functioning in women is signaled at the time of menarche (puberty), generally between ages 10 and 13, by the first menstruation. This age of menarche has been going down over the last few hundred years—since data have been collected—and the age of menopause has been going up (Tanner, 1962). This secular trend—long-term gradual historical change—has been attributed to such factors as better nutrition or hybrid vigor, as discussed in Chapter 2. About 200 years ago, women first started to menstruate at the age of 16. First menstruation is now stabilized at about 12.8 years of age. A study at the Massachusetts Institute of Technology (Altman, 1976) found that girls' average pubertal age has not changed since 1943. The present cohort of adolescents menstruate at about the same age as their mothers did, suggesting that this secular trend has evened off.

As noted, the menstrual cycle is controlled by the female sex hormones of estrogen and progesterone, which are in turn regulated by the pituitary. There are primarily two phases to the cycle: proliferative and secretory. A diagram of the menstrual cycle is shown in Figure 6.7. In the proliferative phase, the secretion of a follicle-stimulating hormone (FSH) by the pituitary gland stimulates the growth of several immature ova (about 400,000 of which have been "waiting" since embryonic days). In turn, the follicle cells in the ovary that surround the growing ova produce estrogen. As the estrogen levels build up, they are secreted into the bloodstream. When they reach a critical level, they trigger the production of luteinizing hormone (LH) by the pituitary and end the production of FSH.

Ovulation, the midpoint of the menstrual cycle, occurs when the level of LH exceeds that of FSH. A single mature follicle is released at this time. It ruptures and ejects the mature ovum into the fallopian tube to await the arrival of sperm. Meanwhile, as part of the preparation for fertilization and pregnancy, the uterine lining is building up to become thick enough for implantation of the fertilized egg.

After ovulation, the follicle that had ejected the ovum is transformed into the corpus luteum, which now takes on the function of producing more estrogen and progesterone to aid in starting the implantation of the new foetus. If pregnancy occurs, even more estrogen and progesterone are produced by the placenta, which encapsulates the developing embryo.

If the ovum has not been fertilized, however, the increased levels of estrogen and progesterone in the bloodstream signal the pituitary to inhibit the production of luteinizing hormone, thus depriving the corpus luteum of its stimulant to prepare more estrogen and progesterone. With the degeneration of the corpus luteum, the two female hormones diminish markedly and menstruation begins. Menstruation—the shedding of the uterine lining through the cervix and vagina—lasts anywhere from three to seven days, on the average.

This complicated interplay of pituitary gland, hypothalamus, ovaries, and uterus produces the

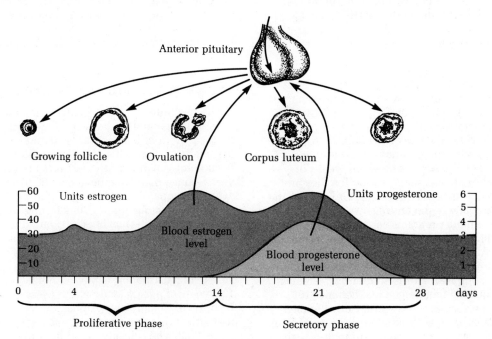

Figure 6.7. The menstrual cycle. *(Source: O'Leary, 1977, after Benson, 1977.)*

28-day cycle shown in Figure 6.7. Although not all women have an invariant 28-day cycle—some menstruate as often as every two weeks and others as seldom as once in several months—the coincidence of the cycle time and the moon phases has been significant to many cultures of the world throughout human history. To many, there is a magical synchronism between the tides of the oceans, influenced by the moon, and the tides in a woman's body. Psychiatrists such as Theresa Benedek (1959) became curious about the relation between crises in women's (patients) disturbed behavior and the phases of the moon as early as the 1930s. Benedek reported that, whereas she found no anxiety themes during the ovulation phase (when estrogen is high), there were many such themes just before menstruation—when both estrogen and progesterone levels are dropping.

More recent research, with women who were not seeking psychiatric help (Gottschalk, Kaplan, Gleser, & Winget, 1962; Ivey & Bardwick, 1968), found high self-esteem and low anxiety and hostility at the midpoint of the menstrual cycle (at ovulation, when the level of estrogen was at its peak) and significant increases in anxiety, depression, and hostility just before menstruation (at the low point of these hormones). Ivey and Bardwick interviewed their college women subjects at various times during the month and report dramatic differences in the content of thoughts. For example, at ovulation one woman said "Well, we just went to Jamaica and it was fantastic, the island is so lush and green and the water is so blue. . . . The place is so fertile and the natives are just so friendly." At premenstruation, the same woman said "I'll tell you about the death of my poor dog . . . my first contact with death and it was very traumatic for me. . . . Then my grandmother died."

Positive emotional feelings have been recorded at other times when hormone levels are high, as during pregnancy. When these hormones drop, we see postpartum depression (O'Leary, 1977) and menopausal depression. We should be wary of premature conclusions, however. It is impossible to separate physiological from socialization effects. As O'Leary (1977) points out, we are dealing with correlational data in all the studies, which tell us nothing about cause and effect. It is just as possible that behavior influences hormone levels as that hormone levels influence behavior—in fact, both probably occur. For example, McClintock (1971) observed that women who live together for a while or who are good friends come to have the same menstrual cycle and menstruate at the same time. Furthermore, most people in our society are more ready to attribute physiological causes to women's behavior than to men's; this is part of the sex-role stereotyping process, which will be discussed in later chapters. The rapid decline of estrogen level preceding menstruation has been associated with several physical symptoms such as water retention and pain or cramping as well as with the emotional symptoms mentioned. The term *premenstrual tension* is often used.

Not all women feel cyclic mood swings. In a study of over 800 "normal young married women," Moos (1968) found that less than half—30 to 40%—reported such swings. Kimmel (1980, p. 144) suggests:

> Many women, perhaps most, either do not experience marked mood changes, are not aware of them as cyclic changes, or successfully cope with them so that they are of minor importance. Certainly, we would expect that personality factors, satisfaction with one's various roles, and general coping ability would be as important in determining the effect of these shifts in hormone levels as the physiological changes themselves. Indeed, we again argue that the effects of physiological sex differences are most usefully seen as an interaction of biological, psychological, and social factors. One woman may feel little change in mood—or little negative effect of the mood shift—because she is involved in ego-satisfying projects. Another may automatically anticipate or adapt to the changes by scheduling her activities to minimize the effects of negative mood and to maximize the effects of positive moods.

Perhaps because of age and sex-role stereotypes, both the quantity and quality of research on both puberty and menopause are woefully insufficient. At this time, we should not even try to base any sound conclusions on available information. Only recently have a few systematic longitudinal studies started on puberty, and so far there are none on menopause that are looking at physiological, hormonal, and psychological variables together.

To confuse matters further, there is even some evidence that men may also experience cyclic fluctuations in hormone—and mood—production (Kimmel, 1980).

MALE PUBERTY

The transition into reproductive maturity in boys begins later than in girls, starting at about age 12 and ending not before 20. Generally, the first signs following the growth spurt are the enlargement of the testes and penis and the growth of fine hair at the base of the penis. Hair in the armpits and on the face does not usually appear until about ages 15 and 18, respectively, and half the boys in the United States have not yet needed to shave at 17 or 18, usually to their embarrassment.

Many secondary sex differences in body size, shape, and tissue structure develop during the adolescent years. The most obvious, beside differences in hair and genitals, are men's greater height and strength, their wider shoulders, and women's breasts and wider hips. Most of these differences emerge during the prepubescent growth spurt, in which practically every muscle and skeletal dimension of the body changes (Tanner, 1962).

Many changes boys experience in puberty, such as sudden erections in public places, acne, "wet dreams," and asynchronous development, produce embarrassment and lower self-concepts, particularly in our society, where parents do not give much sex information. The importance of shared expectations is illustrated by the studies of Mussen and Jones (1957) on the effects of early and late maturing. Although early-maturing boys end up with enhanced self-esteem, late-maturing boys and both extra-early- and extra-late-maturing girls have long-lasting lowered self-esteem.

PREGNANCY

As noted earlier, estrogen and progesterone increase rapidly to very high levels after fertilization and stay high throughout pregnancy (O'Leary, 1977). During the second stage of labor, shortly before delivery, progesterone declines rapidly. Estrogen does not decline until just after the baby is born. It returns to normal level in five to 25 days after birth. These hormone levels have been associated with mood changes in *postpartum depression*. However, depression has also been correlated with the length and difficulty of labor. And being pregnant and giving birth to a child have enormous consequences in a woman's social situation. Thus, it is almost impossible to separate biochemical effects from social effects.

There are wide individual differences at every point. Some women have no trouble conceiving, feel healthy and buoyant throughout pregnancy, and—particularly with natural childbirth practices that remove the helpless, institutionalized feelings from labor and birth—have short, easy deliveries and no observable postpartum depression. Such "lucky" women also are likely to find it easy to produce enough milk to nurse their children adequately. Other women have trouble at every point: they do not get pregnant when they wish or at all. They are ill throughout most of their pregnancy. They miscarry or have protracted, painful deliveries. And they cannot produce enough milk to nurse. Undoubtedly, both physical and psychological factors interact at all these points, as they do for all biological processes.

MENOPAUSE

Degenerative changes in the ovaries and other endocrine glands bring about a relatively dramatic stop to the menstrual cycle—menopause—in women around the age of 50. In part, this change is dramatic because of its association with sexuality and fertility in the minds of most social groups. In part, it is dramatic because it is noticeable. In part, however, it is dramatic because it occurs well before any other obvious physical changes associated with aging. Its association with sexuality and fertility is discussed later in this chapter. First, it is instructive to review what we know—or don't know—about the physiological events surrounding menopause.

Talbert's (1977) review of the human and animal research on the aging of the reproductive system concluded that the menopause now occurs between 48 and 51 years of age for most human populations, but those data conflict as to whether this age has changed over time, as the age of menarche has. There seems to be no relationship between age of menarche and age of menopause. If anything, early puberty may go together with later menopause (Timiras, 1972).

A reduction in the amount of circulating estrogen is associated with changes in the anterior lobe of the pituitary gland. Although there is general agreement that there is an increase in total gonadotrophin in the hypophysis of postmenopausal women, the relative changes in FSH and LH are uncertain (Talbert, 1977). According to Talbert, women approaching the menopause frequently have shorter cycles than they had earlier in their adult life, and this shorter cycle is due mostly to shortening of the follicular phase.

Menopause is followed by some atrophy in the vagina, the uterus, and the breasts, although much of this shrinking does not occur typically for 10 or 20 years after the menses stop and in fact may not be directly related to it. For example, the human uterus grows slowly from birth to puberty, then increases rapidly to the adult (nonpregnant) size of about $8 \times 4 \times .5$ cm. In very old women, it has been observed to be as little as 1 cm in length. Not only do the breasts shrink but their glandular tissue also becomes replaced by fat.

A wide variety of clinical symptoms have been associated with the hormone changes of menopause. Some medical texts, in fact, list as many as 50 such symptoms, taking half a page to present them in paragraph form. Such symptoms include everything from anxiety, depression, and tension to "involutional melancholia," from edema and backache to dizziness and headaches. Some people consider the psychotic accompaniment of menopause inevitable, to some degree at least. Families may attribute any complaint of women "going through the change" to this event. The one clear symptom that can be attributed to menopause is the "hot flash." As the name implies, this is a flash sensation of heat. It is experienced to some degree by perhaps one-fourth to one-third of women at this time, and it varies widely in intensity. Some women may experience three or four "flashes" over a period of several years, and others half a dozen each day. Further discussion of moods and mental health associated with menopause appears in Chapter 16.

Although the degeneration of the ovaries leads to decreased estrogen production, other glands can continue to produce both estrogen and progesterone. Many postmenopausal women continue to have "female hormones" circulating in their blood for many years. This variability in estrogen content could explain the lack of universality in "typical" menopausal symptoms, including "hot flashes."

Even before the menses stop, irregularities in the menstrual cycle, menstrual cycles without ovulation, and premenopausal infertility can occur.

Many medical practitioners now prescribe supplementary hormones—estrogen and sometimes both estrogen and progesterone—when the "natural" production decreases. Although there is considerable disagreement among both researchers and practitioners about the efficacy of this treatment, the consensus seems to be that little, if any, generalized therapeutic value results (Timiras, 1972). It is not clear that it reverses or prevents degenerative changes in the vagina, such as dryness and thinner, less-elastic walls. It is also not clear whether it causes osteoporosis or facial wrinkling and discoloration. In fact, physicians who treat women by prescribing estrogen may be endangering their patients more than helping them. McKinnon (1980) argues that available evidence suggests that a possible benefit of menopause is a limit to the amount of time women are subjected to estrogen. Pregnancy and menopause both cut off oversupplies of estrogen, which are associated with increased risk of cancer. Not only is estrogen replacement therapy associated with higher cancer rates but such higher rates are also found among women who, because of earlier puberty, later menopause, or no pregnancies, have longer exposure to female hormones in a "natural" way (Talbert, 1977).

In a biological model of development, the *climacteric,* or end of reproductive capacity, would probably be considered the end of adulthood. It is significant, therefore, that it is now considered an event of women's middle age. Even rats, under laboratory conditions, spend much of their life in a postreproductive state (Talbert, 1977). Menopause is less significant today not only socially but also psychologically in the life of most American women. Neugarten, Wood, Kraines, and Loomis (1963) found that, although about half of all the 100 normal women they interviewed agreed that the menopause is an unpleasant experience, those who were going through it or were past it were much more likely to associate it with positive changes once it was over. Three-fourths of the menopausal age group (45 to 55) felt that it does not change a woman in any important way and that those who have trouble with it are usually those who "have nothing to do with their time" or who are expecting trouble. Younger women are much more worried about it than middle-aged women who know more about it, although only the over-55 women are not concerned about its unpredictability.

If women are anxious during these years, according to Neugarten (Neugarten et al., 1963), they are more likely to be anxious about changes in their families than about changes in their bodies. When asked to check the worst thing about middle age, over half of those between 45 and 55 said "losing your husband." Only one woman checked "menopause." None of the women was upset by the end of fertility, and many welcomed menopause as relief from menstruation and fear of unwanted pregnancy.

Bart (1971), using the Human Relations Area Files at Yale University as well as ethnographic monographs, found that these descriptions of many societies around the world showed certain cultural patterns and values associated with women's changed status after the childbearing years. Bart assumed that these social changes would be associated with women's reactions to the menopause. Essentially, she found that strong ties to extended kin and important roles in society for older women go together with improved status at middle age. Therefore, argues Bart, women with such opportunities for increased status should suffer less than those primarily devoted to husband and children.

A later study of five subcultures of women in Israel (Eastern European Jews, North African Jews, Near Eastern Jews from Arabian countries, Druze, and Arabs) did not find support for Bart's thesis (Neugarten & Datan, 1974). All the five groups of Israeli women were happy to be done with childbearing, like those in the Neugarten and others (1963) Chicago sample, and only the women from groups in the process of cultural transition (the Near Eastern Jews) showed any distress at this time. Thus Neugarten and Datan felt that it was uncertainty, more than lowered status or decreased social roles, that led to trouble. The prospect of greater freedom than they had had during their fertile years did not make the Arab women any more satisfied or dissatisfied with their postmenopausal states than the prospect of reduced attractiveness made the Western women. It was experiencing different effects than they had been socialized to expect that was traumatic.

MALE CLIMACTERIC

Some writers have been interested in the male climacteric. There can, of course, be no male "menopause." Unlike the relatively rapid changes of hormone level associated with ovar-

ian involution, the decline in testosterone is gradual. In fact, some old men have testosterone levels as high as those of most younger men. Another sex difference is the separation of fertility and hormone decline or potency in men, where these two processes are linked in women. There is a slight and steady drop in plasma testosterone between the ages of 20 and 90 (Doering, 1980), but no noticeable or functional change before the age of 60.

Neugarten and Datan (1974, p. 603) conclude that "although there are exceptional occurrences of abrupt involution comparable to ovarian involution, and occasional reports of symptoms such as headaches, dizziness, and hot flushes, if there is any change at all for the majority of men other than the gradual involution of senescence, the change is neither abrupt nor universal." In fact, so far as hormonal and other physiological effects of the climacteric are concerned, neither women nor men seem to be inevitably distressed by them. Altogether, Neugarten (1968, p. 23) feels that it is the unexpected event in life that is a crisis, not the expected ones: "divorce not marriage; death of a child, not birth of a child." She also concludes that it is the timing of life events that is important—whether they are "on time" (come when expected) or "off time" (come too early or too late).

FERTILITY

In the early formation of the embryo, an initial supply of germ cells migrates from the wall of the *yolk sac* to the newly formed male and female gonads. Present evidence suggests that this initial supply constitutes the total number of

TABLE 6.1 Effect of age of human female on number of oocytes in the ovary

Age in years	Number of cases	Number of oocytes
Birth	7	733,000
4–10	5	499,200
11–17	5	389,300
18–24	7	161,800
25–31	11	62,500
32–38	8	80,200
39–45	7	10,900

Source: Talbert, 1977, after Block, 1952.

ova and sperm—that no new ones are added later in life (Talbert, 1977). Studies by Block (1953) show that the number of oocytes (primitive ova) declines rapidly in the ovary from birth to 25 years or so, then stabilizes until about the age of 38, when a rapid decline is again seen. Nobody has systematically studied this subject in women over 45, although Novak (1970) saw an occasional follicle in women over 50. Block's data are shown in Table 6.1. Unfortunately, the number of cases from which these findings are derived is so small as to be unreliable. The largest number of women studied at any age group was 11! This problem characterizes most of our information about sexual development. Talbert (1977) concludes that most loss of oocytes over life is from attrition or decay and that there is no relation between the rate of ovulation and the rate of decline. After all, only one ovum is lost in each ovulation. It is more probable that some kind of hormone action—perhaps of pituitary hormones—destroys most potential ova.

Women become fertile at the time of menarche and lose fertility at the time of menopause. Both these processes are more gradual than one might think, however. It apparently takes several years for postpubertal women to reach their peak of fertility, just as it takes several years for menopausal women to reach bottom level. Men seem to come to a more rapid peak of fertility than women, even though their puberty starts about two years later on the average. Men's fertility also decreases much more gradually at the later end, with some men being known to have fathered children when they were as old as 70 or 80.

Not only are there fewer ova and sperm

around in later life, but it is also possible that those still in existence are not as viable (Talbert, 1977). Animal research in which ova are transplanted from either a young or an old rodent into the uterus of a young one shows age differences in some species—but not in all. Table 6.2 shows that the age of the mouse from which ova are obtained does not seem to matter but that the age of hamsters and rabbits does.

Deteriorative changes in the corpus luteum (see Figure 6.7), in the ovary itself, and in the uterus are associated with shorter menstrual cycles and miscarriages. An older uterus may not be as good a breeding place as a younger one. Changes in the ova themselves can make offspring of older parents more prone to disorders such as Down's syndrome or other defects of development.

It is on the basis of such data that many physicians advise against pregnancy by older mothers. In fact, there is a commonly held opinion that any mother over the age of 30 is putting herself or her child at risk. This has led to what could be called the "29-year-old syndrome," in which women at 29 rush into childbearing. If not yet married, they accept whatever marriage they can find—some even opt for pregnancy

TABLE 6.2 Effect of age of donor on percentage survival to term of ova transplanted into the uterus of young adults of the same species

	Age of donor			
	Mouse[a]	Hamster[b]	Rabbit[c]	Rabbit[d]
Young adult	48	49.2	45	33.5
Old	54	4.5	26	12.9

[a] Data of Talbert and Krohn, 1966.
[b] Data of Blaha, 1964b.
[c] Data of Maurer and Foote, 1971.
[d] Data of Adams, 1970.

Source: Talbert, 1977.

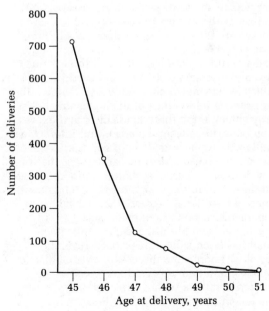

Figure 6.8. Deliveries in women over 44 years of age in England and Wales in 1957. (*Source: Francis, 1970.*)

without marriage—because they think this is their last chance for motherhood. For the vast majority of women, this belief may be harmful. Most women in their 30s and many in their 40s can produce healthy children without risk, and many would make better mothers if they wait for more suitable conditions such as better marriages, more financial security, and the establishment of other life interests, such as jobs. The technique of amniocentesis allows parents to discover the probability of abnormal offspring and gives them an option to terminate such pregnancies if they wish. (See Chapter 21 for further discussion of this topic.)

Talbert (1977) states that socioeconomic factors and contraceptive measures make it difficult to obtain reliable information about potential fertility changes with age in humans. Nonetheless, the abrupt drop in number of children born to women from the age of 45 to the age of 50 (Figure 6.8) is an impressive witness to fertility decline in the late 40s.

SEX BEHAVIOR

Development can be traced in three different kinds of sexual expression: autoerotic activities, or masturbation; homosexual activities, with partners of the same sex; and heterosexual activities, with partners of the opposite sex. We know very little about age differences in other kinds of sexual acts or in celibacy. Both gender and age differences appear in all three kinds of sexual expression just listed, as noted by Laws (1980) in her recent comprehensive review. She stresses the importance of distinguishing not only among these three kinds of sexual expression but also between behavior and interest, as well as between frequency of coitus and frequency of orgasm. Most research on sexual behavior to date is cross-sectional. Most confounds all these variables. Also, most research is confined to traditional heterosexual behavior—to reports of frequencies of coital acts.

What is ignored most are the implications of what has been called the "sexual revolution" for older people. No discussion of sex behavior among youth and young adults would be considered complete without detailed attention to the recent significant changes in attitudes toward sex, including attitudes toward sex as recreation, sexual equality in performance and

enjoyment, choice of occasion and partner, and premarital or extramarital sexual experience. As noted in the more thorough discussion of these topics in Chapters 19 and 20, these historical changes are so extensive that they have affected the attitudes and behavior of older individuals as well as younger. It is hoped that over the next few years more research information will be forthcoming on this "double shift" in sex and sex-role behavior.

Heterosexual sex. Butler and Lewis (1976, p. 10) state that "the act of sex is complex, encompassing the body, the mind, and the emotions. The physiology of sex includes nervous system and hormonal activity as well as specific organs." They delineate four phases in the heterosexual sex act: (1) excitement or erotic arousal; (2) intromission or plateau, in which the penis is placed in the vagina; (3) orgasm or climax; and (4) resolution or recovery. Essentially the same phases apply to both men and women. People are stimulated sexually in a number of ways—through sight, smell, touch, thoughts, and feelings. The pelvic area reacts. Muscle tension and congestion (filling of the blood vessels) occur, especially in the sexual or genital organs.

With the possible exception of the youngest age groups of adult women—those in their teens, 20s, and 30s—most women today have had much less experience with sex than men the same age. This is particularly true for older women. It is therefore rash to generalize about potential sex differences in sexuality. All our data are subject to cohort and period effects, not to mention interactions between cohort and period and between each of these and developmental effects. Keep this information in mind while reading the next few paragraphs.

Men report the shortest arousal periods; the most insistent, frequent, and vigorous orgasms; and the quickest recovery periods during their late teen years, gradually decreasing in all these measures from then on—although not inevitably terminating at any time.

Women start out their sex life—if they start during their teens—with less enjoyment than men. During their 20s, though, women's arousal periods shorten and their orgasms become deeper and more frequent.

The quality of a woman's marriage is related to her development of orgasmic capacity during the first five years of marriage (Clark & Wallin, 1965). Those who reported "good quality" marriages also said orgasmic frequency increased from 65 to 91%. Those who said their marriage was of "poor quality" reported few orgasms and no change over five years. Some women continue to grow more sexually proficient throughout their life. In fact, some women who never experienced orgasms before start enjoying them in middle age—after the menopause and after their children are grown (Pfeiffer & Davis, 1972). This may be true more for current postmenopausal women than for future cohorts who have not worried as much about becoming pregnant.

In general, older people who have led active, regular sex lives earlier continue to lead active, regular sex lives well into old age—although certain changes do come about. In this respect, also, much of our information is probably cohort-specific, influenced by early socialization to the double standard and by attitudes toward birth control or toward success with birth control.

In spite of the many myths about women's reduced sexuality with menopause, there is no evidence that they decline in their physical capacity for sex, either then or later. Masters and Johnson (1968) found that, while men gradually decreased in orgasmic capacity during their adult years, women showed no decrease, at least until their 60s. In late life, the clitoris may become slightly smaller, and the labia may become less firm as fatty tissue is lost from the genital area. However, the clitoris "still remains the source of intense sexual sensation and orgasm, essentially as it was in earlier years. Women in good health who were able to have orgasms in their younger years can continue having orgasms until very late in life, well into the eighties" (Butler & Lewis, 1976, p. 14).

Laws (1980) notes, though, that *Playboy* cartoons depict sexual old men as sleek and plutocratic but depict sexual old women as revolting and ridiculous crones. Considering that older men have enormously greater opportunities for obtaining coital partners than do older women, it would not be surprising if women bent on finding such partners must be more aggressive. Women might also have to turn to other kinds of sexual expression—mostly masturbation, as is discussed later.

According to Butler and Lewis (1976, p. 19), "Most men begin to worry secretly about sexual aging some time in their thirties, when they compare their present level of sexual activity with their previous performance as teen-agers and very young adults. . . . Quite simply, their penises don't work in the same way" and they think they are becoming impotent (unable to have an erection sufficient to carry out the sexual act). Older men take longer to obtain an erection—a matter of minutes after stimulation instead of a matter of seconds—and the erection may not be as large, straight, and hard. Furthermore, they are more prone to premature ejaculation, although this can be controlled. Lubrication is reduced, and also the volume of seminal fluid, which diminishes the urge to ejaculate. "Younger men produce three to five ml. of semen (about one teaspoon) every twenty-four hours, while men past fifty produce two to three ml. Actually this can be a decided advantage in love-making since it means that the older man can delay ejaculation more easily and thus make love longer, extending his own enjoyment and enhancing the possibility of orgasm for his partner" (Butler & Lewis, 1976, p. 21). Butler and Lewis also say that "older men have a choice of an extended period of sexual pleasure with a milder orgasm or a briefer session with a more intense orgasm" (p. 22). On the other hand, younger men can have a second erection in a few minutes; older men may have to wait hours or even days.

Homosexuality. At the beginning of this section, we described the complex nature of gender formation and the fact that it has a compound of genetic, hormonal, and social causes. In the subsequent discussion of sexual activity, the complexities of sexual enjoyment were similarly stressed. There is equal diversity and complexity, probably, in the developments leading to choice of sexual identity, partners, and practices. Until very recently, any deviation from heterosexual partners, preferably joined in legal unions and engaging in coitus in a male-dominant position for the purpose of producing children, was considered both individually and socially pathological.

Freud (1905/1930) was one writer, among many others, who tried to explain the ontogenesis of male homosexuality as an imperfect resolution of a necessary oedipal stage of psychosexual development between the ages of 4 and 6. Most such writers made no distinction between gender identity—whether the person felt himself or herself to be male or female—and preference for same or opposite-sex partners. In the last few years, following on the heels of the women's movement and the gay liberation movement, as well as of shifting attitudes toward sex in general, a number of research investigations have been unable to find any systematic psychological differences between men and women who prefer same-sex partners and those who prefer opposite-sex partners (O'Leary, 1977). A man who prefers another man can be very "masculine" in identity, appearance, preferences, and habits or can be very "feminine." The same can be said for homosexual preferences among women. Some theorists, whose orientation is that of social-learning theory (see Chapter 2), believe that such preferences are primarily a matter of early experiences with people of the same or opposite sex. Happier experiences with women than with men could lead either boys or girls to choose women as sex partners in adulthood, or vice versa.

At the present time, we probably cannot even point to any pathological condition predating the decisions of those (few) individuals who choose to undergo transsexual surgery. The majority of adults who have a choice of partner—if they are not in prison or some other sex-restrictive place—choose a partner of the opposite sex. There are probably wide individual differences here, as in all other areas, with some people being highly heterosexual, some bivalent, and some highly homosexual.

Masturbation.   Marked sex differences exist in age trends for masturbation. Boys start to masturbate early in childhood, usually in the company of other boys who teach and support these practices. During adolescence, the use of pictures and images of women serves as a transition to heterosexual experience. Thus, there is a continuity in masculine sexual development, which is not true for women. Freud's term "latency period" is true more for women than for men. Kinsey and his colleagues report that 88% of their male subjects had masturbated by their midteens (Kinsey et al., 1948), in contrast to only

20% of their female subjects (Kinsey et al., 1953).

Some explain this by the difference in visibility of the sex organs. Every little boy notices his penis. Most little girls have to be told about their clitorises or vaginas—or discover them accidentally. Once women discover masturbation, however, they use it more frequently than men; 40% of Kinsey's 20-year-old women, and 62% of the 40-year-olds, reported some masturbation. During the adult years, masturbation tends to be used less often by men, more often by women. By the age of 40, men and women report equal frequency (Wilson, 1975). Unmarried women report masturbating more than married women: 59% versus 31%, although Hite (1976) suggests that women find out about, or at least turn to, masturbation only after experiencing coitus. When Christenson and Gagnon (1965) reanalyzed some of the Kinsey data on women, they found that, although coitus was higher among married women than among unmarried ones, masturbation was higher among older women who had formerly been married.

Interest in sex.   Not everybody who is interested in sex or aroused sexually engages in sexual activity. Not everybody who engages in sexual activity is either interested in sex or aroused sexually. Data on older people (for example, see Wilson, 1975) show no difference in interest between unmarried and no longer married women, although there are marked differences in activity. Married women continue to experience coitus, at least to the capability of their husbands. Christenson and Gagnon (1965) found, in fact, greater coital activity among women whose husbands were about their own age than among those whose husbands were older. They also found increase in interest among older people, even though coital frequency dropped.

One way of measuring interest in sex is by asking people about their interest level. Another way is by asking them whether they dream about sex at night. Although there was a substantial interest among older women, more older men reported interest in sex than older women: 80% versus 30% (Verwoerdt, Pfeiffer, & Wang, 1969). Some of these sex and age differences may be cohort effects, as is suggested by recent findings that college students no longer show gender differences in sexual arousal by pictures (Sigusch, Schmidt, Reinfeld, & Wiederman, 1970).

Conclusions

The impressive evidence for variability in physical development, as well as for the small amount of actual change in many variables, should help younger people look forward cheerfully to the future. Most people experience no significant bodily changes before the age of 50 or so; for at least three decades, they remain "youthful." Not all the changes of middle age are for the worse, either. Women past the menopause generally improve in health and vitality, for example.

Exercise and diet can forestall many changes in vigor, strength, as well as appearance. Elevations in blood pressure can be corrected by a number of different kinds of techniques, some psychological, others medical. We have come a long way in correcting sensory defects, too. The end of fertility does not mean the end of sexuality, and new attitudes toward variation in sexual expression may make it possible for older people to substitute one activity for another that is lost.

Consider some of the underlying issues described in Chapter 1.

1. *Biology versus environment.* Twin studies suggest that much of our physical development is genetically programmed. Identical twins tend not only to look very much alike but to develop in much the same way throughout life. Thus, in order to estimate what future physical changes might be, people could look at older generations in their families. If their parents and grandparents have become blind or deaf, for example, people might look forward to needing cataract or other eye surgery or might watch for the newest developments in hearing aids. If there is a family tendency toward obesity, diet and exercise are particularly needed. Cardiovascular difficulties among ancestors should alert people to watch their blood pressure from an early age and to adjust their lives to try to avoid such problems—for example, by never smoking.

But biology is not everything. Generational differences as well as socioeconomic differences appear in almost every discussion of physical development. Children are often taller than their parents if they eat different foods. Old men in Africa, where it is quieter, have better hearing than those in America. Middle-class men and women are not as obese as working-class men and women. Older women of today are likely to have less sex activity than older women of tomorrow. Men whose fathers, older brothers, uncles, and grandfathers have all died by 45 of heart attacks can remain living into their 70s and 80s if they seek medical treatment and pay careful attention to their diet and exercise. It is neither our genetic inheritance alone nor our life experiences and circumstances alone that determines our lifelong physical development, but a constant interaction between both.

2. *Change versus development.* The transformational processes in physical development are great. Shakespeare has Jaques say

> All the world's a stage,
> And all the men and women merely players:
> They have their exits and their entrances;
> And one man in his time plays many parts,
> His acts being seven ages. At first the infant,
> Mewling and puking in the nurse's arms.
> And then the whining school-boy, with his satchel
> And shining morning face, creeping like snail
> Unwillingly to school. And then the lover,
> Sighing like furnace, with a woeful ballad
> Made to his mistress' eyebrow. Then a soldier,
> Full of strange oaths and bearded like the pard,
> Jealous in honour, sudden and quick in quarrel,
> Seeking the bubble reputation
> Even in the cannon's mouth. And then the justice,
> In fair round belly with good capon lined,
> With eyes severe and beard of formal cut,
> Full of wise saws and modern instances;
> And so he plays his part. The sixth age shifts
> Into the lean and slipper'd pantaloon,
> With spectacles on nose and pouch on side,
> His youthful hose well saved, a world too wide
> For his shrunk shank; and his big manly voice,
> Turning again toward childish treble, pipes
> And whistles in his sound. Last scene of all,
> That ends this strange eventful history,
> Is second childishness and mere oblivion,
> Sans teeth, sans eyes, sans taste, sans every thing.

[Shakespeare, *As You Like It*, Act 2, Scene 7]

Shakespeare's image is one of such qualitative change, physically, that the metaphor of different roles—different people—seems appropriate. He sees the changes in voice, in shape ("shrunk shank"), and in appetite as too vast to be mere quantitative changes. When we look at photograph albums, and we compare pictures of a child at a tenth birthday party, an adolescent at high school graduation, the bride and groom at a wedding, a grandparent holding a new grandchild, and the celebrants at a golden wedding, we feel sure that we are looking at intrinsically different people. Comparisons of cells or X rays of heart, teeth, and many other body parts at different times of life may also look as if they were from different people.

3. *Retrogressive versus progressive changes.* Clearly, when considering physical development, it is necessary to consider both positive and negative change. Although retrogression need not mean exact reversal and the image of a "second childhood" is not an exact description of the deteriorative physical changes of later life, there do seem to be periods of building up followed by periods of breaking down of processes, systems, and body parts.

4. *State versus process.* With a few exceptions, it is almost impossible to describe a physical state at any given period of life. Suppose we consider people in their 20s. Even if we control for sex, ethnicity, and socioeconomic status, we could not say how tall an Irish man who grew up and lived on the South Side of Chicago is at the age of 25. All we might be able to say is that he is about as tall as he will ever be—a process description. Or even if we were to describe a menopausal woman about 50, we would not be able to state what her symptoms were or how they compared with her symptoms ten years earlier or ten years later. We could, of course, say that her menses had stopped or were soon to stop and that she would no longer be able to become pregnant. That much would be a state description, but the rest would be a process description.

5. *Turning points.* Two commonly cited turning points in the lives of adult women are giving birth and experiencing menopause. These points have received much research attention because it is assumed that they have psychological and social, as well as physical, implications. As we have seen in the review of physical changes in this chapter, their significance is neither clear nor overwhelming. In later chapters, we will look more thoroughly at the significance these events derive from social expectations. Both these events concern women, and no com-

parable turning point is attributed to men's physical development.

6. *Time.* This chapter has been written almost exclusively in the framework of *life time.* Nonetheless, chronological age is not the unit that is most appropriate; "developmental age" would order the sequence of events better. Each person follows a different trajectory of physical development from birth to death, and we need a measure to show how far along this trajectory an individual is at any moment.

Summary

The physical changes in the body past the age of 20 are closely linked to psychological changes, because our culture values youth. The major physical changes in body dimensions are height (people tend to "shrink" a little in old age—women more so than men), weight (people put on weight in middle age—again, women more so than men), and strength (people lose some endurance and mobility with age).

The aging of the endocrine system is of course most strongly apparent in women, who go through childbearing and menopause, with corresponding fluctuations in hormones. However, data on endocrine aging are incomplete; we cannot say that aging entails a consistent breakdown in the endocrine system.

The cardiovascular system, being composed of postmitotic (unrenewable) cells, does tend to break down. Cardiovascular aging may result in constricted blood flow, heart attacks, and high blood pressure. Exercise, weight control, diet, and not smoking all help to preserve functioning.

The senses all may suffer some decline. Hearing and vision losses affect most sharply older people, and these senses are crucial to functioning in society. Taste and smell may also become less acute. Touch-sensation and pain data are contradictory.

Central-nervous-system changes may produce a general slowing down of all functions and processes. Sleep may become progressively lighter and more interrupted.

Changes in appearance involve body structure, hair color, and skin texture, and affect people psychologically in important ways. Women are considered to age less attractively than men in our culture. And working-class people have fewer resources for remaining youthful-looking than do the wealthy.

Sexual changes and behavior development encompass many factors. Gender is hormonal, genetic, and environmental. Menarche initiates a complex hormonal cycle for women that continues, interrupted by childbearing, until the menopause. Male puberty also produces major changes. Both men and women develop secondary sex characteristics during puberty. Pregnancy is a nonuniversal change for women; menopause is universal. The possible male climacteric does not seem to be either universal or as dramatic as menopause, although mood swings (perhaps dictated by culture) may be experienced by both men and women. Fertility does decrease with age, and ends (but not abruptly) with the climacteric (men) or menopause (women).

Sex behavior develops along autoerotic, homosexual, and heterosexual lines. Both gender and age differences appear. Women tend to become sexually active later than do men in our culture, and do not have a continuous heterosexual development. Both men and women masturbate, although men begin earlier; however, once they begin, women may masturbate more than men. Interest in sex varies among individuals. Sexual capacity can continue well into the 80s, although it does decline somewhat. Sex behavior is hard to study and measure because of cultural restrictions on expressing and reporting sex behavior.

7

Health and Illness

Health—or its opposite condition, illness—is generally conceived as a global state. It emphasizes the overall functional competence of a person rather than any specific body part or system. Thus it is possible to be healthy even though many systems, like cardiovascular or digestive, are not working as well as they used to, or as they should by normative standards. It is also possible to be ill even though one's body is in as good condition as that of most people, or as might be required for survival or competent daily functioning.

Health

The constitution of the World Health Organization (WHO) defines health as "a state of complete physical, mental and social well-being and not merely the absence of disease and infirmity" (Dingle, 1973, p. 49). Unfortunately, most literature on health deals primarily with diseases. The Canadian Sickness Survey of 1950–1951 is an example of this tendency to look at illness instead of health. Not all so-called health surveys have the word *sickness* in their title; most use the term *health*. Yet most measure illnesses; they do not ask how many days of good health were experienced.

The Canadian Sickness Survey, which questioned the total Canadian population, found that over the period of an average day about 85% of the population reported no sickness, not even minor ailments (Dingle, 1973). Over the period

of a year, however, that figure went down to about 20%. Thus, only one-fifth of the Canadian population in 1950 had not been sick at all for as long as one year. Conversely, four-fifths had experienced at least some minor ailment. Concentrating on illness is, in a way, easier than concentrating on health. When we are healthy, we do not think about health. When we are ill, we find it difficult *not* to think about health.

In 1970, the U.S. National Center for Health Statistics asked a sample of 116,000 people from all 50 states to report how they perceived their health had been during the past year. This report, shown in Figure 7.1, indicates that the largest incidence of new acute conditions for that year was about two per person and that acute conditions—mostly respiratory infections—were the most prevalent nonhealth episodes reported. Older people's own evaluation of their health tends to be more predictive of their functioning and their feelings about themselves than are ratings of their health by their physicians (Shanas & Maddox, 1976). The longitudinal findings from the Duke University study (Maddox & Douglass, 1973) show that, over time, self and doctors' ratings are congruent. Changes in self-ratings from one round of study to the next predicted physicians' ratings at the second round better than did the physicians' own earlier ratings.

Figure 7.2 illustrates another point we have discussed in earlier chapters—the period, or cohort, effect. By comparing the leading causes of death in 1900, 1940, and 1970, we can see changes wrought by medical technology: primarily, a reduction in the deadliness of infectious diseases. This reduction in turn led to changes in the population profile toward a larger proportion of older people, many of whom earlier would not have survived infectious diseases. This change in turn led to an increase of chronic diseases as more people lived longer.

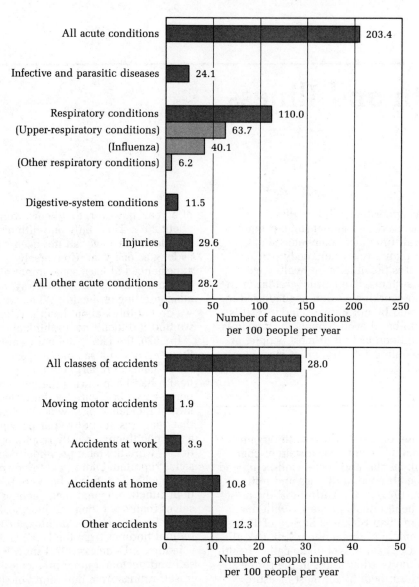

Figure 7.1. Health-survey findings provide a picture of the incidence of disease and accidents in the United States as perceived by the people themselves. The data summarized in these bar charts, published by the National Center for Health Statistics, are derived from a general survey conducted in 1970 of the population of the 50 states. The survey sample was composed of approximately 37,000 households consisting of about 116,000 people. The total number of new acute conditions for the year was 203.4 per 100 people, or slightly more than two per person. Accidents of various types accounted for about an eighth of the total. *(Source: Dingle, 1973.)*

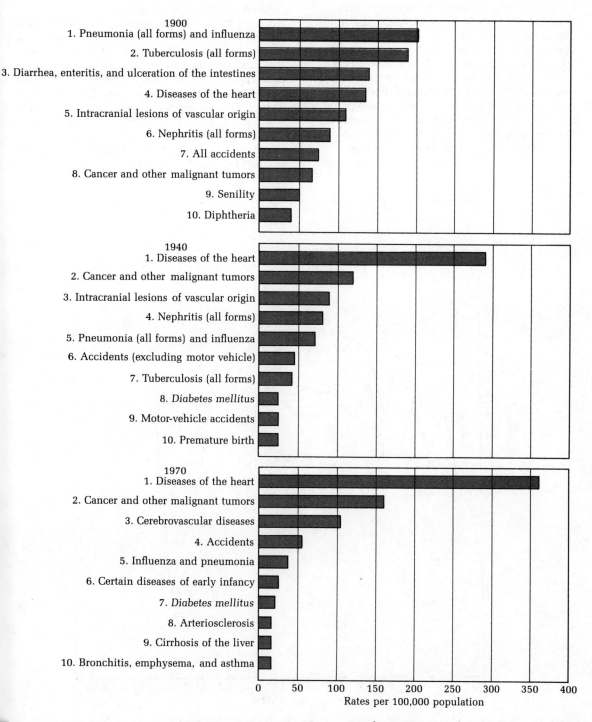

1900
1. Pneumonia (all forms) and influenza
2. Tuberculosis (all forms)
3. Diarrhea, enteritis, and ulceration of the intestines
4. Diseases of the heart
5. Intracranial lesions of vascular origin
6. Nephritis (all forms)
7. All accidents
8. Cancer and other malignant tumors
9. Senility
10. Diphtheria

1940
1. Diseases of the heart
2. Cancer and other malignant tumors
3. Intracranial lesions of vascular origin
4. Nephritis (all forms)
5. Pneumonia (all forms) and influenza
6. Accidents (excluding motor vehicle)
7. Tuberculosis (all forms)
8. *Diabetes mellitus*
9. Motor-vehicle accidents
10. Premature birth

1970
1. Diseases of the heart
2. Cancer and other malignant tumors
3. Cerebrovascular diseases
4. Accidents
5. Influenza and pneumonia
6. Certain diseases of early infancy
7. *Diabetes mellitus*
8. Arteriosclerosis
9. Cirrhosis of the liver
10. Bronchitis, emphysema, and asthma

0   50   100   150   200   250   300   350   400
Rates per 100,000 population

Figure 7.2. Changes in cause of death from 1900 to 1970. *(Source: Dingle, 1973.)*

Figures 7.3 and 7.4 show the declining incidence of respiratory ailments, colds, and allergies at older ages. As infections were conquered, diseases of the heart came to the fore in 1940, which could be considered a watershed year for a shift to chronic diseases as the major cause of death. By 1970, this shift had become established. In Chapter 6, when we discussed the cardiovascular system, we reported that if people live long enough they inevitably die from degeneration of the heart and blood vessels.

Kohn (1973) lists three general categories of illnesses that have age-related patterns. The first category includes illnesses such as arteriosclerosis that are universal, progressive, and irreversible, and that thus are called *primary aging* processes. If one lives long enough, one is likely to die from such an illness, even though age of onset and severity vary widely with genetic constitution, geographic location, and other factors. The second category includes diseases such as cancer, which may occur at all ages but which become more common as people grow older.

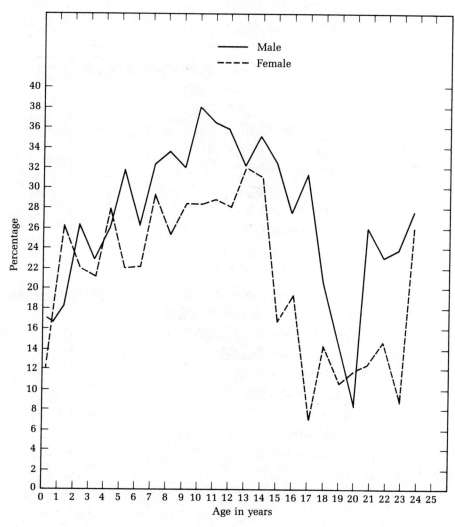

Figure 7.3.   Percentage of U.S. subjects per year of age suffering from allergic symptoms (longitudinal data). *(Source: McCammon, 1970.)*

Such diseases are *secondary aging* processes. Figure 7.5 shows the age patterns for four kinds of cancer. Wilm's tumor is most frequent in young children but becomes rare in the middle teens. Cervical, lung, and stomach cancer all rise from the mid-30s. It is not inevitable that we will develop cancer, but it becomes more probable the longer we live. The third category includes illnesses such as pneumonia, accidents, toxic reactions, and other infectious diseases that are not really related to getting older but that tend to be more severe and fatal for older people—definitely secondary aging processes.

Even though few health researchers are able

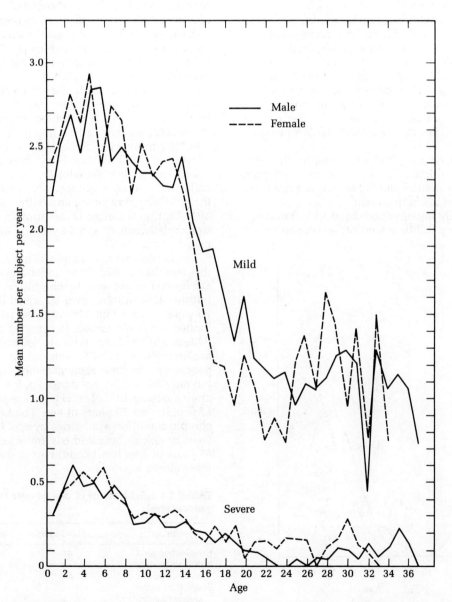

Figure 7.4. Mean number of respiratory infections per U.S. subject per year of age (longitudinal data). *(Source: McCammon, 1970.)*

to stay focused on health as opposed to illness, the longitudinal study of older Americans being conducted at Duke University has developed a six-point scale for measuring "good physical health" (Laurie, 1977, pp. 1–2):

1. *Excellent health:* engages in vigorous physical activity either regularly or at least from time to time
2. *Good health:* no significant illnesses or disabilities and only routine medical care such as annual checkups required
3. *Mildly impaired:* only minor illnesses and/or disabilities that might benefit from medical treatment or corrective measures
4. *Moderately impaired:* one or more diseases or disabilities that are either painful or that require substantial medical treatment
5. *Severely impaired:* one or more illnesses or disabilities that are either severely painful or life threatening or that require extensive medical treatment
6. *Totally impaired:* confined to bed and requiring full-time medical assistance or

nursing care to maintain vital bodily functions

This scale was used to assess the health status of people over age 65 in Durham, North Carolina, and in Cleveland, Ohio. The results are shown in Table 7.1. It is interesting that, even in a population legally classified as "old," less than 10% are severely or completely impaired, and over 40% are in excellent or good health.

A somewhat different scale, based on chronic conditions, was used by Atchley (1977). The distribution of a national sample of all ages is presented in Table 7.2. Half the sample had no chronic conditions at all; each subject in the other half had some chronic condition. This varied by age and sex. It is not too surprising that the percentage that had no irreversible or uncurable chronic conditions declines between adolescence and old age. Sex differences are not linear, because females are better off in childhood and adolescence, worse off during their childbearing years, and better off again after 65. Breast cancer is the primary killer of women between 35 and 54 years of age (Lipman-Blumen, 1975).

The limitations columns in Table 7.2 show that less than 2% of those under 17 years of age are limited in any way by chronic conditions but that 42% of those over 65 are so limited. However, only about 14% of those who are limited are really unable to carry on major activities. Most of those who are severely limited are men. Rosow (1967) points out that 78% of people over 65 have some chronic condition, but only 9% are housebound. Poor health is more characteristic of working-class people and of people over 75 years of age. The kind of chronic condition also varies by age. Under 17 years of age, asthma and hay fever lead. After 45 years of age, heart conditions and arthritis or rheumatism lead.

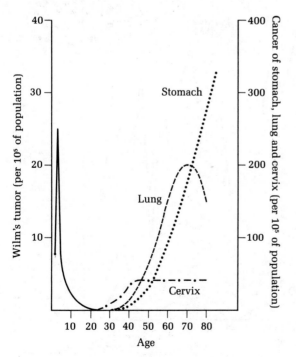

Figure 7.5. Incidence of several types of cancer in humans, by year of age. *(Source: Doll, 1970.)*

TABLE 7.1 Health status of people over 65 (percentages)

Health rating	Cleveland sample	Durham sample
Excellent or good	41	43
Mildly or moderately impaired	53	47
Severely or completely impaired	5	9

Source: Laurie, 1977.

When Kissen (1967) interviewed male thoracic patients between 55 and 64, he found a connection between unhappy childhood and later diagnosis of cancer. Experiencing the death of a parent in childhood, for example, may predispose to cancer. This connection emphasizes the complex interweaving of biological and psychological factors that underlies the human condition.

Age patterns of illness and death influence our thinking about when it is appropriate to be sick or to die. In the United States in 1982, illness after 65 is not as surprising and shocking as before 40 or 50. The timing of illness also affects the patient's response to it. Men under 50 who were recovering from acute myocardial infarctions seldom expected their heart attacks to affect their future lives—their sexuality or their involvement in the world (Goodman, 1972). They were also less depressed and often denied the seriousness of their conditions. Men in their 50s were more in conflict about their hospitalizations. They were even more likely to deny being sick or to admit that they were depressed. Men over 60, who were supposedly less shocked that they had heart attacks, expected greater changes in their lives than did the other two groups. They more readily acknowledged the possibility of imminent death and showed more overt depression.

An earlier study by Rosen and Bibring (1966) found that depression was significantly deeper in the 50-year-olds than in younger and older subjects. As can be seen in Table 7.3, all the men under 39 were judged to be cheerful, and four-fifths of those aged 60 or more were cheerful, but one-third of those in their 50s were noticeably depressed. However, a majority of those 39 and under were considered uncooperative patients as compared with the majority of older men who were cooperative, even though some were clearly anxious and depressed. Again, let us keep in mind that men in older cohorts were more likely to be socialized to be obedient and respectful—and scared—of medical personnel and medical institutions than those who grew up in a more sophisticated or equalitarian era, at least if they were middle-class.

TABLE 7.2 Percentage distribution of people by chronic condition and activity limitation status, according to sex and age (United States, July 1965–June 1967)

Sex and age	Total population	With no chronic conditions	People with 1 or more chronic conditions					
			Total	With no limitation of activity	With limitation but not in major activity[a]	With limitation in amount or kind of major activity[a]	Unable to carry on major activity[a]	Total with some limitation
Both sexes								
All ages	100.0	50.5	49.5	38.0	2.9	6.4	2.1	11.4
Under 17	100.0	77.2	22.8	20.9	1.0	0.7	0.2	1.9
17–44	100.0	45.9	54.1	46.7	2.7	4.1	0.6	7.4
45–64	100.0	28.9	71.1	51.8	5.1	11.4	2.8	19.3
65 and over	100.0	14.4	85.6	39.6	6.5	25.7	13.8	46.0
Male								
All ages	100.0	51.8	48.2	36.1	2.5	6.5	3.1	12.1
Under 17	100.0	75.8	24.2	22.1	1.1	0.8	0.2	2.1
17–44	100.0	47.4	52.6	44.7	2.5	4.6	0.9	8.0
45–64	100.0	30.5	69.5	48.7	4.4	11.9	4.5	20.8
65 and over	100.0	15.6	84.4	31.4	4.6	26.8	21.6	53.0
Female								
All ages	100.0	49.3	50.7	39.9	3.3	6.3	1.2	10.8
Under 17	100.0	78.6	21.4	19.5	1.0	0.7	0.1	1.8
17–44	100.0	44.7	55.3	48.5	2.9	3.6	0.4	6.9
45–64	100.0	27.5	72.5	54.7	5.7	10.9	1.2	17.8
65 and over	100.0	13.5	86.5	45.9	8.0	24.9	7.7	40.6

[a] *Major activity* refers to ability to work, keep house, or engage in school or preschool activities.
Source: Atchley, 1977, after Wilder, 1971.

TABLE 7.3 Age and men's reactions to heart attacks

Age at onset	Overtly depressed	Always cheerful	Uncoop- erative	Coop- erative	Anxious and tense	Re- laxed
39 and under	0	7	4	3	4	3
40–49	3	3	2	4	3	3
50–59	15	7	9	13	14	8
60 and over	3	12	2	13	7	8
Total	21	29	17	33	28	22

Total *(N)* = 50.

Source: Adapted from Rosen and Bibring, 1966. Based on nurses' reports and self-reports.

Common medical problems

CARDIOVASCULAR DISEASE

As reported in Chapter 6, heart diseases kill more than twice as many people as do all forms of cancer. One out of five adult disabilities is related to the cardiovascular system (Hickey, 1980). Furthermore, 50% of victims of heart attacks die within 24 hours. Although most people say they would prefer to die of heart attacks than any other way (Sabatini, 1975), they are also most likely to be afraid of heart attacks.

It is interesting that the symptoms of a myocardial infarction (heart failure) differ by age. Younger people experience chest and back pains, and numbness in the arms. Older victims are more likely to feel generalized weakness, respiratory difficulties, or have associated strokes or other cardiovascular problems (Hickey, 1980). In later years, myocardiac infarctions are one cause of acute brain syndrome, which is a medically related state of confusion and other apparent brain symptoms that is often mistaken for chronic brain syndrome (this will be discussed more fully later). Hickey has found no evidence to suggest that heart attacks are any more severe in older people than in younger, however—or vice versa. He feels that general health status is more important than age in how well victims will recover.

Angina pectoris—sharp chest pain—tends to be a disease of younger rather than older people and is often misdiagnosed for older people. It accompanies strenuous physical exertion in younger people but is more likely to be due to arthritic or respiratory problems, or to gallstones, gall-bladder infections, or hiatus hernias

than to cardiac problems in later ages (Hickey, 1980).

High blood pressure (hypertension), as a disease, is also more prevalent among younger than older people. In fact, older people are more prone to *hypotension*—low blood pressure. In general, telling old people to take it easy and do less is probably the worst thing one could do. Although they may be able to do less than they used to, they need to keep as active physically as they can.

Strokes, or cerebrovascular accidents, are probably among the most disabling illnesses, at any age. They can be due to massive cerebral bleeding or to floating pieces of what Hickey calls "junk" in the bloodstream that can clog an artery and stop blood flow to the brain or other strategic locations in the body. In old age, most strokes are caused by atherosclerosis—thickening and therefore narrowing of arteries and veins. As such, they are more nearly primary aging processes than are cerebral bleeding or blood clots. Previous lifestyle, diet, and activity patterns are all related to whether or not one gets a stroke, or perhaps even to whether or not one gets a heart attack, and also to how well one recovers. Frequent exercise and low-fat diets, for example, prevent atherosclerosis. As in heart attacks, it is most helpful to return to physical activity; inactivity is the worst treatment.

PARKINSON'S DISEASE

Parkinson's disease has become more prevalent in people over 60. Some physiologists feel that this is a cohort effect, the "sleeper effect" of the massive influenza epidemic of the post-World War I period (John Bullock, 1978, personal communication). In younger people, Parkinson's disease is associated with tremors, but in older people it is associated with rigidity and acute-brain-syndrome behaviors.

KIDNEY AND URINARY PROBLEMS

Both structure and function of the renal system deteriorate with age (Hickey, 1980). The kidneys shrink in size, become thicker, and lose cell membranes. Urinary-tract infections are not uncommon in old age, and kidney failure, like heart attacks and Parkinson's disease, produces behavioral symptoms that look like brain disease. Prostate problems are common among older men and are frequently corrected by surgery. Men also are susceptible to cancer of the prostate gland.

ARTHRITIS

Some form of joint degeneration is experienced by many older people. Hickey concludes that this is a primary aging phenomenon, with genetically caused variations in age of onset and severity of symptoms. When arthritis is severe, the pain and crippling can have grave functional consequences.

CANCER

Between the ages of 35 and 55, 7% of American women develop breast cancer, the peak ages being 42 to 47. The rate climbs again from the 50s on, increasing even further among women over 70. Research by Craig (1974) suggests that different kinds of causes and cancers may occur for women under 45 and those over 45. Younger women's cancer seemed to be associated more often with family histories of cancer and with later ages of having their first children. Older women's cancer was more often associated with breastfeeding. Although there has been a higher incidence of breast cancer among White women in the United States than among Black women, the rise in socioeconomic status among Black women is leveling the difference.

Here again, what at first may look like an ethnic difference turns out to be a socioeconomic difference. For most other kinds of cancer, Black men and women are more disadvantaged than White men and women. They get the disease at a younger age, more of them get it, and fewer survive. Recent evidence suggests, though, that the reason is not genetic, but socioeconomic. Blacks are less likely to see a physician, more likely to delay seeing physicians, more likely to work in hazardous places, and less likely to receive competent and careful diagnosis and treatment. As their economic situation has improved, their susceptibility to cancer has come closer to that of Whites.

Because cancer is caused by cell division getting out of control, factors that stop cell division at an early age are likely to remove the risk of cancer. This explanation is tied to such findings

as higher risk for women having no children, or having children late, and for women coming from families that have many cancer victims. The prolonged exposure to estrogen associated with absence of pregnancy could be damaging (McKinnon, 1981). Reactions to breast removal vary widely with marital status and the importance that women or their husbands or lovers attach to the breasts in sexual activities. Breasts are an important part of body image to most women, so their removal can be a blow to self-esteem. Recent advances in prosthetic surgery can help such women.

HYSTERECTOMY

Removal of the uterus (hysterectomy) is the most commonly performed operation in the United States. It is becoming more frequent every year (U.S. Department of Health, Education and Welfare, National Center for Health Statistics, 1978). Only 15% of these operations are to control cancer, however. Most are performed because of uterine prolapse, which is common among women who have had many children. Although any operation is risky, particularly for very old people, this one is considered relatively safe. Feminist health advocates now claim that such surgery is frequently unnecessary, and they advise women to consult at least one other specialist before agreeing to surgery.

OSTEOPOROSIS

The loss of calcium from the bones (osteoporosis) affects millions of women—and also many men. It causes porousness of the bones and greater fragility; bones break more easily. Although some medical practitioners and researchers believe that a major cause of osteoporosis is decline in estrogen following the menopause, others disagree and attribute it to poor nutrition and lack of exercise. It is also more common among smokers. Consistent with their view of what causes osteoporosis, some scientists recommend estrogen-replacement therapy; others recommend diets high in calcium and protein, and regular exercise.

ACUTE BRAIN SYNDROME

Acute brain syndrome is a condition that looks like psychotic breakdown or senility. It is characterized by such symptoms as confusion, amnesia, manic outbursts, and other disturbed behaviors that can—and do—cause many commitments of older people to institutions. The term *acute* means that medical treatment can restore victims to their previous competence. Frequent causes of acute brain syndrome are drug overdose, drug underdose, and poisoning by unfortunate combinations of drugs.

The increase in chronic ailments with age is accompanied by an increase in the number of pills taken regularly. It is not uncommon for older people to juggle three green pills four times a day, four white pills three times a day, and three pink pills once a day, except Sunday. It is also not uncommon, for anyone trying to remember this confusing regimen, to overdose or underdose—in other words, to end up with an acute case of poisoning or electrolyte imbalance. As physicians prescribe new medications for new symptoms, they are too often unaware that their prescriptions are chemically colliding with drugs that their patients may have been taking regularly for 15 years or from several doctors back. The shift toward medical specialists, and away from family or general practitioners who knew their patients over many years, increases this danger, because specialists may

not have access to or know about records of other specialists. For example, an eye doctor may prescribe an otherwise benign medication that combines dangerously with the medication prescribed by an internist, allergist, or cardiac specialist.

Another frequent cause of acute brain syndrome is alcohol. Sometimes the syndrome is initiated by the accumulation of toxic reactions to alcohol over many years. In other cases, it is initiated by a change in sensitivity of the aging organism, so that what was once an innocuous before-dinner cocktail or party "high" can now become dangerous, if not lethal. Although national surveys of American drinking practices (see Peterson & Whittington, 1977) show the lowest percentage of drinkers in the over-60 age group, this may partly reflect the lower longevity for heavy drinkers. Few alcoholics survive to old age.

Use of medical services

The use of medical services by older people is not an exact index of the prevalence of poor health or disability. Many older people were socialized to take care of themselves and are ashamed to ask for help or admit that they need help. Many poor people have learned not to trust middle-class medical practitioners or may not even have medical facilities available to them. Therefore, the figures given in Table 7.4 are probably underestimates of need. Even so, it is clear that people over 65 use more health resources than those between 45 and 64. It is also clear that women use such resources more than men.

Lipman-Blumen (1975) reports that "women are the largest consumers of the nation's health services. They average annually 25 percent more visits to doctors than men, use 50 percent more prescription drugs than men and are admitted to hospitals more often than men" (p. 25). In spite of being sturdier than men at all ages from birth on, women still seek out medical help more than men. Perhaps, feeling generally stronger, they are more sensitive to discomfort and try to remove it. Or, their better use of medical services may help to keep them stronger. It is also possible that the socialization of females in our culture helps them to accept their own vulnerability and thus permits them

TABLE 7.4 Disability and use of health resources (1970)

	Males	Females
Percentage of population visiting physicians one or more times per year		
Age 45–64	63.7%	70.8%
65+	68.1	73.6
Physician visits per year		
Age 45–64	4.1	5.2
65+	5.5	6.6
Hospital discharges per 1,000 population		
Age 45–64	143.0	160.3
65+	254.4	237.2
Average length of stay in hospital		
Age 45–64	11.1	9.8
65+	14.5	14.4
Days of restricted activity per year		
Age 45–64	19.8	20.9
65+	31.7	36.2
Days restricted to bed		
Age 45–64	7.3	7.9
65+	12.7	14.4

Source: U.S. Department of Health, Education and Welfare, National Center for Health Statistics, 1973.

to seek help from others more comfortably than men can.

When older people need medical services—whether medical care, drugs, nursing, or other treatment—their primary source of help is their children. Of those who said they had help available, 42% mentioned their children (Laurie, 1977). The next most frequently cited source was husbands or wives (27%), followed by brothers or sisters (10%), other relatives (9%), and friends (8%). Only about 20% turned to some kind of social or community agency.

Many people feel that an ill or old person cannot be trusted to determine his or her health care. We tend to reduce such people to helpless dependency. A provocative piece of research was done by Richard Schulz (1974) in a long-term institution in North Carolina. When a visiting program was started by college undergraduates, Schulz suggested that visitors be assigned on a systematic basis, and set up four different conditions. In one situation, residents received no visitors. In another, visitors came on a random, unpredictable schedule. In a third, residents were told they would receive visitors and when they could expect them. In the fourth, residents determined both the frequency and the duration of visits. He found that the residents in the group that could predict when visitors would come and those in the group that could determine when they should come both showed improved physical status and increased activity. Residents in the other two groups did not. The element of control thus emerges as a significant factor in physical well-being in old age—and perhaps at any age.

Institutionalization

The word *old* brings to most people in our society an image of homeless, helpless, forlorn derelicts inhabiting park benches, slum hotels, nursing homes, and other institutional ghettos. Several years ago, a young newspaper reporter interviewed me about aging because his editor had assigned him to do a "special" on the subject for the feature section of the Sunday newspaper. Because I had become tired of seeing such specials devoted exclusively to photographs of "Skid Row" inhabitants, I suggested that he look at the older members of his family, older coworkers, and other old people in the

community. He enthusiastically discussed his surprise that he never considered such people old, and he became interested in the developmental progression of a wider array of older Americans. Just before the issue appeared on the stands, however, he called me to apologize for the article he had ended up having to write. Sure enough, it was a series of photographs of derelicts on park benches, of alcoholics sprawled in doorways, and of stuporous people in nursing-home wheelchairs. His editor had said the treatment of aging as "normal" would not evoke the kind of "human interest" he wanted, and had not allowed the reporter to use his earlier draft or photographs.

Because of such prevailing treatment in the media, it comes as a surprise to most people that less than 5% of Americans over 65 years of age (Riley & Foner, 1968) reside in nursing homes, "old folks' homes," or any other old people's institution. Most people labeled "old"—over 65—live with spouses in their own apartments or houses and continue to lead relatively "full" lives with families and friends, and with other independent activities. Even most widows live in their own homes, although probably near at least one of their children. When nursing care is needed, most older Americans still turn to—and get it from—their children (Troll, Miller, & Atchley, 1979). The inhabitants of institutions, therefore, are deviants, not prototypes, of those labeled "old." Even among people over 85, only 17% are institutionalized.

Kastenbaum and Candy (1973) have pointed out that while it is true that only 4 or 5% of older people live in institutions at any given point in time, a larger percentage end up there for at least a while at the end of their lives. Kastenbaum and Candy examined the microfilm records of all death certificates filed in the metropolitan Detroit area during 1971—20,234 deaths over the age of 65. Of all deaths in this age range, 20% occurred in nursing homes, and 24% occurred in extended-care facilities in general. Thus, one in four of us is likely to spend some time—even if only a week—in such an institution before we die if we live to be old.

Although nursing homes and other extended-care facilities are generally seen as places to receive the kind of nursing care we might need at the end of life, only about half the residents of such facilities are mentally or physically impaired (Atchley, 1977). About half the nursing-home residents are ambulatory and continent, and 80% of older people in mental hospitals are equivalently competent.

According to Atchley (1977), one of the key factors in moving to a nursing home or other care facility is the adequacy (or inadequacy) of previous living arrangements. Another is the availability of family. Thus, residents in old-people's institutions tend to have lived alone and to be single and childless. The final decision to enter an institution tends to be the last step in a series of disappointments such as having to leave previous homes because of urban renewal or changes in neighborhood or because of illnesses that prohibit stair climbing or home maintenance. "Admission to an age-segregated institution suggests or confirms to many people the idea that 'it is all over but the dying'" (Kastenbaum, 1967, p. 22). Entry into such a place is a kind of "social death." Many social workers and other staff members of such institutions deplore the infrequency of visiting done by families and friends on the "outside." They assume that nursing homes would not be needed if families "did their duty." What they tend to overlook is the deviant nature of most residents, as just noted, and the psychological and social death that is implied. Where families do exist, institutional placement is usually at the end of a period of marked deterioration and the process of mourning may have preceded the move. To many family members, the nursing-home residents are, in fact, perceived as dead. Therefore, mourning at the time of actual physical death may be much weaker. This topic will be discussed more fully in the next chapter.

In view of most people's perceptions of old-age institutions as the end of the road, it is not surprising that entering them should be accompanied by rising death rates (Lieberman, 1961). The idea of "social death" may not be the only operative factor, however. A number of studies of forced relocation of older people, such as those directed by Norman Bourestom and Leon Pastalan (1975), suggest that removal of autonomy may be significant. Table 7.5 shows that the mortality rate during the year of forced relocation of older patients in two Michigan settings increased markedly: (1) when a nursing home had to close because of budget cutbacks and (2) when another nursing home moved to a new setting. These relocations were compared to the death rate in a comparable nursing home where moving did not take place. The death rate in the nonmoving site was less than 25%; where there was moderate change, it was 37%; and where there was much change it was 43%. Even those patients who survived change became significantly more passive. In each setting, though, patients who had had some hand in the move—if only to inspect the new home before they moved—made much better, nonfatal, adjustments.

Kastenbaum found comparable differences in two wards in an extended-care institution in Massachusetts (Kastenbaum, 1967). In the intensive-treatment ward, which the patients called "Death Valley," 69% of all hospital deaths took place. Only 8% of deaths occurred on the "home ward." "Death Valley" was described thus: "[it] conveys a sense of bustling efficiency, careful scheduling, and readiness for emergency action. . . . Personnel . . . state that they prefer the challenges and requirements of meeting acute medical needs to the management of patients who appear to require chiefly custodial and routine long-term care" (Kastenbaum, 1967, p. 23). Although autonomy of patients in both wards was low, patients were particularly turned into objects in the "Death Valley" ward. Figures 7.6 and 7.7 illustrate the kind of treatment prevalent in many extended-care institutions.

Henry (1963) listed six types of incidents that are found in many nursing homes:

1. Patients being bathed in assembly-line fashion in order to get task done quickly, with no thought to privacy or modesty
2. Attendants never calling patients by name,

TABLE 7.5 Mortality and relocation
Comparison of death rates of relocated patients with death rates of matched nonrelocated patients during period of relocation and readjustment

	Number of patients	Survived	Died	Percentage of mortality
Radical change group	61	35	26	43
Radical change control group	61	49	12	21
Moderate change group	38	24	14	37
Moderate change control group	38	28	10	26

Source: Bourestom and Pastalan, 1975.

Figure 7.6. A "home" for the aged (I). *(Source: Metzelaar, 1975.)*

Figure 7.7. A "home" for the aged (II). *(Source: Metzelaar, 1975.)*

even if the patients have been residents for months

3. The only communication with patients being directions such as "turn over" or "sit down"

4. Disregard of patients' requests for attendants to call relatives to bring them things (no phones being accessible to patients themselves)

5. Several patients being bathed in the same water

6. Patients who caused trouble being tied to their beds or chairs

One study (Prock, 1965) compared three groups of old people: those living in the community and intending to stay there, those on a waiting list for admission to an institution, and those in the institution. The institution in question was considered a "model" one. As far as personality is concerned, the waiting-list people were the worst off. They showed more general anxiety and tension, emotional reactivity, sense of helplessness and powerlessness, depression, and low self-esteem (Prock, 1965). They seemed to be withdrawing actively from those around them and to be showing signs of ego disintegration, as if they were going through the "social death" Kastenbaum suggests. These behaviors had nothing to do with chronological age. These waiting-list subjects were showing more signs of institutionalization than were the people already institutionalized. Was this effect due to the disrupting consequences of transitional status, and did it abate once the reality of the new way of life became established? Or was the group in the institution the hardiest, the survivors? It is hard to say. Apparently, however, a well-run institution, considerate of the dignity of the patients or residents and providing a stable, supportive environment, is not "bad" for all people. These findings, like others mentioned in earlier chapters, underline the importance of helping people through transitional states of life.

Conclusions

Hickey (1980) suggests that members of our society, in recent years, have developed a high degree of technology-based optimism about prolonging life, reducing acute illnesses, and minimizing the disabling effects of chronic illnesses. Encouraged by periodic breakthroughs in medical research, we seem to believe that, even if we may not be able to control eventual death, at least we can remove the hampering effects of illness so long as we live. We also seem to believe that our health is pretty much under our own control—as witness the current flood of books, courses, diets, spiritual programs, and exercises. We are also concerned with toxic damage in the environment, with natural and organic foods, and with meditation and relaxation techniques. We tell ourselves that we are as old as we feel, get angry if a physician blames some ailment on age, and dread becoming sick.

The tone of much of this chapter has echoed this kind of optimistic belief. I have reviewed reports on the shift from acute to chronic illness, on the shift in the causes of death at early and later ages, and on nutrition and exercise techniques for controlling health. Yet the descriptions of some common ailments of late life show that if people live long enough they accumulate not one but generally a large number of health problems and that diagnosis and treatment of these problems can be tricky. We cannot stick our heads in the sand and deny the possibility of trouble to come. When such trouble will come, what kind of trouble it will be, and how bad it will be are all results of the familiar combination of genetic and environmental influences discussed in earlier chapters.

Summary

Most Americans find it difficult to think about health as separate from illness; health is usually defined as the absence of illness.

There are several age-related patterns in illness. There is the cohort effect, for example. As medical technology progresses, certain diseases are either conquered or mitigated. Deaths from infectious diseases, for instance, accounted for more deaths in earlier generations than they do now. Primary aging processes include illnesses that are universal, progressive, and irreversible, such as certain types of cardiovascular disease. If one lives long enough, such diseases may be the cause of death. Secondary aging processes include diseases that become more common as people grow older, such as cancer. And such diseases as pneumonia tend to be more severe and fatal for older people.

Chronic conditions increase with age. Men are less well than women their age except during the childbearing years. And poor people are less well than the wealthy.

Common medical problems include cardiovascular diseases, cancer, Parkinson's disease, kidney and other urinary problems, arthritis, osteoporosis, and acute brain syndrome. Use of medical services by older people varies with cohort and sex. Some older people are socialized not to complain, and men are socialized not to seek help.

Institutionalization involves only 4–5% of the aging, although it involves more people for brief periods at the ends of their lives (those suffering terminal illnesses). After being institutionalized, people die at higher rates. They may suffer social death—not being visited by family or friends and being treated as objects by institution staff. Such treatment lowers morale and the will to "hang on."

Advances in medical technology, coupled with our society's avoidance of death and dying, lead people to optimism about curing all illnesses. This tendency may make us ignore health problems, which accumulate for all of us. And we all die.

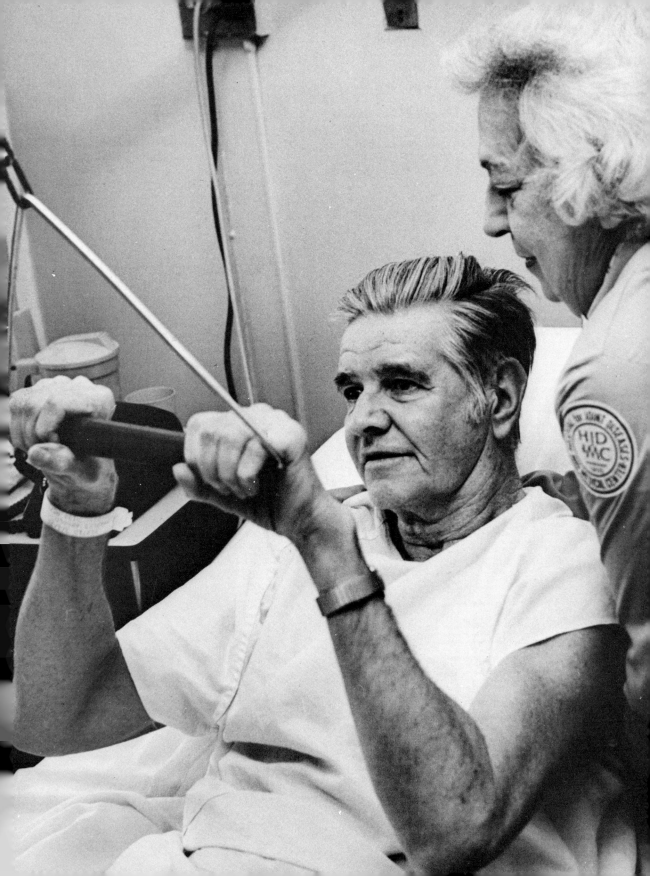

8

Dying, Death, and Mourning

Most humans remember their pasts and envision their futures. They can see that, just as each life has a beginning, it also has an end. All people and all social groups construct some cognitive framework around death, and almost all have evolved rituals to help cope with the emotions death arouses. Until 10 or 15 years ago, our society had been following a course toward privatizing and constraining the experience of dying and bereavement. Even after sex lost some of its secrecy, death remained, for many, a tabooed topic of discussion. Mourning was forsworn. Funerals were considered barbaric, wasteful, and probably antisocial. Recently, however, we have seen a reversal in this trend, accompanied by an accelerating interest in death in both public and scientific communities. With these changed attitudes have come new myths and new rituals. For a comprehensive discussion of this topic, see the new book by Victor Marshall (1980).

We now take it for granted that death is related to old age. This was not always true. When people who are now old—over 70, for example—talk about their early lives, they refer to deaths of siblings, friends, or parents as common events. One man located significant events in his childhood by "That was the year my little sister died" or "That was when my mother died." The statistics in the last chapter showed that until about 1940 most deaths in this country and elsewhere around the world were of infants and very young children. At the beginning of this century, 15% of all children died before

they reached their first birthday, and another 15% died before they reached adolescence. Now fewer than 2% die during their first year, and the vast majority of those who are born live to be over 70 (Morison, 1973).

Another change is in the site of dying and thus in the quality of our experiences with the death of others. At the turn of the century, most dying occurred at home. The average adult had been exposed repeatedly to the sights and sounds and smells of death. The man mentioned earlier not only marked his life by the times of the deaths of his siblings and parents, but by the events of their dying, the "lying in the parlor," and the gathering of family, friends, and neighbors. Today almost all deaths take place in barricaded hospitals or extended-care institutions that do not welcome spontaneous visiting even of family members—particularly not of young children.

Most intensive-care units permit only one person at a time for a hurried, five-minute "look" at the dying person each hour. These visits, furthermore, are rarely private. Beds are grouped for the convenience of surveillance instruments, not human interactions. When my father lay dying, I had a few five-minute turns, alternating with other adult family members. When he saw me come close to his bed, my father looked up in fear and asked me to find out for him what was happening. A doctor and nurse were sitting mechanically in front of a bank of instruments across the large room and looked annoyed when I tried to question them. I went back to my father, held his hand, and said "It's OK." I don't know what I meant. I do know my lie didn't help either of us.

Such procedures have consequences not only for the isolated dying person but also for the socialization of those who survive. If dying is secret, shameful, and mysterious, the value of life is also diminished. Illness and death have become the province of the medical profession, which has surrounded them with a web of designated "health" rituals and taboos reminiscent of ancient priestly ceremony. Unfortunately, the priests and priestesses of this medical cult do not receive appropriate training for their arcane roles and are as often the victims of their practices as are their patients.

Definitions of death

At what point is a person to be labeled dead? When breathing stops? When the heart stops beating? When consciousness cannot be restored? When responsibility for decisions is removed? When involvement in social and family affairs stops? Organ transplants have made such questions critically important today. A kidney or heart cannot be used for another person if it is deteriorated, yet it cannot be removed from the donor body until that body is declared legally dead. Morison (1973) summarizes the dilemma and points out that present consensus seems to be that "what is really human and important about the individual resides in the upper levels of the nervous system, and that these attributes indeed die with the death of the forebrain" (p. 43). Once this point is ascertained, it is no longer necessary to pursue customary heroic efforts to "maintain the spark of life." In other words, machines that maintain breathing, heartbeat, and so on can be unplugged as soon as the valuable organs are removed.

Difficult as it is to define biological death, it is probably even more treacherous to try to define psychological or social death. In many cases, psychological and social deaths can precede biological death by months or even years. A person who no longer relates to other people or events may be considered psychologically dead. A person who is isolated from society by being placed in an institution, and who no longer is involved in the affairs of the world, could be considered socially dead. Even medical personnel confess that they are likely to treat such people as if they were essentially dead, removing both painkillers and the kind of minimal nursing care that would make life bearable (Morison, 1973; Kastenbaum, 1977).

To make definitions even more complicated, it is possible to consider individuals who are physically dead psychologically and socially alive. It is not only "primitive" societies that incorporate ghosts and spirits into their social world. Many bereaved people act as if, and think as if, the person who has died is still with them. This is discussed further later, with reference to bereavement.

Awareness of mortality

Although on the one hand it is probable that even very young children know something about death, on the other hand it seems likely that a conviction of one's own personal finitude does not come until late in life, and then perhaps is felt only for brief moments. We can know that we will eventually die, in the abstract, without truly believing that this will really happen to us. We are not surprised when other people die, but we are stunned when we realize that the bell now will toll for us. Shneidman and Farberow (1957) say that many suicides do not really mean to end their lives; they are unable to imagine their own deaths. They cannot imagine a cessation of experience, a state where there is no more "I." Suicides may not differ profoundly from others in this respect. Freud said that consciousness has no representation of death. Apparently life and death are antithetical.

The European gerontologist Munnichs (1966) was one of the first to call attention to the phenomenon of *awareness of finitude*. He sees it as separating youth from old age: "To realize and know that life comes to an end and adjustment to this fact might possibly be considered the *focal point of the mentality of the aged*" (p. 4).

DEVELOPMENT OF DEATH CONCEPT

There is a developmental progression in children's concepts of death, as first demonstrated by Nagy (1948). The progression she observed generally follows the cognitive developmental sequence described by Piaget (1970). Preschool children (between 3 and 5 years of age) believe that death is just a continuation of life, but on a dimmer level. The dead are only partly alive. They think and feel, although not very well. But even this is thought of as temporary, because after they (the dead) visit a while wherever they have gone (to heaven, to the cemetery, and so on) they will come back. As Kastenbaum and Aisenberg (1972) point out, disappearance of an object (death) cannot be conceptualized before object constancy has been attained. The 5- to 9-year-olds in Nagy's sample in Hungary thought that death could be avoided by doing the right things. Only those older than 9 or 10 years of age believed that death was unavoidable, at least in a general way.

What about children who are themselves dying? Natterson and Knudson (1960) interviewed children dying of cancer at the City of Hope Medical Center in California. The youngest children were most concerned about separation from their parents because of hospitalization. Those between 5 and 10 years of age were most upset by the pain and discomfort involved in their treatments. Only the 11- and 12-year-olds seemed to understand the finality of their dying. In this respect, they have achieved the *mentality of the aged,* to use Munnichs's words. This mentality, then, may have less to do with age than with facing the reality of one's own dying.

In a study of 75 healthy children from 4 to 10 years of age, Childers and Wimmer (1971) distinguished between two aspects of death awareness: universality and irrevocability. By age 10, 90% of the children recognized death's universality, but only one-third said that death was final. In a different small-sample cross-sectional study—the only kind there have been so far in this area—Safier (1964) reports three stages relating to irrevocability. The youngest children she studied (about age 4) seemed to interpret both life and death as a constant flux. She writes "Something goes, then it stops, then it goes on again. There is an absence of the idea of absolutes" (p. 286). Children in the intermediate stage see both life and death caused by outside agents: "Something makes it go, something makes it stop." The boys (all her subjects were boys) at the highest level, about 10 years old, could acknowledge the principle of an internal agent: "Something goes by itself, something stops by itself."

Maurer (1970) asked children a related question: "How can you know if something is alive?" Over 600 subjects in California were asked that question. Of the 131 children in the 5–6 age range, 18 couldn't answer, but most of the rest answered in terms of movement: "Because it moves."

According to Kastenbaum (1977), adolescents and youth live intensely in the present and the immediate future. Neither the far future (adulthood) nor the past is of interest. He points out that this kind of present orientation can go together with romanticism: youth can dream and act out heroic acts that could easily lead to death because death has no reality. Actually, says Neugarten (1968), the turning point in awareness of mortality comes in middle age, when people find themselves thinking ahead to how many years they have left to live instead of thinking back to how many years they have lived. This meaning of death is related to the meaning of time (an issue discussed in Chapter 1), to disengagement theory (see discussion in Chapter 2), and to a theory of life review (Butler, 1963). Butler believes that, when older people come to realize that the time left to them is limited, they begin to take stock, asking themselves "What kind of person have I become?" "Have I been a failure or a success?" "Do I like myself?" This process has much in common with Erikson's (1950) last stage: ego integrity versus despair (see Chapter 2). Two studies of life review (Gorney, 1968; Marshall, 1975) suggest that it is a temporary process, followed by return to a future-time perspective. Among the many questions raised by these somewhat conflicting data is the basic one "Can living people really believe they will cease to be?" Did the dying 12-year-olds interviewed by Natterson and Knudson believe it any more than did the old people discussed by Munnichs?

INDIVIDUAL DIFFERENCES

Wide individual and group differences in awareness of mortality are likely. Kastenbaum feels that death of a parent can precipitate an experience of one's own mortality at any age. He quotes Ben Hecht: "I can recall the hour in which I lost my immortality, in which I tried on my shroud for the first time and saw how it became me. . . . The knowledge of my dying came to me when my mother died" (Kastenbaum, 1977, p. 148). Although Back (1971a, 1971b) did not find age a factor in the meanings

TABLE 8.1 Awareness of finitude in relation to age

Respondent anticipates living an additional	Age		
	Young (64–75) %	Middle (76–84) %	Old (85–96) %
10 or more years	50	28	10
5 to 10 years	43	40	40
Less than 5 years	7	32	50
Total	100	100	100
N =	14	25	10	49

Note: Tau B (difference between groups) = .340; significance = .0003.

Source: Marshall, 1975.

TABLE 8.2 Awareness of finitude in relation to comparative age at death of parents

Respondent anticipates living an additional	Compared to the age at death of his or her parent, the respondent is now		
	Younger than age at death of both (%)	Younger than age at death of one (%)	Older than age at death of both (%)
10 or more years	46	35	7
5–10 years	46	52	29
Less than 5 years	9	13	64
Total	101	100	100
N =	11	23	14	48

Notes: Tau B (difference between groups) = −.426; significance = beyond four places.
Controlling for sex, the following obtain:
  Males: Tau B = −.568; significance = .008
  Females: Tau B = −.390; significance = .0003

Source: Marshall, 1975.

people over 45 attributed to death, Marshall (1975) found that age did affect subjects' estimates of their own "life time." He asked a group of White, middle-class Americans, between 64 and 96 years of age, how much longer they thought they had to live (Tables 8.1 and 8.2). Of the youngest group (64 to 75), 50% said they would live ten or more years, but only 10% of the oldest group (85–96) did.

Note that Marshall found that many of his respondents were using a crude formula to estimate their own life expectancies—a formula based on the ages to which their parents and, secondarily, other family members had lived. One man said "Up to now no men in my family have lived past 70. But a brother is going to be 72. But both parents died at 70. They say you die according to when your parents died." An-

other, aged 81, said "Ha! Ha! Very hard to say. To 90. My father lived to 96, my mother to 72." It is possible that estimates of "life time" (time one expects to live) derive largely not only from progenitors in general but also from one's same-sexed parent in particular. Table 8.2 shows that younger people who are now older than the age at death of both parents are more highly aware of finitude than older people who have not yet surpassed the age at death of their parents. Almost all (92%) of those in the first column, younger than their parents' age at death, expected to live at least five more years. Only about one-third of those in the right-hand column—older than parents' age at death—expected to live that much longer.

Some people, Kastenbaum found, predict that they will live many years even if they are suffering from what are usually considered to be terminal illnesses. In my own experience, I have known older men in a Veterans Administration hospital to rate their health as excellent, brushing off the reason for their current hospitalizations—even brushing off heart attacks. One man said he had no cardiac problems, adding only later, as if it were irrelevant, "except for the one last week." Hard-core unemployed young men whose lifestyles involve unusual peril, however, do not expect to live long (Teahan & Kastenbaum, 1970).

DEATH ANXIETY

A professor at the Harvard Medical School argues that fear of death is the central human anxiety (May, 1973). When asked directly, however, most people say they fear the deaths of others more than they fear their own deaths (Geer, 1965). Let me quote from a term paper by one of my students (Barczon, 1973, p. 3):

As a child the fear of death stalked me constantly. I once had a dream about the end of the world that so frightened me I could not fall asleep at bedtime for several days without worrying that I would not survive the morning. I worried mostly that my mother might die though she was in good health. At times when I was "bad" she would say, "You'll be sorry when I'm dead," or "You're making my heart beat so fast it is going to stop."

I never had a pet that I loved and when I found a dead bird I felt a little sad that it died but I did not feel grief.

I used to occasionally play with a little boy who

hung himself but I didn't feel grief that time either. I went to see him in his casket looking like he had never looked before. He was beautiful in his white suit, one of the few times his face was clean. I couldn't understand, as could no one else, why he hung himself. His death frightened me because in many ways I was "bad" like he was. Maybe I deserved to die too.

Throughout my teen years and early twenties I continued to worry about death. When I married I worried that my husband might die. My child was born and I worried that he might die—and he did. As with the blink of an eyelash, I was faced with the finality and irreversibility of death.

Her remarks illustrate a difference between (1) generalized fears and (2) a reaction to the death of someone close: she felt anxiety and the feeling of finitude of her own life as well as grief. This difference makes it hard to judge the significance of clinical philosophical expressions of death anxiety and of research findings using death-anxiety tests. Where does general anxiety end and death anxiety begin? Are people who show a great deal of death anxiety more neurotic? Is there a significant difference between the two concepts?

Distinctions have been made between *state* anxiety (the result of a particular, presumably temporary situation) and *trait* anxiety (a basic, presumably constant personality component). Although some theories include the concept of a prototypical death anxiety that underlies most other life fears, actual research findings suggest that different people fear different things when they talk about their fear of death. Some are afraid of mutilation, others of abandonment. Some are afraid of the process of dying, of pain and the loss of dignity. Those who hold particular religious beliefs may be afraid of punishment in an afterlife. Others are afraid of extinction or obliteration. Still others fear hurting those who love them, or abandoning those for whom they are responsible. Incidentally, few people seem to be afraid of what will happen to their bodies after death.

Some investigators report that older people, presumably because they are nearer their own deaths or have had more experiences with the deaths of others close to them, have less fear of death than younger adults, even though they think and talk more about death than younger people (for example, see Kastenbaum & Aisenberg, 1972), or are more aware of their own finitude (Munnichs, 1966). Other researchers,

particularly those using one or another of the death-anxiety scales, have not found significant age differences past adolescence (for example, Templer, Ruff, & Franks, 1971). An example of a self-report death-anxiety scale is given in Table 8.3.

A comprehensive clinical study by Feifel and his colleagues in California (Feifel, Jones, & Edwards, 1968; Feifel & Branscomb, 1973) found differences between conscious fears—the kind that would be reported on a death-anxiety scale—and less-conscious feelings. Their subjects were between the ages of 50 and 89, some judged healthy and others who had been told that they had terminal illnesses. Of the 121 people studied, 83% said they were not afraid of death, because it was inevitable, or "God's will"; only 17% admitted being afraid.

Those who knew they were going to die seemed to be most determined to say they were not afraid, but on projective tests they were the most sensitive to death stimuli. The dominant conscious response was repudiation of fear of death, less conscious fantasies showed ambivalence, and at the nonconscious level there was fear. The mechanism of conscious denial served to deal with the underlying fear.

Magni (1972), in fact, found a negative correlation between consciously expressed death fears and nonconscious death fears. The more people said they were not afraid of dying, the

TABLE 8.3 The 15 death-anxiety scale items

Key	Content
T	I am very much afraid to die.
F	The thought of death seldom enters my mind.
F	It doesn't make me nervous when people talk about death.
T	I dread to think about having to have an operation.
F	I am not at all afraid to die.
F	I am not particularly afraid of getting cancer.
F	The thought of death never bothers me.
T	I am often distressed by the way time flies so very rapidly.
T	I fear dying a painful death.
T	The subject of life after death troubles me greatly.
T	I am really scared of having a heart attack.
T	I often think about how short life really is.
T	I shudder when I hear people talking about a World War III.
T	The sight of a dead body is horrifying to me.
F	I feel that the future holds nothing for me to fear.

Note: The answers *(Key)* indicate high death anxiety.

Source: Templer, Ruff, and Franks, 1971.

more they were really afraid. It is interesting that the age period most frequently (35%) chosen as the time at which subjects said they first felt vulnerable to death was the 6- to 12-year-old period—except for the terminally and chronically ill groups, who both said they first felt vulnerable in their 50s and 60s. Most said they wanted to die of heart attacks because such attacks were quick, with little pain. They wanted to die at home because home was familiar and comforting.

Differences have been found between men and women, primarily in the content of death attitudes and fears. Women tend to view death differently from men (Back, 1971a). They are more likely to accept it and see it as peaceful, while men see it as an enemy to be fought. However, 40 years ago, Means (1936) asked 1000 college women to list the things they were afraid of. Death-related items were mentioned most often. A study of college students by Diggory and Rothman (1961) found that men's fears were most concerned with their bodies and their plans—with themselves—while women's were mostly concerned with what would happen to others. Women between the ages of 15 and 39 were most concerned about causing grief to friends, and women over 40 were concerned about causing grief to their dependents. How much these traditional sex-role orientations were cohort related we can only wonder.

When members of the same family have been compared on death anxiety (Templer et al., 1971; Kalish & Johnson, 1972; Nehrke, 1974), significant parent/child and husband/wife correlations are found. The difference between self-reports and attributions by others is shown in the findings about grandmothers, who actually reported less fear of death than did their daughters and granddaughters, even though they were perceived by the younger generations as being more afraid.

Kalish (1976) proposes three reasons for older people's admitting less fear of dying than younger people. First, because older people's lives are valued less, they place less value on their own lives. Second, life expectancy becomes incorporated into their thinking at an early age, and they expect to die at a particular age. As mentioned earlier, with reference to Marshall's study, they feel cheated if they find they are dying before this time and they feel gifted if they find they are living longer than this time.

Third, they become socialized to dying through a process of repeated rehearsals at the times of the deaths of others. The longer they live, the more likely they are to have faced the deaths of people close to them: parents, siblings, spouse, friends. In a British study of bereavement (Cartwright, Hockey, & Anderson, 1973), the proportion of bereaved people who needed help from physicians for shock and anxiety or who reported trouble sleeping decreased with age. Does this mean they were really less bereaved?

One interesting study compared the death anxieties of graduate students in psychology and in religion, Zen meditators, and psychedelic drug users (Garfield, 1974). There was a marked difference between the two student groups at one end and the two altered-consciousness groups at the other. The latter showed less physiological responsivity to death-related stimuli, although no difference in non-death-related stimulation. Kalish (1976) suggests that the blurring of ego lines accompanying an altered state of consciousness, which diminishes feelings of self versus non-self, made subjects in the meditation and drug groups feel there would be less difference being alive and being dead. This suggestion is similar to the theory of Peck (1968), noted in Chapter 2, which proposes that old people should move from body preoccupation to body transcendence and from ego preoccupation to ego transcendence. Could we say that such transcendence is equivalent to an altered state of consciousness and is the necessary foundation for basic awareness of one's own mortality? This question is raised again in the following sections on the dying process and suicide. It provokes a further question: How does such transcendence relate to sacrifice and martyrdom?

The dying process

Elisabeth Kübler-Ross, a psychiatrist, has influenced a large number of both lay and professional people in their attitudes toward death and toward those who are dying. She hypothesizes a five-stage psychological dying process, basing her ideas on about 200 interviews with dying people (Kübler-Ross, 1969). These stages are meant to be considered a normal and desirable sequence and thus fit into the category of stage theories discussed in Chapter 2. That is, people are supposed to follow this sequence in order and to move from the first to the fifth stage to achieve the "right" attitude at the end. Kübler-Ross does state, it is true, that not all people follow the same path and that some never reach the last stage. Her stages are as follows:

1. *Denial* (the first response to the bad news). "No, not me, it cannot be true!"
2. *Anger.* "Why me?" An attempt is made to blame somebody, even God.
3. *Bargaining.* The dying person tries to make a deal with fate, such as asking to live long enough to attend the wedding of a child several months beyond the date of "sentencing."
4. *Depression.* After increased weakness, discomfort, and physical deterioration.
5. *Acceptance.* This is not necessarily a happy state, more devoid of any feeling. It is perhaps the ultimate transcendence of one's own self.

A somewhat different view of the dying process emerges from the investigations of Weisman and Kastenbaum (1968); see also Kastenbaum and Weisman (1972) and Weisman (1974). They adapted a technique called the "psychological autopsy," which had originally been devised by Shneidman and Farberow (1957) to study suicides. One of their first findings was that most terminally ill older people remain mentally alert close to the end of their lives. Kastenbaum (1977, p. 177) stresses that "it would be a mistake to treat the patient as though phenomenologically dead, incapable of understanding or caring about what was left to his life."

Another important finding was that people die in different ways—probably as different as the ways in which they lived. A general classification of "preterminal orientations" consists of acceptance, apathy, apprehension, and anticipation. "Acceptance refers to patients who spoke about death in a dispassionate and realistic way; apathy describes patients who seemed indifferent to almost any event, including death; apprehension refers to patients who openly voiced fear and alarm about death; and anticipation applies to patients who showed acceptance plus an explicit wish for death" (Weisman & Kastenbaum, 1968, p. 22).

Later findings showed that the two most common orientations were feeling acceptance and feeling interrupted. For example, acceptance was shown by "a very independent-minded 90-year old woman ... [who] systematically prepared herself for the end. She decreased her range of interactions and activities, initiated arrangements for her own funeral, and told the staff precisely what she did and did not want to have done for her during the terminal process. As death came very near, she refused medication and insisted that any attempt to prolong her life would be a crime" (Kastenbaum, 1977, p. 177). Another example illustrates feeling interrupted: "An 82-year-old former schoolteacher ... entered the geriatric hospital ... and discovered that life went on ... [she] became an active, popular member of the institutional community. Three years later, she faced death as though it were a regrettable interruption of a still cherishable life" (Kastenbaum, 1977, pp. 177–178). Essentially, she demanded that death "catch her on the run."

Both these common orientations might be considered, in Kübler-Ross's scheme, variations of acceptance. However, Kastenbaum believes that there is no support for Kübler-Ross's proposition that everybody follows the same kind of sequence toward acceptance. Not only do people die in different ways, but also there is no reason to believe that they should die in any "standardized" way.

Suicide

In the beginning of this chapter, I said that all societies construct some framework around death. In our society, we generally feel that death, unless it follows a slow deterioration in advanced old age, is shameful and even wicked. People who have been given their "death sentences"—told they have terminal illnesses—are shunted outside the "chalk circle." They often explain how difficult it is to lead "natural" lives thereafter. Their former friends and acquaintances find them embarrassing. And they can only maintain some semblance of reality if they pretend to others that they are after all not dying, if they talk about everyday things and not discuss their feelings and experiences. We are expected to continue in good health and success.

Illness and failure are shameful. They are

particularly a betrayal of physicians, to whom death is the enemy. If this is true for those who die "naturally," imagine how we feel toward those who have brought about their own deaths. They must either be evil or extraordinarily good—heroes, in fact. And in a way, the history of cultural and religious attitudes toward suicide and murder shows swings between these two extremes. If you take your own life for the glory of God or the good of humanity, you are a hero. If you commit suicide for personal reasons, you are a criminal. If you commit murder for the good of society or your country (as in war), you are a hero. If you do it for your own benefit, you are a villain.

Alvarez (1972), the author of an eloquent book on suicide, starts out his chapter on the background of suicide with a quotation from a letter written in 1860 by a Russian, Nicholas Ogarov, from England. I want to repeat that quotation here because it points up the illogical nature of our attitudes toward suicide. Ogarov's letter describes an execution that actually took place:

> A man was hanged who had cut his throat, but who had been brought back to life. They hanged him for suicide. The doctor had warned them that it was impossible to hang him as the throat would burst open and he would breathe through the aperture. They did not listen to his advice and hanged their man. The wound in the neck immediately opened and the man came back to life again although he was hanged. It took time to convoke the aldermen to decide the question of what was to be done. At length the aldermen assembled and bound up the neck below the wound until he died [p. 43].

Kastenbaum (1977) lists three evils of suicide, as perceived in our culture. First, it is sinful. It is considered morally wrong by all major religions today—although martyrdom was considered specially good at other times and places. Second, it is criminal. Even though Ogarov was describing an execution that took place over one hundred years ago, he could be referring to some legal action we might take today. Committing suicide is against the law in most countries today. Third, it is weakness or madness. Anybody who considers taking his or her own life is considered mentally ill. The Buddhist tradition, however, has an opposite view. Suicide is "the

Great Death" in China and Japan. And Alvarez (1972, p. 64) notes that "the Romans looked on suicide with neither fear nor revulsion, but as a carefully considered and chosen validation of the way they had lived and the principles they had lived by."

People who attempt or succeed in taking their own lives have given a variety of meanings for their actions (Kastenbaum, 1977). Some see death as a reunion with loved people who have died. Others see death as rest and refuge, a "secure harbor" after lives that have been unrelenting and burdensome. Death can be seen as a kind of sleep or vacation. Still others see suicide as getting revenge, at a rejecting lover, at an unappreciative employer, or at parents. Suicide can be seen as a penalty for failure by people who judge themselves and condemn themselves for not living up to their goals, whether of success, of honor, or of virtue. Sometimes suicide is a mistake. Either the people did not really mean to die (just to alert somebody to their need for love or help) or they were ambivalent (part of them wanted to die, but part wanted to be rescued).

Edwin Shneidman, a pioneer and major investigator of the subject of suicide, proposes a classification of all suicidal behaviors (Shneidman, 1963), based on the intentionality of the central act. He uses the term *psyde* to mean "achievement of cessation of living."

Intentional
1. Psyde-seekers, who consciously want an end to all of their conscious existence and go out to achieve this, no matter what method they might choose.
2. Psyde-initiators, psyde-seekers who take an active role in their endings. They are the kind of people who have never been fired; they always quit.
3. Psyde-ignorers, who may seek death but believe that they will continue to lead a conscious existence—to live on in some kind of afterlife.
4. Psyde-darers, the Russian-roulette players and others who take risks and play with the probabilities of life or death.

Subintentional
1. Psyde-chancers, something like the psyde-darers, but taking less risks, thus increasing their chances of surviving.

2. Psyde-hasteners, who unconsciously speed their deaths by abuse or neglect of their health, including smoking, overeating, drug or alcohol abuse, or ignoring prescribed treatment. Their deaths may not be officially classed as suicide, but psychologically such deaths are suicides.
3. Psyde-capitulators, who are so afraid of dying that they bring on their deaths; voodoo deaths would fall into this classification.
4. Psyde-experimenters, who live on the brink of death or in a benumbed or drugged existence. These deaths are often classed as accidental.

Unintentional
1. Psyde-welcomers, those who play no role in their dying but would welcome death. Very old people, especially after long, debilitating illnesses, could be classed as such.
2. Psyde-acceptors, who may not welcome death, but who accept its inevitability. We have discussed this orientation earlier.
3. Psyde-postponers, who realistically expect to die, but not for a long time into the future.
4. Psyde-disdainers, mostly young people who ignore the possibility of dying.
5. Psyde-fearers, such as hypochondriacs who are afraid to die and who are phobic about topics relating to death.

Contraintentional
1. Psyde-feigners, who pretend to commit suicide, but do not intend to die—for example, they may drink from previously emptied poison bottles.
2. Psyde-threateners, who do not intend to die but threaten to do so in order to get the attentions of others.

In a series of investigations that compared successful suicides with those who tried but failed, Shneidman and Farberow (1957) found several interesting trends. First, those who succeeded in killing themselves had different family histories; 33% of those who succeeded had relatives in mental hospitals, as compared with less than 6% of any of the other groups.

Second, the successful suicides used different methods from those who did not succeed: they used hanging or guns, rather than sedatives or wrist slashing. Three-quarters of all the successful and serious suicide attempters had made previous attempts. When the serious suicide attempters were released from the hospital, over two-thirds succeeded in killing themselves within one year.

Third, only about one-third of those who killed themselves left suicide notes. The authors quote Menninger (1938) as saying that all suicides show either the wish to kill, the wish to die, or the wish to be killed. They found that, particularly in men, the wish to kill and the wish to be killed decreased with age, while the wish to die increased. Although women may make more suicide attempts, men are much more likely to kill themselves. The ratio of male to female suicides is between 3 and 4 to 1 at earlier ages, and about 10 to 1 after age 85 (Kastenbaum & Aisenberg, 1972). This ratio holds true across ethnic groups in our own country and across different countries. Part of this difference is due to the kind of method employed. Women are more likely to use sleeping pills or relatively ineffectual poisons, techniques that, as Kastenbaum and Aisenberg point out, "bespeak ambivalence and require but little bravery" (p. 260). Men are more likely to use guns or explosives, methods that "not only [are] more effective but [that] may also possess unconscious masculine or specifically phallic significance as well" (p. 260).

Not only are there sex differences, there are also wide group differences. Dublin (1965) reports that suicide rates for Whites are from two to five times as high as for non-Whites, largely true because of the low rates for Blacks. As the financial security of Blacks has improved, incidentally, their suicide rates have increased, particularly in the wealthier groups (Woodford, 1965). If murder and suicide can be viewed as reciprocal means for solving painful life conditions, it could be expected that groups with high suicide rates would show low murder rates, and vice versa.

Marital status is also related to suicide rates, most obviously for men, among whom the suicide rates are higher altogether. Married men are least likely to commit suicide, unmarried men somewhat more likely, widowers even more, and divorced most. For women, suicide rates go up temporarily right after widowhood but then drop.

Kastenbaum (1977, p. 290) reviews some popular myths about suicide:

1. People who talk about suicide will not actually take their own lives—not true. Approximately three out of every four people who eventually make a fatal attempt give some hint ahead of time.
2. Only a specific class of people commit suicide—not true. People in all income and social-class groups commit suicide.
3. Suicide has simple causes that are easily established—not true. It is more true to say that we tend to be satisfied with easy, simple explanations.
4. Only depressed people commit suicide—not true. Suicide occurs in every psychiatric diagnosis and may not even accompany unhappiness.
5. Only crazy or insane people commit suicide—not true. Many people in their "right minds" do so, particularly in some cultural contexts, as discussed earlier in this chapter.
6. Suicide is inherited—not true. Even though more than one person in a family may commit suicide, there is no evidence for a hereditary basis.
7. Suicide is related to the weather or to such cosmic influences as moon phases, sunspots, or magnetic forms—not true. Research by Pokorny (1968) found little evidence to support such hypotheses, fascinating as they may be.
8. When a suicidal patient shows improvement, the danger is over—not true. The period following an apparent improvement in overall condition is actually one of special danger. Continued therapeutic ties must be maintained for a much longer period of time.
9. People who are under physicians' care or hospitalized are not suicidal risks—not true. Approximately half the people who commit suicide have received medical or psychiatric care within the six months preceding their acts (Pokorny, 1968).
10. Suicide can be prevented only by psychiatrists or mental hospitals—not true. "Some of the most successful suicide prevention efforts are being made by a variety of people in the community who bring concern, stamina, and sensitivity to the task. The human resources of the entire community seem to hold more hope than the limited cadres of professionals or the institutionalization solution."

Kastenbaum (1977) concludes that the suicide rate increases with age for both men and women. However, the rate for women reaches its peak before age 65 and then declines a little, while the rate for men continues to rise into the seventh decade. The big difference between Whites and non-Whites, furthermore, shows up in the later years of life. They have similar rates until their mid-30s. From that point on, the 2:1 ratio (twice as many Whites) is established. Non-White male suicide rates do not change much with age, but White rates continue to rise. White and non-White females have similar rates through their mid-20s, but in the next decade, according to Kastenbaum, "something happens that has yet to be explained satisfactorily" (p. 293). White women between 25 and 34 are more than twice as likely to kill themselves as they were a decade earlier. Suicides of non-White women increase too, but at only half the rate and for only a short period of time. Then the rate returns to the earlier level, while suicides of White women continue to increase for another decade. How much of this may be a period or cohort effect, Kastenbaum does not consider. It could be postulated that the isolation of women in the child-rearing age encourages the altered state of consciousness mentioned earlier. *Or* that the stress of combining work and child rearing is overwhelming. *Or* that this is the group most prone to the androgynous condition espoused by the women's movement and thus most tolerant of masculine impulses.

Is suicide on the increase? According to Pokorny (1968), the reason more people are committing suicide recently is that there are more people in the population. Suicide rates themselves, however, have not increased. The rate was highest in this century during the 1930s—the era of the Depression. There have been short rises and drops since then, but for a long time the rates have changed very little, as shown in Table 8.4 for the four decades from 1940 to 1970. The association between suicide and economic depression should make us look closely at the 1980 figures when they are published. The increased economic hardships of 1980 (compared to 1970) should be associated with higher suicide rates.

Murder

I suggested in the last section that there may be an inverse relationship between suicide and murder. Menninger's (1938) theory of three orientations—wish to die, wish to kill, and wish to be killed—is one expression of this hypothesis. Shneidman's (Shneidman & Farberow, 1957) catalog of orientations toward life's cessation includes kinds of suicides that are entwined with murder. Some people risk murder in a kind of daring or defying of death: those who frequent parts of town that are known to be dangerous, for instance, or who marry violent people. Some people's actions could result in suicide and/or murder: speedy drivers, odd-diet addicts, and cultists. Studies of families of battered children find that parental neglect or violence can often be traced to the past histories of these parents, who themselves experienced neglect or violence or seek a form of unconscious self-destruction in the destruction of their own children (Kastenbaum & Aisenberg, 1972).

The murder rate in our society has increased over the past two decades. Kastenbaum and Aisenberg (1972) report that "of all persons arrested for murder, 9 percent are under 18 years of age, 37 percent are under 25. . . . The overall crime rate among those 21 years of age and under rose 50 percent between 1962 and 1967. . . . More serious crimes are committed by 15-year-olds than by any other age group; 16-year-olds are not far behind" (p. 316).

The ratio of males to females is 5:1 among murderers and 3:1 among victims. A disproportionate number of murders now involve Blacks. They comprise 11% of the population but constitute 54% of the murder victims and 57% of those charged with murder. More murders are committed in the South than in any other part of the United States. Most murderers are not mysterious strangers. In at least two-thirds of the cases, the perpetrators and victims are at least acquainted; 29% are relatives.

Control

Atchley (1977) points out that older people who are dying have less control over their lives than do younger people. "All dying people find that family members and medical personnel, usually with good intentions, take away their free choices" (p. 183). To some extent, older people

TABLE 8.4 Suicide rates in the United States over four decades: 1940–1970

Race and sex (by year)	Rates per 100,000 (by age in years)									
	5–14	15–24	25–34	35–44	45–54	55–64	65–74	75–84	85+	All ages
White males										
1940	0.4	8.4	19.3	28.6	41.6	55.4	57.9	67.3	60.0	22.6
1950	0.3	6.7	13.2	22.3	32.8	44.1	51.9	58.5	69.8	18.5
1960	0.4	8.2	14.6	21.9	33.1	40.7	42.2	55.6	62.4	17.5
1970	0.5	13.8	19.3	23.0	29.0	34.9	37.9	47.2	47.1	17.8
White females										
1940	0.0	4.0	8.1	10.9	13.7	13.1	12.0	8.3	6.3	7.1
1950	0.1	2.6	5.1	8.0	10.2	10.5	10.0	8.2	7.4	5.3
1960	0.1	2.3	5.8	8.0	10.4	10.6	9.2	8.2	4.9	5.2
1970	0.2	4.2	8.7	12.9	13.8	12.2	9.8	7.4	4.4	7.1
Non-White males										
1940	0.2	4.7	10.6	11.0	13.5	12.1	11.4	11.8	6.8	6.8
1950	0.2	5.0	10.3	11.2	11.7	15.9	12.7	12.9	12.5	6.9
1960	0.1	6.5	14.4	12.1	13.6	15.8	13.6	17.6	12.8	7.5
1970	0.3	11.0	18.1	14.2	12.1	10.8	12.4	12.4	13.8	8.4
Non-White females										
1940	0.1	2.8	3.1	2.4	3.3	1.8	2.2	3.1	3.3	1.9
1950	0.1	1.9	2.6	2.5	2.8	2.3	2.0	2.3	0	1.6
1960	0.1	1.9	3.6	3.5	2.9	3.6	2.9	3.0	4.1	1.9
1970	0.3	4.5	6.1	4.9	4.1	2.5	2.7	3.5	4.2	3.0

Source: Linden and Breed, 1976.

cooperate with this dependency. They have been found to be less in favor of being told about their terminal diagnoses than are younger people. They want to be told themselves, that is, but believe that people in general should not be told (Kalish & Reynolds, 1976). Research shows that people tend to die *after* important occasions such as birthdays and holidays significantly more often than they die *before* these dates (Phillips & Feldman, 1973). Kastenbaum (1965) found that in making predictions about how long patients will live, physicians consider patients' "will to live" or "will to die."

The death system

Kastenbaum (1977) has used the term "death system" to include the network of people, places, times, objects, and symbols associated with death and dying. The people are funeral directors, life-insurance personnel, florists, lawyers, medical personnel, food-production and -marketing personnel (the death of animals to provide food), military personnel, religious personnel, scientists designing lethal weapons, and senators voting to approve military appropriations. It is obvious that the list includes almost everybody in our society.

Death-system times are Memorial Day, the Day of the Dead in Mexico, times when prayers for the dead are said, Good Friday, and anniversaries of military events or of the martyrdom of saints. Death objects include hearses and death certificates, wills, newspapers that print obituaries and other news related to death (such as murders and accidents), the noose, the gallows, and the electric chair, telegrams, bug killers, cigarettes, and cancer-producing foods and drugs. Death symbols include black armbands, black limousines, funeral wreaths, slow solemn organ music, and cemeteries.

The functions of the death system include warning and prediction of death, prevention of death, care of the dying, disposal of the dead, social consolidation after death, and making sense of death in general. The role of such a system in providing cohesion for a culture is illustrated in a story told by Ivan Illich (1976): "I asked a man if people over the border, in Mali, spoke the same tongue. He said: 'No, but we understand them, because they cut the prepuce of their boys as we do, and they die our kind of

death'" (p. 39). In traditional societies, each group has a role in the rituals surrounding death, even when the dead person was not a major figure (May, 1973); the society as a whole is involved. In modern society, such functionaries are still present, but their presence has become privatized. Only the family is concerned, although it may invite others. At the same time, fewer people actually die within the folds of the family. In 1958, about 40% died at home; in 1978, only about 20% did.

Funerals and other rituals

Ceremonies to mark important points in the life span are known in practically all societies, including our own. There are rites of passage for birth, puberty, marriage, and death. These rites accomplish at least two major goals: to unify the social group and to celebrate the importance of human life. It may be no accident that avoidance of funerals and other death rituals emerged in the same historical period as did the devaluation of human life (as measured by murder, child and wife abuse, apathy toward others' distress, and so on).

Geoffrey Gorer, in a moving book called *Death, Grief, and Mourning* (1965), describes his feelings when the death of his brother was overtly ignored by everybody who knew the brother, including the widow, who kept a "stiff upper lip" so that she wouldn't embarrass anybody with her private feelings. Kalish (1976) notes:

> There seems little doubt that traditional death-related rituals are in a state of transition today. Many people now request that charitable donations be made in lieu of sending flowers; others desire cremation, with the ashes sprinkled over a mountain or in the ocean, instead of land burial. Neither money donations (which have long been used in many cultures and American subcultures to help the survivors get through what is often a period of acute financial crises) nor sprinkling of ashes suggest a secularization of death. Rather, they point to the development of new kinds of sacred rituals [p. 503].

When I teach classes in death and dying, I encourage the students to make two large lists, one of all the funeral rituals they can remember having seen or heard about, and the other of all the needs experienced by survivors after a death. One blackboard wall is usually filled with one list and another wall with the other list. When we compare these lists, it becomes

TABLE 8.5 Funeral rituals and functions

Rituals	Functions
Attending a wake	Allowing survivors time to recover from shock
Sitting shiva	
Eulogizing	Providing occasion for crying and overt expressions of grief
Singing	
Burying the body	Eliciting overt expressions of grief
Lighting a "perpetual light"	
Marching to the cemetery or dancing	Making the bereaved feel that others are around
Decorating the grave	Remembering the dead
Erecting a memorial stone	Drawing the social group together
Making memorial gifts	
Placing flowers on body and casket	Allaying fear of death
Saying prayers	Allaying fear of ghosts; keeping a spirit from molesting the living
Wearing black attire or armbands	
Signing memorial books	Providing a "shrine" for focusing feelings and activities of mourning
Turning pictures of the person to the wall	
Laying out the corpse and embalming the body	Transforming grief into comfort and hope and joy
Sitting with the corpse	Signaling others that a person is bereaved
Keening and wailing at funeral	Underlining the reality of the death
Sprinkling ashes	Saying goodbye to the dead
Planting a memorial tree	Sending spirit of the dead to the afterlife world
Telling stories about dead person's life	Distributing property and belongings of deceased
Observing memorial days, such as a year after the death	Handing on the family and social roles of the deceased
Staying home from work	Reducing initial anger and hostility toward the deceased
Staying away from social gatherings	
Attending a funeral feast	Honoring the dead
Writing sympathy letters	Handling feelings of anger and aggression
Placing obituaries in newspaper	
Placing anniversary memorial notices in newspaper	
Attending religious services	
Looking solemn and sad	
Reading the will	
Engaging the services of ritual specialists, from keeners to priests	
Isolating the bereaved	

obvious that there is marked overdetermination on both sides. Each ritual on the list can be seen to serve a large number of social and individual needs; each need on the other list can be seen to be served by a large number of the rituals.

Care of the dying

Health care in this country is directed toward the cure of acute illness. This is true equally for physical and mental illness. If somebody has a fever or mysterious set of symptoms that is difficult to diagnose, then physicians, scientists, nurses, and family members are activated to find out what is wrong and get rid of it. Next in order of importance are people who have chronic but not fatal illnesses, who receive some medical attention and probably more nursing or custodial attention. But if somebody is perceived as incurable, as being on the dying trajectory, and particularly if that person is old, we are much less likely to provide the quality of care that might prevent or stop the decline, or even make the last days, weeks, or months tolerable.

A majority of deaths in this country take place in hospital settings—in either acute or long-term care institutions. Glaser and Strauss (1965) surveyed the kinds of care given to dying patients in such places, which are visibly different from the kinds of care given to those who may yet be rescued. Recent innovations in the care of the dying are exemplified by hospices, institutions dedicated exclusively to providing a humane environment for those who are dying and their families and friends. This is, of course, suited more for long dying trajectories, such as cancer, than for short ones, such as heart attacks. The most famous hospice is St. Christopher's, founded by Ciceley Saunders in London. The hospice movement has spread and, unfortunately, is becoming institutionalized. Sometimes it is hard to tell the difference, now, between a hospice and a back or terminal ward in a hospital.

Several years ago, an international task force of specialists on death and dying formulated a series of standards for care of the terminally ill. These consider the needs of the patients, their families, and the hospital staff. The discrepancy between these proposed standards and current practices is wide. Morison (1973) remarks that the big general hospital "is not a very good place to die" (p. 41). The professionals are pre-occupied with administrative matters and the increasingly complicated technical aspects of keeping people alive. The dying patient is more often than not psychologically isolated and lonely and frightened, as well as often physically isolated and ignored except for people rushing in and out tuning up the machines.

Psychotherapy is more and more being considered a legitimate practice with the dying, particularly those with long trajectories. One of the earliest people to try this, LeShan (1969), felt that if dying people could maintain control over their own resources and maximize their strengths they could live out their remaining months as richly as their diseases permitted. Some psychotherapists recommend the use of drugs that induce altered states of consciousness. Insights acquired this way can resolve troubling conflicts and can help patients face their own dying. Such insights can also help patients share their new feelings and attitudes with their families and friends and thus help these loved others deal with present and future losses (Kalish, 1976).

Most older people—and most dying people—prefer to die at home. That they do not do this as often as they wish is attributable to several factors. First, the medical profession is intent on preserving life until the last possible moment, often regardless of the quality of that life, in intensive-care units or large, anonymous general-hospital wards. Also, relatives feel that they wish the best possible care, for which few adult children are trained these days. The time when women learned to be generalists, and could care for the sick, is long gone. Most families are sure that professionals will do the best job—as, in some ways, they will. A third factor is the feelings of the dying people themselves, who fear becoming a burden on those they love, either because it would harm their loved ones or cause them to distance themselves emotionally at the time when they are wanted most.

How professional are the professionals? When it comes to dealing with dying, not very (Kastenbaum, 1967). When personnel in a large geriatric hospital were asked what they say to patients who speak of their own prospective deaths, five types of responses were reported (see Table 8.6). A few gave reassurance with

TABLE 8.6 Self-reported responses of attending personnel to death comments

Type of response	Attendants		LPNs		Total	
	f	%	f	%	f	%
Discussion	11	13.5	24	20.5	35	17.6
Reassurance	12	14.6	14	12.0	26	13.1
Denial	17	20.7	21	17.9	38	19.1
Fatalism	21	25.6	31	26.5	52	26.1
Changing the subject	21	25.6	27	23.1	48	24.1
N		82		117		199

Note: f, frequency of comments; *LPN*, Licensed Practical Nurse.
Source: Kastenbaum, 1967.

statements such as "You're doing so well now. You don't have to feel this way." A few more even were ready to discuss the issue; for example, saying "What makes you feel that way today? Is it something that happened, something somebody said?" About one-fifth used denial: "You don't really mean that. You are not going to die." Another one-fourth changed the subject: "Let's think of something more cheerful." And a final one-fourth gave fatalistic answers: "We are all going to die some time, and it's a good thing we don't know when" (Kastenbaum, 1967, p. 25).

As Kübler-Ross (1969) found, many dying people are eager to discuss their own dying and feel better after they do. It is, therefore, tragic that most relatives and professionals who are near them find it difficult to do so. It can be as hard for survivors as for the dying. Not long ago, a friend whose wife was dying told me how much comfort he got from reading everything he could find on the subject of dying, but how much he would have loved to share this with his wife, who refused to even consider the subject—at least aloud—lest it become a self-fulfilling prophecy.

Bereavement

We experience our own dying only once. We experience the deaths of others many times—if we live long enough. Losses close to our own lives we feel more keenly than those on the periphery. Thus, we even may mourn the loss of a pet who follows us around all day, and jumps on our beds at night, more than that of a parent, sibling, or even child whom we see less frequently. The loss of any treasured object—human or nonhuman—can be felt as the loss of a part of ourselves.

Grieving can be very complex, a mixture of anger, guilt, depression, anxiety and restlessness, somatic distress, and either forgetting of, or preoccupation with, the lost person. In a slow death trajectory, such as occurs with most cancer patients, much grieving can take place before the actual death. Sometimes observers accuse the mourners of being unfeeling when they do not show the strong grief that would be expected. Lindemann (1944) suggests that such bereaved people may have suffered "anticipatory grief." However, a study of 49 widows and 19 widowers, all under age 45, found that such "anticipatory grief" neither diminished the amount of grief experienced when their spouses finally died, nor did it seem to lead to planning for the postdeath period (Glick, Weiss, & Parkes, 1974). The duration of the spouse's illness made a difference, though. Those women who had lived for a long time with the knowledge of inevitable widowhood were more able to "pull themselves together" later.

It is hard to say how far the findings of this study can be generalized to older widowed people or to people who lose parents or children. Some writers (such as Lopata, 1973) have suggested that older widows find the grieving process much easier than young widows do and soon enjoy the companionship of their friends, most of whom have been widows for a long time. This may be more true for those women who have had to nurse their husbands through lengthy illnesses, or whose lives for months or years have revolved around daily visits to hospitals, than for those who have been caught short by unexpected deaths. In fact, Glick, Weiss, and Parkes found that women who found themselves transformed into widows overnight were overwhelmed by grief. They either felt numb and immobilized or cried for hours on end without being able to stop.

There are also sex differences in mourning. The women Glick and associates interviewed expressed a feeling of being abandoned; the men felt dismembered. Earlier in this chapter, in the discussion of generalized attitudes toward death and dying, I reported that women tend to stress their concerns for others, while men tend to express their concerns for their own life ventures. We know that women in our country are socialized to affiliation and to a focus on others, while men are socialized to autonomy and to external mastery. It should be no surprise that these sex-role differences show up in grief reactions, too.

Among the physical symptoms that tend to appear in grief-stricken people are "aches and pains, poor appetite, loss of stamina, headaches, dizziness, and (in younger women) menstrual irregularities" (Kastenbaum, 1977). Sleep disturbances are common. As Kastenbaum describes it, "A widow would go to bed hoping to forget her cares for a while and to wake up the next day with more energy and a brighter outlook. Often, however, she would wake up instead in the middle of the night and remain tormented by grief and the reality of her partner's absence" (pp. 247–248). The typical widower tried to emphasize reality but was more prone to feelings of guilt, such as "I wasn't sensitive enough to her" or "I should have made things easier" (Kastenbaum, 1977, p. 248). (A more complete discussion of husband/wife differences appears in Chapters 19 and 20.)

Perhaps because women, once widowed, tend to remain in that status, there has been more research on widows than on widowers. Considering differential life expectancies, lifestyles, and the tendency for women to marry older men, as well as the greater availability of older women than of older men, it is easy to see why widowers remarry within a couple of years and why widows are less likely to do so.

Among the psychological concomitants of widowhood, in addition to those mentioned in the last paragraph, are obsessional reviews of the past life with the dead spouse, mulling over the whole dying process, and finally idealization of the dead spouse. It is not at all uncommon for people to find it difficult, if not impossible, to realize that the dead person is truly gone. Many bereaved people—if they are not too frightened or ashamed of their reactions—tell of hallucinations they experience in which they hear the dead person moving about in the kitchen, see him or her passing on the street, feel a touch on their head, or feel him or her lying beside them in bed. Parkes (1972) says: "On the whole, grief resembles a physical injury more closely than any other type of illness. The loss may be spoken of as a 'blow'" (p. 5). The "wound" can be said to gradually heal.

(Remember that Parkes is a man and that this type of reaction is found more typically among men than among women.)

In his early study of bereavement, Lindemann (1944) mentioned another tendency of bereaved people that is not often cited: that of taking on the characteristics of the dead person. Adult children who have often criticized their parents for particular behaviors, and have vowed never to be like their parents, find themselves doing the very same acts after their parents have died. Widows or widowers who have long been annoyed by mannerisms of spouses (such as turning back to check if the stove and lights have been turned off or insisting on certain household routines) will find themselves assuming these same mannerisms after their spouses are gone. Lindemann interprets such behavior as attempts to deny the loss by making the dead person part of oneself.

Parkes (1972) identifies four phases of grief. The first is numbness, during which the loss is partially disregarded. (It is during this period that hallucinations of the dead person may occur.) The second phase is yearning, during which the desire to recover the lost person leads to kinds of searching behavior (such as scanning faces in crowds). The third phase is disorganization and despair, when the permanence of the loss is accepted and searching stops. The fourth phase is reorganization of behavior, a transformation of life into a new mode that no longer includes either the real or fantasied presence of the lost person. Kalish (1976) points out that these are descriptive trends, not rigidly defined or exclusive stages.

Consistent with the physical grief reactions noted earlier and with Parkes's description of loss as like having a "phantom limb," statistics show that people who have been bereaved have a higher level of both morbidity and mortality than would be predicted by their actual age projections (Maddison & Viola, 1968; Parkes, 1972). These increased death-risk figures seem to be self-terminating. In Parkes's study of the frequency of deaths of widowers and widows, their death rates returned to "normal" after about five years. Also, Rees and Lutkins (1967) and Heyman and Gianturco (1973) found that old people did not show this heightened mortality rate. Perhaps their increased experience and thoughts of their own deaths and the deaths of people close to them had prepared them for

coping with bereavement. As noted earlier, death anxiety seems to be lower among older people than among younger ones.

Some writers, like Kübler-Ross (1969), stress the near-universality of stages of mourning (as well as of dying). However, recent research by Clayton and her associates (Bornstein, Clayton, Halikas, Maurice, & Robins, 1973) suggests that mourning, like all other behaviors, is related to personality and lifestyle. These latter investigators are finding that widows and widowers who are very depressed one month after the deaths are likely to remain very depressed one year later. And those who do not show extreme symptoms or who show fewer symptoms tend to "recover" sooner.

The Chicago widows studied by Lopata (1973) also varied. About half of them said they were over their husbands' deaths within a year, but 20% said they had never gotten over the deaths and never expected to. These findings are similar to the findings described in Chapter 6 on the menopause. People who are more "fragile" are likely to find any crisis disastrous. People who find it easier to cope with life in general manage to cope with bereavement, too. They are upset and grief-stricken, but they do have techniques for recovery. We must not ignore, also, the quality of the relationship with the dead person. Not all relationships are alike, and the loss of some people may be much harder to take than the loss of others.

I quoted from the term paper of a student earlier in this chapter. Let me conclude the chapter with her description of her mourning process for her son (Barczon, 1973):

It is difficult to write about a death. I suppose if there is a recovery you would not remember a fraction of what goes on around you. After so many years, it seems abnormal that such a memory should remain so vivid. I still wonder why we were isolated in a small room seeing hospital staff only periodically when medication was administered. I can almost laugh now at the thought of the cruel night nurse who insisted on moving furniture and a comatose child because she had been taught in nursing school that the arrangement of the hospital room had to be thus and so. I remember the little girl who recovered from the same illness even though her parents never came to see her. I wondered why we, the "worthy" parents, had been dealt such a cruel blow. What went wrong at that moment when the child died and the doctor became so angry at the nurse? Why was it so important to rush me from that room where death was? Could I not have stayed a moment longer? I wanted to see my child off on his last journey—"Pray, just a moment longer." The doctor did not want me to grieve. Was he uncomfortable in the presence of grief? How could the chaplain be so sure that "all things that God does are good?" How was it that I accepted this explanation so readily then when it makes little sense to me now? Are my thoughts more rational now?

At the moment of death it surprised me that I felt no relationship to that lifeless body and what was once the living personality of my child. It was the immediate severing of affiliation. How odd! Only moments before we had been so close. I grieved for the pleasure of that lost personality— the being.

What ensued in the weeks following death was the realization that no one around me could face death either. They denied its existence by not allowing me to express my grief as the doctor earlier had done. They would suggest I go lie down though I had only just gotten up. Close friends and relatives avoided us so that I began to feel I had a contagious disease. As Clerk says, "Perhaps the bereaved ought to be isolated in special settlements like lepers." This segregation on the other hand precipitated in me an inward-looking and an examination of the death process on those who are not the dead or the dying.

Grief is first a sorrowing for oneself and then, for all those that this death touches. You realize that you have never had such intense feelings before. You have never been so acutely aware. As John Gunther says in *Death Be Not Proud,* "Death always brings one suddenly face to face with life." It forces us to ask, "What is the meaning of life?" Death strips away the superfluous things. You begin to live as you never did before, as you never could before. Such a pity that someone has to die to teach you how to live!

Grief may cause confusion of thought for some who are not mentally healthy to begin with but, on the other hand, for those who have a certain amount of mental maturity it can be a source of strength for the future. If you survive it, you feel you can survive anything even the thought of your own death. Death no longer haunts me, though I know the possibility of its presence every day of my life. Living is what concerns me now.

Summary

Research and theory relating to death and dying seem to have raised more questions than they have answered. However, two psychological aspects can be distinguished: (1) thoughts and feelings about one's own mortality and (2) reactions to the deaths of others. These are not unrelated, of course.

In the face of an almost cultlike movement to encourage us to feel our own mortality in order to enhance our experience of life, a review of the evidence seems rather to underscore the dangers in such activity. There is a suggestion that this is associated with an altered state of consciousness involving loosening of what might be called "ego boundaries"—a separation between self and others that may be prognostic of suicide. Concepts of death seem to follow an age sequence based in part on development of object constancy. But these concepts may be abstract rather than personal.

Grief at the death of people close to one may be seen as an expression of losing part of self. The mourning process may include the incorporation of the lost one's characteristics into the self, particularly if that lost one has been a spouse. The social nature of mourning, symbolized in the funeral and the "death system," may not be as comprehensive in today's society as it was in smaller, more traditional societies. The facts that death tends to come later in life and to occur in institutionalized settings affect the experience both for the dying person and that person's family and friends. Finally, the fear of death on the part of medical personnel suggests a need for retraining to help them fulfill their roles in the death system.

9

Cognitive Development I: Perception and Learning

The issues

Seven of the ten basic issues described in Chapter 1 enter into the consideration of adult cognitive development. Only issues 6, 7, and 8 seem irrelevant here. Let us rephrase these issues in cognitive-developmental terms:

1. How much is intellectual functioning and change after adolescence influenced by biological changes and how much by environmental conditions? Would the number of brain cells or their chemical composition predict competence? Would social expectations for differences in competence at different ages be a more important predictor?

2. How much is cognitive functioning under the control of individuals themselves, and how much is it subject to body or environmental changes outside their control?

3. Given a view of the cognitive system as relatively open or closed, is there a change in this openness after adolescence, or in old age?

4. Are changes in functioning after adolescence merely quantitative, or are there also qualitative developments? Are Piagetians correct in believing that most significant qualitative development ends with the establishment of formal operations during the adolescent years?

5. Are the only changes in intellectual functioning after adolescence retrogressive?

9. How do the parameters of time—chrono-logical age or developmental age—enter into the cognitive-development equation?

10. How universal are developmental changes in intellectual functioning past adolescence? Are there more individual differences than there are similarities?

This chapter and the following one are both on cognitive development. Here I deal with perception and learning; in Chapter 10, I deal with memory and thinking.

Aside from these basic issues, the study of intellectual development in adulthood presents another issue, that of *competence versus performance*. A large body of research shows that older people's scores are lower than younger people's scores. Should we attribute these age differences to performance decline or to competence decline? This question is related to our implicit notion of intellectual development in later life. Three possible patterns of such development are illustrated in Figure 9.1; these patterns could apply equally to competence or to performance.

Pattern A shows continued increase throughout life. At least potentially, according to Pattern A, people could get smarter and smarter so long as they live. Pattern B represents stability of the level reached at the end of adolescence, again either of competence or of performance, or of both. Pattern C represents progressive decline from early adulthood on.

According to Pattern A, lack of observable increase in intellectual performance during adulthood might be attributed to inhibiting environmental circumstances or to conditions that made it more functional or adaptive not to seem too bright. Adults who have changed their lifestyles—entering or returning to college, for example, or undertaking new challenging activities—do seem to become smarter. Has there been accompanying development in potential or competence, as Pattern A would suggest, or has there merely been improvement in performance to bring it closer to potential? People who use the word *senile* for most older people are implicitly assuming that Pattern C holds—probably the most commonly held view.

We not only have an implicit model of direction of intellectual change, but we also have an implicit model of the process of intellectual functioning involved in such change. Roughly, information is *recorded* at an acquisition stage that involves perception and learning. It is then *stored* in memory. Finally it is *retrieved*—remembered—and put into operation. It is, of course, impossible in practice, or in research, to clearly separate the parts of this process. Nevertheless, much research can be categorized in this way, and the discussion in this chapter and the next follows this implied sequence of events wherever possible.

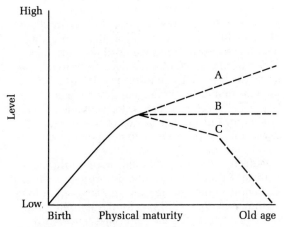

Figure 9.1. Implicit models of life-span cognitive-development functioning or competence.

Acquisition

Acquisition or learning is affected both by the sense organs and by the general state of the organism.

SENSE ORGANS

The profound consequences of sensory deficits have been discussed in Chapter 6. Not only does reduced acuity in vision, hearing, or touch, for example, close out a large part of potential information but, as reported by Palmer (1968), it also has the secondary effect of lowered interest in the environment. Even when there is good physiological acuity in every sense organ, furthermore, there may be lowered sensory processing because of a more generalized sensory sluggishness.

GENERAL STATE OF THE ORGANISM

The general state or condition of the organism—its overall efficiency of functioning—may influence both acquisition and use. Four aspects of organismic *state* relevant to adult cognitive development are (1) speed, (2) arousal, (3) attention, and (4) cautiousness.

Speed of functioning. Until recently, the research evidence strongly suggested that everybody who lives long enough is destined to slow down. This slowing down was considered one of the most solidly established facts about aging. It had been demonstrated both cross-sectionally and longitudinally, although usually only with subjects who were already "past their prime" at first measurement. It had also been demonstrated in both "simple" performances such as reaction time and in more complex cognitive functioning. Slowing down in old age was generally assumed to be caused by slower cerebral activity, slower nerve conduction, and, to some extent, decreased muscular capacity.

Recent research is challenging these conclusions. It looks now as if slowing down may not be inevitable, not irreversible, not true for everybody, not true for all performance, and not caused by the changes it was supposed to be caused by.

Let us first consider the evidence *for* slowing. Some investigators have shown slowing as young as the early teens, others not until middle adulthood 30 years or so later. The pioneer research on slowing was by Surwillo. He reported that electroencephalogram (EEG) alpha periods, a generally accepted measure of speed of functioning, decreased about 4 milliseconds per decade of chronological age from 28 to 99 years of age (Surwillo, 1963). Different investigators found that, when scores on a variety of laboratory tasks were subjected to factor analyses, a speed factor showed up for "old" subjects, but not for the "young" (Birren, Riegel, & Morrison, 1962; Cunningham, 1974). Speed of functioning, in other words, had an effect on the scores of older people only.

In one experiment, younger and older adults were required to decide whether two two-dimensional drawings depicted the same geometrical figure. Either the same drawing was shown in different positions, or mirror-image figures were used (Gaylord & Marsh, 1975). Older adult subjects needed almost twice as much time as younger ones to rotate these figures mentally in order to answer the questions. Furthermore, when stimuli were presented either to one eye (monocular masking) or to both eyes (dichoptic masking), older adults needed about one-third more time to recognize a letter of the alphabet presented both these ways (through a tachistoscope) than did the younger adults (Walsh, 1976). Surwillo suggested that such slowing could be attributed to central-brain functioning and spoke of a biological clock that regulated speed of functioning. In later years, presumably, the clock would be running down.

All the studies just described are cross-sectional. They compare a group of so-called "young" subjects with a different group of so-called old or older subjects. Schaie and his colleagues conducted one of the few longitudinal studies on speed (Schaie, Labouvie, & Buech, 1973). When they compared the performance of the same group of subjects on the different subtests of the Primary Mental Abilities Test over a period of 14 years, they found that the only subtest that showed decrease in scores over time was the one for psychomotor speed. Thus they too concluded that slowing down was part of growing older.

But what really happens? Losses in sensory acuity or in neuromuscular efficiency accounted for only a small portion of the age differences found in response time (Botwinick, 1965). And slowing in speed of nerve conduction rarely accounts for more than 4 milliseconds per meter of nerve involved (Welford, 1977). Other factors that might be handicaps for older subjects also account for only a small proportion of the age differences in speed. These include unfamiliarity with the kinds of tasks assigned, lack of meaning of such tasks for noncollege populations—which older cohorts are more likely to be—and greater cautiousness.

Slowing is most noticeable in those tasks that are characteristic of central-nervous-system processes: discriminations leading to withholding of a response, responding to a series of stimuli, or matching stimuli. When Surwillo (1963) partialed out the alpha period scores from the correlation he obtained between reaction time and age, that correlation disappeared. Older subjects with equivalent alpha patterns acted as quickly as younger subjects did. Thus, general slowing could be attributed to central-nervous-system deterioration; to disease, not to "normal aging." It would be a secondary aging effect—more frequent in older people but not an inevitable accompaniment of aging per se.

That increased response time may be neither inevitable nor irreversible is suggested by the fact that all research that shows average slowing also shows wide individual differences. Some older people are much faster than many younger people. Furthermore, age differences in speed scores have been wiped out by intervention techniques (Hoyer, Labouvie, & Baltes, 1973). Even physical activity showed up accidentally as a contributing factor. In a study at Duke University, where older people were being compared to college students on a variety of cognitive tasks, Botwinick and Thompson (1968) noticed, to their surprise, that as the year of testing went on the college students' average reaction time decreased. And, while there were no clear age differences between older and college-age subjects tested at the beginning of the year, there were marked differences in those tested toward the end of the year.

What was even more curious was the difference between those college students who participated at the beginning of the year and those who participated later. The average scores of the students tested later in the year were much higher than those tested early in the year. In looking over their data, the investigators found that many college athletes, who had been busy in athletic activities early in the year, were volunteering as subjects after the athletic season was over. It was an easy way to fulfill their obligatory research credits for introductory psychology courses. Although the older subjects were clearly slower than the college athletes, they were not significantly different from those college students who were not athletes.

Following up on those Duke findings, Spirduso (1975) compared young and older adults who were or were not engaged in regular athletic activity. As expected, he found that those who did engage in vigorous physical activity regularly—young or old—showed faster reaction time than nonengagers; older athletes were faster than younger nonathletes. Unfortunately, because these studies are correlational, we cannot tell whether those people who do participate in sports, at any age, are those who have faster reaction times to begin with, or whether it is the participation that increases their speed. Longitudinal data on children show that newborn infants differ in general activity level and that these differences tend to persist (Bayley, 1968).

Diana Woodruff (1975) designed an ingenious experiment to test Surwillo's theory that the slowing of aging was related to slowing of EEG alpha waves. (Alpha rhythms in the EEG are in the range of 8 to 13 cycles per second and most apparent in relaxed states.) Woodruff trained both young and old subjects to modify their alpha rhythms by biofeedback. Those who increased their alpha speed also increased their reaction time, whether they were young or old. There was an enormous variability in amount of slowing among the older people. In a different study, Hicks and Birren (1970) found a range of slowing from 20 to 110%.

Alpha rhythm also seems to be connected to survival. When 206 older people were followed over a five-year period (Muller, Grad, & Engelsmann, 1975), those with originally slower alpha waves were more likely to have died by the time of the follow-up.

Arousal.   Intellectual functioning is affected not only by the speed with which one processes information, but also, and perhaps even more fundamentally, by one's state of *arousal* or alertness. One can be highly alerted to the world

around, at one extreme, or asleep, at the other extreme. Research with infants is exceedingly vulnerable to this *state* condition. There is no way to test a sleeping infant or a comatose adult. We all fluctuate during the course of a day in our degree of alertness. Some people are "morning people"; others, "night people." People do their best work at different times because they are differentially aroused at different times.

Psychologists have been wondering whether there are developmental patterns in arousal. Are adolescents more arousable than adults, for example? Are old people less arousable than younger adults? Arousal, like speed of functioning, has been related to brain-wave frequencies. These frequencies are generally slower in older people. But the relation between arousal and performance is complex. Experiments by Eisdorfer (1968), for example, show different arousal patterns for young and old subjects who have been asked to learn something new. Young subjects come quickly to a high state of arousal, perform the task, and then quickly return to their base level. Older subjects take much longer to reach an adequately high arousal level and then, after they have finished their task, take much longer to return to base level too. They may even have a higher base level to begin with (Powell, Buchanan, & Milligan, 1975)—they may always be more aroused than they need be. Eisdorfer suggested that older subjects might have deficient servomechanisms. Figure 9.2 diagrams arousal curves for young and old subjects.

Apparently there is an optimum level of arousal for efficient performance. One does not work well when one is underaroused but one also does not work well when one is overaroused. Figure 9.2 suggests that older people not only have trouble returning to base level but also keep on moving to higher and higher arousal levels (overarousal) before they do drop back again. We all know that practice helps performance. This is particularly true for older people. One reason why practice may help older people perform better is that it decreases their tendency to become overaroused. They get used to the situation and are less anxious, and thus less tense or aroused. At least, this was found to be true in biochemical experiments by Froehling (1974).

Eisdorfer measured arousal by analyzing the

lipid (fat) content of the blood. Thompson and Nowlin (1973) report analogous findings using measures of heartbeats. Generally, the process of focusing attention or becoming aroused is accompanied by slower heartbeats and by

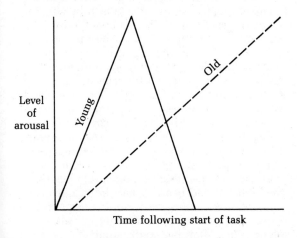

Figure 9.2. Arousal curves.

changes in blood pressure, particularly in diastolic pressure. Figure 9.3 shows the difference in heartbeat intervals found between young and old subjects who had been told that they were soon to be shown a stimulus to which they would have to respond. The different age patterns shown in Figure 9.3 correspond to those found by Eisdorfer in Figure 9.2. During the preparatory interval before the stimulus (s) actually is given (6 seconds before), young subjects—starting at a much lower base level of pressure, incidentally—drop in diastolic pressure. After the stimulus is given and while they are responding, their blood pressure rises sharply. Then, following the response, it drops sharply. Old subjects not only start at a higher level, but also their anticipatory change is shallow, as is their response change.

But not all psychophysiological measurements are different for young and old subjects. Thompson and Nowlin (1973) conclude that "our data allude to comparable alertness or arousal between young and old at the cortical level, but the elderly are significantly less reac-

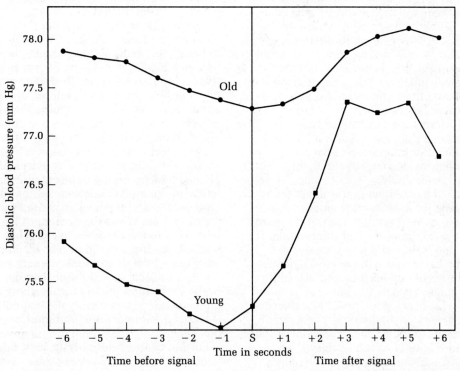

Figure 9.3. Beat-by-beat measures of diastolic pressure for young and old subjects before and after signal. *(Source: Thompson and Nowlin, 1973.)*

tive (and perhaps less aroused) at the autonomic level" (p. 121). Arenberg and Robertson-Tchabo (1977) say further that arousal operates differently for different kinds of functioning—it operates directly on conditioning but indirectly on verbal learning. Thompson and Nowlin conclude, finally, that poorer performance by older people may not be caused by deterioration in either cortical or autonomic systems per se but rather by deterioration in integration or coordination between the two systems. The kind of functioning measured by cardiac reactivity may be canceling out the preparatory effects of cortical activity.

Personality psychologists distinguish between *trait* and *state*. Most of the discussion here has dealt with anxiety or arousal as a relatively transitory state. However, we should also consider the possibility that some people—or people of some ages—are higher in long-lasting *trait anxiety*, which may confound the *state* effect.

Attention.   The term *attention* refers to the manner in which we *focus* on what we are doing, how "tuned in" we are to what is going on around us. Not only do people vary in the degree to which they focus their attention, but they also tend to vary in how wide their *attention span* is. Some people have a very narrow band: they can "take in" only a small amount of information at a time. Others have a very wide attention span: they can "take in" a large amount of information in a unit of time. Furthermore, some information leaves a "deep trace," while other information leaves only a "shallow trace," which could presumably be "wiped out" more easily.

Birren (1969) pointed out that it might be as troublesome to have too narrow an attention span as too wide an attention span. If the span is too narrow, one loses a lot of information. If the span is too wide, one finds it harder to distinguish what is relevant. Such variation is influenced not only by intrinsic individual differences but also by state of alertness, general interest in what is going on, novelty of the surroundings, general mental and physical health, sensory acuity, and other factors. Haviland (1978) found that right-handed subjects recognize facial expression more accurately when pictures are projected to the right visual field. Women are better at recognizing facial expres-

sion than men. Are there systematic age or developmental patterns to attention, too?

People focus attention by selecting out those stimuli that are relevant to their current interests. As Birren (1969) stated, given the almost infinite amount of information available at any moment the important process is to be able to ignore most of it. Focusing ignores the extraneous and concentrates on the necessary. When Layton (1975) reviewed the research on attention, he concluded that with aging there is decreased ability to suppress irrelevant stimuli. Most researchers on this topic present subjects with two or more tasks at the same time and measure how well the subjects can keep from being distracted. For example, Broadbent and Heron (1962) had young and older adults carry out a complex number-canceling task and simultaneously had them report which letters of the alphabet had been repeated during each minute. Young adults were able to perform both these unrelated tasks together fairly well, but older adults often had to drop one task in order to work on the other. Actually, such tasks demand both an ability to ignore irrelevancy and a wide band of attention.

Comalli, Wapner, and Werner (1962) asked children from age 6 to age 19 and young, middle-aged, and older adults to name the ink color in which a color name is typed (for example, in this Stroop Color-Naming Test, the word *red* is typed in blue ink). Older children and young adults were better able to handle the interference between differing names and colors than were younger children and older adults.

The British psychologist Rabbitt (1964) asked young and older adults to sort a deck of cards. He had added varying numbers of irrelevant letters of the alphabet to some of the cards. The time used to sort the deck increased for both young and old when the number of irrelevant letters increased from two to eight, but the older subjects' sorting times increased disproportionately more than those of the younger subjects.

Older subjects scored lower than did children in the Embedded Figures Test—where designs are embedded in random patterns and lines (Markus & Nielsen, 1973) and must be separated out.

Further contradictory results have been obtained with dichotic listening tasks—where different information is presented to each ear and the subjects are asked to report what was presented to one ear before reporting what was presented to the other ear. Craik (1965) found that recall was poorer for older subjects in both ears, particularly in the second one to be reported on. Clark and Knowles (1973), however, did not find that older subjects scored any lower than younger subjects. Between these two extremes, a study by Schonfield, Trueman, and Kline (1972) found no greater loss for Ear 2 than for Ear 1 among older subjects. They did find that older subjects were handicapped by *any* kind of interference, and younger ones only by *some* kinds of interference.

These and other studies suggest that older people's attentive efforts are poorly directed and diffuse, compared to those of younger people. This age difference could not be attributed to more-intensive learning by the older subjects, because Eysenck (1974) found that older subjects did not really *learn* the incidental or irrelevant information. Craik (1965) also reported shallower "traces" and more general loss of information by older subjects. In tests of haptic scanning—requiring subjects to match figures by touch—older people often failed to examine all alternative stimuli before making a decision, used inefficient strategies, and made inappropriate comparisons (Kleinman & Brodzinsky, 1978).

Unfortunately, all this research is cross-sectional and may represent cohort differences at least as much as developmental ones. It has been undertaken in laboratory situations unfamiliar and uncomfortable to older people, and has been based on very small, generally unmatched samples. Although this evidence does suggest aging deficits in attention, we should be extremely cautious in interpreting the evidence as true of all older people on any task and as not reversible by training. We need much better research before we can come to such conclusions.

Cautiousness and rigidity.   The fourth state characteristic—rigidity or cautiousness—is sometimes conceptualized as a style or personality variable and sometimes as an organic variable. Many studies—although far from all—have shown that older subjects, when compared with younger, tend to stick to previous solutions—to perseverate—even if changed circumstances make these inappropriate. Is this because older people (and also older rats) lose

flexibility? Or is it because they have learned many coping strategies, including the advantage of not exerting energy when it is not necessary? Is cautiousness a life-preserving quality or a handicap? So far, some research finds increased rigidity and cautiousness with age, but other research does not.

Supporting the hypothesis of increased rigidity are cross-sectional data by Schaie (1958), in which scores on the Primary Mental Abilities Test correlated with scores on rigidity tests, and both correlated with age. Chown (1961) found that those older people who score poorly on problem-solving tasks also tend to be more rigid. Granick and Friedmann (1967) reported a persistent and rapid decline in general flexibility with age (again, cross-sectionally). Eisdorfer (1968) found that older subjects in learning experiments made more errors of omission, while younger subjects made more errors of commission. If they were not absolutely sure, the older subjects would not answer.

In experiments with rats of different ages, Goodrick (1968) reported that older rats who failed to learn a maze tended to make many perseverative errors (see Figure 9.4). Those who did learn failed to extinguish as rapidly as

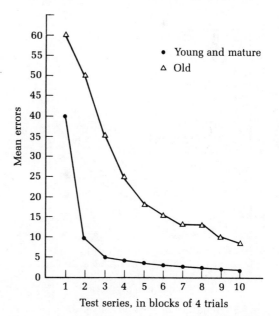

Figure 9.4.   Age differences among rats in errors in maze task. (*Source: Arenberg and Robertson-Tchabo, 1977, after Goodrick, 1973.*)

younger rats—they did not unlearn when they were no longer rewarded for learning. Older rats also showed less exploratory behavior. Finally, techniques such as gentling (touching gently), which improved the performance of younger rats, did not affect the performance of older rats.

If dogmatism can be said to represent rigidity on an ideological plane, then the age differences found by Monge and Gardner (1972) and shown in Figure 9.5 clearly support the idea that rigidity increases with age.

Finally, Arenberg (1974) reported that older men did not devise problem-solving strategies as flexibly as they had six or seven years earlier (longitudinal data).

On the other side of the argument, Rabbitt (1977) and Elias, Elias, and Elias (1977) suggest that what seems to be caused by age differences in rigidity may be instead caused by subjects' trying to solve problems beyond their capacity. Rabbitt says "It is possible to design tasks so complicated that no subjects of any age can grasp what the underlying principles may be. In such situations all subjects will fall back on random, unsystematic strategies (perceiving no relationship to guide them) or will attempt strategies appropriate to other situations" (p. 615).

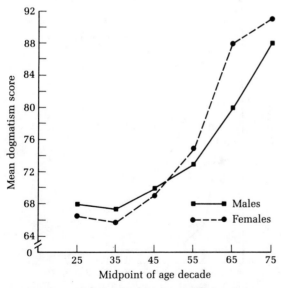

Figure 9.5. Influence of age and sex on the short form of the dogmatism scale used by Monge and Gardner (1972) in the Syracuse-Dade County study. *(Source: Monge and Gardner, 1972.)*

Some studies do *not* support a hypothesis of increasing rigidity with age. Birren (1962) did not find any age differences in rats' learning to solve mazes when the pathways were reversed. When mazes are very complicated, even young rats perseverate (Botwinick, Brinley, & Robbin, 1962). Birren also reported (1969) that, although older humans *prefer* more time for problem solving, they do not *need* more time than younger people. Similarly, Botwinick (1966) found that, if risk taking is necessary, older people do not seem to be more cautious than younger people. When older people (average age 73) had an option to choose either high-risk or low-risk situations, they no longer showed better learning in low-risk ones (Birkhill & Schaie, 1975).

Thus, leading investigators in this field caution against a simple conclusion that rigidity increases with age. Chown (1961), for example, found five different kinds of rigidity and says it is better to talk about rigid behavior as being specific to situations than as being a general characteristic. Furthermore, Monge and Gardner (1972) conclude that it is just as plausible to think of rigidity or cautiousness as adaptive behavior. Ready-made, stereotyped responses conserve energy and avoid trouble. Finally, Elias and his colleagues (1977) point out that what is considered versatile and flexible by the young may be considered rash by older people and that what older people would consider well-thought-out, cautious approaches might be considered slow, ponderous, and indecisive by younger people. That is, we are talking about different, age-associated value systems rather than about fundamental personality or organic characteristics.

Perception

Perception can be seen as part of the process of incorporating new information in the input phase of cognitive functioning. Essentially, it is the process of selecting, out of all the mass of information around, that which is considered relevant. It is thus highly subject to the organic state conditions just discussed, as well as to past experience, present knowledge, and sensory acuity or other physiological conditions.

Elias and his colleagues (1977) and other psychologists who have reviewed the research on perception have ended by asking more questions than by drawing conclusions. Most research so far has confined itself to comparing two small groups—called "young" and "old"—in artificial laboratory situations, using tests involving illusions. Because there is some reason to believe that perceptual development differs among modalities, the following review is subdivided into visual, auditory, spatial, time, and social perception. Affecting all these modalities is the degree of egocentrism or objectivity of the perceiving individual.

EGOCENTRISM

A central theme in Piaget's theory of cognitive development, as interpreted by Elkind (1970), is *egocentrism*. Egocentric people can see only from one perspective: their own. They usually cannot see themselves separately from their environment; they are embedded in it. According to Elkind, early development is characterized by a sequence of gradually achieved objectivity. Infants learn that objects exist separately from them—and that they themselves are separate from objects (including their mothers). Preschool children learn to differentiate objects from symbols. School-age children cannot tell the difference between facts and ideas, while adolescents have to learn to separate the viewpoints of other people from their own. Adults are presumably able to make all these distinctions and to

see that there are many possible points of view. But then, say some researchers, many old people are more egocentric than younger people.

For example, subjects can be told at one point that they are to give directions to very young children and at another point that they are to give the instructions to their parents. The score is based on their ability to make the instructions very simple if they are supposedly talking to very young children or to be terse and concise if they are supposedly directing the parents. Subjects who cannot vary their directions to fit different audiences are judged egocentric. Those who are able to "get out of their own skin" into that of another are judged more objective. This theme appears in most of the perceptual research described next.

VISUAL PERCEPTION

Almost all research on visual perception has measured response to visual illusions. A few studies have used embedded-figures tests, which are another way of measuring ability to "get outside of" immediate contexts. In the

Figure 9.6. The Müller-Lyer illusion. *(Source: Wapner, Werner, and Comalli, 1960.)*

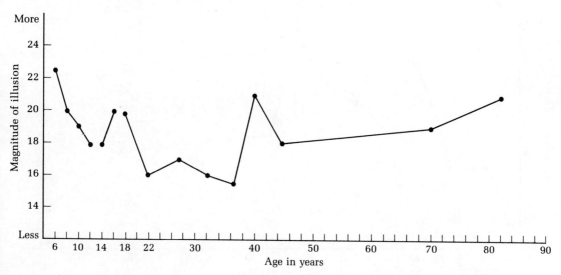

Figure 9.7. Age changes in responses to the Müller-Lyer illusion. *(Sources: Comalli, 1965; Wapner and Werner, 1957; Wapner, Werner, and Comalli, 1960.)*

Müller-Lyer illusion, shown in Figure 9.6, the straight line is actually divided in half by the arrows, but the different directions of these arrows make the line segments look unequal. Egocentric subjects cannot "get rid of" the interfering effect of the arrows; objective subjects can "erase them mentally." A number of investigations (such as Wapner & Werner, 1957; Wapner, Werner, & Comalli, 1960; and Comalli, 1965) all found the same age pattern of susceptibility to this illusion, a reversal in later life back to the level experienced by young children. Adults achieve objectivity but, if we can transform cross-sectional findings to processes, older people lose this ability to distance themselves and see other possibilities. So far as visual illusions are concerned, performance results follow Pattern C of Figure 9.1.

Figure 9.7 shows that susceptibility to the illusion is greatest before age 6 and after age 39. Between the ages of 6 and 20, there is progressively less susceptibility, and between 20 and 39 there is no change. Remember, these are cross-sectional data. When Gajo (1966) used a more analytic research design, he found no perceptible increase in susceptibility before the age of 60. But, as discussed earlier, chronological age is a treacherous index. Therefore, we probably would not be able to say at which age people are likely to become more susceptible again, only that at some point in later life—perhaps starting in their 40s for some people but not until their 70s for others—there is likely to be a return to greater susceptibility to obscuring effects of the environment.

Another illusion is presented by the Titchener circles (Figure 9.8). Age changes found by this test are the opposite of those found on the Müller-Lyer (Figure 9.9). That is, there is an increase in susceptibility during childhood, a plateau during the 20s to the 40s, and a decrease in susceptibility from then on. Research with two other illusions (Ponzo and Poggendorf) showed similar age patterns, with reversals at some point in later life (Comalli, 1970).

Eisner and Schaie (1971) used a cross-sequen-

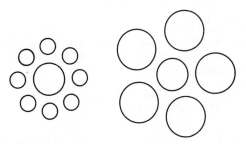

Figure 9.8. The Titchener circles illusion. *(Source: Wapner, Werner, and Comalli, 1960.)*

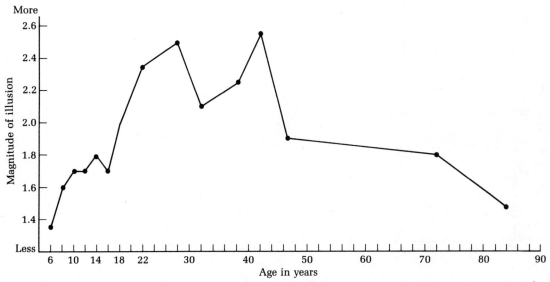

Figure 9.9. Age changes in responses to the Titchener circles illusion. *(Sources: Comalli, 1965; Wapner and Werner, 1957; Wapner, Werner, and Comalli, 1960.)*

tial design with a sample of men from 55 to 77 years of age. They concluded that cohort differences partially accounted for the increase in susceptibility to the Müller-Lyer illusion and that time of measurement (test/retest) partially accounted for the decrease in susceptibility to the Titchener circles illusion. Schaie has repeatedly challenged conclusions of age changes based on cross-sectional data.

In the Embedded Figures Test, a simple geometrical design appears at the left of a row of four more complex designs. The subject is supposed to pick out the one of the four complex designs in which the simple design is hidden. This kind of test can also be used for tactile comparisons; the designs are not seen but are hidden behind a screen and compared by touch. When groups of different ages are given such tests, younger adult subjects generally score better than do older subjects (Basowitz & Korchin, 1957; Axelrod & Cohen, 1961). None of these studies included children for comparison purposes.

Other perceptual tasks involve showing incomplete drawings and asking the subjects to say what they are. As can be seen in Figure 9.10, older subjects, particularly those over 60, have higher failure rates than do younger adults (Comalli, 1963). Wallace (1956) varied this test by showing complete designs and figures moving downward behind a narrow horizontal slit so that only part of the picture could be seen at one time. Although he found no age differences for simple figures, he did for more complex designs. The more the difficulty increased, the more disadvantaged were older subjects.

As noted earlier, when field dependence is measured by the Stroop Color-Naming Test, children and "elderly individuals" seem less able to remove themselves from the influence of the context—are more field dependent—than adults (Comalli, 1965). In a recent study (Schonfield & Smith, 1976), three age groups matched on education—college students and middle-aged and older professors—were asked to find the letters *L, O, V,* and *E* in an array of other letters. Although no significant age differences in scores were found, the oldest group tended to look for words instead of concentrating on the letters and thus made more errors of omission. They missed more letters. Presumably they were more field dependent, more egocentric. In summary, older people's visual perception is not as objective as that of younger adults—for whatever reason.

AUDITORY PERCEPTION

When a sound is repeated over and over, listeners tend to hear it changing. (This is called the *verbal-transformation effect.*) The simpler the stimulus sound, the more likely is it that this kind of auditory transformation will occur (Lass & Golden, 1971). Age comparisons of this effect

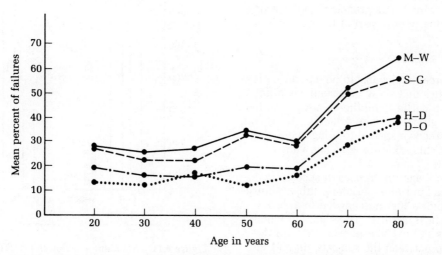

Figure 9.10. Age changes in responses to four perceptual-closure tests: Mutilated Words (MW), Street Gestalt (SG), Hidden Digits (HD), and Dotted Outlines (DO). *(Source: Comalli, 1963.)*

by Warren (1961) showed that children under 8 years heard few or no transformations but that most 8-year-olds did. Transformations became gradually less frequent from the 20s through middle age. Like visual perception, auditory perception seems to follow Pattern C in Figure 9.1. When older people do perceive transformations, they tend to do so gradually. Younger adults are more abrupt.

There is less research on auditory perception than on visual perception, and findings are also less consistent. A study of 156 community volunteers from 46 to 87 (Granick & Friedmann, 1967), for example, found no significant age difference in discrimination of rhythm patterns. However, one longitudinal study of 282 New York adults between 20 and 80 found a noticeable decline in the ability to understand degraded speech signals after the age of 50 (Bergman, Blumenfeld, Cascardo, Dash, Levitt, & Margulies, 1976), particularly after the age of 70.

What about health? Weiss (1971) compared 47 male volunteers over 65 years with 15 young men on a number of auditory perceptual tasks. The healthy older men differed little from the healthy young men, but the less healthy older men needed sharper differences between the two patterns of sound before they could tell that the patterns were different. Whenever more complicated measures were used, however, such as increasing the number of digits in a digit-span test or such as presenting different material to each ear, the older people, even the healthiest, were not as proficient as the young. Health is clearly only part of the explanation.

SPACE PERCEPTION

Space perception seems to be one of the few characteristics that show persistent sex differences—from earliest childhood, boys seem to be better than girls (Maccoby & Jacklin, 1974). Yet, when girls receive special training to equalize experience, this sex difference can vanish (Goldstein & Chance, 1965).

What about age differences in space perception? In one kind of experiment, subjects must judge whether a luminescent rod in a dark room is vertical or tilted. The chairs in which the subjects sit are themselves tilted, and the relationship between the subjects' tilt and the rod's tilt is examined. Six-year-olds say the rod is vertical when it is tilted the same way their bodies are. Twenty-year-olds, however, say the rod is vertical when it is tilted opposite to the tilt of their bodies. This opposite effect was seen among adults until the age of about 60, when the perception of vertical was again in the direction of the body tilt (Comalli, Wapner, & Werner, 1959; Comalli, 1965). Davies and Laytham (1964), however, did not find a regression in old age. And a recent study by Comalli himself (1970), using smaller age ranges, did not find reversal of tilt for men into their 70s.

Other kinds of spatial orientation tests (apparent median plane and apparent horizon) show similar age reversal to the rod-tilt test (Comalli, 1970). It should be noted that women still score lower than men, even in old age; women average four years younger at the time they overcompensate for body tilt (Wapner & Werner, 1957).

Elias and Kinsbourne (1974) asked men and women of two age groups (63 to 77 and 23 to 33) to match verbal and spatial stimuli. Their results are shown in Figure 9.11. Old women were slower to match the visual/spatial stimuli than were old men, but they were faster with verbal stimuli. Some recent theories about hemispheric dominance—verbal processing being controlled by the left cerebral hemisphere and nonverbal

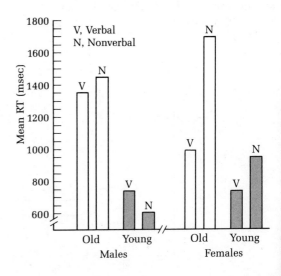

Figure 9.11. Matching reaction times (RT) as a function of age, sex, and verbal (as opposed to nonverbal) stimuli. *(Source: Elias and Kinsbourne, 1974.)*

by the right—were explored for age effects by Elias and Elias (1977). They reported that such asymmetry effects occur only when a task requires competing processes in the left and right hemispheres. Unfortunately, because no evidence of hemisphere asymmetry could be found, they could not test for age by hemisphere interactions.

Witkin and his colleagues have studied many aspects of field dependence that are allied to spatial orientation. They used the Rod and Frame, Body Adjustment, and Embedded Figures tests with children of different ages (Witkin, Lewis, Hartman, Machover, Meisser, & Wapner, 1954) and with subjects of older ages (Comalli, 1962, 1965; Schwartz & Karp, 1967). All these comparisons replicate the reversal of developmental trends, occurring in some cases as early as the 30s (adjustment of body to upright position in a tilted room), or as late as the 60s or 70s (Embedded Figures Test or Stroop Color-Naming Test). Figure 9.12 shows an example.

Piagetian psychologists have used a test of spatial egocentrism that has shown the same kind of mixed results by subject age as do other space-perception tasks. Subjects are asked to show how a configuration of objects would look to people viewing it from different positions. For example, in Figure 9.13 a subject in Position A draws or describes the set of objects on the table. In this position, all the figures can be seen: the two boxes, the kettle, and the cup. The subject is then asked to draw or describe what the array would look like to anyone in Position B, at a right angle to Position A—quite a different picture. When this kind of test was given to a group of subjects between 7 and 76 years old (Rubin, Attewell, Tierney, & Tumolo, 1973), the college-age and middle-aged adults did better than the younger and older subjects. This is the familiar age-reversal effect. Incidentally, no sex differences were found in this study. Schultz and Hoyer (1976) were able to train older people to improve their perspective taking, incidentally, by giving them feedback on their performance.

Hemispheric dominance. It has long been hypothesized that the two hemispheres of the cerebral cortex do not work as a unit and that one hemisphere is likely to control the other. In right-handed individuals, the left hemispheres are dominant. Left-handed individuals, some

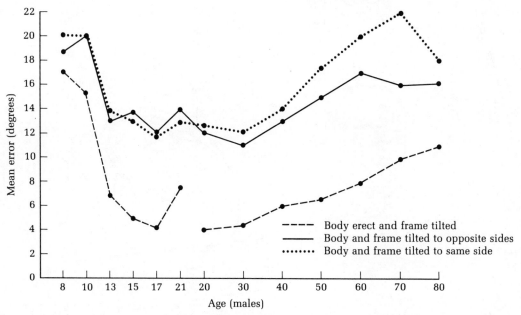

Figure 9.12. Age changes in responses to the Rod and Frame Test. (*Sources: Comalli, 1962, 1965; Witkin, Lewis, Hartman, Machover, Meisser, and Wapner, 1954.*)

think, are divided into those who have right-dominant brains and those who do not have clearly established dominance. Developmental changes in dominance have recently been investigated, and the research findings reviewed by Diana Woodruff (1978). For example, Kimura (1973) found that left-hemisphere dominance is set in both boys and girls by age 4, although children from disadvantaged homes are later in establishing dominance. Clearer dominance is associated with better performance on spatial-perception tasks, and men have clearer dominance than women. Because there is less age-related loss in verbal abilities than in spatial abilities, some psychologists have considered the possibility that the two hemispheres of the brain age at different rates. However, there has been no support for this theory. In general, biological indexes such as EEG wave patterns and hemisphere dominance may be related more to development in the first years of life than in later years. This is in accord with Birren's "dis-

continuity hypothesis," which states that there are different causes for age changes in the beginning of life from causes at the end of life.

TIME PERSPECTIVE

Phenomenologists generally stress space and time as the two basic parameters of personal experience. Less attention has been given to perceptions of time than of space (see the discussion of time in Chapter 1). One question that has been asked is "Do older people, as they face a curtailed future, change their time perception?" Kastenbaum's (1963) research did not find this to be so. Older people (median age 77) were *not* more limited than young people (median age 19) in their general time framework: in knowing time concepts, in estimating time extension (how long something lasted), in time density (how filled a unit of time was), and in coherence (fitting time together with other aspects of thinking). However, older people *were*

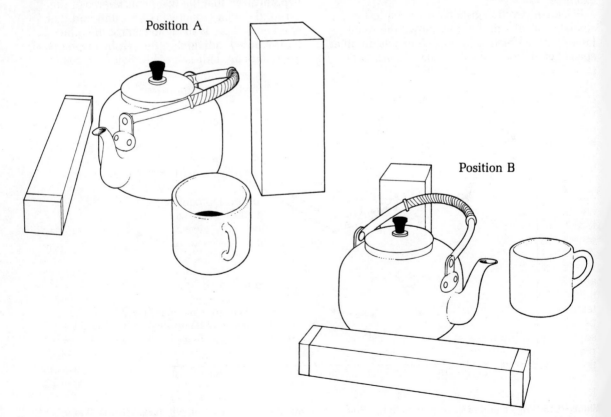

Figure 9.13.   A perceptual-shift test.

more limited in their *personal* time framework. Thus, they could use time concepts adequately except when applied to themselves. This curious contradiction has received surprisingly little attention in developmental literature, as, in fact, has the general area of time perspective. Granick and Friedmann (1967), in one replicative study, found no age differences in objective estimation of brief periods of time.

SOCIAL PERCEPTION

If there is a tendency for people to become more egocentric as they grow older (to be less able to separate themselves from their environment), they should find difficulty not only in distancing themselves from objects (as demonstrated in susceptibility to illusions) but also in distancing themselves from other people. Research in this area has just begun, most of it relating performance on social-perception tasks to amount of social activity in old age (Dolen, 1980). No age comparisons for comparable groups have yet been reported.

In another kind of study, Klein (1972) asked people, while they were being subjected to social pressure, to make judgments about which of two circular disks was smaller. He found that older adults were more susceptible to such social pressure than younger subjects, not only in visual-perception tasks but also in auditory judgments, arithmetic problems, and social attitudes. Incidentally, different groups of younger and older subjects were used for each task.

One possible explanation for this age difference, of course, is that there are cohort differences. The present older generation was socialized to be more conforming and attentive to others than was the present young generation. An alternative explanation is that older subjects were more uncertain about these kinds of tasks and that, like most people in situations of uncertainty, they turned to others for guidance. To test these hypotheses, Klein increased the older people's feelings of confidence. When he did so, most age differences disappeared; the older people were as objective or independent in their judgment as the younger ones.

The accumulation of experiments such as Klein's, which manipulate presumably causal variables, will help us to answer some of the questions asked earlier: "Are these age differences really inevitable, irreversible, and universal?"

Learning

Learning is the final point of input; it is the actual assimilation of what has been selected. So far, most research on learning considers the learner essentially passive and mechanical (see Chapter 1, Issue 2), even though the questions that are being asked may eventually lead to a more organismic view. Can an old dog learn new tricks? Can older people acquire new information and skills, or try new careers? To answer such questions is not easy, because we have to draw inferences about what goes on "inside" from what we can observe outside. There is no way to measure directly how much information is taken in. We have to decide from outward performance. Psychologists have, therefore, resorted to a variety of research strategies to determine whether poorer performance often found for older people should be attributed to secondary factors, such as needs for more time, more reassurance, or more motivation, or to a decline in learning competence as such (the *performance/competence* problem). Some secondary factors that apply particularly to learning are reviewed as follows.

SPEED

Speed of functioning, discussed earlier in the chapter as a "state variable," looms as large in studies of learning as it does in other aspects of cognitive development past adolescence. Most learning studies derive from early association psychology. They typically require subjects seated in laboratories to form connections between two words or nonsense syllables—or any two or more stimuli presented together. These connections are tested by later presenting one of the stimuli and asking the subject to name its pair. The factor of time is central in most of these studies. Its influence has been investigated several ways: (1) how long the words, or other stimuli, are shown; (2) the interval between the presentation of the stimulus and the request for the response; and (3) the time between stimuli. These intervals can be controlled by the experimenter or in self-paced tests by the subjects themselves.

Most studies have shown that younger subjects (young or middle-aged) learn such lists quicker than old subjects, make fewer errors in the process of learning, and learn more difficult lists. However, these age differences are lessened and sometimes even obliterated when older subjects are allowed more time or can self-pace the tests. One of the most prominent of these studies is that of Canestrari (1963). He tested 30 men between ages 50 and 69 and 30 men between ages 17 and 35, all seeking work at a local employment agency. His two age groups were also matched on vocabulary (Wechsler Adult Intelligence Scale), education, and socioeconomic status. Table 9.1 shows the pattern of errors under three time conditions: 1.5 seconds, 3 seconds, and self-paced. The younger subjects made fewer errors than the older under all three time conditions, but the difference between age groups was greatly reduced when they could pace themselves. The older group thus made 39 more errors than the young when the time limit was 1.5 seconds, only 18 more errors when they had 3 seconds to work, and only 9 more when there was no time limit. (Note, however, that older subjects may expect age bias at an employment agency, and thus may be inhibited. Also, older subjects are used to controlling their own lives and thus may resist time controls.)

Eisdorfer, Axelrod, and Wilkie (1963) report another common finding, that older subjects—at least past middle age—benefit more from extra time or self-pacing than do younger subjects. When Monge and Hultsch (1971) systematically varied both time allowed for the subjects to respond and time allowed for subjects to study the task, the older subjects were helped most by increased time to respond. This kind of finding has been used to support the argument that there are no real age differences in learning potential, just differences in speed of response, which is a state-of-the-organism variable. Furthermore, Eisdorfer (1968) found that older people working at a slower speed respond faster than they would need to if the task demanded a faster speed. Therefore, it may not actually be ability to work fast, then, but something about the nature of a speeded assignment that handicaps older subjects. Perhaps it is anxiety provoking, for example.

Arenberg (1965) showed that deficits in verbal learning among older subjects might be a result of more than a lack of sufficient time to respond, however. He compared young (mean age 20) and old (mean age 66) subjects under two anticipation intervals: 1.9 and 3.7 seconds. He also interspersed time-controlled trials with self-paced trials and found that the old group that had learned under the faster time condition made more errors than the old group that had learned under the slower timing. From this, he concluded that older subjects demonstrate both learning *and* performance deficits. In the judgment of Elias and his colleagues (1977), although slower response pacing allows older people—in this case usually after the age of 60—to make fewer errors, it seldom allows them to do as well as younger subjects. The data are so generally inadequate, however, that the controversy over whether performance deficits are connected to timing cannot be settled yet.

Conditioning.   Most of what has been discussed so far concerns associational learning, on which most research in this area is focused. There have been a few conditioning experiments that consider age differences. As early as 1959, Braun and Geiselhart compared three age groups in eye-blink conditioning and extinction: boys aged 8–10, men aged 18–25, and men aged 62–84 years. The eye-blink response occurs naturally to a puff of air and was conditioned to appear when the brightness of a light was increased. The children proved to be the easiest to condition. The two adult groups were similar in the early trials, but eventually the younger adults improved much more than the older ones. The removal (extinguishing) of the conditioned response followed a similar age pattern.

TABLE 9.1 Mean errors and mean time per self-paced trial

Measure	Group	1.5 seconds	3 seconds	Self-paced
Total errors	Young	12.23	7.90	6.27
	Old	50.90	25.90	15.30
Omission errors	Young	10.73	6.10	4.77
	Old	46.57	21.47	9.90
Commission errors	Young	1.60	1.80	1.50
	Old	4.23	4.60	5.40
Time in seconds per trial	Young	—	—	43.14 sec
	Old	—	—	53.08 sec

Source: Canestrari, 1963.

Overall, the oldest group was less conditionable than the two younger ones, between which differences were not significant.

Similar results were obtained with young and old adult groups by Kimble and Pennypacker (1963), who added that their old subjects tended to habituate before they could be conditioned, suggesting arousal or attention problems. In another experiment, brain-damaged older subjects proved even less responsive to conditioning than did healthy older people (Solyom & Barik, 1965).

Habituation (in which subjects stop responding to the stimulus before they become conditioned—perhaps because they lose interest) seems to be characteristic of older subjects in general, regardless of their state of health or cerebral functioning. Botwinick (1970) suggests that the tendency to habituate may be an inverse aspect of general responsiveness. If so, present research data indicate that age seems to bring lowered general responsiveness. As a final confusing note on conditioning and age, when Ayllon and Azrin (1965) tried to increase the adaptive behavior of institutionalized adults via operant conditioning, they found that age presented no barrier to success.

COGNITIVE STYLE

Perhaps the way people process information is important in age differences in learning. A number of different cognitive styles have been investigated, including kinds of categories found (temporal groups, semantic clusters, or hierarchies) and kinds of approach strategies adopted (for example, convergent or divergent thinking, or impulsive versus reflective attacks). In most laboratory studies, older subjects generally seem to use less effective processing strategies than do younger subjects. In fact, they often do not seem to use *any* systematic strategy.

Following Piagetian theory, Kagan, Moss, and Sigel (1963) investigated coding and categorization strategies, using what has come to be a classic task, the matching of familiar figures. They observed a developmental sequence from classifying or grouping on the basis of relationships between objects to classifying on the basis of similarity between objects. Thus, preschool children match a hammer with a nail, which is a relational approach. Older children put a nail together with a screw, which is an analytic/

descriptive or categorical/inferential approach.

The major research on cognitive style in adults and older people has been led by Nathan Kogan, Nancy Denney, and their colleagues. Most life-span findings show the reversal or U-shaped patterns also found in perception studies; older people typically use styles more like those of young children than like those of older children or adults. These studies are far from conclusive, though.

In one study of categorization style, Denney and Lennon (1972) asked subjects of different ages to classify geometric figures. Those between 25 and 55 grouped by similarity. Those between 67 and 95 made graphic designs instead of categories, a behavior more often found in preschool children. Kogan (1974) found similar reversal trends when he asked college students and "old adults" to sort geometric drawings or objects. More older subjects showed relational/thematic groupings than did the younger, who more frequently sorted by categorical/inferential groupings. Yet champion chess players, whom we might expect to be highly analytic, used relational sorts (Johnson, 1971).

One hypothesis is that older subjects are more impulsive in their approach than they are reflective and that thus they are more likely to make mistakes than are younger subjects. Clearly, this hypothesis is the opposite of the other common hypothesis that older people are more cautious and thus are more accurate—although slower. Denney and List (1979) gave a sorting task to people in each decade of life from 30 to 80. Both errors and time to respond increased with age. Thus, the oldest subjects were both more reflective and more inaccurate or were more cautious and more inaccurate. These findings contrast with those of Coyne, Whitbourne, and Glenwick (1978), who report that older subjects took less time to respond and made more errors—were more impulsive.

An interesting longitudinal study—one of the few so far—followed honors science students over four years (Cropley, 1969). Those who "bloomed" in the course of these few years had been no different in ability or achievement from their more everyday classmates. But they did differ from them in style; they were more divergent thinkers.

Clearly, we need much more research in this area before we can even be sure that older people do have cognitive-style differences from younger people, let alone whether there are aging effects in style. Kogan (1973) suggests that the differences found so far may boil down to age differences in speed of response or to cohort-related effects of educational level, occupation, or country of birth. He also wonders whether responses that might be capacity determined in young childhood or late old age might be stylistically determined during the years of top capacity (Kogan, 1974). In a similar vein, Arenberg and Robertson-Tchabo (1977) suggest that older people's approach may help them avoid extra effort, even if they end up being less successful.

LEARNING STRATEGIES

Some investigators have shown older subjects how to use mediators or learning strategies to improve their learning. These mediators, which can be visual images, words, or phrases, provide links between stimuli, thus making them more meaningful. For example, the lines of the musical staff (*E, G, B, D, F*) can be remembered better by thinking of the sentence "Every Good Boy Deserves Fudge." Although this instruction did improve the performance of older subjects (Hulicka & Grossman, 1967), they were still not as good as younger subjects. Table 9.2 shows that some kinds of instruction helped more than others and that different age groups are helped by different kinds of instruction. The young subjects had significantly higher recall scores

TABLE 9.2 Performance with mediators

Age	Type of mediator	Number of pairs recalled	Percent improved over no instruction
Old	No instruction	10.4	—
	Subject-image instruction	15.8	18
	Experimenter-image instruction	13.6	10
	Verbal instruction	14.0	12
Young	No instruction	41.7	—
	Subject-image instruction	48.4	11
	Experimenter-image instruction	46.9	8
	Verbal instruction	42.8	1

Source: Hulicka and Grossman, 1967.

both when they thought up their own mediator images and when they were given images by the experimenter. They were not helped much just by *being* told to use images. The older subjects, however, improved with any kind of instruction. Also, it is clear that the younger subjects performed much better altogether and that the improvement in all cases was far from overwhelming. A different study, by Hultsch (1975), found that older subjects (mean age 75) benefited more from help in organizing words into categories than did younger subjects (mean age 20). Therefore, when instruction applies specifically to the problems of many older people—as in organizing complex material—it may make a difference.

Transfer of training and retroactive inhibition. What is the effect of previous experience and previous learning on new learning? Does earlier experience facilitate new learning, perhaps by providing more meaningful categories into which new information can be grouped? Or, conversely, does it interfere with new learning by providing conflicting associations? Most experimental research in this area is based on tasks requiring the learning of one set of associations, followed by the learning of a second, different set of associations. Presumably, if there is positive transfer, better scores will be obtained on the second set. In an early study by Gladis and Braun (1958), three age groups were compared: 20–29, 40–49, and 60–72. The youngest group showed the most transfer effect—the most improvement. One possible explanation is that the older subjects encountered more interference.

Age differences in initial learning also need to be considered. Their review of the research data led Arenberg and Robertson-Tchabo (1977) to conclude that "when well-established habits are beneficial for learning for the young, they are even more beneficial for the old; and when the well-established behavior interferes with learning for the young, it is even more interfering for the old" (p. 431). The frequent finding that meaningfulness of material is important in the successful new learning of older adults is consistent with this generalization.

One explanation given for the beneficial effects of instruction is that instruction helps subjects "learn to learn." Older individuals presumably have less familiarity with the strange kind of learning required in experiments. Thus, when they are prepared ahead of time or equated for level of first learning, no age differences are found in transfer or retroactive studies. For material that has intrinsic meaning, older individuals also show no age deficits. In fact, associated pairs that have what is called "high associative strength" (more intrinsic meaning) are easier for older subjects to learn than those with low associative strength. There are no age differences on such tasks (Elias et al., 1977). A comparison of reactions to tones versus meaningful spoken phrases showed the age differences in favor of young subjects on tones were not present for spoken phrases (Shmavonian & Busse, 1963).

CRITICAL PERIODS

Ethologists have hypothesized that there are *critical periods* in learning and that material acquired at strategic points of life—generally in early infancy—is learned more efficiently and effectively than that learned later. Elias and his colleagues (1977) state, however, that this hypothesis is now being seriously questioned and that "many types of stimulation presented during the adult portion of the life span have substantial effects on subsequent learning" (p. 163).

TASK COMPLEXITY

Are older learners more disadvantaged than younger learners when the task to be learned is more complex? Complexity has been measured several ways, including by number of choice points, as in maze learning and number of concurrent discriminations that must be made. The research findings in animal studies are far from definitive. Arenberg and Robertson-Tchabo (1977) conclude that, when difficulty is defined as number of choice points, there is support for the idea that older learners are not as good as younger ones. In humans, similarly, when complexity is measured along a concrete/abstract continuum older learners are more likely to perform less well with abstract learning such as forming principles or generalizations. As difficulty increases, perseveration increases in both animal and human subjects. This tendency to stick with inappropriate responses is interpreted by some as behavioral rigidity. As suggested earlier in this chapter, though, all of us perse-

verate where difficulty of tasks exceeds our limits.

INCIDENTAL LEARNING

Botwinick (1970) defines incidental learning as the acquisition of information or skills not relevant to the main purpose of a learning task. So far, research findings do not show age differences in such learning, even though Botwinick points out that older people who find tasks difficult may perform better if they learn to concentrate on the most relevant aspects.

CONCLUSIONS

As suggested throughout this discussion, it is hard to evaluate the intrinsic effect of age on learning because most studies cannot separate out such extrinsic factors as state of the organism, motivation, and measurement. How does one explain findings that age deficits can be erased by handling—"gentling" of rats or encouragement of humans, for example (see Arenberg & Robertson-Tchabo, 1977; Elias et al., 1977)?

A more serious problem is the kind of research used. Birren (1969) raised the question whether measurements used to assess development of children are appropriate for use with adults and older people. This question looms large all through cognitive research, particularly in the area of intelligence testing, which is discussed in Chapter 11.

What can we say about those age deficits we do find in perception and learning? Can we attribute them to inevitable aging processes? Like physical disabilities, they can be more frequent in old age without being inevitable. We cannot say that all older people will have defective perceptual functioning or find it harder to learn. If there are memory losses, we can't blame them automatically on poorer input.

Summary

Before interpreting age differences in cognitive performance as declines in potential, it is necessary to rule out two basic intervening factors: sensory acuity and state of the organism. Dulled senses can keep most information out. Slowed speed of response can affect every step of the cognitive processing. Either under- or overarousal can impede efficient performance. Unfocused attention and rigidity can be as handicapping as sensory deficits are. Slowing of response, attributed by some to central-nervous-system deterioration, may be neither inevitable nor irreversible, however. Physical activity, for instance, seems to be associated with less slowing—and also with better cognitive performance.

Most research on perceptual development is focused on what might be called *egocentrism,* involving the subject's ability to achieve distance from the experience. Most also is cross-sectional. A pervasive age-reversal effect appears, with older subjects performing more like young children than like younger adults or older children. Visual and auditory perception, space perception, and time and social perception have been investigated. One study (Eisner & Schaie, 1971) that is more than cross-sectional attributes most age reversal found to cohort and repeated-measures effects.

Most research on learning is based on paired-associates kinds of tasks. In standard laboratory situations, older adults generally demonstrate both learning and performance deficits, compared with younger adults. Older subjects do better if allowed more time or if allowed to control their own timing, but they still tend to make more errors than do younger subjects. In conditioning experiments, old subjects are harder to condition and also tend to habituate faster than younger adults. Methods of processing information—cognitive style—seem to show the same kind of age-reversal effect as does perception.

It looks as if both biological and social conditions influence adult development in perception and learning. Some changes are at least partly under our control. Certainly exercise seems to affect cognitive functioning at any point in adulthood.

10

Cognitive Development II: Memory and Thinking

A primary difference between living beings and machines is the living being's ability to make use of information in order to adapt to ongoing situations and circumstances. Survival is predicated on thinking out new solutions, based on memory of earlier experiences. Maybe part of survival itself is being able to enjoy both the repetitive and the novel aspects of new experiences, in being able to compare, contrast, and create. For all these activities, it is necessary to retain memories of earlier experience, to retrieve these memories appropriately, and to apply them in a variety of ways. The discussion in this chapter focuses on the possible effect of age or length of living on these intellectual processes. Does age make a difference? Does it impair earlier ability? Or does it increase ability? (Recall the patterns illustrated in Figure 9.1.)

Memory

There are two contradictory popular beliefs about memory changes after people reach adulthood. One is that memories fade gradually over time. The other is that older people find it easier to remember what happened years ago than to remember what happened that morning. It is easier to investigate memory fading than to investigate early memory primacy. We can set up laboratory experiments to teach subjects something at one time, and we can then test their

retention of what they have learned minutes, hours, or weeks later.

It is harder to judge whether memories of years ago are more accurate than those of yesterday. The people who must decide whether it really happened that way were not around then. This is true not only of the longevity claims of geographically isolated people but also of the descriptions by American old-timers of what life was like in Iowa in 1900.

This is not the only problem in studying memory. Just as the only way to see whether something has been learned is to see whether it has been remembered, it is impossible to tell whether something that is not remembered has not, in fact, been learned.

Most adults—particularly those past middle age—worry about losing their memories. At least one member of every audience I have ever lectured to, or been part of, has asked about memory loss. Losing one's past, after all, is losing oneself. In part, this worry is triggered by stereotypes of older people as "losing their minds," and thus many older people get very upset by their occasional lapses of memory, which young people ignore. So far, research results are as contradictory here as they are for perception and learning. Comparisons of the remembering done by older and younger people frequently—but not always—show age differences in favor of the young. Such age differences apply only to some kinds of memories, however, and are often attributable to differences in initial learning or to problems in retrieval.

Classical ways of testing memory are recognition, recall, reproduction, and relearning. Most adult developmental research has involved recognition and recall. A common *recognition* method is to present material learned in an earlier session together with other similar material (digits or words, for example) and to ask subjects to pick out the items learned earlier. A common *recall* method is to ask subjects to report as much of earlier-learned material as they can. A common *reproduction* method is to ask subjects to write or draw the learned items (this test is particularly appropriate for designs or figures). Finally, a common *relearning* test is to see how long it takes subjects to relearn material that had been learned earlier (this test is most appropriate when a long period of time elapses between learning and remembering). Different methods yield different findings at different ages. For instance, most research shows age deficits in recall, but few studies show any in recognition.

PRIMARY AND SECONDARY MEMORY

Before information theory began to displace earlier learning theories, memory was thought to be some kind of stamping in of stimulus traces, probably in some part of the nervous system. More recently, the emphasis has been on the processing of information, even during its storing. For example, Murdock (1967) proposes a three-stage process, illustrated in Figure 10.1. In this model, information is first taken into a sensory store, then moves to a holding system of short-term memory storage, and finally to long-term memory storage. The differences

among these stages are seen to be in capacity (how much can be retained at each step), in encoding characteristics (how much incoming information becomes transformed), and in mechanisms of forgetting.

In sensory memory, there is presumed to be the smallest capacity, information is stored in the same form in which it is experienced, and forgetting is the result of decay. A visual image is stored in its original form—a picture as a picture or a string of letters as a string of letters—instead of being translated into meaningful concepts such as "animal." Capacity is larger in short-term memory and infinite in long-term storage. Information is seen as transformed (or encoded) by the experiencer to fit into his or her previous system of knowledge organization in both short-term and long-term memory. A diagram, for instance, is given a meaningful name such as *house* and remembered that way. Decay for sensory memories is presumed to be very rapid: from ⅓ second to 1 second for visual information and 2 seconds for auditory information. In short-term storage, memories don't fade away; they are pushed out by new information. In long-term storage, although memories endure, they may be difficult to retrieve to consciousness because other stored memories interfere with them.

Waugh and Norman (1965) offer a simpler model than Murdock's, with only two stages. In their model, primary memory is roughly equivalent to Murdock's sensory and short-term memories combined, and secondary memory corresponds to his long-term storage. Primary-memory functioning does not deteriorate with age, but secondary-memory functioning does. The difference is partly due to the reorganization or higher-level processing required for long-term storage and is thus due to the same

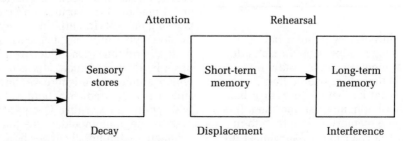

Figure 10.1. A generalized three-stage model of memory. *(Source: Murdock, 1967.)*

problems as for learning complex material. That is, the difficulty appears at the point of entry into storage, not of decay of what has already been stored.

Many studies have failed to find significant age differences in digit span or word span, which are measures of primary memory. Even those studies that have found slight but reliable age decrements in memory span (for example, Botwinick & Storandt, 1974) have not found that the decrements are large enough to represent serious functional impairment. Older subjects do not do as well on backward digits—repeating numbers in reverse order—which requires processing and thus represents secondary memory. Younger subjects tend to receive the same scores on both forward- and backward-repeated digits (Bromley, 1958; Botwinick & Storandt, 1974). We noted in the last chapter that older learners benefit from help in learning how to organize complex material (see Hultsch, 1975).

Secondary memory is considered timeless (Craik, 1977). There is no qualitative difference between what is remembered after 30 seconds and what is remembered after months or years. For secondary-memory material, however, the method of testing does make a difference. Older subjects do not show much forgetting in recognition tests but do in recall tests. This is illus-

trated in Figure 10.2. Cross-sectional comparisons of memory for word lists show no age differences in recognition between 20-year-old subjects and any older groups, including those in their 60s (Schonfield & Robertson, 1966). Recall scores, however, are lower than recognition scores at all ages. Even 20-year-olds do not recall as well as they recognize, and people at each successive decade older show more discrepancy between the two methods. Note, however, that even 60-year-olds have not reached zero level.

Cohort-sequential findings on a test of memory for designs (the Benton visual-retention test), which is a short-term memory test, show double age effects. When Arenberg (1979) plotted the errors made in reproducing designs by age at first measurement, he found not only that the older men remembered less of the designs they had to copy from memory at the first time of testing, in 1961, but also that their performance declined more over time, as measured again in 1975 to 1977. Figure 10.3 demonstrates this double effect, which corresponds to what Schaie and his colleagues have found for intelligence-test performance (to be described in Chapter 11). Because this test is designed to measure brain or central-nervous-system disorders, it may be argued that Arenberg is finding what others have found—that older people have more physiological and health problems. Arenberg remarks that the amount of change was substantial only for the oldest men: the subjects in the top line were over 80 at the time of first testing and close to 100 the second time. Those in the next lower group were over 70 in 1961 and thus near 90 in 1975. The men of the 1933–1940 birth cohort, about age 25 at first testing and age 41 at the second, showed virtually no memory loss. The men in this sample are, incidentally, those older healthy middle-class men who have been volunteers in the National Institute of Aging longitudinal study in Baltimore.

METHOD OF LEARNING

Not only does method of measurement make a difference, but method of learning also affects memory. When information is heard or repeated aloud, it is remembered much better (and also learned much easier) than when it is seen. Although visual sensory memory has been found to last only about 250 milliseconds, audi-

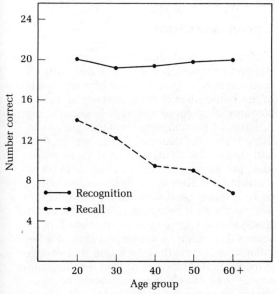

Figure 10.2. Recognition and recall scores as a function of age. (*Source: Schonfield and Robertson, 1966.*)

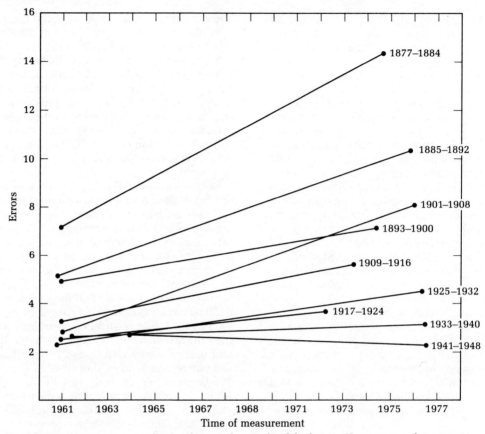

Figure 10.3.   Errors in reproducing designs (longitudinal findings). *(Source: Arenberg, 1979.)*

tory sensory memory may last for as long as 2 seconds (Walsh, 1975). Older subjects get even more advantage from auditory presentation than younger ones do. These data suggest that people who have trouble remembering names, for example, would benefit from repeating them aloud several times, instead of just reading them.

A third factor in age and memory data is type of material learned. Older people have more trouble than younger ones in recognizing as well as in recalling line drawings and pictures (Harwood & Naylor, 1969; Howell, 1972; Arenberg, 1979) as noted in Arenberg's research just mentioned. Events or faces in the news (Warrington & Sanders, 1971) are harder for old people to remember, too. In general, as for learning, older people find it harder to remember complex material such as paragraphs than to remember simple material, such as a list of color names.

NONVERBAL MEMORY

Most memory studies have used verbal material and numbers. Some studies have considered memory of geometric designs such as those in the Benton test or even memory of more meaningful pictorial material. In general, age differences for nonverbal material parallel those for verbal material. There is a decline with age in the ability to reproduce or recognize, but this decline does not seem to be noticeable until after 60 years of age. As noted, there is more age difference for reproduction of designs than for recognition. When Farrimond (1968) showed subjects 25 short silent-film scenes (for example, a 4-second shot of a boy inflating a bicycle tire), he found that younger subjects (under 60 years of age) recalled more scenes than did older subjects (over 60 years of age). Remember the point made earlier in this book about the designation of "old" and "young"—in this case, we see that "young" means under 60, while most studies call anyone over 40 "old."

In another study, subjects learned a series of 40 line drawings (Harwood & Naylor, 1969). After four weeks, the younger group (aged 15–45) recognized 19.0 drawings, and the older group (aged 60–80) recognized 16.1. As noted earlier, such age differences are statistically significant, but they do not show older people really "losing their minds." An example of the difficulty in interpreting research on long-term memory is the findings of Howell (1972). She found that older subjects recognized fewer pictures of common objects and unfamiliar patterns that they had just learned, but they did as well as younger subjects in recognizing pictures reproduced from the 1908 Sears Roebuck catalog.

As noted earlier, a common stereotype about memory in old age is that it is easier to remember what happened 50 years ago than to remember what one had for breakfast. How does one test the validity of such ancient events? Almost all evidence is anecdotal—and there are even graver problems. Schonfield (1972), for example, asked subjects of various ages to recall the names of all their schoolteachers and reported that younger subjects recalled more names than older subjects did. People in their 20s recalled 67%, and those in their 70s recalled 45%. But people in their 20s were recalling 10-year-old memories; those in their 70s were recalling 60-year-old memories. If this can be interpreted to show decay, the time difference is very large, and decay thus very slow. If the deficit is interpreted as an effect of interference, we should remember that 70-year-olds have known many more people than 20-year-olds. Furthermore, how do we know whether the names of the teachers were correct? If I remember that my fifth-grade teacher was Miss Murphy, am I getting her mixed up with a fifth-grade teacher named Miss Murphy, with whom I worked when I was an adult, while my own fifth-grade teacher was really named Miss Sullivan? Because I went to fifth grade in Canada, my teacher was an Australian on a year's exchange, and the school no longer exists, verifying this information would be beyond the means of most investigators. It is impressive that 70-year-olds remembered 45% of their teachers after 60 years.

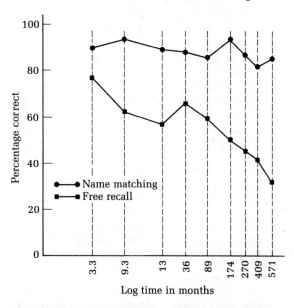

Figure 10.4. Recognition and recall of names and faces of high school colleagues. *(Source: Bahrick, Bahrick, and Wittlinger, 1975.)*

Some of these same criticisms apply to a more elaborate study of old memories by Bahrick, Bahrick, and Wittlinger (1975), who focused on memories of people's high school graduating class, as verified by their high school yearbooks. The results are shown in Figure 10.4. The deficits the researchers found seem to be for subjects over age 50, consistent with results in other studies. Table 10.1 shows decrements in recall and recognition of news items associated with age (40 and older) and time interval (6, 12, and 18 months) (Warrington & Silberstein, 1970). Again, recognition is better than recall, and age differences are more noticeable after 55 than

TABLE 10.1 Percentage retention of public events after three time intervals

	Recall			Recognition		
	Retention interval (months)					
Age group	6	12	18	6	12	18
40	48%	37%	32%	77%	72%	69%
40–54	45	35	31	80	71	68
55+	36	29	26	75	69	68

Source: Warrington and Silberstein, 1970.

before. So far as any of this research shows, we have no basis for concluding that the memories of old people are better for remote events than for recent events. Craik (1977) summarizes his and others' research findings by saying that "when acquisition is equated . . . and when retrieval information is adequate (recognition), age decrements are eliminated" (p. 413).

Like learning, memory functioning is affected profoundly by extraneous factors. These include the subject's attitude toward the task (whether it is perceived as silly or irrelevant), how well the material has been learned in the first place, the pacing of response (whether enough time has been allowed), health, intelligence, and, particularly, interest or motivation. Let me quote the conclusion of Elias and his colleagues (1977) to their chapter on memory:

> Although most people will eventually suffer some memory decline, in most cases the loss will not be severe and may never become recognizable except in a laboratory situation. Perhaps more importantly, memory loss should not be confused with "loss of contact" with reality or disorientation because of the inability to organize one's thoughts in a coherent fashion. These latter processes most likely represent much more severe underlying physiological problems [p. 181].

Retrieval

The poorer scores of older subjects in learning and memory experiments are attributed by some psychologists to retrieval problems. This is a variant of the competence/performance issue. Older people could be as competent as younger ones, but for some reason not be able to perform as well. Their memories may be as good, but they may not be able to get information out of storage as efficiently. Craik (1977), for instance, says that the difference between older people's competence in simpler as compared with more complex material can be attributed to greater retrieval difficulties with complex material. Moreover, these difficulties are not in encoding. For some reason, it is harder to "dredge up" large or more complicated memories.

In one experiment (Craik & Masani, 1969), subjects were presented with word lists in an order alien to normal English usage; the words could not be combined to form a sentence. The investigators scored the number of "chunks" remembered, defining a chunk as a string of words recalled in the same order in which it had been presented. Older subjects recalled fewer chunks than did younger subjects, but they recalled as many words per chunk as younger subjects. Craik concluded that aging had a detrimental effect on retrieval processes (fewer chunks retrieved) but that aging did not affect encoding ability (same number of words encoded into each chunk).

Many people, including many psychologists, assume that the major retrieval problem in later life is that of interference. But what exactly do we mean by interference? In earlier stimulus-response theory, interference meant response competition. It is harder to produce a stored memory when you need to, because other competing memories are simultaneously evoked and you must go through a secondary selection process in order to sort out the particular memory you want.

In information-processing theory, a similar concept is used. Retrieval cues or categories become less effective if more items are included or evoked by them. Craik (1977) points out that, when the number of items becomes too large, retrieval processes are inefficient. It is as if older people are retrieving from larger categories. To counteract this overload and consequent blurring or suppression of memories, one could sharpen the cues or categories so that they differentiate more effectively among the confusion of relevant and irrelevant memories evoked. Furthermore, Hulicka (1967) suggests that susceptibility to retroactive inhibition is a function of the completeness of the original learning. It is more important to "overlearn" as one gets older.

Higher-level thought

It seems incredible that there is so little research literature on the life-span development of higher-level thinking, considering that almost all the world's thinking is done by adults and older people. The words *sages*, *wise men*, and *wise women* all refer to older people. Rodin's "Thinker" is far from a youth. Yet we have many professional journals reporting the development of reaction time, associative learning of simple concepts, and lower-level cognitive processing and only a handful of studies relating to development in solving difficult problems or in wisdom. Labouvie-Vief (1979) points out that, while logical thinking is perfected in adolescence, it is not really put to use before adulthood. Only after individuals become committed and responsible do they use their logical abilities to help them choose the best course of action to solve life problems, to adapt.

I have repeatedly pointed out the artificiality of the distinctions made between components of cognitive functioning. It is virtually impossible, at least in experimental designs, to separate thinking from past learning and memory, which it incorporates. Scholars of problem solving often do not appear to be aware of parallel work going on in the areas of learning and memory. Moreover, intelligence is obviously closely related to higher-level thinking, yet it is treated here in a separate chapter.

One kind of experiment to test problem solving uses switching circuits and asks subjects to deduce the principles underlying them (Bernadelli, cited by Welford, 1958). "Old" subjects identified as many terminals as young, but in the process of doing so they took many more readings. Welford interpreted this to show an aging deficit in memory span rather than in problem solving itself. He pointed out that subjects who see in advance the shortest, and so most informationally productive, sequence of tests to apply in figuring out a problem will have to remember less and thus be quicker (and more successful, if time is important) in solving the problem. There can be a "vicious spiral" effect, however, which Rabbitt (1977) describes as follows:

> The greater the memory load, the greater the time for each operation. The greater the time, the greater the probability of memory inaccuracies. The greater the probability of memory inaccuracies, the greater the probability of incorrect decisions which have to be modified by extra operations. The greater the number of extra operations, the greater the elapsed time and interference by this extra activity, and the greater the probability of memory inaccuracies, etc., etc. [p. 619].

Most data on development of higher mental processes are cross-sectional and thus can merely be suggestive. Let us first look at one of the few longitudinal studies so far. Arenberg (1974) used a display of ten lights to set up problems involving logical relations. He tested 300 well-educated, middle-class men between 24 and 87 at two times, six years apart. (This is part of the longitudinal Baltimore study referred to many times in this book.) His cross-sectional results, comparing men of different ages tested at the same time, show unequivocally poorer performance by men over 60, as well as a generalized decline at younger ages. Men in their 40s used more uninformative inputs than did men in their 30s, and, similarly, men in their 60s used more than did men in their 40s.

In the follow-up six years later, however, which included only 224 men who had succeeded the first time, age changes were observable only for men over 70; they asked significantly more redundant questions. Incidentally, there was a suggestion that the problem-solving effectiveness of men over 70 in the first session was related to their survival over the next six years. Of the 36 men who solved the first problem in the first session, 17% died; of the 13 men who did not solve it, 46% died. The relation between intellectual performance and mortality is discussed in the next chapter.

Arenberg's general conclusion was that, even among these privileged men, there was some decrement in performance over six years—but only at the oldest ages. In view of these longitudinal findings, it is very important to take a hard look at most of our other data. Clearly, we cannot say that higher-level thinking and problem solving stop in old age. We also would not anticipate any decline in brilliance of thinking before the age of 60.

Now let us look at other cross-sectional data. Wetherick (1964) found no significant age differences between 20-, 40-, and 60-year-olds in learning to work a switchboard. This finding supports Arenberg's conclusion that most cross-sectional age declines tend to be for ages older than 60. Collins (1964) also found no age differences on a complexity task, however, and his subjects ranged between 17 and 85.

Nehrke (1971), with a much larger sample (1151 people between 20 and 70 years old), reports that age, sex, education, and number of trials all produce significant differences in solving syllogisms. In a different study (Jerome, 1962), which asked subjects to judge the relationship of premises to conclusions, the better-educated got the best scores in each age group. However, even among the better-educated, average scores were lower for each older decade. Furthermore, old problem solvers asked far more questions along the way, and their questions tended to be more redundant than those of younger problem solvers.

The issue of task difficulty has emerged at several points. Thus, Wetherick (1964) felt that Jerome's findings were partly due to the excessive difficulty of the task he assigned. When Wetherick devised a simpler set of tasks that he gave to subjects matched in nonverbal intelligence, he did not find that older subjects asked more redundant questions. There was also no age difference in either the easiest problem or the hardest—but there was on problems of intermediate difficulty. Younger subjects tried to guess on these intermediate-level problems and ended up getting better scores than the older subjects, who rarely guessed. The older subjects were more cautious.

James Birren has long said that what we should be studying is the kind of cognitive strategies people of different ages use. Cognitive strategies include guessing and asking questions. They also include selecting different kinds of cognitive styles to approach different problems, as well as degree of impulsivity. For example, young people, knowing that they can function quickly, may be more likely to use relatively inefficient methods such as trial and error—to be more impulsive. Older people, finding that they are sometimes slower, may be more efficient. They may tend to think through a problem first, so that when they go to work they could use fewer trials; they would be more reflective.

Such logic is at least partly supported by data that show no age differences in complex task solutions when unlimited time is available. Presumably, the extra time taken by older people is used for planning and deliberation. When Birren (1969) interviewed 100 successful older professional people, he found that most had not only long-range goals but also tactical insight into how to achieve them. Some of their strategies were conservation of their resources and control of their emotions. In general, they were more focused on what they had decided was important than younger people tend to be. Again, we must remember that these are mid-dle-aged, not old people, and that it is dangerous to call everybody over 30 or 40 "old."

CAUTIOUSNESS

If older people are less willing to take risks, as many psychologists conclude, this could affect their success in complex problem-solving tasks. As mentioned earlier, Botwinick (1966) found that young adults between 18 and 35 were less cautious than older ones between 67 and 80. However, when he adjusted the appropriateness of the tasks to the age group (Botwinick, 1969) and forced older subjects to choose alternatives to which some risk was attached, he no longer found age differences.

Instead of considering cautious behavior as caused by rigidity, we might consider other explanations, such as an interest in conserving energy. Labouvie-Vief (1979) goes further and suggests that the label *rigidity* may be a misnomer. Its pejorative implication may be misleading, certainly from the adaptive view of the society. The exploratory curiosity of younger people may be detrimental to the group as a whole if it is not balanced by the wisdom or cautiousness of older group members.

Nehrke (1971) tried a somewhat different approach. He administered a syllogism test to volunteers in "senior citizens' centers." Half the items were emotionally toned—such as issues dealing with Vietnam, communism, or Yippies, at a time when these were hotly debated—and half were not; half were valid, and half were not. He found that, although men got higher scores than women, there was no age effect with respect to emotionality of items.

Wetherick (1969), however, found that older subjects tended to handle disconfirming evidence as if it were actually confirming. They could be described as more prone to *cognitive dissonance*—accepting only that evidence that confirms their own previous beliefs. A similar observation was made by Weir (1961), who noticed that subjects over 70 seemed to become emotionally involved with test items and less able to differentiate fact and value.

COMPETENCE/PERFORMANCE AGAIN

The difference between competence and performance applies to problem solving, as it does to most other cognitive endeavors. Sanford and

Maule (1971) asked subjects of various ages to make observations related to the inspection and correction of intermittent responses in "machines." Their older subjects learned the probability bias, which helped improve performance, as well as the young, but they did not use this knowledge as efficiently. Although the best strategy was to test a "frequent-fault" machine every time, only the young subjects actually did.

Experiments with animals have found that age differences in problem solving can be minimized with treatments such as air ionization, certain drugs, increased sensory stimulation, and distributed practice. This kind of reversal suggests that some cause other than aging may account for older animals' disadvantages.

Can older people who do not have efficient cognitive strategies be helped to develop them? Some recent research says yes. Labouvie-Vief and Gonda (1976) tried three methods of training on a task using alphabetical-letter sets with 60 women between 63 and 95 recruited from a housing development. In comparison with the control group who received no training, those who were given either cognitive or anxiety-alleviating training (being shown how to follow procedures to overcome anxiety) performed significantly better on an immediate posttest (after training). In a delayed posttest (two weeks later) the antianxiety training still helped, but an open-ended training procedure proved better in the long run than a modeling procedure.

Creativity

Problems of definition plague the studies of creativity. To begin with, are we talking about ability, personality, or cognitive style? Is a person who produces many "creative" works more creative than one who produces fewer? Are we interested in productivity or capacity? in ability or performance? Is creativity different from general intelligence? Is qualitative change of cognitive structure, following Piaget's theory, an example of creativity? Can we thus consider anybody who reaches the *formal operations* stage a creative person? Or is a creative act more specialized and limited—perhaps we should say more elite? Can we consider transformations of personality and lifestyle creative acts?

Over and above these definitional problems are those related to life-span developmental issues. Most research in this area has been confined to the early years of life. Piagetian theory suggests that qualitative cognitive development ends during adolescence, that the only changes after adolescence are quantitative—or regressive.

Flavell (1970) suggests that an act of creating starts with confrontation with new information for which there is no existing category. If so, it would not necessarily be a decline in capacity for structural change that limits creativity after adolescence, but the adult's desire to maintain the stability achieved so laboriously at the end of the rapid changes of adolescence. Adults would try to ignore such new information. When events necessitate a restructuring of thinking, however, creativity can occur even among older adults. We could therefore say that there is a plateau in creative *capacity*, even though there is a decline in creative *performance*. The fact that most scientific and artistic productions occur in late adolescence or the early 20s may not be because that is the time of greatest potential but because that is the time of entering jobs and careers. Consequently, fresh viewpoints are brought to the existing body of skills and knowledge. Should there be more career changes in later adulthood, we might see more old-age, as well as nonlinear, patterns of creative output.

The classic work on life-span creative achievements was done by Lehman (1953). He tabulated the output of notable people whose works were part of the public domain and announced that major creative achievements occur relatively early in people's productive careers, somewhere between their 20s and 40s, varying with their field. Furthermore, although their achievements may continue for many years after their peak, their later work is generally recognized (by other experts) to be less outstanding and significant than their early work. He assumed that people produce their best work when they are producing their most work.

Lehman's findings have been challenged. Dennis (1966), for example, reviewed the productivity of 738 scholars, scientists, and artists who had all lived to at least the age of 79. His findings are summarized in Table 10.2. For most disciplines, the most productive (or almost the most productive) decade was the 40s; only in

TABLE 10.2 Percentage of total works between ages 20 and 80 that were done in each decade

	N	N	Age decade					
			20s	30s	40s	50s	60s	70s
Scholarship	**Men**	**Works**						
Historians	46	615	3	19	19	22	*24*	20
Philosophers	42	225	3	17	20	18	*22*	20
Scholars	43	326	6	17	*21*	*21*	16	19
		Means	4	18	20	20	*21*	20
Sciences	**Men**	**Works**						
Biologists	32	3456	5	22	*24*	19	17	13
Botanists	49	1889	4	15	*22*	*22*	*22*	15
Chemists	24	2420	11	21	*24*	19	12	13
Geologists	40	2672	3	13	22	*28*	19	14
Inventors	44	646	2	10	17	18	*32*	21
Mathematicians	36	3104	8	*20*	*20*	18	19	15
		Means	6	17	*22*	21	20	15
Arts	**Men**	**Works**						
Architects	44	1148	7	24	*29*	25	10	4
Chamber musicians	35	109	15	*21*	17	20	18	9
Dramatists	25	803	10	27	*29*	21	9	3
Librettists	38	164	8	21	*30*	22	15	4
Novelists	32	494	5	19	18	*28*	23	7
Opera composers	176	476	8	30	*31*	16	10	5
Poets	46	402	11	21	*26*	16	16	10
		Means	9	23	*26*	21	14	6

Note: Maximum values are shown in italics.

Source: Dennis, 1966.

music was the 30s decade more productive than that of the 40s. Dennis also showed that scholarly productivity was maintained at a high level through the 60s, with only a slight decline in the 70s. Scientific productivity was also maintained through the 60s, but decline was more marked in the 70s. Artistic productivity declined gradually from the 40s through the 70s.

Dennis interpreted the difference among the various fields in terms of individual effort versus assistance from others and the length of the training period. Artists today usually work alone; laboratory scientists usually have teams of assistants and students.

When Taylor (1969) studied critics' reviews of noted pianists, he found the most-cited age changes to be (1) an inability to control complex materials, such as fugues, and (2) a lessening of "pounding" and fast tempos. (Age changes are not all bad, then!) Critics do not expect declines before the artists enter the 60s. Like Dennis, Taylor mentions overlearning, early learning, and frequent repetition of material as aids to maintaining repertoires. Also, such strategies as

scheduling less frequent concerts and repeating old material are noted.

Dennis also considered distance from age of death and said that significant decline in creativity was not apparent until the decade before death. See the discussion on *terminal drop* in Chapter 11. An interesting longitudinal study of master chess players (Elo, 1965) regressed later performance on earlier performance and found an inverted U-curve, peaking at about the age of 35. Performance levels at age 63 were comparable to those at age 20. These data replicate those of Lehman. When Charness (in press) varied both age (16–64) and skill of master chess players, he found that older players searched for problem solutions less extensively than younger. However, older players are no different from younger players in rate of search or the quality of the moves selected.

Lehman's findings were also evaluated by Butler (1967), who cited the association between productivity and decline in time available for work. As people gain eminence, they are invited to enter administrative or honorary positions and thus effectively diminish their creative output. Scholars and scientists, for example, become department heads and deans. Artists become teachers.

Butler's second point is that, when abilities are exercised, they do not decline. There are more within-age differences than between-age differences. One could cite such notable examples as Pablo Casals, who was still playing the cello brilliantly at 95; Pablo Picasso, who was painting in new ways at 90; and P. G. Wodehouse, who published one of his best books at 90. Also, there are many instances of people who did not even begin their notable work until their later years.

Finally, Butler questions various aspects of Lehman's methodology. For example, Lehman combined people of different longevities (Dennis considered this point in his study) and defined creativity in terms of quantity of products. Furthermore, his sampling was biased.

Probably the most profound analysis of life-span creativity so far has been done by Kogan (1973). To begin with, he defines three different approaches to its study: the product-centered approach of Lehman (1953) and of Dennis (1966), the psychological-assessment approach of MacKinnon (1962) and of Barron (1963), and the process-centered approach of Guilford (1967). Guilford developed a set of divergent thinking tests that included testing for fluency, flexibility, and originality. These tests have been used—almost exclusively with children—to examine the complex relationship between intelligence and creativity. Essentially, Kogan suggests, they may have the same kind of sequential (or necessary but not sufficient) relationship that exists between cognitive level (Piagetian) and moral judgment (Kohlberg). That is, one must be at a particular cognitive level in order to be able to achieve a particular level of moral judgment, or, in this case, of creativity. However, just being at that cognitive level does not automatically guarantee that one will also be at the comparable moral judgment or creative level.

Kogan also considers several factors that may moderate creative activity. Flexibility (or rigidity) and fluency are particularly relevant for performance in later life. Chown (1961) found that tests of spontaneous flexibility were not significantly related to age, however, although they were to general intelligence. Flexibility was most evident among Chown's young subjects, interme-

diate for her oldest subjects (the age range was 20 through 82), and lowest for her middle-aged group. Whether this is a developmental or a cohort effect—or both—one cannot say.

Another study looked at conceptual-sorting task performances of subjects between 17 and 75. Older subjects produced fewer responses than younger ones. Furthermore, the productivity difference was more notable for original kinds of responses than for popular or commonly produced responses (Bromley, 1967). This follows Kogan's distinction between unusualness of response and originality of response. The former, unusualness, is very much like verbal fluency. Similar results were found in an investigation of teachers (Alpaugh, 1975). Although older teachers were not different from younger in intelligence, they *were* less creative—both in ideational fluency and in originality. By raising older people's perception of their own competence, Klein and Birren (1973) increased their originality.

Generational differences certainly exist in terms of opportunities and interests. If a culture emphasizes engineering at one point in history, for example, potential musicians—those who would be more creative as musicians than as engineers—are lost, becoming mediocre engineers. Such cultural emphases can shift quickly, too. Young people who turn creatively to physics when it is a challenging area in college may find opportunities closed ten years later, when there are more jobs in interpersonal fields—or vice versa.

Aside from career considerations, the issue of creativity is central to leisure time and retirement policies and practices. Can people who have devoted their lives to practical, convergent thinking shift to more divergent, creative pursuits and thinking? A number of challenging experiments have been conducted with retired older people in the last few years. The success of Kenneth Koch (1978) in teaching poetry writing to deteriorated old people in nursing homes challenges many stereotypes and points to the adaptational component in most intellectual functioning.

Wisdom

A wise person is more than a smart person. For one thing, one needs a body of experience in order to be wise. This should make wisdom one of the topics adult developmentalists would want very much to research. Yet, although it is sometimes mentioned as an important unexplored topic, there are hardly any studies in this area.

Vivian Clayton (1975) attacked the preliminary question "What is wisdom, and what age and sex of person is supposed to be wise?" She found that most subjects said they would prefer to go to a middle-aged man for advice. Then she asked young, middle-aged, and older subjects to list the five most salient characteristics of a wise person they had known, and she selected the 33 most frequently chosen adjectives. The 40 men and 40 women were divided equally into four cohort groups (young adults, 23 years; adults, 35 years; middle-aged, 54 years; and older people, over 72 years). All subjects were asked to rate a person they had designated as wise on the chosen adjectives, which included *concerned, introspective, thoughtful, peaceful,* and *experienced.* One interesting finding is that it was impossible to obtain a set of factors in a factor analysis, because individual differences were so large. Different people believe different qualities constitute wisdom.

The people nominated as wise, incidentally, ranged from 60 to 67 years of age, and thus might be considered middle-aged rather than really old. Middle-aged respondents chose a person of their own sex, but people of other ages did not discriminate by sex. It is to be hoped that this preliminary work is followed by much more attention to this topic.

Summary

Although much research on information acquisition shows relatively strong support for a hypothesis of decline in the later years of life, the data on storage of information and cognitive processing reviewed in this chapter are less clear. A model of memory includes at least two stages: (1) primary memory, which involves initial taking in information; and (2) secondary memory, which involves storing information.

Most life-span developmental psychologists would not agree that there is deterioration in primary-memory processing, that older people do not encode new information as well as younger people. But there is little evidence for deterioration in "deep-storage" memories. If older people have trouble remembering, the problem is likely to be in retrieving information from deep storage or in inadequate acquisition or learning. Older people might be advised to take more time to code or classify new information and then to "overlearn" it—repeat it more times than they used to in youth. In a way, this would be the cognitive strategy associated with greater cautiousness—the wisdom of the old.

Higher-level thinking, the province of adults, has received much less attention than one would expect. Available data suggest that people who solve problems well in their early years continue to solve problems well in their later years. Although there may be some deterioration, it does not seem to show up before the ages of 60 or 70. Again, cautiousness is a significant factor. Lowered performance may result from conserving energy and avoiding risks, rather than from lowered competence itself. Creating, like other higher-level cognitive processing, has been widely considered to deteriorate in later life, but recent evidence suggests that we should not jump to this conclusion.

There is no evidence for progressive closing of the cognitive system with age. The same kinds of retrogressive processes noted in Chapter 9 can be seen in memory and problem solving, but they are not as noticeable. If wisdom and caution really increase, this should be adaptive for both individual and society, offsetting and balancing the impulsiveness and risk taking of the young. Because memories seem to remain intact if they can be retrieved, the presence of older people within a group can ensure the transmission of rare kinds of information that are not part of everyday experience. Finally, older people are more unlike each other than like each other in memory and higher-level thought. Individual differences far outweigh similarities.

11

Intelligence Tests

Cognitive psychologists—before and after Piaget—have investigated life-span development by using a variety of experimental approaches. Meanwhile, an almost independent body of research has accumulated that uses intelligence tests. In fact, during the years when IQ was a political issue and intelligence testing was charged with being elitist and biased in other ways, such tests were providing significant clues to the problems of aging. Calls for sophisticated research designs came first from psychologists who were testing adults of different ages (such as Schaie and his colleagues). This body of research is thus, in many ways, years ahead of the laboratory-based results. The two bodies of data are not proving contradictory, however. Recent communication between the proponents of the two approaches is influencing both sides. In the decade of the 1980s, we should reap the benefits of a synthesis between the two kinds of information. Because the research has been so independent, however, it is reported separately in this chapter. Comparisons with the findings presented in Chapters 9 and 10 will be included wherever possible.

Intelligence testing had an empirical origin, rather than a theoretical origin. It started as a procedure to screen or classify people—mostly children—on the basis of their presumed abilities to learn. It almost always assumes hierarchical (originally, age-graded) abilities; higher scores indicate superiority. Originally, there were also assumptions of an underlying "general intelligence" (g). More recently, following the

work of Thurstone (1935), a multidimensional view of mental abilities has been accepted. Some research has even shown that there may be a developmental pattern from general to multidimensional intellectual functioning. General intelligence (if you're good in one ability, you're likely to be good in all others) is thus characteristic of young children and old adults, and multidimensional or specialized abilities are characteristic of adolescents and young adults.

From the first Binet test to the present Wechsler Adult Intelligence Scale (WAIS), intelligence measures such as the IQ (intelligence quotient)* have been believed to represent a composite of separate abilities. However, there is little agreement on the degree of interrelatedness of these separate abilities. There are also questions about how much intelligence-test scores predict functioning and about how stable they are from one testing to another.

Age patterns

Tests of general intelligence—sometimes referred to as "omnibus" tests—derive a single overall score, such as an IQ, by combining scores on diverse subtests. Examples of such tests that have been used to study adult intelli-

---

*IQ is obtained by dividing the mental age, or MA (score on age-graded tests), by the chronological age, or CA. Some IQ estimates do not use MA scores but estimate directly from raw scores to IQ scores. The WAIS is an example.

gence over the life span are the Stanford-Binet, the Army Alpha, the Otis, and the Wechsler. The most common way of using this kind of measure to assess development is to test groups of people of different ages at the same time. As pointed out in previous chapters, such cross-sectional studies show age differences. However, they may not show age changes because different age cohorts can have had different kinds of educational backgrounds as well as different experiences with test taking. By testing and comparing people now in their 70s with those now in their 50s and now in their 20s, we find that, on the average, the younger subjects get higher scores. But we do not know whether they will get lower scores when eventually they turn 50 or 70.

Cross-sectional findings

Cross-sectional studies with omnibus measures usually show that the highest overall intelligence-test scores occur at some time between the late teens and the late 20s. People in their 30s, 40s, and 50s tend to score somewhat lower than those in their 20s. From their late 50s on, people score markedly lower. (See the upper part of Figure 11.1.) These are, it should be emphasized, average scores for all people of a given age group. Many older people may have much higher IQs than many younger people.

In the early 1930s, Jones and Conrad (1933) gave the Army Alpha to 1000 rural New Englanders between 10 and 60 years of age—the total mobile population of a New Hampshire village. At that time, 16-year-olds scored the highest, and older and younger people scored progressively lower. However, there was more variation among people of the same age than across ages. The difference between the highest scores and lowest scores of any age was greater than the difference between the average score for that age and the average score for the next older or next younger age.

It is necessary to proceed cautiously in interpreting such cross-sectional intelligence-test results. We must take into account not only individual differences, but also the effects of such factors as education, feelings about being tested, speed, cohort and period effects of many kinds, sex, and type of subtests used. There is a correlation between number of years of school completed and general intelligence level. The more education people have, the higher their scores are to begin with and the higher they will continue to score throughout life, compared with others of their own age. Because most younger people over the last few decades have had more education than their parents and grandparents, they get higher IQ scores. By the time they are the same age as their parents and grandparents, they still will have higher IQs than their parents when they were that age.

Some of these age-cohort differences reflect a *secular trend*—a slow, persistent historical trend—toward higher ability, similar to those trends found for increased height, size, health, and onset of sexual maturity. It may be of interest to note that, when the first edition of the Stanford-Binet intelligence test was developed in 1917, the ceiling age at which intellectual growth presumably stopped was 12. In successive revisions over the following 40 years or so, this ceiling rose to 16 and then to 21. Similarly, Jones and Conrad found the peak of test performance to be about 16 in the early 1930s, but more-recent cross-sectional studies have reported peaks at 30 and, most recently, at 50 years of age (Botwinick, 1967).

I noted in Chapter 9 that overall speed of performance often decreases as people get older. Some age differences noted in cross-sectional studies can therefore be attributed to speed factors. When time limits are removed from omnibus tests, in fact, age differences are often wiped out. Ghiselli (1957) found no age effect in 1400 subjects 20 to 65 years old when he removed time limits from tests and used well-educated subjects. In an earlier study, Lorge (1936) matched older and younger subjects on a test that had no time limit (the Thorndike CAVD), and then gave them the Army Alpha, which does have a time limit. The younger subjects did better than the older ones on the timed test.

The effects of cohort and period can be seen in Figure 11.1, which presents the results of testing three independent samples from the same general population of West Coast medical-plan members between 21 and 70 years of age (Schaie et al., 1973). The diagram in the upper part of the figure shows the cross-sectional gradients obtained by comparing the people of different ages who had been tested at the same time. These age comparisons are not identical

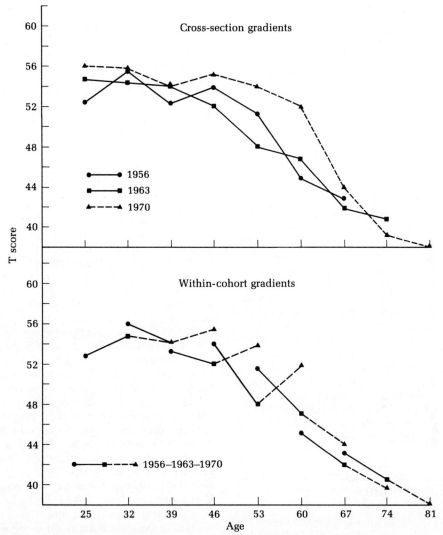

Figure 11.1. Age, cross-sectional, and within-cohort intellectual changes. *(Source: Schaie, Labouvie, and Buech, 1973.)*

for the three times of testing (1956, 1963, and 1970). However, the differences among people the same age for different years of testing are not very noticeable for those younger than 53. As far as age differences are concerned, there is a plateau between 25 and 46 and then a gradual drop.

The lower part of Figure 11.1 shows the within-cohort gradients: the differences in scores between groups of people born at the same time but tested at different ages. Clearly, age cohort

(see Chapter 1) influences intellectual performance. Those born most recently did not change much over the 14 years between their first and last tests. But those born before the turn of the century—a period that may have been a watershed in American history—show dramatic drops from one test period to the next. Compare these findings with those of Arenberg, shown in Figure 10.3. Arenberg found the same cohort influence in memory for designs that Schaie and his colleagues did with intelligence tests.

The kind of lives led by people born since 1900 has produced several generations whose intellectual performances have been more durable than those of their parents and grandparents. Perhaps intellectual performance is more central to our modern way of life. Perhaps, also, future generations who value education and intellectual pursuits less—as suggested by recent drops in national averages on academic-achievement tests—will show drops in intelligence-test scores compared to their parents and grandparents. If they do, cross-sectional curves of intelligence will look as if people became smarter as they aged.

The kinds of tasks that make up intelligence tests were selected originally to intrigue children in order to induce their best performance. They may not be the kinds of tasks that would induce the best performance of adults and older people. Children also are accustomed to showing adults that they are doing well and growing up; they are used to being evaluated. But adults often interpret examinations as indications that they are somehow wanting, and they are not likely to feel comfortable or to perform at their best when their competence is challenged. Adults are presumed to have arrived at maturity, at competence, and shouldn't have to prove it. And older adults may not be in the habit of pushing their limits. They are more likely to underuse their full strength, whether in physical effort or in intellectual exercise.

Longitudinal findings

Many factors that influence the performance of older people as compared to younger cohorts in cross-sectional studies are also present in longitudinal studies, of course. If we follow the same group of people along over the years, however, we are in a better position to estimate the extent of age *changes*, even though we now face other kinds of problems. Such problems mostly involve repeating the same tests.

Repeating can cause learning; it can also cause boredom. Learning increases scores, boredom decreases them. Do these two effects cancel each other out? It is hard to say. In the following paragraphs, I examine the findings of the relatively large body of longitudinal studies with intelligence tests that now exist.

AGE

It is strategic to divide the longitudinal studies reviewed into three groups: those that follow subjects from childhood to early adulthood (about 30 years of age), those that follow subjects to middle age (about 60 years of age), and those that follow subjects past middle age to very old age. The four studies of the first group all found increases in intelligence-test performance over time (Bradway, Thompson, & Cravens, 1958; Honzik & Macfarlane, 1973; Schaie et al., 1973; Eichorn, 1973). The six studies in the second group (Kangas & Bradway, 1971; Bayley & Oden, 1955; Tuddenham, Blumenkrantz, & Wilkin, 1968; Owens, 1953; Cunningham, 1974; Schaie et al., 1973) found either continued increase or plateau, depending on the kind of task, sample, and so forth. In one such study, done with Army veterans (Tuddenham et al., 1968) nonverbal performance declined before middle age. The nine studies in the old-age group, those following people past the age of 60, show three separate patterns. First, they show the classical aging pattern of Botwinick (1977), namely stability of verbal tests and decline in performance tests. Second, they show a regression to the mean, with those who score lower in the beginning improving and those who score higher declining. And, third, they show a general decline of both verbal and nonverbal scores. These studies include those done by Eisdorfer and Wilkie (1973); Jarvik, Kallmann, and Falek (1962); Blum, Fosshage, and Jarvik (1972); Rhudick and Gordon (1973); Gilbert (1973); Schaie, Labouvie, and Buech (1973); Berkowitz and Green (1965); Troll, Saltz, and Dunin-Markiewicz (1976); and Riegel and Riegel (1972). Possible reasons for these different patterns are explored in the next few paragraphs.

Although there may be statistically significant increases or decreases over time, it is important to note that almost all these changes are small. In practically no study did the scores of older people drop to their early-adult level. In other words, it is Pattern B of Figure 9.1 that is supported here, not A or C.

ABILITY LEVEL

Do smarter people—or those who score higher on tests in early years—keep their levels up longer than those who are not so smart? In cross-sectional research, this does seem to be true (Botwinick, 1977). People with higher education and thus presumably greater ability do get higher scores in old age. In longitudinal studies, however, the evidence is less clear.

When Owens (1959) retested college students 30 years later, he found no relation between initial scores and final scores. However, his sample was restricted; all were originally college students. In general, most follow-ups for the early years of adulthood are based on superior samples, and most of them report increases to the ages of 30 or 40. The better educated samples followed to middle age also show increases more than do average or less-educated samples. As noted, however, the picture for older ages is more of regression to the mean. How much decreases in intellectual activity accompanying the physical and social deficits of old age contribute to this effect, we cannot now say. Some new research on reversals of cognitive aging deficits are discussed in the following sections. "Use it or lose it!" may also apply to intellectual endeavors, not only physical ones.

RETEST INTERVAL

As noted earlier, one problem of longitudinal research is the very nature of retesting or repeating tasks. Rhudick and Gordon (1973) focused on the length of the retesting interval. They found that for verbal tests it did not seem to matter whether the second testing was less than two years, between two and six years, or between six and eight years. However, for performance, or nonverbal, tests, the longer the interval, the greater the decline—among subjects over 60. Because verbal scores tend to show less decline altogether, one might conclude that more vulnerable abilities are more susceptible to testing conditions and benefit less from repetition. Experimental research has shown that, unless repetition is accompanied by help in improving processing strategies, it does not improve performance.

OTHER FACTORS

Health and type of environment have both been found to be related to stability of test performance. Those in poorer health show greater declines, which should not surprise us, in view of the importance of health noted in most pre-

vious chapters. In fact, intelligence-test performance is a surprising predictor of imminence of death (see discussion of terminal drop, later). Institutionalization is also related to poorer performance. Of course, people in poorer health and less adequate mental functioning are more likely to be institutionalized.

Honzik and Macfarlane (1973) examined the personality characteristics of 7 men and 13 women who gained the most (eight or more IQ points) on the WAIS between the ages of 18 and 40. Compared with those whose IQs did not change, the gainers tend to have been children who were not gregarious, not highly sex-typed, and not liked or accepted. At age 30, they were less satisfied with their appearance and less likely to be asked for advice and reassurance. In general, therefore, they were more likely to be dissatisfied with their current lives and thus more likely to try harder and keep on trying harder.

Differential abilities

So far we have been looking at omnibus tests, or combined measures of ability. Changes with age are a function of the kinds of abilities measured. Among the nine subtests of the WAIS, for example, those which require quick thinking—such as the Digit Symbol Test—show an age-change pattern similar to that for many perceptual abilities described in Chapter 9. They reach a peak in the 20s, plateau for a decade or two, and then decline steadily. Tests of stored information, such as vocabulary or general information, may continue to increase almost to the end of life. Certain types of reasoning tests, such as arithmetic reasoning, show an intermediate pattern: essentially, a plateau through the adult years. Most recent attention to adult intellectual development has focused primarily on these differential patterns, particularly on the model proposed by Cattell (1963) of a division between *fluid* and *crystallized* intelligence.

Fluid intelligence has been defined as an underlying or basic ability resulting from the interaction of physiological capacity and early—and perhaps also later—experiences. All active processing of information, whether coding during the acquisition phase or higher thought processes such as problem solving, involves fluid intelligence. The curve of growth and decline in this kind of ability would parallel that of various biological processes, perhaps declining steadily from the late teens.

Crystallized intelligence is the product of the action of fluid intelligence on life experiences. It can be defined as knowledge. Horn (1970) calls it a "precipitate out of experience." This kind of ability continues to increase throughout adulthood.

Because an omnibus measure such as IQ measures a mixture of fluid and crystallized intelligence, it can remain stable through the adult years. As the proportion of fluid intelligence goes down, the proportion of crystallized intelligence goes up; the average remains constant (see Figure 11.2).

Hooper and Storck (1972) compared cross-sectional data on the Raven Progressive Matrices Test (representing fluid intelligence) and the Stanford-Binet Vocabulary Subtest (representing crystallized intelligence). The age patterns for the two tests closely approximate these curves hypothesized by Horn (1970). That is, adolescents (ages 14 to 17) have the highest scores on the Raven, and older people have successively

lower scores; there is no appreciable age difference in vocabulary. The correlation between the Raven and the WAIS was significantly lower in a group of older people than in a group of young adults (Cunningham, Clayton, & Overton, 1975). Again, this suggests differential developmental patterns in fluid and crystallized intelligence.

Quantitative versus structural change in intelligence

Two kinds of age changes in intelligence can be considered, related to Issue 4, change versus development. The simplest kind is a quantitative change: increase or decrease in the amount of whatever intellectual abilities existed before. For example, a quantitative change in memory results in the capacity to retain ten digits recited in a row, instead of only eight digits, as at an earlier age. The reverse is also a quantitative change: a decrease in retention with age from ten digits to eight digits.

A more profound kind of intellectual change is alteration in cognitive structure—a qualitative transformation. One kind of structural change is the appearance or disappearance of kinds of abilities. For example, children who had not previously been able to remember any numbers show structural change when they first become able to do so. Conversely, old people who were previously able to repeat a series of digits show structural change if they are no longer able to do so.

Another kind of structural change is in the composition of the components of intelligence. For example, people who had previously remembered a series of digits as isolated and discrete units show structural change when they begin to cluster these digits into groups or categories, with consequent improvement in memorizing ability.

A third kind of structural change is new combinations of preexisting components of intelligence. For example, if different kinds of memory functions were integrated into a more complex kind of storing function, the result would be a major structural change.

Although all intellectual changes can conceivably be developmental if they follow a temporal pattern, most theorists (for example, Flavell, 1970) feel that only quantitative changes—

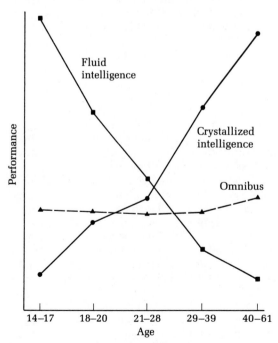

Figure 11.2.   Fluid- and crystallized-intelligence patterns with age. *(Source: Horn, 1970.)*

growth in crystallized intelligence—occur during adulthood. Flavell also believes that even quantitative intellectual development is smaller in adulthood than in childhood and comes about mainly as the result of major life experiences. These experiences could be "programmed" (such as education or psychotherapy) or "unprogrammed" (such as marriage, child rearing, or job experiences). They could be normative—expected and anticipated (such as marriage)—or unexpected (such as divorce). Remember Issue 7?

Balinsky (1941) and others have found that factor analysis of tests of adolescents and adults shows differentiation in late adolescence (many unrelated abilities or specialized abilities), followed by what Balinsky calls "reorganization towards a 'flexible complexity' " (or more integration of abilities) in adulthood.* These psychologists suggest that adults can continue to show qualitative as well as quantitative structural change in intelligence when they have to cope with situations that demand new approaches. In fact, Plemons, Willis, and Baltes (1975) found that it was possible to improve fluid intelligence by a cognitive training program.

Horn (1970) points out that one can learn the intelligence of one's culture and be intelligent in one sense of the term, without being particularly insightful or intelligent in another sense of the term. For example, tests of intelligence, which are successful in predicting school achievement, fail to predict success in adult life if success is measured by other than intellectual standards (such as income, occupational status, or interpersonal competency).

Sex differences

Intellectual development during adulthood seems to be very different for men and women in our country. All test findings agree in this respect. Girls are more advanced than boys in the preschool years, the sexes are the same during early and middle school years, and boys score higher starting with high school (Maccoby & Jacklin, 1974). Kangas and Bradway (1971) report retests spanning 38 years on the Stanford-

*Increasing differentiation is shown by factor structures that have a greater number of factors, a less dominant general factor, and lower factor intercorrelations. The reorganization of adulthood reverses differentiation, showing fewer factors and greater factor intercorrelations (Baltes & Labouvie, 1973).

Binet for 48 men and women between the ages of 12 and 50. Men who had higher IQs at 12 gained more in IQ by the mid-20s than did those who started with lower IQs, but women who had higher IQs at 12 gained less than those with lower IQs. Eichorn (1973) reported an increase in general IQ for men between 16 and 36 and a slight decline for women from 26 to 36 years. It is as if women use their intelligence to grow dumber, at least in the early years of adulthood. It could be adaptive (see Issue 9) for women to seem less competent than the men they seek to marry—and do marry—in a society that encourages men to "marry down" and to feel good about themselves if they are smarter than their wives. This subject will be discussed more fully in Chapters 19 and 20.

Bayley (1968) and Honzik and Macfarlane (1973) present the most recent follow-up testing with the two Berkeley longitudinal samples: the Growth Study and the Oakland Growth Study, respectively. Sex differences emerged in both correlational analyses. The largest gain on the WAIS between ages 18 and 40 is that made by women on verbal IQ (over seven points). This gain is really a return to the equality found in childhood, because the women at 18 scored much lower than the men. The same general effect holds for the full-scale IQ.

Schaie and his associates (1973) administered the Primary Mental Abilities Test to three independent samples of adults of all ages and found very stable and significant sex differences, at all ages and in all analyses. These differences varied in direction according to the particular mental ability tested. Women were superior in verbal meaning, reasoning, and word fluency; men were superior in space, number, and general intellectual ability (overall score).

Sex differences were particularly pronounced in the childhood personality antecedents of adult intelligence (Honzik & Macfarlane, 1973). For one thing, more of the girls' than the boys' early characteristics correlated with their intelligence at age 40. Honzik and Macfarlane suggest that the greater variety of men's occupational experiences produces more changes in their behavior. Women tend to change less. Those women who had the highest IQs at 40 had been productive, complex, self-doubting little girls and independent, interested 30-year-old women.

A Fels Institute longitudinal study (Sontag, Baker, & Nelson, 1958) of 72 women and 59 men, using the Otis test, found that those women who were highly social and dependent were more likely to have declining IQs than were those who were less characteristically sex-typed. From the standpoint of our new hard look at data on sex differences in achievement and performance, it seems more likely that we are dealing with the effects of sex-role socialization, which Matina Horner (1970) has dramatically called "fear of success," rather than with any basic sex differences. In other words, we are dealing with adaptation to the realities of adult sex-typed life rather than intrinsic sex differences. The same new perspective on class, ethnic, and racial differences in adult intelligence makes us suspect that sex differences also reflect socialization and culture-related expectations and experience. Issue 10, referring to the effect of adaptation to varying conditions on development, is involved here.

Terminal drop

In a longitudinal study of older men, Kleemeier (1962) discovered that those men who did not survive to the last rounds of testing, over a period of 12 years, showed a drop in their intelligence-test scores before they died; those who survived maintained the level of their scores on the Wechsler-Bellevue over the years. Lieberman (1965) and Riegel and Riegel (1972) replicated these results with progressively larger samples, and so have others since—for example, Jarvik and Falek (1963), who tested sets of identical twins. What at first seemed a mere curiosity now seems to be a noteworthy phenomenon. Intelligence-test scores—or at least drops in such scores—seem to be predicting time of death. Note that this kind of finding can only be obtained from longitudinal research, because the drop is from the subjects' own previous levels.

Lieberman interpreted these findings partly as a general systemic decline; presumably system decline leads to death. This harks back to the theory of Schrödinger (1962) that the essence of life is meaning, system, and organization and that disintegration of order and meaning leads to a condition of chaos, randomness, or death. Schrödinger derived his theory from the second law of thermodynamics. Lieberman further sug-

gested that withdrawal from life, or from participation in life activities, in the later years could result from people's attempts to cope with an experience of inner disintegration. This disintegration would probably thus precede the reduced emotional investment in the affairs of life that Cumming and Henry (1961) called "disengagement." People may limit their activities in an effort to "hold themselves together"—to reduce the experience of chaos. Among other things, they would not want to be tested at all if they felt this way. Riegel, Riegel, and Meyer (1967), in fact, found that people who dropped out of their longitudinal study, refusing to participate any more, had shown some decline at the last testing. The drops in intelligence-test scores are not always large; what is significant is the pattern of decline and the fact that this decline occurs from one to five years before death.

Riegel and Riegel suggested that the increasing variation in test scores found with age may be due to the presence of increasing numbers of predeath subjects. Their increasing prevalence in older samples may also account for the declines in performance noted in cross-sectional studies including older people.

The interpretation of terminal drop has been challenged by Palmore and Cleveland (1975) and by Wilkie and Eisdorfer (1974), whose findings with the Duke sample of older men suggested that most of the drop could be attributed to health. On looking back over the test scores of those subjects who died, they found that physicians had assessed their health as essentially poorer than the health of those who survived. All the nonsurviving subjects had a chronic disease, whereas the survivors were relatively free of chronic disease and only 17% had a history of acute disorders. Botwinick, West, and Storandt (1978) found that discriminative score cutoffs correctly classified 66% of 300 healthy men and women over 60 as to their survival status.

The possibility of predicting death by means of repeated intellectual measurement would have its uses, although the problems surrounding such procedures could easily outweigh any advantages. Riegel (1971), incidentally, observed that the relation between retest drops and longevity was greater for subjects under 65 and suggested that death may be more predictable at younger ages and more random at older ages.

Intervention and reversal

Until recently, deteriorative processes in older people were assumed to be "natural." Therefore, nobody tried to treat them other than by institutionalization or other kinds of maintenance procedures. But in the last few years there has been some interest and hope in reversing cognitive declines. Various drug therapies have been used, such as Eisdorfer, Nowlin, and Wilkie's (1970) experimentation with propranolol to decrease the heightened autonomic arousal assumed to produce poorer performance. No clear evidence for success with any drugs has yet been obtained (Eisdorfer & Stotsky, 1977). General verbal psychotherapy is also becoming more prevalent with older people as psychotherapists change their preconceptions about the modifiability of behavior in late life.

These procedures are generally difficult to evaluate. Behavior-modification techniques have been used by a number of psychologists (such as Plemons, Willis, & Baltes, 1978), directed to training and transfer of training. Plemons, Willis, and Baltes, for example, trained older subjects on figural relations, which is a fluid-intelligence measure. Then they examined the persistence, over one week, one month, and six months, of the changes they had induced. They also looked at transfer effects to other fluid-intelligence measures and even to one test of crystallized intelligence. They report that their training program was successful in enhancing performance for the following six months, and transferred to other measures for shorter periods. Unfortunately, most such intervention procedures seem to have only a short-run influence. Although intellectual performance at any age seems more modifiable than we used to believe, it may have limits.

Life change and stress have a major effect on IQ performance. Schwartz and Elonen (1975) found shifts of 13 points or more at the time of major life events (see Chapter 1). They also found that the scores of emotionally unstable people had many ups and downs. Baltes and Willis (1978) feel that only nonnormative life events such as health or other personal crises cause marked change in intelligence scores. Expected events are not so upsetting. Because they are anticipated and prepared for, they do not entail the kind of stress and adaptation that unexpected events do.

Summary

Whatever intelligence tests measure, they do not contradict experimental results but extend them. IQ scores on omnibus tests are remarkably stable in longitudinal research. People maintain the same score into advanced old age and seem to decline only a few months or years before death. This *terminal drop,* whether due to systemic disorganization or declining health, may lead to disengagement in order to offset a feeling of chaos.

Two different kinds of intelligence are described. *Fluid intelligence,* basic to active cognitive processing, seems to decline through the adult years. *Crystallized intelligence,* or the result of interaction between fluid intelligence and life experience, continues to increase until almost the end of life. The average of these two kinds of scores is the IQ. Combining the declining curve of fluid intelligence with the increasing curve of crystallized intelligence results in a stable IQ over the years.

Sex, ethnic, cohort, and educational differences all attest to the interaction of biological and social factors in adult intellectual development. If the fluid/crystallized dichotomy is true, people cannot do much about improving "fluid" processes except what has been noted in the past two chapters, such as develop better strategies. However, they can enhance the growth of crystallized intelligence by maintaining intellectual pursuits during their adult years. Biological declines may "close in" certain kinds of sensitivity to the environment, but such declines seem to be of a remarkably minor order of magnitude so far as intelligence is concerned. Terminal drop may be considered evidence for a major turning point of this kind, but it is perhaps the only one. Terminal drop also highlights the importance of *life time*—developmental age, or distance from death. Finally, the evidence from intelligence tests is strongly against a hypothesis of universality of intellectual development. Variability is the rule.

12

Work and Achievement of Men

Work, particularly for men, is organized around jobs. Sometimes a job is a career. It can offer low status or high status; can pay nothing, just a little, or a fortune. A job or career can be so repetitive that the worker's mind can wander in any and all directions or so new and challenging that it calls for complete attention and commitment. It can have been the same throughout history or just created today. People can do the same things throughout their working lives, or they can move through a connected sequence of jobs, or they can shift from one kind of activity to an almost totally unrelated kind at various points, while keeping the same job title. Sometimes jobs end at specified points in life and sometimes they continue to the end of life.

It is against this kind of diversity that we attempt to chart occupational development. This chapter will review the research on job development of men; Chapter 13 will treat job development of women. Until recently, attention has focused almost exclusively on men's employment. Only in the last few years have women been studied. Because job development of men and women is different in many ways, it is meaningful to treat them separately.

Kinds of job development

Almost everyone's life is organized by jobs. Where people live, the kind of homes they live in, the kind of clothes they wear, the hours they wake up and go to bed, the kind of food they eat, the people they meet, their friends, their recreation, their participation in informal organizations, even their self-esteem and health are all related to the kind of job they or some member of their immediate family holds.

Adulthood itself—at least for men—is defined by working at a job. It is presumed to begin with entry into a first job and to end with retirement. Both Freud and Erikson recognize the importance of the job in their concepts of maturity and mental health. A good man, to Freud, is one who is able to love and to work; a good woman, he thought, is able to be loved, but also to work, although at a different kind of occupation. For Erikson, the stages of intimacy and generativity define adulthood—again, love and work. Family and job are intertwined in psychoanalytic thinking and also in the lives of men and women, as will be seen in this and subsequent chapters.

From early childhood, we plan the kind of job we are going to have "when we grow up." Every boy, almost as soon as he can talk, is asked "What will you *be* when you grow up?" It is as if *being* is synonymous with working. It also implies that for each individual there is only one job. In our country, it is expected that children, in the course of "growing up," will pass through a sequence of ideas about what they will be and that these ideas will fluctuate a great deal before they gradually consolidate into a small number of possibilities that can be tried out for size.

Our educational system is our primary occupational training ground, not only developing skills but also separating children according to their future occupational tracks. Johnny becomes recognized as good in mathematics and encouraged toward scientific occupations. Billy is a "natural leader" and is helped to dream of politics or executive status. George is "good with his hands" and sent to technical or trade school.

Tyler (1968) noted that high school students knew about more occupations than they considered possible choices for themselves. They chose first on the basis of intrinsic factors—what they wanted to do or felt they'd be good at—but they rejected some of these choices on the basis of extrinsic factors such as money, security, or prestige.

When an acceptable level of proficiency has been reached, individuals are expected to enter their first job and from there "work up," hopefully to the "top." This level of proficiency may be no more than knowing how to carry a load and sign a paycheck. Or it may involve elaborate accumulation of knowledge and skills.

But what if a man can't get the right first job, the one that leads up the ladder to success? Or what if that job evaporates as the company folds or is absorbed by a larger corporation or moves to another part of the country? What if his skills, which he worked so hard to perfect, become obsolete in ten years? Or what if a group of younger people with newer skills becomes available for employment and he is declared outmoded? What if he gets bored doing the same thing all the time and wants to try his hand at something new? What if he isn't hired, or is fired, or receives lower pay, or receives subtle kinds of unpleasant treatment because he is not the right color or age? Extrinsic and random factors probably play a larger role in job development than they do in most other areas.

Defining job development

It is harder to conceptualize development in work than development in other areas of life, such as intellectual abilities, personality, or the family. An uncomplicated definition would merely refer to any systematic changes with age (Neugarten, 1968). For example, at least from cross-sectional data, job satisfaction increases with age as job mobility decreases with age. We could then say that job development during the

adult years consists of settling into a job and enjoying it more, or of finding a job that is satisfying and settling into it.

Another way we could define job development is in terms of directional movement along a path. For example, some people (although probably no more than 30% of workers) move up systematically in the status hierarchy of bureaucratic organizations, from bottom positions at the time of entry to higher positions after a suitable number of years. In countries such as ours, where many still believe in unlimited opportunity for all, such a progression is the ideal, even though not the common pattern. Because bureaucracies are pyramids, there is little room at the top, and most of those who start at the bottom stay near the bottom. Wilensky (1961) would call regular upward progression an *orderly career*.

Over the last hundred years, according to a historian (Hareven, 1976), we have moved toward greater orderliness of careers, even though less than one-third of today's workers experience such systematic progression. In 1900, nearly half of all gainfully employed men were between 16 and 34 years old. The kinds of jobs they held were closely related to their age. Men between 20 and 40 worked in industry. Those who were younger and older worked on farms or in unskilled jobs. After years of hard labor, even highly skilled workers had to "retire" to lower-paying but less demanding jobs, often temporary and unskilled. Working-class families moved into and out of poverty all their lives, being worse off when they were young parents with too many children and during what we today would call middle age but what to most of them was a worn-out old age.

In some cases, an orderly progression is simply additive, involving a given number of years at each step in order to qualify for promotion to the next step, as in the army or the civil service. In other cases, a certain amount of qualitative transformation in cognitive or personality structure is expected to take place during the process. The junior executive is supposed to gain expertise and wisdom as he gains experience, thus becoming a different *kind* of executive, before he moves into a senior post. One way that Atlantic Telephone & Telegraph (AT&T) executives changed over 20 years was in their attitudes toward the company. From an unquestioning enthusiasm when they first began, in their middle to late 20s, they moved to a more realistic appraisal—even though still positive (Howard, 1978).

In the additive (ladder) model, the additions may be steps to a predetermined goal—whether that goal be money, status, or a particular position, such as president of the company or the country. Goals such as these are usually extrinsic characteristics of jobs. That is, the actual work done day by day has less meaning than reaching the goal, although this does not mean that the work itself cannot be enjoyed too.

In the transformation model, the focus is more likely to be internal rather than external. We can speak of stages or sequences along the way, instead of rungs on a ladder. Artists or artisans can enjoy this kind of job development, provided they measure progress not quantitatively—by so many pictures or books each year—but qualitatively—by transformations in the pictures or books as one follows the other, or in their vision of the world as it becomes expressed in their products.

All these definitions deal with development of individuals or their products. We might also consider development of the work group or of the productive society. From the time such a group assembles, it can continue to grow, in both complexity and coping power. It can learn to work more smoothly, with fewer overt communications, and to differentiate into a variety of functional positions that are integrated into a more effective unit. Perhaps, in moving toward more rapid job changes to meet changing conditions, we are losing the benefits of interpersonal, prosocial production-group development, which comes with association over time. A study by Burns (1955) found age differences in the nature of work groups. Younger, more mobile men got together for power, to plot mutual political advantage. Older men formed cliques for protection and reassurance.

Most empirical and theoretical literature on jobs, work, and careers has been concerned with industrial settings. Only a few studies have dealt with development in such nonbusiness careers as art, science, and the helping professions (for example, Bécker, 1951; Becker, Geer, Hughes, & Strauss, 1961; Henry, Sims, & Spray, 1971; Lopata, 1971; Roe, 1961). Finally, our rigid definitions of jobs and work have warped our views of the nature of leisure occupations, which to some people are more central than is paid employment. Trends toward greater automation, fewer meaningful "jobs," and earlier retirement alert us to a broader view of the area of work, one that can include job development along multiple pathways. This is discussed more fully in Chapter 14.

Jobs versus careers

Most adult men and over half of all adult women either have jobs or they are trying to find jobs. They are thus technically included in the *labor force*. Such jobs are usually expected to take them outside their homes, to have regular schedules, to involve specifiable activities, and to provide money. When current jobs are related to previous training and previous jobs, as well as to future, anticipated jobs, they can be considered *careers*. The concept of career, though, can be broader than jobs. It is applied to life career, family career, and so on. The next few pages focus primarily on jobs in the more limited sense. Later I will deal with development in careers.

Why we work

Anyone talking about the subject of working must begin by reading Studs Terkel's arousing book called, simply, *Working* (Terkel, 1972). Work, he says, is "a search for daily meaning as well as daily bread, for recognition as well as cash, for astonishment rather than torpor; in short, for a sort of life rather than a Monday through Friday sort of dying. Perhaps immortality, too, is part of the quest" (p. xiii). A few pages later, he quotes one of the women he interviewed: "I think most of us are looking for a calling, not a job. Most of us, like the assembly line worker, have jobs that are too small for our spirit. Jobs are not big enough for people" (p. xxix). Terkel confesses that he was "constantly astonished by the extraordinary dreams of ordinary people. No matter how bewildering the times, no matter how dissembling the official language, those we call ordinary are aware of a sense of personal worth—or more often a lack of it—in the work they do" (pp. xxix–xxx).

Work has different meanings for different people. For some, it may be a source of prestige and social recognition, a basis for self-respect and sense of worth. For others, it is an opportunity for social participation or a way of being of service. For still others, it is enjoyment of the activity for itself or for creative self-expression. Or work may be merely a way to earn a living. There are age differences and age changes in such job orientations. There also seem to be family similarities and lifetime stability in at least some aspects of job orientation.

Although general attitudes toward working may be transmitted partly within the family, they are susceptible to early life experience; to generational "keynote themes" of new, upcoming generations; and to early on-the-job experience. The effect of early life experience is dramatically apparent in the cohort of men and women who were teenagers during the Great Depression of the 1930s. When Glenn Elder (1974) followed the careers of some Oakland, California, boys and girls from their early teens to their 40s, he found that the amount of relative deprivation of their families during the Depression had an enduring influence on their work values. Those California boys whose families experienced marked deprivation relative to their pre-Depression standard of living were likely to have found jobs at an earlier age than those whose families were less affected. Note that this is relative deprivation, not absolute. Most of the families were better off than the general U.S. population at that time. The boys became adults earlier, in this way, and valued dependability and industry more than the less deprived during the rest of their lives.

Social class did not seem to make a difference, although the subjects from blue-collar families in this California study did not experience severe deprivation that would restrict options to the point of hopelessness. The men from the deprived families, regardless of class, chose their future careers while they were still in high school and ended up in more-orderly career patterns than did those from the less deprived families. It is important to note that this cohort experienced the Depression in their teens and World War II in their 20s. This made it possible for them to make up for inadequacies in education by using the GI Bill after the war. Older cohorts were more damaged by the Depression.

In a 1964 follow-up, when these men were in their 40s, most of them said that the most important arena of their lives was work (see Table 12.1). There was no difference in this respect between those who were deprived in their youth and those who were not. The events of adulthood wiped out class and deprivation differences so far as orientation toward work is concerned. However, as the table shows, these events do seem to have left their mark on other aspects of life, such as family involvement and leisure activities. These arenas are discussed later in this book.

Members of the generation that came of age during the 1960s, many of them probably children of the Depression generation, adopted as one of its generational "keynote themes" a rebellion against the "Protestant ethic" of their parents. They devalued dependability and industry and emphasized more intrinsic, self-fulfilling attitudes toward work. Some seemed to be turning away from a work orientation alto-

TABLE 12.1 Activity preferences[a] of middle-class Oakland longitudinal-study men at time of 1964 follow-up, by Depression deprivation status

Family deprivation	Activity area			
	Work	Family	Leisure	Community
Nondeprived (N=19)	3.9	1.8	2.1	1.0
Deprived (N=16)	4.0	3.2[b]	1.5	0.6

[a] The term refers to activity enjoyed most, activity subjects would like to devote more time to, and activity providing the greatest sense of accomplishment.

[b] Significant difference between deprived and nondeprived ($p < .05$ on two-tailed test).

Source: Elder, 1974.

gether and to be "dropping out," although this proved to be a temporary phenomenon restricted to a small, elite segment of that generation. In their review of generational similarities within the family, Troll and Bengtson (1979) noted that there was more generational difference with respect to work attitudes than there was for religion or politics.

One of the earliest studies of family background and work orientation is that of Reuben Hill and his colleagues in Minneapolis, who studied 100 three-generation families during the late 1950s, each including three sets of couples (Hill, Foote, Aldous, Carlson, & Macdonald, 1970). They found that, in 47% of the male lineages, grandfather, father, and son all remained in the same general occupation and had the same orientation toward work. The fact that half of these families kept the same kinds of jobs and attitudes toward jobs over the generations during a time of rapid industrial change when youth were supposed to find new paths is remarkable. Two separate studies under my direction found significant correlations between parents and their children in how much they value achievement (Troll, Neugarten, & Kraines, 1969; Troll & Smith, 1972), again showing family transmission in the work area.

Thomas and Stankiewicz (1973) found a curious cross-sex correlation on the valuation of work security, sons agreeing with their mothers and daughters with their fathers. However, they did not find family agreement on achievement values. The younger-generation members they studied were "forerunners," and so, because they led the way, they differed temporarily from both their parents and their peers (Troll & Bengtson, 1979; Bengtson & Troll, 1978). The conclusion, from a review of the data, was that five years later this "generation gap" would diminish in the forerunner families, perhaps, and increase in the nonforerunner families. The combined influence of family, generation, and historical period is notable throughout.

Job experiences

Several recent longitudinal investigations of men's occupational development find that the first few years on the job are strategic so far as later job attitudes and behavior are concerned. Elder's (1974) study of the Depression cohort,

Bray and Howard's reports on AT&T executives, and Kanter's (1977) study of corporations all find that these first few years either wipe out earlier distinctions, like economic deprivation, or separate men who start out alike (Bray & Howard, 1978).

A 20-year longitudinal study of AT&T executives (Bray & Howard, 1978) found that the more successful men, measured by job-status level, increased in their need to accomplish difficult tasks and to solve difficult problems, and that this major shift occurred during the first eight years on the job. The success of their early efforts led to increased desire for success. It also led to a gradual move from extrinsic to intrinsic achievement motivations. Kanter (1977) reports similar trends from other studies. When early efforts do not meet with success, however, perhaps because of the luck of early job placements, men with high achievement needs may look to other kinds of arenas to satisfy these needs.

Cross-sectional studies have repeatedly found age differences in men's orientation to work. Older men differ from younger ones in wanting to control and manage more and to do their work their own way—to be more independent (Veroff & Feld, 1970; Friedmann & Havighurst, 1954; Strong, 1959).

Veroff and Feld also found that men with high affiliation motive, defined as a desire to avoid aloneness, tend to seek jobs that include social participation. They are distinctly absent from farming jobs. Older affiliative men are likely to be supervisors.

Although high achievement motivation, defined as a desire for recognition of accomplishment, was not associated with particular jobs for younger men, it was correlated with jobs of high prestige among older men. It may be that psychological factors such as motivation have more predictive power on job behavior over the long run than they do in the early work years. Generally, though, Veroff and Feld's findings (and those of others, such as Voydanoff, 1977) show that motives have less relevance to the work *satisfactions* of older men than they do to those of younger men.

As executives get older, they become more and more autonomous and also more aggressive, feeling freer to express hostility. Although the AT&T executives learned more about the business over the years, they did not really improve in their basic management abilities. In some ways, they had reached a plateau at the end of 20 years of work. Most were satisfied with the level they had reached and with their material success. They no longer had the same push toward upward mobility or promotion they had had when they started, even though they enjoyed doing difficult jobs well more than they ever had. The more successful executives— those who had reached higher job levels—differed from the less successful, not in life satisfaction, but in job commitment and forcefulness and dominance (Bray & Howard, 1978), as well as in achievement motivation (see Table 12.2). When they just started out, in 1956–1960, the average score for all beginning managers in achievement motivation was 63%. Those who had not been promoted past the first three management levels scored 78% in 1976–1977, 20 years later, and those who had reached Levels 4–5 scored 89%. Both successful and less successful men thus increased in achievement-motivation scores, but the more successful increased more.

Studies such as that by Veroff and Feld (1970) show strong age differences in orientation toward working. Of those men who said they would have liked to be doing some other kind of work (52% of those aged 21–34), the younger ones complained of poor achievement opportunities; the older men, of economic problems. Younger men said "There's no chance to show my ability." Older men said "The pay is low." Veroff and Feld concluded that younger men have more direct emotional investment in their work, are "more committed to the actual ongoing psychological life at work, including achievement activities and affiliative relation-

ships, while older men are more concerned with the extrinsic aspects of the job role" (p. 217). This finding differs from the AT&T study, particularly when compared with the attitudes of more successful executives.

A life-transition study of lower-middle-class San Franciscans (Lowenthal, Thurnher, & Chiriboga, 1975) found that high school seniors interviewed had little awareness of the course their occupational careers would follow. Many spoke as if they were describing "fantasy trips." They talked about "making it big" and then retiring early to "really live." The next older men, recently married, spoke of purpose to their education and were more realistic, like the beginning AT&T executives. They were also more aware of the nonmaterial aspects of working and wondered what they would like to spend their lifetimes doing. Most of the middle-aged men seemed to believe that their work should have been more important to them than it actually was. Remember, this was a lower-middle-class sample, not a managerial sample. The men had clearly reached a plateau and wondered whether their lack of "success" was their own fault. Apparently they had not found rewards in non-job arenas, as had the less successful managers. The men facing retirement seemed to be using a work orientation in planning their retirements, and they stressed economic security and control.

Apparently, general vocational interests tend to stay much the same over the adult years; they also tend to be repeated from parents to children. Lowenthal (1972) sees job orientations as aspects of lifestyles. Changes such as loss of job or retirement are compensated for in ways that serve to retain fundamental patterns. We can even predict the way people will react to retire-

TABLE 12.2 **Average motivation scores**

Need for	New managers		Middle-aged managers		
	1956–1960	1977	Levels 1–3 1976–1977	Levels 4–5 1976–1977	Levels 4–5 1978
Achievement	63%	67%	78%	89%	84%
Aggression	55	55	69	71	76
Autonomy	57	66	82	85	82
Affiliation	56	58	36	29	24

Note: From Edwards Personal Preference Schedule; norm group = 585 Bell System college recruits, 1958.

Source: Bray and Howard, 1978.

ment on the basis of their previous job behaviors. For example, self-determining people will find new situations in which to continue expressing themselves, and passive people will wait for new supervisors to take care of them. Retirement is discussed further in Chapter 14.

Measurement

Stability in job orientation has been measured both by personality tests that look at motivations and interests and by the kinds of jobs people hold. Jobs have been classified by status or pay, by actual performance, or even by presumed underlying personality requirements. Holland's (1973) personality-based classification of jobs has been used in longitudinal research to show remarkable stability in people's job category over a period of five years (Gottfredson, 1977). As shown in Figure 12.1, even among the most mobile 21- to 25-year-olds, almost three-fourths

moved among jobs in the same category. Over 90% of people over 50 stayed in the same job category.

Most of our discussion so far has assumed that social conditions remain static. Yet we know that there have been dramatic historical changes in work opportunities, working conditions, and work attitudes over the past generations. In 1955, and again in 1977, Swedish men were asked "What gives your life the most meaning—your family, your work, or your leisure?" (Yankelovich, 1978). The answers are shown in Figure 12.2. Although "family" remained the most frequent answer, work dropped and leisure increased from 1955 to 1977.

American men have followed the same path. For American women, however, the trend is reversed: the symbolic significance of work has greatly increased for them. It is true, points out Yankelovich, that many women stress the economic gains from working; they are the sole

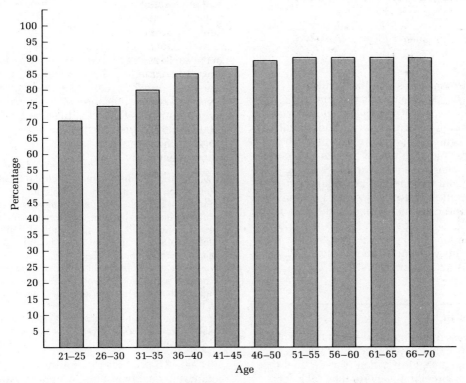

Figure 12.1. Percentage of employed men who remained in some occupational category, in Holland's classification scheme, between 1965 and 1970. *(Source: Gottfredson, 1977.)*

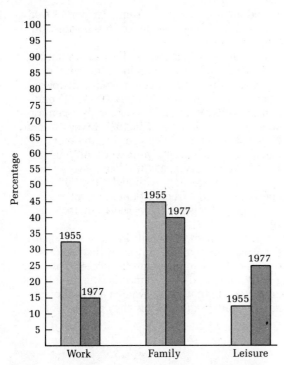

Figure 12.2.   Answers to the question "What gives your life most meaning?" *(Source: Yankelovich, 1978.)*

support of themselves and their children. People whom Yankelovich calls the "new breed" say that the aspect of working most important to them is "being recognized as an individual person" and being given the opportunity to be with pleasant people with whom they like to work.

Finally, some recent research is shifting our attention from the effect of personality on job orientation to the effect of jobs on personality, or the reciprocal effect of personality and work. Men may choose jobs on the basis of personality, but the jobs they work at change their personality. This was partly true of the AT&T executives (Bray & Howard, 1978).

Job satisfaction

Being jobless and poor rarely breeds satisfaction. The primary objective of jobs for most people is income. Only when workers feel they are earning enough money do they look for more-intrinsic rewards. The lower the position

of workers in the occupational hierarchy—skilled, manual, and below—the more they are likely to be motivated by extrinsic factors such as pay and job security. It is usually higher-status or higher-paid workers—business, professional, and white-collar—who value the more-intrinsic qualities of achievement, recognition, responsibility, and self-fulfillment (Friedmann & Havighurst, 1954; Crites, 1969).

Most jobs are satisfying in some ways and not in others. Some factors contribute to satisfaction (the positive end) such as achievement and recognition, while others contribute more to dissatisfaction (the negative end) such as company-policy manipulations and working conditions (Herzberg, Mausner, & Snyderman, 1959). In general, good working conditions are not by themselves likely to make a job highly desirable, although bad working conditions will make it very undesirable.

Terkel's (1972) respondents repeatedly spoke of their dissatisfactions and questioned the "work ethic" they had been brought up to. In the face of automation and mechanization, they said such things as "I'm a machine," "I'm caged," "A monkey can do what I do," "I'm less than a farm implement," "I'm an object," and "I'm a robot." Terkel suggests an age pattern when he says "Ralph Werner, twenty, is far more amenable to the status quo and certainly more job conscious than Bud Freeman, sixty-seven" (p. xxvii). Stagner (1975) notes the diversity of attitudes—that what to some workers may be intolerable boredom, to others may be a soothing monotony and security. A U.S. Labor Department study found that

> when asked to identify the individual facets of the job which were of greatest importance to them, most workers in a national sample gave high ratings to the availability of the resources needed to perform well and to the challenge of their jobs and lower ratings to financial rewards and "comfort" factors. Blue-collar workers, however, tended to consider pay more significant than the challenge of the job, while women workers were somewhat more interested in "comfort" than were men. . . . The "average" American workers appear to seek many things simultaneously (e.g., good pay, interesting work) from each job [Quinn, Staines, & McCullough, 1974, p. 3b].

Table 12.3 presents the findings of a study comparing quality of employment in America in 1969, 1973, and 1977 (Quinn & Staines, 1979).

TABLE 12.3 Frequency and severity of selected work-related problems (1969, 1973, and 1977)

Problem area	Percentage of workers reporting one problem or more in each area[a]			Percentage of those reporting the problem who regarded it as "sizable" or "great"		
	1969	1973	1977	1969	1973	1977
Inadequacy of family income for meeting monthly expenses	26%	21%	21%	63%	55%	57%
Desire for additional fringe benefits, all workers	39	40	46[b]	43	39	40[b]
Wage and salaried workers only[a]	45	45	55[b]	43	39	40[b]
Exposure to one or more health and safety problems	38	42	78[b]	46	40	32[b]
Work-related illness or injury during last three years	13	14	15	56	48	44
Occupational handicap(s)	9	9	10	39	30	29
Inconvenient or excessive hours	30	39	34	38	34	36
Age discrimination	5	4	6	35[c]	35[c]	34[c]
Sex discrimination, all workers	3	5	5	44[c]	37[c]	33[c]
Women only[a]	8	14	12	44[c]	37[c]	33[c]
Race or national origin discrimination, all workers	3	3	6	53[c]	52[c]	51[c]
Blacks only[a]	17	15	16	62[c]	68[c]	37[c]
Unsteady employment	11	9	9	36	26	27
Transportation problems	35	40	34	40	37	33
Unpleasant physical conditions[d]	33	40	37	38	36	37

[a] An indented-row description indicates that the percentage is based on the subsample thus described. Otherwise, the percentages are based on all workers for whom the information was obtained or confidently imputed.

[b] The 1969 and 1973 data are not comparable to those from 1977.

[c] $N < 100$ in 1969 or weighted $N < 140$ in 1973 or 1977.

[d] Includes only those who work at one place or building.

Source: Quinn and Staines, 1979.

There are notable differences in several areas: desire for fringe benefits went up over the three time periods, particularly among wage and salaried workers, and concern over exposure to health and safety problems doubled. Three problems stayed about the same: inconvenient or excessive hours, transportation, and unpleasant physical conditions, each mentioned by about one-third of the workers surveyed. When the 1977 responses are grouped by problem area, health and safety hazards and work schedules draw the most complaints; over 75% of the people answering listed them. Fringe benefits and inadequate time for leisure activities are each mentioned by about half the respondents, as are difficulty in getting duties changed and shortage of jobs in the worker's line of work.

This picture looks different, however, when the respondents were asked whether they would rather have 10% pay raises or improvements of the conditions they didn't like. In this case, the only thing they would prefer over pay raises is better retirement benefits.

The influence of the worker's age on job complaints is shown in Table 12.4; different age

TABLE 12.4 Overall job satisfaction by study year and chronological age

Age	1969	1973	1977
Under 21	−40[a]	−42	−41
21–29	−21	−26	−49
30–44	5	11	−20
45–54	12	11	− 4
55–64	19	17	− 2
65 or older	23	63	11

[a] The job satisfaction index is transformed to a mean of 0 and standard deviation of 87 in 1969. Negative figures indicate deviations below the 1969 mean, or, in other words, job *dissatisfaction*.

Source: Staines, 1980.

effects showed up in each of the three years of the study. In general, there is more job satisfaction among older workers, particularly in the first two years surveyed: 1969 and 1973. Job satisfaction was higher among older than younger workers in 1977 too, but workers of all ages were dissatisfied that year. Only the very oldest group, those over 65 years of age, approximated the mean level of 1969. This profound drop in job satisfaction in 1977 had been heralded by writers for a number of years. Such "blue-collar blues," however, had not shown up in earlier research findings, even in a five-year longitudinal study of a large national sample (Parnes, Adams, Andresani, et al., 1975). Staines's youngest group, those under 21 years of age, did not change across the three times of study; they were clearly and consistently dissatisfied. Black workers also showed negative satisfaction all three years, and their dissatisfaction deepened in 1977. Sex differences were not pronounced, however, nor were, on the whole, educational differences. We might conclude that those most likely to experience poor working conditions and least likely to experience the delights of working—unskilled workers, minority groups, and women—are likely to emphasize those aspects of their jobs that make the difference between the jobs being miserable and being "OK."

Sheppard's (1971) findings on job seeking among unemployed workers point to the influence of personality on job satisfaction. The greater the need to achieve, the more vigorously unemployed workers search for new jobs and the more chance they have of finding such jobs. High achievement desires may lead people to

Tell me something about your work.

Grandfather, age 78
There was a Greek fellow who was cooking with me in the army; he was running the cafeteria. He told me to come over there. Then they opened a place on the Avenue, and he wanted me to take over the cash register there. So I did that for a while. Then I worked making bearings for cars. So I had a lot of ups and downs this way and that. I worked at Packard Car Company. I worked at Midwest Tool for six years on machines. When we came back from the farm, I went to work for Fisher Body for three and a half years until I was laid off. Then I worked at Bundy Tubing for three years and retired at 65. Now I do the housework; I'm a "nanny." I like to work on cars, whether I understand it or not. And another thing—I like anything with any machine work. I'm an idealist. I invented quite a number of things while I worked at Fisher Body. At one time I designed a gauge for a bore, and from that time on we never scrapped a job.

Father, age 51
Went to work for Vickers Tool Company in 1939. At that time my folks moved to East Detroit. Went to work for Chrysler in the summer of 1942. I met Jean [wife] in 1941, then went into the service in 1942. I was in the cavalry for six months, then they mechanized the cavalry, and I drove all army vehicles, except tanks. I heard about a machinist job, so I took a test and passed, even though I didn't know anything about machines. Then I transferred into a machinist company and drove a machine-shop truck. I got married in 1945. Before getting married, I went to the Tank Arsenal to apply for a job. Then I got a job at Dodge Truck.

Son, age 23
I've had a good life. I was never deprived. I admire successful people. I mean, happy, successful people, not just financially successful—probably because I'm trying to achieve that kind of success right now myself.

select jobs not so much for specific characteristics as for the opportunities they provide for advancement. Frustrated desires to achieve can lead to job mobility or second careers or, eventually, to searching for fulfillment in other aspects of life. Because younger workers can still hope for success, they may be more sensitive to the success components of jobs. Most blue-collar industrial workers, however, look to nonwork areas for fulfillment, perhaps especially those with high achievement aspirations (Dubin, 1956). In this way, they resemble the less-successful managers described earlier.

Job satisfaction seems to be independent of job or career change or mobility (Herzberg et al., 1959). In fact, workers can like some things about their jobs and dislike others, yet neither like nor dislike by itself will affect their job performances, their job changes, their feelings about the company or co-workers, or their mental health.

The relationship between job satisfaction and education is complicated. Workers with grade school education express greater job satisfaction than do those with more education, up to a college degree. Starting college but not finishing—or not going on to graduate school—makes one less satisfied with one's job than if one had much less educational experience. Sex differences, which are also complicated, are discussed in Chapter 13.

Job mobility

As noted, job mobility is related to, but distinct from, job satisfaction. Unlike job satisfaction, it is highest at the beginning of work life and gradually decreases from then on. Mobility can refer to moves within an organization (horizontally or vertically) or to moves from one place of employment to another. Moves up the occupational ladder are discussed later. Here I consider only location moves.

Parnes, Nestel, and Andresani (1972) found that about one-fifth of the men who were employed in 1966 changed employers over the next three years. More than three-fifths of these changes were voluntary, not the result of being laid off. Furthermore, these changes were concentrated among a minority of highly mobile individuals. That is, certain workers tend to move from job to job, leaving each one a few months after beginning it. The longer a man remains on a job, the more he is likely to stay with it. Those on a job less than 5 years are seven times more likely to change than those working 20 years or more; they are also three times more likely to be fired.

More recent data quoted by Arbeiter (1979) show the mobility rate of employed people moving into new occupations at 8.7% per year. The marked relation between mobility and age

is shown in Table 12.5. Over a third of young workers changed jobs, only a quarter of those in their 20s did, and fewer and fewer at older ages until only 3% of men over 45 did.

In the middle years, Black and White men show differences in the rates of voluntary job change. Among Whites, voluntary movement drops from 12 to 9% of all job moves between the 45–49 age range and the 55–59 age range, while involuntary changes remain at a constant 6 or 7%. For Blacks, there is less age-related variation in voluntary change, but an increase in involuntary—from 5 to 8% as they get older.

Middle-aged men—both Blacks and Whites—prefer to stick to their jobs, but Black men are more vulnerable to being fired. The exception is men with 20 or more years of service, who increase in voluntary changes. This phenomenon may be attributable to their opting for early retirement and subsequently changing to new or part-time jobs; more blue-collar workers show this pattern. Almost half the White men in the construction industry who were surveyed in 1966 were with different employers in 1969. In general, mobility is related to wages. Those whose hourly rates were less than $2 per hour (in 1969) were almost three times as likely to make voluntary job changes as those earning more. Having a pension works in the opposite direction: it tends to decrease mobility.

Hill's three-generation data (Hill et al., 1970) show a steady increase in job mobility from the oldest to the youngest generation. The grandfathers were apt to have still been on their first jobs until the second half of the first decade of marriage (and they did not marry before they were about 25). Almost half of their sons were on their second jobs by the second year of their marriage, and 40% were in at least their fourth jobs after ten years of marriage. Their fathers had taken their whole lifetimes to go through

TABLE 12.5 Occupational mobility rate for men in 1975

Age	Rate
18–19	37.3%
20–24	24.9
25–34	12.4
35–44	6.2
45–54	3.5

Source: Arbeiter, 1979, after Byrne, 1975.

this many jobs. During the year of longitudinal observation of this sample, the grandchildren showed the most job mobility of all. Almost 60% had changed jobs; of the men, 76% had. The greatest mobility was shown among men in semiskilled and minor clerical jobs, suggesting that the lowest job satisfaction occurs in these categories, which is consistent with findings in all other studies. In all three generations, job change was associated with periods of prosperity. It did not seem to be associated with individual planning; overall, little planning was reported. Therefore, to a large extent, changes could be attributed to opportunity more than to motive.

That changing jobs can represent positive work orientation is suggested by Elder's (1974) data, described earlier. Only 5% of the men who had experienced deprivation in their teens changed jobs during their adult years, in contrast to 28% of those who had not suffered so much during the Depression. Yet the blue-collar men interviewed by Lillian Rubin (1976) had held as many as six to ten jobs by the time they reached 25—having worked almost eight years. By 30, half had worked in the same places for five years and would stay there until they retired—if they were not fired, an experience that would not be unexpected.

A changing economy

Toffler, in *Future Shock* (1970), emphasizes the acceleration of change in our modern economy. He speaks of increasing frequency of job changes associated with an advanced technology that requires drastic changes in types of skills and personalities. Specialization increases the number of different occupations and reduces the life expectancy of any given occupation. In a *Fortune* survey (cited in Toffler, 1970) of 1003 young executives in major corporations, one-third were holding jobs that had not existed until the executives stepped into them. Another large group were in jobs that had been held by only one person before them. Even when the name of the job stays the same, the content of the work does not. A U.S. Labor Department survey of 71 million people in the labor force (cited by Toffler) shows that they had held their current jobs an average of 4.2 years, compared with an average of 4.6 years in a survey only

three years earlier. Toffler feels that, instead of thinking of a career, modern men should think of "serial careers." The impressive quality of the degree of change is underscored by the fact that change statistics do not even include changes within the same company or plant or shifts from one department to another.

The highest turnover rates are among the least-skilled groups. The poor are the last hired and the first fired. People in the middle range of affluence and education, although more mobile than agricultural populations, are, compared with the poor, stable. It is the groups most characteristic of the future—scientists and engineers, highly educated professionals and technicians, and executives and managers—whose turnover rates are showing the most spectacular increases. For management, the relative advantage of experience or knowledge is rapidly decreasing (Toffler, 1970). Rosabeth Kanter's (1977) description of life in a large corporation confirms Toffler's prediction. A job's importance to managers on the rise is its usefulness as a stepping stone toward higher rank. This means that loyalty and length of service are irrelevant and in many cases that moving around becomes an end in itself.

Occupational-mobility patterns are reflected in household-mobility patterns (Arbeiter, 1979). In 1978, 44% of 20-year-olds moved, 56% of 25-year-olds, and 40% of 30-year-olds, but only 27% of 35-year-olds and 18% of 45-year-olds.

Discrimination

As noted in Chapter 4, older people, women, and Blacks all have difficulty in finding work commensurate with their education, in getting the same pay as others doing the same work, and in holding on to jobs when they do get them.

A 1965 report by the U.S. Labor Department (Smith, 1966) documents that more than half of all private employers in states without age-discrimination legislation used age limits in hiring. Half of all job openings were barred to applicants over 55 years of age, and one-fourth were barred to those over 45, regardless of education or skill. A 1962 Detroit study of hard-core unemployed found that, even when other factors were controlled, age was significantly related to unemployment status (Wachtel, 1966). A 1977 review (U.S. Commission on Civil Rights, 1977) shows age discrimination in federal retraining and reemployment programs. The only factor slightly more important than age is education (but most older workers also have little education). Older workers are less successful in finding new jobs, and they receive lower wages when they do, even though there are no age differences in the numbers applying to employment services (Sheppard & Belitsky, 1966). It may take many years before new legislation removes these more subtle age-discrimination situations.

Periods of unemployment grow increasingly longer with age. Older workers who are unemployed must compete with younger job seekers and face bias on the part of employment agencies as well as on the part of employers. Education makes no difference in the reemployment of older manual workers (Wilcock & Franke, 1963; Sheppard & Belitsky, 1966). Neither does skill. Age cancels ability, in the eyes of most employers.

Sheppard and Belitsky (*The Job Hunt*, 1966) studied 309 male blue-collar workers looking for jobs. Older workers waited longer than younger ones in starting their job hunts and used fewer job-seeking techniques. But, even if they used as many techniques and started as soon as younger workers, their job-finding success was lower. They were referred to fewer jobs by the employment service, and they got fewer jobs of those they were referred to. And only 10% of people age 45 and over are included in retraining programs, although 25% of the unemployed are in this age group.

Racial inequality has been so long taken for granted, and its effects have been so pervasive in our country, that, in spite of affirmative-action legislation, several generations may pass before it can disappear. Employment figures still show racial differences in rates of unemployment, and wage differentials are probably comparable. Whether the new cohort of young advantaged Blacks is the first wave of a sweeping tide or a short-lived historical event cannot be judged. As this cohort ages, will others follow in its footsteps? Will this be a watershed era in race bias in the United States? Can we even be sure that this cohort will maintain its advantage throughout its lifetime? Certainly wage improvements have affected Black men much more than Black women. Among Black couples in which both husband and wife are employed, the husbands earn more than their wives for the same kind of work just as with White couples.

The career ladder

At the beginning of this chapter, jobs, as discrete units, were distinguished from careers, as interconnected or interrelated work experiences over time. This section deals with the career sequence.

DEVELOPMENTAL SEQUENCES

Some theorists feel that the process of socialization for careers follows a necessary sequence. For example, Ginzberg and his associates (Ginzberg, Ginsberg, Axelrod, & Herna, 1951) say that occupational choices shift from being based on fantasy between ages 6 and 16 to becoming more realistic at 17 or 18.

Super (1957) offers a five-stage developmental sequence for occupational orientation, starting in adolescence:

1. *Crystallization* (ages 14 to 18): emergence of awareness about career choices
2. *Specification* (ages 18 to 21): onset of job training
3. *Implementation* (ages 21 to 24): entry-level position
4. *Stabilization* (ages 25 to 33): establishment in a field
5. *Consolidation* (ages 35 on): reweaving and embellishment of vocational direction

In adulthood, says Osipow (1972), vocational selections are more a matter of rejecting some of the alternatives considered earlier than of coming up with totally new ones.

Choices and options. People differ greatly in the ways they come to their occupations (Veroff & Feld, 1970). Some are forced into the job market long before they finish high school or have enough education or training for the work they would like to do. Others apparently stumble into the job market, unconcerned about preparation, either because they don't understand how important preparation is or because they consider it irrelevant to success in life. Still others plan their careers very carefully and persist in acquiring the necessary education and preparation in the face of economic hardship. In general, the higher the social status of the families they come from, the more people are able to and likely to plan careers, or at least the general outlines of careers.

Entry into the work world has become increasingly difficult over the past few generations, partly because there are more types of jobs from which to choose and less information about each job on which to base a choice. Because of the increasingly complex nature of many jobs, training has also become longer and more expensive. Our society tends to believe that freedom of choice is important. Therefore, adolescents feel great responsibility for choosing well. The consequences can be serious: one's options can be many or few, depending on the state of the economy and one's position in it. During economic depressions, even the most elaborately trained workers are lucky to find any jobs. And even in times of economic abundance, many untrained people, such as young Black men and those with outdated skills, have no choice. There is no meaning in vocational choice unless there is a range of available jobs.

Vocational psychologists such as Holland (1973) stress the matching of personality characteristics to characteristics of the job under consideration. Such matching is seen to be a conscious activity prior to job search that is best assisted by vocational counselors trained in the use of a variety of techniques for assessing personality as well as job characteristics. In Holland's scheme, this kind of conscious matching is seen as appropriate throughout adult life, because both workers themselves and job requirements change constantly.

Becoming a worker: Prejob development.
The foundations of occupational development are laid down long before adulthood. Before people start thinking about a choice of vocation, they have a well-established orientation toward the importance of work in life, know the general kind of work they should aspire to, and have rehearsed the way they should behave as workers. Furthermore, social class, ethnic background, and school experiences all have profound influence on the options available in the job market. Some positions require such specific training that they can be filled only by people

from particular schools or firms, to which access is regulated. Some jobs are filled only from the lower ranks within an organization, others only from outside an organization. Obviously, people cannot even consider a job unless they know of its existence, and this knowledge may be restricted, as pointed out in the earlier section on bias.

Job preparation and training proceed on many levels. In a broad sense, the whole educational progression from kindergarten on is a process of vocational selection and training—and not only for middle-class occupations. University curricula are broadening to include specific training for a variety of careers whose preparation was once handled in technical schools or on the job. Many of these new programs train people for occupations that did not exist a few years ago.

JOB INITIATION

Not all job selection and training can precede entry into the job world. Even though Hill and his associates (1970) found that men who follow their fathers' and grandfathers' occupation are more likely to succeed, the family can be of only minimum help in training because children don't always enter the same occupation as their parents—in part because social change often makes the parents' occupation obsolete. The school cannot help completely because, in many cases, occupational choice or job availability is not determined until the end of schooling. There may also be a lag between training programs and job-market changes. Therefore, the first years in the labor force are typically a time of trial and error for the new worker.

The first year on the job can be seen as a critical period. In some ways, it is a period of initiation, accompanied by fears about competence and self-worth and by the use of such coping strategies as rehearsal and strict adherence to rules (Becker, 1964).

MOVING ALONG

After a man gets a job, he has to keep it or, even better, get ahead in it. This kind of development may depend on all kinds of informal and subtle in-service training (Becker & Strauss, 1956). Coworkers already on the job may teach new workers some of their trade secrets, but not until they feel the new men can be included in their group. Superiors may serve as sponsors or mentors and may arrange for certain kinds of experiences that will train for what they know will be the next step ahead—a step that they may, in fact, maneuver at the appropriate time.

Kanter (1977) refers to "fast trackers"—men who are marked out almost at the beginning of their careers for rapid advancement. The opposite are "dead-enders." Career men learn what is considered the right amount of time to stay at one level and learn how to grasp opportunities as they arise.

Because the work group is important to how men feel about their jobs—and because people's careers are interdependent—awkward and delicate situations occur when subordinates or colleagues move ahead. Different people can be important at different stages of a career. At one point, age mates are crucial, even if only as competitors. At another time, it is superiors who are most important. Because men who fail usually disappear from the scene, the longer men

remain in jobs, the more likely they are to interact only with those who are also succeeding. One effect of length of stay on a job is the formation of a strong and cohesive job culture. In fact, loyalty to such a group can work against job mobility.

When Elder (1974) analyzed the factors that led to occupational status of the men who had gone through the Depression in their adolescence, the most important contributor was access to higher education. Although the most successful members of that cohort were higher in IQ and family status than the less successful, these factors were important primarily because they contributed to educational opportunities. Figure 12.3 diagrams the contributions of the various factors: family status in 1929 (pre-Depression), IQ, achievement motivation, and educational attainment in job status. The numbers show the relative importance of these factors in leading to occupational status. Notice that the various factors affect each other as well as occupation. Educational attainment (X_4) has a path

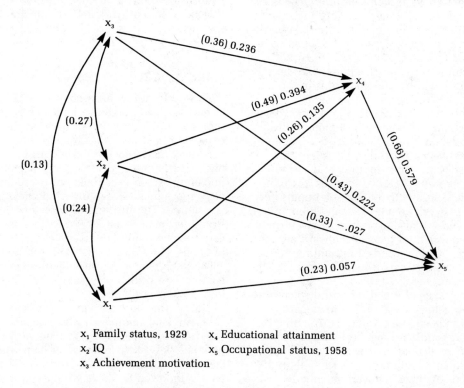

x_1 Family status, 1929 x_4 Educational attainment
x_2 IQ x_5 Occupational status, 1958
x_3 Achievement motivation

Figure 12.3. Paths relating occupational and educational status in adulthood to achievement motivation, IQ, and class origin (1929). *(Source: Elder, 1974.)*

coefficient of .66 toward occupational status and is thus a more important influence than achievement motivation (X_3), whose path coefficient is .43, and IQ (X_2), whose path coefficient is .33. Bray (personal communication, 1978) also had found that education was important to the success of AT&T managers, some of whom had started out as college graduates and others been promoted on the job.

Kanter (1977) lists three ways in which opportunity can be blocked to produce "dead-enders": being in low-ceiling occupations, failing to reach the high ceiling possible, and taking the wrong route to a high-ceiling job because of poor background. These three ways, she feels, have different consequences for the attitudes of the workers involved. Men in the low-ceiling occupation, because they don't expect to be able to climb, are not generally disaffected and usually turn to other sources of enjoyment in working, such as association with colleagues. Individuals who fail feel very badly and turn for their social life to people outside their organization, who may not know of their job failure. Those who have taken the wrong route are intermediate in disaffection. They tend to turn to subordinates or less advantaged people for social companionship. The job orientations of men with low opportunity structure are much like those of women. More will be said about this in the next chapter.

Great opportunity, states Kanter, breeds competitiveness, an instrumental orientation toward personal relationships—"using friends"—and being excessively absorbed in work. All these characteristics are noted by Bray and Howard (1978) in successful AT&T executives. Incidentally, Kanter suggests that too much opportunity, therefore, may run counter to many human and humane values. It also turns people away from intrinsic enjoyment of their jobs toward an emphasis on extrinsic rewards, thus ending up making the most successful people more like the least successful in job attitudes.

The importance of social skills and social interaction in getting ahead in the managerial world is documented by Kanter (1977). She notes that research in England found that executives spent 80% of their work time talking and that Robert Dubin found that less than a quarter of this talking involved making decisions. Corporations demand from their executives a personal attachment and a generalized,

diffuse, unlimited commitment that extend way beyond stated working hours and that include entertaining and being entertained at home as well as outside the home. A survey of sales managers showed that they placed loyalty highest of all their job strengths, much higher than ambition. Frequent geographic transfers that cut down on personal ties and commitments just served to increase such diffuse company loyalty.

An interesting example of transformational job development is described by Henry, Sims, and Spray (1971) in a study of mental-health professionals—psychiatrists, social workers, and clinical psychologists. At some time during their training years and subsequent therapeutic work, they underwent marked changes that turned them all into psychotherapists. This led them to share beliefs and ways of behaving and to share a common ideology that superseded the beliefs of any specific school of psychological thought. Although they started out with very different educational backgrounds, they ended up similar in their use of work and leisure time, in their patterns of interests at work, in their social interactions both at work and at home, in their systems of belief and explanations of behavior, and in the kinds of people they met as patients.

RETRAINING AND SECOND CAREERS

The world of the job is constantly changing. Occupations and organizations change in structure and in the direction of their activities. They expand or contract. Old functions and positions disappear, and new ones arise. An individual once clearly destined for a particular position finds no position or a choice of two new ones. New specialties emerge for which new training is required. The Institute of Directors in Great Britain estimated that 2000 directors and managers became redundant each year as the result of mergers and dismissals (Belbin & Belbin, 1968). Such people find it difficult to get new employment if their experience has been geared to particular positions.

Considering the consequences of technological change for manpower obsolescence, there are two possibilities for displaced workers. One path is followed by many older men who reclassify themselves as early retirees. The other path is followed by those who prepare for new careers. So far, our socialization does not prepare people to think of a lifetime of multiple careers, although Toffler (1970) thinks we should be moving in this direction. For one thing, there are institutional obstacles, such as pension plans, seniority rules, and early-retirement programs, that militate against making any kind of change if one doesn't have to. When Sheppard and Belitsky (1966) interviewed 140 workers in Pennsylvania, only 49 (35%) were interested in second careers. Belbin and Belbin (1968) found that most adults they tried to recruit avoided entering retraining programs. They were more willing to accept job downgrading than to train for new jobs. When a group of 115 recently unemployed middle-aged managers and engineers in Los Angeles were interviewed (Dyer, 1972), most were not interested in new careers, although half did consider using their current skills in self-employment.

People who are interested in retraining and career change differ from those who are not. They tend to be more interested in the social-psychological characteristics of jobs. They also tend to have higher achievement motivation combined with lower perceived mobility chances and lower job satisfaction (Sheppard & Belitsky, 1966). That is, they want to get ahead or do good work, but they don't see any chance of doing so where they are.

Community colleges have boomed across the nation in response to the demands of less skilled men and women for improving their employment opportunities. In 1920, only 1% of students in higher education were enrolled in junior or community colleges; in 1965, 15% were (Tickton, 1968). Most were studying job-related subjects. More people over age 25 are now going to college altogether. The percentage of college students who are over 25 rose from 28% in 1972 to 36% in 1977. The increase is particularly noticeable for women.

Multiple careers may be related to personal development and creativity if they include opportunities for acquiring new perspectives. It may be that there is an optimal duration for any one pursuit. After 15 years, for instance, a person may have "drawn out" all the "juice" from one activity but may start a whole new cycle of creativity by shifting to a different arena. Some

of the dramatic productivity of women in recent years who have returned to careers after a period spent in child rearing suggests that regular switching of arenas of achievement may encourage cognitive and creative development in many people.

Summary

Individual development in thinking, creativity, and skills is contrasted with occupational development measured in terms of money, status, or recognition. Development in any of these senses is contingent on economic and social conditions that affect opportunity and choices. Even among the privileged executives studied by Bray and Howard, luck at the beginning of their work history determined future success. Because education is an important precursor of job success, any systematic discrimination, such as by age, sex, or ethnic group, that bars access to job opportunities at any point along the way, from school experience to knowledge about jobs to acceptance on the job, limits job development.

Jobs affect almost all aspects of lives. During the adult years, there is progressive decrease in job mobility and progressive increase in stated job satisfaction, although these two variables are not in themselves correlated. People either look for and find the kind of job to which they are best suited and thus become more satisfied, or make the best of the situation they find and look for satisfaction from other arenas in their life, such as friends, nonjob pursuits, and family. Achievement motivation, however measured, is related to job satisfaction and also to job mobility, because men who are highly achievement oriented tend to look for jobs that allow them to express this need, including entering retraining programs or going back to school.

Other personality variables also seem related to job behavior, in that shifts in jobs stay within a personality category. Finally, there is a marked tendency for men to follow the same job categories as their fathers; when they do, they tend to be more "successful."

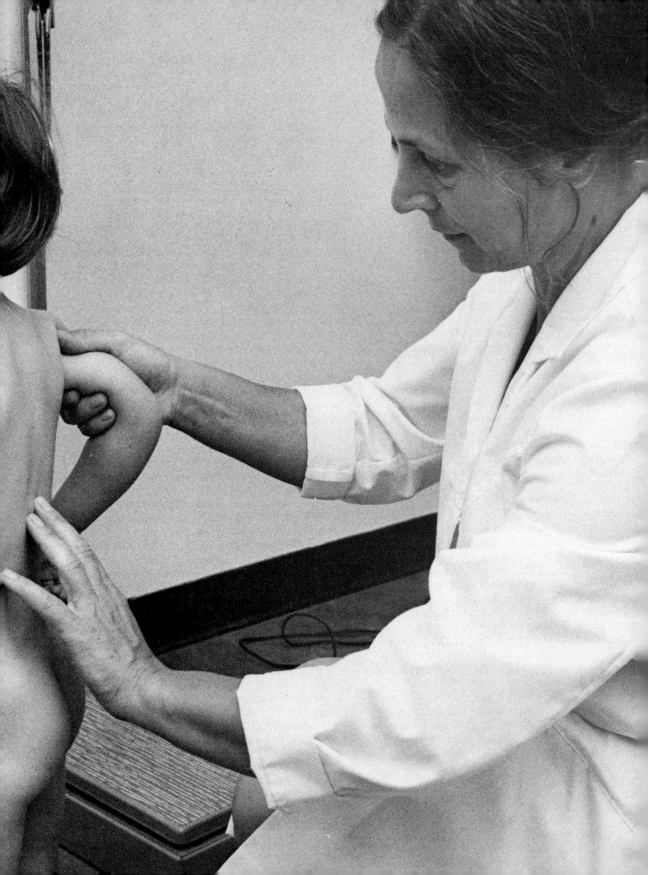

13

Work and Achievement of Women

Although some see women's employment as a remarkable, new event, it is not. Women have always worked. As the old proverb says, "A woman's work is never done." Women have also worked outside their homes. In fact, in the early years of the Industrial Revolution, whole families worked together in factories—husbands, wives, and children of all ages. Migrant worker families today still work together, in the fields. One of the first acts of the 19th-century enlightenment movement was to protect children from the exploitation of such work, which led in turn to the privatization of the home and the seclusion of women from what came to be considered the men's world of work. Later, other legislation, protecting women who had to work, also turned into rules to keep women out of "men's jobs" as much as possible. Social policy meant to correct one evil can thus be said to create new evils. The significance of women's employment during the 1960s and 1970s was its new meaning, not its new existence.

Labor-force participation

During the second half of the 19th century, few married women in the United States worked outside their homes. In 1893, only 5% did so, and these were mainly from the slum districts—Blacks and immigrants. Between 1900 and 1969, this percentage more than doubled—from 20% to 42% of the adult female population (Sheppard, 1971). By 1974, it was 45%.

In 1948, although it was customary for unmarried women to have jobs, only 22% of married women did. Less than a generation later, in 1969, nearly 40% of married women had jobs, and the percentage of married women employed exceeded for the first time that of widowed, separated, or divorced women. The needs of World War II brought many married women into the factories and offices, but this was only temporary. After the war, it was again considered inappropriate for them to work outside their homes unless their families needed the money. Three million women left the labor force in the two years between April 1945 and April 1947 (U.S. Department of Labor, Women's Bureau, 1969a). It was a teacher shortage, caused by the growing number of children in the population—the "baby boom"—that drew back to work married women who could teach (Helson, 1972); others followed rapidly. Table 13.1 presents the sex distributions for 1968, 1973, and 1978.

Hill and his associates (1970) report that women who became adults about the turn of the

TABLE 13.1 Changes in labor-force participation rates by sex

	1968	1973	1978
Men	80	79	78
Women	42	45	50

Source: U.S. Department of Labor, Bureau of Labor Statistics, 1979.

century—the grandparent generation in the Minneapolis study—had few opportunities for employment except for home-based industries. Also, they were kept busy as wives and mothers for a longer period of their lives. Not until after child rearing—which came later than it did for their children's generation—did as many as 20% of this generation hold jobs outside their homes. In contrast, 20% of the next generation of women were in the labor force when they married. Although about half of them dropped out for childbearing, they returned to work in about five years and stayed there for at least a decade. Half of the married women in this middle generation were working again after their children left home, but this proportion gradually dropped off to 30% about ten years later. Over 60% of the wives in the third generation, who were young adults at the time of the study, began marriage while working. Although some left the labor market for a few years to have children, not all did, and those who left did not stay home very long. Four years after the wives in the third generation were married, almost 40% were working.

Of the more than 25 million women who worked at some time in 1967, 74% worked full time. These were mostly younger women (20 to 24 years old) and those between 45 and 64. Table 13.2 presents the dramatic changes between 1940 and 1976. The two peak ages more than doubled in these 36 years, and all ages doubled in labor-force participation during the period.

These increases in women's employment are attributable to a combination of demographic, economic, and social developments. For example, the ratio of women to men increased. An increasingly service-dominated urban economy made physical strength no longer a significant factor in job performance. Homemaking became easier, marriage occurred earlier (although this trend has probably reversed), childbearing occurred earlier, and fewer children were born to each couple.

Some women who are about to retire or who have already retired have worked all their adult lives at full-time jobs. These women have generally had the same anxieties and financial pressures as their male counterparts. For example, a study of workers in a garment factory in Bayonne, New Jersey, found that 61% were 50 or older and had worked in the same factory

TABLE 13.2 Percentage of the female population in the labor force, by age and year of employment

		Year			
Age	*1976*[a]	*1970*[b]	*1960*	*1950*	*1940*
16+	54.5	41.6	35.7	29.9	26.9
16–19	59.1	35.3	32.7	31.1	26.9
20–21	75.8	55.9	48.3	46.1	47.8
22–24		56.5	42.6	41.0	44.0
25–29	66.1	45.7	35.0	32.6	35.5
30–34		44.6	35.5	31.0	30.9
35–39	64.7	48.7	40.1	33.8	28.3
40–44		52.4	45.3	36.4	26.0
45–49	60.7	53.3	47.4	34.8	23.7
50–54		52.4	45.9	30.8	21.2
55–59	52.6	47.6	39.7	25.9	18.5
60–64	40.6	36.4	29.4	20.6	14.8
65–69	20.7	17.2	16.5	13.0	9.5
70–74	6.8	9.1	9.6	6.4	5.1
75+		4.7	4.3	2.6	2.3
45+	38.8	34.8	31.5	22.6	16.4

[a] Data for 1976 are from Special Labor Force Report 201, "Work Experience of the Population in 1976," Bureau of Labor Statistics.

[b] Data for 1940 to 1970 are from 1970 U.S. Census, Subject Report, "Employment Status and Work Experience."

Source: Fischer, Carlton-Ford, and Briles, 1979.

since their youth (Goodman, 1978). Their greatest concern was that the factory might close, and they felt the most important function of government was to provide jobs.

Both income (husband's) and education are related to women's employment. In 1969, most working wives had husbands whose incomes were between $5000 and $7000 (U.S. Department of Labor, Women's Bureau, 1969a). A smaller percentage of wives of poor men (income under $3000) held jobs outside the home. Few wives of very rich men did. Yet the more a woman is likely to earn, the more likely she is to be employed (Fischer et al., 1979). Not surprisingly, the longer a woman is employed and the more satisfaction she gets from her job, the more committed she is to it (Haller & Rosenmayr, 1971). Daughters of women who had been employed during their youth are more likely to work and also to combine jobs and families. Although, as a general rule, men are most likely to encourage traditional femininity in their daughters, high-status fathers tend to encourage achievement, particularly for oldest girls or when there are no sons (Hoffman, 1974).

Another way to visualize the age patterning of

women's work today is illustrated in Figure 13.1. Men show a much more regular pattern than women. They also clearly have a much higher percentage in the labor force. Women's participation shows a bimodal curve. After a peak in the 20s, women's participation rates drop for almost a decade and then rise again to the same level as before in their mid-40s.

The more education a woman has, the more likely she is to have a job outside the home. In 1948, when 42% of all women were in the labor force, 71% of women with five years of college and 48% of women with only high school education were employed, as compared with only 30% of those who did not go beyond the eighth grade. An interesting finding from a longitudinal study of employed women between 30 and 44 is that their wages are more predictable from

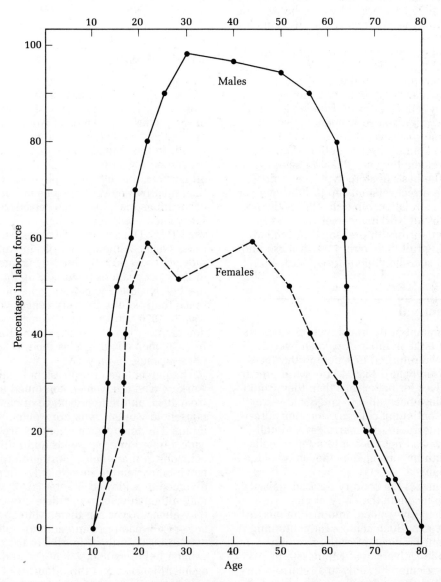

Figure 13.1. Labor-force participation rates by age (United States, 1970). *(Source: Atchley, 1977, after U.S. Department of Commerce, Bureau of the Census, 1973.)*

their educational level, occupational status, and work experience than are those of men (Parnes, Shea, Spitz, Zeller, & Associates, 1970). In other words, they are more likely to be paid strictly by the rules than are men.

Some women hold jobs for the first time in middle age. Others return to jobs similar to those they held before or during their early years of marriage. In 1966, the U.S. Labor Department forecast that by 1980 at least 60% of all women 45 to 54 years old would be working. This peak was reached two years earlier than predicted.

In spite of all this, women are the first to be laid off, and they find it far more difficult to get new jobs than do men in the same situation. They also average only half the number of years on any job. One-third of unemployed workers are middle-aged women, mainly in lower income brackets (Sheppard, 1971). A more subtle kind of discrimination affects professional women: they are likely to be assigned to jobs on the basis of stereotyped sex roles.

Age has a direct relationship to full-time work because of its relationship to health. Although about half of all working women 45 to 64 reported that their health prevented or limited their working full time, only 11% of those under 45 reported such limitations (Sheppard, 1971).

Back to school

One concomitant of the revolution in women's work is the large number of women over 25 years old who returned to school in the 1960s and 1970s (see Figure 13.2). Many were preparing themselves for better jobs than they would otherwise have been able to get. Some were starting or continuing college educations prevented or interrupted by marriages and children. Others had not been interested in college in their youth but changed as they grew older— or times changed.

Colleges across the country devised special programs to facilitate the entry of older students, particularly women, into institutions designed for youth. Such centers for continuing education mushroomed after the first one opened at the University of Minnesota in 1955. They were oriented not only to a return to formal education or jobs but also to a search for new identities. Many women felt their return to

the labor force was a new start on life, bringing with it sharp discontinuities in manner of daily living and in ways of relating to husband, children, parents, and neighbors.

Of course, the rise in employment among 40-year-old women may be as much a historical change as an age change. Perhaps the "returning woman" just happened to be 40 at a point in time when it became customary for women to go back to work and when jobs became available.

Kinds of work

Although the figures just quoted show an impressive number and proportion of American women working, they do not show another side of the picture—the kinds of work and the kinds of prestige and status women have in the job world. In the United States in 1966, women accounted for only .5% of all engineers, 3% of all lawyers, and 6% of all physicians. In addition, men had moved into jobs in a number of occupations that were once considered "safe" for women—teaching, library work, and social work (U.S. Department of Labor, Women's Bureau, 1969a). Although the rise in women's employment was accompanied by greater variety in their occupations (Figure 13.3), the high-status, highly skilled jobs were more out of their reach than before. In every census year from 1900 to 1970, most working women were in predominantly "female" occupations (Kanter, 1977). In 1970, men could be classified in 63 occupations; women, in only 17.

The percentage of professional and technical workers who are women continued to go down from 1940, and the percentage of clerical and household workers who are women went steadily up. The few women scientists are apt to be concentrated in a few fields and in the lower echelons of these fields. Furthermore, women move into scientific careers only after becoming divorced or widowed. Kanter (1977) points out that, although women populate corporations, they almost never run them. Men constitute 96% of all managers and administrators earning over $15,000. In three-fourths of the companies, women hold less than 2% of the middle-management jobs, and in three-fourths of the companies they hold none of the top-management jobs.

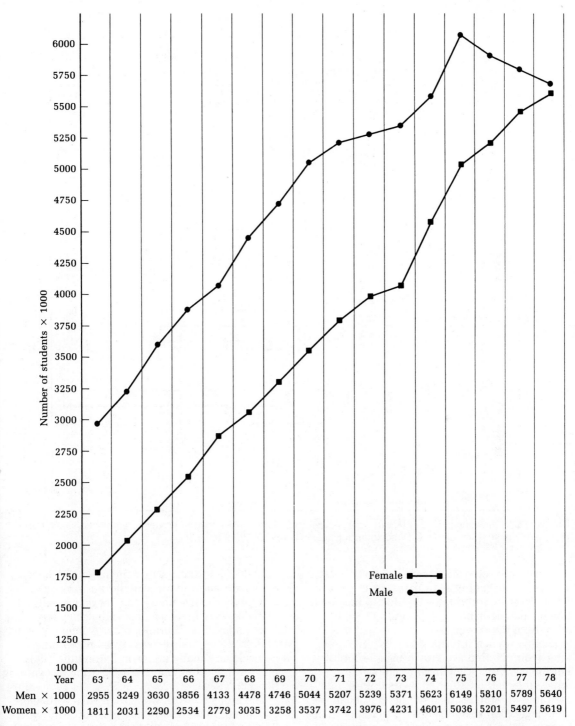

Year	63	64	65	66	67	68	69	70	71	72	73	74	75	76	77	78
Men × 1000	2955	3249	3630	3856	4133	4478	4746	5044	5207	5239	5371	5623	6149	5810	5789	5640
Women × 1000	1811	2031	2290	2534	2779	3035	3258	3537	3742	3976	4231	4601	5036	5201	5497	5619

Figure 13.2.   More people over 25 are going to college.   *(Source: U.S. Department of Health, Education, and Welfare, National Center for Education Statistics, 1980.)*

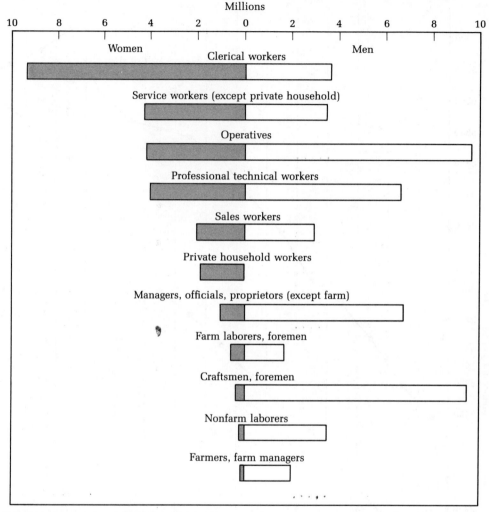

Figure 13.3.   Seven out of ten clerical workers are women (major occupation groups of employed women and men, April 1968). *(Source: U.S. Department of Labor, Women's Bureau, 1969a.)*

Women are secretaries, men are their bosses, and the occasional woman manager is just a token. Women are usually shunted to the "emotional," people-handling jobs and are kept far away from the power.

Finally, women returning to jobs and careers after their children are grown usually find it hard to catch up. They have to go back to where they left off 10 or 15 years before; the men in their cohorts, meanwhile, had been developing expertise and status all that time. Thus women go back to the level of a younger age cohort, their skills are rusty, their information

outdated, and their status anomalous. Women of a younger age cohort, who did not "drop out" for family involvement, may not be as well along as their male age mates, but they too overshadow the returning older women. Nevertheless, many middle-aged women continue to go back, and many are even finding the challenge exhilarating enough to fight for recognition and rewards.

The kinds of work women do vary with age, education, race, where they grew up, and where they live (Sheppard, 1971). For instance, White women have more white-collar jobs than do

Black women. They are also likely to earn more, although this depends on city size and age. Young Black women in big cities are less likely to be domestics than are older Black women or younger Black women in small cities. Only in large cities did Black women earn more than $2000 in 1966. There are complex interrelated effects of the variables of city size, age, and race. Generally, older women seem to be more polarized in income and job status than younger women, regardless of the size of their city and their race. Older women who are not top earners are likely to be at the bottom of the range, and they are not spread as evenly over the income range as are younger women. However, even those women who are top earners are not likely to earn as much as average-earning men.

It is remarkable that the burgeoning numbers of married women in the labor force during the 1950s and 1960s went almost unnoticed, both by the women themselves and by (male) commentators. Such is the power of normative expectations! Even in the late 1960s, with a near-majority of married women aged 35–54 in the labor force, employed married women regarded themselves as deviant. Professional women who worked and college women who wanted careers were considered pathological. Only after 1970 were women's career motivations seen as positive (Astin, 1976; Helson, 1972; Sedney & Turner, 1975).

Bernard (1975) suggests that "when a pattern becomes modal it tends to become normative, even coercive" and that the "tipping point" for labor-force participation of married women with school-age children (women aged 35–54) occurred in 1972. In 1974, when 59% of wives with college degrees were in the labor force (Haghe, 1977), it was not only no longer deviant for them to hold jobs, but was the right thing for them to do.

It is worth noting that the labor-force participation rates of White women now approximate the rates of Black women, which have historically always been high. Only a decade ago, Black and poor women were expected to work—and did. Now both Black and White women work (Turner & McCaffrey, 1974). By 1990, labor-force participation may be normatively prescribed as part of the wife/mother role constellation. The particularly swift increase in labor-force participation among mothers of pre-schoolers—from 13% in 1960 to 33% in 1970 to 37% in 1974—highlights the changing expectations. Child-rearing norms, buttressed by lack of child-care facilities, still proscribe employment for this group. But these norms are very likely in the process of changing too.

Job orientation

Most studies report sex differences in general orientation to work. Women are seen to be more interested than men in the interpersonal and extrinsic factors of jobs and less interested than men in the status and achievement factors. They are less inclined than men to say that they would continue to work if they were freed from economic necessity; only 57% of the women would work if they did not have to, but 75% of the men would (Crowley, Levitin, & Quinn, 1973).

In the Lowenthal, Thurnher, and Chiriboga study (1975), the working women (lower-middle class) were not highly committed to their work. Getting jobs was for them secondary to their primary activities as wives, mothers, and homemakers. Lillian Rubin (1976) found the same thing when she interviewed working-class women. These women were satisfied with financial rewards that were lower than those of men, because they were just adding to their husbands' income in order to maintain their families' lifestyles. They said they would pass up chances for advancement if it meant increased obligations that would drain their energies and leave less for their family roles. They never really tried to succeed in their jobs, and retirement did not have the significance for them that it had for men in the sample. However, remember that these women were part-time, often temporary workers. Those middle-aged women in the same study who had worked steadily for years said that their work *was* important to them. In fact, they had a feeling it was more important than it should be.

Are women working because they need money or because they are lonely? Are they more concerned about interpersonal relationships than accomplishments? From their survey of the literature, Stein and Bailey (1973) conclude that, in fact, women are as motivated as men to achieve, but that the areas in which they achieve are different. They have a more social

---

Tell me something about your work.

Grandmother, age 74
I like to sew, quilt, knit, crochet, gather dried things for arrangements. Just to have them around, I guess, and to be busy. I don't like to loaf around. I don't like to cook very well, and I don't like to iron. Just put them off and don't interest me as much.

Mother, age 47
I like my job—secretarial work. That's what I always wanted to do when I was young. I like to sew—make clothes for myself and my daughter—and to cook. I like to see the end result and create things; I like to do my work because it's a challenge. I like to redecorate my house and finish things. I don't like housework. Not only it's monotonous, but it's a waste of time; next week you have to do it all over again. Same with washing dishes. I hate to clean out closets and cupboards, because it doesn't really show that it's been done; the door is closed.

Daughter, age 20
I like to create things. I like to sew, cook, paint, read, go horseback riding and camping. Sports that you can do alone. I like them because they're the things that don't bore me, and they make me feel like I've accomplished something. I don't like housecleaning or creative things—painting or drawing—when there are no new ideas yet. I don't like work in general, unless I have to or unless it's something special, something I really enjoy. I would rather spend my time doing things I like.

---

pattern of achievement behavior than do men. Furthermore, the reason they direct their achievement behavior to a social area is that they receive more social approval for doing so than do men. They also receive less censure than if they try to achieve in areas that are classified as masculine.

College-educated women (Eyde, 1968) studied over a five-year period showed not only stability of motive but also reasons other than money for working. Gifted women first studied as children by Lewis Terman, when followed over the years, turned out to be much more satisfied with their lives if they had careers (Sears & Sears, 1978).

The effects of age, marital status, and education are perhaps even more important in women's orientation to jobs than in men's. Thus, independence and recognition by others are

valued more by nonmarried, educated, and older women than by married, less educated, and younger women (Bickel, 1968). Interesting activity is most desired by married women, by middle-aged more than by younger women, and by part-time workers more than by full-time workers. More women who have just started to work outside their homes say that they want interesting jobs than do those who have worked for a long time. Married women are least interested in the economic aspects of working, and so are older and better-educated women.

It would be naive to assume that all women have the same attitude toward working. They do not. Nor do all men. Furthermore, many women may put their work in second place because they feel their job options are limited. In the Crowley et al. (1973) study cited earlier, the reason women may have said that they did not want to be promoted is that they saw no possibility of being promoted. They may have been more interested in the interpersonal surroundings of their jobs because they were more likely to be assigned to person-oriented positions.

Many employed women who work primarily because of financial need wish that they didn't have to—like blue-collar men with "blue-collar blues." Those who got jobs for other reasons— the other half of employed women—are not so likely to want to quit. Furthermore, Sobol (1963) found that, although 48% of working wives he interviewed said that they worked because their families needed money, there was no significant relationship between their work commitments and their husbands' current incomes, their own incomes, or their future work plans. Instead, the factors related to their work commitments were, in order: need for accomplishment, meeting people or occupying time, helping in family businesses, acquiring income, and acquiring assets. Like men, those who worked because they wanted to "accomplish something" tended to have more education than the others and also better jobs and younger children. The "needing-money" group had the least education and the lowest-status jobs.

Hoffman (1963) reports that the first answer a woman gives when asked why she works is usually "money." But if she is asked to elaborate she adds "boredom," "insufficient work at home," or being "nervous" at home—or she mentions good things about her job. In fact, says Hoffman, industrial psychologists know that inarticulate and unacceptable frustrations and desires of workers are expressed overtly in terms of wage demands, although money may not be the core problem.

In the last chapter, we referred to Elder's (1974) study of men who had been economically deprived during their adolescence in the Depression. Let us now look at the women of that cohort. Like the men, they had grown up fast, started work early in their teens, and shown more dependability and industriousness than women who had come from families that experienced less deprivation. Instead of going to college after the war when affluence and the GI Bill enabled the men to make up for lost educational opportunity, however, the women generally continued to work to put their husbands through school and then went home to have babies. They shared the "feminine mystique" ideology of most women who were adults during the 1950s. Betty Friedan's book *The Feminine Mystique* (1963) could have used them as its basis. Although four-fifths were working until 1945, more than half were out of the labor market ten years later. When asked to rank their preferred activities, they overwhelmingly listed family activities first (Figure 13.4). This pattern was characteristic of even the most active women, as well as of those who were not happy in their marriages. Compare this picture

with that of the men shown in Table 12.1, and with a later survey by Yankelovich shown in Figure 12.2, also for men.

A substantial number of those women who responded so predominantly in favor of the priority of family commitments were already employed. Others were planning to go back to work. Those women who put work first had the most education and the most job experience. They may have been, then, the luckiest in terms of getting what they wanted from their jobs. The others, like the less successful AT&T executives, turned to—or stuck with—nonjob pursuits for personal satisfaction. Interestingly, husbands' status was not relevant to the women's plans. Those who had been most deprived in youth and who had assumed large family and household responsibilities during the Depression to help their working mothers were least likely to be oriented toward working themselves. Their past experience had clearly not encouraged them to think of working as challenging or fulfilling.

A different study found that women who chose not to marry in early adulthood became more invested in their careers. A follow-up study of college students 12 years later found that those who were committed to careers after 12 years had married later, had fewer children, and completed more years of education (Harmon, 1970).

Fogarty, Rapoport, and Rapoport (1971) make an interesting suggestion with regard to attractiveness and women's careers. They refer to Alice Rossi's findings (personal communication, 1966) that short, fat girls were more likely to consider themselves unattractive, less likely to marry, and therefore more likely to pursue careers than were their taller, thinner peers. Attractive girls may be secure enough in their heterosexual relationships to be able to devote major attention to work tasks—particularly during the courting phase of development. Other factors may operate to favor attractive women later on in their careers, too, such as more support from male superiors. Judith Bardwick (1971) refers to the contingent nature of women's career success. In a footnote, she notes—like Fogarty and her associates—that women graduate students in psychology achieve much better if they are married, particularly if they are married to men in higher-status occupations than psychology—such as medicine or mathematics.

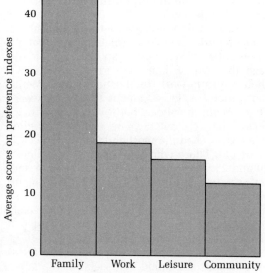

Figure 13.4. Activity preferences of women (*N* = 52). *(Source: Elder, 1974.)*

Attitudes of husbands as well as community facilities such as nursery schools and flexible shopping hours can be important to women's job development. The male helpmate who supports the dedicated professional woman is a rare bird—much rarer than the wife helping her dedicated husband. The fact that their husbands' support is a particularly prominent feature of women's success emerged from the findings of a longitudinal study of older women returning for a graduate degree at the University of Chicago (LeFevre, 1970). Practically all the 35 women studied said their husbands shared their values and supported their decision to return to college. Otherwise, they said, they could not have continued. These women were fortunate. Most mention that there is a direct conflict between their husbands' wishes and the demands of school or jobs. The section on household division of labor, in Chapter 18, discusses this issue further. Turner (1964), however, argues that married women who choose to work leave material ambitions to their husbands and are bipolar in their goals. They intend either just to supplement their husbands' incomes, or, conversely, to look for intrinsic gratifications from their jobs.

Development

Stein and Bailey (1973) point out that sex differences favoring men in achievement motivation and achievement itself begin to emerge in adolescence. Until that time, more boys are underachievers than are girls. After adolescence, boys gradually outstrip girls until by college there is a clear advantage on the men's side.

During high school, girls have much hazier and less realistic future goals for their adult lives than do boys (Douvan & Adelson, 1966). They don't say they want to be housewives, but they name careers too fanciful (such as "movie star") to allow them to be realistic in planning for such careers. Horner (1972) states that, as a woman nears the end of her college career, she may switch to more "feminine" subjects and exhibit signs of "fear of success."

Although boys and girls enter primary school in approximately equal numbers, girls start dropping out in early adolescence. From 14 to 24, there are fewer girls in school than boys of the same age. Since 1900, women are less likely than men to enter college, despite the fact that they are more likely than men to complete secondary school. Look back at Figure 13.2 for a graphic illustration of this sex difference.

Adolescence may accentuate sex-role conflicts in many girls, but longitudinal data (Kagan & Moss, 1962) show that it does not create entirely new patterns. Young women's responses to social expectations in adolescence depend on earlier patterns of achievement-related behavior. In data from the Fels Research longitudinal study, achievement striving in adulthood was highly correlated with observed achievement behavior in middle childhood and early adolescence (Crandall & Battle, 1970; Kagan & Moss, 1962). Some women remain stable in achievement desires, major in "masculine" subjects, and select jobs that are not traditionally feminine. They are *role innovators,* to use Tangri's (1972) term. Significantly, they are more likely to be role innovators if their mothers are too.

Although more women than men obtain master's degrees, few obtain Ph.D.s. This is as true in Great Britain as in the United States (Fogarty et al., 1971). In England, the professions were opened to women during the 1920s, and the number of women in architecture, medicine, government, and so on increased. By the 1950s, a number of women who had come through these doors 30 years before had established themselves as accepted senior practitioners, but there was a drop in new entrants that has continued to this day.

A study of Radcliffe graduates by Baruch (1967) found a significant relationship among the number of years they had been out of college, the level of their motive to achieve, and their return to work. Intellectual achievement motivation was lowest among those who were 10 years out of college, but it was higher for those who were out 15 years, even though the latter group had the most children under 8 years old. Those who had been out of college 20 and 25 years showed a high and stable need for achievement. In fact, those with the highest scores on achievement need had generally returned to work, particularly if their achievement scores on the Thematic Apperception Test (TAT) were centered on female figures.

When Baruch repeated this study with a less elite sample, she found that social class made a great difference among the older women. Older respondents in her broader-based Survey Research Sample showed less need achievement than did younger women—perhaps this is a cohort difference. In fact, one wonders whether present rates will hold up in another 10 years.

Satisfaction

The data on women's life satisfaction as it relates to employment are confused. Huston-Stein and Higgins-Trenk (1978) summarize them as follows. First, employed women are more satisfied with their lives than are housewives. Second, middle-aged career women, whether single or married, have higher self-esteem than homemakers in every domain, even feeling more adequate as mothers. Third, older women with blue-collar jobs and women with more than three children are less satisfied when employed. Fourth, life satisfaction generally remains stable across ages, but employed women's life satisfaction increases with increasing age. And, fifth, employed working-class women have lower marital satisfaction than working-class housewives; middle-class women who are employed have marital satisfaction equal to that of middle-class housewives. Overall, they conclude that the problems associated with combining family and work roles are more a function of role overload than of role conflict. Even when they have as much education as men, women's annual median earnings as full-time workers are only 80% that of men; 95% of working women earned less than the average man (Levitin, Quinn, & Staines, 1971). Yet only 8% reported that they felt discriminated against. They took the inequality for granted.

An Austrian study of satisfaction with work, marriage, and household activities found much more complex processes. Women who worked for intrinsic reasons—because they themselves wanted to—were altogether more satisfied than those who worked in order to help their families (Szinovacz, 1973).

The secretary

The majority of working women are secretaries or clerical workers, and almost all secretaries and clerical workers are women (see Figure 13.3). A secretary is expected to bring the "feminine" aspect of life into an office. Secretaries serve their bosses as they would—and usually do—serve their husbands, and they brighten the corners where they are. But they have little direct power (Kanter, 1977).

Kanter notes that, in the large corporations she studied, secretaries' desks were surrounded by splashes of color: postcards, posters, and cartoons. Managers' (men) desks were supposed to be clear except for the obligatory portrait photographs of wives and children. Secretaries remembered birthdays, made coffee, and looked after the comfort of visitors and bosses. Their derived status was shown by the fact that their ranks depended on the ranks of their bosses, although there was considerably less variation among secretarial ranks. In one corporation studied, 25% of the secretaries had worked for the company over 15 years, but only 12% had held more than three jobs, and over half earned less than $11,000 (1970 standards). They often started out in a secretarial pool, where both dissatisfaction and turnover rates were higher than when they worked for individual bosses. Their routes to any higher positions were almost entirely dependent on the decisions of other people—their supervisors first, and ultimately the men who chose them as their personal secretaries. Kanter tells of one male executive who refused to select a particular woman as his secretary when he found out that her credentials had also been reviewed by another executive. He was incensed that she might be the one to decide between them. No matter what the details of personal relationships are, it is clearly appropriate to label secretaries "office wives."

A prominent issue in women's rights is sexual harassment on the job. Attitudes of men—and many women—on appropriate behavior toward women are so ingrained and pervasive that the cases that surface in the media and the law courts can represent only the tip of the iceberg. Not only are secretaries "office wives," but they are also partly "office mistresses." How many times has an otherwise businesslike man said in passing, "I'll have my girl take care of that." The implications of ownership and gender distinction need be extended only slightly to expectations of direct sexual favors.

Cohort differences are apparent, however. Kanter describes the older secretary as knowing her place, serving with a smile, being willing to be the scapegoat for her boss's mistakes, and not presuming. Young women are more likely to refuse to do "housework" and to participate in defining relationships as they want them to be, even making their jobs more clearly administrative. No matter how "liberated" they may be in these respects, though, they are still dependent on their bosses. If a boss leaves and doesn't take his secretary with him, she has to start all over again, renegotiating a new one-to-one relationship.

A comparison between women and men in the general clerical categories of the company that Kanter studied shows, first, that men have higher expectations of advancement and want to advance and, second, that women have many fewer supports for advancement (Homall, 1974). Table 13.3 shows the unequal number of men and women in the clerical ranks: 88 women to 23 men. Furthermore, the women were largely lower-level clerical workers or junior secretaries—dead-end jobs. The men were accounting clerks—jobs that were on the ladder to management. The men were younger, had worked fewer years, and had already had supervisory experience. In the lower half of the table are shown ratings of amount of encouragement: the higher the number, the more the support. The men had significantly more help in ascending the career ladder than the women had. When they were asked to rate possible outcomes of promotion on desirability and likelihood, the men saw such outcomes as both desirable and likely; the women saw them as desirable but

unlikely. It is no surprise that women, on the whole, were less committed to their jobs than were men. Like the AT&T executives who found themselves at a dead end, most women who work in corporations turn to other sources of gratification—friendships and outside preoccupations.

Because women in large organizations—and small ones, too—do not have explicit power, they can only advance through the help of others, particularly men. Those few women who have made it to top executive positions stressed the essential roles their male sponsors played in their rise (Henning, 1970). Women's relative lack of power as bosses—when they get to be bosses—is associated with their tendency to be rules-minded, authoritarian, nagging, and conservative. The vicious circle is demonstrated by the responses of 1000 men and 900 women executives, one-fifth of whom said, in 1965, that they would feel uncomfortable working for women. And 51% of the men said that women are temperamentally unfit for management positions (Kanter, 1977).

Women who are clerical workers are poorly paid, given few possibilities for advancement, allowed little say in what their work will be—and dissatisfied. A recent study by Suzanne Haynes also found that, while working women as a whole have no higher rate of heart disease than housewives, women employed in clerical and sales occupations do. Their coronary-dis-

TABLE 13.3 Situations reflecting opportunity differences for men and women nonexempt personnel at one company

	Men (N=23)	Women (N=88)	
Proportion under 25 years old	44%	30%	
Proportion with the company less than 5 years	65%	40%	
Proportion who have *ever* held a supervisory position	57%	20%	
Mean rating on scale of 1–9 of			
Amount of encouragement received from superiors to improve	7.62	6.20	$p<.05$
Amount of encouragement received from superiors to advance	7.18	6.32	$p<.05$
Amount of company awareness of one's contributions	7.15	6.10	$p<.05$

Note: Figures reported with the permission of G. Homall (1974).

Source: Kanter, 1977.

ease rates are twice those of other women (Goodman, 1979).

Group differences

The effect of race on women's job orientation has been explored by Turner (1972) with University of Massachusetts students. On the whole, career preferences of Black and White women students are similar, but many more Black women expect to work full time than do White women (54% of Blacks versus 16% of Whites). Tangri (1972) found that University of Michigan students whose mothers had careers were more likely to plan on having careers themselves. Because more Black women than White can be said to hold dual careers, their daughters would be more likely to adopt such a pattern. (The Rapoports, in a 1969 study, use the term *dual career* to describe all women who are responsible for both outside jobs and homes.)

Poor women have long worked away from home—in the homes of others, in factories, in the streets. Therefore, poor families who "better themselves" take pride in the wives' being able to restrict themselves to "feminine" activities. Many working women, as in the Bayonne garment factory studied by Goodman, would not mind staying home. However, men with equivalent monotonous, difficult jobs are also happy to stop working if they have enough money to do something more to their liking. For many traditional men whose mothers had to work during their sons' childhoods, the ability to support wives and raise them to housewife status is an important sign of success. Middle-class families have usually had a different history. Only the educated woman, who is more able than the less-educated to find an interesting, challenging, and rewarding job, can feel superior to "just a housewife."

Conflicts between work and family life

An analysis of the Quality of Employment Survey (Pleck, Staines, & Lang, 1980) shows that one-third of men and women who are currently married and have children under 18 living at home report moderate or severe interference between their job and their family lives. Surprisingly, there are no sex differences in these reports: men report as much conflict as women. The three most common responses are "excessive work time," "schedule conflicts," and "fatigue and irritability." Men report more "excessive work time," though, and women more "schedule conflicts." In an earlier survey, Quinn and his associates (1974) had reported lowest job and marital satisfaction for both men and women when their children are preschoolers.

Weingarten and Daniels (1978) have been examining ways in which couples coordinate work and family roles. They distinguish between sequential and simultaneous patterns. In sequential patterns, women first have children and then work, or first work and then have children. In simultaneous patterns, child rearing and work occur at the same time. The presence of young children while both parents are struggling to establish their separate careers seems to produce the most stress, so that either sequential pattern is easier than a simultaneous one. The study of women executives by Henning (1970) shows the advantages, for women intent on success, of delaying marriage and childbearing. It helps marital relations if the husbands are able to reach a middle level of success before parenting starts. Although most research shows no increase in the men's participation in household work after the birth of children or after the women return to work (Pleck, Staines, & Lang, 1980), at least there may be greater economic security.

Years ago, only single women were career women. This picture has not changed completely, as illustrated in Table 13.4, which presents the number of single, married, widowed, and divorced women in a variety of occupational classifications. By their mid-20s, those women who have not married are likely to be professional women—or, three times as many of them, clerical workers (1 million, compared to almost 3 million). Thus there is a bimodal distribution of working single women, one age group being young and uneducated and the other group being older and better educated (Donelson & Gullahorn, 1977). Other marital categories seem to be more evenly distributed.

Neugarten and Hagestad (1976), in speaking of cohort differences in the timing of role transitions, point out marked changes in the work cycle. "The twentieth century has seen a steady decline in the proportion of men's lives spent in the labor force, with entry into work roles delayed because of prolonged education and with exit accelerated because of a drop in age of retirement. . . . For women there are often two periods in the labor force, one before and one after the early child-rearing years. While in a given calendar year, work-force participation by age forms the shape of an inverted U-curve for men, it forms the shape of an M for women" (p. 47). This M-curve is illustrated in Figure 13.1.

Mothers of preschool children tend to be employed less frequently than mothers of older children, even though the percentage of work-ing mothers has gone up over the years for both groups (see Figure 13.5). Furthermore, mothers of preschool children who do work tend to find their jobs difficult and unsatisfying. Child rearing can be a highly involving experience for most parents. Having to attend to other aspects of life—such as earning a living—can be disturbing, particularly for mothers who have been socialized to expect protection from society (for example, by husbands) at this time and who might to some extent resent working even though they themselves have chosen to do so. Attitudinal change can lag behind behavioral change.

A number of options are thus open to women

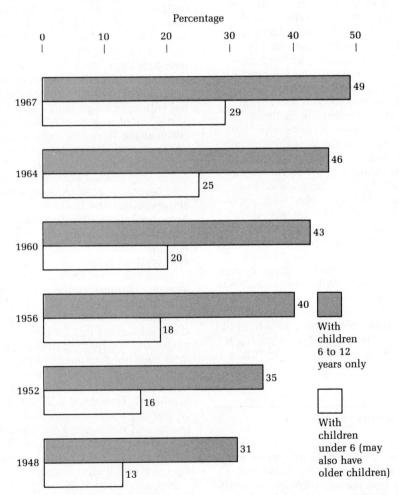

Figure 13.5. Mothers are more likely to work today than ever before (labor-force participation rates of mothers, by age of children, selected years 1948–1967). *(Source: U.S. Department of Labor, Women's Bureau, 1969a.)*

TABLE 13.4 Occupations of employed, single, and married women (percentages)

Major occupational group	Marital status		
	Single	Married, husband present	Other[a]
Professional/technical workers	15.4	16.1	11.6
Managers/administrators	3.2	5.2	6.5
Clerical workers	38.5	34.1	29.1
Sales workers	6.5	7.2	5.6
Operatives	9.5	15.1	14.6
Household/service workers	24.2	18.6	29.1

[a]Widowed, divorced, or separated.
Source: U.S. Department of Labor, Women's Bureau, 1975.

with high achievement motivation. First, they may follow careers that are not "feminine" and not marry. Second, they may marry and have dual careers (both job careers and housewife/mother careers). Third, they may marry and follow serial careers (leave the job for the years of early child rearing and then return). Fourth, they may not start employment until after the early child-rearing years are over. Or they may follow some variation of these options.

However, they may (fifth) pursue "feminine" careers or even (sixth) obtain their achievement gratification vicariously through their husbands' or children's accomplishments. A discussion of women's various modes of achievement appears in Chapter 16. Lipman-Blumen (1972) surveyed about 1000 young, college-educated married women. Most said that their husbands' accomplishments were more gratifying than their own. This attitude was more common for women with traditional roles than for those with more liberated views. Incidentally, on the TAT, women who choose "feminine" occupations are more likely to tell achievement stories in response to pictures of men than in response to pictures of women (Stein & Bailey, 1973). They are primarily oriented toward vicarious gratification, even though they may also hold jobs.

There are other solutions for the femininity-versus-career conflict. Women may see to it that their work remains mediocre or that they do not accept promotions. Or they may adopt what Stein and Bailey call the "superwoman" role, compensating for their achievements by also being superfeminine.

It should be noted that, if a married woman—especially if she has children—becomes em-ployed, she is adding on jobs, not substituting one for another. She usually remains responsible for the care of the home and for the raising of the children, even though she may pay other people to do some of the actual work. The employed man is better able to separate his family and work lives. At least, his family needs do not impinge on his work time, although his job has an important influence on his family's welfare. The employed woman is less able to separate family and work life, and her family needs *do* impinge on her work time.

The topic of household division of labor and sex-role specialization in family life is treated in greater depth in Chapter 18, on couple development. The reader is referred to the discussion there for more details about the home side of the working woman's development.

The housewife

A housewife, according to Helena Lopata (1971), is a woman responsible for running her home, whether or not she does all the work herself. She is customarily married or once was married. The functions and status of housewives have been pushed into prominence by the women's movement, which assumes the desirability of women's moving out of the home into the world of employment, as well as sharing home management with husbands.

Ann Oakley (1974) has labeled the housewife the "invisible woman" as far as research—and social thinking and planning—is concerned. Only two books have come out about the housewife, both published since the 1970s, one British, one American. Yet 85% of all British women are homemakers, and so are almost all American women—whether or not they also work on a job.

In her study of 40 British housewives in their late 20s (20 middle class and 20 working class), Oakley found that they all define housework as labor, just like any work on a *job*. What they valued most about the job of homemaker was the autonomy it provides—the feeling that one is one's own boss. They also said they worked harder than their husbands did and that their work was—as the old adage says—never done. Even if they were visiting or their children were sleeping, they were still *responsible* for their children, in addition to other tasks they performed at such times.

Different kinds of tasks are involved in housekeeping: cleaning, shopping, cooking, dishwashing, clothes washing, and ironing, among others. Ironing was disliked the most because it was the most monotonous. Cooking was considered the best because it was the most creative.

Overall, 70% of the housewives Oakley interviewed were dissatisfied with their job (of housewife). The higher their social class, the more dissatisfied they were. Of the low-social-status women, 62% were dissatisfied with housework, 67% of middle-status women, and 100% of high-status women. They complained not only of monotony but also of loneliness and the low status that being "just a housewife" brings. One of their unstated problems revolved around rewards for their work. Their husbands did not praise them—husbands only commented when something was wrong—nor did other members of their family, although their mothers were the most significant people in defining their attitudes toward and standards for housework. Sometimes the women tried to be like their mothers; sometimes to be the opposite. So they tended to set up standards by which they rated themselves and gave themselves pluses and minuses for meeting their goals. These standards may have served to give them some pride in their work, but the standards also boomeranged by setting up demands and accompanying stresses to meet these demands. In this way, the part of the work the women said they valued most—their autonomy—was effectively canceled out.

Lopata's earlier findings on several large samples of Chicago women in many differing circumstances are not essentially different from Oakley's. One major theme was the dependence of the housewife's whole style of existence on the man she had married. Yet social-class differences in definitions of women's work are surprisingly small. One factor that has helped to equate the colonel's lady and Mrs. O'Grady is the disappearance of servants. Today, middle-class women not only are responsible for most household management and work but also tend to do most of it themselves. The proliferation of mechanical household appliances has been found to affect the arduousness and duration of housework very little. In spite of middle-class ideology that supports husband and wife sharing of household work, middle-class families differ little from more traditional families in what work is actually shared.

The peripheral role of housewives in our society is underlined in their financial status in later years. The plight of the displaced homemaker has been brought to national attention by the women's movement. Women who have been full-time housewives can and often do find themselves abandoned and penniless at the will or whim of their husbands. Most retirement pensions do not automatically provide for widows, and many men select options for greater benefits during their own lives rather than for lesser life benefits with provision for their widows should they die. Such choices are often made without consulting their wives. Not long ago, middle-aged women who had been divorced were not entitled to share their husbands' retirement benefits unless they had been married more than 20 years (and this shift down to 20 years occurred only in 1977). In 1980, however, the number of years of marriage was cut to 10. In spite of media notoriety given to the small percentage of women who receive large amounts of alimony, most divorced women receive none at all—and must support their children by themselves, to boot. A report by the International Woman's Year Commission states that only 14% of divorced women are awarded alimony and only 44% are awarded child support. Fewer than half collect either regularly (Hendy, 1978). If they have no occupational skills other than housewife, if they have young children left to raise, and if they are advanced in age, they are truly disadvantaged.

Efforts to provide a financial base for housewives by such methods as having them employed by men who are their neighbors while the neighbors' wives are in turn employed by their husbands do not change the low economic value placed on such services. Other suggestions have included half shares in the husband's income. So far, none of these suggestions have been implemented legally. If housewives were paid for the highest level of their contributions—for psychological comfort and nurturance—they should be reimbursed at least at the level of a psychiatrist's income.

The corporate wife, a middle-class subspecialty of housewife (Kanter, 1977), is supposed to prove her husband's "normality." She is expected to raise children but not interfere with company activities. She must have social skills for entertaining other company executives and their wives and for being entertained by them. Kanter says that it is often hard to know where such wives fit into the organization, whether to consider them insiders or outsiders. The fact that they are included in retirement-planning sessions underlines this ambiguous position. Some wives are actually directly involved with the organization, some are involved only through their husbands, and others are completely uninvolved. Kanter identifies three phases in the career of a corporate wife:

1. *Technical,* when her husband is premanagement and on the early rungs of the management ladder, and she provides technical assistance or personal support. The technical assistance is fairly menial, such as typing his papers or running errands.
2. *Managerial,* when her husband enters the middle- and upper-management levels and she takes on social, "people-handling" tasks, becoming involved in the informal political structure of the company. She learns such rules as not inviting superiors in rank before they invite you, never turning up at the office, and never appearing too outstanding.
3. *Institutional,* when her husband is at the top of the organization and must represent it to the outside. She becomes a diplomat, an official hostess, and a leader of other company wives.

Summary

Women's employment is not new. For the working-class woman, particularly the Black woman, it has been the accepted way of life, as it has for many single women. What has been shifting over the past century are middle-class attitudes toward employment and the conditions of combining work outside the home with work in the family domain. During the 1970s, over half of American women were in the labor market full time. The age profile of their employment differed from men's in being bimodal rather than an inverted U-shape. The majority of women still tend to withdraw from the labor market during the early years of their children, although more and more mothers of infants and preschool children are now employed.

Changing expectations for and by women that are associated with the women's movement are worked out differently by young and middle-aged women of today. Young women are confronted with a triple choice: (1) remaining unmarried, or at least childless—an old pattern; (2) taking on wifehood, motherhood, and career simultaneously; or (3) taking on wifehood and motherhood first and career later, or career first and motherhood later—a sequential pattern. For most young married women, the result is a dual career, because husbands' sharing of household tasks rarely approaches equality, particularly after the birth of the first child. Middle-aged women of today are more likely to have withdrawn from jobs at the birth of the first child and to have returned to the labor market only after their children were almost grown. This cohort has often experienced a marked shift in attitudes toward employment and has flooded continuum and counseling centers over the last quarter century in an effort to accommodate changing goals and life conditions. They have become a significant portion of university students. Once launched in careers or jobs, they face a variety of problems: rusty skills, starting points well behind their male age mates and even behind their young adult daughters, marital and social problems related to transitional status, and retirement looming just as they hit their stride.

Few women, especially few "returning" women, reach high levels of their occupations, partly because of age and sex discrimination. They are mostly found in clerical and other white-collar jobs, which consistently show the lowest levels of job satisfaction. Like men who do not "succeed," they are not likely to become highly attached or committed to their jobs and consider jobs second to families in priority. The job of housewife is self-defeating, of low general social status, highly monotonous, and low in recognition for achievement.

14

Retirement and Leisure

People have always aged, but only recently
have they retired. This apparent "overmaturity,"
as Belbin (1972) calls it, has no exact counterpart among other species of primates.

The first retirement program was probably
one designed in England in 1810, for civil servants. Such civil-service pensions were not begun in this country for another hundred years,
in 1920. A national retirement policy, the Social
Security Act, took another decade, probably
speeded by the Depression of the 1930s. This
legislation declared that people had *earned* the
right to guaranteed income after many years of
employment. It also led to industrial retirement
programs that, by instituting compulsory age
limits, carried the message that people over
these age limits were no longer wanted in the
job world.

Because this legislation was passed as part of
a national recovery program from the Depression, it set as early a retirement age as it
could—65. Perhaps if it had been begun at a
time of financial prosperity, a higher age would
have been set. Later legislation extended the
retirement age to 70 years without removing the
compulsory nature of the event, although in
many cases greater flexibility was provided by
allowances for "early" retirement. There are
many implications of these policies for economic and political conditions, and the reader is
advised to turn to more detailed discussions
(such as Atchley, 1975b, 1977; Schulz, 1976;
Foner & Schwab, 1981).

By the mid-1960s, most adult Americans expected that they would eventually retire, most
before the age of 60 (Harris, 1965), and only a
few looked forward to this event with dread.
Eighty-six percent of both the general public
and the older population felt, however, that
people should be able to continue working if
they wanted to (Harris & Associates, 1975).
Compulsory retirement is not a popular policy.
About two-thirds of those who retired between
1958 and 1963 did so voluntarily, and this proportion is increasing (Atchley, 1977) as options
for early retirement expand. Most of those who
do retire "early" state that their reason is poor
health. In spite of the popular assumption that
retirement leads soon to death, it is possible that
the facts are more the other way around. Poor
health—and imminent death—leads to retirement.

Position, process, or event

Retirement may be viewed as a position, as a
process, or as an event. Until recently, it has
been assumed that, because the work role is the
chief focus of people's lives and provides both
identity and social position, then being retired
must be nonidentity and the retired person a
social nonperson. It has also been assumed that
retirement is automatically disagreeable because
it is associated with aging and death. From this
perspective, retirement is not only social death
but also a sign of approaching physical death.
Like assumptions about the disastrous effects of

the menopause, however, these assumptions have proved to be greatly exaggerated. Only about 15% of people near retirement or already retired feel badly about it (Atchley, 1975b), and those who do are more affected by the compulsory nature of their retirement than by retirement itself. Schulz (1974) believes that if retirement were not mandatory, even highly work-oriented people would accept it as just a way station in life. After all, working does not carry the same status for all people. For some, it is a central identity, but for others it is marginal or even undesirable.

As a process, retirement suggests change over time: withdrawal, leaving the scene of action, or at least shifting to a new scene of action. Atchley (1975b) has suggested a seven-stage sequence in the retirement process:

1. *Early preretirement* occurs in early middle age, when the event seems remote.
2. *Near preretirement* is the time when the event seems scary. The worker may start to plan and look around for what to do next. This may be a process of mutual disengagement, when the worker gradually severs ties by such procedures as taking longer breaks between assignments or work periods, longer vacations, and so on. There is a final rite of passage: the retirement ceremony.
3. The *honeymoon period* is when workers feel "Finally, I'm free!" and indulge in fantasies about what they will do next.
4. *Disenchantment* is when retirees feel let down, empty, or depressed. The onset of this stage may be connected with health or money problems.
5. *Reorientation* is a time when retirees might seek assistance in future planning.
6. *Stability* is when retirees realize that they have some adjusting to do and begin to schedule their time and plan their lives. Different personality characteristics affect different patterns of adjustment at this time.
7. *Termination of retired role* comes by death, chronic illness (assumption of the invalid role), or entry into a new career—either a new job or a new leisure involvement.

Atchley's sequence is not to be considered invariant or irreversible. People may go through it differently, some skipping stages, others repeating parts of the sequence several times. Many even reverse themselves and start over by going back to work again, starting new jobs from which they will eventually retire to start the sequence again.

Above and beyond the social aspects of retirement is the economic aspect in today's society. For the working class, and for most women, retirement means a drastic reduction of income, often to or below the poverty level. In fact, a person whose work life has been irregular or drab and routine and whose lifestyle has revolved more about nonwork activities and settings may find the economic aspect of retirement the only difficult one. Women are generally more disadvantaged than men. Not only have they accumulated less reserves, but even pensions discriminate against them. Sylvia Porter (1980) points out that the average private pension received by a retired woman is less than $81 a month, or $970 for a full year. Fewer than 2% of older widows receive benefits from their husbands' private pension. Although 54% of American women work, fewer than 20% currently receive pensions.

Lowenthal (1972) found that social withdrawal and retirement are relatively unrelated. Many people continue to work well into old age (Stein & Travis, 1961), and many, particularly women, do not technically enter or leave the work force at all. People who work part-time are also among those labeled *retired*. One-third of the men over 65 whom Palmore (1967) surveyed had worked for some time the previous year. People who are self-employed, such as independent craftspeople, professionals, or farmers, are much more likely to continue working so long as they wish and are physically able. Farmers, however, may not wish to continue working so much as being compelled to because their children and other possible younger replacements have moved to the cities.

Attitudes toward retirement

Studies of reactions to retirement agree that these reactions depend on previous lifelong personality patterns (Lowenthal, 1972; Gutmann, 1972). Retiring is more upsetting to people whose life goals are more "instrumental/material" than "ease/contentment" and to those whose goals involve long-term projections into the future than to those focused on the present.

Some people may benefit from retirement. They can be relieved from abrasive contact with those who control them and from difficult or monotonous work. Yet they would lose the external structures that organize their lives, as well as their salaries, which, aside from economic necessity, symbolize reward for virtue. If social agencies or social insurance took over the function of supplying funds, direction, and even companionship, many retirees could be freed to seek out new kinds of lives.

On the whole, there is no relationship between job satisfaction and attitude toward retirement (Glamser, 1976). Glamser attributes this to an adaptive loosening of commitment toward jobs. Presumably, people who are most adapted to jobs are making use of their adaptive skills to adapt to what comes next. He too found that financial situation and social activity level are more related to life satisfaction than other factors.

Expected income and also present income strongly affect people's attitudes toward retirement (Harris, 1965). Those with high incomes look forward to retirement much more favorably than those with low incomes. They expect to be financially secure, at least, even if their income is cut in half. Such people, of course, include those at higher educational and occupational levels. Those who feel they have achieved what they wanted in life are also much more likely to favor retirement; those who are still trying to reach their goals are less likely to want to stop (Atchley, 1971), although they may not be actually antagonistic to doing so. Highly career-oriented women who have returned to the labor force in middle age would thus be among those least ready to retire.

Older people seem to look forward less happily to retirement than younger adults (Katona, 1965; Streib & Schneider, 1971). They may worry more about reduction in income, be less socialized to the idea of retirement, or be closer to the reality. In a study of people over 58 by the Social Security Administration (Sheppard, 1976), nearly one-half of the men and two-fifths of the unmarried women said they would not retire. Evidence for cohort change comes from a longitudinal study by Parnes, Nestel, and Andresani 1974). In 1966, 28% of middle-aged employed

men said they planned to retire within five years. Five years later, 39% of the same men said they wanted early retirement. Because they were now five years older, we might have expected the opposite finding—namely, that *fewer* men at the follow-up would plan to retire early.

Since the Social Security Act was amended to allow early retirement—in 1956 for women and 1964 for men—more than half of all retirees covered by Social Security elected to retire early (Morgan, 1972). Morgan's review of the Survey Research Center data led him to conclude that there now are two different groups of people in the process of retirement: one that is doing so willingly, often early and with adequate income, and another that is doing so unwillingly, without adequate income and only because of poor health or compulsory regulations.

Desire for early retirement is related to the kind of job. Those men in heavy labor wanted a much younger retirement age than those in lighter work; they also said their health was poorer (Jacobsohn, 1972). Less than half the workers in individualized jobs were ready to accept compulsory retirement, but three-fourths of those in mechanized jobs were. Even though Jacobsohn's subjects were British, the same results would probably be found in the United States. American automobile workers, men 50 years or older, followed a similar pattern (Sheppard, 1976). Blue-collar workers were much more ready than white-collar workers for early retirement—if they were assured of adequate incomes. If they were faced with compulsory retirement within five years, men in middle-income occupations looked forward most readily to this event, more readily than those in either upper or lower income brackets (Kerckhoff, 1964). American blue-collar women workers in a Bayonne, New Jersey, clothing factory varied in their attitude toward retirement by age, as shown in Table 14.1. Half of the women under 40, and three-fourths of those between 40 and 49, wanted to remain on the same job. However, women between 50 and 59 were split between wanting to stay on the same job and wanting to stay home altogether. Those over 60 mostly wanted to stay home (Goodman, 1978). Like Parnes's subjects, these working-class women looked forward to retirement more as they became older.

Jaslow (1976) surveyed attitudes toward retirement of 2398 women 65 and over. Those who

TABLE 14.1 Age differences in attitudes toward retirement (percentages)

Age	Wanted same job	Wanted another job	Wanted to stay home
Under 40	50.0	25.0	25.0
40–49	76.5	23.5	0
50–59	46.4	7.1	46.4
60 and over	5.3	15.8	78.9

Source: Goodman, 1978.

were still employed had higher morale than those who had retired, at least if their annual income was over $5000. In part, these findings show that the women who were working were younger, healthier, and financially better off than those who had retired—similar to findings for men. The worst-off group consisted of those who had never worked. They were older, sicker, poorer, and more miserable generally.

As noted earlier, job commitment is not consistently related to attitude toward retirement (Atchley, 1977; Glamser, 1976). Men whose attitude toward their jobs improved over five years of a longitudinal study (Parnes et al., 1974) were more likely to lower their expected age of retirement. Another longitudinal study, in Iowa, that interviewed men in 1964 and again in 1974 (Goudy & Barb, 1975), found an opposite situation. More Iowans expressed satisfaction with their work ten years later, fewer said they would retire early if they were given annuities, and most moved their desired retirement age to a later time. Men who had retired during this time, however, changed to a more positive attitude toward retirement. Either they convinced themselves that what they had must be good or they found themselves enjoying life more than they had anticipated.

Ellen Robin (1971) calls attention to the deviant nature of the "almost aged," those between 60 and 65. When she studied a sample of 720 adults in a Michigan county, she found that the people in this age range behaved differently from those who were younger and those who were older. The anticipation of a major life change such as retirement comes not during the year before and after the event, but at least five years before. Similar findings had been reported ten years earlier in a California study (Reichard, Livson, & Peterson, 1962). The term *anticipatory socialization* suggests that preparatory rehearsal is common to most expected major life events.

Retirement planning

Despite the fact that most people can expect to retire if they live long enough—and if they don't lose their jobs—it is startling to find in study after study that very few actually make plans for this eventuality. Preretirement programs are increasingly common in large corporations or organizations and in community adult education. However, only a small proportion of those who are eligible attend. Yet some kind of preparatory activity, even exposure to news media, does seem to be related to favorable attitudes toward retirement. How much this is the result of the programs or information acquired, and how much is the reverse (that people who look forward comfortably to retiring are more likely to avail themselves of these programs), it is hard to say. One study (Cokinda, 1972) found that the one factor that discriminated between company employees who attended preretirement programs and those who didn't was having a lifelong habit of preparing for the future.

When group and individual preretirement programs were compared (Glamser & De Jong, 1975), individual programs had little effect, but people who participated in group programs increased their information about retirement issues and also increased their preparatory activities. Another study (Wexley, McLaughlin, & Sterns, 1975), which compared people's feelings about having their needs satisfied, found that those people nearer to compulsory retirement placed less importance on self-actualization and autonomy needs. In general, they started worrying about retirement four to seven years before the event and began to change their goal patterns to fit their inevitable future. Plans for early retirement correlate highly with economic responsibility for children and declining health. Barfield and Morgan (1978) and McPherson and Guppy (1979) found that mandatory retirees made fewer plans than did voluntary ones.

Effects of retirement

Everybody has heard about such common retirement stories as the sudden and immediate death of previously healthy and vigorous men as soon as they retire. And everybody has heard about the feelings of uselessness and depression that follow retirement. In their masterful chapter called "Adjustment to Retirement" in the second edition of the *American Handbook of Psychiatry*, Friedmann and Orbach (1974) call such stories *myths*. They review the research relevant to these myths by topic, and I will follow their lead. A word of caution here, though—most of the research has been with men.

PHYSICAL HEALTH

There is no support for the myth that healthy people sicken and die on retirement. Friedmann and Orbach say that longitudinal studies show the same pattern of health changes in both retired and nonretired people of the same cohorts. People in poor health are more likely to retire, and to retire early. In fact, many people improve in health after retirement.

MENTAL HEALTH

Again, there is no support for the myth that mentally competent people deteriorate after retirement. People who "fall apart" at such times are, like those who "fall apart" at other major life events, also likely to have had trouble with earlier life transitions.

Streib and Schneider (1971) found that retirement did not affect life satisfaction significantly. Similarly, Cottrell and Atchley (1969) found that depression was rare among retired teachers and telephone employees. They found, as did Thompson (1973) in a study of 1589 men, that life satisfaction following retirement is related more to family situation, past job history, and other personal factors (such as health, age, and income) than to the event of retirement. In fact, self-esteem of retired people was higher than that of high school students. How much this age difference should be attributed to the particularly high stresses of adolescence and how much to cohort differences is hard to say.

Longitudinal data show that occupational prestige affects satisfaction with retirement (George & Maddox, 1977). Less prestigious jobs are associated with increasing dissatisfaction after retirement; more prestigious jobs with general satisfaction. Education is negatively correlated with "adjustment" to retirement. The bet-

ter educated, the less satisfied retirees are. It is possible that people with formerly prestigious jobs are never truly out of the mainstream. The day after the retirement party, when they have slept late, lingered over breakfast, and just decided to walk through their gardens, their phones ring and they are urged to assume new, prestigious roles as community leaders or consultants. Those whose jobs were challenging but who don't have this eminence may have to look harder for equivalent sources of satisfaction.

More evidence on the impact of retirement comes from personality research (Back & Guptill, 1966). Three dimensions of self-concept derived from the Semantic Differential Test were involvement, optimism, and autonomy. Although retirement made no difference on optimism or autonomy, it did lead to lower involvement. Even the healthiest people, who had many personal interests, never seemed to fill the gap left by their jobs. Retired people with the highest feelings of job deprivation were likely not to have looked forward to retiring, not to have achieved their job-related aspirations, and not to have adequate retirement income (Simpson, Back, & McKinney, 1966). In another study, the percentage of people who said they felt "useless" increased from 12 to 27% after retirement (Streib & Schneider, 1971). Three-quarters of all the retired people they studied, however, did not say they felt useless. Furthermore, only a small minority of retired people showed decreases in social participation (allied to loneliness and isolation), and showed even fewer if widowhood was controlled for.

Because social participation is related to social class, particularly among men, a higher proportion of working-class retired men may become isolated than of middle-class men or women (Rosenberg, 1970). This is true in spite of the fact that working-class men generally derive less gratification from their jobs than do middle-class men (Dubin, 1956). They derive less gratification from their other activities, too, according to Lillian Rubin (1976).

In Cottrell and Atchley's (1969) study of telephone company and teacher retirees, the majority of respondents considered themselves well-adjusted to being retired. There were large sex differences, however. More women than men felt that they would never get used to it, and women who did feel adjusted generally took longer to get there. This was most true of the retired women teachers, who also were more likely to say they felt lonely. Women who had once worked for the telephone company were more likely to feel anxious, however. Telephone-company employees may not derive as much social satisfaction from their jobs as schoolteachers do. They may also have a harder time financially.

Atchley (1977) concludes from available research that "most people continue to do in retirement the same *kinds* of things they did when they were working" (p. 158). This agrees with Lowenthal's (1972) conclusions about persistence of lifestyle. About one-third of the retirees studied by Simpson and her associates (1966) increased the level of their non-job-related activities to fill the gap; about one-fifth decreased their activities. Male social scientists interviewed by Havighurst, McDonald, Maewen, and Mogel (1979) generally continued their life patterns into retirement. Professors who had published a great deal continued to do so, and those who had published little showed diversified activities.

Retired people tend to be less "adjusted" to retirement if they have financial or health problems (Sheppard, 1976). Yet the longitudinal data of Streib and Schneider (1971) show that most people found retirement less unpleasant than they had expected. After five years, only 4 or 5% felt that retirement was worse than they expected, and one-third actually said they found it better than they had expected.

FAMILY RELATIONSHIPS

After retirement, there is a high degree of continuity in family relationships, conclude Friedmann and Orbach (1974), and there is certainly no "crisis" in relationships. If anything, people tend to retire *into* the family, to see relatives more, visit and interact more, and become closer in feelings. Streib's Cornell study (Streib & Schneider, 1971) found that although the retirees' children did not see much change in their fathers' family relationships, the fathers themselves said they now placed greater emphasis on family life.

The picture with women retirees may be considerably different. For one thing, many women now among the retired group have never married: 19% of Ohio Telephone Company retirees and 37% of retired teachers, as compared with

only 2% of retired men in either group (Cottrell & Atchley, 1969). These topics are discussed in more detail in the later chapters on the family.

SOCIAL RELATIONSHIPS

Friedmann and Orbach (1974) state that "broad general findings based on cross-sectional data have shown, in different populations, under different social and situational conditions, and in different areas of social interaction, both patterns of increment and decrement of activity and satisfaction" (p. 628). Notice the many qualifications needed to discuss the process usually called *disengagement*. In essence, the effect of retirement on activity patterns is complex and varied, depending on many other situations and circumstances, and is in no way directly related to the event or process of retirement itself.

As Friedmann and Orbach say, most Americans are coming to view retirement as a normal event of life that follows a delimited period of working and has its own activities and rewards. An alternative viewpoint and process is suggested by Sheppard (1976), though. On the one hand, he speculates, future cohorts of people approaching retirement will tend to be better educated and to have worked more in white-collar jobs; thus they will be less eager to retire. On the other hand, the current suggested trend for multiple careers may increase, and these more "sophisticated" workers may then turn to new jobs—or careers—to maintain their incomes. However, so many other variables can affect future work history and retirement—for example, energy depletions or inflation—that it would be almost impossible to try to predict such a process.

Atchley (1975b) thinks that we should consider people's hierarchy of personal goals. Those who place their jobs high in their order of what they want are more likely to seek other jobs or job substitutes after retirement than are those who value other goals more. People who retired from university teaching or administration reported a variety of attitudes, feelings, and activities but did not generally look for second careers (Ingraham, 1974). One respondent said "Retirement is the best thing to happen since the invention of the wheel" (p. 6). This attitude is highly contingent on financial security, as shown by a study of older applicants for public housing in 1959–1960 (Carp, 1968). Those who were working were significantly more satisfied with life than either those not working or those volunteering. When people are at an economic level that makes them eligible for public housing, they want money, not occupations to keep them busy.

Retired women who had been housewives have a higher "affect balance" in retirement than do those who have been employed (Fox, 1977). But should we call them "retired" in that case? Most still work as homemakers. Working women have been used to more social life outside their families, whereas housewives have been used to more contacts around their homes. After a period of time, retired women formed new extrafamilial contacts or increased the frequency of older ones. Fox's data are from the Duke longitudinal study.

One subject that has not received much attention is the synchronization of retirement times between husband and wife. Because women usually are married to older men, who are thus more likely to reach retirement age before they do, they often find "themselves being rushed into retirement at an even earlier age than their husbands, although women may in fact be better suited to a later retirement age than men" (Ragan, 1977). Because more than half of current preretirees are women, many issues around synchronized retirement emerge. Among middle-class couples, I know of cases where both husband and wife retire with suitable fanfare in each one's sphere and move to their dream retirement home—where the husband "putters" while his wife looks for a new job. Among blue-collar workers, if the wife continues to work for the same reason she has all along—money—she could end up being the sole or major breadwinner, often upsetting the traditional dominance of the husband.

Leisure

In a way, leisure is to work what health is to physical development. Both leisure and health are considered important, yet leisure is commonly defined only as the opposite of work and health as the opposite of illness. Having so defined them, researchers then concentrate on working or on disease.

In a sense, the increased numbers of retired people in our society today have pushed the topic of leisure into prominence. If people are not nominally working, may we ask whether they are *leisuring*? Most of today's retirees have not been socialized for leisure in any sense and thus can be considered pioneers in this domain. They are exploring for themselves what they want to do, or what they can do, and they are also leading the way for younger cohorts. At the same time, a historical trend toward devaluation of the work ethic may be making the youngest adult cohorts more ready to accept leisure than are their parents and grandparents.

Robinson (1979) points out that as a nation we are singularly inept in leisure, prey to artificial and commercial purveyors of recreation that often leave us bored or dissatisfied. The market has caught on to the vast possibilities of this ineptness and has come forth with all kinds of mechanized, routinized, and packaged "recreation." At the same time, many adult educators have spread the idea that we are facing longer periods of nonwork time and that it behooves us to learn "leisure skills." This last statement is misleading, though, in implying a general increase in time for leisure. It is true that men's work years have shortened as they enter the labor market later and retire earlier, but so far the number of hours worked per day has not changed since 1948 for nonstudent males (Owen, 1976). The apparent shortening of working time is an artifact of the number of part-time workers who are students or housewives. Thus, the working man's available time for leisure is limited, although it is not as restricted as that of the employed woman's.

WHAT IS LEISURE?

In the beginning of his book on the psychology of leisure, Neulinger (1974) says:

Leisure has been the concern of men through the ages. While in antiquity, it represented man's ultimate goal, a life of tranquility and contemplation, in modern days, it seems to be turning into man's ultimate problem: how to cope with a life that has set man free from the daily struggle for survival, but has not taught him to be himself and take advantage of never-before existing opportunities.

The metamorphosis of leisure from goal to problem was paralleled by a change in the meaning of leisure. Leisure once meant a way of life, a state of being. Today, leisure is generally defined in opposition to work, as time left over, as a residue [p. xi].

Some writers equate leisure with free time, others with what you do without pay, or what you derive pleasure from, or what you yourself choose to do as opposed to what you *have* to do, or what you do in your nonwork time, or play. Neulinger also says that the problem of leisure is that we have become alienated from our work, that it has lost meaning for us; otherwise, our work could be our leisure. Most modern researchers have unfortunately moved away from a view of leisure as a meaningful state or activity to counting what people say they do in nonjob time. Although this has made measurement possible, it has altered what is being measured.

Tell me something about the things you like to do.

Grandfather, age 79
I like to travel and see different places. And I like gardening because it relaxes me and lets me use my hands. I also like to drive when I can.

Father, age 53
I like to watch almost any type of sporting event, live or on television. I like to swim, and I read all types of books and magazines, when I have the time. I love to drive a car and travel to different towns and cities in the state.

Son, age 20
My main interests lie in meeting people, listening to music, and traveling. I like to meet people because every person is a unique individual and has something to offer. I like to listen to music because it relaxes me, or cheers me up, or lets me isolate myself from everything else. I like traveling (although I've done very little) because I think there is a lot of beautiful places in this world that everyone should try to see.

LEISURE AND RECREATION

In considering what we mean by leisure, we might also consider what its relation is to recreation. Taken in its most literal sense, recreation refers to *re-creation*, or the remaking of self. If leisure is the process of enhancing the meaning of life, it should thereby promote recreation.

This sense is somewhat different from the first implication of Neulinger's quotation because it implies that, no matter how much meaning our work has, we need to balance it, to offset it by other activities or states. Thus we

are referring to the rhythm and balance of life, not only in the long term, but over the short term of weeks, days, or even hours. Here the opposite of leisure is not work, not obligatory occupations, not even monotonous occupation, but unvaried occupation—doing the same thing constantly instead of doing a variety of things. The most committed or creative artist or scientist, in this last sense, must take time out for doing something altogether different, no matter what that is. Recreation can be swimming or jogging or sex or reading something unrelated to one's work, going back to school to study something new, or even pursuing a different art or science. Recreation may be done alone or in the company of others—friends or family or even strangers. But it is *different*. And in this sense, we turn full circle to reconsider the simple definition of leisure as *free* time—as time away from one's main activity, as *other* occupation.

Neulinger makes the point that there can be no leisure unless there is free time; free time is necessary but not sufficient for leisure. The converse may also be true. There can be no leisure without some occupation (in its most general sense); occupation too is necessary but not sufficient for leisure. This point is important in studying or planning leisure for retired people. *If time has no structure, it cannot be patterned.*

A rapidly growing field called "leisure therapy" or "leisure counseling" is appearing, largely in response to public concern about the lack of meaning in the life of many retired people. Many leisure or art therapists or counselors are concerned with developing new skills in writing, painting, or other so-called *arts*, on the assumption that these will provide absorbing occupations for the idle and handicapped of our nation. But Neulinger (1978) points out that before such skills are introduced, the counselors should be prepared to help their clients discover their own leisure interests—to find themselves. In other words, clients need to see what would be a variation from regular activity and therefore first need to see what is regular activity.

LEISURE AND PLAY

Leisure is sometimes equated with play. Other writers see play as only one kind of leisure (Gordon, Gaitz, & Scott, 1976), that having to do with "pretend" or fantasy. A semantic-differential study by Neulinger (1974) found three major parameters related to the meanings of leisure for a sample of New York City residents: recreation/play, leisure/free time, and work/labor. In this study, leisure or free time is distinct from recreation or play. The subject of play has been studied across animal species, across cultures, and across ages among humans. The variety of meanings attached to leisure, recreation, play, and free time makes simple discussions or comparisons impossible.

ORIENTATIONS AND TYPOLOGIES

When there are several conflicting definitions of a concept, three possible solutions can be used: (1) to try to combine all the definitions into one composite definition, (2) to choose one as the correct definition and discard the others, and (3) to decide the concept is nonunitary, and separate it into a number of unrelated concepts. All these solutions appear in the leisure literature. Gordon, Gaitz, and Scott (1976) adopt the first solution. They define leisure as "personally expressive discretionary activity, varying in intensity of involvement from relaxation and diversion at the low end of the continuum, through personal development and creativity at higher levels, up to sensual transcendence at the highest levels of cognitive, emotional, and physical involvement" (p. 316).

Many other investigators adopt a unitary definition; for example, "leisure is what is done in nonwork time." So far, no one has suggested using different constructs, which assume that work and leisure are unrelated, although in some research this attitude seems implicit.

In Figure 14.1, Gordon et al. place what they consider the five major objectives of leisure—derived from the literature—into an ordered sequence in terms of expressive involvement. It is assumed that solitude, resting, and sleeping are leisure activities that demand very little involvement or feeling, while sexual activity, drug experiences, and highly competitive games demand almost total personal involvement.

FORMS OF LEISURE ACTIVITY

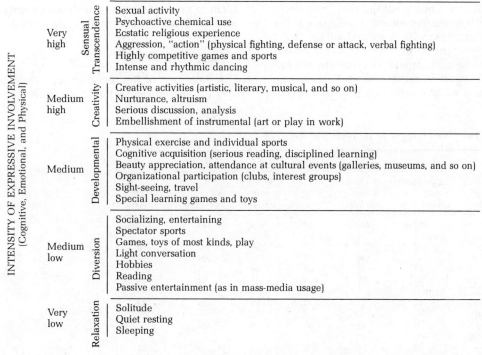

Figure 14.1. Qualitatively varying forms of leisure activity (expressive primacy in personal activity), according to intensity of expressive involvement. *(Source: Gordon, Gaitz, and Scott, 1976.)*

Gordon et al.'s theory derives from Parsons's (1955) division between instrumental and expressive behavior. Work is considered instrumental, goal directed, and serving no purpose of existence. Trying to hold to this dichotomy in studying leisure, particularly from a developmental perspective, is difficult.

Consider Gordon et al.'s (1976) developmental stages of leisure. For infancy and childhood, they believe the main form of leisure would be play (any "pretend" action) and games (play with a structure of rules). Gordon and associates see both play and games as forerunners of adult competence in higher-order cognitive functioning. These activities fall into the "medium low" category shown in Figure 14.1 and thus should show low intensity of expressive involvement. These assumptions could be challenged, however. If there is an instrumental component to children's leisure activities, can they truly be defined as leisure? And can we demonstrate that children are less expressively involved in play than adults?

The instrumental component of play and leisure, Gordon et al. believe, is even more conspicuous for adolescence than it is for infancy and childhood. They point out that "leisure for adolescents tends to concern developing skills and competences to be rewarded within the youth culture and so provides an alternative to the school-based competences that are rewarded later in adult social structures. Sexual competence and other interpersonal skills foster so-cial acceptance and later interpersonal intimacy" (p. 320).

According to their scheme, in youth and young adulthood, subculture features such as desire for variety, autonomy, and sensory experience through music, clothes, sexual indulgence, and drug use color the leisure characteristics of the period and serve to segregate youth from other age groups.

In early maturity—the 30s and 40s—the most frequent leisure activities are home and family centered, including television viewing, visiting, and hobbies. Men are more active in their activities than women. They see the differentiation between work and leisure as significant at this point in life and varying by social class.

In full maturity—age 45 to retirement—leisure is described as more home centered and personally expressive.

Finally, after retirement, the range of leisure activities narrows altogether, although there is more time devoted to leisure.

It is possible that the instrumental/expressive dichotomy may not solve the problems of defining what leisure is. Nevertheless, the model of Gordon, Gaitz, and Scott made it possible for them to investigate kinds of developmental patterns in leisure, which will be presented shortly.

TIME BUDGETS

A large part of the research on leisure consists of time and money budgets: how free time

TABLE 14.2 Time budget, in minutes per day

	Men			Women		
Activity	Executives and professionals	White-collar workers	Laborers	White-collar workers	Laborers	Housewives
Sleeping	492	498	540	492	498	516
Working for pay	372	384	354	354	402	6
Eating	106	114	101	116	109	106
Visiting	79	81	94	94	74	151
Reading	74	61	95	43	38	84
Being entertained	15	45	35	48	29	44
Engaging in sports	40	34	35	19	20	16
Participating in clubs	10	8	0	3	0	61

Source: Lundberg, Komarovsky, and McInerny, 1934.

is divided up, and how money is apportioned to various leisure pursuits. Table 14.2 is an example of a time budget. According to these data, suburban people in 1934 spent ten times as many minutes in nonleisure activities—as sleeping and working were defined—as they did in leisure activities. Eating, the most time-consuming activity assumed to be leisure, took one-fourth less time than sleeping and one-third less than working for pay.

An equivalent time budget for middle-aged and older people is shown in Table 14.3. This was derived from the responses of 261 men and 241 women between the ages of 46 and 71 (Pfeiffer & Davis, 1971). The subjects could account, on the average, for 96 waking hours per week. Employed people could account for more hours than nonemployed. And work, including work-related travel, accounted for the largest number of hours per week. Watching television was next. Presumably, many of these respondents were retired.

The justification for time budgets is that time spent on any activity has been shown to be a valid index of preference and enjoyment of that activity (Robinson, 1979). In his analysis of the University of Michigan's Survey Research Center's 1965 and 1975 studies of how Americans use their free time, Robinson found a strong relationship between time spent and expressed enjoyment. Not surprisingly, this correlation was higher for activities that were less obligatory, but it was still positive for activities such as work and child care. People who said they enjoyed reading spent 51 minutes per day reading, compared with only 9 minutes spent by those who didn't enjoy it; those who liked being with friends spent an average of 64 minutes per day with them, compared with the 48 minutes of those who didn't enjoy it.

The national survey of aging conducted by Louis Harris and his associates (1975) on behalf of the National Council on Aging (NCOA) found age or cohort differences in time spent at a variety of activities. Table 14.4 shows that watching television is the only activity at which people over 65 spend much more time than those between 18 and 64.

Gordon et al. (1976) went one step further than the Harris study. They interviewed Houston adults over the age of 20 about their leisure activities. The study was carried on in 1969–1970, using a stratified sample of 1441 people, balanced by sex, ethnicity, and occupational status. The age patterns they found for frequency of different activities are shown in Figures 14.2, 14.3, and 14.4. Activities that increased from age 30 to age 94 (cross-sectionally) are shown in Figure 14.2; those which remained at relatively the same level are shown in Figure 14.3; and those which decreased are shown in Figure 14.4. In general, there were lower levels at

TABLE 14.3 Mean hours spent per week on various activities

Activity	Men	Women
Working	36.8	34.5
Eating	9.8	9.8
Caring for oneself	7.7	8.4
Watching television	11.6	13.2
Reading	8.3	9.0
Engaging in sport hobby	3.9	3.4
Engaging in sport in person	0.6	0.3
Attending church and meetings	2.3	2.9
Volunteer work	0.7	1.1
Socializing	4.8	7.2
Doing activity around house	5.7	3.6
Doing other activities (specified)	0.7	0.6
Just sitting around	3.3	2.6

Source: Pfeiffer and Davis, 1971.

TABLE 14.4 "A lot of time" personally spent doing various activities by public aged 65+ compared with public aged 18-64 (in percents)

	18-64	65+	Net difference
Socializing with friends	55%	47%	− 8
Caring for older or younger members of the family	53	27	−26
Working part-time or full	51	10	−41
Reading	38	36	− 2
Sitting and thinking	37	31	− 6
Gardening and raising plants	34	39	+ 5
Participating in recreational activities and hobbies	34	26	− 8
Watching television	23	36	+13
Going for walks	22	25	+ 3
Participating in sports, such as golf, tennis, swimming	22	3	−19
Sleeping	15	16	+ 1
Participating in fraternal or community organizations	13	17	+ 4
Just doing nothing	9	15	+ 6
Doing volunteer work	8	8	—
Participating in political activities	5	6	+ 1

Source: Harris and Associates, 1975.

older ages in the more vigorous activities and those that required going out of the home, although there were also lower levels in reading and cultural production. The Duke study, however, had found that reading was significantly greater among older than among younger people (Pfeiffer & Davis, 1971). Some of these age differences are undoubtedly due to aging, but others, such as for reading, could be attributed to cohort or group differences in education.

Social and community activities tended to be of equivalent frequency at all ages among Houston respondents, and Pfeiffer and Davis similarly report no age differences in church attendance. Solitary activities and cooking were more frequent among older people, although there is a clear sex/age difference. Older wom-

en cook less than younger women, older men cook more than younger men.

Older social workers (Seltzer & Atchley, 1971b) preferred autonomous leisure activities more than did younger ones, who tended to engage more in activities that involved other people. However, Havighurst (1961) found no age effect on any of his social scales (noted earlier).

Vacations, according to Pfeiffer and Davis, are highly institutionalized among older people. Almost all men and women took them. For most people, vacations consisted of trips.

In the San Francisco study of four age cohorts (Lowenthal et al., 1975) the high school seniors and newlyweds engaged in the greatest *variety* of leisure activities, were involved in them

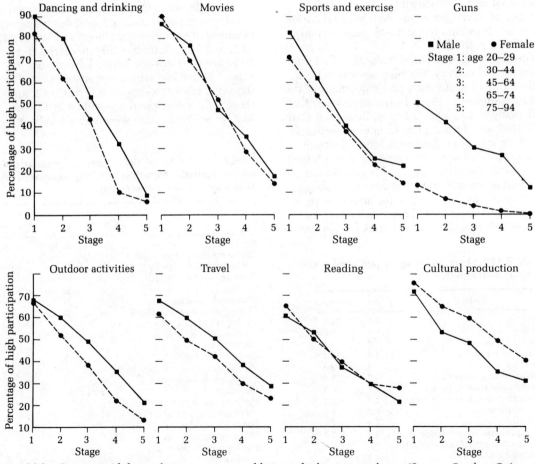

Figure 14.2. Patterns with lower frequency among older people, by stage and sex. *(Source: Gordon, Gaitz, and Scott, 1976.)*

more often, and even mentioned them as important sources of stress in their lives. The middle-aged men had the least variety. Although they may have retained membership in clubs and church, their participation was more symbolic than real. This was also true for AT&T executives in their 40s (Bray & Howard, 1978), at least those who were more successful (reached higher corporate levels), as well as for the middle-aged successful men studied by Elder (1974) and Kanter (1977). Middle-aged women, many working primarily in order to increase their family incomes, also tended to be centered on their families so far as leisure activities were concerned.

Hess and Markson (1980) point out that what older people might wish to do with leisure time is restricted by what they *can* do. In general,

older people report watching television or "doing nothing." Gordon et al. (1976) found more variety than Hess and Markson did, though. Those older people who do have many different kinds of activities show higher life satisfaction (Peppers, 1976)—in agreement with the Kansas City studies on disengagement and morale.

In the study conducted at Duke University (Pfeiffer & Davis, 1971), women between the ages of 46 and 55 said they had too little free time, but men between the ages of 66 and 71 said they had too much free time.

Most Duke respondents found the question "When was the last time you really had fun?" intriguing. Two-thirds of the men and women said they had had fun within the last day or week, but 16% said not for months or years. This response was not related to age, but was

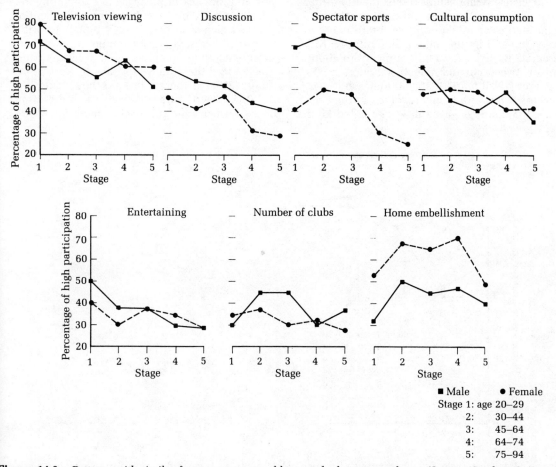

Figure 14.3. Patterns with similar frequency among older people, by stage and sex. *(Source: Gordon, Gaitz, and Scott, 1976.)*

slightly related to working for the men—77% of the working men had had fun recently, as compared with 56% of the nonworking men.

RELATION BETWEEN WORK AND LEISURE ORIENTATIONS

Two opposing theories about attitudes toward work and play have been considered. Havighurst (1961) suggested that people can get the same satisfaction from leisure as they do from work. He based this theory on his research with New Zealand and Kansas City residents. This has been labeled the "spillover" hypothesis. Its opposite is the "compensation" hypothesis, that leisure activities provide balance for jobs, fulfilling needs not met by jobs. Research findings are contradictory, pointing to several types of work/leisure relationships rather than to either the spillover or compensation position alone. Some studies show similarity of interests between job and leisure, others dissimilarity. Most research, in fact, shows no significant relationships between job and nonjob activities.

Parker (1965) found that youth and child-care workers, who were highly involved in their work, frequently engaged in work-related kinds of leisure. Bank officers, however, were low in job involvement and generally selected leisure activities that were completely different from their work. People who enjoy interpersonal interaction appear to look for it in both jobs and play. Those who want to be independent want to be independent in leisure as well as on the job. And those who like to be challenged intellectually look for challenge in all spheres of life. The AT&T executives who were highly involved in their work did not turn to leisure much, but those who were not highly involved sought their satisfactions largely from leisure.

Among the more interesting findings from a University of Michigan Survey Research Center study (Quinn & Staines, 1979) is the pleasure people take from "personal maintenance" activities of eating, sleeping, washing, and dressing and the lack of pleasure in commuting to work. Another major point is the enjoyment of work, which is surpassed only by talking with friends. Most said that they enjoyed work and leisure activities about equally. Twice as many people said that they would like to work more hours (20%) as those who said they would like to work fewer hours (10%), although Robinson (1979) suspects the prospect of more income

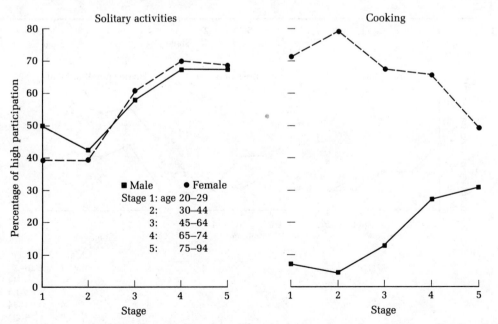

Figure 14.4.   Patterns with higher frequency among older people, by stage and sex. *(Source: Gordon, Gaitz, and Scott, 1976.)*

may enter into this judgment. In fact, there is a general negative relationship between free time and life satisfaction. Except among employed women, Robinson notes that people with the highest life satisfaction have the least amount of free time. This is largely true for those in the middle of the free-time range, though. People with "time on their hands" as well as those who can never catch up are both lower in life satisfaction.

People vary in how they rank the meaningfulness of job and leisure activities. They may rank both high in meaning, attach more meaning to one sphere or the other, or find meaning in both spheres to be low. Dubin (1956) based his idea of *central life interests,* for example, on his finding that for many people nonjob activities are much more important than job activities. This is particularly true for industrial workers. Orbach (1963) found this also to be true for four out of five nurses he studied, and Oliver (1971) found it true for people who retired early to an Ozark recreational life. Obviously, the kind of job one holds has much to do with one's central life interest, as noted in Chapter 12. The opposite can also be true; if one's central life interest is recreational, one is likely to select a more perfunctory job, designed mainly to finance more central interests.

RETIREMENT AND LEISURE

Atchley (1971) points out that leisure activities can serve as a bridge between pre- and postretirement life. Miller's (1965) identity-crisis theory states that, because people derive identity from their job, they will face an identity crisis when they retire. Nevertheless, data from the Scripps Foundation study of retirement (Atchley, 1977) indicate that, although it is true that men and women lose their sense of involvement, this loss is not related to other self-concept variables. Many retired people still value work highly and maintain a strong work orientation, but this orientation is not connected with anxiety, depression, dislike of retirement, or withdrawal from activity in general. According to Cottrell's (1970) data, as the concept of retirement gets incorporated into the culture, work will more and more be seen as a temporary part of life, and the meanings derived from work may become more generalized to other life pursuits.

Retirees, according to the ads, should be leaving their cares and responsibilities behind them and taking off for the communities called "leisure villages." These are ideally located in the Sun Belt: Florida, Arizona, and California. The migration is not as overwhelming as the popular belief would indicate, though. Older people move only half as much as the population in general (Biggar, 1980). One-fourth of Americans over 60 changed dwellings between 1965 and 1970. More than a million crossed state lines, though, and represent a sizable number of migrants. Like movers of any age, these Sun-Belt immigrants represent the best-off portion of their cohort. They have better health, more money, higher socioeconomic status, and more education. Biggar points out that their moves deplete the areas they left and enrich those they entered. Older people who do not move are, like those who migrate across the country, most likely to be married. Those who just move locally, however, often tend to be widows moving in with, or at least closer to, children. Incidentally, one of the reasons given for migration is better recreational facilities.

SEX DIFFERENCES IN LEISURE

When Elder (1974) asked the men and women of the Oakland longitudinal study what their activity preferences were (Figure 14.5), the men whose families had not experienced marked deprivation during the Depression of the 1930s preferred leisure activities next to work and over community and family, but those who had been deprived clearly put families next to work and over leisure. The women (see Figure 13.4) put leisure behind work, in third place, as did the deprived men. Elder adds that men in high-status occupations were likely to mix play and work; they said "My job is my recreation" (p. 189).

Most American (and Western European) women today hold two jobs, one of them being that of homemaker—whose work is never done. It should therefore come as no surprise that women tend to incorporate their leisure into their work time (Havighurst, 1961) and also tend to wish they had more leisure (Neulinger, 1974; Pfeiffer & Davis, 1971). Men are generally more satisfied with the amount of leisure they have. Havighurst also found that men seemed more achievement oriented and physical in their leisure than women, who rated service to others higher than did men. However, the corporate wives described by Kanter (1977) combined leisure with their (homemaker) jobs as much as did their husbands. Sex-role differences pervade leisure, as they do most other areas of life.

SOCIAL-CLASS DIFFERENCES IN LEISURE

Social class encompasses income, education, and occupation. All these elements make a difference in leisure style and practice. At the lowest income and educational levels, only about 2% of money left after taxes is spent on recreation or leisure (Ennis, 1968). When the income is $15,000, between 5 and 6% is spent—at all educational levels. And 5% of $15,000 is much more money than 5% of $5,000. Social-class differences also were clear in Havighurst's (1961) Kansas City data. Middle-class respondents—both men and women—were more likely to choose a recreation because it had some bearing on their personal lives. The lower classes were more likely to choose a recreation because it was near to their homes. Middle-class respondents were more innovative; they did and tried more new things instead of habitually repeating old things, and they were also more likely to pick leisure activities for their enjoyment value instead of just to kill time. They were more achievement oriented—more interested in de-

veloping skills and talents. Altogether, they were more vigorous and active pleasure seekers.

Tell me something about the things you like to do.

Grandmother, age 80
I love to read, that's my hobby. You miss something if you don't like to read.

Mother, age 50
Sleep. The way things are now I don't have the time to do a lot of things. I'm tired when I get home from work. I don't have a car, so that's limiting. I watch TV, listen to my daughter sing, and go to church, of course.

Daughter, age 22
Music! It's not just what I like best to do; it's something I *have* to do. If I didn't have music, I'd lose my mind. I like to date. I like to associate with people, ride bikes, walk on a summer day.

PERSONALITY

Leisure style is an aspect of lifestyle. We can describe individual personality differences in terms of the ways people spend their leisure and the goals they express. As mentioned earlier, some people are instrumental or extrinsic oriented. They do very little for its own sake but rather for what it will get them—skills, recogni-

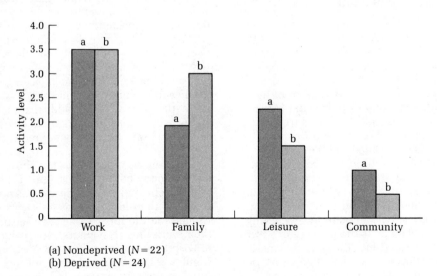

(a) Nondeprived (N = 22)
(b) Deprived (N = 24)

Figure 14.5. Activity preferences of California men, by amount of economic deprivation during adolescence. *(Source: Elder, 1974.)*

tion, friends, business contacts, and so on. Other people enjoy the doing, the playing of the game rather than the winning. They do not care whether their trip gets them anywhere or widens their horizons or allows them to purchase conversation pieces. If they are exploring, to use an example of Neulinger, they don't care whether they get anywhere but enjoy the act of exploring for its own sake.

When Maas and Kuypers (1974) studied the lives of a group of people in their 70s, they divided the people into types in terms of their central lifestyles or, if you will, leisure styles. There were four such types for the men: family-centered fathers, hobbyists, remotely sociable fathers, and unwell/disengaged fathers. All their subjects had been first studied when their children were selected to be part of the Berkeley longitudinal study in the 1920s. The family-centered fathers were highly involved with their wives, children, and grandchildren, and most of their high satisfaction could be attributed to their marriage and their grandchildren. They said their relationships with their wife and children had improved with age and were currently very close. About one-third also visited siblings frequently. Practically all their leisure was spent with other family members; they were rarely alone. Not only were their late lives family centered, but so had most of their earlier lives been.

The hobbyists, however, had never spent much time visiting either family or friends. They were highly engaged in getting things done: reading a manuscript, playing the organ, working in the workshop, making an itinerary for a trip, laying tile in the basement.

Although socially busy, the remotely sociable fathers were not involved in close relationships with people. They took old friends to the doctor, chatted with former coworkers on the street, played bridge with acquaintances who dropped in for the evening.

The unwell/disengaged saw themselves as withdrawing from this world. Some kept up a high involvement in the church, but in general saw themselves as having changed and as not being happy about it.

The women in the study could be grouped in six different categories: husband centered, uncentered, visiting, work centered, disabled/disengaging, and group centered. The husband-centered women were not too different from the family-centered men, although it should be mentioned that the type of lifestyle of one spouse was not usually the same as that of the other. A husband-centered woman could be married to an unwell/disengaged man, a work-centered woman to a hobbyist man. The uncentered were usually widows in poor health. Although they saw both their children and grandchildren, they were not highly involved with them. They were preoccupied with their unsatisfying health or finances.

The visiting women, although usually married, were less focused on their marriages than they were on being hostesses, guests, parents, or group members. They had close and meaningful relationships with a variety of relatives and friends, as well as many recreational interests, some of which they pursued alone.

The work-centered women were mostly no longer married and were highly involved with their jobs. They also had many recreational interests, not to mention their involvement with their children.

The disabled/disengaging women resemble the unwell/disengaged men. They focused on their illnesses and had notably decreased their activities.

Finally, the group-centered women resembled the remotely sociable men. They had many recreational interests and did many of them alone. None of their satisfactions lay in the family arena, either. They seemed remote and formal.

This work by Maas and Kuypers used lifestyles as an index of personality. Other research has used more discrete variables, such as traits or motives. Veroff and Feld (1970) found differential patterns when they considered the relationship between men's leisure activities and their ratings on three motives: achievement, power, and affiliation. For example, affiliation tendencies seemed to be expressed directly in leisure activities, although they were expressed differently by men of different ages.

They were also influenced by the men's job status. Younger men with high affiliation motives seemed to seek gratifying relationships through membership in social organizations if they had low-prestige jobs, but older men in the same position looked for more intimate relationships. Middle-aged men (these would be classified as adults, not middle-aged, by the general criteria used in this book) in high-status jobs usually said they didn't have enough friends.

Veroff and Feld suggest that such men probably turn to their family. They could begin to look like the family-centered men described by Maas and Kuypers. In general, older men in high-status jobs were more likely to report affiliative leisure activities than were those in low-status jobs. Overall, the relationship between affiliation motives and leisure seems to be largely a function of low prestige particularly among the younger and older men.

Perhaps the most interesting finding is that the men high in achievement motivation (as rated on the Thematic Apperception Test) did not try to express this motive in their leisure activities. They looked for the kind of job that would enable them to show achievement. Even if they could not be satisfied through job achievement, they did not turn to leisure pursuits for such achievement. These findings do not support Havighurst's (1961) findings of similarity of orientation in job and leisure.

So far as the power motive is concerned, only older men in high-prestige jobs seemed to look for power in leisure. Veroff and Feld (1970) suggest that these men may be looking forward to retirement and the consequent loss of their job power by seeking to obtain power in other arenas. The lifestyles of the much older men studied by Maas and Kuypers (1974) do not express power motives, even though many of these men held high-prestige jobs before they retired.

GENERAL TRENDS

The importance of leisure to both the individual and the society has been stressed by a number of writers recently. De Carlo (1974) found that subjects between 79 and 91—surviving members of twin pairs—showed a positive relationship between continued participation in recreational activities and successful aging (assessed by a number of physical and mental health measures). Cognitive recreational activities were most likely to go with "success aging," as shown in Table 14.5. How much this is due to the greater survival chances of more "intelligent people," we cannot say.

An anthropologist (Clark, 1972) speculates that there has been a shift in our culture from a work morality to an activity morality; activity of any sort is valued over inactivity. Thus leisure is valued if it is active leisure. The "institutionali-

TABLE 14.5 Correlations among criteria of successful aging and total life recreative activity

	Criteria of successful aging			
Activities	*Physical health*	*Mental health*	*Intellectual performance*	*Total criteria*
Motor	.11	.34	.19	.29
Cognitive	.28	.28	.52	.48
Affective	.01	.30	.28	.30
Total	.14	.45	.42	.48

Source: De Carlo, 1974.

zation" of leisure activities would be a natural consequence of such a value on extrinsic goals, as would adult education and skill acquisition. Such interests also are consistent with our value of independence. The "hobbyists" described by Maas and Kuypers are developing talents and skills and are relatively independent of other people. They are also fulfilling a third value high in our culture, that of "self-actualization."

As leisure becomes increasingly more acceptable and more money is invested in leisure activities, says Eisdorfer (1972), workers should find that time spent away from jobs is more enjoyable than the time spent on jobs. However, the leisure of the wealthy and the recreational pursuits of holidays are still seen differently from retirement (Rosow, 1967). Eisdorfer suggests that, if retirement income becomes more adequate, more people will retire early and attitudes toward retirement activities will change. In fact, he predicts many workers will adopt a "sour-grapes" attitude toward working.

In the future, we may turn to measuring what Atchley (1977) calls "leisure competence" with the same zeal as we have measured achievement motivation and achievement behavior. We may worry about incompetent leisurers and try to change their ways as we reward the competent by praise and recognition and perhaps even money. Leisure will then have become fully instrumental.

Summary

The nonjob years at the end of life are longer than they used to be. Some people retire because of compulsory regulations, others because they have accumulated enough money to turn to more central activities in their lives. Retirement can be seen as a process that begins years before the event and ends with death, disabling illness, or entry into a new job. Attitudes toward retirement vary with life goals, financial concerns, age, health, kind of job, and general job commitment. Women, on the average, find retirement more difficult than do men. Not many people attend preretirement programs, although some kind of preparatory activity is associated with more favorable attitudes toward retirement. Poor health is more likely to cause early retirement rather than retirement to cause deterioration in health.

There are many definitions of *leisure,* from *free time, nonobligatory activity,* and *nonwork activity* to *recreation* and *play.* Insofar as leisure is seen as an attitude toward activity rather than any specific activity or absence of activity, leisure activities can vary widely among individuals. Gordon, Gaitz, and Scott propose a scale of the five major objectives of leisure in terms of expressive involvement. The least ex-

pressive are solitude, resting, and sleeping, and the most expressive are sexual activity, drug experiences, and highly competitive games. In general, younger adults choose more vigorous activities that involve going outside the home, while older people choose less vigorous, more home-bound activities. Some people have the same orientation toward their work as toward their leisure—a "spillover" pattern. Others have opposite orientations toward work and leisure— a "compensatory" pattern. Most research findings show little relationship between job and leisure activities. Many retirees of today retain an instrumental orientation toward leisure, seek to "get things done," to compete with others, and to demonstrate competence. The retirees of today, along with members of the youth culture of the 1960s and 1970s, who adopted what might be called a leisure attitude toward work, may be the pioneers in the leisure world. They may lead the way to more meaningful kinds of leisure in the future.

15

Personal Development

Many of my students in adult development and aging are concerned about what may happen to their bodies or their memories as they get older. But, most of all, they worry about personality changes. Although it seems impossible that they will not always be themselves, they occasionally wonder whether they will someday feel differently about themselves and their world from the way they feel now. Will they become interested in different kinds of things, different kinds of activities? They see themselves as distinctly different from their parents and wonder whether, when they get to be their parents' age, they will become more like their parents. They read about midlife crises and senile dementia and hormonally related personality changes in women. Taking a course in adult development and aging is a little like going to a fortune-teller or reading Tarot cards or casting the I Ching. What will the future hold?

Personality development is much harder to write about than is either physical or cognitive development because personality is an ambiguous, controversial, and conglomerate construct. The research and theory come from such disparate perspectives that putting them together is a Herculean task.

Issues

Some of the thorny issues confronting us have been outlined in Chapter 1. Let me first review five issues that are particularly pertinent to this chapter.

1. *Genotype/phenotype.* Does the behavior we label *aggressive* in early childhood really represent the same psychological process as the behavior we label *aggressive* in middle age? Is biting equivalent to insults? If biting children grow up to provoke everyone around them, does this mean they have remained basically the same throughout their lives?

2. *Universality of turning points.* Can all humans expect to change in the same ways at specific times of life? Does getting married make everybody more responsible, for example? Does the "empty nest" make everybody mournful? Does retirement make everybody sick?

3. *Biological determinism.* What is the relationship among physiological, cognitive, and personality processes? Do physiological changes affect personality processes or cognitive functioning?

4. *Personal determinism.* To what extent can people shape their environments and their destinies, and to what extent is their behavior shaped by external events?

5. *Discontinuity of explanations.* To what extent can we apply the principles and findings derived from the study of early life to adult life? Is adult development essentially different from child development? And to what extent do events of adult life alter early tendencies and shape later ones?

Self

A half century ago, George Herbert Mead (1934) distinguished two parts of the *self*: the *I* and the *me*. The *I* is the core or center; it unifies diverse feelings and experiences as well as past, present, and future, and makes one feel that one is the same person throughout the passage of time. Mischel (1969) says that this sense of sameness, of *I*-ness, acts "like an extraordinarily effective reducing valve that creates and maintains the perception of continuity even in the face of perpetual observed changes in actual behavior" (p. 101).

Several writers suggest that, if we did not have this sense of continuity, of *I*-ness, we would be unable to function. Erikson (1968) says "No one who has worked with autistic children will ever forget the horror of observing how desperately they struggle to grasp the meaning of saying 'I' and 'You' and how impossible it is for them, for language presupposes the experience of a coherent 'I.' By the same token, work with deeply disturbed young people confronts the worker with the awful awareness of the patients' incapacity to *feel* the 'I' and the 'You' " (p. 217). Weinberg (1956), a psychiatrist who has pioneered in the treatment of older people, reflects the view of most psychoanalytic thinking about aging. He suggested that pathological symptoms of aging are defenses against the dissolution of ego boundaries. Such dissolution leads to loss of ego intactness and oneness. Aging people give up certain powers in order to maintain this sense of identity. The aged exclude stimuli, conserve energy, and even regress intellectually to accomplish this purpose. Mischel (1969), a leading developmental theorist, essentially agrees: "[The] experience of subjective continuity in ourselves—of basic oneness and durability in the self—is perhaps the most compelling and fundamental feature of personality . . . the loss of a sense of felt consistency may be a chief characteristic of personality disorganization" (p. 1012).

As early as three or four months of age, the infant develops a sense of "existential" separateness from others, a sense of "I" as separate from "you" and "them" (Lewis & Brooks, 1975). We seem to tend "toward consistency in our perceptions of ourselves" (Clausen, 1972, p. 502). This feeling of being the same people all along is so stable and so pervasive that reunions with old friends or classmates can be profoundly shocking. When we discover that our images of those people are not what those people are like now, we must face the fact that we too have changed. However, we may soon find that the changes that impress us are relatively superficial. After a few minutes of conversation, we may go right back to where we left off, again seeing both our friends and ourselves as having remained the same people over time.

Maintaining a sense of continuity, of *I*, may become more crucial as people get older (Lowenthal et al., 1975). Times when multiple changes in body and in social position occur may be times when it becomes particularly important—but more difficult—to keep one's identity.

The *me*, postulated Mead, is the part of the *self* that results from interaction with others in society. This categorical sense—it consists of descriptive categories or classifications—does not start to develop, according to Lewis and Brooks, until about two years of age. It requires sufficient cognitive maturity to be able to classify: to compare ourselves with others and to combine the characteristics that others attribute to us with those we attribute to ourselves. Because these views of ourselves incorporate the views of others around us, the *me* should be more likely to change with changing associations and experiences than the *I*. For instance, if we see, as we get old, that most people we know now consider us helpless, we are likely to define ourselves as helpless. And then we would change our behavior to fit this new self-definition: we would act helpless.

In Erikson's theory, identity formation is—or at least is expected to be—completed early in adolescence. However, there are probably recurrent "identity crises" throughout the rest of life. Only a few people may really *complete* their identity formation by 15 or even 20 years of age. Erikson himself stresses that the process is ongoing. Identity formation may be the most important task faced by adolescents, but it may also be a task faced by older people, particularly by those whose life circumstances change. According to Erikson, this sense of being distinct individuals, and the distinct definitions of ourselves that we form, must agree with the definitions other people have of us. Some psychologists (such as Mischel, 1968) feel, however, that by early adulthood most people have long known who they are and what they are like. These images of themselves remain remarkably stable from then on, almost as stable as the sense of *I*-ness. Psychotherapists have documented resistance to changes in self-definitions, even among people who come to them for the purpose of changing. If we believe we are incompetent, we will need much rethinking and many new experiences to prove to ourselves that we are really competent. And we will fight that change all the way. In order to maintain the integrity of our self-definitions, we may go to great lengths to warp or mold our experiences. We select out evidence to confirm our self-perceptions, and we discard contradictory evidence. We surround ourselves with people who confirm our beliefs, and we put ourselves into situations that enable us to live up to—or down to—our self-definitions.

Byrne (1966) reported stability in self-descriptions over time, as did Kelly (1955) and Woodruff and Birren (1972). The subjects in Woodruff and Birren's study were originally administered the California Personality Inventory in 1944 when they were college students and were given it again in 1969, 25 years later. Curiously enough, they described themselves very much the same way in 1969 as they had in 1944, even though they claimed they had changed a great deal. Their descriptions, at age 45, of what they had been like as college students were very different from the way they had actually described themselves when they were students. Apparently, most of us want to think we have changed—usually we want to think we have improved over time—and we often have not.

Other research suggests that the self-descriptions of older adults tend to be more differentiated than those of younger adults (Mullener & Laird, 1971). Older people attribute more different aspects and characteristics to themselves; younger adults are relatively more global. Thus, older people might describe themselves as responsible, caring, imaginative, athletic, orderly, and ambitious, while younger people might just say they are kind and strong. Men showed a greater discrepancy than did women between who they felt they were and what they imagined other people thought about them.

STABILITY AND VARIABILITY

The *me* part of the *self* consists of our self-definitions, self-images, or self-concepts. It

includes a wide variety of individual characteristics, from temperament to need for achievement. We use these characteristics as labels in defining ourselves and others. And others use these characteristics in defining us. We are aware of, or conscious of, some of these traits and can tell others about them. We are unaware of some; they are unconscious. If life does not shake us up too much or too abruptly, most of us manage to maintain these systems of characteristics pretty much unchanged over time. For many people, the *me* is almost as persistent as the *I*. Yet we do not act the same or feel the same in all situations.

Mischel (1979) emphasizes the distinction between *stability* over time and *variability* from one situation to another. He says that "people change as the conditions of their lives change and these changes are genuine, not merely phenotypic" (p. 15). Figure 15.1 shows a diagram of this distinction. At Time 1—let us say, in early adulthood—the person we are analyzing shows three kinds of behaviors in Situation A (*l*, *m*, and *n*), one kind of behavior in Situation B (*m*), and two kinds of behavior in Situation C (*n* and *o*). This person is thus more variable in Situation A than in Situations B and C. At Time 2, perhaps 20 years later, and Time 3, perhaps another 20 years later, this same person shows the same behavior in Situation A as he or she did in youth: still *l*, *m*, and *n*. Measurements of the personality of that person done in Situation A would show exact similarity of performance over the years and would justify a conclusion of stability of personality over time. But look what would happen if the measurements were in Situation B. The person would show personality change from youth to middle age, adding on *p* characteristics to his or her earlier *m* characteristics in the adult years. But he or she would keep these characteristics into Time 3. If we drew conclusions about stability from Situation B, we would conclude that people change during early adulthood but then stay the same into

	Situations		
	A	*B*	*C*
Time 1	l, m, n	m	n, o
Time 2	l, m, n	m, p	n
Time 3	l, m, n	m, p	q

Figure 15.1.   Stability and variability of behavior.

old age. If the measurement were of Situation C behavior, there would be *no* apparent stability over time at all.

We are just beginning to recognize these problems in the longitudinal measurement of personality. Psychologists now are sensitized to the problems of cross-sectional comparisons, but few have yet learned to look critically at assumptions derived from single-characteristic or single-situation (or -test) measurement.

In the following paragraphs, I review the findings of available research. Some of the information comes from cross-sectional comparisons, some from long-term—though usually small and biased-sample—longitudinal research. Some comes from follow-up studies, some from within-family generational comparisons. No matter what research design has been used, they all measure characteristics defined by the investigator and judge them from the investigator's point of view. Almost all studies ignore what Gordon Allport (1937) called the *idiographic approach*. They do not look at what the world looks like to the individuals whom they are studying. Nor do they try to derive their measures from those individuals themselves.

Longitudinal studies

During the 1920s and 1930s, longitudinal studies of human development were begun in several locations across the United States. More recently, there have been some in Europe as well. Most of the studies selected subjects in early childhood (even newborns and prenatals) and followed them—or, at any rate, the survivors— over time. More recently, a few studies started with measurements of adults or even older adults.

Three long-term studies in California began with infants or children: Terman's study of gifted children (Sears & Sears, 1978; Terman & Oden, 1959); the Berkeley Growth Study (Elder, 1974; Livson, 1976; Maas & Kuypers, 1974); and the Oakland Growth Study (Honzik, 1964; Clausen, 1972). Most subjects in these studies are now middle-aged, and their parents, who were also studied in some cases, are old. Follow-ups of these people have yielded interesting data on adult development (for example, see Elder, 1974; Livson, 1976; Maas & Kuypers, 1974).

The Fels Longitudinal Study in Ohio was the basis for Kagan and Moss's (1962) report *Birth to Maturity*. Two longitudinal studies of older men—one in Baltimore, now under the auspices of the National Institutes of Aging (for example, see Costa & McCrae, 1976) and the other at Duke University (for example, see Palmore, 1968)—are yielding information about aging processes. So is a unique study of twins started by Kallmann and continued by Jarvik and her associates (Kallmann & Jarvik, 1959). In the early 1980s, follow-ups of several large-scale samples will be yielding important longitudinal information.

The earliest longitudinal report on adults was done by Kelly (1955). Kelly tested several hundred engaged couples in the early 1930s, when their average age was in the mid-20s, and then retested them 20 years later. This study set the stage for almost all later findings. Kelly found that some measures were remarkably stable over time but that others changed a lot. The most stable were values tested by the Allport-Vernon Scale of Values (esthetic, religious, economic, social, political, and theoretical). Even on these most stable measures, however, about half the subjects showed some change. The least stable traits were particular attitudes, such as toward marriage, church, child rearing, housekeeping, entertaining, and gardening. Thus, more-general orientations toward life persisted, and more-specific subcategories changed. In general, also, husbands changed more than did their wives—a gender difference noted repeatedly. Presumably, the more variable lifestyles of men, and the multiplicity of their experiences, induce more change.

Temperament

Basic differences in temperament or activity level mold most other individual differences in personality. Some babies move quickly, some are placid. Some adults rush through everything at a fast pace, and some are serene. Quickly moving adults were probably quickly moving babies (Honzik, 1964).

In follow-ups of adults in the Berkeley and Oakland longitudinal studies (Haan & Day, 1974), activity level proved to be one of the characteristics that stay most stable over the life span. Rapid-tempo children generally become

come rapid-tempo 40- and 50-year-olds. The most active members of an age cohort retain their relative speediness, although their absolute tempo may not stay at the same high level. If quickness is an outstanding characteristic in early life, it is usually an outstanding characteristic in later life, too. Even if active people slow down as they age, along with their peers, they tend to remain among the quickest of their peers to the end. Activity level in this sense should not be confused with cognitive speed, however. A speedy person is not necessarily a quick thinker.

Affect

Do feelings or emotions change over life? Are they stronger at some periods than at others; stronger in adolescence than in old age, for example? And how do we define *emotions*? Are we thinking about visceral activities (excitement that can be measured in heart rate or amount of adrenalin), or about facial expressions (looking sad or looking happy), or about experiences (feelings of fear or joy)? Whatever our definition, we can agree that emotions are important regulators of behavior, not only among humans but also among other animals. Our interpretations of facial and gestural expressions of people from widely different cultures can be remarkably accurate, and so are the meanings we assign to the expressions of gorillas and other anthropoids (for example, see Ekman & Friesen, 1971; Malatesta, 1980).

Several psychologists suggest that facial expressions of affect may be more overt in children than in older people. Development during childhood and adolescence is accompanied by the suppression of facial displays of emotion and by the substitution of symbols for the actual motor activity (Izard, 1971). Haviland and Myers (1979) asked children, young adults, and older adults to construct faces (out of features drawn on paper, like eyes, nose, and mouth) for children, young adults, and older adults. Most subjects constructed children's faces that were more open and expressive than those they constructed for adults. The ages of the subjects themselves did not seem to make much difference. These results suggest that people have age stereotypes of expressiveness. Some people suggest an opposite effect (cited in Malatesta, 1980),

which Haviland has labeled "crystallized affect." This effect is the molding of a person's facial features by that person's dominant expressions over life. A person who has been primarily happy will have a "happy face," and one who has seen much sorrow will have a "tragic face." Actors and painters often prefer to represent older people because it is both easier and more interesting to portray their strong expressions.

When Rosen and Neugarten (1960) administered the TAT to people between 40 and 71 years of age, they found age differences in a number of affective measures, including activity/energy and affect intensity. They concluded that older people tend more toward inactivity and passivity and tend less often to perceive emotion as important parts of life situations. Using a different projective test, Lakin and Eisdorfer (1960) also found age differences between young subjects (mean age 24) and old subjects (mean age 73). They found no difference in intensity level, although they did in number of affects and in activity level. Even though Lakin and Eisdorfer concluded that their results were consistent with decline in affective energy with age, Malatesta (1980) suggests that they were confounding experiential and expressive aspects of affect. Older people may feel the same emotion, but may show it less.

In some recent innovative research, Csikszentmihalyi, Graef, and Larson (1979) asked men and women between 13 and 65 years of age to report their feelings at the time they were signaled by an electronic pager they carried with them. One finding was an *increase* in the intensity of involvement with age. These results thus are counter to those of Rosen and Neugarten and to those of Lakin and Eisdorfer. It is true that Csikszentmihalyi and his colleagues did not use subjects who were as old as subjects in the earlier studies. The increase was remarkably consistent, however, as shown in Table 15.1. Older adults reported greater concentration, less distractibility, and less wish to be doing something else. In view of my earlier discussion about variability, it is interesting that the older people in this study saw themselves as more self-consistent over time than did younger people. Their feelings in one situation were less unique and more like their feelings in other situations. This effect, which was particularly notable in activity level, agrees with the often-

TABLE 15.1 Age differences in self-reported involvement in daily experiences

Measures of involvement	Age	Number of subjects	Means	"p" level (one-way ANOVA)
1. Task difficulty (challenges)	13–18	75	3.57	NS
	19–30	38	3.55	
	31–40	31	3.92	
	41–65	35	3.89	
2. Coping ability (skills)	13–18	75	5.26	NS
	19–30	38	5.22	
	31–40	31	5.68	
	41–65	35	5.24	
3. Ability to concentrate	13–18	75	4.70	.004
	19–30	38	4.89	
	31–40	31	5.37	
	41–65	35	5.67	
4. Distractibility (difficulty in concentrating)	13–18	75	2.20	.0002
	19–30	38	1.41	
	31–40	31	1.67	
	41–65	35	1.37	
5. Investment (wish to be doing something else)	13–18	75	4.02	.0001
	19–30	38	3.54	
	31–40	31	3.46	
	41–65	35	2.51	

Source: Csikszentmihalyi, Graef, and Larson, 1979.

voiced statement that we grow more like ourselves as we grow older. Youth traditionally is seen as a time of extreme mood oscillation; old age is seen as a time of serenity. Perhaps there is something to this view. Adult changes in affect, therefore, may or may not exist. We need much more research before we can start to draw any serious conclusions.

Personality characteristics

Most adult-development studies have looked at personality characteristics that could be called *traits*. These are either behaviors that can be observed and tallied or values, attitudes, and opinions reported by interviewees. Although some consider these traits to be components of the self-definition or self-concept, others see them as parts of a repertoire of behavior. Such characteristics are rarely measured in an idiographic way.

There are many possible classifications for such characteristics. The following presentation is neither consistent nor logical but arises more or less from the literature.

RELIGION

One problem in studying age changes in religiosity is the lack of consistency in the constructs investigated. There could be age differences or age changes in church *affiliation* or membership, in regularity of *attendance*, in *beliefs* and *strength of belief*, in so-called religious *experience*, or in *participation* in church activities. It is generally assumed that old age is a time devoted to religion. Attempts to see whether this is true are confused by the many ways religion is measured. Also, some decades of the past century have been times of general decline in many aspects of religion, while others have been times of general increase. That is, there have been rapidly oscillating period effects.

A review of generational literature shows that religious affiliation is the area of strongest cross-generational transmission (Troll & Bengtson, 1979). Two-thirds of the Minneapolis families studied by Hill and his associates (1970) showed three-generational continuity in affiliation. Both religious affiliation and religious orientations seem to be basic family themes. If parents are highly religious, so are their children; if parents are irreligious, so are their children. Actual practices and beliefs, however, may vary from one generation to another.

Cross-sectional studies show conflicting results, although a majority indicate more religion of all kinds among people in their late 60s than among those in their late 20s. People in their 70s or older, though, have lower church attendance than younger cohorts. One explanation is problems with transportation and health. Many older people maintain church membership, however, and when they find it difficult to get to church they turn to religious services on television or radio, praying, Bible reading, and meditating (Moberg, 1972). They also are likely to hold more traditional religious beliefs.

There have been a few longitudinal studies. A large sample of college students (originally 3749, and 893 in the follow-up) was tested originally in 1936 and retested in 1950. Over these 14 years, the majority maintained its attitudes toward church, Sunday observance, God as a reality, and God as related to conduct (Nelson, 1956). A group of 84 Dartmouth students, however, increased significantly over time in religious-value scores on the Allport-Vernon Scale of Values (Bender, 1958). I noted earlier that Kelly's subjects were much more stable in religious values than in attitudes toward the church. Research with somewhat older samples (Moberg, 1972) shows either persistence of attitudes and behaviors or increased interest in religion over time.

As contrasted with middle-class subjects, a group of 369 Indiana farmers studied by Ludwig (1965) lost, over time, much of their faith in the future, their belief in their mastery over external events, and their faith in a benevolent God. Moberg concluded that religion as a set of rituals apparently decreases in old age (over 70). But religion as a way of feeling humanity's relationship to God apparently increases among religious older people. This conclusion does *not* mean that people who were not religious in their earlier years turn to religion as they age.

In view of the widespread charismatic religious movements during the late 1960s and 1970s, we should hesitate to generalize from past cross-sectional data that suggest a latency period in religious interest among people in their 20s, followed by an increased interest when these people are parents and socializing their children. We do not know how much the cult members and devout youth of today, many of whom do not have religious parents, will retain their religiosity over their lifetimes, or how many will transmit these beliefs and practices to their children and grandchildren.

POLITICS

Like religious affiliation, political-party affiliation tends to be transmitted within families and maintained over most of the members' lives (Troll & Bengtson, 1979). However, political affiliation shows more period and cohort effects over the past few decades of study than does religion. In times of general conservatism, more young adults and high school students shared conservative parents' Republican Party affiliations. In times of general liberalism more children of Democratic Party voters say they are Democrats. In *Children of the Great Depression* (1974), Elder reports that the children of parents who experienced deprivation at that time, and who consequently switched from the Republican to the Democratic Party, retained their Democratic affiliation. In this sample, fathers and children agreed on party affiliation in four out of five cases.

New political-party affiliation or political attitudes tend to arise during youth. A systematic comparison of cohort and period effects of voters' attitudes (Meddin, 1975) found that the cohort or generation effect was stronger than the period effect. This relative strength is demonstrated in Figure 15.2, Figure 15.3, and Figure 15.4. The two times of testing were 1964 and 1970. Four age cohorts were tested: Group 1 (g_1), 21–28; Group 2 (g_2), 29–44; Group 3 (g_3), 45–60; and Group 4 (g_4), 61 and older. Figure 15.2, which concerns trust in the government, shows that all people lost trust between 1964 and 1970 (lower scores show more trust). In 1964, the two youngest cohorts were the most trusting. The oldest group was the least trusting. Six years later, trust was much lower in all groups and was lower exactly in order of age. Figure 15.3 shows similar age effects with racial attitudes, although in the opposite direction—all cohorts became more racially tolerant, with the youngest remaining the most tolerant. In Figure 15.4, the cohort effect is seen even more clearly. The three older groups remained about the same in their beliefs about the political efficacy of citi-

	1964		1970
75			
77	$\overline{X}$		$\overline{X}$
79	3.85	g⁴	3.85
80	3.80		3.80
81	3.75		3.75
82	3.70		3.70
83	3.65	g³	3.65
84	3.60	g²	3.60
85	3.55	g¹	3.55
86	3.50		3.60
87	3.45		3.45
88	3.40		3.45
89	3.35		3.35
90	3.30		3.30
91	3.25 g⁴		3.25
92	3.20		3.20
93	3.15 g³		3.15
94	3.10		3.10
95	3.05 g¹, g²		3.05
96	———		———
97	3.12		3.67
98			

Figure 15.2.   Trust in government, by age (total sample). *(Source: Meddin, 1975.)*

	1964		1970
104			
106	$\overline{X}$		$\overline{X}$
108	3.00 g⁴		3.00
109	2.95		2.95
110	2.90		2.90
111	2.85 g³		2.85
112	2.80		2.80
113	2.75		2.75
114	2.70		2.70
115	2.65		2.65
116	2.60		2.60
117	2.55	g⁴	2.55
118	2.50 g¹,g²	g³	2.50
119	2.45		2.45
120	2.40		2.40
121	2.35		2.35
122	2.30		2.30
123	2.25	g²	2.25
124	2.20		2.20
125	2.15		2.15
126	2.10		2.10
127	2.05		2.05
128	2.00		2.00
129	1.95	g¹	1.95
130	———		———
131	2.72		2.33
132			

Figure 15.3.   Racial tolerance, by age (total sample). *(Source: Meddin, 1975.)*

	1964		1970
138			
140	$\overline{X}$		$\overline{X}$
142	3.65	g⁴	3.65
143	3.60		3.60
144	3.55		3.55
145	3.50 g⁴		
146	3.45		3.45
147	3.40		3.40
148	3.35		3.35
149	3.30		3.30
150	3.25	g³	3.25
151	3.20 g³		3.20
152	3.15		
153	3.10		3.10
154	3.05	g¹	3.05
155	3.00		3.00
156	2.95		2.95
157	2.90 g²	g²	2.90
158	2.85		2.85
159	2.80 g¹		2.80
160	___		___
161	3.10		3.20
162			

Figure 15.4. Belief in political efficacy, by age (total sample). *(Source: Meddin, 1975.)*

zens over the six years. However, the youngest group, which started out believing most in political efficacy, changed the most. Yet it still did not reach the level of disillusionment of the two older groups.

Older people are politically conservative if they were socialized in an era of conservativism. Present cohorts of old people, thus, who grew up at the turn of the century, are more likely to be conservative, because in their youth it made some sense to believe in the rewards of thrift, hard work, and isolationism. Future generations of old people are likely to be more politically conservative than their younger contemporaries if they were so in their youth.

Douglass, Cleveland, and Maddox (1974) examined public opinion between 1940 and 1970. They found that older cohorts were more conservative than younger only in family matters. There were no significant age differences on economic and national issues. Either the younger cohorts of this sample were more conservative than those Meddin (1975) studied, therefore, or the older cohorts were less conservative.

The flexibility of older people's political attitudes is demonstrated by Cutler's (1973) findings that those who are poor or who feel that growing old diminishes prestige are more likely to approve national legislation for the benefit of the old. We might predict, finally, that the forerunner young people of the 1960s and 1970s will be more liberal than are their children and grandchildren if present trends toward conservatism persist. If so, in the year 2020 cross-sectional studies could show that people get more radical as they get older.

CONVENTIONALISM AND MORALITY

Popular belief holds that people become not only more religious and more politically conservative as they get older but also more conventionally moral. Over 50 years ago, a study by Anderson and Dvorak (1928) found that their older subjects said they would make many more decisions on the basis of absolute ideas about right and wrong than did college students. The college students said they would base decisions on logic and intelligence. How much can we attribute such findings to cohort differences related to amount of education?

Longitudinal studies from childhood through middle age (Haan & Day, 1974) show that unconventional adolescents do not usually become more conventional with time. When these data were extended into older ages, however, older men (mean age 69) differed from older women and from themselves when younger in how much they stressed conventionality of thought (Haan, 1976). Given men's shorter life expectancy, one wonders how much these differences may be attributable to the beginning of a constricted intellectual functioning as a defense against perceived intellectual decline. (Remember the earlier discussion about rigidity and cautiousness.)

The relation between moral judgment and education is demonstrated in an Oregon study of 185 men and women between the ages of 25 and 74 (Dortzbach, 1979). The study found a clear pattern of increase in the level of moral reasoning—based on Kohlberg's model (see Chapter 2)—with increase in education. Table 15.2 shows that the percentage of people who used principled reasoning increased from 10% for those with only grade school education to almost 50% for those with graduate or professional education. The progressive decrease in moral-judgment scores with age (shown in the same table) can be explained almost completely by the correlation between age and education. We may find it distressing, though, that more than half of our well-educated citizens use lower-level moral judgments.

Haan's findings may be related also to sex-typed behavior. Girls tend to become more conventional during adolescence, but they become less so in early adulthood and thus become more like men their own age. During the adult years, men and women remain about the same in this trait, although women seem to become less conventional than men in middle age, and the men become more conventional.

Generational comparisons (Hill et al., 1970; Troll et al., 1969; Troll & Bengtson, 1979) suggest that unconventional adolescents and young adults tend to be the children of unconventional middle-aged parents, or that conventional middle-aged parents tend to have conventional children. However, Hill and his colleagues feel that this finding may not be a constant generational process. Times of rapid change may be recorded in family generation gaps, just as such historical events as droughts, plagues, and cold spells can be observed in tree rings. In their Minneapolis study, Hill and his colleagues found a marked generational shift away from earlier traditional values between their grandparent generation and their parent (middle-aged) generation. They concluded that this shift is probably associated with the fact that their middle-aged and young-adult generations had significantly more education than their oldest generation. The fact that there was much less change from their middle generation to their young generation suggests that a new, less conventional culture was becoming stabilized, at least for a generation or two. A new wave of conventionality in the upcoming adults of tomorrow would result in a switch: older people would be less conventional than younger people.

TABLE 15.2 Use of moral-judgment principled reasoning: Means by age and education

Subgroup	Mean	N
Age		
25–34	48.8%	50
35–44	33.9	34
45–54	34.6	37
55–64	31.9	39
65–74	24.3	25
Education		
Grade school	10.0%	5
Junior high school	28.3	2
High school	28.2	44
High school and vocational school	33.6	24
College (2 years or more)	37.4	64
Graduate or professional	47.3	46
Total sample	36.3%	185

Source: Dortzbach, 1979.

SEX BEHAVIOR AND ATTITUDES

Almost all norms for sexual behavior have changed during the last few decades. Younger adults tend to be much less restrictive than youth of earlier times, than their parents, and than older people in general (Bengtson & Starr, 1975; Zelnick & Kantner, 1977). Many older people, of course, have also shifted with the times. They are more permissive now than they were 10 or 15 years ago (Bengtson & Troll, 1978). Some of this shift seems to be a *period effect*—showing the influence of historical changes in the society as a whole. Some is probably "reciprocal socialization"—youth influencing their parents. Middle-aged mothers of "avant-garde" youth admitted to an interviewer that their attitudes had changed as a result of trying to accept the "freer" sexual behavior of their children

(Angres, 1975). The pull of family ties is strong. Rather than condemn their children or become estranged, parents reexamine their own attitudes in the light of their children's attitudes. Grandparents may also shift in order to accept grandchildren's behavior, although perhaps less than parents (Hagestad, 1978).

ACHIEVEMENT MOTIVATION

In Chapter 12 we concluded that there is an impressive amount of stability over time in orientation toward work and achievement. The longitudinal data on AT&T executives (Howard, 1978) suggest that, although the first job experiences may alter initial attitudes or values of work, orientations remain stable thereafter. The Berkeley longitudinal data (Haan, 1976; Elder, 1974) show even more consistency. Generational research, however, hints at a recent cohort shift toward valuing intrinsic aspects of jobs more than extrinsic aspects. If so, and if these new values are not modified by early job experiences, we may see a future emphasis on achievement and creativity over money and status.

In *Birth to Maturity*, Kagan and Moss (1962) reported that the motive to achieve is acquired early in childhood and tends to remain stable into the 20s. They found correlations (in age periods 6–10 and the mid-20s) of .68 for boys and .49 for girls between childhood achievement behavior and adult concern with intellectual competence. This finding sets the theme for most adult sex differences in this area.

Comparison of college students' achievement needs with that of their parents (Troll et al., 1969) shows significant correlations among all four parent/child dyads (father/son, .45; father/daughter, .39; mother/daughter, .30; and mother/son, .27). The greater consistency in the male line can be attributed to historical shifts in women's achievement motivation. Otherwise, women should be as much like their mothers as men are like their fathers, as may be the case for the next generations of mothers and daughters.

Matina Horner's (1970) findings with college students have been widely reported. University of Michigan students, she found, were sure that a woman who was at the top of her medical-school class would be ugly and miserable, and a failure both as a woman and in her career. However, a man described similarly would be seen as having a glowing future ahead of him. Not only did men believe this, but also women. The "will to fail" and the "fear of success" that Horner alerted us to have not stood up to later research, and, while they are interesting clinical concepts, they are hard to find in reality. They may, in fact, be submitting already to historical changes and may not be exclusive to women.

A study of Radcliffe graduates by Baruch (1966) points to the persistence of motive to achieve, as a trait, across an intervening period of submerged expression. This is what Kagan and Moss called the "sleeper effect." It reflects the competence/performance dilemma. Baruch found a significant relationship among the number of years a woman had been out of college, the level of her motive to achieve, and her return to work. As measured by responses to the TAT, the need to achieve was lowest for women 10 years out of college with very young children. But it was higher among women out for 15 years, even though this latter group had the most children under 8 years old. Women who had been out of college for 20 and 25 years showed high and stable needs for achievement. In fact, those with the highest scores had generally returned to work, particularly if their achievement stories were focused on female figures. Curiously, if their stories dealt with men who were achieving, the women were not likely to be working. Presumably, this latter group of women could have their achievement needs fulfilled through the efforts of the men in their lives—husbands or sons, for example.

Achievement, affiliation, and power motives may operate independently in shaping the kinds of lives men try to lead or the kinds and amounts of satisfaction they derive from their lifestyles. In women, these three motives may be interrelated in complex ways. Women may express their achievement needs either directly, through their own actions, or indirectly, through the actions of others. If women express these needs directly, they may be operating more like men, with achievement motives independent of power and affiliation motives. But, even if they are expressing achievement needs directly, their modes of expression may be quite different from those of men. Outside the job world, women may achieve by doing community work, gourmet cooking, decorating and gardening, or even superior packaging of their bodies for glamor. If they express their achievement needs indirectly, they may be just as satisfied by the successes of their husbands and children as by their own products. If they express such needs directly, it may appear superficially as if they were expressing affiliation motives (wanting to be close to their husbands and children) or power motives (wanting to influence husbands and children), when instead they are really expressing achievement motives (wanting to excel). Figure 15.5 presents a hypothetical framework for examining the various modes in which women might express achievement motives.

Switzer (1975) compared three generations of women—grandmothers, their daughters, and their granddaughters—on achievement-related variables. Interesting generational differences emerged along with intrafamily continuity. First, when the combined level of achievement motivation was considered, the correlation between the grandmother and her daughter was .26; between daughter and granddaughter, .42. The larger gap between the two older generations is partly attributable to the educational difference. Only a handful of the grandmothers had any college education. In fact, most did not complete elementary school. One-fourth of their daughters, however, had some college, as did one-half of the young-adult granddaughters. The level of achievement motivation went up progressively from the oldest to the youngest generation.

Taking the four achievement modes separately (Figure 15.5), Switzer found that different generations stressed different modes. The oldest generation most valued achievement via task mastery; the middle generation, achievement via interpersonal influence; and the youngest generation, achievement via creativity.

There have been cohort shifts not only in education, in level of achievement motivation, and in mode of achievement desired but also in locus of control. The grandmothers and most of the mothers showed external locus of control— they felt the power to control their lives resided in people or forces outside themselves. The granddaughters felt the power rested in themselves (internal locus of control).

Blood and Wolfe (1960) report that wives of successful men do not tend to go back to work in middle age to the same extent as wives of less successful men. Presumably, those wives of successful men who are achievement oriented will express their needs vicariously or in more traditionally feminine arenas. More data are needed before these issues can be clarified.

The effect of social class is highlighted in Baruch's (1967) attempt to replicate her Radcliffe study with a less elite sample—763 wom-

Achievement modes

Approach and arena	Achievement as task mastery	Achievement as recognition or status	Achievement as interpersonal influence	Achievement as creativity
Direct				
Home and community	Good housekeeper— clean, efficient, skilled	Best-dressed woman Beauty queen	PTA president	House decorator Gourmet cook
Traditional "feminine" job	Fast typist Good classroom manager	Secretary of top executive Principal	Social worker	Artist
Innovative "masculine" job	Skilled surgeon Successful lawyer	Dean of college Popular magazine writer	Executive in industry	College professor Theoretical writer
Indirect	Husband good salesman or financially successful	Expensive house in exclusive suburb	Wife of powerful political person	Patron, "angel"

Figure 15.5. Expression of achievement motivation in women.

en from Gurin, Veroff, and Feld's (1960) Michigan Survey Research Center sample. In the latter case, need achievement was lower in older women, particularly in those over 55. The profile of college women in the Survey Research Center sample looked like that of the Radcliffe alumnae—those who were between 35 and 39 showed higher achievement need than did those older and younger.

In the Michigan sample, the effect of education interacts with that of age. High school graduates between 21 and 25 years old showed the highest achievement need; those between 30 and 39 showed a lesser need, and those in the 40s showed a little higher need than did those in the 30s. For women with less than a high school education, achievement need declines steadily with years out of school. Thus, the more education a woman has had, the more likely she is to need achievement once her child-rearing years are past. Those with little education—and probably less achievement need to begin with—tend to show even less need for achievement after their children are grown. New trends toward women working more and delaying marriage and child rearing may alter this picture, of course.

At the present time, and given very insufficient data, it seems possible that motives and needs, although they expand and contract over life, remain in the same general domain for each individual. People who have a high need for achievement or power may wax or wane in the expression of this need. But they tend more than others their age always to want to achieve or exert influence over others and to express such wants whenever appropriate.

OTHER VALUES AND INTERESTS

Lifestyle themes such as intellectualism, humanitarianism, estheticism, or practicality tend to become increasingly more important from late adolescence to early adulthood and then tend either to remain stable or to increase a bit more through the adult years (Haan & Day, 1974). These adult themes show the same patterning over time from childhood through old age (Haan, 1976). Well-functioning, financially secure men and women remain dependable, straightforward, giving, warm, and sympathetic, and they continue to arouse liking. However,

notes Haan (1976), the intimate, more-tender interpersonal attributes of likability, givingness, warmth, sympathy, and straightforwardness have more important roles in older people's hierarchies than they did when these people were younger.

Generational studies (Troll & Bengtson, 1979) also suggest that such characteristics are often shared by members of the same family across generations. By their late 20s, for example, people settle into their basic value and interest patterns, and on the whole these patterns tend to be very much like those of their parents. Intellectual parents can look forward to having intellectual children, although the particular areas of study their children pursue may be very different from those the parents pursued.

An examination of the values that appear to be least stable over generations suggests that these are the lifestyle traits used to highlight the unique status of an age or an age cohort. For example, college students in 1965 stressed self-realization, estheticism, and humanitarianism (Troll et al., 1969). Troll and Bengtson (1979) refer to these characteristics as "generation-keynote themes." For example, child-rearing values were those that changed most from the grandparent to the middle-aged parent generation in the Minneapolis families studied by Hill and his associates (1970). Permissive child rearing was a "keynote theme" of the forerunner youth of the 1940s.

Cross-sectional comparisons of older and younger middle-class subjects on the Strong Vocational Interest Blank show that older (middle-aged) men tend to like new activities less, to prefer cultural (rather than physical) activities, and to like solitary activities more than do younger men. Older men express as many likes and dislikes as younger men, for both people and things. But the older men more intensely like those people and things that they like than do the younger men, and they more intensely dislike the people and things they dislike.

This observed increase in "executive" interests during adulthood is consistent with Havighurst's (1957) finding that middle-aged men spend more time reading newspapers than reading books or magazines. They also read editorials rather than sports, crime, or disaster stories. They read more history and love stories than they used to, and fewer science and sports books. Krohn and Gutmann (1971) report that men between 30 and 54 years old dream about work more than do older men.

The San Francisco study examined four groups of men and women at presumed turning points of the adult years—high school seniors, newlyweds, "empty-nest" parents, and pre-retirees. The researchers found that the 40- to 50-year-old empty-nesters were interested primarily in people and feelings. The 50- to 60-year-old preretirees were interested more in ease and contentment (Lowenthal et al., 1975). Some of this difference may be due to cohort change, however.

Most of the attitude change with age exhibited by Kelly's subjects was toward increased interest in whatever they were previously interested in (compare with Havighurst's subjects, mentioned earlier). There was one exception: although both men and women said that they liked housekeeping before they got married, both felt much less favorable toward it after 20 years of marriage.

Kimmel and Stein (1973) found age differences in self-reported personality needs. Adolescents indicated that their foremost needs were sex, nurturance, counteraction, succorance, sentience, deference, and dominance. Middle-aged respondents showed a very different pattern. For them, needs to be dominant and to have others defer to them were much more salient, while needs for sex and feeling (sentience) were much less salient. Thus, in later adulthood, the need to be helped is weaker and the need to help is stronger. On the whole, though, sex and socioeconomic status make more difference than does age in these results.

Kalish (1975) points out that, although some studies show less need for affiliation among older subjects than among younger ones, this finding could be because older people whose friends and associates have died or moved away say they have less desire for others. They feel there is no chance to find new friends or associates, and they try to deny their loneliness. And not all data are consistent: some studies show no age differences in such traits between middle-aged and older samples.

In summary, changes in the content of adult life from youth to middle age seem to be more in the nature of consolidating and narrowing of

range than in shifting in kind. With age, likes and dislikes become stronger and more stable.

Sex differences in personality

Perhaps the most impressive finding in Haan and Day's (1974) data on interests and values is the relatively small number of differences according to gender. Those differences that do exist in adolescence seem to even out during adulthood. Even though the men and women in the sample differed in education and, undoubtedly, in lifestyle, they tended to share basic interests and value orientations.

Troll and her associates (1969) found that parents of college students are more like each other in values than either parent is like their children. And their children are more like the parents than like other members of the children's age cohort. There are some sex differences. Estheticism was a value more likely to be shared by women college students and their mothers, while humanitarianism and materialism were values more often shared by sons and their parents. Parent/child correlations on conventionality are particularly intriguing. Grotevant (1976) found that mothers and daughters tended to be similar, as were fathers and sons. But mothers and sons, and fathers and daughters, were not similar. A conventional mother has a good chance of producing a conventional daughter, but it is not nearly as predictable that her son will also be conventional—particularly if her husband is not.

SEX-ROLE CHARACTERISTICS

Differences between men and women are emphasized in almost every human culture. Men are encouraged from infancy on to behave in certain ways considered "manly," and women are encouraged to behave in "womanly" ways. What is labeled manly will differ from one society to another, as Margaret Mead illustrated vividly in her early books on cross-cultural differences. In some parts of the world, a man is supposed to be nurturant and artistic. In other parts, he is supposed to be aggressive and independent. Modern Western societies also emphasize sex differences even though we have become aware that most of these characteristics and their prejudicial effects are not biologically inevitable. Before we were born, our parents were ready to find us vigorous, hardy, aggressive, and independent if we were born with penises; and fragile, delicate, sensitive, and dependent if we were born with vaginas. All through our lives, both our parents and the rest of the world in which we have moved have reaffirmed same-sex characteristics whenever they appear and have discouraged opposite-sex characteristics.

Longitudinal correlations from childhood to adulthood, over a 20-year period, are moderate and sometimes statistically significant for such traits as dependency and aggressiveness (Skolnick, 1966a, 1966b). Kagan and Moss (1962) found these traits most stable if they were congruent with prevailing sex-role stereotypes. Thus, dependency was more stable for girls and aggressiveness more stable for boys.

It is interesting that correlations about the same size as those found in these longitudinal studies have been found between two generations of related adults, particularly mothers and their daughters. Grotevant reports parent/child correlations ranging from .24 to .43 for being dominant, realistic, investigative, and artistic. But there were no significant correlations for being sociable or enterprising, which are not part of the sex-role definitions. Father/son correlations were not significant for being dominant, realistic, investigative, and artistic, but were significant (.31 and .34) for being sociable and enterprising.

A study of the moral development of Harvard-graduate professionals (Gilligan, 1980) found different developmental patterns for men and women. Women started out concerned about relationships and only later became concerned about integrity and individuation. Men moved in the opposite direction: they started out concerned about issues of justice and individuation and only later became concerned about issues of caring.

Personality types

Until this point, I have considered personality characteristics more or less independently, grouping them by content but not by clustering or typing within individuals. A number of psychologists have been interested in the possible stability of trait clusters. Do people who score high on one kind of characteristic also score high on another, and low on a third? Are there types of lifestyles? Some developmental theorists, such as Lowenthal, point to lifelong consistency in lifestyle patterns.

Most studies on personality type are based on cross-sectional data or on aggregated longitudinal data—all the people's scores being pooled together at each time of testing instead of individuals being followed separately. Also, most analyses have begun with mental-health measures rather than value-free descriptions of behavior, so that the types derived are more relevant to mental health than to personality development per se. Nevertheless, some research points to little change in general lifestyle. It looks more as if the change may be in the satisfactions received from particular styles. Apparently, people tend to maintain their general modes of dealing with life, at least over the adult years. But men whose modes are "instrumental," "adjusting," or "independent" will be rewarded more in middle age than in old age (Lowenthal et al., 1975). And women who are passive and dependent are rewarded more in youth than in middle age (Livson, 1976). Old people of both sexes are rewarded for valuing "terminal" goals (satisfying in themselves instead of leading to other ends) rather than instrumental ones and for being inclined toward a "rocking-chair" or "passive/dependent" mode.

Disengagement theory

The first book to come out of the University of Chicago Kansas City study of aging, by Cumming and Henry (1961), reported a linear relationship between age (at least past 50) and involvement in life affairs. It suggested that gradual disengagement is a universal process and attributed disengagement to preparation for death. Therefore, it implied that old people who disengage the most should have the highest morale. This theory had a profound influence on gerontologists. For one thing, it contradicted the prevailing "activity theory," which held that, the more active and involved old people are, the better their morale and health.

Further analysis of the Kansas City data

showed that, in fact, not all older people disengaged. The mature "integrated" and the "armored," for example, remained highly involved in life around them. What is more, the "integrated" had high morale and the "armored" did not. Disengagement did *not* seem to be allied to morale, then, but personality did. The "integrated" generally coped well with life and usually had coped well in earlier years. At the time of retirement or other potential crises of later life, they might show temporary distress but then they rearranged their life for continued successful adaptation and usually continued to be involved. Havighurst, Munnichs, Neugarten, and Thomas (1969) found that many schoolteachers forced to retire because of school-system policies embarked on new careers that earned them more money and gave them greater satisfaction than teaching had ever done. Few of them disengaged. The "armored" type also continued engaged, but they did so with desperation, as if cutting down activities would destroy them. They were engaging with gritted teeth instead of with enjoyment.

Then there were some people who disengaged with as high morale as the "integrated" who remained engaged. These were called the "rocking-chair" people, who could hardly wait to ease up, let go, and let other people take over and take care of them. Finally, the unintegrated, unhappy, and self-hating members of the sample were not that way because they had disengaged but because they had been that way long before.

An almost-identical typology had emerged from a study of men before retirement (Reichard et al., 1962). Vaillant's (1977) study of coping styles of Harvard men, followed longitudinally over 30 years, found remarkable consistency in the way these men approached life. Although some of them changed superficially, the ways they reacted to what happened to them in life could be traced to their early behavior. Similar stability in lifestyles is reported by Maas and Kuypers (1974) in their follow-up of the parents in the Berkeley longitudinal study sample. Livson (1976) reviewed the histories of the now-middle-aged women from the Berkeley study who had *not* made the shift in middle age from "feminine" to "androgynous" (combining both so-called masculine and feminine characteristics). She found them to have

been more fragile and dependent in childhood, as well.

Orientation to life

The same Kansas City study that led to the theory of disengagement also led to a different kind of personality theory. When the subjects were given TATs instead of behavioral or self-report measures, their responses showed interesting age differences of a more covert kind. Neugarten and Gutmann (1964) referred to these differences as *mastery styles*. Sex differences were clear. Younger adult men—until about their 50s—seemed to show an *active-mastery* mode. If they wanted something, they were inclined to go out and try to get it. Their orientation was outward, toward the external environment, which they were intent on manipulating to the best of their abilities. During their 50s, perhaps as a result of less success in using an active mode, men turned inward, becoming more interested in their feelings and ideas and using a *passive-mastery* mode. They seemed to be trying to get what they wanted by appealing to powers greater than themselves. The oldest men, perhaps not finding even passive mastery successful, turned to *magic mastery*. They distorted events and their own wishes so as to make themselves believe they had gotten what they wanted, when they had not.

Women seemed to show a different pattern. Younger women tended to use passive mastery. After all, women are trained from childhood to get what they want through the active efforts of others, especially men—fathers, husbands, or sons. In middle age, though, these efforts may no longer work—some say because of loss of sexual attractiveness or charm (for example, Kastenbaum & Symonds, 1977). At any rate, while men in their 50s apparently are turning to passive mastery, women of that age show more-active mastery. They turn outward while the men turn inward, and they become more comfortable with their assertiveness. Note that the era in which this research was done was also the period during which the influx of women into the labor market—particularly of middle-aged women—was remarkable. Again, we do not know to what extent such changes are developmental and to what extent they are due to cohort changes. Old women, however, like old men, are likely to turn to magic mastery. Sex differences in mastery disappear with the general loss of power in old age.

Livson (1976), reporting on the Berkeley longitudinal data, found that many nontraditional women—so far as "feminine" personality characteristics went—who had been leading traditional lives in their early adult years became more assertive or nontraditional in midlife. Monge (1975) found age differences in a number of self-concept components derived from analysis of semantic-differential responses. Figure 15.6 shows his findings, which agree with the mastery theory for the transition from active to passive, or passive to active. At least men, during their 50s, decrease somewhat in the achievement/leadership component of personality, increase sharply in congeniality/sociability, and decrease in masculinity. Women, at the

same time, increase in achievement/leadership—more sharply than men decrease. Women's age patterns on the other two components are not consistent with mastery theory, however. Women increase in congeniality/sociability and in femininity.

Ryff and Baltes (1978), with cross-sectional data, found that middle-aged women were more instrumentally oriented and that old women were more terminally oriented. Instrumental orientation involved preference for values of ambition, capability, and courage. Terminal orientation involved preference for values of desirable end states of existence, sense of accomplishment, freedom, happiness, and so on.

Other research findings are also less clearly supportive of mastery theory. Costa and McCrae (1976) factor-analyzed Cattell's personality-test responses of 969 men of different ages. They found that young men appeared to have a domi-

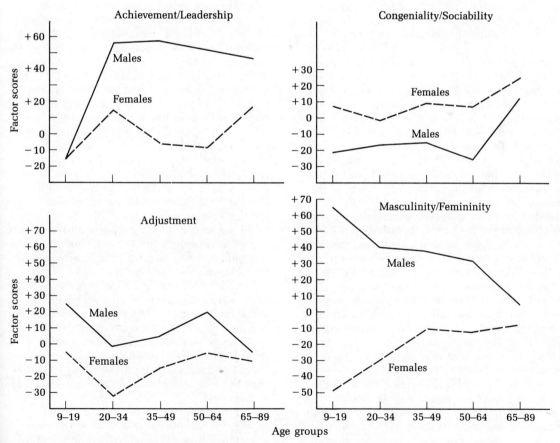

Figure 15.6. Sex and age differences in four components of the self-concept. *(Source: Monge, 1975.)*

nant feeling function and middle-aged men a dominant thinking function, while old men integrated both.

Gutmann's mastery theory is not very different from Jung's (1930/1971) concept of expansion/constriction, expressed also by Buhler (1968) and Kuhlen (1964). Jung felt there was a gradual expansion of interests and activities and goals during early adulthood and gradual constriction from then on. Buhler (1968), for example, divided the life span into phases of goal setting. She saw the first 20 years as a period for establishing goals, and she saw the next period, of less-determined duration, as a time for fulfilling them. When these two periods are over, some people reexamine and set new goals, but others opt for stability and retirement.

Similarly, Kuhlen (1964) defined certain motives as expansion seeking (achievement, power, creativity, and self-actualization, for instance) and others as restricting or contracting (passivity, vicariousness of achievement, less investment in life). His cross-sectional study of the goals of schoolteachers (Kuhlen & Johnson, 1952) found both age and sex differences in the kinds of goals mentioned when teachers were asked "What would you most like to be doing ten years from now?" As can be seen in Figure 15.7, young single women want most to marry, and young married women want most to have homes and be housewives. Both these goals are presumably considered expansion goals. After age 30, single women focus more on career advancement than on getting married (still expansion), but after about age 45, they are most interested in retiring. After about 35, most married teachers' goals were constricting. They want to stay on the same job and, after 40, to retire. Thus, single women's goals may be seen as expanding longer than those of married women. Married men stayed career oriented until, after 50, more of them said that they looked forward to retiring (thus holding expanding goals longer than either single or married women). Notice that Kuhlen's research took place at the beginning of the "feminine mystique" era when most women were adopting home-oriented goals.

The most noticeable difference between the earlier and later life stages investigated by Lowenthal and her colleagues (1975) was in the expansiveness or constriction of their orientation to life—again enforcing the theme introduced by Jung. The two younger groups—high school seniors and newlyweds—were more likely to refer to success and self-fulfillment. The two older groups were more likely to caution against setting goals too high. Remember here that these subjects were of the lower middle class.

High school boys and girls—and also newlywed men—placed the highest value on personal achievement and happiness. The men were likely to think in terms of occupational and personal success. A typical statement by a high school boy is quoted by the authors: "I figure that I'll be working for the most of my life, so I want to get a good job that I'll be able to enjoy. So then I'll be able to enjoy my life, because that will be my life. Of course, you can't really enjoy life unless you have a lot of money" (p. 178).

The high school girls focused on self-actualization and self-fulfillment. One of them said "I think if people want something bad enough, they should go after it and prove themselves" (p. 178). Newlywed men responded not much differently from high school seniors, but newlywed women were more likely to stress giving oneself to others. One said she wanted "to bring good into the world. I find now that my main purpose is to please my husband, my family, to find happiness in life myself" (p. 179).

The middle-aged men and those facing retirement responded in a dry and conformist way about the dual tasks of earning a living and raising a family: "Well, I'd say probably earning a living. . . . I just think it's the responsibility that the husband should have to his family, to see that they're taken care of" (p. 179). Women of the same age, whose youngest children were high school seniors, tended to speak of "living a good life and bringing up your family well so they have a good life" (p. 180).

The men and women in the preretirement stage were more likely to mention humanitarian and moral purposes. The men also mentioned leaving a legacy, and the women mentioned some religious themes. Thus, a man said, "I think [a man] does well if he makes himself a decent and satisfactory part of society, with at least the sort of contribution that is recognized or recognizable."

The question of whether or not lifestyles change over lifetimes returns us to the genotype/phenotype dilemma. If people select dif-

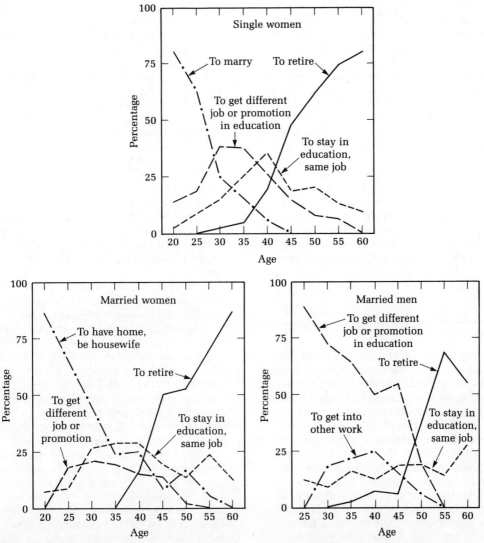

Figure 15.7. Changes in goals with increasing adult age as reflected in the responses of public school teachers to the question "What would you most like to be doing ten years from now?" *(Source: Kuhlen and Johnson, 1952.)*

ferent individual traits at different times to maintain consistent styles in the face of change, both description and explanation are difficult. Neugarten (1977) concludes that the major lesson so far from the Berkeley longitudinal studies is the demonstration of "individual differences: that persons (or types of persons) maintain their recognizability and that, in this sense, there is continuity of personality over time" (p. 641). In her follow-up study of a group

of women first studied when they were between 45 and 57 and then reinterviewed ten years later, a variety of measures, including coping abilities, showed relatively high consistency over time. In a cross-sectional study by O'Connell (1979), age was not relevant to the lifestyles of women between 30 and 58. Whether or not women were traditional was related to personality and other factors, but not to age.

In general, we could conclude from an overall look at research now available that there is a complex pattern of effects of change and stability of personality that includes both apparent resistance to change and "adaptation" to change. A recent cross-sequential test of the stability of adult-personality measures by Schaie and Parham (1976) on subjects between 21 and 84 years of age reported that all factors were stable except for excitability and humanitarian concerns, both of which increased with age. These authors suggest a three-part model to account for differential stability of factor scores. The first includes *biostable* traits, which show sex differences that are reliably maintained throughout adulthood. The second includes *acculturated* traits, which show no sex differences but do show differences between age groups. The third includes *biocultural* traits, presumably based on genetic differences that are modified by universally experienced life-stage expectancies.

Egocentrism

Underlying the concepts of mastery and instrumentalism are two basic orientation-to-life constructs that have so far received only minor attention in the psychological life-span literature. These are *egocentrism* and *locus of control.* Looft and Charles (1971) define egocentrism as an embeddedness in one's own point of view or as an inability to "decenter" to other perspectives. In Piaget's theory, from which Looft and Charles's definition stems, egocentrism is supposed to diminish after the acquisition of formal-operational thought, normatively in adolescence. Little attention has been given to its presence, let alone its possible waxing or waning, in the later years of life, beyond generally held beliefs that old age is characterized by both heightened egocentrism and self-centeredness.

In a crude exploratory study using Piagetian tasks with college students and older people, Looft and Charles did find that the college students were significantly less egocentric than were their older subjects. However, the subjects had to cooperate in a social-interaction task in which the more they could communicate to their partners—and therefore be able to see their partners' viewpoints—the better their score. The only significant age difference

proved to be one of time taken to complete the task. The older subjects were slower, but not more egocentric. It is clear that we need much more research on egocentrism.

Gutmann and Neugarten's mastery theory is analogous to Rotter's concept of locus of control. Both refer to feelings of control over the environment. Rotter (1966) pointed out that some people, whom he calls *internals*, perceive that their own actions can have an effect on their lives. Others, called *externals*, feel that they are essentially powerless, controlled by powers outside themselves. That is, some feel that control is internal to themselves, others that it is external. If one believes that there is little one can do to change one's circumstances (external locus of control), one is likely to become passive and to depend on others to take care of one. This pattern is believed to be particularly true of old people.

So far, studies of age differences in locus of control are not in agreement. Staats (1974) reports that older people are more internal than are younger people. Bradley and Webb (1976) found that people over age 60 are more external than are younger adults. Kuypers (1972) administered a shortened version of Rotter's scale to 64 parents in the Berkeley longitudinal study. These 25 men and 39 women were sent the questionnaire by mail. Kuypers could find neither sex nor age differences in locus-of-control scores. The internals, however, showed "higher" coping mechanisms than did the externals. They were more talkative, had a wider range of interests, were concerned with philosophical problems, enjoyed esthetic experiences, and so forth. The externals were more defensive and closed off from the environment. Kuypers concludes that "for the elderly as for all other ages, existence is more than a series of responses to changing conditions. The individual carries within himself a context against which events are anticipated, experienced, and handled. The control dimension is one of these contexts and perhaps a critical one" (p. 173).

Two other studies also found no age differences (Nehrke & Reimanis, 1978; Duke, Shaheen, & Nowicki, 1974). Nehrke and Reimanis found, further, that institutionalization per se does not lead inevitably to externality. They studied men living in a Veterans Administration Domiciliary. These men were more *internal* than men and women of the same age living in the community. This finding runs counter to most literature on the effects of institutionalization. The finding may perhaps be attributable to the self-selection among veterans who knew how to manipulate the VA system in order to succeed in being admitted to the relatively desirable domiciliary.

Generational research

Traits that stay the most stable over time within individuals also tend to be transmitted across generations, particularly within the family. In a review of generational research, Troll and Bengtson (1979) suggest that there is a relation between individual and family persistence of traits and societal stability. Other things being equal—in the absence of accelerated social or historical change—adults tend to remain constant in personality, or to resist change. Adult stability may be understood in part if we consider that adulthood follows adolescence, and that adolescence is the time of life when change is greatest and fastest—and thus the most difficult to assimilate as well as the most stressful experientially. Individuals who have succeeded in achieving the identity resolution that marks adulthood are not eager to seek out more change. The kinds of personality changes just summarized look like shifts in relatively peripheral characteristics that do not "rock the boat," as alterations in basic belief patterns would.

According to Troll and Bengtson, change can be understood as the result of interactions between four generational effects: (1) individual development, (2) cohort or age group, (3) historical period, and (4) family transmission. In other words, social climate, through either historical or generational effects, can temper and modify individual developmental and family effects. In the absence of societal change, individual developmental change will be the kind that is most noticeable. During the adult years, when there is developmental pressure for stability, there will be little change, not only in the individual, but also in the person's family from one generation to the next. Furthermore, pressures are not one-way but reciprocal. Change in an individual can upset people with whom that individual interacts. These people in turn may then exert pressure on the individual to resist change. Conversely, change in youths could

pressure their parents to change along with them, in order to maintain ties.

There may be particular times of life, such as adolescence, during which there is strong pressure for change. Adolescents are supposed to establish their unique identities in the face of rapid physiological change, on the one hand, and in the face of strong expectations by parents and others for them to "grow up," on the other hand. Moreover, studies of the activist students of the mid-1960s (Flacks, 1967; Haan, Smith, & Block, 1968) found that these students, who were the forerunners of their generation, came from particular kinds of families, with particular kinds of "family themes," to adopt a term of Hess and Handel's (1959).

Haan, Smith, and Block (1968) compared three groups of college-age youth in California: radical activists in Berkeley, children of "authoritarian-personality" parents, and members of the Berkeley longitudinal study. They found that the activist students were more likely to have parents who, like them, valued social change and were dedicated to idealist philosophies. Both the activist students and their parents, furthermore, made more cognitively complex moral judgments (Kohlberg, 1973) than did subjects in the other two groups. During late adolescence, these "forerunner" students, who shared their parents' general orientation, were impelled to establish their own identities separate from their parents. They therefore transformed their parents' attitudes and beliefs into relevant new forms. They created a set of "generational-keynote characteristics" to underline generational difference, while keeping the basic family orientations.

During this transition, these late adolescents tended to drop in their level of moral judgment. This drop was temporary, however; eventually, they matched the high moral levels of their parents. The authoritarian-raised youth made no moral or value transformations at this point in their life. In fact, they tended to remain at their high school level in moral judgment and other beliefs. In adulthood, they too matched the level of their parents, which they had reached at a younger age because the level—"conventional" moralism—was lower than that of the forerunner children and their parents. The third group, the Berkeley longitudinal subjects and their parents, had moral levels in between the two other groups.

Data such as these suggest a three-step process of generational and reciprocal historical change (Troll & Bengtson, 1979). In Step 1, a new age cohort of "forerunners," on reaching maturity, turns to new ways of expressing the general orientation (for example, dedication to causes) received from families. These forerunners will be less like their parents in specific attitudes (which we could label "generation-keynote effects") than the rest of their age mates are like *their* parents.

In Step 2, if the new generation-keynote theme meets the needs of the rest of the generation, it is adopted by the generation as a whole. It is also adopted by the parents of the forerunners, either through reciprocal socialization or because they, like their children, are attuned to this new orientation. Parents, even those susceptible to particular ideas, take longer to adopt new orientations because they are perhaps less ready to change. After the forerunners' parents and peers have adopted the new orientation, the parents and children of such families are more alike than are the parents and children of other families.

In Step 3, if the once-new attitude is adopted by most of the society and a new cohort of forerunners is espousing a new keynote theme, the families of these forerunners again show a larger "generation gap" than their nonforerunner peers and *their* parents.

Forerunners are not necessarily more liberal than their elders. They are more liberal only in times of societal swings toward liberalism. It is commonly believed, for example, that old people are more conservative than young. This pattern is demonstrated in the findings of Glamser (1974), shown in Table 15.3, although his age groups did not include particularly old subjects. Note that there is little age difference in number of conservative opinions; the greatest difference is in the liberal column. The early 1970s were a time of swing toward liberalism and the youth were the ones to swing first. A decade

later, the swing went the other way, and the youth led again.

Although it is easier to see this "forerunner effect" operating for "pioneer" groups of youth, a similar process may occur in pioneer cohorts at any age. Large numbers of middle-aged women today, for example, are living longer than did previous generations of women because of the life-expectancy changes described in Chapter 5. These women live longer than their mothers and grandmothers, and so are pioneers in that they do not have models of older women before them. They have also lost serving roles as mothers and wives while they are still healthy, vigorous, and able to be economically independent because of labor-market shifts favoring women's employment. Such a cohort could have as much impact on society today as forerunner cohorts of youth did 15 years earlier. We may find, in addition, that members of such a "generation unit," to use Mannheim's (1952) term, like the mid-1960s youth, come from particular families and backgrounds that are conducive to adopting a pioneer status. Also members of such a unit are similar to activist youth because they have had to become independent and find new identities. Retirees and healthy older people of the 1970s represent a similar pioneer cohort, searching for new ways to lead a nonwork life and reversing the attitudes of the work-oriented younger members of their families in reciprocal socialization.

Possible reactions to change

There are four possible ways to react to major or abrupt life changes:

1. *Denial.* We could act as if no change has occurred. It is possible, for example, to look in the mirror each day as we brush teeth or hair and to see, not the faces actually reflected there, but the faces of an earlier age. Many husbands and wives continue to try to interact with spouses as if the spouses were the same as they were at the time of marriage, even though the years have wrought important changes. Many parents continue to treat their children as if they were still four years old—when the "children" actually are in their 30s, 40s, or even 50s. Many adult children continue to perceive their parents as the omnipotent people they

TABLE 15.3 Political and social opinions, by age

Age	Liberal	Moderate	Conservative
20–29	55%	39%	6%
50–65	21	69	10

Source: Glamser, 1974.

seemed when the children were young, even though the parents may now actually be powerless and confused. This kind of reaction may make functioning difficult, because it runs counter to reality. It can certainly lead to confused and discordant interpersonal interaction.

2. *Homeostatic readjustment.* We can modify our behavior just enough to return almost to the condition we were in before the change had occurred. If we lose friends, jobs, or relatives, we may substitute other friends, jobs, or relatives as close in character to the ones lost as possible. Although we may not deny such losses, we may try to maintain our own self-images and ways of interacting. This mode of reaction is not confined to losses. If we are promoted or advance to more prestigious or more advantageous situations, we may repeat earlier modes of looking at ourselves or others, with only minimal alterations. We may increase the quantity of our activities or interactions without changing our modes of behavior. Or we may change some behavior patterns, but not more than we have to in order to "adjust."

3. *Fragmentation.* Instead of denial, we could welcome change so much or induce change of such a massive order that we lose our sense of "I-ness" or our ability to feel control over ourselves and our environment. Psychotherapists might label such a reaction a "breakdown," a "psychosis," or an "ego fragmentation." It is no accident that the onset of schizophrenia (a disease characterized by fragmentation of personality) is often in adolescence, because adolescence is a time of enormous changes in body as well as in social expectations and demands. Many schools of psychotherapy that became popular during the 1960s and early 1970s thought it necessary to disrupt previous behavior and identities, to abandon previous ways of thinking and acting and embrace totally new self-images. The incidence of "breakdowns" among followers of these approaches was high (for example, see Lieberman, Yalom, & Miles, 1973). It was higher in group therapy than in individual treatment, perhaps because the group therapist had less opportunity to promote self-continuity among group members.

4. *Development.* Faced with new experiences, few people seem to evolve, to re-create or transform themselves into more-complex and more-differentiated human beings. People who develop this reaction do not lose their sense of

I-ness. What they do is change their *me,* their *ways* of behaving.

Turning points

Chapter 1 noted that life crises, major life events, or universal transition points are controversial issues in life-span developmental theory. Some psychologists believe that particular ages or particular life events bring on particular kinds of behavior. Others are not convinced of the universality of such general points of change. Although many major life events may challenge previous self-images, most people probably deny such challenges or make some minor adjustments that will return them to homeostasis. Probably few adults break apart, and few develop. We tend to maintain our self-definitions to a remarkable degree.

A major investigation of life transitions (Srole & Fischer, 1978) found that when people were asked to name turning points in their life—defined in terms of heavy blows—about 50% of the respondents reported at least one. Half of those who did said that the blow was a turn for the better and half for the worse. The "empty nest" and retirement are presumed to be two major turning points in life. Yet neither of these events showed any influence on responses to the question "Who are you?" (Back, 1971b) in a study of 502 men and women between ages 45 and 70.

A life transition, according to David Chiriboga (1979a), has a sequence. First, a precipitating event upsets the previous equilibrium. This *marker* event precipitates a "quest for a more satisfying paradigm" that in turn will produce reequilibrium. The successful quest is followed by a period of consolidating that new equilibrium. Note that Chiriboga is assuming the homeostatic response to change, rather than any of the other three responses just suggested. However, the new equilibrium could be a transformed state and thus could constitute development.

MIDLIFE TRANSITION

Some hypotheses are so inherently attractive that failure to verify them does not deter their persistence. Among these are the many theories about senility and other universal deteriorations of old age; the importance of birth order as an antecedent personality variable; the primarily biological determinism of behavior, particularly for women; and the existence of a midlife crisis. There are many others.

The midlife transition is seen, by some theorists, to be precipitated by awareness of one's own mortality. Other theorists consider it to be brought on by the termination of the "parental imperative" that dominates adulthood from late adolescence to the "empty nest," or perhaps by the menopause, depending on the stress the theorist places on biological determinism. The "parental-imperative" view has been espoused by David Gutmann (1975). Basing his conclusions on the responses of men and women of different ages and cultures to the TAT, Gutmann feels that psychological characteristics are reversed after the demands of parenting are over. His conclusions about changes in mastery style over life were described earlier in this chapter. At that point, I did not discuss his sex-role implications. Primarily, he sees the midlife transition as one from masculinity or femininity toward androgyny.

Driven by the needs of parenting, says Gutmann, young men seek pleasure mainly in sex. This pleasure has a productive goal: "the production of sons who will aid the father in his work and will be his social security in old age" (p. 45). Young women must be confined to the home site in order to care for and protect children, so they must be passive, sensual, and tender. Gutmann says that the lack of balance induced by this extreme differentiation is compensated for psychologically in marriage. The young man benefits from his wife's feminine qualities, and she benefits from her husband's managerial, achievement-oriented, and relatively tough-minded "masculine" qualities. After the shift to the "normal" androgyny of midlife, "Both sexes can . . . afford the luxury of living out the potentials and pleasures that they had to relinquish earlier in the service of their particular parental assignment" (p. 53). The old man can become sensitive and compliant, the old woman dominant. Gold (1960) reports that 14 out of 26 societies studied by anthropologists show a midlife shift toward greater female dominance. The other cultures show no shift. No culture showed a shift toward greater male dominance with advanced age.

For some theorists, this midlife shift in sex-role characteristics is seen primarily as a change in direction or an emphasis on different characteristics. For others, it is an unearthing of preexistent characteristics, a return to the essential androgyny of preadolescence.

Gutmann sees the end of the "parental imperative" as the precipitator of this midlife shift. Other theorists, primarily those who developed the disengagement theory, see an awareness of mortality as the precipitator. Neugarten, for example, has spoken of the shift from looking at life as time since birth to looking at life as time left to live.

Most proponents of the "midlife crisis," such as Levinson, are most concerned about the stress and psychopathology that mark the event. This aspect of the theory is discussed in Chapter 16, on quality of life. Finally, many make the point that the middle of life is a time of particular openness, when, as Chiriboga has said, people seek new ways of living. These issues have been discussed more fully in Chapter 1.

What can we conclude about personality development in adulthood and old age? Maybe we can conclude that, if the context or situation does not change, neither does the person, in most respects. But where there is a precipitating event, people can change in a variety of ways. Sometimes they truly develop.

Summary

Both aspects of the self seem remarkably stable during the adult years: the feeling of being oneself—the *I*—and the way one describes oneself or is described by others—the *me*. Other personality characteristics are also consistent over time, even over generations in the family.

The time of major changes seems to be adolescence, which is probably the most turbulent and stressful period of the life span. After this point, outer or inner events that call for change are rarely welcomed and are met, on the whole, with resistance—with denial or at least the most-minimal adjustment that will allow a return to a previous equilibrium. In spite of a number of persuasive theories about universal turning points such as the "midlife crisis," the evidence so far is ambiguous at best.

Individual and generational changes seem to be mediated by historical and cohort changes.

Generational forerunners or pioneers, such as adult women returning to the labor force, face new circumstances for which they have no models. In times of rapid social change, their experience becomes the model for other generations, older and younger.

16

Happiness, Coping, and Mental Health

How can we judge the quality of a person's life? One can be symptom-free, and therefore be in good mental health, yet one can also feel that one has failed to live up to one's standards, and thus have low self-esteem. One can be very unhappy on Monday, but very happy on Tuesday. One can find life exciting, but fail to adjust to the requirements of the society one lives in. One can use primitive coping mechanisms, yet be highly esteemed by associates and be very successful at survival.

This chapter deals with some of the very different indexes that have been used to assess quality of living: self-esteem, happiness, zest, life satisfaction, morale, ego mechanisms, adaptation, adjustment, and mental health. No apology is offered for the confounding of indexes in much of the literature. After all, these indexes are not separable in the people who are studied.

Self-esteem

How well people like themselves is usually measured by matching their self-descriptions to their descriptions of their ideal person. Early research on self-esteem found that older people in general don't like themselves as much as younger people like themselves (Mason, 1954; Kogan & Wallach, 1961). Mason compared three unmatched groups: 30 young parents of clinic patients, 30 middle-class people over 60, and 60 poor people over 55. Even though her middle-

class group was the best off economically, the younger people liked themselves better. It should come as no surprise that the poor old people liked themselves the least.

Kogan and Wallach's (1961) study was somewhat more sophisticated, even though their four groups were also unmatched. Like many later investigators, they used the semantic-differential technique to contrast feelings about real self with feelings about an ideal self. They found, to their surprise, that even though the older subjects had lower self-esteem than the younger ones, these older people did not set their ideal selves as high as the younger ones did—were not as perfectionistic. Thus, methods of assessing self-esteem at different ages may not be measuring the same thing. This kind of measurement problem was discussed in Chapter 2.

Later studies—also almost all cross-sectional—found the picture much more complex than the original picture of a linear downward path of self-esteem with age. In some studies, self-esteem is higher for middle-aged than for younger and older subjects (Hess, 1970; Bloom, 1961; Lowenthal et al., 1975; Grant, 1969; Bray & Howard, 1978; Back, 1971b). Mullener and Laird (1971), like Kogan and Wallach (1961), found age differences in the way people were rating themselves. Adolescents gave relatively global judgments, adults, relatively differentiated ones. Asking people to draw a human figure is sometimes used as a projective test of self-definition and self-esteem. Tuckman, Lorge, and Zeman (1961) found that the drawings of older

people were incomplete, disorganized, disproportionate, and bizarre. In this case, the older
people were closer to the age of 90, the younger
closer to 55—most studies would call this "younger" group old.

Lowenthal and her associates (1975) found
that the high school seniors studied had the
lowest self-esteem; the older subjects had progressively higher self-esteem. When men and
women were looked at separately, however, the
curves looked different. The newlywed men
and the oldest women liked themselves the best
of the eight age/sex groups. The age pattern of
the men was more irregular than that for the
women. The young-adult men had higher self-
esteem than did the adolescent men; the
middle-aged men had slightly lower self-esteem
than the adolescent men. The women, however,
showed progressively higher self-esteem with
age.

When these same subjects were reinterviewed five years later, there was no change in
self-esteem for the middle-aged women. Noberini and Neugarten (1975) found similar stability
for middle-aged women in a ten-year follow-up.
The middle-aged men in the Lowenthal study,
however, showed a continued move toward passivity (Thurnher, 1977). Whether passivity is
analogous to low self-esteem may be debated, of
course.

The San Francisco high school boys were
painfully aware of their social inadequacies.
One said "Socially I have lots of room for progress. I'm the kind of person that most people
don't think one way or the other about"
(Lowenthal et al., 1975, p. 69). The high school
girls were no different: The authors said "They
are even more likely to question their ability to
lead an independent life" (p. 72). It is interesting to compare these feelings with those found
in a large national investigation ten years earlier. Young people who had been asked about
their past and future lives in a 1959 Gallup poll
(Bortner & Hultsch, 1976) saw both the past and
future as better than the present. Thus, while
they were currently "down in the dumps," they
didn't expect to stay there forever. To the extent
that we can compare San Francisco lower-middle-class youth in 1970 with a national sample
drawn in a more stable and affluent era, the
low self-esteem of the San Francisco youth may
be low only in contrast to their high aspirations
for the future. Their ideal selves were perhaps

exaggerated, so their evaluation of their current
state could only be low.

The newlywed young men felt great confidence in themselves, greater than did the newlywed women. This sex difference is consistent
with findings generally reported, particularly
among married adults. Women are more critical
of themselves and devalue themselves much
more than do men (Lowenthal et al., 1975; Back,
1971b; Gurin, Veroff, & Feld, 1960). Bortner and
Hultsch (1976) found more of the pattern they
called "great expectations"—exaggerated hopes
for the future—among young adults the age of
the San Francisco newlyweds than among the
other age groups they studied, even the adolescents.

The San Francisco middle-aged men described themselves as dull, reserved, and lacking a sense of humor; they did not like themselves as much as the newlyweds liked
themselves. The middle-aged women were not
much more pleased with themselves than their
male contemporaries. But the preretired men
and women, who were ten years older (around
60), seemed much more comfortable with themselves. A woman at this time of life said "I can
say what I feel, I am not embarrassed by many
things any more, and my personality is better"
(p. 74). Bortner and Hultsch found, however, an
"anticipating-deprivation" pattern most common
at this age. The pattern called "all downhill"
was the fate of people about 70 and older. The
middle-aged feeling of ease and self-liking must
thus be seen against a backdrop of doom. It is
the *Götterdämmerung,* the "twilight of the
gods."

Women tend, on the whole, to derive their
feelings of self-worth from family circumstances; men, on the whole, derive their worth
from job circumstances. Nowak (1976) found
that middle-aged women, in addition, were sensitive to their appearance and didn't like themselves much when their skin began to sag and
show other signs of aging. Others have suggested that men have similar sensitivity to their
declining strength and power. It is interesting
that the men's self-esteem is related not to the
prestige or financial rewards of their job, but to
their occupational achievement relative to others with similar education (Luck & Heiss, 1972).

It is hardly surprising that older people who
have more-negative attitudes about old age, as
well as poor health, should have lower self-

esteem than other people their age who don't devalue old age and feel in better health (Ward, 1977). But which is the chicken and which is the egg? It may well be that poor self-esteem would lead older people to think more negatively about old age and even to exaggerate their health problems.

Response biases may explain both age and sex differences. Gurin and her associates (1960) found that women over age 55 were less self-critical than those under 55, but were still more self-critical than men their age. Gove and Geerken (1977) found that, when those response styles characteristic of our oldest cohorts, such as tendency to agree or contradict, were controlled, neither age nor sex differences were significant.

Another factor related to self-esteem is locus of control, discussed in Chapter 15. High external control—feeling that one's rewards depend on luck, fate, or outside forces—is related to negative self-image and to large discrepancies between real- and ideal-self ratings (Breytspaak, 1974). This becomes important in interpreting sex differences. For example, there is less sex difference in locus of control among college students (Palmore & Luikart, 1972) than among middle-aged men and women. There may even be a period effect of increasing internality in women over the last 20 years, as suggested in the last chapter.

Happiness

A 1969 Gallup poll asked people "Is your life exciting?" (Alston & Dudley, 1973). The percentages of those who answered yes are shown in Table 16.1. Clearly, older people (although 50 is not very old) felt less excitement in their lives than did younger ones. The only noticeable sex difference, incidentally, was in the youngest group: women in the child-rearing years found life duller than men of the same age. Three-quarters of men in their 20s felt that life was exciting. Fewer men *and* women over 50 thought life was exciting—only two-fifths. Again, before we conclude that life gets duller as one goes along, we should consider the effect of the self-actualization movement and its stress on excitement in life. In 1969, that movement was relatively new and thus would have had its greatest impact on youth. A 1982 poll asking the

TABLE 16.1 Percentage saying that life is exciting, by age and sex

Age	Male % (N)	Female % (N)	Total % (N)
20–29	75 (117)	65 (138)	70 (255)
30–39	56 (121)	55 (144)	55 (265)
40–49	48 (153)	49 (157)	48 (310)
50 and over[a]	40 (310)	36 (240)	39 (550)
Total	50 (701)	49 (679)	50 (1380)

[a]Previous analyses indicated no statistically significant changes in proportions saying that life was exciting by ten-year intervals after the 50-year-old level.

Source: Alston and Dudley, 1973.

same question might find less age difference in this respect.

Although exciting lives may be more possible for youth than for their elders, an unexciting life is not necessarily unsatisfactory or unhappy. One can have high life satisfaction and high morale and be neither happy nor unhappy. Serenity is not exciting, but it is not depression. For example, the youngest San Francisco group, the high school seniors, were the least happy, the most lonely, the lowest in life satisfaction, and the highest in negative experiences reported—but they also reported the most happy experiences! We could call their lives both exciting and complex. When they weren't up, they were down. Their lives were rarely calm.

The newlyweds were a little less complex. Overall, we could call them the happiest group. They were highest in life satisfaction and reported a majority of positive experiences. They were, however, the second highest in reported negative experiences, next to the adolescents, and they were lonelier than the middle-aged subjects. Their lives were not as exciting as those of the teenagers, but were next to the teenagers' lives in excitement.

On the whole, the middle-aged parents of high school seniors were in the middle on most quality-of-life measures. The women's life-satisfaction scores, though, were the lowest of all age/sex groups. Overall, they were not as happy as the newlyweds, but were happier than the subjects who were their children's age.

The oldest group, in late middle age, was happier than those who were ten years younger. It was as high in life satisfaction as the newlyweds (particularly the men), but had lower affect, either positive or negative, than did younger groups.

The oldest Kansas City study subjects (up to 71 years old) showed the lowest affect intensity in TAT responses (Rosen & Neugarten, 1960). However, old subjects (average age 73) tested by the Lakin and Eisdorfer (1960) on a different projective test (Reitman stick figures) did not have lower affect intensity than young subjects, whose average age was 24. The very "coolness" of the older San Francisco subjects may have contributed to their satisfaction and contentment, as suggested by the fact that those with broader interests in this group had lower satisfaction than those with narrower interests. We might conclude that our society penalizes our more complex and more involved citizens, particularly when they are older. Or conversely, we might conclude that more complex people are not so easily content with the lower rewards from life that old age offers.

LIFE SATISFACTION

Most research on life satisfaction compares middle-aged with older people. One exception is Lieberman's study (1970), which found no difference between college students and old people. The young subjects, however, answered in terms of the present and the future, while the old ones answered in terms of the past. This finding is reminiscent of Bortner and Hultsch's (1976) self-esteem findings. The use of different time frames at different times of life skews all such age comparison.

Dwelling in the past is not an inevitable condition of old age, however. The findings of Lehr (1967) and Spence (1968) indicate that subjects until the very oldest ages report plans for their futures. Elder's (1974) longitudinal data show that adults' retrospective reports of the trend of happiness in their lives are affected by their early experiences. If their adolescent years were deprived, their adult years look good; everything seems to be going up.

Life satisfaction in old age seems to be relative to past and present circumstances. This contextual contribution makes it hard to draw conclusions from existing research data. Many investigators find a downward curve, although further analysis often suggests that such mediating factors as socioeconomic status and health are responsible, rather than aging per se. Old

---

Tell me something about where and how you would like to live.

Grandfather, age 71
I'd stay in Michigan and spend the summer up north. I would possibly have a home in Florida during the winter, someplace warm. I would travel more. There would probably be no changes in material things.

Father, age 45
I would continue to live in Michigan. I'd like to go south for a vacation but stay in Michigan every summer. I would continue to work. I don't think I would change material things.

Son, age 15
I'd probably live in the Rocky Mountains and get back to nature. I'd learn to provide for myself, using only what's really necessary.

---

people with good health and plenty of money continue to enjoy their lives. Other studies find a U-shaped pattern, with morale down in middle age compared with youth and old age. Longitudinal studies, however, often find marked stability in well-being over time, suggesting that if you want to have a satisfying old age you should start out by having a satisfying childhood, adolescence, and adulthood. In fact, one large-scale cross-national study (Cantril, 1965) found no relation between life satisfaction and age. These findings thus duplicate those on self-esteem in their lack of consistency.

Ego mechanisms

Turning now from the phenomenological *self* to a different concept of personality, let us consider possible development in ego functioning past adolescence.

COPING

Freud (1927) introduced the construct of the ego to denote that part of the self that handles adaptation to the environment. The ego supposedly is made up of processes that help us adjust to the world around us by controlling our more primitive impulses and by modifying the rigid rules we learned from our parents in childhood. Freud's daughter, Anna Freud (1946), took her father's theory a step forward by describing a set of mechanisms used in this process of managing life. Subsequent psychologists, notably Norma Haan (1963), have distinguished between coping mechanisms, the "normal" ways to adapt, and defense mechanisms, the pathological ways. Her model is presented in Table 16.2. The ego mechanisms given in the first column can be expressed either positively, as coping mechanisms, or negatively, as defense mechanisms.

According to Haan, coping mechanisms involve choice and are realistic, flexible, and purposive. Defense mechanisms are rigid, distort reality, and are primitive. Haan (1972) compared the coping of adolescents with their own coping when they were 30 and 45 years of age. She reported that, over time, behaviors reflecting fantasy and reaction formation decreased and those reflecting altruism and suppression increased.

Among the other ego systems proposed, that of Vaillant (1977) is relevant because he used it in a longitudinal study of adult men. His list is seen in Table 16.3. There is a hierarchical order to Vaillant's mechanisms, from "psychotic" (at the bottom) through "immature" and "neurotic," to "mature" (at the top). "Normal" children under age 5 are seen as using "psychotic" mechanisms; children between 3 and 15, "immature" mechanisms; and "healthy" people between the ages of 3 and 90, "neurotic" mechanisms. Only people over the age of 12 use "mature" mechanisms. The equivalence between pathological and early-development processes, although convenient in classifying adult men, is unfortunate from a developmental perspective.

Vaillant followed a group of Harvard men and described them as using more-mature defenses with the passage of years. Figure 16.1

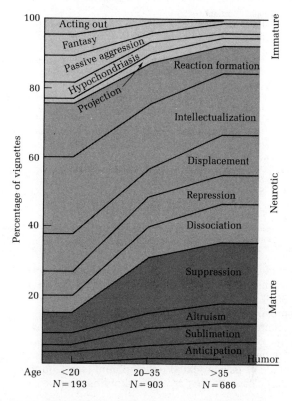

Figure 16.1. Shifts in defensive styles during adulthood. *(Source: Vaillant, 1977.)*

TABLE 16.2 Ego mechanisms: Coping and defense

Ego mechanism	Defense mechanism	Coping mechanism
Discrimination	Isolation[a]	Objectivity
Detachment	Intellectualization	Intellectuality
Means/ends symbolization	Rationalization	Logical analysis
Delayed response	Doubt	Tolerance of ambiguity
Selective awareness	Denial	Concentration
Sensitivity	Projection	Empathy
Time reversal	Regression	Regression in the service of the ego
Impulse diversion	Displacement	Sublimation
Impulse transformation	Reaction formation	Substitution
Impulse restraint	Repression	Suppression

[a]Exclusion of a problem area from everyday (normal) thought processes.
Source: Haan, 1963.

TABLE 16.3 Defense mechanisms (Vaillant's system)

Level 1. "Psychotic"
Delusional projection: having frank delusions about external reality, usually of a persecutory type
Denial: denying external reality, including use of fantasy
Distortion: grossly reshaping external reality to suit inner needs

Level 2. "Immature"
Projection: attributing one's own unacknowledged feelings to others
Schizoid fantasy: using fantasy to indulge in autistic retreat
Hypochondriasis: transforming reproach toward others into self-reproach and then into pain and illness
Passive/aggressive behavior: indirectly expressing aggression toward others
Acting out: directly expressing unconscious wishes

Level 3. "Neurotic"
Intellectualization: thinking about instinctual wishes in formal, bland terms
Repression: failing to acknowledge input from sense organs
Displacement: redirecting feelings toward less-cared-for objects
Reaction formation: behaving directly opposite to an instinctual impulse
Dissociation: temporarily modifying one's sense of identity

Level 4. "Mature"
Altruism: giving vicarious service to others
Humor: seeing what is funny about life's dilemmas
Suppression: deciding to postpone paying attention to conflict
Anticipation: planning for the future
Sublimation: indirectly expressing instincts

Source: Vaillant, 1977.

shows the proportion of the different mechanisms at three ages: under 20, 20 to 35, and over 35. The labels in the right margin classify the mechanisms as "immature," "neurotic," and "mature." Vaillant further analyzed age changes by comparing two groups: "perpetual boys" and "generative." Basing his analysis on Erikson's scale of psychosexual development (see Chapter 2), he saw the first group as showing no progression into the adult stages and the second group as having developed. Frequencies of immature, neurotic, and mature mechanisms are shown for the first group in Figure 16.2 and for the second group in Figure 16.3.

It is interesting that the "perpetual boys" showed more mature mechanisms in adolescence than did the "generative" group. Vaillant sees this result as consistent with Anna Freud's

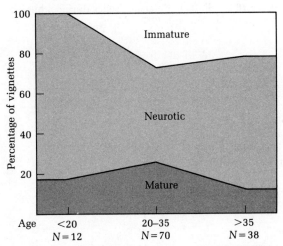

Figure 16.2. Mechanisms used by "perpetual boys." *(Source: Vaillant, 1977.)*

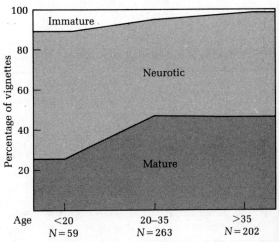

Figure 16.3. Mechanisms used by maturing men. *(Source: Vaillant, 1977.)*

theory that it is "normal" for adolescents to be rebellious and immature; that adolescents have to go through this regression or they cannot truly mature later. Both Haan, Smith, and Block (1968) and Kohlberg (1973) report analogous "deterioration" in moral judgment among youth who later reach the highest levels on Kohlberg's moral-judgment scale (see Chapter 2). Those who did not deteriorate at this time remained at a lower, conventional level, as noted in Chapter 15.

When they compared the efficiency of ego functioning among different age groups in their San Francisco study, Lowenthal and her associates (1975) noted better instrumental behavior in the older subjects. They were less absent-minded, disorderly, lazy, and restless than the younger ones. The middle-aged people were also more skilled in interpersonal relations, less suspicious, and less embarrassed. They used fewer misrepresentations and manipulations and less guile, shrewdness, and drama. They appeared more frank and open and were less likely to use conflict-evoking behavior such as sarcasm or stubbornness.

Vaillant believes that "maturation of defenses, like morality, is linked both to cognitive maturation and to the evolution of impulse control" (p. 340). He uses the cogent example of jokes: "They evolve from *passive aggression* (the sado-masochistic pratfall and the hilarious thumbtack in the chair) through the *displacement* of cartoons, puns, and schoolyard smut, to the more sophisticated *displacements* of parody and Broadway comedy, to the subtle mitigation of reality present in the adult humor of the *Punch* or *New Yorker* cartoon" (p. 340). Slater and Scarr (1964), incidentally, found that older educated respondents (between 50 and 90) were less impulsive and had greater intellectual control than did college students.

When Symonds (1961) compared adolescents' TAT scores with their scores in their late 20s, he found that themes of criminality went down and that themes of guilt and depression went up. Symonds feels this reversal shows increasing maturity. Both Neugarten and Havighurst have reported high levels of the ego qualities of "executive" function and competence in middle-aged people.

Not all research has found individual change in ego functioning, however. Srole and Fischer's (1978) 20-year follow-up of their mid-Manhattan study found cohort improvement but found no individual, age-related improvement. Those who were studied in 1954 tended to show neither improvement nor decline over 20 years, but 50-year-olds in 1974 functioned better than 50-year-olds in 1954. This improvement turned out largely to be for women; men were essentially stable.

Neugarten (1977) writes "Whether or not the relationship between personality and adaptation remains generally the same in successive periods of adulthood is a complex question, complicated by the fact that the psychological issues and the preoccupations of adults change over time" (p. 638). When the Kansas City study subjects' scores on various coping and defense mechanisms were factor-analyzed, only four of the resultant personality types showed any relation to age. Among the men, passive/dependent and constricted types were present only among the younger (middle-aged) subjects. Among the women, self-doubting and competitive types were also found only at these comparatively younger ages (Neugarten, Crotty, & Tobin, 1964).

Daydreaming is usually considered the opposite of or absence of coping: one *dreams* one is doing instead of actually doing. Daydreaming is thus usually considered more characteristic of adolescents than of older adults. When three age groups were compared, 18–29, 30–39, and 40–49, the older ones reported successively less daydreaming (Singer & McCraven, 1961). Giambra (1973) extended the age range of investigation to 77, comparing college students at the youngest end—ages 17–22—with participants in the longitudinal study on aging (135 men altogether). He looked at attitude toward daydreaming, frequency of daydreaming, and content of the dreams themselves. One of his first findings was the high incidence of daydreaming at all ages, although the youngest age group daydreamed the most. Successively older groups daydreamed less, except for the men past retirement, who reported a higher frequency. Almost three-fourths of the men regarded daydreaming positively—72% of each age group. Actually, the youngest group was the least positive; perhaps they were more action-oriented. The majority of respondents said that they had continued daydreaming all their lives. There was no tendency for daydreams to be more past-oriented with increased age, although the 66- to 77-year-old group showed the strongest tendency to think about the more distant past. Finally, daydreams about heroic action and personal advancement declined steadily with age; in fact, were common only among college students. A similarly predictable result was the decrease of personal achievement daydreams among the oldest men. In other words, daydreaming may be tied to coping behavior, not a substitute for it.

ADAPTATION

Not all psychologists have found the psychoanalytically based ego model useful. Some have looked at adaptive mechanisms in a more generic way. For example, Spence and Lonner (1972) used "career set" in studying adult adaptation. The careers they refer to may be occupation or motherhood but resemble Freud's defense mechanisms in that they are seen to mold the behaviors of men and women throughout life. The career set of motherhood, for example, may determine choices and reactions many years before women actually become mothers. Little girls may retreat from scholastic achievement and learn ways to attract males long before puberty. Motherhood as a career set may also determine choices and reaction long beyond the time of the "empty nest."

Livson (1976) used other terms to describe the changing coping styles of the Berkeley longitudinal subjects. Different ways of coping were adaptive at different ages and for men and women. In youth, mentally healthy men were ambitious and intellectual and mentally healthy women were aggressively flirtatious. At the same period, less healthy young men were more likely to be rebellious, hostile, and impulsive; less healthy young women were more likely to be unassertive, gregarious, and conforming. In adulthood, healthy men were rational and narrower in their interests than they had been in youth; healthy women were expressive, open, and nurturant. Less healthy adult men were productive but irritable; less healthy adult women were about the same as they had been in youth. In middle age, healthy men showed a rise in nurturant and expressive behaviors, both men and women were more dependent and expressive, and women were more fearful and self-defeating.

Because Livson's subjects had only reached middle age, she turned to their parents for information about adaptive behavior at older ages.

These older people relied more on relations with others in organizing their lives than their children did, a trend similar to that noted recently by Veroff and Depner (1978), discussed earlier. Otherwise, they did not differ from their children so far as general ways of coping were concerned (Haan, 1976).

The greater use of interpersonal ties by older people was also found important by Lowenthal and Haven (1968). Old San Francisco residents who had confidants were more successful copers. Having such confidants enabled them to survive in the community. Old people who landed in the psychiatric ward lacked such resources.

Reminiscing by older people may be an adaptive technique and may even predict successful coping. A somewhat similar mechanism, experiencing, refers to the introspective examination of one's own feelings. This strategy has also been found to be related to good adjustment in old age (Gorney, 1968). However, because experiencing is more common in settled situations (after admission to an institution) than during transitions (being on the waiting list), it could be a consequent rather than antecedent to good coping.

The AT&T executives studied longitudinally by Bray, Campbell, and Grant (1974) were divided into those who showed *enlarging* adaptive styles and those who showed *enfolding* styles. Both styles were equally adaptive so far as life satisfaction was concerned, although different in terms of occupational success and focus of life interests. Enlargers emphasize extending their influence out into the community, seek expanding responsibilities, and are not too tied to their past. Enfolders value old ties and tend to deepen them.

Perlin and Butler (1971) have even suggested that lifelong pathology could be adaptive in old age. It is not a shift from pathology to health but a shift in environmental requirements that changes the consequences of particular strategies from poor to good coping. Because coping is presumably characteristic of proactive rather than reactive people, we might conclude that each of us has a repertoire of coping mechanisms at our disposal. We bring different coping mechanisms to play at different points of life, as well as in different situations at the same time of life. Lieberman (1975) describes the "adaptive paranoia" of old age: bastards and bitches are more likely to survive than are "nice" people. (Remember the old proverb "The good die young.") At the end of life, if most physical and psychological systems are operating close to the edge of reserve capacity, a good strategy would be to retreat and conserve resources rather than to fight. Thus, combativeness may itself be a sign of greater strength.

STRESS AND TRANSITION

In Chapters 1 and 15, I presented four possible ways to react to major life change: fragmentation, denial, minimum readjustment to preserve homeostasis, and development. About 20 years ago, psychologists were searching for universal life events that would inevitably be accompanied by stress and inevitably induce change. Then empirical studies challenged this assumption. For example, Frenkel-Brunswik, whose work was completed by her colleagues after her death (Reichard et al., 1962), found that one such major life event, retirement, was often not stressful, at least at the time, and often did not lead to changes. The empty nest and the menopause, other presumably universal change points, also have failed to show inevitable breakdowns. Only widowhood perhaps can still be considered a classic stress point, although maybe more so for young women and men than for older (Weiss, 1976b; Noberini & Neugarten, 1975). Neugarten (1977) suggested that we see none of the expected signs of stress at times we expect to because people *anticipate* and rehearse for these major life events or turning points. We must therefore distinguish between normative, expected events and nonnormative, unexpected ones. There is anticipatory socialization for the normative, but not for the unexpected.

One problem in investigating life stresses is finding adequate measures. Most research to date has adopted the scale of Holmes and Rahe (1967), presented in Table 16.4. This scale assumes that good events are as stressful as bad; for example, that outstanding achievement is as stressful as in-law troubles. Note that widowhood is at the top of the list, having 27 more points than divorce, the next most stressful item. When I discuss widowhood, in a later chapter, I will return to this point.

There are several problems with this kind of scale, even though it spurred on much life-span

TABLE 16.4 Life-change scale

Event	Stress value
Death of spouse	100
Divorce	73
Marital separation	65
Jail term	63
Death of close family member	63
Personal injury, sickness	53
Marriage	50
Dismissal from job	47
Marriage reconciliation	45
Retirement	45
Illness in family	44
Pregnancy	40
Sex difficulties	39
Arrival of new family member	39
Change in business	39
Change in financial state	38
Death of close friend	37
Change in line of work	36
Change in number of family fights	35
Mortgage over $10,000	31
Mortgage or loan foreclosed	30
Departure of grown child from home	29
Change in job duties	29
In-law troubles	29
Outstanding achievement	28
Wife begins or stops work	26
Beginning or end of school	26
Change in living conditions	25
Revision of personal habits	24
Trouble with boss	23
Change in work hours or conditions	20
Move to new home	20

Source: Holmes and Rahe, 1967.

research. One is its repetition of the universality error. What is stressful to one person may not be stressful to another.

More-idiographic approaches have been used recently in several investigations. Coyne and Lazarus (1979) asked their respondents to fill out questionnaires each month, listing their stressful encounters. Their 100 middle-aged subjects had an average of 13 such encounters each month. In line with other findings on sex differences, those encounters listed by men tended to revolve around work and those listed by women, around family and health. Some were what the investigators labeled "hassles"; others were "uplifts." Older subjects listed more hassles than uplifts. Women reported more intense and more frequent uplifts; there were no significant sex differences in hassles.

One of Coyne and Lazarus's major hypotheses is that psychological symptoms and life events are transactional in nature, rather than having a straightforward cause/effect nature. Rather than events leading to depressive complaints, for example, depression could lead to major life events. For example, a depressed person could make friendship or marriage miserable and job performance poor, leading to loss of friends, spouse, and job.

In their follow-up of the Midtown Manhattan Study, Srole and Fischer (1978) asked respondents to report their idea of what their major turning points in life were. The question was "They say that life is the school of hard knocks that we all have to take. As you think back over your life, what heavy blows have hit you the hardest and upset you the most for some time afterward? What happened and how old were you at that time?" (p. 16). Their subjects ranged in age from 40 to 79. The most frequent blows listed were family deaths and illnesses (more than half the illnesses were psychiatric), marital disruptions other than widowhood, events in job or career, and experiences in World War II. Incidentally, only half perceived these blows as turning points in their life. Of these people, only half saw them as being "for the worse."

Parron (1978) asked golden-wedding couples to describe their reactions to three presumed major life events: marriage, birth of first child, and departure of last child. Their responses indicated that these times were not as significant as others they themselves mentioned. At least in retrospect, personally important life events were not necessarily socially defined major events. They were more likely to attribute change in their lives to the Depression or to war than even to the birth of their first child. It is unfortunately true that retrospective data tend to be warped by current events and feelings, so that we cannot know how the people felt at the time of occurrence.

Lowenthal and her associates (1975) were led to develop a typology of stress in their San Francisco study. When the men and women of the four life stages were asked to fill out a life-evaluation chart indicating ups and downs in life satisfaction, both sex and stage differences emerged in the areas they considered stressful. The most prominent stress areas for women were education (mentioned by 71%), families (55%), health (51%), and dating and marital relationships (50%). There were only two areas in which half or more of the men reported stresses: education (69%) and work (50%).

The two younger groups reported more situations they considered stressful than did the two older groups. The newlyweds were the only group reporting highly positive and negative stresses, although positive stresses predominated. Thus the stress reports differed somewhat from the self-esteem and happiness data mentioned earlier. This ratio was reversed for the middle-aged, for whom negative stresses predominated. Table 16.5 shows the stresses listed for the previous ten years, collapsing the four age groups into two (older and younger) and combining positive and negative stresses. Incidentally, there was no relation between changes experienced in the past and changes anticipated in the future.

Stress in middle age was analyzed by Parent (1978) in interviews with Louisiana men and women between 45 and 64 years of age. Like Lowenthal and her associates (1975), Parent used a self-identified set of stresses by asking respondents to identify stressful events in their lives over the past year. Table 16.6 shows the age distribution of these stresses, by system affected and type of stress. Family stresses, and the threat of family stresses, clearly predominated in this sample. No significant sex differences were found, incidentally; men were as concerned about their children—primarily their sons—and about possible deaths of relatives as were women. Body stresses accounted for only a quarter of all stresses and, during the 55–59 period, dropped to lowest place. At least in this sample, interpersonal concerns superseded physical ones. During this same five years, family concerns were higher than for other ages.

The oft-noted sensitivity on the part of women to other people is also evident here. Of the 58 events in the lives of others, 38 were reported by women. Parent concludes that "threat, reflecting anxiety about impinging danger, is most noted by those with greatest coping advantages: the young, the more affluent, and the men; while losses and chronic stress were the curses of older people, lower classes and of women" (p. 12).

Possible steps followed by people after stress have been suggested by Hultsch and Plemons (1979). These authors believe that stressed people try to recreate congruity with their environ-

TABLE 16.5 Stresses (including positive and negative) over last ten years (percentage mentioning at least one such stress)

	Younger			Older		
	Men	Women	Total	Men	Women	Total
Education	71	80	76[d]	2	9	6
Residential	33[a]	40[a]	36[d]	9	4	6
Dating/marriage	33[a]	50[a]	40[d]	2	12	8
Friends	27	44	35[d]	13	5	9
Family	24	36	30	13[a]	26[a]	20
Marriage	18	28	23[c]	9	12	11
Health	10	22	16	13[b]	38[b]	27
Work	22	14	18[c]	45[b]	21[b]	32[c]
Leisure activities	35[a]	12[a]	23[d]	6	2	4
Military	27[b]	2[b]	14[d]	0	4	2
Death	14	12	13	18	19	19
Finances	6	4	5	18	11	14

[a]Differences between men and women within the cohort are significant, with $p < .05$.
[b]Differences between men and women within the cohort are significant, with $p < .01$.
[c]Differences between young and old are significant, with $p < .05$.
[d]Differences between young and old are significant, with $p < .01$.

Source: Lowenthal, Thurnher, and Chiriboga, 1975.

ments. Their previous experiences with stress have led them to accumulate a repertoire of coping strategies. From this repertoire, they select the particular coping strategy or strategies they believe will suit the immediate context of their present situations. Because older people see their world as more constricting than do younger ones, they will be more likely to use intrapsychic strategies than to use direct action (remember the active-mastery/passive-mastery theory).

TABLE 16.6 Percentages of stress system and type by age (N = 243)

	Age			
	45–49	50–54	55–59	60–64
System				
Body	20	22	11	25
Family	42	35	45	38
Socioeconomic	22	22	24	21
Personality	16	21	20	16
Type				
Loss	22	25	33	32
Threat	56	57	40	53
Chronicity	22	18	27	15

Source: Parent, 1978.

One factor in determining the sequence of responses is the degree of the perceived threat. If the threat is considered strong, there could be a decrease in variability of attempted maneuvers, and consequently an increase in stereotyped behavior, especially such defensive maneuvers as avoidance and denial. If strategies prove adequate, the situation will return to stability or homeostasis, according to the model of reaction to change presented in the last chapter. If the stress is not alleviated, however, a highly unstable period can result, often accompanied by confusion, frustration, disruption of usual behavior, and greater likelihood of pathology. Such failure, though, could result in search for and acquisition of new coping strategies for a happier ending.

Women in midlife. Once it was thought that women were supposed to fall apart at the time of the menopause. Chapter 6 presents the evidence against this belief. Next, women were supposed to become depressed and mournful because of the empty nest. The evidence against this is presented later, in Chapter 19. There is a persistent underlying conviction that midlife is a period of unusual stress for women. If neither menopause nor empty nest is the reason, could there be another one—that is, if women are indeed more stressed at this point? Four such reasons have occurred to me; I have identified them by Greek mythological characters: Cassandra, Tantalus, Procrustes, and Penelope.

Cassandra, the Trojan princess, worried a lot. Like her, the middle-class, middle-aged woman today is a worrier *par excellence*. From infancy, she has been socialized to be "tuned in" to the feelings and attitudes of others. Thus, she gives a lot of attention to the woes of her family. First, she worries whether her young adult children are turning out "right." Are they settling into a career, marrying and having the appropriate number of children at the appropriate ages? If not, then she may feel that she has done something wrong in raising them, that she has not been a good mother.

The shift in the prevailing ideology toward "doing one's own thing" often means that middle-class young adults feel it is less important to take serious jobs and marry. This can be stressful on their parents, even though many of the parents eventually go through "reverse socialization" and accept their children's values (Troll & Bengtson, 1979).

The Cassandras of today also worry about their husbands, whose jobs may be in jeopardy or losing impetus; whose health may be precarious, raising the possibility that (like many middle-aged women they know) they may become prematurely widowed; or whose love may wane (like the husbands of many women they know who have left them for younger, less familiar women). As Lopata (1973) notes, it is not as bad being a deserted woman when you are 70 or older as it is when you are 30, 40, or 50.

These Cassandras are also worried about their parents, who perhaps show signs of aging and may actually need lots of care. Most studies show that, when older parents need help, their daughters are their chief caregivers (Troll, Miller, & Atchley, 1979). Finally, Cassandras are worried about their own self-fulfillment, now that their children are supposed to be out of the nest (although many wonder whether their children will ever leave). This brings us to the second Greek myth.

Tantalus was forever "tantalized." Every time he reached for some of the good things that surrounded him, they withdrew just beyond his reach. The modern midlife middle-class woman

---

Tell me something about where and how you would like to live.

Grandmother, age 69
I'd like to live in Florida in the wintertime and up north in the summertime. And how? Not in a flamboyant way. Just a normal way of living, but I'd like to be able to help people in many ways.

Mother, age 51
That's funny, I've never phantasied that. I'd love to live where there's sun. But first I'd go around and visit all the places and pick the one I want. And I'd never do any housework. I know what I *have* phantasied: someone who comes in, cooks the dinner, sets the table, lights the candles, and serves the dinner . . . and does the dishes, of course. Oh, yes, I'd enjoy a chauffeured car.

Daughter, age 27
I'd love to live in Massachusetts. I haven't been any place more glamorous. I've spent a vacation there when I was going to school in New Hampshire. But I'm really happy here. I'd like to live in a nice, contemporary-styled home, right near the ocean. I'd like my husband not to have to work . . . just when he wants to.

---

has been led to believe that she should be actualizing herself. Some women find fulfillment outside family relationships by resuming old careers or pursuits or quickly advancing in new ones. But many reach for something which they later find to be beyond them. They cannot make up for years spent as housewives, which for many women meant near—or total—isolation from public life, or they hit retirement when they are just getting into their stride. Research shows that women find retirement much harder than men do (Atchley, 1976).

Procrustes was an innkeeper who insisted that his guests fit into his standard-sized bed. If his guests were too long, he cut them down to size. If they were too short, he stretched them to fit. Many prescriptions and descriptions of midlife women use a Procrustean approach, leaving inadequate room for individual differences. Fitting a rigid standard can be painful. During the last two decades, middle-class women whose children departed for college felt pressured to go out into the world and do *"their* own thing"—particularly to resume or to assume a career. This course of action suits many women but it does not suit all. The Procrustean demand for self-expression leads many middle-aged graduating college women to tell me wistfully that they suppose they should go on to graduate school, but that they really would prefer to be free to travel with their husbands, and generally to spend more time with their husbands in a relaxed fashion.

Penelope, wife of the constant traveler Odysseus, wove her cloth during the day and unraveled it each night. Many midlife women today seem to be destroying what they have woven earlier. Like Penelope, perhaps they are trying to forestall the end of hope. It takes a long time to build up the fabric of a life, to create a network of relationships and activities. Turning to new pursuits in midlife can sometimes destroy this delicate structure. The high value our culture places on change and progress can often blind us to the possibly equal value of treasuring what we have. Sometimes our desire to create something new represents a need to feel that we can still create and change, and does not benefit us, either in the present or future.

Today several prominent writers claim that middle-aged women go through a transition, usually a crisis accompanied by stress and anxiety. Such statements are often Procrustean. Rather, research suggests that most transitions women experience tend to be more gradual than abrupt. Their impact is diminished by the processes of rehearsal and anticipatory socialization (Neugarten, 1968). Some suggest that midlife transitions may be neither qualitatively nor quantitatively different from transitions at other times of life.

For most women, one change or transition is not overwhelming. However, many changes coming together could be stressful. Life could be easier if barriers in the Tantalus situation could be removed, making available (to those who wish them) education and jobs, as well as voluntary retirement at a later age for women than for men, because, on the average, women live longer and stay healthier longer than men do. Middle age could be easier if some of Cassandra's burdens were lightened—primarily exclusive concern and caring for aged parents. Daughters do not abandon their parents and may in fact assume more responsibility than is good for them or for their parents. Additional community facilities may benefit daughters even more than their parents.

ADJUSTMENT

Adjustment involves two parts: (1) the individual's coping and (2) the situation's demands. If these are incongruent, the individual cannot adjust. It is not surprising, therefore, that adjustment can vary with age and other factors that put people out of line with their environments. If there is any developmental curve of coping strength similar to that for physical health, its pattern might be obscured by the timing and severity of environmental stresses. And such stresses may themselves vary with age changes in coping strength. More-vulnerable people may bring on more disaster than those who are stronger and better able to manipulate circumstances to their advantage. Or coping strength may increase steadily throughout life, but social and health factors may increase stress even more steadily.

Two studies have examined antecedents of adjustment. In the AT&T study of managers (Bray & Howard, 1978), five measurements in the initial testing session, when the managers were in their 20s, correlated significantly with adjustment 20 years later. As shown in Table 16.7, these are high scores on ascendancy, self-confidence, and emotional stability, and low scores in mental ability and heterosexuality. In other words, self-confident and emotionally stable young men become well-adjusted middle-aged men if they are neither very intelligent nor very interested in women. The members of the Berkeley longitudinal study who were well-adjusted in adulthood (Siegelman, Block, Block, &

TABLE 16.7 Twenty-year predictors of life satisfaction

	Correlation with adjustment	Correlation with happiness
Ascendancy	.25	.23
Self-confidence	.38	.35
Emotional stability	.37	.31
Expectations	.21	.27
Standardized test scores	−.13	−.26
Mental ability ratings	−.30	−.34
Heterosexuality	−.29	−.27

Note: $r \geq .22$, $p < .05$; $r \geq .28$, $p < .01$, $r \geq .36$, $p < .001$, $N = 80$

Source: Bray and Howard, 1978.

Von der Lippe, 1970) had well-adjusted parents and happy homes during childhood. Unlike the AT&T managers, however, Berkeley people with high IQ were more likely to be well-adjusted later. The discrepancy so far as IQ is concerned may be explained by the restricted nature of the AT&T sample, and also by the fact that the managers have not yet reached the ages of the Berkeley subjects. Thus, there is some evidence not only for continuity in adjustment in an individual's life but also for continuity over generations in the family.

A nine-year longitudinal study of older people by Britton and Britton (1972) used judges' ratings of adjustment in three interview times: 1956, 1962, and 1965. Women were rated higher than men, on the whole—a finding contrary to sex-difference findings for self-esteem and happiness. Old age may not demand as much of women. In general, there was little consistency of the subjects in relation to each other over time; the better-adjusted people at one time of measurement were not necessarily better adjust-

ed at the next interval. As far as longitudinal trend scores are concerned, a majority of the men and women decreased in adjustment over the nine-year period. About one-fifth changed for the better, though, and quite a number did not change at all. Regarding factors related to change, the only significant one seemed to be church attendance; women who changed positively attended less than once per week. This may just mean, of course, that less-adjusted women sought the solace of religion more often.

Only aggregated or grouped scores on adjustment have been reported for the Kansas City study (Peck & Berkowitz, 1964). These show a low point of adjustment for people in their 50s. People in their 50s were lower than those in their 40s and those in their 60s. The authors interpreted this as a sign of a middle-age crisis. Because these were not only grouped but also cross-sectional data, we cannot make age/ change predictions safely. Another cross-sectional study, of values (Antonucci, 1974), found that those older men who share the general

TABLE 16.8 Number of resident patients and resident patient rates, state and county mental hospitals (United States, 1955 and 1968)

Age in years	All mental disorders		Schizophrenia		Mental disorders of aging		All other mental disorders	
	1955	1968	1955	1968	1955	1968	1955	1968
Number								
All ages	558,922	399,152	267,995	194,922	73,772	49,158	217,155	155,072
Under 15	2,301	6,365	374	1,774	—	—	1,927	4,591
15–24	17,276	25,315	8,156	10,887	—	—	9,120	14,428
25–34	57,634	36,546	36,819	21,531	—	—	20,815	15,015
35–44	96,304	52,623	63,269	31,314	—	—	33,035	21,309
45–54	117,500	71,166	65,895	41,815	—	—	51,605	29,351
55–64	109,622	86,997	50,302	46,689	8,672	4,924	50,648	35,384
65+	158,285	120,140	43,180	40,912	65,100	44,234	50,005	34,994
65–74	92,223	66,177	31,396	27,450	24,842	15,067	35,985	23,660
75+	66,062	53,963	11,784	13,462	40,258	29,167	14,020	11,334
Rate per 100,000 population								
All ages	344.4	202.0	165.1	98.7	45.5	24.9	133.8	78.4
Under 15	4.7	10.7	.8	3.0	—	—	3.9	7.7
15–24	86.1	79.9	40.7	34.3	—	—	45.4	45.6
25–34	246.0	157.8	157.1	92.9	—	—	88.9	64.9
35–44	427.2	226.4	280.6	134.7	—	—	146.6	91.7
45–54	622.8	312.2	349.3	183.5	—	—	273.5	128.7
55–64	753.7	486.7	345.8	261.2	59.6	27.5	348.3	198.0
65+	1,125.1	627.9	306.9	213.9	462.7	231.2	355.4	182.9
65–74	979.4	561.5	333.4	232.9	263.8	127.8	382.2	200.7
75+	1,419.8	734.9	253.3	183.3	865.2	397.2	301.3	154.4

Source: Kramer, Taube, and Redick, 1973.

societal devaluation of old age are better adjusted than those who value more involvement in life. This finding generally replicates that of Lowenthal and her associates (1975), who found that those preretired men whose interest structure resembled the well-adjusted middle-aged men were lower in adjustment scores than those with more-limited interests. What makes for good adjustment at one age is not what makes for good adjustment at another.

Mental health

The preceding pages have examined quality of functioning from the standpoint of goodness. The present section starts at the other end, at obviously poor functioning. To get mental-health statistics, one can look at the number of patients in different kinds of treatment institutions (federal, state, county, or private) or in outpatient clinics. One can look at the ages of new admissions in a given year. One can look at suicide or accident or alcoholism figures.

There are sex, social-class, ethnic, and age differences in use of different mental-health facilities. Table 16.8 shows all the patients that were in state and county mental hospitals in the United States for two years, 1955 and 1968. The drop in institutional residence over 13 years followed social-policy shifts that said such people could be rehabilitated better outside institutions. As a result of this policy shift, nursing homes and foster homes expanded at the expense of larger, more formal institutions. Unfortunately, this shift did not usually result in improved care. So far as age is concerned, it is obvious that most inhabitants of mental hospitals in 1955 were over 65. This age group also experienced the biggest drop between 1955 and 1968, although it still represented the most patients in 1968.

Figure 16.4 shows another side of this picture: the age distribution of patients in different facilities—outpatient psychiatric clinics, general hospitals with psychiatric facilities, private mental hospitals, Veterans Administration hospitals, and state and county mental hospitals. Younger patients are less likely to be in mental hospitals than are older ones. They are presumably considered amenable to short-term, partial treatment.

Figure 16.5 shows new admissions instead of

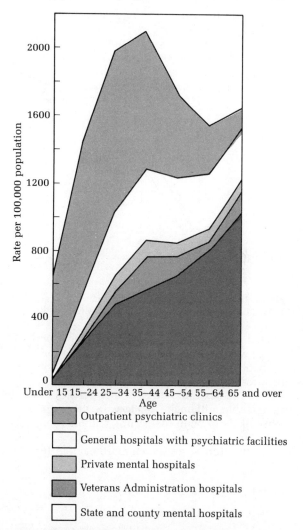

Outpatient psychiatric clinics

General hospitals with psychiatric facilities

Private mental hospitals

Veterans Administration hospitals

State and county mental hospitals

Figure 16.4. Number of patient-care episodes per 100,000 population in psychiatric facilities by type of facility and age (United States, 1966). *(Source: Kramer, Taube, and Redick, 1973.)*

current patients. The effect of social policy is clear with respect to people over 45 or 55. In 1962, this age group represented the most new admissions. By 1972, middle-aged and older people were being admitted at a rate lower than that of adolescents; they were being sent instead to nursing homes and foster homes. The reasons given for admission to outpatient psychiatric services in 1969 are presented in Figure 16.6. That year, people 18 to 24 were mostly being

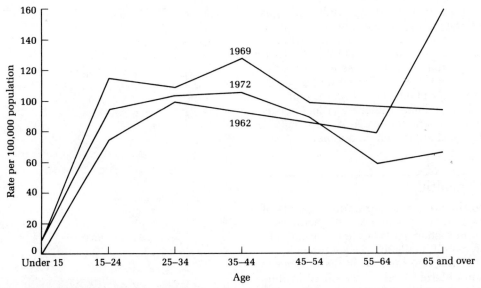

Figure 16.5. Changes over time in rate of first admissions to state and county medical hospitals, by age (1962, 1969, 1972). *(Source: National Institute of Mental Health, 1973.)*

treated for drug-abuse disorders, or for "condition[s] without manifest psychiatric disorder"— probably people who were unhappy but not manifesting any symptoms that could be labeled. The sex differences at this age were not remarkable, although women were somewhat more likely to be in the group "without manifest disorder."

Sex differences are much more evident for

those five to ten years older, between 25 and 34. Men this age are still mostly treated for drug disorders and are treated at the same rate as their juniors. But women are now mostly treated for "personality disorders" or for the anomalous "without manifest psychiatric disorder," although adding alcoholism and drug-abuse rates together makes their substance-abuse rate as high as their "personality-disorder" rate.

A marked cohort difference can be seen when we look at the next older category, the 35- to 44-year-olds. Here the men are being treated for alcoholism instead of drugs, but what is more interesting is the disproportionately high number of women needing alcoholism treatment. And the oldest group in this figure, the 45- to 64-year-olds (remember, older people are not customarily treated in outpatient psychiatric services), looks different again. For one thing, the percentages by age increase sharply—at this age, more people altogether are being treated. For another, sex differences are not as marked as they were in the next younger group. Two-thirds of the men being treated are diagnosed as having "major affective disorders" and one-half as having "other psychoses." Alcoholism is still prevalent. The women are equally divided between "major affective disorders" and "other psychoses." Drug abuse is higher for them than is alcohol abuse, although presumably we are

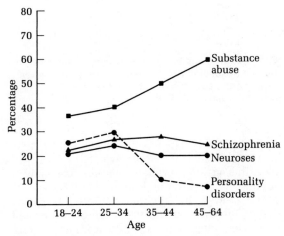

Figure 16.6. Admissions to outpatient psychiatric services (United States, 1969). *(Source: U.S. Department of Commerce, Bureau of the Census, 1970.)*

TABLE 16.9 Suicide rates in the United States for 1970, by age, sex, and race

Age range	White males	White females	Non-White males	Non-White females
15–19	9.4	2.9	5.4	2.9
20–24	19.3	5.7	19.4	5.5
25–29	19.8	8.6	20.1	6.0
30–34	20.0	9.5	19.4	5.6
35–39	21.9	12.2	13.9	4.5
40–44	24.6	13.8	11.4	4.1
45–49	28.2	13.5	16.5	4.0
50–54	30.9	13.5	11.3	5.1
55–59	34.9	13.1	12.3	1.8
60–64	35.0	11.5	8.4	2.8
65–69	37.4	9.4	11.5	3.2
70–74	40.4	9.7	8.2	3.9
75–79	42.2	7.3	5.7	3.1
80–84	51.4	7.2	22.9	3.2
85+	45.8	5.8	12.6	6.4

Source: U.S. Department of Health, Education, and Welfare, National Center for Health Statistics, 1974. (a)

now talking about a different kind of drug abuse, that resulting from physician overprescription or patient forgetfulness.

Suicide is often considered an indicator of poor mental health. Table 16.9 shows the suicide rate by age, sex, and race for 1970. As can be seen, older White men have much higher suicide rates than people in any other category. In general, men are more likely to commit suicide than are women, White men more likely than non-White men, and older White men than anybody else.

If we distinguish between suicide attempters and suicide completers, we find that attempters tend to be young women, while completers (as noted earlier) are older men. Because most suicide attempters are depressed, it is legitimate to look at the rates of such attempts by age. Across the world, these rates have risen for people under 30 years of age. Rates for women are twice as high as for men. Women are also most often diagnosed as "neurotic," while men are most often diagnosed as having "personality disorders." This sex difference can be linked to our Western socialization process, which reinforces "neurotic" (internalized) behaviors in women and reinforces acting-out behaviors in men. Incidentally, although the number of psychiatric symptoms reported is greater for women than for men, this number goes down over time for older subjects (Britton & Britton, 1972), as can be seen in Table 16.10.

In 1954, a cross-sectional study of the health,

TABLE 16.10 Health changes in older people by percentage over time

Item	Men			Women		
	1956	1962	1965	1956	1962	1965
Self-rating on health (N)	(16)	(16)	(17)	(27)	(27)	(29)
Excellent	6	—	—	11	15	7
Good	38	63	41	52	59	52
Fair	44	38	53	26	26	34
Poor or very poor	13	—	6	11	—	6
Number of serious physical problems (N)	(17)	(15)	(16)	(28)	(27)	(29)
Five or more	—	7	6	7	7	7
Three or four	29	47	31	29	44	38
One or two	59	40	56	54	37	41
None	12	7	6	11	11	14
Number of physical difficulties (N)	(17)	(16)	(16)	(28)	(26)	(27)
Five or more	18	25	13	29	31	30
Three or four	41	31	25	32	35	26
One or two	41	31	56	21	23	22
None	—	13	6	18	12	22
Number of psychosomatic ailments (N)	(17)	(15)	(15)	(28)	(27)	(28)
Five or more	12	7	7	32	11	21
Three or four	12	13	27	36	33	39
One or two	65	67	53	18	44	29
None	12	13	13	14	11	11

Note: Dash indicates no data.

Source: Britton and Britton, 1972.

TABLE 16.11 Midtown Manhattan mental-impairment rates, follow-up panel (N = 695)

		A b. ±1900 (N = 134)	B b. ±1910 (N = 199)	C b. ±1920 (N = 195)	D b. ±1930 (N = 167)
		Cohorts (decade of birth)			
1954	Age	(50–59)	(40–49)	(30–39)	(20–29)
	Rate	22%	16%	14%	7%
1974	Age	(70–79)	(60–69)	(50–59)	(40–49)
	Rate	18%	12%	10%	8%
	Difference	−4%	−4%	−4%	+1%
	Significance of difference	NS	NS	NS	NS

Note: NS = not statistically significant.

Source: Srole and Fischer, 1978.

both mental and physical, of 1660 Manhattan residents between 20 and 59 found that mental health went down as age went up. Twenty years later, 695 of those located from the original sample were reinterviewed. They were now between the ages of 40 and 79 and had scattered across the world. The follow-up data did not match the original findings. There was no sign of an intraindividual decrease in mental health. Men stayed pretty much at the levels they had been at earlier, and women's conditions even improved. Cross-sequential comparisons are presented in Table 16.11 without regard to sex. Group A (born about 1900 and in its 50s in 1954 and its 70s in 1974) changed from 22% rated mentally impaired at the first round of study to 18% at the second round, a nonsignificant difference. Comparing Group A (in its 50s at the first round) with Group C (in its 50s at the second round), we see that there was improvement: from 22% to 10%.

When men and women are considered separately (Table 16.12), we see the marked drop in mental impairment for female 50-year-olds from the first to the second round of the study: from 26% in 1954 to 11% in 1974. The same is true for 40-year-old women, but not for men. What has been happening is that women, who had much higher rates of mental illness than men before, have been moving over to rates comparable to men.

Elder's (1974) longitudinal comparisons of mental or physical problems of children of the Depression show complex interaction effects between social class and deprivation. Table 16.13 shows that the children from the nondeprived

working class and the deprived middle class were in the best health 20 years later. The most striking effects are seen for psychosomatic illness and behavior disorders. The nondeprived working-class subjects were most likely to develop psychosomatic illnesses. The nondeprived middle-class subjects were most likely to develop behavior disorders such as alcoholism. The working-class subjects were more likely to be described as vulnerable and brittle than were the nondeprived middle-class subjects, who were judged adaptive and competent. Finally, those subjects who had experienced deprivation in adolescence were more likely to change in anxiety or emotionality scores during adulthood than were those who had experienced no deprivation. The latter showed stability over time:

TABLE 16.12 Midtown Manhattan mental-impairment rates, follow-up panel (N = 695), by generation-separated pairs of like-age cohorts and gender subgroups

Cohort	Men	Women
A (aged 50–59 in 1954)	15%	26%
C (aged 50–59 in 1974)	9%	11%
Difference	−6%	−15%
p	NS	<.01
B (aged 40–49 in 1954)	9%	21%
D (aged 40–49 in 1974)	9%	8%
Difference	0%	−13%
p	NS	<.02

Note: NS = not statistically significant.

Source: Srole and Fischer, 1978.

TABLE 16.13 Diagnostic classification of men and women (1954) by economic deprivation and class origin, in percentages

Health groups	Middle class		Working class	
	Nondeprived	Deprived	Nondeprived	Deprived
Relatively symptom-free	11	38	18	13
Anxiety and tension states	11	7	27	21
Psychosomatic illness	29	21	36	17
Behavior disorders	26	7	9	25
Somatic illness (serious)	20	19	9	17
Psychotic reaction	3	7	—	8
	100	99	99	101
Total number of cases	35	42	11	24

Source: Elder, 1974.

those who had been anxious adolescents were anxious adults; those who had not been anxious also did not change.

Could it be that the women who improved so much in the Mid-Manhattan study were exhibiting the same kind of deprivation effect? Opportunities opened up to women during the 1960s and 1970s; women had a chance to adapt and improve. Because those opportunities had already existed for men, no change occurred for them.

Similar findings are reported by Livson (1977a). Middle-aged women in the 1970s who became more androgynous—more balanced in sex-role characteristics and thus more flexible and adaptive to opening opportunities—were judged in good mental health. In fact, their mental health was better than earlier in their adult years. All the men had moved toward androgyny, incidentally, and all were judged in good mental health. However, the women who clung to their femininity and who did not change in middle age were judged in more precarious mental health. A review of their earlier records showed that they tended to have been the more fragile girls.

Almost any psychiatric or medical text one opens is likely to say that psychopathology is rampant in old age and that there are two types: organic and functional. Diagnoses of organic disorders assume that brain deterioration of one kind or another leads inevitably to predictable "senile signs." Some medical diagnosticians assume that some kind of organic cause underlies all unwanted behavior change in later life. Other diagnosticians, who are more liberal, feel

that some problems can be explained without reference to physiological processes, that they are personality disorders similar to those in earlier life, whatever their cause may be. Some psychiatrists state that it is rare to find a new schizophrenic patient—one who never has had schizophrenic symptoms before—in old age. Such psychiatrists attribute pathological behavior to the losses and disadvantages of later life.

Gurland (1973) is the most iconoclastic theorist. He says "Taken singly, each criterion of psychopathology can be found wanting. Personal distress could be a perfectly reasonable transient response to bereavement. Discomfort caused to others could be a reflection of the latter's hypersensitivity.... Change from a previous state might be for the better rather than for the worse [even in old age]" (pp. 344–345). He points out that "there is a high consensus of opinion that psychopathology is being manifested when an old person contemporaneously expresses distress, disturbs others, is incompetent, and shows a change from his previous state (especially when this change is rapid and marked)" (p. 344).

The more uncommon a behavior, the more likely it is to be viewed as psychopathological. When Perlin and Butler (1971) evaluated 47 so-called normal men over the age of 65, they found that 29, or about two-thirds, showed "functional psychopathology." Depression was the most common symptom. Somewhat happier findings come from two other studies, one in Cleveland and the other in Durham, North Carolina (Laurie, 1977). About two-thirds of both these samples were rated as being in excellent or good mental health, and only 4% were rated as being severely or completely impaired.

An intensive investigation was made of older San Francisco residents who land in San Francisco General Hospital's psychiatric ward (Simon, Lowenthal, & Epstein, 1970). The study found that older patients who undergo a psychiatric crisis for the first time after the age of 60 generally suffer from massive disintegration, both physical and mental. There was no convincing evidence that age-linked universal crises such as widowhood or retirement had anything to do with this breakdown. Different constellations of characteristics described different age/sex groups. For example, the younger men, those close to 60, were of low socioeconomic status, native-born Protestants, and very much isolated. They tended to live alone and to have no close relatives. This was less true of older men on the ward and of women. So far as improvement on the ward was concerned, the degree of impairment when patients were admitted didn't seem to have much to do with improvement or deterioration subsequently. Those who had been diagnosed as having chronic brain syndrome (attributed to cortical deterioration) were least likely to improve. Those diagnosed as having psychogenic disorders were most likely to improve. Those with fewest pathological symptoms were more likely to improve.

Particular pathological symptoms are not inherent in any particular disease. They are determined by context, by the expectations of the people around the individual. Symptoms given the same diagnostic label differ for young children and for adults and old people. Psychopathology that occurs for the first time in old age has no common life history. As noted, symptoms cannot even be classified by reference to brain disorder. Autopsy studies have repeatedly demonstrated that there is no one-to-one relationship between signs of deterioration in the brain and the behavior that is labeled *brain syndrome*, whether acute or chronic.

As noted several times in this book, there has been a period effect of rising anxiety and depression over the last few decades. The cross-sequential study of Woodruff and Birren (1972) showed stability of neurotic scores in individuals over 20 years longitudinally, but an increase in neuroticism from the college students of 1950 to those of 1970. The large-scale follow-up surveys conducted by the University of Michigan (Veroff & Depner, 1978) showed similar findings, greater increases in pathology for younger Americans than for older. These authors say that "the elderly are experiencing less agitation than they did a generation ago, and compared to the young, have not become as depressed by the last twenty years. Instead, they seem to have a slightly increased experience of immobilization, especially among the pre-retirement group" (p. 14).

It seems to be much harder to get going in adult life during times of sharp transition than to keep going once your adult pattern is set. Coping skills probably accumulate over the adult years. In fact, therapists generally are surprised to find that older patients are easier to treat than are younger patients, even though the opposite was once held to be true. Although older people respond well to therapy—of almost any kind—most therapists still are reluctant to treat them. Furthermore, both private and governmental programs for increasing mental-health services admittedly suffer from age bias (Troll & Turner, 1978).

Summary

The many different indexes of how well people live do not necessarily agree. Self-esteem, or how much one likes oneself, is one such index; it depends on one's concept of what one should be like. This ideal self changes over time. Further, women, on the whole, derive their self-worth from family circumstances and men from job circumstances. Negative evaluations of old age are related to lowered self-esteem among old people. Other indexes, such as happiness or excitement, seem to decrease linearly with age from young adulthood onward, although lack of excitement is not the same as unhappiness, or depression. Life satisfaction may not vary systematically with age, although younger people look toward the future for their source of satisfaction and older people look toward the past.

Most investigators conclude that coping mechanisms become more "mature" and less impulsive or fantasy dominated as young adults grow older. A 20-year follow-up study published in 1979, however, found that most of the improvement is the result of today's women improving in coping over those of 20 years ago—a period effect. Longitudinal data suggest that re-emergence of preadolescent opposite-sex characteristics produces a "healthier" androgyny in late middle age. It is even possible that certain behaviors labeled *pathological* in younger people—such as paranoia—become *adaptive* in old age.

Neugarten makes the distinction between expected life stresses, which do not produce intense maladaptive reactions because they are anticipated and rehearsed, and unexpected life stresses, which are accompanied by customary signs of stress. The context and combinations of stresses may be more significant than any particular kind of stress by itself.

Use of outpatient services by age shows that substance abuse is the most prevalent reason for treatment at all ages and shows that personality disorders decrease with age. In general, men are more likely to commit suicide than women, White men than non-White men, and older White men than anybody else. Older patients who undergo a psychiatric crisis for the first time after the age of 60 generally suffer from massive disintegration, both physical and mental. Symptoms differ for the same diagnostic labels at different ages, and psychopathology that occurs for the first time in old age has no common life history.

If anything, people seem to gradually build up a repertoire of coping skills that give them survival power—at least so far as mental health is concerned—in old age. Older people can endure greater stress than younger and respond to therapy more quickly. A secular trend for increased anxiety and depression over the past decades is noticeable more among younger adults than older ones.

17

Friendship

How many people do we see or know? In what different contexts are they seen or known? Are there developmental or age patterns: do adolescents know more people than do the middle-aged or old? Do we turn to others more at certain times of life than at others? Does the quality of our relationships change, becoming more intimate at some times of life, for example, and more gregarious at others?

The last two chapters were concerned with personality processes "within" individuals and paid little attention to the social aspects of personality. This chapter looks at the person as a social being and at interindividual processes. Many, if not most, intimate social interactions take place among family members, and these interactions will be treated in subsequent chapters. This chapter will look only at nonfamily associates, such as friends, neighbors, and colleagues.

The social system

We are social animals; all of us are embedded in society. According to G. H. Mead (1934), we could not become or remain human if we were not social. Yet there are variations in this embeddedness, and, according to disengagement theory, there are developmental processes associated with these variations. Sociologists such as Rosow (1967) see people tied together by (1) shared values, (2) memberships in formal and informal groups, and (3) social roles. In this

chapter, I treat social ties in inverse order of intimacy: the more superficial ties of formal organizations first, then the more informal social networks, and, finally, friendships.

Formal interactions

Examples of formal social organizations are employment situations, religious groups, and community organizations. Participation in these organizations, although it can also be or become intimate, is generally not. One can be active in such organizations and still keep high fences around one's self—can remain very private. The number of group involvements and the strength of these involvements tend to increase during the childhood years and to reach a peak in early adulthood. This is followed by a plateau during the adult years and a decrease during the last years of life—as per disengagement theory. Figure 17.1, derived from a California survey of social connections (Stueve & Fischer, 1978), shows that people's social worlds continue to shrink after a peak in early adulthood (18 to 35 years of age).

Also, sex differences are marked. Men have more *total* social contacts than women in early adulthood, and somewhat more than women until age 50, but somewhat fewer after 50. As far as their *organizational* contacts are concerned, men have more than women until they reach 50. However, this kind of interpersonal behavior forms a very small part of anybody's

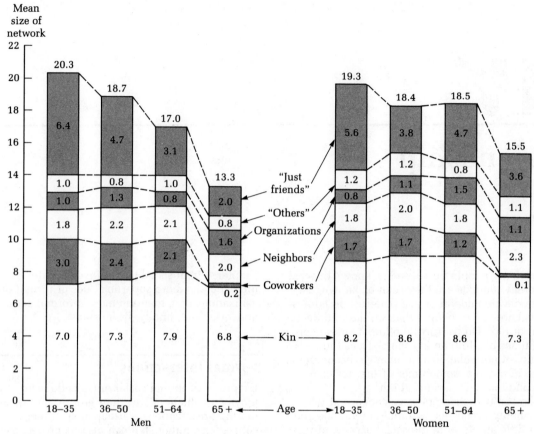

Figure 17.1.   Social-context composition of networks, by age and sex. *(Source: Stueve and Fischer, 1978.)*

total social activity and is characteristic of only a small percentage of the population—primarily the economically successful middle class. In old age, although men are outnumbered by women, they participate more in formal groups, but less than younger men do.

One of the earliest reports from the Kansas City Study (Cumming & Henry, 1961) looked at social-role involvement. It was this report, remember, that proposed disengagement theory. The findings are similar to those of Stueve and Fischer, although limited to people over 50. These are shown in Table 17.1. The organization column in Table 17.1 shows an irregular pattern of increases and decreases for men, with a final clear drop after 70. Very few men in Kansas City were involved with organizations after 75—at least during the late 1950s.

The pattern for women is different. Women's involvement is highest between 60 and 64—

more than twice as high as men their age and about the same amount as men five years younger. Also, the later decline for women is not as great as for men. In general, the Kansas City men, like the men in California studied by Stueve and Fischer a quarter century later, showed less organizational participation than did women their age.

Now, let us compare this with involvement as workers. Notice that all the men studied were working between the ages of 55 and 59—at the same time that they had the highest community participation. Only four-fifths were working five years later, and only one-third five years after that. One-fifth was still working after 75, though. Men and women showed one pattern in common. The peak of their involvement in the work force was also the peak of their involvement in community activities. However, women reached this peak five years later than men—

TABLE 17.1 Percentage of older people having various active roles, by age and sex

Age and sex	N	Roles (percent)						
		Spouse	Household	Kin	Friend	Neighbor	Worker	Organization
Males	107							
50–54	19	89.5	100.0	68.4	73.7	68.4	94.7	36.8
55–59	18	88.9	94.4	61.1	50.0	66.7	100.0	55.6
60–64	19	84.2	84.2	63.2	73.7	47.4	78.9	21.1
65–69	12	91.7	100.0	83.3	83.3	66.7	33.3	33.3
70–74	25	64.0	76.0	76.0	72.0	48.0	24.0	20.0
75 and over	14	78.6	85.7	71.4	71.4	35.7	21.4	7.1
Females	104							
50–54	17	82.4	82.4	64.7	70.6	58.8	82.4	35.3
55–59	16	62.5	87.5	87.5	75.0	75.0	31.3	43.8
60–64	15	60.0	86.7	80.0	66.7	73.3	53.6	53.3
65–69	19	36.8	57.9	52.6	63.2	57.9	26.3	36.8
70–74	25	28.0	52.0	56.0	60.0	52.0	16.0	32.0
75 and over	12	16.7	50.0	50.0	83.3	50.0	16.7	25.0

Source: Cumming and Henry, 1961.

and at a considerably lower frequency. Community involvement did not compensate for work involvement but did parallel it.

Both the California and the Kansas City investigations were cross-sectional. Decreases in formal-organization participation were found at younger ages for the AT&T managers studied longitudinally by Bray and Howard (1978). However, the more successful managers cut down their community activities less than did the less successful ones. Again, we see that greater involvement with job brings greater involvement with formal organizations. Wilensky (1961) found that "orderly careers" were correlated with greater community participation.

Britton and Britton's (1972) longitudinal data for old age are presented in Table 17.2. Again we see that men's organizational involvement, as measured by time spent, decreased from age 55 to approximately age 65 and then remained stable during the next two interview periods, over approximately nine years. The amount of time spent by women in informal-organization activity tended to stay about the same over the whole period in this small-town sample. Men almost never attended club meetings, but women attended once or twice a month. Men attended church once a week or more during the first two interview periods, but never in 1965. Women continued to attend church once a week or more.

Following their extensive review of the gerontological literature, Riley and Foner (1968) concluded that most old people do not belong to any voluntary associations except church. Church membership tends to continue well into the age of the 70s, although participation in church activities declines earlier.

In general, participation in organizations is related more to sex, to social class, and to general activity than it is to age as such. In fact, studies of older people who join senior centers find that such people tend to have had lifelong patterns of organizational involvement. So far as social class is concerned, those with higher incomes, higher-status occupations, and better educations tend to participate more in community organizations at all times of life than those with lower levels. Higher socioeconomic status (SES) also goes together with better health and generally higher activity level. Thus, older people of higher socioeconomic status are more likely to be involved, and involved for more years of their life, than older people who are less well off.

In their analysis of the lifestyles of the parents of the Berkeley longitudinal subjects, Maas and Kuypers (1974) describe the kind of men and women whose major involvement is formal organizations. In this middle-class sample, only one-quarter of the men and one-tenth of the women fit this pattern. The men were labeled *remotely sociable;* the women, *group centered.* As young adults, these remotely sociable men came from upper-status occupations and were comfortably well off. Throughout most of their

TABLE 17.2 Friendships, activities, and religion of longitudinal subjects, by percent

Item	Men			Women		
	1956	1962	1965	1956	1962	1965
Number of friends (N)	(15)	(15)	(14)	(28)	(27)	(29)
10 or more	93	93	70	89	100	93
5–9	—	—	7	7	—	7
1–4	7	7	14	4	—	—
0	—	—	7	—	—	—
Number of close friends (N)	(11)	(10)	(12)	(25)	(23)	(26)
10 or more	45	50	33	12	9	15
5–9	27	20	17	12	17	12
1–4	18	30	33	48	43	38
0	9	—	17	28	30	35
Number of free-time activities (N)	(17)	(16)	(15)	(28)	(27)	(29)
7 or more	6	44	60	14	59	76
3–6	23	50	33	32	41	21
1–2	59	6	—	36	—	3
Just sit and think	12	—	7	18	—	—
Frequency of attending club meetings (N)	(17)	(16)	(16)	(28)	(26)	(28)
Once a week or more	—	6	—	21	19	18
Once or twice a month	12	31	13	29	35	36
Less than once a month	23	6	13	18	15	14
Never	65	56	75	32	31	32
Time given to organizations (N)—in 1956, compared to age 55; in 1962, to 1956; in 1965, to 1962	(16)	(16)	(15)	(27)	(27)	(25)
More now	13	—	—	33	15	—
About the same	38	88	67	37	67	56
Less now	50	13	33	30	19	44
Church membership[a] (N)	(17)	(16)	(15)	(28)	(27)	(28)
Yes	71	69	73	89	93	82
No	29	31	27	11	7	18
Frequency of attending church (N)	(17)	(16)	(17)	(28)	(27)	(29)
Once a week or more	41	50	29	61	56	52
Once or twice a month	6	—	—	11	11	3
Less than once a month	35	31	29	21	22	14
Never	18	19	41	7	11	31

[a]Except for one man who defined his own religion, all subjects were Protestant.

Note: Dash indicates no data; usually, no responses in that category.

Source: Britton and Britton, 1972.

adult lives, they had large social networks but no intimate relationships. Even their marriages tended to be formal and not very satisfying. They were always highly independent. Although they had had close relationships with their children in youth, they were not very involved with their children now, in old age. They were not likely to express affection and altogether were very private about their experiences.

One of the six lifestyle clusters of women was group centered, similar to the group of remotely sociable men. This style included 11 of the 95 women studied. These women were involved in

clubs and other formal groups, church, and politics. Even though they were about 70 years old at the time of the last interview, they attended meetings frequently and were often leaders of their groups. They expressed great satisfaction with these activities. Like the remotely sociable men, these group-centered women were minimally involved with their families, and the authors describe them, too, as remote and formal people. They enjoyed being grandparents, in a formal way. In early adulthood, they had been more involved with their families, but their present greater remoteness was felt by them and by the investigators to be much more compatible with their personalities. Even though two-thirds of them were still married, marriage did not seem to be very important to their lives. They, like the community-involved men, came from relatively affluent backgrounds. Their early adult years were marked by conflict with parents, husbands, and children. In fact, they were closer to their children in old age than they had been earlier and were more informal with their grandchildren than they had been with their children.

Ethnic differences are shown in another study on the relation between personality and older people's membership in a Jewish center (Guttmann, 1973). Those members from American backgrounds preferred activities enabling them to express their individuality, while those of Eastern European backgrounds wanted activities that gave them a sense of belonging. An example of the low importance of organizations in most lives is shown by the fact that, when middle-class, middle-aged couples move (Hess, 1972), the women do not use organizations—even churches—in finding new friends.

Organizational activity has been found to have the greatest effect on life satisfaction—after health—among people over 60 (Palmore & Luikart, 1972). The researchers feel that this is probably a two-way effect: being involved in organizations leads to life satisfaction, and depressed people with little life satisfaction tend to withdraw or not get involved in organizations. A similar finding was obtained in a study of widows (Pihlblad & Adams, 1971): formal-group participation was even more related to satisfaction than was contact with friends.

SOCIAL NETWORKS

Although participation in organizations is just what formal people need and want, informal social interactions do more for many others. General gregariousness involves "letting down the barriers" more than formal group interaction does. It therefore allows other people to come close and to lend support when necessary.

Some theorists believe that people have a basic social need, which is stronger in some individuals than in others. Weiss (1976b) stresses the special nature of primary-group relationships; without constant interactions within primary groups, we would "drift into a state of normlessness or anomie" (p. 18). On the basis of

his clinical experience with several couples who had recently moved, Weiss concluded that both primary and network kinds of relationships are necessary. These couples needed both close marital ties and looser network supports for good functioning.

Other theorists believe that each individual has a constant "fund of sociability" that can be expended in different ways. For example, there can be as much satisfaction from intense contact with a few as from less intense contact with many. Most studies show that, while some people thrive in primarily formal relations, others do better with more informal, visiting kinds of contacts, and still others in tightly knit intimate units. And some are most at ease in near isolation (Lowenthal, 1964). Lifelong isolates tend to have average or better-than-average morale and are no more prone to hospitalization for mental illness in old age than are other old people. Generally, though, Lowenthal found, in her study of the number of social roles and the level of social interaction of older community residents in San Francisco (Lowenthal & Haven, 1968), that there was a clear statistical relationship between social interaction and mental health and morale. Low levels of social interaction were related to depression.

In a later paper, Lowenthal and Robinson (1976) have suggested that a rhythm of oscillation between social involvement and interaction may be established early in life. Some people may have daily rhythms, others weekly, monthly, or even annual. In fact, it may be because they prevent the expression of such rhythms that institutions are so deadly.

Recent exploratory research on the characteristics of social networks has looked at such variables as dimensionality and density (Hirsch, 1980). Relationships are unidimensional if the people involved do only one kind of thing together—for example, attend classes or work together in the PTA. They are multidimensional if the people involved do a number of different kinds of things together—for example, work together in PTA, belong to the same church, live on the same block, are parents of children who are friends, and work in the same business organization. A network is dense if its members are all interconnected. In his early work, Hirsch has found that members of less dense and multidimensional networks give each other more support in crises and are associated with better mental health. Hirsch suggests that less dense groups may be more adaptive under conditions of change such as life crises and that having diverse role partners may enhance ability to cope with change.

A number of theorists propose a sequence from undifferentiated social responsiveness or gregariousness (just wanting to be with others) to differentiated and discriminating social responsiveness (wanting particular characteristics in particular people). Haan and Day (1974) reported such a progression through the adolescent years, and in childhood. Bray and his colleagues (1974) found a similar effect during adulthood.

Because one inevitable concomitant of old age is the progressive loss of family members and friends, a person who lives long has survived others. Gerontologists such as Rosow (1967) have examined the conditions under which integration into local—usually informal—groups can be facilitated. Among these is living in a relatively stable, homogeneous, unchanging neighborhood for a long period of time. Not many people in today's rapidly changing society can meet this condition; it is particularly hard for aging people to do so. Rosow's large-scale study of Cleveland old people looked at the age homogeneity of their neighborhoods and found that the more other old people they had around them, the larger their social network and, at least initially, the easier their acceptance of aging. He noticed several types of network associations. First there were the *cosmopolitans* (32% of the sample), who resemble the remotely sociable and group-centered men and women in the Berkeley study (Maas & Kuypers, 1974). Like them, these were largely middle-class people in good health, most of whose social life was outside their immediate neighborhood. They had a moderately large circle of friends, with whom they actually had little contact. The second group was the *isolated* (23%), who had few social contacts and said they would like more. The third group was *the merry widows* (about 25%), who had many contacts in the neighborhood and did not want any more. The fourth group was the *insatiable* (10%), who had much social contact but wanted still more.

Sex differences in social activities are noticeable from early childhood onward. Maccoby and Jacklin (1974), in their comprehensive review of sex-difference literature, conclude that

girls' friendship patterns are more intimate and boys' more gregarious. This childhood difference continues to hold true for adolescents and adults (Douvan & Adelson, 1966; Unseem, 1969).

Most people distinguish between family and nonfamily interactions. Ethnic and class differences highlight this distinction. Thus, working-class people see friends and neighbors as equivalent. Friends are neighbors, and neighbors are friends. Middle-class respondents talk about relationships with three groups: kin, friends, and neighbors. But working-class people refer only to kin and neighbors—and even these may be the same in many communities.

Ethnic differences in nonfamily interactions were found by Dowd and Bengtson (1975) in a Southern California study. Nonfamily interaction was greatest for Anglos, less for Blacks, and least for Mexican-Americans. Because interactions with kin were in the inverse order, the authors come to the same conclusion as Weiss: people have an optimum level of social interaction and look for substitutes when their primary category is depleted. Rosow had likewise reported an inverse relation between family interactions and friend interactions. Figure 17.1 shows that women in the post-child-rearing years increase their interactions with friends.

However, more-informal or more-intense relationships or social networks are not requirements for good mental health. There are strong individual differences, and for many older people formal interactions are more conducive to life satisfaction than informal ones (Palmore & Luikart, 1972). If formal relations are the kind one has been used to all one's life, one is not going to feel comfortable or get any personal pleasure from new kinds of relationships. Senior centers and nutritional sites are popular with lower-middle-class or working-class people who have been oriented to informal neighborly interactions. More-formal organizations, such as the Association for Retired Teachers, are better for other people.

Friends

Some psychologists prefer to describe and explain intimate dyadic relations, such as those of lovers, husband/wife, parent/child, or friends, in terms of the same dynamics that pertain to less intimate relationships. Other psychologists see qualitative differences. Formal-organization activity can be described as primarily impersonal. Informal social interactions can be described as primarily gregarious or generically affiliative. And dyadic relationships can be described as intimate, often similar to the close bonds in infant/mother attachment.

Alternatively, we can use a fence metaphor, hypothesizing a range from high to low fences around individuals or around dyads and other groups. Individuals who maintain high, impermeable fences around themselves probably find it easier to participate in formal groups. But high fences interfere with more-intimate dyadic interaction. Some groups may have higher fences around them than do others—families may have higher fences than do work groups, for example. Some dyads may also have higher fences than do others.

Maas and Kuypers's (1974) descriptions of remotely sociable older people suggest that such people have high individual fences; they may, however, have either high or low group fences. Some fanatic religious or political groups may have low individual fences but high group fences. Members of such groups may feel almost closer to each other than to themselves and may only trust and want to interact with other members. Nonmembers may be seen as heathen or alien—as outsiders. Some lovers or married couples are more intimate than others, not only letting down their "barriers" physically but also sharing most other parts of their lives. Other lovers or married couples may be physically close but maintain individual separateness. I am assuming here that the friendship dyad has relatively low individual fences and a light dyadic or group fence. At least, this could be true for "best friends."

Lowenthal and her associates (1975) name our types of dyadic relationships: (1) acquaintanceship, (2) friendly interaction, (3) friendship, and (4) intimacy. These types are listed in order of how much the friends know about the unique individuality of the other or others. Friendship can differ by number (how many friends a person has), age, sex, relation to subject's spouse, and length and frequency of contact. Figure 17.1 shows a clear decrease in interaction with friends from youth to old age, for both men and women (Stueve & Fischer, 1978). Although friends are second to kin in importance at all ages and for both sexes, the relative

importance decreases from close to 1:1 for those who are 18–35 years of age to 7:2 for men and 2:1 for women over 65 years of age.

The subjects in the San Francisco study (Lowenthal et al., 1975) reported a range in number of friends from 0 to 24, with a mean of 5.7. This mean is higher than that found by Booth (1972), whose subjects reported a mean of 3.7 friends. But Booth's subjects tended more to be working-class and to be older. Of the four stages studied by Lowenthal and her associates, the newlyweds had the most friends (mean of 7.6), the oldest group second (6.0), and the early middle-aged and high school seniors least (4.7 and 4.8). One reason why the newlyweds reported the most friends is that they counted a couple as two friends, while the other groups usually considered only the same-sex member of the couple as a friend. At all ages, women reported more friends than did men (means of 6.3 and 5.2, respectively), and this was even more true of middle-class women than of working-class women. If you look back at Table 17.2, you will see that Britton and Britton's (1972) old longitudinal subjects reported fewer friends as they got older. This was true for both men and women, but the women started and ended with more friends than did the men.

The San Francisco high school seniors saw their friends the most—they saw most of their friends daily. The other age groups reported weekly or monthly interactions.

The older the respondents, the longer they had known their friends. About three-quarters of the friends reported by the high school group were of less than five years' duration, while 90% of the older men and women had friends of more than six years' duration. In an exercise on friendship conducted by my students a few years ago, older women had known the friends they named since they were about 20 years of age. The older men dated their friendships back even further. In another student study (Jones, 1974), women college students dated their friendships from the time they started college; men students dated theirs back to early or middle adolescence.

Finally, there is an intertwining of friends and spouses over the years of marriage. Newlyweds start out with their premarital friends and gradually establish "couple friends," shared by both husband and wife. Such couple friends, furthermore, tend to be recruited by the husband through his work associates rather than to be recruited by the wife, even if she too has a job (Babchuck & Bates, 1963). Most of Lowenthal's San Francisco respondents named friends their own age and sex. Affluent husbands and wives who were middle-class, middle-aged managerial migrants named different "best friends." They had almost no overlap (Hess, 1972). Wives mentioned as friends women from earlier residences, or new neighbors. Men were more likely to name business associates. However, Parron (1979) found considerable overlap between the friends of the husband and wife in golden-wedding couples.

FUNCTIONS

What are friends for? What functions do they serve? A recent review of the literature by Kathleen McCormick (1982) identifies seven such functions:

1. *Liking, or affection,* an unconditional expression of approval, whether merited or not
2. *Self-disclosure,* the sharing of secrets with someone who knows one well and can provide support or approval—as distinct from "telling all" to a stranger one meets on a bus or airplane
3. *Stimulation,* or the providing of new experiences
4. *Respect*
5. *Trust*
6. *Utilitarian aid,* whether advice, goods, or services
7. *Obligation*

A factor-analytic study found three major friendship functions: intimacy/assistance, status, and power (Candy, 1977). These factors emerged from both men's and women's responses, although their relative importance varied somewhat by age and sex. Thus, as Duck and Spencer (1972) pointed out, friendship is not a unitary concept. Its meaning to people alters as they develop. In the earliest stages of life, friendship is essentially reactive; the "friend" is an interesting stimulus object to which the young infant or child reacts as to any other object (Sutton-Smith, 1973). Later on, there is more mutuality. Younger nursery school children play alongside or watch other children

(Parten, 1932). Older nursery school children play *with* the others.

Theoretically, the *egocentrism* of children—their inability to see the other's independent existence—could make true friendship rare among them. But egocentrism and its consequences for mutuality of relationships are not confined to children. Many adults, of all ages, see only their own point of view, and their intimate relationships are consequently shallow. Their friends are no more real than are those of infants. Some observers note similar shallowness in relationships among very old people.

Bigelow and la Gaipa (1975) graded children's friendships and concluded that they progressed with age from *egocentric* to *sociocentric* to *empathic.* However, any child can have all three kinds at the same time, just as any adult can have formal- and informal-group interactions and intimate dyadic ones at the same time.

A similar progression can be observed during adolescence (Douvan & Adelson, 1966). As noted earlier, the developmental process from early adolescence to middle age is a shift from simple gregariousness to more-interactive behavior (Haan & Day, 1974). Weiss and Lowenthal (1975), reporting on the four-stage San Francisco study, said that their middle-aged subjects were involved in more helping and understanding relationships than were their adolescent or newlywed subjects. All the adult groups, however, including the newlyweds, had some intimate, supporting, sharing relationships.

Although friends may originally be attracted to each other because they find they are alike in many ways, people who have stayed friends for many years tend to stress psychological support over similarity. That is, one's friend makes one feel good (Bailey, Finney, & Heim, 1975). Izard (1963), in a cross-sectional study of college students, found less similarity among friends for seniors than for freshmen. He suggests that, with maturity, one has less need to have one's characteristics reflected in one's friends. Yet the subjects of the San Francisco study (Lowenthal et al., 1975), regardless of their ages, put similarity as the most important characteristic of an ideal friend. They said, of their own friends, "We've gone through a lot together" or "We're the same type of personalities so we get along" (p. 53). Like Izard's subjects, however, older people found this quality less important than did younger ones. Men stressed similarity more than women.

Candy (1977) found no age differences among men for any of the three friendship functions: intimacy/aid, status, and power. Although women show no age differences for intimacy/aid, there is a bimodal age pattern for *status* (decrease from adolescence to middle age, then increase) and a consistent decrease with age for *power*. Men and women of all ages say they turn to the people they named as friends for sharing confidences as well as for more-concrete kinds of help. Men of all ages derive satisfaction from being associated with a person of high status. Young and old women also do, but middle-aged women are less likely to. Men of all ages like to give or get advice and influence their friends. Older women are less likely to want this from friends than are younger women—regardless of the sex of the friends.

Reciprocity and mutuality, particularly in helping and support, are also noted by many investigators as being essential to friendship (Lowenthal et al., 1975). Respondents use phrases such as "mutual understanding," "total acceptance," "someone to confide in," and "mutual trust." Because such qualities in a friend are mentioned by people of all life stages (at least from high school senior to preretirement), Lowenthal and her associates conclude that such requirements may be established at an early age and maintained throughout life. Women found reciprocity even more important than did men.

Five different developmental trends in friendship have been mentioned: (1) in turnover, from frequent changes of friends to persistence; (2) in number of friends; (3) in importance of friends vis-à-vis family; (4) in reciprocity and mutuality; and (5) in function. Not all these trends are linear. In fact, cross-sectional data show U-shaped or inverted U-shaped curves in four of these trends: in number, in importance vis-à-vis kin, in reciprocity, and in function. Young and old respondents have fewer friends who are less important to them than are kin, with whom they reciprocate functions less, and who serve status and power functions instead of intimacy functions. Only in persistence is there an apparent linear trend.

Troll and Smith (1976) postulated an inverse relationship between attraction and attachment in close relationships. In the beginning of any relationship, attraction dominates. We form new friends because they are interesting, intriguing, or novel. Over time, however, if the relationship persists, attraction—which is dependent at least partly on novelty—must wane. It is often replaced by attachment, based on "going through a lot of things together," "feeling comfortable with each other," or "trusting each other." There also seems to be a trend, at least at older ages, toward choosing friends of one's own age (Stueve & Fischer, 1978; Lopata, 1977). Stueve and Fischer's California data show a decrease in age similarity during middle age and an increase later on. Lowenthal and her colleagues (1975) found no age differences in this respect, but their oldest group was younger than the old samples of the other two studies.

SEX DIFFERENCES

Girls have more friends than boys do, and girls' friends are more likely to form a complex network of interrelationships (Bigelow, 1977)—to be more *dense*, in Hirsch's terms. Some psychologists interpret this to mean that girls have stronger affiliative needs and require both more friends and greater diversity of friends. In adolescence, same-sex friends are more important than opposite-sex friends, particularly for girls (Douvan & Adelson, 1966), perhaps because boys' friendships are not as intimate or mature as those of girls. College students are different, however. Both men and women in the later teens care less about and tell fewer secrets to their same-sex friends than to their opposite-sex friends (Pederson & Higbee, 1969).

Adult men and women look for different things in choosing friends. Women look for both men and women friends who think the way they do. Men want like-mindedness only in their men friends (Duck, 1973). Older men report more friends than older women, but they spend less time with close friends than do women and are less likely to replace lost friends (Powers & Bultena, 1976).

In general, women are influenced more by sharing of confidences (Walker & Wright, 1976). Although men say they confide most often in their wives, they do not name their wives as their best friends (Candy, 1977).

There are also cohort and ethnic differences that could account for some of the sex differences. People of the oldest cohorts were often brought up to believe that friendship outside the family was dangerous, that secrets should be kept in the family. Many older widows who never confided in anybody except their family members do not make friends easily when they are alone and could use some (Lopata, 1977). Only about 10% of the widows Lopata interviewed said that they confided in their "close friends." Traditional women, therefore, may not differ so much from men; as with the majority of men, their confidant is their spouse. In her study of golden-wedding couples, Parron (1979) found that some men said they discussed personal problems with "no one."

CROSS-SEX FRIENDSHIP

Men have consistently reported more cross-sex friendships than have women (Booth, 1972; Stein, 1976). Considering women's greater affiliativeness, one might conclude, with Stein, that it is easier to be friends with women than with men. Cross-sex friendships among adults have traditionally been viewed with suspicion. Poets are not the only ones who snort at the idea of platonic relationships. In an exploratory study, both men and women said they had nonsexual cross-sex friendships (Zimmerman, 1978). Some women admitted that what had started out as nonsexual relationships had become sexual— and that they had thereby lost the men as friends. In marriage, cross-sex friendships are regulated by becoming joint couple arrangements (Hess, 1972). The presence of the spouse supposedly allays suspicion and anxiety.

Only in old age, when people are not seen as sexual beings, is this caution considered unnecessary. Unfortunately, the supply of potential cross-sex friends at this age is limited, particularly for women. Men over 45 years of age reported more cross-sex friendships than did women in that age group (Booth & Hess, 1974). People who were no longer married, particularly widows (Lopata, 1977), reported much fewer cross-sex friends than did their married age mates.

SELF-DISCLOSURE

Self-disclosure—the sharing of information one would otherwise keep to oneself—may not be the only function of friendship. However, it is an important function, at least in the begin-

ning of a relationship and during critical transition periods (Jourard & Lasakow, 1958; Lowenthal & Haven, 1968; Candy, 1977). Having a confidant seems to be the most significant distinguishing characteristic between older people who live independently in their communities and those who land in psychiatric wards (Lowenthal & Haven, 1968). Losing one's confidant leads to depression; if you still have one, you can survive other losses. Men and women of all ages define friendship primarily in terms of sharing, either of confidences or of help (Candy, 1977).

DENSITY

Do a person's different friends have the same characteristics or serve the same functions? Hirsch (1980) found that, the more interconnections among friends and the more each served several functions, the better the friends' mental health. Lowenthal and her associates report less homogeneity among friends of high school seniors and preretirees than among friends of newlyweds and the middle-aged. Half the high school students described their three closest friends in the same way, but only two-fifths of the newlyweds, one-quarter of the "empty-nest" group, and three-quarters of the preretirees did so. Middle-aged respondents had fewer friends and used them for fewer functions than respondents of other ages.

The data just reported are not highly consistent with those shown in Figure 17.1. Women's friends were more diverse than men's. Old people have fewer friends than younger people. The friendship ties of old people may also be shallower, consistent with the importance of family in old age, at least to people who are now old (Rosow, 1967). Again, there may not be a straight age pattern here. Family may be more important than friends during transitional periods or times of crisis, but friends may be more important when help is not needed. Until we have more longitudinal data on friendship, we cannot attempt to understand some of these conflicting patterns.

SOCIAL CLASS

Social-class differences are important. As noted earlier, working-class people are likely to make no distinction between neighbors and

TABLE 17.3 Percentage reporting numbers of good friends in same neighborhood or section of town, by length of residence, according to social class

Social class	Years of residence	Number of friends			Total respondents
		None	*1–3*	*4+*	
Working class	1–4	45%	26%	29%	167
	5+	42	31	24	98
Middle class	1–4	30	30	40	354
	5+	23	31	46	450

Source: Rosow, 1967.

friends, and their "friends" may often just be acquaintances. Because working-class people are less mobile than middle-class people, most friends of working-class people live in their neighborhoods. Although working-class people may not travel as far to visit family or friends, however, they do move their residences more often, which operates to make their friendships more transient than those of middle-class people, who can get together with friends on vacation or cross-country visits. On the other hand, old working-class people are more likely to live in neighborhoods in which there are other old people, which makes it possible for them to meet more people like themselves (Rosow, 1967). Table 17.3 shows class differences in number of friends by length of residence. It is evident not only that middle-class respondents have more friends than do working-class respondents but also that they have proportionately more friends in their own neighborhoods. They also have more in other places; friendship is more a part of their lives—as are all close

TABLE 17.4 Percentage reporting number of new friends in past year, according to social class and residential density

Social class and density	Number of new friends			N
	None	*1–3*	*4+*	
Working class				
Normal	59%	22%	19%	152
Dense	30	14	56	147
Middle class				
Normal	55	19	26	244
Concentrated	57	17	26	290
Dense	51	18	31	229
Hotels	62	16	22	61

Source: Rosow, 1967.

interactions. It is not surprising that older people are more likely to make new friends if their neighborhoods have more people their own age, as can be seen in Table 17.4.

MARITAL STATUS

People who are married—who in a way may be said to have built-in friends, their spouses—are also more likely to have nonfamily friends than are single, widowed, or divorced people. These friends are more likely to be of longer duration, because married couples are not as likely to have been uprooted as much as widowed or divorced people have been. The golden-wedding husbands and wives studied by Parron (1979) were with each other all day but also lived highly social lives, phoning and visiting relatives and friends every day. Much middle-class social life is based on couples, so that single people, particularly women, are at a disadvantage.

The husband-centered wives in Maas and Kuypers's (1974) study were least likely to have made new friends since the age of 60. Like most married older people, they are less influenced by density of age mates in their neighborhoods than are widowed or divorced older people.

ISOLATES

Retired people are more affected by density of age mates than are people who are still working. All in all, one-third of the Cleveland sample of people over 65 years of age (Rosow, 1967) said they wished they had more friends. Less than 5% were what Rosow called the *phlegmatic* type, characterized by little contact with neighbors and no desire for more friends. Not only were these phlegmatic people older and in poorer health, but they also tended to have been socially isolated most of their life, like Lowenthal's isolated San Franciscans. Other isolates, however, had not chosen their lot and did want more friends (23% of sample). Another one-fourth, the *sociable,* had high contact and were satisfied. The *insatiable,* about 10%, also had high contact but still wanted more. Rosow's typology bears some resemblance to Maas and Kuypers's (1974). In both cases, it is clear that older people are not alike in their social preferences and pursuits. Some are sociable, some are not. Some want to be, some do not. As in all age-related phenomena, variation is wide.

Lowenthal and Haven (1968) differentiated between *marginal isolates* and *lifelong isolates.* Marginal isolates had tried but failed to achieve close relationships, and lifelong isolates had never tried. In general, marginal isolates had lower morale than the lifelong isolates, who apparently had never wanted close friends. The number of friends that one is satisfied with may thus be a lifelong characteristic.

SATISFACTION WITH NUMBER OF FRIENDS

Data on satisfaction with number of friends, from national surveys made 20 years apart, are shown in Table 17.5 (Antonucci & Bornstein,

TABLE 17.5 "Enough friends": Differences in percentages, 1957 versus 1976

Cohort				
Year	Age	Satisfied	Dissatisfied	N
1. 1957	21–29	55	47	450
1976	40–49	57	43	338
2. 1957	30–39	58	42	581
1976	50–59	63	37	341
3. 1957	40–49	58	42	512
1976	60–69	57	43	306
4. 1957	50–59	63	37	388
1976	70–79	63	37	179
5. 1957	60+	67	34	498
1976	80+	68	33	68

Source: Antonucci and Bornstein, 1978.

1978). Overall satisfaction with number of friends seems to have declined between 1957 and 1976, particularly for people in their 20s and in their 60s. Forty-year-olds remained about the same. More older than younger respondents felt satisfied both times, perhaps because they wanted friends less.

Friends made more difference to widows' life satisfaction than did children or siblings (Pihlblad & Adams, 1971). However, friends did not contribute to the satisfaction of AT&T managers (Bray & Howard, 1978). To confuse matters further, having a confidant was moderately related to life satisfaction among aging men in the Duke longitudinal sample but was negatively related to life satisfaction among the women. Clearly, more research is needed.

Summary

Social interaction can vary from formal groups to intimate dyads. Present evidence suggests that what kind is best depends on the person and that the dominant mode of interaction tends to stay the same for each person most of adult life.

There are five possible developmental trends for friendship. First, there may be rapid change or turnover of friends in youth to persistence in later adulthood. Second, one may have fewer friends in youth and old age than in the intervening years. Third, friends are less important than family in early youth, and again in old age, but are at least as important in the middle years. Fourth, reciprocity and mutuality increase as friends and friendships mature. Fifth, some functions of friendship remain constant over the years; for example, intimacy and assistance.

Adolescents and old people use friends more for status and power functions than do middle adults. Having a confidant has been found to be important in continued functioning in old age. However, people who have always been isolates can be equally content. Women tend to have closer friends than do men, particularly if the women are middle class and married.

18

The Couple: Love and Marriage

Since the 1950s—and, incidentally, while the baby boom was still going strong—family theorists were convincing each other that the family was dying, that only the isolated nuclear family survived as an atavistic appendage of society, and that it too was fragmenting. A wide variety of social ills, from violence in the schools to nursing-home abuses, have been attributed to this demise.

The first swing back of the theoretical pendulum followed gerontological research that demonstrated without question that old people, at least, are surrounded by families. The decade of the 1970s has seen repeated evidence that people of all ages live in families, even though not necessarily in the same households. In a recent national survey conducted by the University of Michigan Survey Research Institute (Douvan, 1979), respondents of all ages and of both sexes said that their family roles were their most important roles. In fact, the percentage of people saying so in 1976 was even greater than that in an earlier, matching study in 1957. In spite of alarming increases in divorce, ideological norm shifts toward individual self-fulfillment, and geographic mobility, therefore, we can conclude that the family lives.

Although families are best seen as wholes or as systems, most existing research has focused on individuals or dyads. Therefore, this chapter and Chapter 20 deal primarily with couples, Chapter 21 deals with parent/child dyads, and Chapter 22 deals with more-extended kin.

Much of the meaning and drama of adult life takes place within the family. Although the family has many forms, and these forms change to adapt to changing historical conditions, the family is the most basic primary social group. "Families differ from other groups in having powerful bondings, special rules, homeostatic mechanisms, telegraphic styles of communication, private meanings, myths, regressive features, alliances, loyalties, and dynamic influences from previous generations" (Framo, 1979, p. 4). Relationships with kin are models for most other intimate relationships. In fact, many close relationships are given a kin name: "Aunt Jane" is not necessarily a parent's sister but may be a parent's close friend.

The family is often thought of as the woman's domain—as the job is considered the man's domain. Yet this distinction is not completely true now, has probably never been completely true, and will probably be even less true tomorrow. Being married is also not a requirement for membership in a family. Single, widowed, and divorced men and women have relatives. In fact, when an important family relation is lost—as by death, divorce, or moving away—another may be substituted out of a reservoir of more-distant relatives.

Until recently, census figures showed that overwhelming proportions of Americans were marrying, more than at most other times in past history and more than in other countries. Until 1956, there was a trend for earlier age of first marriage, as well as a trend for increasing divorce (Lipman-Blumen, 1975). These events, in-

cidentally, tend to be related: the younger people are when they first marry, the more likely
they are to divorce. Both these trends have either reversed or stabilized over the last two
decades, although it is really too soon to tell
whether or not such changes are temporary os-
cillations.

According to Glick (1979), women who married for the first time in 1977 were about a year
older (21.0 years old) than those who married in
1967 (who were 19.9 years old). Furthermore,
20-year-olds in the 1970s were postponing marriage and were living together without marriage.
Women who did not marry accounted for one-
third more of the women 20 to 24 years of age
in 1978 than in 1968, and they accounted for
even more of the 25- to 29-year-olds (Glick,
1979). In part, this trend could be a temporary
historical effect caused by a "marriage
squeeze": baby-boom women were ready to
marry before the baby-boom men were old
enough. However, those who delay too long often never marry.

As for divorce, Glick (1979) says "The long-
time upward trend in divorce became an upsurge between 1965 and 1975, when the U.S.
divorce rate per 1,000 married women nearly
doubled, from 10.6 per 1,000 in 1965 to 20.3 in
1975" (p. 3). Since 1975, though, the divorce rate
has been rising much more slowly. Divorce will
be discussed in a later chapter.

Demographic shifts can be responses to historical events, such as economic affluence or
depression and wars, or to ideological movements. People tend to marry more and to marry
at earlier ages in times of economic prosperity,
for example, or when social norms do not require preparatory economic "nest building." A
couple can catch up on furnishing a home during the early years of marriage if both husband
and wife earn money and do not have children.
Sigmund Freud repeatedly soothed his impa-
tient fiancée by reminding her that they still did
not have enough linen ready. In those days, it
was taken for granted that household goods had
to be acquired before marriage, because the
couple was expected to start child rearing,
housekeeping, and entertaining right after the
wedding (Jones, 1953). The couples who married
in the 1950s also may have had added motivation to marry early because of their own deprivation as children in the Depression of the
1930s (Elder, 1974).

These kinds of period and cohort effects (see
Chapter 4) influence the timing of all phases of
what some have called the *family cycle*. The
changing rhythms of family life events can be
observed in generational differences that will
be discussed in Chapter 21.

Premarital beginnings

The development of "family careers" starts to
shape boys' and girls' behavior in early childhood. Development of heterosexual attitudes
and relationships is manifest in early adolescence in modern American society. Along with
secular trends for earlier puberty, there has
been a matching trend toward earlier couple
formation over the last 50 years.

Dating is an American innovation. It originat-
ed in urban and college settings during the
1920s, moved down into the high schools in the
1930s and 1940s, and since then into junior high
school (Moss, Apolonio, & Jensen, 1971). Not all
dating is courtship for marriage, of course. Dating can be recreation, socialization for sex-role
identity, and status seeking, as well as courtship.

Choices have multiplied in love, sex, and
marriage behaviors (Fox, 1975a). And, with options available, there are more decision points
along the way. The result is greater complexity
in the conduct of life and more-conscious control over decisions.

More than half of college women in the late
1970s no longer saw virginity as a valuable asset
in acquiring a husband. The average American
woman today is sexually knowledgeable—or at
least has had some sexual experience—by the
time she marries. A national survey by Zelnick
and Kantner (1977) showed that 55% of never-
married young women had engaged in sexual
intercourse before they were 19 years old. In
1953, Kinsey found that only 20% had been
sexually active before the age of 20. Thus there
has been an increase of 25% in approximately
25 years. Similarly, men no longer must demonstrate economic capability before marrying.

One aspect of the marriage game has changed
little, though. Because more decisions must be
made and because women are less skilled at
making decisions, women are still disadvantaged and thus are vulnerable to greater stress
than are men. Another consequence of having
many choices is their reversibility—it is now

easier to change one's mind. This reversibility can blur choices. No one choice or decision is irrevocable, and thus no one choice is very important. In a way, marriage itself is of less strategic importance than it once was; the distinction between marriage and singlehood is less acute.

Although the time allowed for getting married has lengthened somewhat, there is still a definite time limit for women during which the mate-selection process must occur, particularly if children are desired. This limitation adds to the stresses of decision making.

The changes just mentioned can be understood both in terms of mathematical models of availability and in terms of exchange or marketplace models of bargaining. Goode (1964) points up the difference between a "good *match*," in which the partners are evenly balanced in what they offer each other, and a "good *catch*," in which one partner gets a lot for a little. The changes mentioned can also be related to norms of whom one must marry and whom one must not marry. When more women than men are available, as has been the case for many years now, we can expect that more desirable women than desirable men will be "left over." Jessie Bernard (1973) says that unmarried women are the "cream of the crop" and unmarried men the "bottom of the barrel." Because the excess of women over men increases with each decade of life, there are bound to be—and are—more unmarried older women than unmarried older men. Widowed or divorced men are thus much more likely to remarry than widowed or divorced women—particularly if they are older.

Mate-selection norms traditionally include what has been called the *mating gradient:* whatever the woman has or is, the man should have more of it—height, weight, age, IQ, education, experience, social status, or income. Men are also supposed to search for, initiate contact with, and make the final selection of their wives. Women are supposed to attract, accept, and retain men. Women thus have greater value when they're attractive and young; men have greater value when they're older and more successful.

In the 1957 Institute for Social Research study (Veroff & Feld, 1970), four-fifths of all respondents thought only sick or immoral people would not want to marry. In the 1976 repetition of this study (Douvan, 1979), only one-quarter of

the respondents thought not marrying was wrong. Among college students, particularly those with feminist orientations, the norm shift is even more marked. Mandle (1975) found that only 78% of nonfeminists hoped to marry, and only 38% of feminists did. These findings are in sharp contrast to studies only a few years earlier, which were still finding that over 90% of all American women hoped to marry and did marry. As more and more women are choosing, if only temporarily, such options as career over marriage, different bargaining rules are emerging. Among them are shifts in the valuation of men, away from economic to personal attractiveness. Thus, Fox believes, sex may have been taken off the market. She hopes that greater equality between men and women will eventually result.

Over a decade ago, Wake (1969) compared parents' reports of their sex behavior when they were young with what they would approve for their children. Of a sample of mothers, 30% reported having had premarital coital experience, but only 9% thought that their sons should have it, and only 3% thought that their daughters should. Of the fathers, 51% reported having had premarital sex, but only 18% thought that their sons should have it, and only 9% thought that their daughters should. Apparently, at least in the 1960s, as soon as people got married, their approval of premarital sexual activity dropped sharply. When their children reached puberty, it dropped even more. In general, the greater their responsibility for other family members and the less they themselves were courting, the more likely they were to disapprove of sexual permissiveness. Reverse socialization by children of their parents is taking place, however, leading to a period effect of greater permissiveness in the whole population (Bengtson & Troll, 1978).

Every little girl and her parents know that her beauty—or lack of it—is important to her future life options. Yet the amount of research on attractiveness is astonishingly meager. Elder (1974), for example, studied women of the Depression cohort who had married successful men and who thus themselves would have been considered successful, by their own standards. These women were, regardless of their class or economic origin, among the most attractive and well groomed of their groups. More-attractive girls also tend to have more sex experience

(Kaats & Davis, 1970). Over half of the most attractive girls these researchers studied were nonvirgins, while only 31% of the moderately attractive, and 37% of the least attractive, were nonvirgins. The most attractive also had the most sex partners. The attractive girls tended, of course, to marry earlier.

Development of the marital dyad

In traditional couple formation, there is often a sequence from casual dating to steady dating, going steady, engaged to be engaged, and engaged. This sequence has a number of filter or choice points along the way. Initial idealization of the partner (Pollis, 1969) tends gradually to give way to a more realistic appraisal. Partners who start dating at an early age and who see each other often are more likely to go through the dating progression quickly and to marry young.

Children of unhappy marriages tend to start dating earlier, to date more people in junior and senior high school, to date more frequently in college, and to marry earlier. Thus children of unhappy marriages are likely to choose partners on the basis of more-primitive attributes and end up having unhappy marriages, just like their parents.

Residential propinquity and similarity in background and values are major influences in the choice of dating partners in the beginning. Even in the United States, where traditional patterns presumably have broken down, boys and girls generally select partners from the same social class and family background (Lopata, 1971). Murstein (1967) found similarity among courting partners even in mental health. Well-functioning young people select well-functioning partners, and the poorly functioning are drawn to others who are functioning poorly.

Before dating itself begins, a developmental sequence can be observed in heterosexual attitudes and orientations that Adams (1979) calls "being attracted to marriage itself." Broderick and Rowe (1968) proposed a five-step process, based on their studies of about 1500 12-year-olds. This process, they feel, reflects movement from the general to the specific and from the universalistic to the particularistic. These are their steps:

1. A recognition, following the experience of being in love, of the heterosexual relation in marriage
2. Viewing marriage as a positive element in the future; expressing a desire to marry
3. Singling out a person of the opposite sex and labeling him or her "boyfriend" or "girlfriend," sometimes without the target knowing about it
4. Desiring companionship with the opposite sex
5. Beginning to date

One problem in determining developmental sequences in mate selection is that most such sequences have been based on marriage as the validating end state. Yet relationships may develop over time without ending in legal marriage. In fact, the actual event of marrying may be precipitated, not by the stage of the dyadic relationship reached, but by such random or accidental factors as graduation, getting a job, pregnancy, parental strictness, death of a parent, or even urging of a parent. The domino effect may also be observed. Partners who have not seriously considered marriage before may begin considering it if they are the last of their crowd left unmarried. Conversely, partners who might otherwise consider marriage might hesitate to be the first of their friends to do so. Although marriage may not be the best way to validate a dyad-formation process, it is true that couples who split up are no longer developing their relationships.

Almost 20 years ago, Kerckhoff and Davis (1962) observed "seriously attached" college-student couples over a period of six months. Using their findings, Adams (1979) constructed the following sequence:

1. Attraction to marriage itself—a conscious, expressed desire to marry
2. Propinquity
3. Early attraction, based on such surface behaviors of the partner as
   a. Gregariousness
   b. Poise
   c. Similar interests and abilities
   d. Physical appearance and attractiveness, particularly in girls
   e. Similarity to one's ideal image
4. Perpetuation of attraction, aided by

a. Reactions of others, including being labeled as a couple
b. Disclosure, opening oneself up to each other
c. Pair rapport, feeling comfortable in each other's presence
5. Commitment and intimacy, establishing a bond
6. Deeper attraction, enhanced by
   a. Value consensus or co-orientation, providing validation of each other's viewpoints
   b. Feelings of competence reinforced
   c. Perception of other similarities in the partner, such as
      Attractiveness
      Levels of emotional maturity
      Affective expressiveness
      Self-esteem
      Race, ethnic group, or religion, if important to members
      Birth-order matching
7. Deciding that this is "right for me" or "the best I can get"
8. Marriage

Once "dyad crystallization" occurs, there are still the reactions of others to consider. And there are barriers to breaking up, such as the effort involved in forming a new relationship and the problem of hurting one's partner. These barriers help to move the sequence to the final step.

Because Adams derived his theory primarily from research on college students, it may be less applicable to people of other ages and classes. Marriage of adolescents, for example, is usually precipitated by pregnancy (De Lissovoy, 1973) and may occur before the sequence is completed. We know almost nothing about the later-life formation of couples except what McKain (1969) reported about remarriage after 55: that it tends to occur between people who have known each other for many years.

In a longitudinal study of couples (Paris & Luckey, 1966), those who continued their relationship over two years were more likely to have scored higher on role fit and achievement of dyadic crystallization at the beginning of the study. They started off "ahead of the game."

Identity as a couple is analogous to Erikson's (1950) concept of individual identity. It assumes

recognition both by the partners themselves and by other people in their social world, especially family and friends. Lewis (1973b) found that couples were more likely to stay together longer than 10 weeks and to develop their relationship if they were recognized as a couple by others.

Love and attraction

A recent focus in developmental research has been on the formation of primal bonds or "attachments" between infants and their caretakers. Out of these studies and others on interpersonal interaction have come a few hypotheses about the nature and formation of interpersonal bonds. Gewirtz (1972), for instance, makes an emphatic distinction between *attachment*, defined as a two-person reciprocal relationship, and *dependency*, defined as a relationship with a set of (perhaps) interchangeable others. Attachment involves person-to-person bonds, and dependency involves person-to-group bonds. The tight psychological space of a two-person system may foster more-intense relationships than may the wider space within which groups of friends or relatives exist. Thus intensity of relationship may be inversely related to the number of people included. Parent/child, lover, best-friend, and husband/wife relationships may be strong and persistent as compared to relationships with extended kin, peer groups, and networks of friends and neighbors.

Not many psychologists have studied love and attachment among adults, even though Maslow (1955) wrote about it a quarter of a century ago. He distinguished between D-love (deficiency love) and B-love (love for the being of another person). He also distinguished between intrinsic and extrinsic functions of a relationship. Fox (1975a) distinguishes between *love as fission*, or explosion, and *love as fusion*, a strong binding force. Rougemont (1956) has made another distinction, between *being in love*, a feeling, and *loving*, an act.

Western culture has been dominated by a strong myth of romantic love. Fulfillment, in romantic love, destroys that love; reality intrudes on fantasy and destroys the fantasy. Cozby and Rosenblatt (1971) report that many societies encourage privacy for newlyweds as a way of isolating them from the everyday affairs of life in order to strengthen their bonds. We have our own, similar, custom of the honeymoon.

An examination of long-term relationships—parent/child, sibling, old-friend, and long-married couple relationships—suggests that there may be an inverse relationship between attraction and attachment. In the beginning of a relationship, attraction is high, because part of its impetus is novelty and discovery. But attachment is low, because bonds are not yet cemented. A breakup of the relationship at this stage would cause only temporary distress, and substitutions for loved objects would be relatively easy—there are many more fish in the sea! In the course of repeated interaction, however, novelty is gone and attraction is reduced—but attachment may have become very strong. The two members of the dyad have become part of each other; they have achieved a joint identity. A breakup at this time may never be completely overcome. No substitution of loved object may be possible, and a "phantom-limb" pain may persist.

An interesting study of types of marriages among successful Americans describes five ways of expressing love, if not attachment (Cuber & Harroff, 1963):

1. *Conflict-habituated:* conflict and tension become part of an ongoing pattern. This can (and does, for some) last a lifetime.
2. *Devitalized:* no serious tension, but no zest either. There may be aspects of marriage that are satisfying, such as children, property, or family tradition and occasional

feelings of sharing something, if only memory.
3. *Passive/congenial:* passively content, not disillusioned with what is there.
4. *Vital:* vibrant and exciting sharing of some important life experience, such as sex, work, child rearing, creative endeavor, or even a hobby.
5. *Total:* like vital, but multifaceted. All important aspects of life are shared. This type of relationship is rare.

Reedy and Birren (1978) studied 102 happily married couples. They concluded that there are two main types of loving: a *companionship* type, based on expression of love, communication, and respect, and a *traditional* type, based on mutual material and emotional investments. As seen in Table 18.1, the companionship type is most common among young adults and the traditional type among older adults. In part, this is probably a cohort difference. However, it is probably also in part a developmental change. Intense communication and self-disclosure may be more important to affectionate bonding early in a relationship. Loyalty, investment, and commitment to the relationship—the traditional way of loving—may develop over time. This pattern is analogous to the attraction/attachment paradigm, or to the "cooling-off" effect seen over time in Cuber and Harroff's data.

SEX DIFFERENCES

Sex differences tend to pervade all courtship. They showed up in an intriguing study by

TABLE 18.1 Frequency distribution of styles of loving by age

Style of loving	Age group			
	Young adult	Middle-aged adult	Older adult	Total
Companionship	48[a]	36	19	103
	(47%)[b]	(35%)	(18%)	(50%)
Combination/transitional	10	17	16	43
	(23%)	(40%)	(37%)	(22%)
Traditional	10	15	33	58
	(17%)	(26%)	(57%)	(28%)
Total	68	68	68	204
	(33%)	(33%)	(33%)	(100%)

[a]Frequency.
[b]Row percentage.

Source: Reedy and Birren, 1978.

Coombs and Kenkel (1966) of computer dating among first-year college students. The women had more-rigid standards than the men had for selecting and judging their dates and had higher expectations of them. They wanted their dates to have socially desirable characteristics such as seriousness, intelligence, occupational potential, and general capability. They were much more cautious than the men in deciding whom to date and in stating whether they would like to date their partners again. The men limited their specifications to physical attractiveness. They were more easily satisfied with their dates and more ready to date them again. For most women, getting married and having children is a very serious decision. Because the man a woman marries defines much of her future life, she is more emotionally involved and goal oriented in dating. This also makes her more vulnerable and allows her less control over the whole marital process.

When Douvan and Adelson (1966) asked high school boys what they wanted to be when they grew up, the boys usually had no trouble responding. But girls usually answered "It depends." What it depends on, of course, is whether they marry and whom they marry. Bardwick (1971) remarks that women graduate students who are married—and married to men with more status than they—are much better students than other women. They can let themselves achieve.

Historically, men have usually had more control over marital choice than women. The cost of abstaining from marriage is still greater for women than men, even though, as Bernard (1973) eloquently points out, the negative consequences of marriage are also greater for women. Some reasons for men's greater power in this sphere are as follows. First, women "marry up" because their marriages are seen as conferring social status. Second, marrying up or down applies to age as well as to social class, intelligence, and education. Third, women have a shorter age range of marriageability and a longer life span, factors that put them in a position of greater supply and lesser demand.

The man usually takes the most active role in asking for a date, makes most of the decisions about what to do on a date, and makes the final decision about getting married. Once a woman accepts a man as a legitimate suitor, he is expected to shoulder most subsequent responsibil-

ities. It is not surprising, therefore, that women are much more sensitive to the characteristics and wishes of men than men are to the characteristics and wishes of women. In fact, the progress of courtship can be predicted from the woman's ability to sense her partner's perception of himself (Murstein, 1972). Because the man has more options all along the way, he does not risk as much at each choice point. He can always withdraw.

Getting married is considered an important event that changes the lives of both partners. Even during the height of the youth movement, about 80% had a religious ceremony (Lopata, 1971). There have been pendulum swings back and forth for and against formal weddings. The innovative and off-beat weddings of the late 1960s and 1970s are again yielding to more traditional ceremonies. Today's ceremonies have been modified slightly by new ideas but are more like the old than like the new—even though the couple may have been living together for years. I have observed that few couples now disappear dramatically in the middle of the wedding party. As one of them said, "It's our party. We want to stay to the end!" Separation of the *sexual* rite of passage from the *social* rite of passage seems to be one of the more permanent legacies of the sexual revolution. If you have been cohabiting for three years and more, you are in no hurry to get off to the hotel room.

Many women still change from "Miss" to "Mrs.," signifying instant transition to a new role. This ritual persists in spite of attempts to minimize the importance of being married by using "Ms." and by keeping maiden names in jobs.

Unfortunately, outside the dating relationship there may be little preparation for the new roles of husband, wife, or parent.

Being a husband

The average man becomes a husband at about 23, although this age is probably moving up. Traditionally, in our society, he is expected to support his family and to mediate between it and the outside world. Recent surveys have shown that, in spite of ideological pressure for more egalitarian husband/wife behavior, most husbands remain traditional. What is more, most husbands *and* wives like it that way (Pleck, 1975).

Blood and Wolfe (1960) reported that Detroit-area women said that their husbands participated very little in washing the evening dishes, straightening up the house, or preparing their own breakfasts. They participated more in grocery shopping and in keeping track of financial assets and bills. Fifteen years later, after the impact of the women's movement, another study in Detroit (Duncan, Schuman, & Duncan, 1973) found remarkably little change. There were small adjustments in assigned work, but no change in overall separation of roles. The men were more likely to make their own breakfasts but were less likely to repair things around the house. A 1970 Harris poll (Yankelovich, 1970) found that fixing things around the house was the husband's most frequent household activity—the only one he spent more time at than watching sports on television.

A time/motion study of Syracuse, New York, families (Walker, 1970) and a multinational time-use study (Szalai, 1972) both found that husbands spent an average of about an hour and a half per day altogether in family work. Their wives' employment made a difference on men's housework only if they had babies under 1 year old. Thus men's family participation is not only small but also rigidly and arbitrarily limited (Pleck, 1975).

Commitment to this traditional role varies with education and personality needs. Grade-school-educated men who want to achieve tend to be not very involved with their marriages. As long as they provide for their families, they can look elsewhere for feelings of accomplishment and self-worth. College-educated men have greater role conflicts because they have a more ambiguous role (Veroff & Feld, 1970). They are expected not only to be successful providers but also to spend considerable time at home with their wives and children, sharing in housework and child rearing. Over the past few decades, as more married women—even married women with young children—have been employed outside the home, expectations that men should be the sole providers have been decreasing among noncollege families, too. Concomitant changes in other husband behaviors and expectations may evolve in the future.

So far, both cross-sectional and longitudinal data show that, over the years of marriage, hus-bands seem to participate less and less in household activities (Pineo, 1961). They also show decreasing interest in families and households and engage in less sexual activity with their wives as their preoccupations with jobs and activities outside their families increase. What they value in marriage, if they are generally successful in their occupational careers, is companionship and mutual understanding. Those who are less successful are, curiously, as interested in children as they are in companionship (Elder, 1974). Table 18.2 shows the value middle-aged men placed on various family goals. Valuing children did not necessarily lead to having more. Men from families that were not deprived at the time of their adolescence had an average of 2.3 children, compared with an average of 3.4 in families that were deprived.

Being a wife

In 1975 (U.S. Department of Commerce, Bureau of the Census, 1977), the average woman became a wife at age 20. Women's traditional roles include those of housewife and mother, companion, and partner. In the beginning of marriage, the companion role is usually at its peak, partly as a carryover from the courtship relationship. Young wives turn to their husbands both for sympathy and in anger. But as time passes—and particularly if children intervene—intimacy wanes, anger is held in, and wives turn to God, other people, and housework.

A nonemployed wife who has young children at home is markedly restricted. If she does not live near her mother and sisters, she depends on her husband for help, companionship, and news of the outside world. A woman in one of my classes said that she felt our discussions of friendship among housewives were meaningless, because she never met anybody outside her family—and she was even taking courses at the university. As children get older, many women tend to reach out more, partly through activities around their children's broadening world (for example, PTA and Scouts). They are more likely then to help their husbands "get ahead" by earning some money, by giving husbands emotional support and encouragement, or by entertaining husbands' friends and business

TABLE 18.2 Most valuable aspects of marriage as rated by men, by economic deprivation and class origin, in percentages

Aspects of marriage	Middle-class origin		Total sample		
	Nondeprived (N = 16)	Deprived (N = 13)	Nondeprived (N = 19)	Deprived (N = 21)	Total (N = 40)
Home					
The standard of living —kind of house, clothes, and so on	6	8	5	10	8
The security and comfort of a home	6	16	16	14	15
Children					
The chance to have and rear children	13	46	10	48	30
Relations with wife					
Sexual relations	30	15	30	19	26
Companionship in doing things	71	46	70	50	59
Mutual understanding of each other's problems and feelings	70	69	70	64	67

Source: Elder, 1974.

associates. These activities vary by social class, but not in a simple fashion, because personality, family background, and other factors are also important influences. Entertaining in order to help a husband's career, for example, is a high-status role. Lopata (1971) found such entertaining more common among suburban women than among inner-city housewives.

As noted earlier, Kelly (1955) reported that housekeeping loses its allure over the years of marriage. A generation ago, only about one-third of female high school graduates showed any interest in domestic arts, and less than one-fifth of college women did (Bernard, 1975). Bernard believes that the figures would be much lower today. Fortunately, most of Lopata's housewife respondents said that they had some help with cooking, child care, and household finances. Only 46 out of 205 women interviewed did all of the cooking with no help from their husbands, and some got help from other people. Fast-food chains have multiplied throughout the land, for example. Only 19% had no help with child care. Of the helpers, 75% were their husbands. Housewives also handle finances—21% completely, and 37% jointly with their husbands. Only 37% said that this was completely their husbands' job.

Although being a housewife today is not personally rewarding to many women, Veroff and Feld (1970) found that some do find this role fulfilling. Those with strong achievement motivation can express these strivings through fostering their husbands' careers and participating in successes, if the husbands are successful—an indirect approach to achievement. The traditional marital role also seems to satisfy grade-school-educated women with high power needs. If other arenas of displaying power are limited, running a house and directing young children can be gratifying.

The women in the Oakland longitudinal study (Elder, 1974), who were adolescents during the 1930s Depression, are representative of women who do enjoy housework and being housewives. As Figure 18.1 shows, they preferred their family role over all others, even if they were active in other roles and even if they were not happy with their marriages. More than half of them thoroughly enjoyed taking care of their homes and rejected the statement that cooking, sewing, and cleaning are just jobs that have to be done. Only 10% clearly disliked the duties of homemaking. Women from deprived backgrounds liked housekeeping even more than did those from nondeprived backgrounds.

Starting in the late 1960s, and perhaps precipitated by such feminist books as Simone de Beauvoir's *The Second Sex* (1953) and Betty Friedan's *The Feminine Mystique* (1963), the

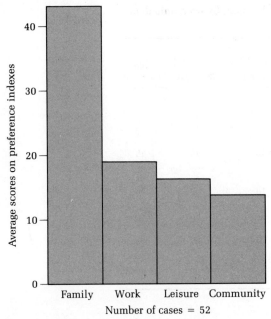

Figure 18.1. Activity preferences of women. *(Source: Elder, 1974.)*

women's movement has become a major influence on the American scene. There is a burgeoning literature that is in part a protest against the traditional inequities and burdensomeness of women's lives and in part an exploration of options for other ways to live. Suggested alternatives range all the way from rejection of childbearing and heterosexual relationships altogether, to equal husband/wife sharing of child rearing, housekeeping, and providing income. Some plans for sharing involve the interchangeability—either simultaneously or sequentially—of home and job roles between both sexes (see Rossi, 1964). Others stress the need for community provision of child-care facilities and centers that would free parents of young children from confinement to the home, for at least part of the day or week. Still others opt for communal living (see the discussion in the next chapter). It is too soon to determine the possible long-range effects of emerging new perspectives on being a wife. Research so far has dealt mostly with job and career aspects, perhaps because these have been evident for a longer period of time. Being a wife may be a very different experience in the 1980s from what it was in the 1950s and 1960s.

Development of the couple

In 1890, a marriage was expected to last less than 25 years before one of the partners died. During this time, children were almost always in the home. Death of one spouse terminated the marriage about two years before the marriage of the last child. By 1970, the average life expectancy from the time of marriage had risen, so that couples married in their early 20s could expect to stay together—if they didn't separate—for 45 years. Furthermore, there would be no children in the home for the last 20 years or more.

Tell me something about a woman you know well.

Grandfather, age 85
Well, I guess it'd be my wife. She's one of the loveliest things on earth. She stays home and takes care of her family—good cook. She's got a lot of good habits.

Father, age 50
My wife is a very beautiful woman; she has brown eyes, and she's medium height, very slender, probably underweight. She has a very nice figure. Her mannerisms are very nice, and she is a joy to be with. She is a bit self-conscious, and at times she is self-depreciating. Probably she has an inferiority complex, and she shouldn't, because she gets along with everybody. She is intelligent, articulate, and very good company.

Son, age 23
I know this one girl; as I said before, she's my roommate. She's the most beautiful girl I have ever seen—in soul and heart and in looks. She's very intelligent, very intellectual, extremely versatile in many things. She's very loving. She's a little bit shy. I like that in her. At times, though, she could be just a little bit more aggressive.

Most young men and women enter marriage with a formal commitment to engage in an enduring relationship. They look forward with excitement and pleasure to shared activity and interest and to total involvement. Partners expect to be each other's main companion, concerned with all aspects of life and feelings, and to leave relatives and friends behind.

Some of these hopes are fulfilled for some couples. When Veroff and Feld (1970) asked their respondents to evaluate their marriages, a majority felt that they had made the right decision and that marriage is a legitimate and positive condition. The following paragraphs treat different aspects of the couple relationship over time. Unfortunately, we still do not have data based on a life-span development approach that focuses on evolving, transformational processes in marital interactions or holistic family dynamics. Lewis's work with premarital couples needs to be applied to couples beyond marriage or at least after formation of the dyad.

ECONOMIC DEVELOPMENT

Other things being equal, the economic condition of married couples follows a cyclical curve. But different generations start out at different economic levels. Compared to their parents and grandparents, young couples of the 1970s began married life in relative comfort. The young married couples studied by Hill and his colleagues in Minneapolis in the late 1950s had a collection of durable goods nearly as large as the collection their parents and grandparents had acquired after 20 years of marriage (Hill et al., 1970). These young couples lagged somewhat behind their middle-aged parents in housing adequacy and financial security, but in that respect also they were generally ahead of what their parents had had when their parents were first married. In eras of lower affluence, this generational pattern would once more be reversed. Young couples in the 1980s might start out more like their grandparents, who got married during the Depression.

Once a couple has children, its standard of living usually declines. Because economic recovery does not begin until the oldest child can start earning money, working-class couples may recover their peak economic level earlier than middle-class couples—if they do not have more children to offset this gain. In wealthier or more socially striving families, this recovery is postponed because of commitment to lengthier education for the children.

After retirement, there is frequently another downswing, to more restricted economic circumstances—in fact, to below the poverty level, for many retired couples. Hill and his associates (1970) found that the grandparent generation averaged the fewest rooms per person, paid the least rent, had the lowest financial security (77% had no investments for retirement), and owned the smallest number of durable goods.

Premature marital and parental careers can offset family-cycle economic rhythms, becoming a trap for both younger and older generations. Early marriage—and, even more, early pregnancy—is associated with living with parents and with being of the lower class. Families with "such a rapid generational turnover barely have time to get over the economic drain of raising one generation" before they have to take on the problems of "supporting a growing set of grandchildren followed by the problems of supporting declining parents" (Fischer, Beasley, & Harter, 1968, p. 299). This "telescoping of generations" prevents the economic recuperation during the middle years that families with later marriage and parenthood find possible.

One reason newlywed and childless couples enjoy a relatively high standard of living is that both husbands and wives are likely to be working. Lacking other major responsibilities, they buy more cars, furniture, appliances, clothes, meals out, and recreation than at any other time of life. This buying spree, Aldous (1978) notes, ends with the arrival of the first child. Then comes a time of buying homes, washers and dryers, food and medicine, and toys and children's equipment.

Some—but not all—investigations find an upswing in marital satisfaction after the children are grown. One contributing factor here is probably the being freed from expenditures on children as well as an absolute increase in economic resources, at least for middle-class couples who are at the peak of their earning power. A majority of middle-aged women are employed, and the heavy financial burdens of child rearing are at least diminished. Giving money to grown children becomes more of a voluntary contribution than a demanding responsibility. But, as Aldous points out, this period can be truncated by a new set of financial responsibilities for ill and aging parents or even for ill or aging husbands or wives. Some couples survive to old age with sufficient funds or securities to continue to live comfortably, particularly if they reduce their wants and particularly with our present policies for Social Security, Medicare, and Medicaid, meager as they are.

The amount of money couples have to spend on their own needs and desires clearly influences the way they live and the way they feel about their lives. This applies not only to the absolute amount available to them but also to the *income pinch* they experience: the amount they have relative to the amount they need to spend. Other things being equal, young couples raising children are more pinched than couples who do not have children and those whose children have become relatively independent economically. Postretirement couples are usually more deprived economically than before retirement. The percentage of households below the poverty level is almost twice as great over age 65 as between 22 and 64.

ROLE DIFFERENTIATION

As with all topics in the analysis of development during the long years of adulthood, changes in marital interaction are combinations of individual development and generational effects. For example, grandparent partners do not share each other's values as much as do parent and adult-child partners (Hill et al., 1970), but they look on each other in a more kindly light. Yet how much of this effect should be attributed to the effect of many years of learning to tolerate differences? How much should be attributed to historical changes in sex-role socialization, resulting in more-ambiguous definitions of marital roles?

One way of looking at marital interaction is along a role-differentiation dimension. In traditional marriages, a husband is expected to earn a living and protect his family from the outer world, while a wife is expected to raise children and maintain a smoothly running, comfortable home. Little is expected in the way of love or warmth or emotional support or shared thoughts and interests. The husband finds his friends among his work associates or neighborhood bar cronies; the wife finds hers among sisters and neighbors. At the opposite end is the expressive, shared relationship, in which love, warmth, and companionship are primary expectations. In such marriages, role differentiation is at a minimum. Husband and wife are supposed to share all and to be able to interchange roles as much as physical and economic conditions permit.

Ethnic, social-class, and generational differences exist among couples with respect to sex-role differentiation. The more traditional social groups—lower classes, less-educated people, and older generations—tend to expect a high degree of role differentiation. The more modern groups—urbanized middle and upper classes,

---

Tell me something about a man you know well.

Grandmother, age 74
My husband. He is gone 23 years now, He was a good man. He was a good provider, good to his children, good to everybody. Good is good.

Mother, age 48
My husband—he's the one I know best. He is a very sincere person. "Easy going" doesn't really describe him, although he is easy to live with. He is very accommodating. He is not a person to highlight birthdays and anniversaries, though. More often than not, he says to take the checkbook and get what I want. And if he does buy me a special gift, he forgets from year to year what he has given me before. But I've always had all the material things I needed, and the fact that he is casual about special, tangible remembrances has never disturbed me—this is not the way he shows his consideration. He is kind, thoughtful, and considerate in all our interactions. He is very easy to live with. He is the kind of man who never adds up his wife's checkbook expenditures. In all our married life, he's never questioned or complained about the way I've managed household finances.

Daughter, age 22
Bill, he's really a nice husband. He's my best friend. He is so easygoing. He makes me laugh, he listens to what I say, and he questions his actions and thinks things out. He is considerate, understanding. He is always trying to be aware of everything he does, all his actions and all his motives. He is really a beautiful person. But Bill, too, does not really know all there is to know about himself, and he is still unsure about what he wants. I guess that is why we get along so much better now. Before we were just in love, and we had to have plans and know where we were going. Now we are really happy, and our friendship is so important to us. We really enjoy going everywhere together. We love to ride our bikes and to pick fresh fruit in the country.

---

more educated people, and younger generations—expect little role differentiation. A high level of role differentiation has been associated with the existence of the extended family, because the woman who gets companionship and daily help from her mother and sisters is not as dependent on her husband for household services. Conversely, if her husband shares her work, she need not turn to her mother and sisters for help. Within an isolated nuclear family, the absence of supportive relatives makes it necessary for husband and wife to lean more heavily on each other (see Bott, 1957/1971).

Just as we have had to modify our predictions about the demise of the extended family, we must also modify our predictions about the demise of traditional marital-role differentiation. Present-day husbands and wives are probably neither as differentiated in function or behavior as some family theorists believe, nor as interchangeable as other theorists assert. Furthermore, *perceptions* of role changes may be greater than the actual changes. For example, the younger couples in Hill's sample describe their marriages as markedly egalitarian and as being different in this way from their parents' and grandparents' marriages. But their behavior, as described by the interviewers, did not seem very different from that of their parents and grandparents. More change has probably taken place in ideology than in behavior. Of course, ideology can be the forerunner of new behavior.

Our understanding of the distribution of household work between husband and wife, unfortunately, is clouded by errors in the data. For one thing, the kinds of tasks that have been considered, such as those used by Blood and Wolfe (1960) in their classic study of marriage, are not representative. They looked at who did most household repairs, mowed the lawn, shoveled the walk, kept track of money and bills, shopped for groceries, washed the dishes, and so forth. A second problem is that wives' reports of their husbands' participation are not consistent with their husbands' own reports and, what is worse, with actual time/motion studies (Walker, 1970). Bahr (1973) concluded that employed husbands of employed wives performed significantly more household tasks than did employed husbands of full-time homemakers. But Walker's data show that employed husbands spend 1.5 hours per day in household work compared with 5 hours per day spent by employed wives.

All studies agree that wives are responsible for and actually perform almost all janitorial services, child-care tasks, and meal preparation. Husbands are responsible for and generally perform a very few "masculine" tasks that, in any case, occur less frequently: minor repairs, shoveling snow, and mowing the grass. Emptying the garbage is an exception; it must be done more often. Most studies do not even consider

kin-keeping functions performed by wives such as visiting, keeping contact with, and writing to all geographically distant relatives (and friends).

Over the life course, there is somewhat more sharing of household work before the first child is born, and there is greater specialization after the first child (Hoffman & Manis, 1978). Hoffman and Manis's findings agree with earlier work by Blood and Wolfe (1960), who reported increasing specialization by sex from early marriage to retirement. The relative *amount* of housework done by wives as compared with husbands in Blood and Wolfe's large cross-sectional Detroit sample remained relatively constant after the children were of school age.

A later study, by Campbell, Converse, and Rodgers (1976), found, further, that the more children a woman has, the more housework she does. Only after the birth of the fourth child do husbands increase their contributions to work around the home. Husbands do not increase their family work when their wives are employed, either (Pleck, 1977). Although it is true that occupational and family work are inversely related to each other for both sexes, employed men still do only a fraction of the family work (one-third) that fully employed women do. As noted in Chapter 13, men's family roles do *not* intrude into their work lives, but women's family roles *do* intrude into *their* work lives. Conversely, many husbands take work home; not many wives do.

Many adults in our society dislike housework, especially men and college-educated women, and this trend may be increasing. Therefore, we may find that less housework will actually get done, that standards for cleanliness will decline, or that new lifestyles will be found that minimize the need for housework.

Many marriages are still based on either implicit or explicit expectations of traditional role differentiation. Moreover, marriages that start out with egalitarian ideologies and practices shift, at least in practice, after the birth of the first child. At that time, husbands turn to their jobs and careers, leaving their wives with primary responsibility for the families. This means that truly egalitarian marriages are usually those that do not have children.

There are few signs that couples return to egalitarian family orientations once their pattern has shifted after the birth of the first child. Wives take on almost all the family responsibilities that their husbands might otherwise have to share. In addition, they emotionally—and often practically—support their husbands in their husbands' work roles.

The evidence for household work sharing by retired husbands and wives is ambiguous. One early study (Lipman, 1962) found that many retired husbands work together with their wives in chores that require little specialized skill and knowledge, such as washing dishes and shopping for groceries. Another study, which compared retired husbands with employed husbands of the same age (Ballweg, 1967), found that retired husbands do not share even this kind of household activity any more than employed husbands do. Ballweg's retired husbands were slightly more likely to assume full responsibility for a few tasks already socially defined as "masculine," such as washing the car; they did *not* perform "feminine" tasks—and the wives in this study said they were generally satisfied with this condition. In other words, the men continued the tasks they had performed before retirement; they did not add on any new ones. The women who write to Ann Landers complaining about their retired husbands following them around the house all day, watching everything they do, or doing their work before they—the wives—have a chance to do it thus share the attitude of Ballweg's wives, that they don't want their retired husbands getting in their way.

Cohort differences undoubtedly cause some of the variation in findings. An ongoing study of retired couples by Atchley and Miller (Troll, Miller, & Atchley, 1979) is finding a great deal of household-task sharing. Although they find that there is often a division of labor between husband and wife, this division is not based on sex-stereotyped lines, but on what each prefers or feels competent in.

Summary

Most American adults have, at least at some time of their lives, been married. Marriage is more important to women and more beneficial to men. Generational differences in age of marriage and in economic circumstances vary with general economic opportunities.

Recent cohorts of young couples have married younger than their parents and grandparents, although this has changed again in the past decade. They have also started off in better economic circumstances, with more money and durable goods. This situation, too, may be changing.

The distribution of household work between husband and wife seems to have changed little: actuality has not caught up with ideology. Women are both responsible for and carry out most household work, even if they work full time, even if they have children and work full time, and even after the men have retired.

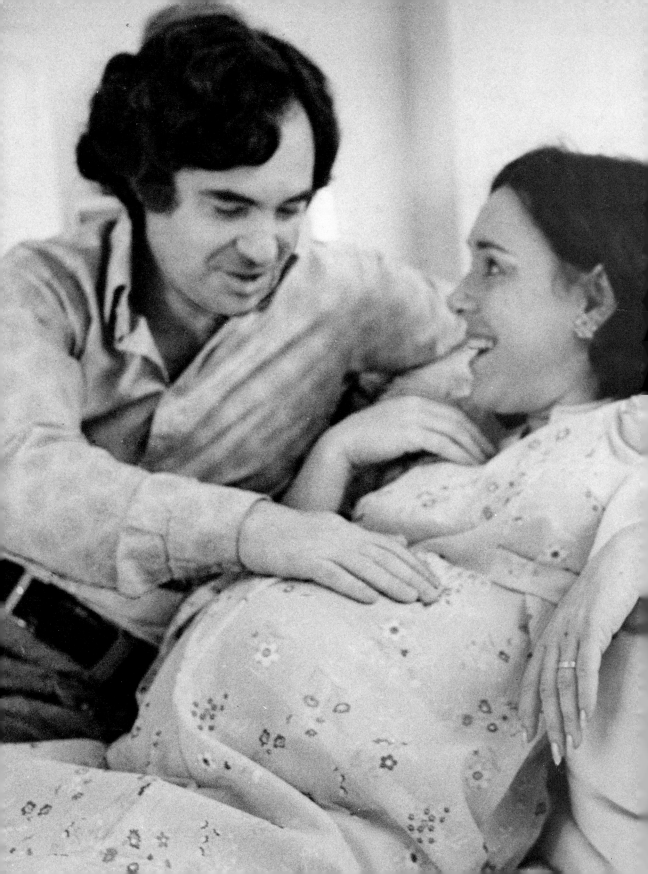

19

The Couple's Development

Not all adults in the United States are parents, but a vast majority are. For those who are, becoming parents is one of the important events of their lives. Parents generally have different developmental trajectories from nonparents, at least in the older cohorts of adults alive in the 1980s. In this chapter, the lifelong effects of parenting are reviewed.

The effect of parenting

What is there about being parents that makes marriage so different for parents and nonparents? Also, why should the birth of the first child be so important? Life-span developmentalists have been intrigued with these questions for almost 30 years, and philosophers for centuries.

THE FIRST CHILD

The birth of the first child has repeatedly been shown to be the most significant event in the development of American couples. Over 20 years ago, LeMasters (1957) called this event a "crisis." Many reasons have been offered for its enormous impact on couple relationships, and they will be discussed in the following pages. More recently, research has been focusing on the kinds of impact that can be observed.

An ongoing study on family/career transitions in women's lives (Weingarten & Daniels, 1978) finds a dramatic difference in the effect of par-

enthood on women's and men's work histories. Regardless of generation, educational level, or family timing pattern, parenting alters women's lives much more than it does their husbands' lives. The first child almost always draws the mother back into her home. No man in Weingarten and Daniels's study dropped out of school or left a good job on account of becoming a father. In fact, the men reported that becoming fathers gave them an impetus to "make it" on their jobs and intensified their sense of financial responsibility. Thus, the baby drew its mother into the home and pushed its father out.

Women accommodate their work lives to meet the needs of their families. As discussed in Chapter 13, some adopt a sequential pattern: either having children early and starting a career later or first pursuing a career and then having children. Others adopt a simultaneous pattern: making daily transitions from one sphere to the other.

The sequential pattern provides a more radical transition. It is interesting to note that most of the simultaneous-pattern women were college-educated *late* first-time mothers. Those mothers who were able to choose the timing of their entry or reentry into the work world did so in relation to their children. But the early years of parenting were used by many women also to forge new identities, including occupational identities. The mothers and grandmothers of today's younger women saw their first children as the end of their job careers and the beginning of home careers that would last the rest of their lives. But the newer generations of women do not see their wife and mother roles as the end or the only major roles in their lives. They have a broader life-span view that includes later roles, too.

Some couples find that trouble begins in the pregnancy period (Masters & Johnson, 1966; Meyerowitz & Feldman, 1967). The restriction on sexual activity and feelings about loss of attractiveness in pregnant women are major contributors to this trouble. Newly married couples chose sex as one of the important aspects of marriage—men chose it as the most important. After the birth of the first child, sex dropped to the least important aspect for the women and to second place for their husbands (Reedy, 1977). Golden-wedding couples' retrospective reports confirmed this trend (Parron, 1979). However, many husbands showed increasing solicitude toward their pregnant wives and took over more household tasks than at any other time of marriage. In fact, they would have been willing to do more than their wives let them do (Feldman, 1971).

A number of explanations have been offered for the crisis nature of the first birth. One is the shift from dyad to triad. Small-group psychologists have demonstrated that the triad in human groups tends to be unstable, with the weakest member forming a coalition with one of the two stronger members. In the case of the mother/father/newborn triad, this usually results in the baby and mother becoming the strongly knit element, leaving the father out (Freilich, 1964).

The new mothers whom Russell (1974) studied worried about their appearance and their poor physical condition. They complained of fatigue, exhaustion, loss of sleep, and being unable to keep up with housework. They worried about being competent mothers and at the same time resented being tied down. Their husbands also lost sleep and had to adjust to new routines and responsibilities. And then there was money—the burst of new expenditures that sends young fathers out to increase their income.

However, Aldous (1978) says most couples "negotiate the transition period with no great sense of crisis" (p. 162). Factors that help make the transition easier include adequate preparation for parenthood, a strong marital bond that can weather the intrusion of a third person, adequate finances, and enough preparatory time—at least three years between wedding and baby. Couples that found time to be alone to-

gether in the evening and in which the husband got up at night with the baby reported fewer problems.

THE CHILD-REARING PERIOD

During the ensuing child-rearing years, the theme is one of separation of interests and activities between husbands and wives. Husbands, particularly if they are successful, grow increasingly immersed in their jobs and personal interests. Wives immerse themselves primarily in home and family and secondarily in jobs, if they have jobs.

The presence of children is critical. Feldman (1964) compared couples at different family stages with couples married the same length of time who had no children. On the one hand, children were associated with lower communication and satisfaction; on the other hand, they were associated with higher values placed on marriage, on being needed and being in love, and on children being more important than money or an orderly home. Couples with no children were more concerned with getting ahead, cultivating intellectual capacities, and developing personal interests. Such partners were able to express both conflict and affection more freely and openly than couples surrounded by children. Of course, those child-free couples that stayed married and so were available for study were more likely to be harmonious. Less harmonious couples are more likely to divorce. In the absence of children, divorce is easier to consider.

The parents of high school students in the San Francisco study (Lowenthal et al., 1975) believed in being married and having children, and they also appreciated their children. But the disruptive effect of their children on their marriages and their lives was a recurrent theme in their interviews. Childless couples who had been married about the same length of time as these parents had (Feldman, 1964) were more like newly married couples in their interactions. Moreover, women who are most heavily involved with parenting and have not turned to other, more personal interests about this time tend to be more troubled (Spence & Lonner, 1971; Bart, 1970). Bart used the vivid phrase "Mother Portnoy" to describe those women who have put "all their eggs in one basket"—namely mothering.

When the couples of the Burgess and Wallin (1953) longitudinal sample were interviewed by Pineo (1961) after they had been married 20 years, they showed gradual decreases in sexual relations, in companionship, and in demonstrations of affection. They had fewer common interests, didn't agree so much on basic values and opinions, and had less faith in the permanence of their unions. Pineo called this trend *disenchantment*. Because the personal adjustments of the individual husbands and wives were not related to their marital maladjustments, Pineo concluded that what was happening was a progressive loss of fit between them

as partners. When they got married, they had been at the peak of being well matched, because American marriage is by personal choice. As each partner changed and developed over the years, however, they may not have developed in the same way or in the same direction. Any change in either partner was bound to decrease the amount of fit. After 20 years, they might be matched no better than if they had been joined by chance.

Figure 19.1 shows the conditions under which a good fit could—or could not—be maintained. Either partner could become more complex, less complex, or stay the same. According to this

Development of husband	Development of wife		
	None (stable)	Becomes more complex	Becomes less complex
None (stable)	Match should remain good. Perhaps dormant while children intervene, but, when they leave, may get a "second honeymoon."	Match deteriorates. Wife's needs no longer met.	Match deteriorates. Husband's needs no longer met.
Becomes more complex	Match deteriorates. Husband's needs no longer met.	Relationship has chance to develop if individuals' changes are on same path. But they could each develop in different directions and would no longer match.	Match deteriorates. Husband's needs no longer met.
Becomes less complex	Match deteriorates. Wife's needs no longer met.	Match deteriorates. Wife's needs no longer met.	Relationship has chance of staying matched if negative developments of both are synchronous; could be like "cooling off." But if not, synchronization will disappear.

Figure 19.1. Possibilities for husband/wife matching over years of marriage as a function of personality development in either or both. *(Source: Troll, 1975.)*

model, if both husband and wife remain stable in personality over the years of their marriage, their match can remain good. This positive match may not be apparent while their children are present: the fit was just between the two of them. After the children leave (or at least become somewhat less intrusive), however, the original good match can shine through. Incidentally, in other kinds of societies, where marriages are arranged by extended families for the benefit of a larger unit, the couple relationship may even be enhanced by the arrival and presence of children.

If both husband and wife develop toward greater complexity over time, their fit can remain good—or perhaps even improve—only if they both develop "on the same wavelength." However, husband and wife may grow apart instead of together. In fact, those who are able to grow in unison may be rare exceptions. The same conclusions may be drawn for couples who decrease in complexity or deteriorate over time. If they deteriorate in the same way (for example, if both "cool off"), they may remain well matched.

The same process of decreasing fit could come about by any kind of individual-change process in husband and wife. For example, Neugarten and Gutmann (1964) noted shifts in personality during the middle and later years that were associated with perceptions of ability to control one's own destiny.

The kinds of changes noted by Pineo are also found in cross-sectional studies (Blood & Wolfe, 1960; Feldman, 1964). This diverging or "cooling off" is not necessarily associated with unhappiness or lack of satisfaction with the union. Some people whose relations were cooler reported that they were highly satisfied with their marriage. From a developmental point of view, it is interesting that there could be an increase in marital comfort in middle age based on kinds of interactions different from those present 20 years before.

Couples who never have had children also seem to experience a cooling-off process, although perhaps not to the same extent as do parents. Couples who marry when they are older (Blood & Wolfe, 1960) seem to show the same pattern of initial euphoria and high emotional interaction followed by gradual cooling, although the time sequence may be different. Couples married in high school follow this trajectory at a markedly accelerated pace (De Lissovoy, 1973). They reach "disenchantment" after only 18 months of marriage instead of after 20 years. Furthermore, Kelly (1955) found that partners who are not close to each other when they are engaged are not likely to be brought closer together after 18 years of marriage.

The interaction patterns of younger or newly-wed couples are markedly consistent across studies. Feldman (1964) reports that partners talk to each other about subjects close to their hearts: their homes, their children, and their parents. They often get very excited when they talk, and they can easily get into fights. Whether or not they fight, their interactions usually make them feel warm and close to each other. The younger couples also go out more together and have more fun, particularly if they are middle-class.

Disagreements between younger partners are mostly over in-laws. Later on, when the wives quit their jobs to have babies, the partners fight more over money. Later still, they fight over the absence of joint recreation. They don't report fighting over their children until the children are old enough to get into deliberate trouble—in adolescence, usually.

The interactions of couples married about 20 years are markedly different from those of younger couples. The partners talk about objective subjects: home repairs, religion, news, culture, and sports (Feldman, 1964). Their conversations are much calmer. They neither criticize each other nor run out slamming the door. They don't go out much with each other but are more sober and sedentary. This may partly be a cohort difference, of course, because this is cross-sectional research. Couples now older may not have been as recreation oriented even in the beginning of their marriages.

THE EMPTY NEST

As noted earlier, the number of years that partners are likely to have alone together again after the children are supposed to leave home has increased greatly over the last century. Today the empty-nest transition occurs in middle age rather than in old age. Furthermore, many nests never truly empty, or empty in a nominal rather than an actual way. One woman in the San Francisco sample suggested that the empty nest is surrounded by telephone wires. Others remarked "What empty nest?" Their children continue to hang around in fact, even though they have moved out in theory. A study of newlyweds by Ryder (1968) found that although some newlyweds do have little contact with their parents, others visit and telephone often and still use their parents' closet space, checking and charge accounts, cars, and so on.

Feldman (1964) finds that partners in the "launching stage," when one or more children are still at home, say their relations with each other tend to be calm and objective more than emotional—like Cuber and Harroff's (1963) *passive/congenial* relationships. Their focus is still on their children. They spend a lot of time talking about their children, and much of their interaction involves them. They still fight, but, while their early fights tended to end with lovemaking and increased happiness, they now tend to look back without much pleasure on the course of the marriage. Women at this time are more likely than are men to express concern about the coming transition (Lowenthal et al., 1975). They are also more likely to look forward to increased freedom and to see their children as new social resources (Hagestad, 1977).

The lengthening of the period when the couple is "alone again" has been accompanied by a number of new relationships between husbands and wives, most of them still unstudied. Many contradictory statements appear in the family literature. For example, there are popular reports that marriages are more likely to break up when the children leave home, with a second peak in divorce rates comparable to that for beginning marriages (so far unsupported by any demographic data). These reports are counterbalanced by other reports of second honeymoons. There are statements that women are more affected or more changed in their feelings and behavior by the emptying of the nest than their husbands, but nobody has done systematic research on how husbands are affected. Do couples now have greater opportunity for sharing both household chores and leisure activities? If so, does this greater sharing lead to greater enjoyment of the marriage?

There are reports that sexuality terminates for most couples at this time, counterbalanced by reports of revitalized sexuality. There are reports of heightened marital satisfaction—but these are often tied to reports of cooling interpersonal interactions. Unfortunately, most of our research information is still so tenuous for these later years that we must proceed cautiously in drawing anything but tentative conclusions. It would not be too far-fetched to presume that diversity of marital style in later years is even greater than in earlier years. After all, variation increases in almost every other measure with each succeeding decade of life. It is possible that many of the preceding reports are true—each for a different segment of the population.

Feldman's "empty-nest" couples are even less satisfied with their marriages than are couples who still have children at home. They place the highest values on calmness and companionship and place a low value on more-romantic emotional factors. In Reedy's (1977) and Parron's (1979) Q-sort data, sex was at the bottom in importance and loyalty and emotional security at the top. Partners' discussions now are restricted in range to conventional topics such as religion and home repairs (Feldman, 1964). They are preoccupied with health. The partners rarely have fun away from home, and their marital interaction is low. The wife at this time has the highest degree of power relative to her husband—perhaps because she is in better health. On the whole, though, an outstanding characteristic of this group is a general feeling of peacefulness, lack of stress, and expressed satisfaction with marriage, whether or not they have raised children.

Most of the post-empty-nest people in the San Francisco study (Lowenthal et al., 1975) felt that they had experienced positive changes in their marital relationships. They were twice as likely as the pre-empty-nest group to say they had experienced any change (33% versus 15%). And they were less likely to report negative changes in their marriages (14% versus 38%). See Table 19.1.

TABLE 19.1 Changes in past relationships with spouse during two life stages

	Relationship	
Changes	Empty nest (N = 54)	Preretired (N = 60)
Positive	47%	53%
No change	15	33
Negative	38	14

Source: Lurie, 1974.

Timing is important (Harkins, 1978). Mothers of off-time children are not as content as mothers of on-time children. This finding fits the Cassandra syndrome, mentioned in Chapter 16. The mothers of off-time children had more time to worry about those children.

The San Francisco late-middle-aged group expressed renewed interest in their spouses. Of both men and women in this stage, 82% described them positively, and felt that their marriages had improved since their children left home. This was particularly true for the men. People in this stage experienced greater companionship and closeness and did not expect this improvement to dissipate during retirement.

Retirement

Most writers assume that retirement happens to husbands, not wives, and that it is significant for marriage because it brings the husband back into the home. They have examined the wife's feelings about the intrusion of the husband into her domain and the husband's feelings about moving into a female domain. As far as the San Francisco study preretirement couples are concerned, neither wife nor husband relished such a prospect (Lowenthal et al., 1975).

The diversity of lifestyles and marital-interaction patterns among retired couples reminds us again of the rule of thumb that variance in everything increases with age. Maas and Kuypers (1974) and Fengler (1975) both use typologies in describing such diverse patterns. Maas and Kuypers note, furthermore, that most respondents seem to have followed their lifestyles for many years; they did not begin with retirement.

An intensive study of 22 golden-wedding couples (Parron & Troll, 1978) noted diverse patterns of sharing of activities after retirement. One couple, for example, began the day with a joint breakfast, followed by an hour of separate morning activities. During that hour, the wife phoned two of her children while her husband read the morning paper. From then on, they spent their time together in a sequence of social activities. The opposite pattern is a predominantly unsharing couple, with each spouse engaging in separate pursuits and not even eating meals together. This latter style is a rarity, however, because togetherness tends to be the rule.

In a study of 25 couples where the wives had retired generally within a year of their husbands' retirement (Szinovacz, 1978), household-task allocation was predominantly sex-role segregated. Wives prepared dinner, did the laundry, and cleaned the house; husbands undertook small repairs and washed the cars. Of the couples, 36% said they had not changed the distribution of their household responsibilities on retirement. Another 28% said the wives had increased their household work. Only 20% said the husbands now did more work around the house.

When the retired husband ends up sharing household tasks, his feelings about it depend on his value system. If, as is true of many working-class husbands, "woman's work" is considered demeaning, the man who shares such work feels devalued. This attitude is less common among middle-class men (Lipman, 1962) than among working-class men.

The retired men studied by Kerckhoff (1964) had become more involved in household tasks. Moreover, this change seems to be welcomed by the middle- and upper-status wives but not by wives of men with lower-status jobs. Another study found that working-class women felt sorry that their husbands had retired (Heyman & Jeffers, 1968). A husband often retires because of poor health, and it would not be surprising if his poor health itself had an adverse effect on the marriage. Maas and Kuypers (1974) found no evidence that retirement as such created marital problems for middle-class husbands.

Fengler (1975) studied wives' attitudes toward their husbands' coming retirement. His sample fell into three roughly equal categories: optimists (39%), neutralists (29%), and pessimists (32%). The optimists saw retirement as a time for sharing exciting new lives characterized by more companionship and shared activities. The neutralists expected retirement to change their marriages very little. The pessimists tended to fear that their husbands would find themselves with too much time on their hands and would intrude into their own domestic domains.

Of the 47 upper-middle-class California men studied by Maas and Kuypers (1974), about 40% were highly involved with their wives and happy with their marriages. Another 23% were involved at a slightly lower level. The remaining 36% showed low involvement in their marital relationships; their marital satisfaction was low and in many cases declining. Among the women in the study, about half were no longer married (most were widows); another quarter were husband centered; and about 17% showed low involvement in their marriages. Furthermore, there was no evidence that these aging couples, who had been married over 40 years, patterned their lifestyles in any reciprocal fashion. What the husbands did with their time had no relation to what the wives did. This finding clearly differs from the "togetherness" of the golden-wedding couples studied by Parron (1979), who were somewhat lower in socioeconomic status.

Some older couples are filled with hostility. The spouses blame their husbands or wives for all their troubles, and wish that they could somehow terminate their marriages. Religious orthodoxy, such as the strong Catholic policy against divorce, has no doubt kept many such couples together. The same could be said of social pressure in the community: the stigma of divorce has kept people together for years under a more or less armed truce. The onset of illness or feebleness in such couples can truly bring disaster. Managers of "old-age homes" have noted that their "couples' rooms" are not in high demand. One reason why a member of a couple would enter such an institution is separation from a disliked spouse. Otherwise, the usual arrangement is for the healthier spouse to care for the sick one, at home.

Generally, when both husband and wife become feeble, they share work on an idiosyncratic basis: each does what he or she can. The reciprocity between them becomes so intimate that the term *symbiotic* seems appropriate (Clark & Anderson, 1967; Cumming & Henry, 1961). In fact, when one partner dies, the other partner rarely survives.

On the average, women at this time of life tend to be stronger and healthier than their husbands, particularly if they married men older than they. Given the tendency for many middle-aged men to deny even life-threatening signs of ill health (see Chapter 7), it is not surprising that married men live longer than single men—their wives take care of them. Vigorous unmarried women in their 40s and older complain that all the men they meet want wives to take care of them in their declining years.

Not only do wives monitor diet and exercise and medical attention for their husbands but they are also responsible for much of the terminal nursing care at home (Lopata, 1973). Almost half of the Chicago widows Lopata studied had taken care of their husbands, some for over a year. This kind of wifely power is limited, because it is associated with severe curtailment of the wife's freedom of movement.

Sex differences

Sex differences in marital behavior appear to be profound. Bernard (1973) concluded that marriage is an institution that benefits husbands but not wives, although women are the ones for whom it is of prime social importance. Women seem to worry much more than men do about their families, especially in middle age. Middle-aged women constitute the age/sex group most critical of husbands and most prone to reporting difficulties in getting along with them (Lowenthal et al., 1975). Although four-fifths of all men and the same proportion of newlywed and older women evaluated their spouses positively, only two-fifths of middle-aged women did.

A recent study of the primary ties of men over 45 replicated what most of the sex-difference literature has shown—that men most often name their wives as their primary friends and confidantes (Babchuk, 1979). Table 19.2 shows these men's feelings of relative closeness to their wives, children, parents, and friends. Even if children and parents are combined, their wives come first.

Interestingly, while the middle-aged San Francisco men stressed their wives' virtues, only one-third of them thought they were meeting their wives' expectations. Thurnher reports (in Lowenthal et al., 1975) that middle-aged men did not question their adequacy as providers. But they seemed aware—although not necessarily contrite about it or moved to change—that they were often inconsiderate and unheeding of their wives' desires for attention, companionship, or diversion. The women mentioned their husbands when they described their daily activities, but the men did not usually mention their wives. In fact, the men tended not even to mention the everyday domestic interactions that the women described. Like the working-class and upper-middle-class men described by Rubin (1976), then, these lower-middle-class middle-aged men tended to be psychologically absent from their homes even when physically present.

TABLE 19.2 Relatives identified as primary, or as both primary and confidants, by 275 men 45 and older

Number of respondents	Relationship of relative	Number who list no relatives as primary	Number who list relatives only as primary	Number who list relatives as both primary and confidants
231	Wife	43	6	182
208	Offspring	63	39	106
275	Parent	209	11	57
275	Sibling	134	44	98

Note: Of the men, 44 were not married, and 23 of those who were married did not have any children.

Source: Babchuk, 1979.

Many older women in the San Francisco study (Lowenthal et al., 1975) felt that their husbands were overdependent. Among the newlyweds, the husbands were more likely to express the feeling that their wives were overdependent. Whereas the men tended to describe their dependent feelings as tender, the women described their husbands as clinging. In their TAT responses, middle-aged men and women both yearned for warmth and intimacy in the marital relationship. But women seemed less hopeful of achieving such qualities, expecting at best relationships that provided support and staved off loneliness.

Social-class and race differences

Economic, health, and other demographic factors all influence marital interactions. There are class differences in values and expectations. Research on Black couples, unfortunately, is not only rarer than that for White couples but frequently has not distinguished between middle class and lower class. Poor Black couples are too often compared with middle-class White couples. Generally, Black couples tend to be poorer, to have poorer health, and to live fewer years than White couples. Thus, fewer older Black women live with their husbands, particularly in the South, and this racial differential has been increasing rather than decreasing over time (Jackson, 1977). Fewer Black women than White marry, and, if they do, they are likely to be widowed at an earlier age. There is also some evidence that the mother/child bond is valued more highly in Black families than is the husband/wife bond (Bell, 1965). However, Par-

ron (1979), who compared Black and White golden-wedding couples matched for socioeconomic status and education, found no significant differences among them. It is possible that most Black/White family differences would be wiped out if economics were considered.

Health factors in marital relations

Concern with health comes to the fore in the middle years of marriage. It looms large in conversation between middle-aged and older husbands and wives. Neugarten, Wood, Kraines, and Loomis (1963) feel that middle-aged women are concerned about their husbands' health, rather than their own health. They do not want to be propelled into widowhood before their time. These investigators' research on middle-aged women's attitudes toward menopause found much concern about health but no evidence that they were worried about their *own* bodies. As discussed elsewhere in this book, wives have real reason to be concerned; the consequences of having to nurse husbands or of becoming widowed are both unpleasant.

The paramount importance of having a spouse is seen in advanced old age. A study of 249 people over 70 (Tobin & Kulys, 1979) asked people to name whom they would designate a "responsible other"—who would be responsible if they needed to be admitted to a hospital, for instance. Of the respondents, 88% named family members—specifically spouses—if available. The only times spouses would not be named were if they were also ill or were newly acquired. Yet not all the people named "responsible other" were the ones listed when respondents were asked to whom they felt closest. Of the 36 spouses named as "responsible other," 15 (nearly half) were *not* named as "closest"!

The couple as a system

There is more than one way to view a family over its lifetime. We can focus on the individual members, in this case the husband or wife. We can also shift our focus to the couple as an interactional, bounded system. As noted earlier, a system can react to change in one of four ways: it can deny change, it can alter just enough to return to equilibrium or a homeostatic status, it can fragment and fall apart, or it can "develop."

Denial could operate thus: in spite of changes in a husband or wife, or in any strategic part of the situation in which they interact, the marriage could continue as if there had been no changes. For example, partners whose children were adults and living in their own homes could continue to focus their relationship on their children as much as when the children were still in need of a great deal of parental care. Or, to return to equilibrium, the marriage could change just a little. For example, a husband and wife could act toward each other as if the other were the children who had left, and thus could treat each other with extra nurturance and protectiveness. Or the marriage could fragment and end in divorce or alienation between spouses. Marriages do exist in which one partner has not talked to the other for years. Finally, the marriage could develop and improve in any of a number of ways. This last alternative would imply not only a second honeymoon, but would also imply an even richer relationship than during the first honeymoon, being now based on the more mature personalities of both spouses.

The theory of the family as a system has come from psychotherapists who deal with the families of patients suffering from schizophrenia and other behavioral disorders. The focus has been on communication patterns. Many therapists discovered when the symptoms of one family member are cured or alleviated, these symptoms show up in another member. Jackson (1957) used the term "family homeostasis" for this phenomenon. According to family-system theory, a marriage can be helped only by changing the communication and interaction patterns of both husband and wife. Hess and Handel (1959) were among the few psychologists who avoided the pathology emphasis; they called their book *Family Worlds*, although they stressed the intertwining of family members. Their "family worlds" are family systems.

Jackson's concept of family homeostasis is spelled out in Haley's (1962) "first law of relationships": *when an organism indicates a change in relation to another, the other will act on the first so as to diminish and modify that change.* The mechanism involved is the cybernetic concept of feedback, whereby an informational loop is formed by output data becoming a source that affects input. Negative feedback operates to offset change and to maintain steady states in systems. For example, attempts on the part of a husband to modify his original relationship with his wife will be met by countermoves on her part to return them to their original balance. Men and women often use different strategies to accomplish this, because they have different socialization histories. Change in relationships over time—development—comes about by *positive feedback*. For example, the action of the wife could enhance her husband's move toward change.

Winter, Ferreira, and Bowers (1973) found that married couples showed greater "spontaneous agreement" without consulting each other than did "synthetic" couples (men and women paired randomly). The married couples also required less explicit informational exchange and reached joint decisions in a shorter time. The better the spontaneous agreement, furthermore, the longer the duration of the marriage and the higher the satisfaction with the marriage.

Raush, Barry, Hertel, and Swain (1974) provide us with some valuable longitudinal data. They followed 46 young couples from their fourth month of marriage for about two years. First, they noticed that these couples had established stable and characteristic communication patterns by the fourth month. Second, these patterns were maintained over the duration of the study. In fact, these couple patterns were more stable over time than were the individual patterns of either husband or wife. Raush, Greif, and Nugent (1979) conclude that the behavior of individual family members can be understood only within the context of their family systems and that change in individual behavior patterns must be accompanied by change in patterns of interpersonal communication among family members.

Stability and satisfaction

Marriages are usually assessed according to two separate criteria: happiness and stability. People who have happy marriages can get divorced, and people with very unhappy marriages may stay together for 50 years. Although stability of a marriage is no indication of its being satisfying to either partner, stability does have value in our culture, which stresses success. A stable marriage—one that lasts—is seen as a successful marriage. Partners who manage to survive together to their fifth, tenth, 25th, and, above all, 50th anniversary are accorded not only congratulations but also respect. Unhappy, unsatisfying marriages where the partners might be much better off separating are seen by other people as successful if such marriages endure at least superficially.

Happiness and duration are not the same; nevertheless, Lewis and Spanier (1979) feel that the single best predictor of marital stability is marital quality. That is, good quality is a necessary but not sufficient precursor of marital duration. Marital quality involves such premarital resources as good mental health, education, social class, and degree of acquaintance. It also involves a high level of skill in interpersonal relations, and good physical health. Good parental models are important, as is the support of significant others. The women in Elder's (1974) sample were happiest in their marriages if their husbands were successful. Lewis and Spanier also cite emotional gratification as part of high-quality marriages. Such gratification is achieved by expressions of affection, respect, encouragement, emotional interdependence, and sexual satisfaction. Congruence between perceived and ideal spousal characteristics and feelings of identity as a couple are both important. Finally, reciprocity of support (instead of unilateral giving or receiving) has been correlated with higher morale in Coyne and Lazarus's (1979) longitudinal study of stress.

Happiness in marriage depends as much on the partners' expectations as on their actual relationship. Highly educated men and women who stress self-actualization and romantic love may not tolerate a relationship that would seem good to a working-class wife who is satisfied with an occasional paycheck and not being beaten. Findings from three studies (Westley & Epstein, 1960; Aller, 1962; Cutler & Dyer, 1965) all show that couples with traditional expectations for marriage say they are happier than do those with more-expressive expectations. Perhaps the rules are clearer in traditional marriages, and other options more limited.

Generations differ widely in attitudes toward divorce (Spanier, Lewis, & Coles, 1975), and there are many problems in measuring marital satisfaction over time. For example, self-reports, which almost all investigations have used, are extraordinarily vulnerable to such psychological-distortion processes as *cognitive dissonance* (resolving the discomfort of confronting opposing facts by choosing one fact and denying the other). One may be likely to evaluate one's marriage as satisfactory when one perceives few other options or when being married is the basis for all other aspects of one's life. Bernard (1973) points out that resignation often is reported as satisfaction. And Veroff and Feld (1970) found that those most likely to feel that their marriages were good were women who had the least education—and thus had few other options.

SEX DIFFERENCES IN SATISFACTION

In general, husbands tend to find marriage more satisfactory than do wives. When Veroff and Feld (1970) asked respondents to list things about their marriages that they did not like, 45% of the married men said "nothing," as compared with only 25% of the women. Husbands' satisfaction did not decrease over time, as their wives' did (Luckey, 1961). When men do say that they are dissatisfied with their marriages, they are more often reflecting discontentment with their life situations—with their children or their jobs—than with their relationships with their wives. The more educated the men are, the happier they tend to be with their marriages, because their lives are likely to be more comfortable all around. Younger men, particularly those with children, are more unhappy about their marriages than older men; younger men are more likely to be financially disadvantaged. Finally, when a husband is unhappy, the couple is unhappy; but a wife's unhappiness does not seem to transfer to her husband in the same way.

Wives report more marital stress than their husbands do, but they also report more overall satisfaction. Bernard (1973) believes that wives have to pay more for companionship and sociability. Love seems to be so important to women that they are willing to pay an exorbitant price for it. They learn before marriage to become sensitive to their men's thoughts and feelings. Keeping a husband happy can become a full-time career. Whereas men generally say that they are satisfied with their marriages if their overall lives are going well, women who are dissatisfied with their marriages are unhappy in all other areas of life. Marriage is secondary to a man's self-esteem but is primary to a woman's. Happiness in marriage is related to congruence between the wife's perception of her husband and his own self-perception (not necessarily between her perception and others' perceptions of him). But happiness is not related to the husband's perception of his wife or to *her* own self-perception (Luckey, 1960). Similarly, Stuckert (1963) found that it was important for marital satisfaction that the wife understand her husband but not that her husband understand her.

Ross (1973) studied first-year women students at Michigan State University who were in the top 1% of their class and followed up the study a few years later. Those who had married tended to have lost their independence and "impulse expression" and to have become more submissive and conservative. Because women have more at stake in marriage, they make more of the adjustments. And they often constrict their personalities in order not to displease their husbands.

Jessie Bernard, in *The Future of Marriage* (1973), writes that, even though marriage is a condition desired more by women than by men, it is much more beneficial to men. Married women have worse mental health than do either single women or married men. But married men have better mental health than either married women or single men. Single women are spectacularly better off than married women so far as psychological-distress symptoms are concerned—either women may start out with an initial advantage, which marriage reverses, or men may prefer to marry women with poorer mental health, or both. Bernard quotes Gurin,

Veroff, and Feld's (1960) findings that more married than single women feel that they are about to have nervous breakdowns, experience psychological and physical anxiety, blame themselves for their lack of general adjustment, and exhibit phobic reactions, depression, and passivity.

Although marriage tends to protect both men and women from suicide (or perhaps suicidal people don't marry), it protects women less. In middle age, more married women than single women are alcoholics. Much of this unhappiness may be attributable to lack of choices and to restrictive environments rather than to being married per se. This explanation is suggested by the significant improvements in the mental health of women over the past 20 years, as noted in the Srole and Fischer Mid-Manhattan study (1978) discussed in Chapter 16.

Veroff and Feld (1970) found that just getting married and being married are themselves important sources of gratification of affiliative needs for many women. But these sources seem to function only in the beginning of marriage. Another study (Blood & Wolfe, 1960) found that, of women married less than two years, 52% were very satisfied, and none were very dissatisfied. For those married 20 years or longer, only 6% were very satisfied, and 21% were conspicuously dissatisfied. Newlyweds were the most likely to say their marriages have improved; middle-aged men were next most likely to say so (Lowenthal et al., 1975).

Paris and Luckey (1966) followed 31 satisfied couples and 31 dissatisfied couples from 1957 to 1963. The satisfied couples tended to decrease in satisfaction, and the dissatisfied increased somewhat in satisfaction, suggesting a "regression to the mean." Nevertheless, there was an overall trend toward decreased satisfaction over time.

Marital problems are not directly related to marital unhappiness. Younger women, particularly those with children, have more marital problems than do older women. But older women, particularly those who have only a grade school education, report greater marital unhappiness (Veroff & Feld, 1970). (Remember the discussion of happiness, excitement, and life complexity in Chapter 16.)

Honeymooning couples are the group most satisfied with their marriages (Feldman, 1964). The next most satisfied age group is the elderly, followed by those in the "launching phase" (when their children are leaving home). The least satisfied are parents whose youngest children have just entered school and parents of teenagers. Many "postparental" couples report that they get along better after their children leave (Deutscher, 1964; Blood & Wolfe, 1960). For them, this time is like a second honeymoon; they recapture the joys of undivided companionship. Only after the children leave are parents comparable to the childless couples in satisfaction. Of course, child-free couples who were not happy had already separated by this time.

Husbands assume a less significant role as audiences and friends for their wives when there are children in the home (Blood & Wolfe, 1960). Yet reported satisfaction with love is higher when children are preschoolers than at other times. The presence of young children may increase the emotional bonds of understanding and love between the parents, even though it depresses their standard of living and limits their companionship. Or the wife may be so unhappy that a little love goes a long way. Mothers in the launching stage are often bitter about the loss of their husbands' affection and companionship. Only after the children are gone does the second honeymoon occur—if it occurs at all.

Stinnett, Collins, and Montgomery (1970) investigated older people's perceptions of how well their marriages fulfilled six emotional needs: love, personality fulfillment, respect, communication, finding meaning in life, and integration of past life experiences. The older men (age 60 or older) felt that more of these needs were satisfied than did the older women. Significantly, men felt they were not getting enough respect; women felt they were not getting enough communication.

AFTER CHILD REARING

The post-child-rearing couples Feldman (1964) interviewed reported higher satisfaction with their marriages than did couples in earlier stages. This "upswing" seemed to be even more pronounced among the oldest couples in Feldman's study. Similar findings are cited by Stinnett, Carter, and Montgomery (1972). But not all research has found such results, and at present the support for a "second-honeymoon" effect is shaky.

Does unhappiness, dissatisfaction, or disenchantment increase linearly from the honeymoon for the rest of the marriage, with the only solace being that after a while nobody cares? Or does the return to the dyad reverse this trend?

Burr (1970) and Lowenthal and her associates (1975) did not find any systematic general decline in marital satisfaction with length of marriage. They did find a gradual increase in satisfaction after the children were beyond the school-age years. Bradburn and Caplovitz (1965), however, found that marital tensions decreased, particularly after children left home, with concomitant increases in marital happiness. Gurin, Veroff, and Feld (1960) found a clear curvilinear trend, as did Rollins and Feldman (1970): a decrease in satisfaction until children leave home and then an upswing afterward. Masters and Johnson (1974) mention the emotional poverty of middle-age relationships. And Peterson (1973) notes that many middle-class couples in a retirement community were looking for marriage counseling.

In one study (Stinnett, Carter, & Montgomery, 1972), older subjects rated their marriages as having become better over time. In another study (Glenn, 1975), post-child-rearing couples reported more happiness than did still-child-rearing couples. And Birren, Butler, Greenhouse, Sokoloff, and Yarrow (1971) found that one-third of older healthy men in a longitudinal panel said they had poor and deteriorating marriages. Bray and Howard's (1978) middle-aged AT&T executives liked their work very much but were often troubled about their marriages.

Gilford and Bengtson (1979) have shed some light on these troubled waters by breaking down the marital relationship into positive and negative components. The positive marital component is related to interaction, and the negative component is related to feelings. Figure 19.2 shows that, while the positive component is highest for the youngest generation and lowest for the middle generation, it goes up again for the oldest generation. At the same time, the negative component goes down steadily over the three generations. In other words, both marital interactions and good feelings about each other are highest in the youngest adult generation, but are not so clearly related to each other in older generations. Good feelings about the spouse may never come back to the peak of the honeymoon era, even though husband and wife increase their contact in the later years.

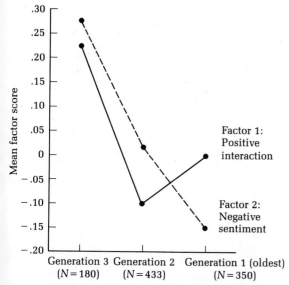

Figure 19.2. Marital satisfaction: Means of each factor score by generation. *(Source: Gilford and Bengtson, 1979.)*

As Lowenthal, Thurnher, and Chiriboga (1975) noted for their four stages of life, youth are highest in both positive and negative affect, not only when viewed as individuals but also when viewed interpersonally, as couples. Feldman (1964) noted that newlyweds fight a lot but also love a lot—or love a lot and also fight a lot. Middle-aged couples don't love as much and are not happy about this state of affairs. Older partners may find their interactions more positive than their middle-aged children find *their* interactions. And older partners value this small amount of good news—they don't complain about what they don't have.

In the Michigan time-sequential study mentioned earlier (Veroff & Depner, 1978), there was a significant positive correlation between being married and being happy among older men in 1976. But there was no such correlation for older men in 1957—or for women in either 1976 or 1957. Apparently, marriage became of greater benefit to older men over these years than it did to older women.

Sexual behavior

We have witnessed a "sexual revolution" over the past decades. Diversity of sexual values and practices is accepted more now. However, a new mandate for sexual skillfulness may be superseding the old one for sexual naiveté—at least for women. In this chapter, I focus primarily on sexual behavior between husband and wife.

According to Robert Bell (1975), the traditional view of sex is that it must have a purpose, either for procreation or to express affection. Thus, the greatest change has been a shift from extrinsic to intrinsic value. Sex has become a pleasure instead of a duty—unless what has happened is that it is now a duty to get pleasure. Yet blue-collar women still learn to negotiate what they want from their husbands before sexual intercourse—sex gives bargaining power (Komarovsky, 1964).

In the early months and years of marriage, of couple formation, sex is a predominant issue. Data collected by Kinsey and his associates (1948, 1953) show that the initial high frequency of coitus for both men and women gradually declines. Unfortunately, these data are not available for married couples; we can only assume that the patterns shown in Figure 19.3 for married people also represent those married to each other. Because the patterns are similar for married and single men and for married women, but not for single women, women's sexuality seems to be contingent on men's—or at least that was so 30 years ago.

The effect of pregnancy and childbirth on sexuality is pronounced (Masters & Johnson, 1966). Seventy-nine middle-class wives were interviewed three times during pregnancy, and both they and their husbands were seen again after delivery. Of the 43 women who were pregnant for the first time, 33 said they had lost interest in sex and were less effective in sexual performance during the first three months of pregnancy. However, they felt heightened eroticism and activity during the next three months. This increased sexuality during the middle trimester of pregnancy was also reported by women having second or later children. During the last three months, a combination of physical symptoms and doctor's advice led to decreased sexual activity and, for some partners, cessation. Physical discomfort at all stages of pregnancy was more common among women who already had children, because of increased fatigue—they had their other children to take care of.

Even after the birth, one-half the women reported less interest and activity in sex for at least three months more. However, some wom-

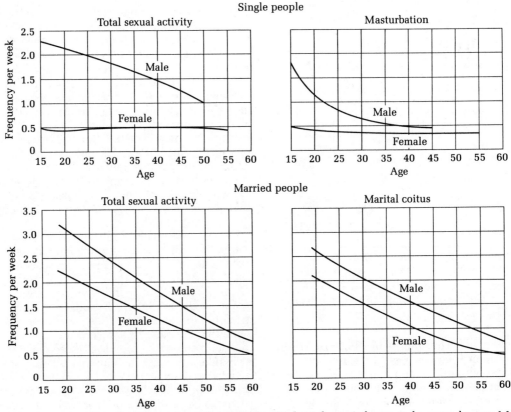

Figure 19.3. Comparison of patterns of sexual activity for single and married men and women by age: Median frequencies of all orgasms and of orgasms resulting from masturbation and from marital coitus. *(Source: Kinsey et al., 1953.)*

en, either because of their own heightened interest or because they wanted to satisfy their husbands, resumed intercourse as early as three weeks after birth. The husbands' reports were consistent with those of their wives. Most mentioned a decrease in sexual activity, and most who did said they decreased activity because of concern for the coming baby.

A few men did say that they were not attracted by their wives during this time, and some of these men turned to extramarital sexual activity during the later prenatal and early postnatal months. Not surprisingly, their wives were not happy about this situation, and this factor alone accounted for much of the perinatal stress (both before and after birth) mentioned earlier in this chapter.

Another study of sexual intercourse among pregnant couples (Meyerowitz & Feldman, 1967) found similar effects. The average rate of inter-

course was three times per week during mid-pregnancy, but only once every other week during the last month. During the first month after birth, most couples had had intercourse at least once. However, the predelivery rate of three times a week was not reached until the infant was five months old. The corresponding drop in reported marital satisfaction may be self-explanatory.

Most couples are able to negotiate the first pregnancy successfully (Aldous, 1978). It helps if the marital bond is strong and if the husband participates in the process—is deeply interested, shares work, and perhaps attends birth and child-care classes. Some couples, however, never recover. Most research suggests that the disruptive effects increase with later pregnancies. In Pineo's study (1961), mentioned earlier, couples followed for 20 years reported progressive loss of intimacy and pleasure in marriage. And both Reedy (1977) and Parron (1979) found that sex was rated highest in importance to marriage among newly married men (and second among newly married women) but was rated lowest by both men and women later on.

As far as sex in marriage is concerned, Clark and Wallin (1965) conclude, on the basis of longitudinal data, that women who have mutual love and respect in their relationships with their husbands are relatively high in sexual responsiveness and become more responsive with increased coital experience. Women whose marriages have had a persistently negative quality tend to remain relatively low in responsiveness. Shope and Broderick (1967) found that sexual experience before marriage was not necessarily conducive to good sexual adjustment in marriage.

Much has been said about the sexual boredom that goes along with long-lasting marriages—at least in this culture, where sexuality has been given much attention in recent years. Masters and Johnson (1966) prescribe variety in positions and foreplay. Some authors recommend open marriage and extramarital explorations. Others recommend serial marriages with reappraisal and easy divorce built into the marital contract.

Masters and Johnson (1974) suggest that the often-reported second honeymoon of middle age may be partly due to the unleashing of sexual desires in previously inhibited women who no longer fear getting pregnant. The women's upsurge of sexual interest may then induce renewed sexual interest in their husbands. Another possibility is that there may be a baseline of pleasure and stability in the sexual component of marriage to which many couples can return after the interfering preoccupations of child rearing are removed.

Again, the phenomenon of renewed sexuality in middle age may show a cohort effect, because a generation that started sex life and marriage with "the pill" would not be as hampered by pregnancy risks as earlier generations were. A different reason for a woman's greater satisfaction with her sex life in middle age may be her husband's decreased sexual activity. If her husband's earlier sexual appetite was greater than hers, his decrease with age may match them more comfortably, so that they can now be more pleased with each other and thus also with themselves.

Summary

Marital happiness and satisfaction are greatest at the beginning of marriage and go downhill from then on, particularly after the birth of the first child. Some of this decline is attributed to progressive loss of fit over time. And some may be attributed to the disruption of the dyad by children, to the financial pinch that children bring, and to a variety of other causes.

The cooling down of original ardor is not necessarily associated with reported dissatisfaction, however. Attraction can be replaced by attachment, and an emphasis on sex can be replaced by an emphasis on emotional security and loyalty.

Whether or not there is a second honeymoon after the children are "launched" is debatable. It may depend on the nature of the original relationship between husband and wife.

When the positive and negative components of marriage are examined separately, the positive component decreases from the youngest to the middle generation but goes up a bit in the oldest generation. The negative component decreases linearly with age. Sexual activity shows the same curve as does satisfaction, going down markedly during the first pregnancy and recovering only slightly thereafter.

20

Couple Splits and Variations

The previous two chapters dealt with the development of the dyad, both from the viewpoints of the husband and wife singly and from the viewpoint of the dyad as a system. This chapter is concerned with dyadic splits such as divorce and widowhood and with the formation of second-time dyads by remarriage. It also briefly discusses new or alternate forms of dyads aside from traditional marriage.

Conflict and divorce

At the present time, the U.S. divorce rate is one of the highest in the world. There were 32 divorces per 1000 married women 14 to 44 years old for the years 1972 to 1974 (Norton & Glick, 1976), or 20 per 1000 married women of all ages in 1975 (Glick, 1979). This is double the rate of a decade earlier. Since 1975, however, the divorce rate has risen more slowly, reaching 22 per 1000 by 1978.

Although dissatisfaction and unhappiness in marriage may be necessary precursors of divorce or separation, they are far from sufficient causes. Many couples who are very unhappy with their marriages have never considered divorcing. The decision to divorce is a function of many factors, such as religion, value placed on the family, socioeconomic status, and personality.

Figure 20.1 shows that in 1972 the highest number of divorced people (not remarried) was for Black women, particularly between the ages

of 30 and 34. The lowest number was for White men, particularly those in their teens but also for all other ages. Although Black couples are more likely to terminate their marriages at any time than are White couples, the sex differences among both Blacks and Whites must be attributed to remarriage frequencies. Fewer Black women remarry; they stay divorced, and swell the number of divorced people. White men may get as many as or more divorces than White women and all Blacks, but if they remarry soon they aren't counted as divorced.

The age differences shown are no doubt partly cohort effects and partly survivor effects. Older cohorts do not share the belief held by the young that marriage must be happy or else it is not worth maintaining. Older couples may live with conditions that younger couples find intolerable. Increases in life expectancy may also play a part. If you are not too content with your spouse but believe you have only ten more years to live, you may not be so likely to go to the trouble of divorcing as you would if you felt you had 40 more years to suffer.

There has been a steady rise in the divorce rate over the last 50 years. There is also a trend toward earlier age of divorce. Monahan (1962) analyzed all the divorces in the state of Wisconsin since the middle 1800s. He found that most separations occur during the first year of marriage, and most divorces occur within the first three years. The frequency drops markedly from the third through the seventh year and continues dropping thereafter. One-half of di-

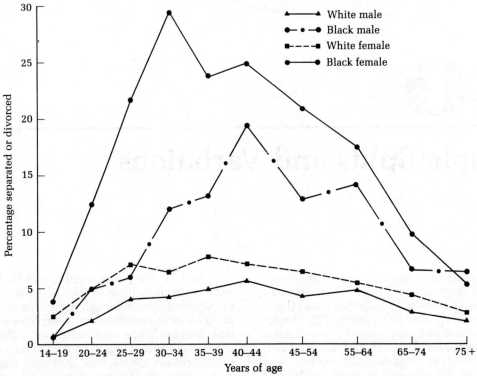

Figure 20.1. Percentage separated or divorced, by age. *(Source: U.S. Department of Commerce, Bureau of the Census, 1976.)*

vorces after first marriage occur within seven years after marriage (Glick, 1979). One-half of those after remarriage occur within three years. More recent data show a slightly longer period between marriage and divorce. The slowing in the rise of divorce is partly due to the rise in cohabitation of unmarried couples. The break-ups of such couples do not enter divorce statistics.

Age at marriage is related to duration of marriage. Men who marry before age 21 and women who marry before 19 are least likely to stay married. Men who marry when they are over 30 tend to stay married, even though they may say they are unhappy. Partners whose income is low or who have children soon after marriage are more likely to divorce (Norton & Glick, 1976). There were eight divorces per 1000 married men who earned less than $8000 but only four per 1000 married men who earned more than $8000. Women who had children before two years of marriage had an average divorce rate of 24 per 1000 while those whose first child

was born after two years of marriage had a rate of 12 per 1000. Finally, divorce can be said to run in families. Children of divorced parents tend to marry children of divorced parents, and they too are likely to end their marriages in divorce (Landis, 1962).

Patterns of conflict management were studied in 48 White, middle-class, newlywed couples (Raush et al., 1974). Those couples who don't divorce continue these patterns into the later years of their marriage. When the couples were put into situations designed to elicit conflict, what one partner did was related to what the other partner did. In fact, both tended to use the same kind of response. If one spouse acted emotionally or coercively, so did the other, and the conflict was therefore likely to escalate. Those couples who were committed to the continuation of their marriages were more likely, however, to get out of this spiral by using negative feedback mechanisms. Thus, if one of them said something rejecting, the other would not respond by rejecting. The more happily married couples were less likely to use rejecting or coercive statements than were the less happily married ones and were more likely to provide information about the issue in question or to suggest a solution. The difference was even more noticeable among husbands than among wives. The more-happily married husbands were more likely to initiate peace-making statements. The less happily married couples were more likely to get into power struggles in which neither partner listened to the other and both resorted to personal attacks.

Chiriboga (1979b) concludes that there are stages in the transition experience of divorce: (1) segregation, in which the individual is isolated from previous associations, (2) transitional, in which the individual has no clear social identity; and (3) aggregation, in which the individual is reestablished in the social order. Thus, divorce is like a rite of passage. His study of 125 men and 185 women between 20 and 79 who were in the process of divorce found that most divorces followed this process.

What happens after divorce? Hetherington, Cox, and Cox (1976) compared 48 divorced couples with 48 still-married couples over a period of two years. The greatest amount of readjustment and unhappiness occurred in the first few months after the divorce was granted. Men who had depended on their wives' care now had to learn to take care of themselves. Their wives were also learning to assume the tasks their husbands had performed. Relations with their ex-spouses occupied most of the time and energy of both ex-husbands and ex-wives. Two-thirds of these encounters followed the interaction patterns of earlier times. Conflicts were particularly bitter over finances, which now had to be spread over two households instead of one. Husbands tried to work harder to get more income but found it difficult to work at all because they were so upset. Their wives may also have had trouble working, either at home or on the job.

Curiously, not all the continuing interactions were negative. Old affection patterns also persisted. In fact, 6 of the 48 divorced couples had sexual intercourse during these first two months. And most of the men and women said they would turn first to their ex-spouses if they needed help in a crisis. Remember the hypothesis of attachment versus attraction? Although divorce may result from loss of attraction—or

shifts in attraction—or from unhappiness and conflict, attachment is not so easily dissipated (see Weiss, 1976a).

The dissolution of a marriage is almost always accompanied by enormous stress for both partners. It involves changes in role and status and reexaminations of identity. These strains can be particularly acute for women who have primarily defined themselves as being their husbands' wives and who must now figure out who they are on their own. Also, such women must do so at a time when they have lost most of their social ties, who were "family friends" connected to their husbands' occupations. These difficulties are even further enhanced by feelings of failure and by financial crisis.

A woman traditionally measures her success and derives her feelings of worth from first capturing a man and then holding onto him. In spite of the changes in women's self-perceptions resulting from the "consciousness raising" of the women's movement, most divorced women are still subject to derision as failures and are vulnerable to self-accusations by the same standards. In Douvan's (1979) Michigan study, the two groups in the American population showing notable symptoms of stress were divorced women and single men. This was as true in 1976 as in 1957. According to Douvan, the divorced woman, particularly if she is raising children alone, faces poverty and role overload that are so oppressive that the social stigma of divorce pales by comparison.

Divorced women face grave financial problems. Only 14% of American women are awarded alimony, and less than half of them get it regularly. Only 44% are awarded child support, and less than half get it regularly (Lake, 1976). Furthermore, older women who have been brought up to believe that getting married means economic security, and who have few employable skills or experience, find themselves on a steep downward curve socioeconomically. Remember that the middle-aged women studied by Elder (1974) were most satisfied with their marriages—and often their lives—if their husbands were successful. A husband's success is no longer relevant to his ex-wife after the divorce.

Chiriboga (1979b) found that, while both women and men experienced much stress during the divorcing process, the men seemed even worse off than were the women. In part, he attributes this finding to the fact that men get more out of marriage than do women, and thus have more to lose. Age was also important; divorced men and women in their 50s and 60s were significantly lower in overall happiness than were younger respondents. Actually, sex differences were complicated. Men experienced a lower sense of overall well-being, but women reported greater emotional turmoil: feeling angry, being unable to get going, feeling there was too much to do, and feeling uneasy. Older people of both sexes were more disrupted socially than were younger people. The ages of the 50s and 60s are times when some couples enjoy being together again after their children are less intrusive, and a separation at this time can be particularly distressing.

Starting to date again can be awkward, and it is often complicated by the disapproval shown by the divorced person's children. There are no social norms or socialized expectations for the transition to "once married." Therefore, each person must go through the process feeling alone, lost, and deviant. Organizations such as Parents Without Partners attempt to create a kind of subculture and to evolve guidelines for handling common problems. In general, however, as long as the unit of adult friendship and social life is the couple, anyone who is single or becomes single again is automatically considered a deviant.

In the long run, divorced women are more disadvantaged than divorced men for a number of reasons, particularly if they retain custody of children. Their reasons for feeling that they are failures have been mentioned. Their identity crises are more acute, particularly if they are traditional women who derive identity and social status from their husbands. Their husbands still can define themselves in terms of job identity. Because there are more eligible women than eligible men, women are less frequently included in couple gatherings as extra guests. They feel responsible for socializing their children to conventional sex behavior, so they worry about setting the wrong standards if they are overtly sexual in dating. Besides, their children may disapprove of their dating for a number of reasons: jealousy, insecurity, or feelings that their mothers' dating is age inappropriate. Men have greater options for remarriage, and, when they do so, for divesting themselves of responsibility for the children of their previous mar-

riage, financially as well as personally. Occasional staggering alimony settlements are given much publicity, but most divorced women are expected to assume most of the support for themselves and their children if they do not want to accept drastically reduced standards of living.

Every year, nearly 10,000 Americans 65 years old or over are divorced. This statistic does not imply a new peaking of divorce in later life, because the age profile of divorces has not changed. It does suggest that older couples are not immune to the tenor of the times, which makes divorce almost imperative for unhappy marriages. In fact, we may have reached a "tipping point," a reversal in general attitudes, a general belief that marriages that are not happy should be terminated. Once partners felt obligated to stay together even if they were highly incompatible and unhappy, and they were ashamed if they did divorce. Now such couples feel apologetic if they *don't* divorce.

A number of family researchers suspect that many divorces may cause more problems than they solve. One problem group that has come to national attention is the group of *displaced homemakers*. Such women, trained primarily for the job of housewife, have been discarded by their husbands in middle or later life, often with no financial provisions that can be enforced and with no skills that could lead to jobs.

Until very recently, such women were not entitled to Social Security benefits unless they had been married over 20 years, nor are they eligible for their ex-husbands' private pension benefits. Recent legislation spurred on by women's advocacy groups has at least lowered the length of marriage necessary for benefits from 20 to 10 years. Many women who are not entitled to retirement benefits in their own right are forced to accept welfare. In a current study of the perceptions of income adequacy of women age 50 and over, Sheila Miller (1977) found that the divorced women felt much worse off than even the widows. This applies not only to financial matters but also to self-esteem and relations with others. Widowhood is more likely to be seen as a sad experience, divorce as a sinful or shameful one. Thus, widows may even increase in self-esteem, while divorced women decrease. In addition, the divorce of older parents can be expected to have an impact on relations with adult children and other kin, who are often forced to take sides and who may avoid both parents. This area of research in gerontology is one of the most neglected.

Widowhood

The effect of a spouse's death has been discussed several times so far in this book, principally in Chapter 8. The focus here is on the family aspects of widows and widowers.

THE WIDOW

In the United States, there are at least 90,000 men and women under age 60 who are widowed, and half of them are under 45. This number does not include those who have remarried. Thus widowhood is not necessarily an old-age phenomenon. Women tend to marry older men, and many men die at relatively young ages. Middle-class men die from cardiovascular causes, and lower-class men die from the rigors of difficult lifestyles. Figure 20.2 shows the ages of women at the time their husbands died, for two years, 1900 and 1964. The period effect shown in the figure is as interesting as the age effect. Women tended to be considerably younger in 1900 when their husbands died than they were in 1964.

A younger widow is apt to be lonelier than an older widow, who is more likely to have many friends in the same position. Furthermore, older people might be better prepared psychologically for widowhood because they have had occasions (the deaths of friends and relatives) to "rehearse" for the deaths of spouses.

"Anticipatory socialization" had not occurred for the 40 Kansas widows studied by Gibbs (1979), however. They had little preparation for widowhood, even though all were over 50 years of age. Intensive interviews with widows of three age groups (30–40, 41–59, and 60 and older) revealed some common problems as well as some problems that differed by age (Wyly & Hulicka, 1975). All complained of loneliness and of difficulties in maintaining homes and cars. The two younger age groups also mentioned problems with decision making, child rearing, sex, and money. The oldest widows had trouble learning how to manage money, finding transportation, and fearing crime. Although some younger widows acknowledged that they felt more independent and free than they had while married, the oldest widows saw no advantages to their condition.

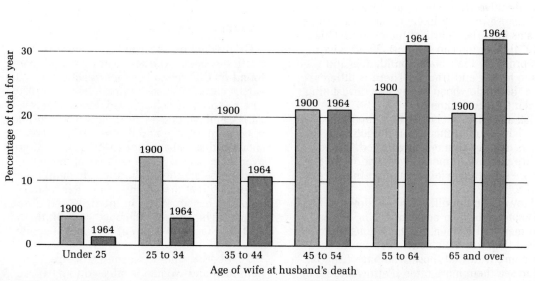

Figure 20.2. Age distribution of new widows in the United States, 1900 and 1964. Includes allowance for deaths of husbands in the armed forces overseas during 1964. *(Source: Kimmel, 1980, after Jacobson, 1966.)*

To some extent, cohort differences are more important here than age differences. For example, younger women are more likely to have participated in money management and to have driven cars. Other investigators feel that, while younger widows have lower levels of well-being, they are more likely to remarry (Cleveland & Gianturco, 1976). Wyly and Hulicka's older subjects reported nothing good about their state—but a Los Angeles study (Morgan, 1976) found that older widows had higher morale than did older married women.

THE WIDOWER

The impact of widowhood on men has received little systematic attention, and the role of widower is probably even vaguer than that of widow. Because widowers who have not remarried are not very common in the community until after age 75, they are not as likely to join each other in groups. Like widows, they are expected to preserve the memories of their wives and are expected not to show interest in other women. Indications are that many widowers adhere to the former but ignore the latter, as can be inferred from the remarriage rates cited earlier.

Because men traditionally acquire their identities only partly from being husbands, widowers are probably not as apt as widows to face acute identity crises when they lose their wives. Yet, because they are likely to have seen their wives as important parts of themselves (Glick et al., 1974), they too can feel lost. Their wives were probably their main confidantes and their links to family and friends. There is little evidence that widowhood is any less devastating for men than for women.

Glick and his associates (1974) report that widowers have more difficulty on the job than do widows during the mourning period. Because jobs are primary in men's lives, widowers may be more sensitive to job disruption than are widows.

Widowers do not differ from widows in feeling isolated from kin or friends. Nor are widowed men and women, on the whole, more isolated than are their married peers. In fact, after being widowed those who have friends tend to see them more often (Petrowsky, 1976). When Atchley (1975c) controlled for social class, he found that widowhood tends to increase contacts with friends among middle-class widowers and to decrease them among lower-class widowers. It could be that the large surplus of women in senior centers and similar social groups for older people—generally used more by working-class people than by middle-class people—may inhibit working-class widowers from developing new kinds of community activities. Widowers tend to be embarrassed and even to feel harassed by the competition among widows for their attentions. Moreover, they are unaccustomed to participating in such preponderantly female gatherings, where women dominate discussions and other activities. Petrowsky (1976) found that widowers were less involved in religious activities than were widows, an effect that is probably due to a continuation of religious-participation sex differences established earlier in life.

Between the ages of 65 and 74, widowers in general are slightly more likely than widows to live in group quarters such as hotels or rooming houses rather than in independent households. After age 75, there is little sex difference in type of residence. Widowers who live in their own homes are slightly more likely to live alone than are widows and are only slightly less likely to be living with their children. When they live in multiperson households, however, widowers are much more likely to be considered heads of such households.

GRIEF

Grief is not necessarily less intense if the death has been expected. Most research has found no difference between reactions to acute versus chronic causes of death (George, 1980). The research of Schwab, Chalmers, Conroy, Farris, and Markush (1975), however, did find grief more intense and disorganizing when spouses' deaths were unexpected. Even if grief over an expected death is intense, though, it tends to be shorter in duration. It should not be surprising that the quality of marital relationship also has an effect on intensity and duration of grief. The stronger the couple bond, the harder it is to face the death of a spouse (Lopata, 1973).

That bereavement is a source of stress for both men and women is attested to by Parkes's (1964) data, which show that the life expectancy of a surviving spouse is shortened for about five years following his or her partner's death. By simply following the vital-statistics records of surviving spouses, Parkes found that the survivors' death rates were higher than would be predicted for their ages. Eventually, however, death rates for those who survived returned to the average of other people their age. The same effect is illustrated in Figure 20.3. Of four marital-status categories—married, widowed, divorced, and single (presumably never married)—of men and women between the ages of 15 and 64, non-White widowers have the highest death rate by far. The only people who come close are non-White divorced men. Obviously, marriage is a particularly life-preserving institution for the otherwise-disadvantaged non-White men. Or perhaps only the healthiest non-White men marry. Lopata (1973) found that living in closely knit ethnic communities helped widows.

White married women have the lowest death rate during the adult years. But, then, White women of all marital categories live longer than any other group—non-White women and all men. We must be cautious in interpreting these data. For one thing, they do not show all people who have ever been widowed or divorced, but only those who have stayed widowed or divorced.

A different way of assessing the process of bereavement is by looking at mental health. A 13-month longitudinal study (Bornstein et al., 1973) found that 35% of widows (men and women) were diagnosed as depressed one month after the death of their spouses, but only 17% were diagnosed thus after one year.

For women past 50, widowhood is usually a permanent status, although not necessarily a preferred one. Only 5% of women who become widowed after age 55 ever remarry (Cleveland & Gianturco, 1976). In contrast most widowers remarry if they are under 70. As can be seen in Table 20.1, there are thus many more older men who have wives than older women who have husbands.

Young widows are soon considered to be single again rather than considered to be widows (Lopata, 1973). Because they are so much in the minority among their age peers, however, they tend to feel stigmatized. In contrast, older wom-

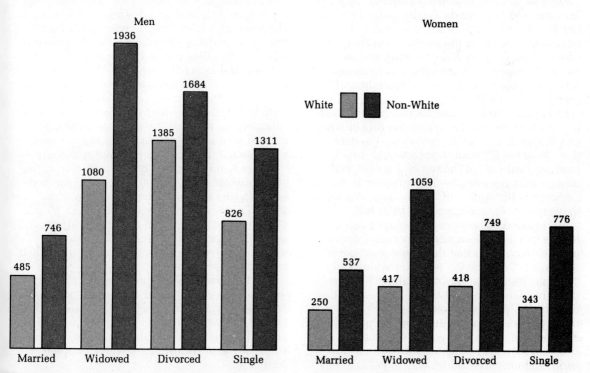

Figure 20.3. Death rates by marital status. *(Source: Carter and Glick, 1970.)*

TABLE 20.1 Marital status of Blacks and Whites, by age and sex: United States, 1975 (percentages)

	Men						Women					
	Age											
Marital status	16–25	26–35	36–45	46–55	56–65	66–75	16–25	26–35	36–45	46–55	56–65	66–75
White												
Never married	75	14	5	5	5	5	60	9	4	4	5	7
Married, living with spouse	22	77	79	79	77	74	34	70	71	67	56	38
Remarried	1	9	15	16	18	21	2	12	16	18	18	19
Divorced	1	4	4	3	2	1	2	6	6	5	3	3
Widowed	0	0	0	1	3	8	0	0	2	6	16	34
Black												
Never married	80	22	8	7	5	5	73	19	7	5	5	6
Married, living with spouse	17	58	62	54	52	43	21	48	47	44	33	23
Remarried	0	0	17	26	27	33	1	7	17	23	29	33
Divorced	1	4	7	3	4	3	2	8	9	9	5	3
Widowed	0	0	0	3	7	10	0	2	6	11	22	32

Source: U.S. Department of Commerce, Bureau of the Census, 1976.

en see widowhood as more normal. Even as early as age 65, a third of all women are widows. Thus, the prevalence of widowhood in later life combines with low expectations for remarriage to produce a more definite social position for the older widow.

Even so, the role of older widows is vague. Ties with their husbands' families may be drastically reduced, yet they are supposed to be interested in keeping the memories of their husbands alive. They are also not supposed to be interested in men but are supposed to associate primarily with other widows or with their children (Lopata, 1973).

Becoming a widow changes the basis of identity for those women for whom the role of wife and mother is central. In answering the question "Who am I?" such women would usually have put "wife of" at the top of their list. But many—although not all—find it harder to do the same with "widow of." They have also lost the very people who supported their self-definition. Husbands who were best friends and confidants may have been very important in making their wives feel that they were good people. And it is not uncommon for older widows to "consult" their dead husbands about whether they are "doing the right thing" ten years after they died. This kind of loss can be felt even if the dead spouse was an antagonist. One widow said that she only knew where she stood on an issue after she had fought it out with her husband, and now she had no way to validate her judgment.

Lopata (1973) found that widows cope with this identity crisis in different ways. Role-oriented women can turn to other roles, taking jobs or increasing their investment in jobs they already have. They may also become more involved in civic or social organizations. Those who need confirmation of their personal qualities may become more involved with friends and family. However, in a later study Lopata (1977) found that those widows who had not had friends outside their families before their husbands died did not tend to acquire any after their husbands' deaths. Widows who base their identities on things rather than on people are often in trouble because they find that their incomes are substantially reduced. All these orientations may, of course, be present in the same person and may continue earlier personality patterns.

A follow-up study was made of 56 women out of an original group of 100 who had been studied ten years earlier (Noberini & Neugarten, 1975). Those women, now aged between 55 and 67, who were widowed in the interim did not show any significant difference in mood tone, sense of self-worth, sense of accomplishing their goals, or sense of integrity.

Clearly, women vary in the extent to which the role of wife is central to their identities. For many, motherhood supersedes wifehood. Others had never developed close, intimate relationships with their husbands. Thus, it is not surprising that widows vary widely in their adaptations.

Loneliness is presumed to be common among

widows, the divorced, and the old. Living alone, however, is not the same as feeling lonely, feeling isolated, or feeling desolated. Many people—young and old—who live alone do not feel lonely, isolated, or desolated. And many people who live with spouses or other relatives *do* feel lonely, isolated, and desolated. Many widows quickly grow accustomed to living alone; more than half of older widows do so and apparently even prefer to do so. They miss their husbands, both as people and as partners in many activities (Lopata, 1973; Blau, 1961), but if they become involved with groups of other widows they tend to miss their spouses' companionship less. In residential areas with a high concentration of older widows, widows report loneliness much less frequently than in areas where such widows are more isolated. In fact, Atchley, Pignatiello, and Shaw (1975) found that widows had higher rates of interaction than did married older women.

Older widows in Kansas spent most of their time at home alone—but then this may also have been true of their lives as housewives. When they did spend time with others, it was mostly with kin—children or siblings—and mostly with other women (Gibbs, 1979). Those who lived in more-urban communities, where formal organizations were more available, spent time at meetings, which also tended to be women's groups.

The amount and kind of social disruption caused by widowhood depend largely on what life activities had been shared with husbands. For example, a middle-class woman is more likely than a working-class woman to have seen herself as part of a husband/wife team. Therefore, a middle-class woman would be cut out of a wide variety of activities by her husband's death. Churches and voluntary associations organized around interests can provide avenues for increased social contact for widows, because these activities do not usually depend on having a spouse or being accompanied by a member of the opposite sex. Single-sex groups are often more comfortable than heterosexual groups because they do not confront widows, particularly younger ones, with being the lone single woman, or widowers the rare man.

Social class is also a factor in adjustment to widowhood. Middle-class women are more likely than working-class women to have balanced their roles as wives, companions, and mothers.

Therefore, the loss of comradeship can often be traumatic for middle-class women. However, middle-class women also tend to have more social options, more nonfamily friends, and more organizational activity, not to mention more personal resources in general. They usually have more-secure incomes, more education, and more job skills. To balance this advantage in a small way, many working-class women tend to emphasize their mother role more than their wife role, and thus may experience less personal loss. But we must not forget that working-class women have fewer friends, fewer organizational memberships, less money, and fewer personal resources. On the whole, then, we would expect working-class widows to be much more isolated and lonely than are middle-class widows.

Among low-income elderly, the widowed were consistently more negative in their self-reports of life satisfaction (Hutchison, 1975). Widowhood is a more important factor among low-income people (but not among the lowest) than among those at the poverty level. At the poverty level, apparently, the grim problems of surviving may have lessened the likelihood of emotional closeness between husband and wife. Furthermore, poverty often leads to lowered social participation outside the home (Atchley, 1975b). In fact, a five-country investigation (Harvey & Bahr, 1974) found that the major long-term negative effects of widowhood were primarily associated with poverty.

Class differences were particularly large among Blacks. Working-class Black women tend to become widowed at even earlier ages than working-class Whites. However, overt hostility between the sexes is more prevalent among Blacks, and therefore widows sanctify their husbands' memory less. As a result, widowhood brings less emotional distress to working-class Blacks than to working-class Whites (Lopata, 1973).

There are also considerable ethnic and foreign-birth differences in the impact of widowhood. These differences are complex and are tied to expectations and to the congruence between these expectations of the older and younger generations in the family. Foreign-born older widows are much more likely to have had traditional expectations for respect and care in old age, which conflict with the different values of their Americanized children.

Remarriage

As can be seen from Figure 20.4, remarriage rates vary by sex and age. Young divorced women—under age 30—have the greatest chance of remarrying. After 30, however, divorced men have the advantage, and they retain this advantage from that age on. Black women have an even lower rate of remarriage than White women.

Because men have better chances of remarrying than women, those men who stay unmarried probably are in poorer mental or physical health. The lifestyles of unmarried men—particularly non-White unmarried men, who may be economically as well as personally or emotionally disadvantaged—are often harmful to health.

Remarriage also depends on attitudes toward prospective suitors. A woman who was married before and is now dating someone who was not married has a shorter courtship than a man who was married before dating a woman who was not. A previously married woman seems to be readier to remarry. Divorcees are particularly easy to please. Widows often glorify their dead spouses, but divorcees are likely to do the opposite. In 1960, every eighth person in the United States had been married more than once. In 1971, over 10% of American men (10.1% White and 12.5% Black) and over 14% of American women (14.1% White and 19.2% Black) had been married at least twice. Glick (1979) notes the increasing proportion of marriages that are remarriages.

As noted earlier, the older the divorced or widowed person and the longer since the divorce or death, the less likely is remarriage. Also, both low income for men, and children for women, reduce remarriage chances.

Aldous (1978) suggests that in some respects first marriages that end in divorce can be seen as socialization for second marriages. Because about five-sixths of all divorced men and three-fourths of divorced women remarry, on the average within three years of divorce, they obviously are not disillusioned with the idea of marriage. However, the difference in marital happiness between first- and second-marriage couples, while not very large, favors those who are still in their first marriages. These differences are statistically significant for women

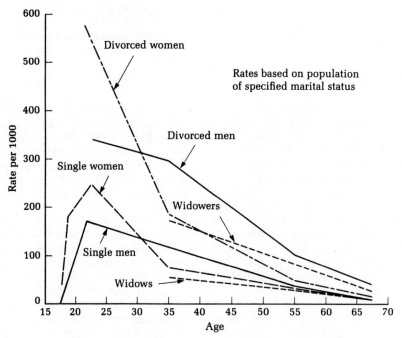

Figure 20.4. Remarriage rates. *(Source: Carter and Glick, 1970.)*

(Glenn & Weaver, 1977). Apparently, once-divorced couples learn that divorce is an option. What they haven't learned is how to get along more comfortably. Somewhat different findings come from another study of remarried couples (Hetherington et al., 1976). These couples were as happy as a matched group of still-married couples, but the remarried couples' self-esteem and sense of competency with the opposite sex was lower than that of the still-married.

A prominent factor in remarriage is the excess of older women over older men. Over age 65, there are about 75 men to 100 women. It is not surprising, therefore, that in 1970 older grooms outnumbered older brides two to one. Of the 31,000 men over 65 who got married in 1970, 59% married women under 65. Of the 15,000 women over 65 married in 1970, only 15% married men under 65. A happy remarriage may ease the pain of widowhood or divorce, but this option simply is not available to most middle-aged or older women.

In a study of 100 couples who married in later maturity, McKain (1969) found that companionship was by far the most frequently given reason for remarriage. Previous good experience with marriage helped. Few of the couples he interviewed believed in romantic love. Besides companionship, they wanted lasting affection and regard. As McKain (1969, p. 36) said, "The role of sex in the lives of these older people extended far beyond love-making and coitus; a woman's gentle touch, the perfume of her hair, a word of endearment—all these and many more reminders that he is married help to satisfy a man's urge for the opposite sex. The same is true for the older wife." A few older people remarried to allay their anxiety about their own poor health. As discussed earlier, it is likely these were men looking for nurses. Some remarried to avoid having to depend on children.

Many older people tended to select mates who reminded them of previous spouses (McKain, 1969). In fact, many married someone they had known for many years, often in the setting of an earlier couples group that had included their now-dead spouse. For example, a widower would marry a widow who had been part of the same social group when his wife and her husband were living. They thus followed the same pattern of homogamy as did young couples, marrying those from similar back-grounds in socioeconomic status, religion, ethnicity, education, and even personality. About three-fourths of older new marriages include widowed people (Treas & Van Hilst, 1976). Widows may be preferred to divorced people, although in this age cohort there are probably more who are widowed than divorced.

McKain (1969) studied the results of such unobtrusive measures as displays of affection, respect and consideration, obvious enjoyment of each other's company, lack of complaints about each other, and pride in their marriage as indicators of successful marriage. He found that these factors were more common among partners who had known each other well over a period of years than among those who had met recently. Probably the prime reason that long friendship was so strongly related to successful remarriage in later life is that intimate knowledge allowed better matching of interests and favorite activities.

Approval of the marriage by family and friends was important for the success of these late marriages, as it was in earlier life (McKain, 1969). Many older couples face considerable social opposition to marriage. There is a belief that they do not need to be married, because marriage is primarily an institution for reproduction and child rearing. Their children may also be concerned about what might happen to their inheritances. Because older people generally share the beliefs of their generation, they are often very sensitive to such pressure. Encouragement from children and friends can be strategic in the decision to marry.

There also appears to be an element of personal adaptability that influences adjustments to late-life marriages. McKain found that, unless both the bride and groom were reasonably well-adjusted individuals, marriage in later life was not likely to be successful. Financial factors were also important. It helped if both partners owned homes, for example. In part, the importance of dual home ownership (each partner owns a home) was symbolic, indicating that each partner brought something concrete to the marriage. The same principle applied if both had sufficient income. Arrangements for pooling property or giving to children were similarly symbolic, indicating the priority a partner held in the eyes of the other. When the marriage partner had priority over children in the distribution of resources, the marriage was more likely to be successful.

The never-married

Many studies of marriage contrast married people with single people, including in singleness those who have once been married but are married no longer as well as those who have never married. As noted at the beginning of Chapter 18, present cohorts of Americans are probably the most married, not only in the world today, but also in human history. The percentage of those who have never married, particularly at older ages, has been very small. However, Glick (1979) predicts that present 20-year-olds who delay marriages, and who may end up never marrying, will constitute a larger never-married cohort in the future. Peter Stein (1978) notes that most texts treat singlehood as a transient state; it is rarely investigated. The incidence of never-married people in 1976 is shown in Table 20.2.

Among singles, both sex and age differences are marked. Thus, 91% of men aged 18–19 have never married, contrasted with only 78% of women that age. These statistics just mean that women marry younger. By their early 30s, only 12% of men and only 7% of women have never married. Over 65 years of age, 4% of men and 6% of women have never married. Old men who have never married do not have as great a chance of survival as do old men who are married.

Stein (1978) distinguishes between voluntary and involuntary singlehood and between stable or temporary singlehood. A comparison of 20 never-married men over the age of 35 with 20 men who first married after 35 (Darling, 1976) suggests that voluntary stable bachelorhood is primarily situational rather than psychological. I pointed out in Chapter 18 that, as often as not, people marry because of shifts in their social condition, such as changes in reference groups, in relationships with their families, or in their careers. Thus, some voluntary stable bachelorhood may be "chosen" because of situational stability. Shifts that might have prompted marriage have simply never occurred.

Cohort effects are evident in age of marrying. In 1960, 28% of women between 20 and 24 had never married. In 1976, 43% had never married. For men of the same age, the move was less dramatic: from 53% in 1960 to 62% in 1976 (Stein, 1978). One reason for the increase in unmarried young women was the availability of other options, such as education and careers, which made remaining unmarried relatively comfortable, at least economically. A different reason is their decreased chances of finding marriageable men, because the women born during the post-World War II "baby boom" reached adulthood before the men of that boom. It takes men longer to mature. Also,

TABLE 20.2 Marital status of the population (age 18 and over) by sex and age, 1976

Marital status	Total population (× 1000)	Percent of population	18–19	20–24	25–29	30–34	35–44	45–64	Over 65
Men									
Never married	14,656	21.4	91.1	62.1	24.9	12.3	7.2	5.6	4.4
Separated	1,353	2.0	0.1	1.5	2.3	2.5	2.3	2.1	1.6
Divorced	2,703	4.1	0.2	1.8	4.1	5.7	5.4	5.0	2.7
Widowed	1,793	2.6	—	0.1	0.1	0.1	0.3	2.4	13.7
Married	47,854	69.9	7.1	33.4	68.0	78.4	83.7	83.8	76.4
Total	68,439	100.0							
Women									
Never married	11,515	15.1	78.3	42.6	14.8	7.0	4.7	4.6	5.9
Separated	2,405	3.2	1.5	3.8	4.2	5.0	4.3	2.7	1.1
Divorced	4,403	5.8	0.6	3.5	7.4	8.4	8.6	6.3	2.8
Widowed	10,019	13.2	—	0.1	0.4	1.0	2.5	12.7	53.0
Married	47,684	62.7	18.3	48.6	72.3	78.0	78.9	72.7	36.8
Total	76,026	100.0							

Note: Dash indicates no data.

Source: U.S. Department of Commerce, Bureau of the Census, 1977.

women that age are sought by an older (there-fore smaller) cohort of men. The "bad publicity" given marriage by increased divorce rates also led to greater uncertainty about the desirability of marriage. A large proportion of single people, particularly women, tend to live alone or with temporary partners and tend to live in large cities.

Men and women who remained single into their 30s reported that their middle to late 20s were a time of great difficulty (Stein, 1978). They felt intense parental and societal pressure to marry and also were not completely sure that they liked their jobs or their living arrangements.

Interviews with 73 college-educated single men and women over 30 (Schwartz, 1976) suggest six different lifestyles. The three most common are (1) the professional, a strong identification with occupational role; (2) the social, focusing on personal relationships; and (3) the individualistic, emphasizing self-direction and self-growth. Men were more likely to fall into the first category, the professional. Women were more likely to fall into the second, the social. This conformity with sex-role stereotypes is not surprising.

Middle-aged women who have never married are much better off, in terms of education, finances, and mental health, than are men that age who have never married (Bernard, 1973). Old people (over 65) who have never married are described by Gubrium (1975) as *lifelong isolates*. They are not especially lonely and are more positive than divorced or widowed old people; thus they are comparable to the still-married. Perhaps because they have been spared the desolation caused by the loss of a spouse, they are even relatively advantaged.

Many more Black men and women than Whites never marry. Between 25 and 29 years of age, about 33% of Black men, compared to 25% of White men, have not married. About 30% of Black women, compared with about 10% of White women, have not married. One complaint voiced by never-married Blacks is that they don't have a place where they can meet possible partners (Staples, 1977).

Although one might expect that older men and women who had never married would be isolated and cut off from potential sources of help in old age, Clark and Anderson (1967) did not find this to be true, at least in San Francisco. Apparently such older people learned very

early in life to cope with loneliness and to look after themselves and were successfully autonomous and self-reliant in their later years. People who never marry may miss a lot of the "good" parts of life, but they also seem to miss some of the "bad" (Gubrium, 1975).

Older people who have never married might be expected to have more contacts with extended kin than do those who married. However, Atchley, Pignatiello, and Shaw (1975) found that such contact depends a great deal on social class, at least for women. Never-married older women teachers interacted with extended kin significantly more than those who were married. But older telephone workers who never married had much lower levels of interaction with extended family than did those who were married. They had relatively more contacts with friends who were not relatives. Single older women who had been telephone-company employees had much higher interaction levels than did married women employees.

New forms of marriage

Many forces in today's world operate to weaken the appropriateness and satisfaction of traditional monogamous marriage. Let's examine just a few. First, increasing life expectancy makes "till death do us part" a much heavier commitment than it was when 20 or 30 years of marriage, rather than 40 or 50, was the rule. Second, overpopulation makes the bearing of many children "bad" rather than "good." Third, decreased infant mortality makes it more likely that each child born will grow up, and thus a large supply of children becomes less necessary to ensure family continuity and help. Fourth, much new technology does not require physical strength. Therefore, the work of women is as good as the work of men; women who can get jobs as easily as men can do not need to depend on husbands for economic benefits. Fifth, the supplementation and substitution of home services makes a professional housewife an option instead of a necessity for each man. Sixth, increased mobility has led to superficiality in human relationships and to the absence of socialization for deep commitment and involvement. Seventh, there is a spirit of searching for new ways and a distrust of old ways.

During the last few years, a small number of

young, largely urban culture leaders have experimented with a variety of alternatives to traditional marriage, and these ventures have received wide publicity. Writers such as Toffler (*Future Shock*, 1970) and Bernard (*The Future of Marriage*, 1973) point out the irrelevance or imperfections of old forms of marriage. They also consider possible new forms. So far, the radical new styles that have received most attention have been rare and transitory. However, some patterns, such as serial monogamy and unmarried cohabitation, are growing in frequency.

SERIAL MONOGAMY

Serial monogamy has long been an accepted form of marital arrangement. It used to be the result of death rather than of divorce, but in both cases remarriage occurs after the termination of a previous marriage. Norton and Glick (1976) found 16% living in second marriages 20 or more years after first marriages, and 2% in third marriages. These percentages are increasing. (For further discussion, read again the section on remarriage.)

SWINGING

Swinging is a relatively simple and not very revolutionary modification of marriage that ensures both security and (presumably) sexual excitement. Couples exchange partners for limited encounters. Most swingers are young (in their 20s and 30s), married four or five years, and parents. The women are usually housewives; a few are teachers. The same kinds of race, age, and class criteria are used to select partners that are used for traditional marriage partners (Bartell, 1971). Swingers are mostly middle-class suburban couples who lead otherwise conventional lives in separate, isolated households and who keep their swinging activities hidden from their neighbors. This lifestyle is most common on the West and East Coasts, where couples may travel great distances to find each other. Bernard (1973) sees the effects of swinging as generally benign. On the other side of the ledger, it is male oriented, and wives tend to be bartered by husbands for the wives of other men. Many couples—especially the men—find that they can't live up to the sexual expecta-

tions, become jealous, are infected with venereal disease, or become disillusioned by the mechanistic nature of such sexual experiences.

INTIMATE NETWORKS

In intimate networks, there is greater commitment and involvement than in ordinary swinging, and there is an emphasis on close emotional relationships, openness, and honesty. Although this arrangement also does not pose much threat to marriage, it is more of a threat than is swinging because it is less impersonal. Constantine and Constantine (1973) describe such networks as "a cluster or chain of families maintaining separate domiciles and family identity, but coupled by intimate relationships between families" (in Bernard, 1973, p. 224). The ideal is to maintain relationships—usually sexual—over time and to get together whenever possible or convenient. This style seems essentially an extension of the "couple-friends" relationship described in Chapter 17.

MÉNAGE À TROIS

A ménage à trois usually consists of one man and two women, with only one of the women legally attached to the man. It is usually the man who initiates this arrangement. And, as one would expect, he is likely to get more out of it than do the women.

GROUP MARRIAGE

In multilateral marriage, or *group marriage*, three or more people commit themselves to one another and consider all to be married to each other, with hopes of genuine intimacy and affection. They hope for permanence but provide for opting out and have no commitment to exclusivity. This arrangement provides sexual variety and also security. It relieves the men of sole responsibility for supporting the combined families and relieves the women of sole responsibility for child rearing and housekeeping. Bernard (1973) feels that, as in other male-initiated arrangements, it gives lip service to equality between the sexes but is really under male leadership. This arrangement can become enormously complex and time consuming as the number of people included increases. Homosexuality is sometimes permitted but occurs rarely, because it adds to the already burdensome complexity of relationships.

These extreme forms of quasi-marital living are the kind that receive wide publicity. Less extreme forms also exist. A common one is the *dual-career* family, in which both husband and wife are equally committed to employment and child/household careers. Like the extreme forms, this one tends to be more nominal than actual. When push comes to shove, the husband's employment takes priority over the wife's, and the wife's responsibility for the children takes priority over the husband's (Rapoport & Rapoport, 1969). The husband will rarely give up his job to follow his wife in a promising career move to another city. It is equally rare that an emergency call from a child—or a parent—is responded to by the husband instead of by the wife. One hears stories about fathers who participate in cooperative nursery schools or bring their infants to work with them, but one suspects that the wide publicity given such stories attests to their rarity and curiosity rather than to their frequency.

HOMOSEXUAL PARTNERSHIPS

Homosexual partnerships are little studied, in part, perhaps, because "coming out of the closet" is so recent. One anonymous study of a "nonprobability sample" reported that most male homosexual partnerships are transitory, as much from preference as from accident. The peak of committed gay liaisons—59% of a sample of gays interviewed—is for men between 46 and 55 years of age. We seem to know even less about lesbian relationships, although they may be more enduring and committed.

COMMUNES

Communes are distinguishable from intimate networks in that they are more inclusive and rarely imply sexual interchanges. Stein, Polk, and Polk (1973) distinguish between religious and nonreligious communes and between rural and urban communes. Many rural communes incorporate commitment to some religious or political/religious ideology and also are restricted by the necessities of agricultural living. Most seem to be more transitory than urban com-

munes, which are also not very stable (Levine, Carr, & Horenblas, 1973). Each of these studies involved loosely organized interviews and observations of about 30 communes. Their descriptions are consistent, however.

Most urban-commune members are young adults (with a few as old as the 40s and 50s) and some preschool children. Most are of middle-class, White origin and contain one or two couples mixed with singles, about 55% of all the members being men. Most are situated in large, old houses in downtown areas near a university. Most include financial and work sharing. Interestingly, Levine and associates (1973) note that meal preparation and handling of money tend to be allocated to particular members, although other tasks are rotated. The issue of food and meals is reportedly emotion laden. Those communes that survived moved toward insistence on privacy and on exclusion of factors that could be disruptive, such as transient, uncommitted, or disturbed individuals and such as drug use. As in marriages, the departure of a member tends to be highly disturbing, but, unlike marriages, the arrival of a new commune member does not. Like other alternative family forms, communes are rare and temporary.

Although alternative family forms would theoretically seem to be a good answer for isolated older people, such alternatives are even rarer among the old than among the young. Hochschild (1973) described one in *The Unexpected Community*, but the commune that she described does not seem to have inspired many others. In the 1970 census, over 18,000 couples aged 65 and over listed themselves as unmarried and living together (Dressel & Avant, 1978). But other variations of noncouple intimacy such as polygamy and homosexuality are not most older people's "cup of tea." Perhaps later cohorts of older people will create alternative versions more readily than do today's cohorts.

Summary

Divorce has been increasing across the board over the past few decades, but the age pattern has not changed. It is most frequent at the beginning of marriage, and there is no peak at any later age. Divorce is almost always stressful and has more severe economic consequences for women than for men, particularly if they have children.

It is harder to be a young widow than an old one, although chances of remarrying are better for the young. Because men have better chances of remarrying than women do, there are fewer old widowers than old widows.

Although the number of never-married men and women is increasing, it has so far been so low that the never-married state is generally ignored in research or is treated as transitory. Although those who never marry miss some of the benefits of marriage—which are greater for men than for women—they also miss some of the problems. Living alone is not synonymous with feeling isolated or desolated. People who chose isolated lifestyles early in life are better off than those who have loved and lost.

Many new forms of marriage or cohabitation have been tried, but none have become widespread. And none are used widely by older people, who might benefit most from such alternatives.

21

The Generations of Parents and Children

In our society, husbands and wives at least pretend to choose each other. Therefore, there may be some justification for considering couple relationships as if they were independent of other family members. However, it is a rare child who is born into a social vacuum, or even to a mother alone. Bilateral or multilateral influences abound, both direct and indirect (Lewis & Feiring, 1978). Children's crying changes the behavior of parents, and parents' responses to crying change children's crying. These are *direct* effects. The effect of children's crying can also be influenced by parents' previous experiences with crying—for example, of the parents' younger siblings or previous children. Family rules (sometimes transmitted through their own parents) can also affect parents' decisions about whether or not to pick up crying babies. These are *indirect* effects. Other indirect influences include the relationship between the mother and father, which can affect both parents' interactions with their children. Similarly, the child's demands on parents can influence the relationship between the parents.

It seems that parents remain parents throughout their lives—often beyond their own lives, throughout their children's lives.* Offspring always remain children to their parents. Even when offspring are called on to take care of ill and dying parents, they do so from the perspective of children. There is no evidence that they reverse their roles to become parents of their own parents, except in the most limited sense.

Another theme that emerges in parent/child relations is the importance of both mother and father. It is true that, in our culture, many fathers have more indirect than direct effects, but their contribution cannot be ignored. American families are not much different from most families around the world in that much early child care is by the mother. Only in a minority of families are the roles of mother and father interchangeable.

Generations in the family

The rhythm of development within the family has altered over the last few generations; indeed, over the last two centuries. Before 1900, only about 40% of American women went through what was later considered the "ideal" family cycle of leaving home, getting married, having children, launching children, and surviving with their husbands into old age (Hareven, 1977). The rest (60%) never married, never reached marriageable age, died before childbirth, or were widowed while their children

*It would be useful to have terms that distinguish between children as people in the first years of life and children as offspring of parents. The word *offspring* is awkward but must suffice.

were small. More people today live out their full life spans, more parents limit the number of their children, and economic affluence permits more young couples to get married before they are economically independent. The grandparents of today's young adults, who married early in the 20th century, were married longer before they had their first children than were the next two generations. However, they had children at closer intervals and continued having children for a longer period of time (see Figure 21.1).

The next generation got married during the Depression and had to delay having children. Of the three generations of adult couples studied by Hill and his associates (1970), the grandparents had spent the most years raising chil-

dren. Table 21.1 shows the progression in age of first marriages from 1900 to 1970. In 1900, women married at 21, on the average (Glick, 1977), and men at 26 (Glick, Heer, & Beresford, 1959). Brides were one year younger during the 1950s and 1960s (20 years old on the average) but went up to 21 years of age again in the 1970s. The difference between the mother's age when she got married and her age at the birth of the first child has remained remarkably steady over the last 80 years. With an average of 1.7 years, its shortest time was in the 1960s—1.3 years— and its longest time in the 1930s—2.1 years. The major differences are in the mother's age at the birth of the last child, the marriage of the last child, and the death of the spouse. The mother's

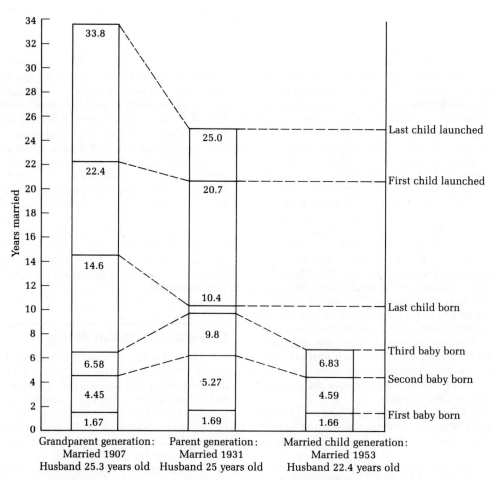

Figure 21.1. Profile of the timing of family-composition changes, by generation. (*Source: Hill, Foote, Aldous, Carlson, and Macdonald, 1970.*)

TABLE 21.1 Median age of mothers at selected stages of the family life cycle

Stage of the family life cycle	80-year aver-age	Period of birth of mother							
		1880s	1890s	1900s	1910s	1920s	1930s	1940s	1950s
		Approximate period of first marriage							
		1900s	1910s	1920s	1930s	1940s	1950s	1960s	1970s
Median age at:									
First marriage	20.9	21.4	21.2	21.0	21.4	20.7	20.0	20.5	21.2
Birth of first child	22.6	23.0	22.9	22.8	23.5	22.7	21.4	21.8	22.7
Birth of last child	31.3	32.9	32.0	31.0	32.0	31.5	31.2	30.1	29.6
Marriage of last child	53.5	55.4	54.8	53.0	53.2	53.2	53.6	52.7	52.3
Death of one spouse	62.8	57.0	59.6	62.3	63.7	64.4	65.1	65.1	65.2
Difference between age at first marriage and:									
Birth of first child	1.7	1.6	1.7	1.8	2.1	2.0	1.4	1.3	1.5
Birth of last child	10.4	11.5	10.8	10.0	10.6	10.8	11.2	9.6	8.4
Marriage of last child	32.6	34.0	33.6	32.0	31.8	32.5	33.6	32.2	31.1
Death of one spouse	41.9	35.6	38.4	41.3	42.3	43.7	45.1	44.6	44.0
Difference between:									
Age at birth of first and last children	8.7	9.9	9.1	8.2	8.5	8.8	9.8	8.3	6.9
Age at birth of and marriage of last child	22.2	22.5	22.8	22.0	21.2	21.7	22.4	22.6	22.7
Age at marriage of last child and death of one spouse (empty nest)	9.3	1.6	4.8	9.3	10.5	11.2	11.5	12.4	12.9

Source: U.S. Department of Commerce, Bureau of the Census, 1976.

age at the birth of the last child has gone down steadily since the 1930s—from 32.9 to 29.6—as has her age at the marriage of the last child—from 55.4 to 52.3. Meanwhile, the age at death of spouse has gone up steadily—from 57.0 to 65.2. In all, the difference has been in the terminal phase of childbearing and child rearing, not in the initial phase of that process. Primarily, the time the couple is alone together after child rearing has increased markedly. These changes are illustrated in Figure 21.2.

The American family profile has been changing. In 1960, the percentage of children remained about the same as in 1900, but there were fewer family members between 20 and 35 and more older people. It does not require much imagination to see the consequences for family life of different family compositions. For instance, if a large number of children must be cared for by a small number of adults, more work and responsibility will be delegated to older children. A smaller adult/child ratio is also more likely to be associated with authori-

tarian practices, because there is little time or energy for parents to consider the individual needs of particular children at particular times.

Adults today are not all of one generation—as they tended to be at the turn of the century—but are of three or even four generations (for example, parents, grandparents, and great-grandparents). Therefore, adult interrelationships are more complex and provide a variety of models for the growing children. If there are more children than adults in a family, children have much less value than if there is one child on whom several generations of adults focus hopes, wishes, and attentions. Husbands and wives who have only one or two children are freer to pursue activities other than child rearing and to examine their own relationships. They are also likely to be less upset when their children grow up and leave home.

Two separate generation effects have been mentioned: different timing of events and greater complexity of relationships. A third generation effect is the replication or replacement of a

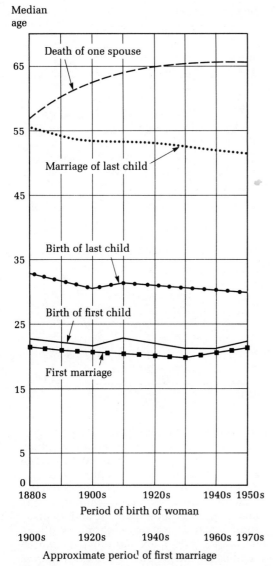

Median
age

Figure 21.2. Median age of mothers at the beginning of selected stages of the family cycle. *(Source: Glick, 1977.)*

pattern of roles, positions, and personality characteristics as each new generation succeeds the preceding one. As older family members die, their emotional, intellectual, cultural, biological, material, and personal legacies continue through a *generation spiral* (Duvall, 1971). Their children now become the oldest generation, taking on many of the preceding generation's char-

acteristics, and their grandchildren become the second generation.

The three generations of Minneapolis families studied by Hill and his associates (1970) interact with each other continually. They share activities, visit back and forth, and help each other in many ways. The middle generation (parents of married children) is the *lineage bridge* between the older and the younger generations. This generation helps and is involved with both other generations. Each generation turns to the kinship network for the help it needs: grandparents for care in illness and household management, middle-aged parents for emotional gratification, and young married couples for assistance with finances and child care. Table 21.4 (p. 354) shows the percentages of help given and received by all three generations over a year's time. It is clear that the family is both major donor and major recipient of help. The popular notion of the modern family as a vulnerable, isolated, nuclear unit of husband, wife, and young children is not supported. Instead, these generational units form a modified extended family with a rich network of interactions.

A developmental interpretation of parenting

The development of parent/child dyads (mother/child and father/child) may follow a pattern like that postulated for the husband/wife dyad in Chapter 19. We can look at combined effects of separate development of each parent and his or her child. Or we can look at the development of each of the parent/child dyads as systems. Or we can consider the family (mother/father/child or children) as the system. Or we can look at even larger units.

Most family-development descriptions so far have followed the first approach. The development of the child has been followed along one track and that of each of the parents—although usually only the mother—along parallel tracks. A growing body of research has focused on the attachment of infants to mothers (for example, Ainsworth, 1969; Bowlby, 1969). Hartup and Lempers (1973) also point out that attachment is probably mutual. The parent becomes as attached to the infant as the infant does to the parent; the interaction is reciprocal. Because most longitudinal studies on relationships have not gone beyond a year or so, we must wait for future research to help us understand the nature of social bonds and social networks over the life span.

The dyadic or family system makes strenuous efforts to maintain stability, or homeostasis, in the face of the enormous changes accompanying the development of a child. The presence of a child or children in a family may make it imperative for the family system as such to develop *or else*. Divorces may reflect not just the failure of the husband/wife system to deal with change. It may also reflect the failure of the total family system to function.

Mothering

The American mother—particularly the American urban middle-class mother of today—is supposed to be the primary child rearer. This has been the norm since the middle of the 19th century (Hareven, 1979). Before then, the separation between job world and family world was smaller, particularly for working-class families. Family members were more likely to function as a unit, both at work and in what are now called "family matters."

The burden of the housewife/mother of today, according to Lopata (1971), is a consequence of several factors. First, modern American society is strongly child oriented—at least in some respects. Second, it is difficult to learn and carry out complex child-rearing and housekeeping procedures without training either by parents or schools. Third, there is the belief that mothers alone should be responsible for raising their children. Fourth, there is the notion that if mothers are sufficiently competent they can— and must—raise superior children. Children who are less superior are the mother's fault. Fifth, there is a belief that all problems should be handled rationally, systematically, and calmly—which is almost impossible in the highly emotional process of raising infants and children. Sixth, rapid social change and social heterogeneity present conflicting norms.

The belief that the mother is the primary parent pervades our culture to the extent that both new mothers and new fathers acknowledge it. Shapiro (1978) reports that first-time mothers ad-

mit that they want to be credited as *the* parent. They tend to denigrate their husbands' parenting competence in order to highlight their own tenuous successes. A new father in one of my classes admitted that he would not pick up the baby when the infant cried at night without first getting his wife's permission. He had to "go through channels." Feldman (1971) found that more of the fathers he studied would have been willing to participate in care of their infants than were allowed to by their wives.

Being a mother and knowing how to be a mother are so much part of a woman's self-affirmation that the events of pregnancy and childbirth are highly charged. Another side of this coin, unhappily, is the fact that most new mothers are profoundly ignorant about details of what to expect from their babies and of what to do for babies. Yet pediatricians—male, particularly—seem to assume that mothers *must* know about such things because, after all, they are mothers. What they learned in early biology classes—that there is no "maternal instinct" that includes specific, built-in knowledge of how to nurse, diaper, and care for babies—seems to have made no impression.

In part, the physicians themselves may be ignorant of these everyday details, which aren't likely to be taught in medical school or observed in hospital wards. It is no wonder that publishers profit from the multitude of "how-to" books for mothering and that the media in general find parenting advice a good way to get large audiences. Women from tightly knit kin networks such as described by Bott (1971) find mothering much more familiar and comfortable (Aldous, 1978). After all, they have probably assisted aunts, mother, older sisters, or cousins in these jobs, and they also have all these relatives on hand for advice and help.

Couples who try to establish cooperative households are partially motivated by the demands of young mothers for more sharing and companionship. Other forms of supplementing maternal care, such as community child-care facilities, are not providing the quality care they promised a decade ago or that similar facilities provide in other countries. More options for the care of infants and preschool children, including trained child-care workers and foster grandparents, could make this relatively short period of intensive maternal stress one that approaches closer to the ideal that having a baby is a joy. The country does not seem to be moving that way, however. College students, both women and men, expect that they and their spouses will work at the same time as they raise children. They do not often think about how they will manage child care.

Many women claim that the greatest change in their lives is not marriage but the birth of the first child—when they become mothers. LeMasters (1957) feels that the entire period before and after birth should be considered a crisis in mental health, because the shift of roles and statuses is abrupt and without previous preparation. As with any crisis, not all aspects of the event are negative. For some new mothers, the positive aspects compensate for the negative.

Most new mothers—and fathers—are proud of their new status. They say that having children changed them into adults (Hoffman & Manis, 1978). In contrast, young people who were not parents checked "supporting yourself" as the most important thing in making them feel they were really adult. Parenting is such an agent for change in the lives of young adults that most couples find their old friendships strained (Bram, 1974). In fact, many adults name as their closest friends the parents of their children's friends.

Mothers of newborns interviewed by Russell (1974) were worried about being emotionally upset and about having a poor physical appearance. They complained of exhaustion, loss of sleep, and inability to keep up with housework. They worried about being able to be competent mothers; at the same time, they resented being tied down. Almost all mothers of young children feel restricted: restricted to the geographic boundaries of house and immediate neighborhood and restricted to the companionship of small children. They are particularly eager for their husbands' support and encouragement—and above all, companionship—at this time. Mothers who live close to their own mothers and sisters are, of course, less likely to suffer such isolation.

Hoffman and Hoffman (1973) summarized the reasons people give for their decisions to have children:

1. Children confirm adult status by their presence and give parents, particularly mothers, recognized social identities.

2. Children provide a means for continuation of the self, a kind of immortality.

3. Children tie parents to their communities through children's activities in schools, public recreation programs, and neighborhoods.

4. Children show, according to religious doctrine, that couples are moral beings, because the parents place others' welfare before their own and contribute to the continuity of the group.

5. Children protect parents from loneliness in an impersonal world.

6. Children supply novelty and fun to family life, which keeps life interesting.

7. Children, with their attendant socialization requirements, develop competencies in parents and give them a sense of accomplishment.

8. Children provide scope to parents for demonstrating creative child-rearing strategies.

9. Children permit parents to exercise power over others, as well as to gain prestige, because parents usually receive more social approval than do childless people.

10. Children give some parents a sense of vicarious achievement through their accomplishments.

11. Children can be of economic use, especially to older parents who need financial aid or a place of residence.

PREGNANCY

Pregnancy is a psychobiological/social event, a period of conflicting feelings and experiences. To begin with, it is an event with extreme age proscriptions. It is not supposed to occur either too early or too late. As discussed in Chapter 6, there is a prevalent dictum that the first child should be born before the mother is 30. The dictum has become so firmly entrenched that many women who are not married, or who have not had a child by then, go through a "29-year-old crisis."

This rule is supported by the medical profession, which warns of the increased probability of birth defects beyond this age. Yet a look at Tables 21.2 and 21.3 shows that this is not so. The percentage of infant deaths in the over-30 age groups is even lower than in the high-birth years of 25–29 (see Table 21.2). Furthermore,

TABLE 21.2 Distribution of fetal deaths, by age of mother (percentages)

Age of mother	Percentage of infants dying × 100,000 live births
Under 15	0.6
15–19	16.4
20–24	30.5
25–29	28.8
30–34	14.6
35–39	6.5
40–44	2.3
45–49	0.3

Source: U.S. Department of Health, Education and Welfare, National Center for Health Statistics, 1977.

TABLE 21.3 Infant mortality rates, 1968 and 1976

Cause	1968	1976
All causes	2178	1524
Anomalies (defective children)	316	263
Down's syndrome	3.4	1.8

Note: Figures are × 100,000 live births.

Source: U.S. Department of Health, Education and Welfare, National Center for Health Statistics, 1977.

abnormal births—at least those leading to the death of the infant—went down from 1968 to 1976.

Age norms and age proscriptions were discussed in Chapter 3; the biological aspects of pregnancy in Chapter 6. Therefore, only parenting aspects are treated here.

First-time pregnancies are different from later pregnancies in more than one way. They are unknown and ambiguous; it is not surprising that many primiparous (first-birth) women are anxious (Loesch & Greenberg, 1962; Shapiro, 1978). The first-pregnancy women whom Shapiro interviewed were less likely to express their anxiety than those who had been pregnant before, however. They may have been too defensive to admit such feelings, even to themselves.

Arbeit (1975) noticed that many primiparous women reevaluate their relationships with their own mothers, feeling closer to them than they had for many years. The complex effect of parenting on relationships with older generations is a challenging topic for research. Also, during pregnancy, women gradually define the fetus as a child and begin to differentiate themselves from this unborn "other."

Preliminary reports of the research of Yarrow and his colleagues (Soule, 1974) indicate that much of the pregnancy experience is shared by both parents. It is a "couple experience," although it is physically more *direct* for the woman than for the man. Many women are unhappy about their appearance at this time (Feldman, 1971) and feel uncomfortable in public; others are proud and pleased with the way they look.

During the 1960s and 1970s, perhaps because of the various "movements" of the time, a variety of new or renewed childbirth practices were tried out. So far, little systematic evaluation of these methods exists. In general, these "radical" approaches point to the importance of childbirth for many couples even though—or perhaps because—there are apparently contradictory ideologies for women's employment and for limiting population size.

The thrust of these new practices has been to remove pregnancy and childbirth psychologically from the medical realm, which tended to automatically classify such events as "diseases." Anderson and Standley (1976) feel that, when a wife in labor talks to her husband, she is less likely to feel pain. Perhaps in part this is a kind of "Hawthorne effect." The new methods change the frightening and impersonal "labor" and "delivery-room" atmosphere to a more familiar, more personal, and socially more open experience. This change may lessen tension and pain no matter what else occurs.

Support for the idea that fear of the unknown may contribute to childbirth pain comes from differences in experience between first-birth and later-birth women. It is true that a first birth, particularly in a very young woman, may be more difficult physiologically. Yet primiparous mothers describe feeling strange, distant, and unfamiliar, even in their attitudes toward their babies (Robson & Moss, 1970), and later-birth mothers are much more comfortable. This difference suggests that the psychological component is important. Shapiro (1978) reported that the first-time mothers found labor and delivery so fatiguing and stressful that they "distanced" themselves from the experience, were numb or in shock, or were simply worn out. They felt a discontinuity between the pregnancy and the birth.

In contrast, the second-time mothers, regardless of medication, said that they were more able to attend to and enjoy the experience and felt more available to make contact with the infants moments after birth. In general, the new mothers felt that the labor and delivery experience marked both a painful separation from the pregnancy and infant within themselves and a new kind of attachment to the infant outside themselves. This pattern was particularly true for the nursing mothers. Incidentally, those women who had difficulty breastfeeding reported feelings of not being well enough taken care of and helped by their own mothers. The second-time mothers breezed in and out of the hospital and saw the period as a brief respite, followed by "business as usual." They also were more able to consider their own needs for rest and solitude and were less likely to want to room in with or to spend all their time with their babies.

Are women biologically primed for motherhood? Do they have built-in mechanisms that make them more natural or more desirable parents than are men? If so, at what point does this priming take place? These questions are central to several current theories. Psychobiologists would answer yes to the first two questions. And most would claim that hormonal mechanisms were involved. Thus, puberty would "turn on" maternal feelings, and menopause would turn them off.

Gutmann (1975) hypothesizes that a "parental imperative" pushes men toward stereotypically masculine traits and women toward stereotypically feminine traits. His social theory proposes that women become more "maternal" at the end of adolescence, the appropriate time to bear a child. They become less "maternal" when their children are grown, at the time of the "empty nest."

A third theoretical perspective is that of social-learning theory, which suggests that both men and women are socialized to an interest in babies when they become parents. They lose this interest when they are no longer parents of babies. Shirley Feldman and Sharon Nash (1978, 1979) devised an ingenious set of experiments at Stanford University to test these hypotheses. In one study, young adults who were either cohabiting, married and childless, pregnant, or parents of infants were confronted with an infant and mother in a waiting room. They were also given some tests involving pictures of people of various ages, including infants.

The results showed marked sex differences. In most measures, women showed much more sensitivity to infants than did men. But the only women that showed this sensitivity were themselves mothers of infants. In fact, the pregnant women conspicuously ignored the babies. A second study by the same investigators used the same situations and measures, but with older men and women: with parents of adolescents, with empty-nesters, and with grandparents. The grandparents—the only ones who were personally involved with babies—were much more "tuned in" to the babies in the waiting room.

Essentially, thus, neither the sociobiological nor the parental-imperative theories were confirmed. However, the grandfathers' move toward accepting "femininity" is what Gutmann would predict. The social-learning theory is the closest to explaining the mothering effect in the study. Having a baby makes one interested in babies. It makes women interested in all babies, but men, apparently, only become interested in their own. This difference is harder to explain than is the "simple" increase of interest.

Fathering

Complicated as the mother/child relationship is, the father/child one may be even more so. Many people believe that fathering is at best an indirect activity, that a father's main function is to support the mother economically and emotionally so that she can carry on her job of bearing and raising children. There are, however, direct functions in the fathering role, even at its beginning.

For those who look to primate behavior for clues or support for human behavior, let me note that there is wide diversity in the behavior of adult primate males toward the young. Behavior can range from extreme hostility to extreme nurturance (Mitchell, 1969). Pleck (1975) concludes that, while hormones may facilitate the development of parental behaviors (presumably only in mothers), such behaviors can also develop in the absence of hormones, even if more slowly.

Observers of couples during pregnancy have not noticed much difference between the attitudes of the father-to-be and the mother-to-be toward the coming event (Soule, 1974). In general, the 67 husbands studied by Yarrow, Waxler, and Scott (1971) were less ambivalent about the pregnancy than were their wives, and they anticipated fewer life changes in the immediate future. In a way, this expectation was realistic. The ten first-time fathers studied by Shapiro (1978) felt intensified financial pressure but it was their wives who made drastic lifestyle changes.

First-time fathers described themselves as elated during and after the first birth. Those going through a second birth were still pleased, but not as emotionally involved. After the first birth, they said that they had felt physically excluded during the pregnancy. They enjoyed the moment of birth because the baby became directly available to them.

There is no evidence, incidentally, that the presence of the father at the birth facilitates father/infant bonding (Greenberg & Morris, 1974). Some men who participated at the births did not develop strong attachment to the babies; others did. The fathers in Shapiro's sample had different responses to their wives' efforts to exclude them from the care of the newborns. Some were relieved, some withdrew from the scene altogether, some were angry, and some actively competed for contact with babies. Yet most fathers felt much more removed from babies' crying and were able to tune it out or ask their wives to do something about it.

Not until the second month did most fathers report feeling "hooked" on parenting. At this time, they spent more and more time with their infants, primarily in play. As noted earlier, Feldman and Nash's (1978, 1979) research showed that fathers' interest in babies seemed confined to their own babies.

Although the first-time mothers were not ready to turn babies over to fathers for care for the first several months, second-time mothers appreciated fathers' help from the beginning. Fathers were closest to their firstborn children after the birth of their second-born ones. The sex of the children did not make any difference. Lamb (1978) points out that, because fathers generally show more interest in sons, the displaced firstborn girl is most likely to benefit from her father's special attention after she has a sibling. A mutual bond is formed when the displaced older child turns to the father in anger and resentment over the new birth.

A series of studies by Parke and his colleagues (Parke & O'Leary, 1975; Parke & Sawin, 1975) found that both first-time mothers and first-time fathers were eager to hold and interact with their newborn babies. The one notable difference was that fathers did not smile at their babies as much as mothers did. Also, most infants form relationships with both parents at about the same time (Lamb, 1978), although they show clear preference for their mothers at about one year of age.

An interesting *indirect* effect of fathers was observed by Parke and O'Leary. Mothers seemed more interested in their babies when the fathers were around. This pattern was particularly true for their baby boys, who were touched much more when the fathers were there. Some of these recent research findings on fathers' influence in infancy may, of course, be a cohort effect, influenced by the movement toward joint parenting. When men try to participate in family work, they are more likely to accept child-care responsibilities than other household work (Pleck, 1975).

A study of the importance of parenting to a group of fathers (Heath, 1978) found that less than half of the fathers showed very strong parenting desires or effects. Those that were affected by becoming fathers were described as better adjusted and more mature adults. Feldman (1971) reported that men said becoming fathers had made them less selfish. It may be that the age and maturational point at which a man becomes a father are more important to his reaction than they are for the mother. As noted earlier, the high school fathers in De Lissovoy's (1973) study seemed to remain boys, busy at school and with friends. Nydegger (1973) reported from a study of older first-time fathers that "late fathers are great fathers."

The way fathers play with their children tends to be different from the way mothers play (Lamb & Lamb, 1976). Fathers are more vigorous and use unusual and unpredictable movements. Babies tend, therefore, to enjoy playing with their fathers more than with their mothers.

After the child is about one year of age, fathers tend to play mostly with their sons. Much of the sons' sex-role modeling, however, depends on the way mothers picture fathers to their sons, particularly if fathers are not around much. There is a difference between saying "Daddy is away on a trip, but he misses you" and "You behave just like your father!" (Lewis & Feiring, 1978). Fathers' absence, which used to be considered harmful to sons, may sometimes lead to greater cognitive development. Or maybe the fathers who are away more are brighter and have brighter children. Cognitive distancing, considered a sign of more-analytic thinking, is more common in middle-class families. According to Sigel (1970), such distancing results from intermittent object presence. Brooks and Lewis (in press) found that infants label pictures of their fathers earlier than they label pictures of their mothers, just as they say "Daddy" before they say "Mommy" (Jakobson, 1962).

Late fathers—those whose first children are born when they are about 40—tend to remain involved with their babies longer than do young fathers, perhaps partly because of greater economic security. They see their role as a model and a transmitter of qualities they value, and they are more dispassionate, objective, and accepting of differences. Early fathers are more likely to see their role as a teacher of skills, a problem solver, or a buddy (Nydegger, 1973).

The effects of education and social class are marked in fathering, as they are in mothering. Lower-status fathers are perhaps less involved (Bowerman & Elder, 1964; Veroff & Feld, 1970). Having a child may be seen as a sign of potency, and the duties of a father may be seen as symbols of physical security. Although there has been some cultural shift away from paternal authoritarianism, lower-class fathers are still likely to follow this pattern. Furthermore, Veroff and Feld believe that the less education a father has, the earlier his discomfort with fathering, because his child will find out earlier that he has lower status than do other people the child meets. In this respect, college-educated fathers are better off. Grade-school-educated fathers become uncomfortable when their children are in grade school, high-school-educated fathers when their children are adolescents, and college-educated fathers when their children are grown (Veroff & Feld, 1970).

Fathers tend to exercise more control over sons than over daughters, whereas mothers control daughters more. This distinction is particularly true for the lower classes. The more children in the family, the more controlling and authoritarian the father is and the less he is likely to communicate with his children (Walters & Stinnett, 1971). Middle-class fathers tend

to use reason in dealing with their children and to appeal to guilt. Lower-class fathers tend to use physical punishment (Rosen, 1964).

Some research has suggested that the departure of the children from the home (the empty nest) does not seem to affect fathers to the same extent that it affects mothers. However, Lurie (1972) points out that the joys as well as the difficulties of parenthood reside in interaction with children. When the children have left home and founded their own families, fathers find less conflict with them, of course. But they also derive less pleasure from them.

The oldest group of fathers in the San Francisco study (Lowenthal et al., 1975) expressed as much concern over their sons as did the oldest mothers. Of course, mothers also were concerned about their daughters. Curiously, middle-aged women were not as pleased with their mothers as they were with their fathers. If approval of one's same-sexed parents is an index of how well one likes oneself, this finding would add to the mass of data about the low self-esteem of middle-aged women. At least, it would add to the data about this cohort, which was socialized to feel that men were superior but that women should strive for the same things. Although earlier cohorts probably shared the message that men were superior, they had more consistent values. Future cohorts of women may be gradually removing some of the inconsistencies in sex-role socialization that make achieving women's lives so difficult.

Because adult-parent/adult-child interaction appears to be carried on more through the female linkage than through the male, the father of adult children may assume an even more peripheral role than he had when his children were small.

An ongoing cross-sectional study of fathers aged 45 to 80 (Nydegger & Mitteness, 1979) shows developmental changes in fathering even after their children become adults. According to the investigators, these changes are transformations, rather than losses. The number of functions fathers perform drops from eight or nine when their children are preadolescents to one or two when they are adults. No new functions are added. The first function to drop out is authority, followed by protecting, teaching, providing, and last, if at all, counseling. The one function that remains, and that is developed, is friendship. These findings thus are in agreement with those of Hagestad and Snow (1977), mentioned earlier in the book.

A national study of male kinship (Klatsky, 1972) found that the age of sons did not affect patterns of contact with fathers who lived in another city but did affect contact with fathers who lived in the same city. Contact with their fathers was lowest for men under 45. Although contact with fathers seemed higher for sons between 45 to 65, further analysis showed this was due to varying probabilities of having a living father and of sharing a household with him. When these factors were controlled, sons between 45 and 64 whose fathers lived in the same city had the lowest rate of contact with them. Apparently, middle-aged men do not feel impelled to visit fathers simply because the fathers are alone, but they do go out of their way to visit if necessary. Presumably fathers in the same city could call in emergencies, but distant fathers need surveillance. Distant fathers might also be more interesting to visit.

Parents of infants

The middle-aged subjects in the San Francisco study (Lowenthal et al., 1975) looked back to the time when their children were infants as the period of greatest parental happiness. We cannot tell how much of this effect should be attributed to the golden haze of memory, how much to the glorification of their own youth, and how much to the feeling of power they felt vis-à-vis the helpless infant.

Much research on parenting infants shows the importance of the baby's character. Mothers of more alert infants are more attentive than mothers of less alert ones (Osofsky & Danzger, 1974). Infants modulate interaction in other ways, too. For example, they avert their gaze when their mothers' stimulation is too intense (Stern, 1974). When mothers are unresponsive, infants intensify their efforts to get attention, eventually either crying or withdrawing. Talking (by the mother) or vocalizing (by the baby) is more likely to continue if either the mother or the baby responds (Vietze, Strain, & Falsey, 1975). By the end of the first year, a strong mother/infant attachment is present in most families (Ainsworth, 1969).

Even though both first-time mothers and first-time fathers are eager to hold and interact with their new babies, according to Parke and O'Leary (1975), mothers are far more likely to feed the babies, even if they are bottle-feeding. And mothers are more likely to assume all the other work, too. Shapiro's first-time mothers were highly sensitized to the babies' cries. During the first month, at least, the mothers felt that crying put a demand on them and indicated that they were not sufficiently competent. Feldman's (1971) longitudinal data show that those couples that said their babies brought them closer together were the ones who at one month had been able to handle the crying or not to feel threatened if they could not stop it. They were also likely to feed the children according to the children's needs instead of their own. Babies who cry less and smile more, who respond nicely to cuddling, and who coo on schedule are more likely to induce mothers' feelings of well-being and competence than are babies who are fretful, ill, or developing poorly (Robson & Moss, 1970).

Although the older San Francisco subjects said the infancy period was best, the older subjects interviewed by Veroff and Feld (1970) selected the preschool period as their favorite. So did the subjects in Lois Hoffman's cross-national study (Hoffman & Manis, 1978). Some writers stress mothers' resistance to and resentment of their children's growing independence and diminishing need for them. However, the small amount of research data currently available—admittedly with more recent and thus more "liberated" cohorts of mothers, who may be more eager to resume their own independence—do not bear this out. Both mothers and babies have been found to tolerate greater physical separation in public parks as the babies get older (Rheingold & Eckerman, 1970).

The degree of matching of mothers' and infants' characteristics affects much of their subsequent relationships. Parents who prefer lively babies tend to be more responsive to lively babies. Those who prefer placid babies tend to be more responsive to placid babies.

Although there is a growing body of research and theoretical literature on reciprocal parent/child interaction, most of it so far is limited to the infancy period, and to the mother/infant dyad. Lewis and Feiring (1978) feel that the addition of each new member to a family complicates family interactions. The birth of a second child, for example, adds a child/child dyad to the three dyads already existing within the child-rearing unit: mother/child, father/child, and mother/father. Of course, it also adds two new parent/child dyads, because no parent interacts with different children in the same way. Number and spacing of children have been seen to affect their IQs (Zajonc & Markus, 1975). Primiparous mothers spend much more time with, talk more with, and generally stimulate their infants more than do mothers of later-born children. Not only do mothers have less time and energy for later-born children, but also the older children in the family are likely to interfere and intervene directly in such interactions. Feldman (1971) had noted earlier that the more children there were, the lower the marital interaction frequency and the lower the marital satisfaction.

Parents of older children

Parents of older children often express negative feelings toward schools and teachers (Klein & Ross, 1958), presumably because they feel rivalry with them. An analogous effect was noticed by Veroff and Feld (1970). The less education parents had, the more discomfort, rivalry, and displacement they felt as the children got older.

Adolescents are notably difficult for their parents. They interfere with parents' privacy (Hoffman & Manis, 1978). They stay up later at night, join their parents' conversations, and are attuned to their parents' sexuality. They seem to take over the house. The middle-aged mothers in the San Francisco study (Lowenthal et al., 1975) mentioned conflict over tidiness, study habits, communication, and lackadaisical attitudes. The same parents who complained also praised, however. And very few parents would ever consider separating from their children, even their adolescent children. Both parents and adolescent children, in fact, will go to great length to maintain their family ties. Hagestad (1979) found the use of "demilitarized zones"— pacts concerning what *not* to talk about. Troll (1972a) observed an analogous strategy of being careful about what they fight over. Both college students and their parents said they fought over hairstyles and clothes (relatively trivial issues) but not over serious moral or core values.

Often the demands and burdens of child rearing are so immediate and overwhelming that

mothers do not look ahead to their inevitable ending. Most women who are approaching the "empty nest," however, do not view it as a disaster. They are more inclined to look forward to greater freedom and a new phase of life. Anyway, mothering rarely ends with the departure of the children from the home. For most, ties continue throughout life.

Parents of adults

Parents are supposed to "launch" children when they are through raising them. In our society, this time comes when children complete their education or training for economic self-sufficiency. Working-class families generally expect their children to leave when they finish high school, middle-class families when they finish college or sometimes graduate or professional school. According to the nuclear-family norms described by Parsons, parental cords should then be cut, and only formal relations should continue.

These expectations seem to be more norm than reality, however. Of young people between 18 and 25 who are not married, 60% live with their parents (Glick, 1975). (It is true, however, that this percentage was higher a decade earlier.) The frequency of visiting and helping is correspondingly high, as is the strength of affectional bonds.

Although most so-called empty-nest parents probably do not regret continued visiting and love, many parents of modern youth who have delayed marriage and child rearing have had to accommodate themselves to this divergence from expectations. Spence and Lonner (1972) suggest that they do so by "striking a bargain" in some way, often by redefining their expectations so that they feel it is all right for their children to deviate. This redefinition is an example of reciprocal socialization; the children socialize their parents into new norms. According to the discussion of generational influence in Chapter 15, some parents—those whose values are more in tune with such possibilities— may find this readjustment of expectations easier than others. In fact, children who are the most age deviant may come from such families.

In one study, of rural Pennsylvania families, both mothers and fathers report a mixture of loss and gain in launching their children (Barber, 1978). The mothers tended to be more extreme, some reporting more loss than did any men and some reporting more gain.

The gain was an increased sense of personal freedom and relief from parental responsibilities. The loss of the children in the home was often exacerbated by concurrent biological changes (menopause for women) and career changes (reported more by men). Women tended to have anticipated this event more than did men and thus to be better prepared. Some men are faced with the independence of their children just when they are beginning to be ready to get close to the children.

Barber's sample may not represent the majority of launching parents. A national survey (Borland, 1979) found no evidence for the idea that the empty nest was a crisis or even a time of loss. Other research (Hagestad & Snow, 1977) reports that most parents interviewed saw this event as a distinct gain. They gained freedom, and they also gained a new set of resource people: their children.

This latter gain was different for mothers and fathers and different for sons and daughters. As with most findings, the mother/daughter dyad was unique in many ways. One of Hagestad and Snow's (1977) respondents said "It's great! You don't have any little ones to worry about. . . . The joy of adult children is mammoth! It's a friend to a friend—sharing as adults" (p. 3). A mother said "I haven't lost a daughter, I have gained a confidante" (p. 3). Practically all the mothers and fathers felt that their now adult children were sensitive to their feelings and moods. However, mothers were about three times more likely to discuss personal problems with children as were fathers.

Three-fourths of the mothers and one-third of the fathers admitted that their children had tried to change them in some way, with at least partial success. Mothers reported influence in activities outside the home, in work, education, or leisure. In fact, several mothers reported that their children had been a major influence in the mothers' returning to work or to school. Fathers were influenced in views on current issues and also in improving their physical appearance. One father said "You know, not infrequently, I find myself in situations where I ask myself how Steve might handle it if he were me" (Hagestad & Snow, 1977, p. 4). In general, mothers were more open to being influenced than were fathers. Perhaps mothers had stronger emotional ties with their children. Although mothers were influenced more and had more intense interactions with their children, there was no sex difference in support received from children.

The mother/daughter dyad was perceived by Hagestad and Snow (1977) as the most balanced or reciprocal. The father/daughter dyad was seen as the most imbalanced, with the daughter giving much more than receiving. Mothers and daughters also saw their relationships in the same way. Their consensus was stronger than for other parent/child dyads.

Most studies have found that over 80% of present-day middle-aged and older people who have ever married have living children (for example, see Murray, 1976). It is intriguing to realize that about 10% of those over age 65 also have children who are over 65. And most adults are not at all isolated from their parents and children.

Four general kinds of information are used in the analysis of parent/adult-child relationships. The first, *residential proximity,* involves how near they live to each other. The second, *interaction frequency and type,* involves how often they visit, phone, or write to each other. The third is *mutual aid,* whether in household services, gifts, or money. The fourth, *feelings,* concerns love or obligation as well as a variety of other subtle and qualitative indexes such as valuing the family, solidarity, attachment, loyalty, transmission of values, and intrinsic meaningfulness to each other.

RESIDENTIAL NEARNESS

There is a widespread belief that emigration from "old countries" or from rural to urban environments led to separation between parents and adult children. However, historical evidence shows that, when people moved, they moved into areas where other relatives had settled earlier. After sons and daughters established themselves, they usually sent for their parents (Hareven, 1976).

Almost all surveys on residence show that older people prefer, whenever possible, to live in their own homes but near their children. This preference is particularly true if they—the parents—are still married. In a recent tabulation of 1970 U.S. Census data, 9% of those older people who live with a child are men and 81% are women. The men are more likely to have living spouses. Parents move in with children only if they do not have enough money to live alone, if their health is so poor that self-care is impossible (as with very old parents), or if their spouses have died (less frequent). It is not a favored solution.

Of people aged 65 and over who do live with their children, more are likely to live with unmarried children than with married ones, more with daughters (65%) than with sons (35%). In most of these cases, furthermore, the parent tends to be the *head of household*. The unmarried son or daughter moves in with parents—or remains with parents—rather than older parents moving in with children.

Finally, such joint households usually involve two generations, not three or more. The oldest generation moves in with a younger one usually after the grandchildren have moved out. Fewer than 8% of American households are true three-generation ones, with grandchildren in them. A recent study of three-generation households (Newman, 1976) shows mixed benefits and disadvantages. Benefits include affection, enjoyment, household help, and relief from worry. Disadvantages include reduction in social activities and loss of privacy. Nearly 60% of the adult children said there had been no change as a result of their parents moving in, however.

Although joint households are the exception rather than the rule, related nuclear households tend to be near each other, particularly among urban working-class families. Shanas, Townsend, Wedderburn, Friis, Milhoj, and Stehouwer (1968), in a study of old people in three industrial societies, found that 84% of those over 65 lived less than an hour away from one of their children. Similarly, Adams (1968) found that one-third of his North Carolina sample of young adults (average age, 33) live near their parents. However, it is hard to compare his figures with Shanas's because different kinds of measurements were used.

It may be that there is a period in the life course—when parents are middle-aged and children are beginning their own family households—when the two generations are most geographically distant. This pattern may be particularly true for middle-class families. When the parents retire and grow old, though, they may migrate to be near one of their children (Bultena & Wood, 1969). Generally, because success has been associated in our culture with frequent geographic moves, older parents whose children are not living nearby seem to be happier than those whose children do. If unsuccessful children stick around, their presence may serve as a constant reminder of their lack of success and, thus, of the parents' own lack of success in raising them properly. This explanation may be more true for fathers than for mothers, who may still enjoy having such children around (Pihlblad & Adams, 1971).

There is some evidence that people in their middle years return to the geographic areas where they grew up (Lee, 1974). In addition, when older parents need more aid in maintaining their households, some adult children move closer to them. When Gray and Smith (1960) studied migrating families, one of their incidental findings was that marital problems could be attributed to the separation of a wife from her relatives.

The desire to be close to parents and children is not only related to need for help. Recent surveys suggest that executives are not as eager to move as they used to be, and moving companies report decreases in company moving. A curious reversal of "empty-nest" feelings was reported recently in a column of the *New York Times* (Kreiss, 1979). The author wrote about her anger and grief when her parents "shook our roots loose" by selling their home in the suburban family enclave and moving to Florida. Kreiss says "They taught me the value of family, urged me to settle in town, nurtured the love of my children and then they left!" (p. C7).

INTERACTION FREQUENCY

The findings on interaction between parents and their adult children parallel those on residential proximity. Most see each other often. If, as in many middle-class families, they live too far apart for regular weekly visiting, they maintain contact by telephone and letter writing and then get together when they can for extended visits.

Shanas and her colleagues (1968) made a large-scale study of old people in three industrial countries (United States, England, and Denmark). Of the American respondents with living children, 84% had seen at least one of their children within the previous week, and 90% within the last month. Families in England and Denmark were not very different. In Hill's sample, 70% of the married young adults saw their parents weekly (Hill et al., 1970).

Often, visiting between older parents and their children involves no more than brief conversations "catching up on the time of day." Sometimes, in the case of aged parents, visiting may be a kind of monitoring—checking to see that all is well. Often such visiting also includes other activities: shopping, commercial and outdoor recreation, or religious activities. Parents and children who do not live near each other maintain contact by telephoning and letter writing; by periodically getting together for family ritual occasions such as birthdays, anniversaries, weddings, and funerals; and by exchanging visits at holidays such as Thanksgiving and Christmas, or during vacations. Types of contact vary over the life cycle. Much visiting is done by telephone even if they live nearby.

A study of newlyweds by Ryder (1968; Ryder & Goodrich, 1966) found that some have little contact with their parents, but others visit and telephone often and still use their parents' closet space, checking and charge accounts, car, and so on. Those who have the closest contacts with parents are more interested in becoming parents themselves. Those who have cut themselves off most from their parents are more interested in "expressive sexuality" and less in having children. It would be interesting to see if these patterns persist as the newlyweds get older. Aldous (1965) reports that those Minneapolis lineages that were most alike in values and behavior tended to visit each other most. Adams's (1968) Greensboro, North Carolina, parents and children, however, visited each other regardless of similarity of values.

The *visiting linkage*, like the residential linkage, is generally stronger along the female line. In fact, husbands are more likely to be in touch with their wives' parents than with their own, unless the wife arranges contact. Younger women visit their mothers more than do older women (perhaps more have mothers still living). The order of frequency of interaction among New York Jewish families is with wife's mother, husband's mother, wife's father, and husband's father (Leichter & Mitchell, 1967). Couples who remarry in old age tend to visit their children along a same-sex line, according to McKain (1969): fathers with their sons and mothers with their daughters.

AID

Mutual aid is considered by many writers to be a critical variable in determining extended-family status. Aid may be either in the form of services, such as baby-sitting, shopping, or housecleaning, or in money or money equivalents, such as gifts. For dying parents, it may also include nursing care or payment for such care. Brody (1977) estimates that 70 to 80% of the care provided old people is by their children.

A study of the kind of help old people get from their children (Bracey, 1966) found that shopping and housework were most frequent, followed by cooking and advice about financial and maintenance matters. Help was specific, not generalized. It was given when needed, not routinely.

Riley and Foner (1968) state:

Contrary to the often-held theory of a one-way flow of contributions to old people, the flow of support between aged parents and their adult offspring appears to be two-directional, from parent to child or from child to parent as need and opportunity dictate. Altogether, the proportions of old people who give help to their children tends to exceed the proportions who receive help from their children [pp. 551–552].

Their conclusion is based largely on data collected by Streib (1965) and by Shanas and her colleagues (1968).

Mutual-aid patterns differ considerably by the type of aid being exchanged. Hill's findings are shown in Table 21.4. We are usually quite willing to assume that the differential between help given and help received would be greatest in the economic sphere. Yet the grandparents got much more than they gave in other areas, such as emotional gratification, household management, and care in illness. The middle generation was the one that apparently gave the most economic aid. Hill's findings are less likely to be applicable to upper-middle-class families, where the oldest generation might continue to control the most resources.

QUALITY OF RELATIONSHIP

Proximity, interaction frequency, and mutual aid are important indices of adult parent/child

TABLE 21.4 Comparison of help received and help given by generation for chief problem areas

	Type of crisis		Emotional gratification		Household management		Type of crisis			
	Economic						Child care		Illness	
	Gave (percent)	Received (percent)	Gave (percent)	Received (percent)	Gave (percent)	Received (percent)	Gave (percent)	Received (percent)	Gave (percent)	Received (percent)
Total	100	100	100	100	100	100	100	100	100	100
Grandparents	26	34	23	42	21	52	16	0	32	61
Parents	41	17	47	37	47	23	50	23	21	21
Married children	34	49	31	21	33	25	34	78	47	18

Note: Percents may not total 100 because of rounding.

Source: Hill, Foote, Aldous, Carlson, and Macdonald, 1970.

relationships. However, qualitative aspects of such relationships, such as degree of closeness, similarities in beliefs, or strength of feelings (affection or dislike), are perhaps more revealing.

Intergenerational continuity.   Troll and Bengtson's (1979) review of the available literature on generations concludes that there is substantial but selective intergenerational continuity within the family. Parent/child similarity is most noticeable in religious and political affiliations, least in sex roles and personality. Social and historical forces—cohort and period effects—serve as moderator variables. Similarity is greater in areas where social forces encourage such values or behavior. It is less in areas where social forces counteract them. The sex of the child does not appear to be a relevant variable in parent/child similarity. In general, the relative influence of parents and friends appears to be complementary rather than oppositional. People appear to choose friends who reinforce their families' values or personality styles. Furthermore, even when they disagree, parents and children continue to see each other. Finally, the effect of parents' or children's age or position in their life courses cannot be separated from historical effects, so far as similarities between parent and child generations are concerned. Hagestad (1979) refers to a new phenomenon, *social-age peership,* in which both parents and their adult children can be students, workers, retirees, and even fathers of young children at the same time. She mentions that it now is often difficult to tell mother from daughter, both in youthfulness of appearance and in life circumstances.

Feelings.   Many writers assume that closeness is synonymous with liking or loving and that estrangement indicates negative feelings—that we love those relatives we feel close to and hate those we feel distant from. There is evidence, however, that we cannot separate positive from negative feelings this way. Where feelings run high, they are rarely only positive or only negative. Where love is to be found, so is hate.

Furthermore, there is probably an ebb and flow in most family feelings. People may feel warm and loving in the morning and neutral or hostile when they are tired or disgruntled in the evening. Adults may feel very close to their parents at the time of an anniversary or when things are going well but may feel overburdened and even hostile at other times—for example, at times of illness or economic difficulty. Parents of young children may adore them when they are asleep or are shining in a school play but may hate them when they destroy a treasured possession or are brought home by the police for doing wrong.

These intense feelings, on the part of both parents and children, can continue to swing back and forth if grown children continue to live at home. "Although years of separate residence and greater self-knowledge may erase some of the minor difficulties and blunt the edge of some of the major ones, struggles for control, patterns of blaming, disappointments about achievement and such, may linger to undermine the possibility of a comfortable relationship between parents and children in the later years," say Hess and Waring (1978, p. 251).

Times of crisis can reawaken conflict. One

might say there is a continual push and pull of attachments throughout life. Most middle-aged and older parents admit they prefer "intimacy at a distance." Their feelings of closeness carry with them a need for some separateness.

In general, most parents and children report positive feelings for each other at all ages. Even high school students rarely say they do not feel close to their own parents (Kandel & Lesser, 1972; Douvan & Adelson, 1966; Bengtson, 1970). Studies of college students (Troll et al., 1969; Bengtson & Black, 1973b) show that they and their parents may think there is a generation gap in society as a whole, but they rarely perceive such a gap in their own families. This finding was as true of student radicals as it was of more-general samples. Most middle-aged parents in the San Francisco sample (Lowenthal et al., 1975) felt good about their children. About half had only positive things to say about them. Only about 10% of the middle-aged and none of those in their 60s had any strong negative comments. Yet, when a sample of middle-aged men and women were asked about the sources of stress in their lives (Parent, 1978), both mothers and fathers put their children high on the list. Obviously, love and stress are not mutually exclusive. Mothers were concerned about a variety of children's problems; fathers were most concerned about their sons.

For older ages, Bengtson and Black (1973b) found high levels of regard reported both by old parents and by their middle-aged children. It seems that parents remain important to their children throughout the lives of the children. When adults of all ages were asked to describe a person, they tended spontaneously to refer to their parents more frequently than to any other person (Troll, 1972b). The oldest members of Troll's sample, in their 70s and 80s, were still using parents as reference people.

A Boston study (Johnson & Bursk, 1977) found a significant correlation between ratings of their relationship provided by older parents and by one of their adult children. Occasionally, parents rated their relationship to the child higher than their child had. Both generations felt better about each other when the parents were in good health and able to be financially independent. There was also a positive correlation between the ratings and the parents' positive attitudes about aging. Whether the good feelings

were engendered by absence of trouble or whether they induced better health and well-being, it is not possible to say.

Cumming and Henry (1961), with a Kansas City sample of people over age 50, were also interested in the quality of family relationships. Respondents were asked whom they felt closest to; in most cases, they felt closest to their child or children. They felt almost as close to their parents, if the parents were alive. This parental or filial attachment—with *ascendant/descendant* rather than *collateral* kin—was stronger than that toward siblings and spouse. It did not extend to grandchildren, concerning whom the feelings reported were much weaker. Grandparenting is discussed in Chapter 22.

Although friends sometimes substitute for lost siblings, they rarely substitute for missing children (Rosow, 1967). The reciprocal is also true. Dobrof and Litwak (1977) found that *adult* children who had placed their parents in nursing homes felt strained, guilty, and bereaved. Such a decision represents a state of crisis to the family (Tobin & Kulys, 1979) and reawakens many old issues. It is not uncommon for the sibling who has been least loved by the parent to emerge as the caretaker because of that sibling's wish to try for that love one more time, even at the cost of much sacrifice.

We have said that the transitions of aging reawaken many old feelings. Hess and Waring (1978) mention imbalances between socialized expectations for particular kinds of help and societal value shifts that stress other practices. They also mention the unhappiness of older people who must depend on the largess of their former subordinates (their children) even though their own self-images are based on mastery and independence. This shift would therefore be even harder for men in our society than for women, and harder for authoritarian parents than for more democratic ones. Most parents gradually relinquish control over adult children, although they usually end up as friends. When the needs of one family member conflict with those of another, the self-absorption of each can limit helping or can generate resentment, as in the case of a mother who becomes widowed when her daughter is in the process of divorce.

In helping aging parents, offspring also rehearse for their own futures. Conversely, the aging parents, having already lived through middle-age transitions, can serve as role models and sources of advice. In many ways, adult offspring have an "anticipatory stake" (Waring, 1975) in their parents' aging gracefully just as parents have a "developmental stake" (Bengtson & Kuypers, 1971) in their children developing successfully.

Kulys and Tobin (1978) interviewed old (over 70) Chicago people and the children they had designated as "responsible others" when they needed help. The study unearthed some interesting feelings. Of these children, 20% said they did not feel their parents understood them. Yet they tended to feel that they would know their parents' wishes in the event of a parent's serious illness. There seemed to be less explicit communication of future concerns by the parents, but more explicit understanding by the children. The investigators felt that this finding may be related to the finding that parents wish more emotional closeness, while their children would rather perform instrumental tasks. Altogether, there was less agreement between parent/child dyads than between parent/nonchild pairs on such issues as closeness, willingness to sacrifice, and giving help or advice. These findings differ from those of investigations of middle-aged parents and their children. It is obviously easier to feel close to parents who are not in need. In fact, perhaps the very emotional nature of many parent/child relationships makes children the worst possible caretakers of their parents.

Duty.   Not all relations between parents and their children are characterized by affection and emotional ties. Many times, feelings of obligation or a sense of duty underlie care. There may be shame that others would consider one delinquent in expected duties, or there may be a more internalized guilt. For example, Lozier and Althouse (1974) found that in one Appalachian community adult children were heavily involved with their parents because they knew that negative community opinion would follow from failure to meet their obligations.

Kohlberg (1973) sees the higher states of moral development as resulting from having had to make irrevocable moral decisions or choices. Adult children may achieve filial maturity when they must assume responsibility for some aspects of their parents' lives and must live with the results of acting on related decisions. In helping parents, children often learn more about them. It is much less easy to assume that you "know" someone when you must create conditions that will fit that person's attitudes and preferences.

Blenkner (1965) believes that filial maturity occurs in middle age. At this point, we first see our parents as real people. Erikson (1959) also speaks of middle age as the time of changing perspective in feelings toward our parents, when we can first truly appreciate them and see the relevance of their lives for our own lives. So far, there is little research evidence for this assumption.

Adams (1968), who compared friendship and kinship ties in terms of Parsons's interaction theory, postulated that relations between kin are dominated by intimacy and *positive concern*. These attributes lead to feelings of obligation or duty and tend to persist over time, spatial separation, and occupational mobility. Relations with friends, on the other hand, are characterized by *value consensus*. While friendships may be more desired at the moment, they less often persist over time and mobility. Adams compared the interactions reported by his North Carolina respondents with their best friends, parents, nearest-age sibs, and best-known cousins. Interactions with parents were the closest and most obligatory, and those with friends were the highest in value consensus. Interactions with sibs were in the middle. We need further research into qualitative differences in relationships both in and out of the family. Until then, we can only speculate about the significance of a parent/child attachment that may persist throughout life and that may be transferred to the next generation of parents and children, but not to more-peripheral relationships—even sibs and even grandchildren.

Adams (1968) found that, when parents lived nearby, affectional closeness had little effect on interaction frequency. Neither affection nor agreement on values influenced visiting frequency. Among "close" sons, one-third saw their parents often; among "distant" sons, one-third saw their parents often. Yet the reasons for keeping in touch varied according to the degree of affectional closeness to either or both parents. Obligation or a combination of obligation and enjoyment were much more frequent reasons given by children who said they did not feel close to either parent. Children who felt close to one or both parents were more likely to say they visited because of enjoyment or because of a combination of enjoyment and obligation.

The obligatory motive in interaction between aged parents and their adult children is commonly assumed. For example, Schorr (1960) speaks of filial obligation or responsibility and at one point equates the adult-offspring/older-parent situation with the parent/young-child situation. In both, a balance must be achieved between family obligations and aid. When a mother is widowed, contacts with her children increase for a time. In the long run, the mother/daughter relationship is smoother and closer than the mother/son relationship. Perhaps mothers and daughters can reciprocate services, but mothers and sons cannot. Consequently, mutual enjoyment and affection between mothers and sons tend to decrease following the mother's widowhood.

Few widowed mothers wish to move in with daughters, however. Lopata (1973) explains this finding as partly due to the mother's reluctance to become a subordinate in someone else's house—perhaps particularly her daughter's. She may also be reluctant to get involved anew in child rearing. Sons of widows were more likely than daughters to say that they kept in touch because they enjoyed the contact. Both sons and daughters, however, said that they felt less close to their parent than before their parent's widowhood. Does an increased feeling of obligation act to diminish closeness? Is the possibility of reviving early mother/son intimacy threatening to both? Middle-aged mothers admit that they feel differently about their sons and daughters. They expect more interaction and help from their daughters and are upset when they don't get it. They expect much less from their sons and are delighted with anything they get (Hagestad, 1977).

Sex and birth-order differences

Sex and birth order function as intertwined influences on maternal behavior (Walters & Stinnett, 1971). Boys are allowed to ask for more comforting and get more praise, particularly if they are firstborn. In general, mothers are more involved with first children—more likely to give them help and more anxious that they do well. They more often praise firstborn boys (and second-born girls), and they more often tell firstborn girls (and second-born boys) that they have done wrong. They control daughters more than they do sons. But love and affection do not differ by birth order. They love one child as much as another, even if they treat the children differently—or so they say.

Whether a mother loves or hates a child is a more persistent influence over the child's life than whether she is permissive or controlling (Bayley, 1964). A mother who loves her children when they are infants or preschoolers will continue to love them in adolescence. But she may be very controlling when the children are preschoolers and much more permissive when they are adolescents. Mothers of boys show even greater consistency in loving or hostility over time than do mothers of girls. But they show less consistency in controlling behavior. That is, their control over girls does not decrease as much when they get older as does their control over boys, who are more readily released from the nest. Fathers, however, tend to be more permissive toward daughters than toward sons, particularly with regard to both aggression and dependency (Rothbart & Maccoby, 1966). Parents whose sex roles are highly differentiated are more permissive with opposite-sexed children. Thus traditional "feminine" mothers are more permissive with their sons, and traditional "masculine" fathers are more permissive with their daughters.

Hoffman and Manis (1978) report that parents in general are more worried about daughters than about sons, particularly when they are adolescent. Their primary concern is still the traditional one about sexuality. Sometimes they worry about daughters' reputation, sometimes about their vulnerability to sexual attack, sometimes about premarital pregnancy.

As suggested earlier, the adult-child/older-parent relationship may be influenced by whether the relationship is mother/daughter, mother/son, father/daughter, or father/son. The literature is fairly consistent about the solidarity among women in the family; from adulthood on, mother/daughter ties tend to be stronger than mother/son ties. Among the second-generation Italians in Boston studied by Gans (1962), the mother/married-daughter tie is the only viable cross-generational one. With this exception, kinship interaction tends to be confined to relatives of the same sex *and* same generation.

Lowenthal and her associates (1975) report that both men and women—in every age group—said they felt closer to their mothers almost twice as often as they said they felt close to their fathers. However, women in their 50s and 60s experienced more-satisfying relationships with their daughters, and older men preferred their oldest sons. When Tobin and Kulys (1979) asked people over 70 whom they would name as the "person responsible," most widows named a child. If a son was named as the responsible other, usually he would not be named as the person to whom the mother felt closest. If a daughter was named, she would be put into both categories—responsible and close.

Not all research has found as strong a sex link as did Lowenthal. Adams (1968) found relatively little sex differentiation in kinship interrelations except for patterns of mutual aid. Greensboro, North Carolina, women shopped with their mothers and *received* babysitting and gifts. More men than women *gave* help in both money and services (work in the house) to their parents and joined them in out-of-the-home recreation. Similarly, Albrecht (1962) found no preference for sharing rituals with the mother's side of the family over the father's side in a middle-class sample of 252 extended families, one-third of which included people over age 70.

Maas and Kuypers (1974) found a variety of parent/child relationships among mothers. To begin with, and contrary to other findings, only about 21% had very high satisfaction and involvement with their adult children. About 65% had relatively low involvement with their children (compared to other involvements), and 13% of the older mothers even had strained parent/child relationships.

A final note on sex differences is provided by Adams's (1968) finding that, even though women may not agree with their parents' values, they still feel close to them and visit them often. This pattern is less true for men. Adams also found a curious sex difference in feelings about parents. Daughters' affections for their fathers were related to their fathers' occupational positions. They appreciated their fathers more if the

fathers had higher status. Sons, however, related to their mothers in terms of the sons' own status. The more successful the son, the more he appreciated his mother.

Social-class and ethnic differences

Patterns of child rearing vary among different social classes. But what is middle-class behavior in one generation may become working-class behavior a generation later. Less educated mothers feel particularly negative about their parental role. They are less likely to have planned their maternity, are more often raising their children without a husband, and are likely to have more children than they want. Yet college-educated mothers don't come off much better, for they have higher standards for achievement all around. They must be perfect mothers, and their children must be outstanding children.

The importance people attach to having children affects the satisfactions they derive from them. Value systems also affect socialization practices. Three kinds of practices were observed by Baumrind (1972) when she visited the homes of 150 four-year-olds. She labeled their parents authoritarian, authoritative, or permissive. The *authoritarian* parents gave their children little leeway; children had to follow the rules laid down by the parents without explanation, discussion, or discretion. The *authoritative* parents gave their children reasons for the rules and permission to question them, although they also insisted on obedience. The *permissive* parents were generally accepting of all behavior by children, unless it led to physical harm.

Value systems such as those Baumrind described are related to social class. Working-class parents place higher priority on conformity (Kohn, 1969). Middle-class parents want the children to learn how to make their own judgments and decisions. Working-class parents are more apt to discipline their children on the basis of direct and immediate consequences of their children's acts or for refusing to do what they are told. Middle-class parents are more likely to discipline on the basis of the children's intent.

Less educated parents are more likely than are college-educated parents to see children as an asset to their marriages (Hoffman & Manis, 1978). However, social-class, education, or ethnic differences are not generally as significant as sex differences when family relationships among adults are concerned.

In middle-class samples, considerable help continues to flow from old parents to middle-aged children down the generation line. Among blue-collar families, more help goes from middle-aged children to old parents as well as to young-adult children. Working-class parents give services, middle-class parents give financial aid. Giving services is restricted to children or parents who live nearby, but financial help is not as geographically limited. Therefore, middle-class families are not as affected by geographic mobility as are working-class families. Thus, Litwak's (1960) proposition that the modified extended family continues to give family aid despite geographic separation may be more appropriate for middle-class than working-class populations. However, Adams does suggest that, because it is usually easier for working-class people than for middle-class people to find jobs nearby, they are not likely to move far from kin unless they are already estranged. Middle-class families sometimes find it necessary to move about in order to establish careers, no matter how they may feel about leaving their relatives and even if they tend to return close to them again later. There is even a value difference that flows from this: middle-class families expect scattering of relatives; working-class families feel punished by scattering.

Sex segregation is stronger in working-class families. Fathers are closer to sons, and mothers are closer to daughters. This trend runs counter to the more general pattern of female sex linkage. When Dykers (1974) questioned foreign students attending a U.S. university, he found that those roughly classified as Western (North and South American and European) felt that their mothers' families were more important. Students roughly classified as Eastern (African and Asian) felt that their fathers' families were more important.

Variations among Black, Anglo, and Hispanic groups in the United States complicate the social-class patterns to which they are tied. More middle-class Black and Hispanic families live in separate dwellings and provide help down the generational line than do lower-class and poorer families (Jackson, 1977; Cantor, 1977). Furthermore, the more "manual" the work done by the Black family, the stronger its female gen-

erational linkage. What poorer Black families can provide for their young-adult children, such as more education, more often goes to daughters than to sons. Cantor's study of New York City elderly found that the Spanish were the most likely to have ongoing contact with at least one child, as compared with White and Black residents. A smaller study of Hispanic families living in Kansas (Bastida, 1978) used more-discriminative measures of ethnicity. This study found that more-"ethnic" families—those with no intermarriage, who spoke Spanish, who shared values, and so on—were most likely to maintain cross-generational association. It is interesting to note, however, that almost none of these families lived in joint households. In the absence of ill health and poverty, the American pattern of independent households prevails. It also mattered which sex had married outside the group: if women did, there was less change in family behavior than if men did.

Divorce

The number of children involved in all divorces has been increasing steadily. But the average per couple has been declining, probably as a result of declining birthrates (Glick, 1979).

Of the 77 million children of all ages living with ever-married parent(s) in 1970: 55 million lived with both parents (who had been) married (only) once; 11 million lived with one divorced parent (7 million of whom were formerly divorced but currently remarried); 3 million lived with two formerly divorced but currently remarried parents; 4 million others lived with one or both parents currently or formerly widowed, and 4 million lived with a parent married once but currently separated [Glick & Norton, 1975, p. 1].

In spite of the large numbers of children affected by divorce and the consequences for their future development—we know that they are more likely to get divorced themselves, for example—there is remarkably little research on reconstituted families or parenting after divorce. One significant study was done by Hetherington, Cox, and Cox (1976). They found that, during the period of divorce between separation and decree, the parents are too absorbed in themselves and each other (see Chapter 20) to be interested in parenting. The children are most neglected at this time. One year after the divorce is final, however, the mother tends to become much more concerned about the behavior of the children and "cracks down" on them with increased discipline. At the same time, the father—who generally is not around as much—becomes increasingly indulgent, apparently in an effort to tighten the waning ties with his children. Two years after the decree, the father has virtually disappeared from the scene, usually remarrying and becoming involved in a new family. The mother, left with the major responsibility for the children and no longer having to react against the father's indulgence, returns to a more balanced kind of parenting, resulting in a more harmonious parent/child interaction.

If the mother remarries, though, new turmoil can occur. The new man in the picture may be resented as an interloper trying to undermine the children's loyalty to their own father. The stepfather's attempts at "true fathering" can lead to angry rebellion. If the children are adolescent, the aura of sexuality between the newly married partners can be disturbing to children who are trying to adjust to their own awakening sexual feelings. The remarried mother is happy, but the home scene is not. We know even less about what happens to other family ties. Divorce after the children are adult may have other consequences, but again we have only questions.

The rise in single-parent households poses many questions. In 1978, 19% of the 63 million noninstitutionalized children in the United States were living with only one parent (Glick, 1979). Of these, 90% were living with mothers. Two-thirds of these single-parent children had divorced or separated parents; the other third had either a widowed parent or a never-married one. A trend of the 1970s toward mothers keeping children born out of wedlock—part of the "sexual revolution"—has added another group of single mothers. Heretofore, this pattern had been largely confined to Black or lower-class families, so that evaluating such families was confounded by other kinds of deprivations. One question we have for future research is the efficacy of single parenting, inside or outside of extended-kin networks. Is it only in divorced families that parenting is better by one consistent person than by two discordant people?

The handful of studies on single parents, mostly middle-class, show curious similarities between men and women (De Frain & Eirick,

1979) and a few significant differences. Among the similarities are the dedication and commitment to their children. Although fathers said they dated, many did not consider cohabitation because it would not be good for their children. In fact, one of their greatest concerns was sex education and female models for their daughters.

Another similarity between men and women as single parents is the time and work pressure created by trying to balance jobs and child raising. Another is the feeling that family life is better now than during the stormy period of separation and divorce. Perhaps the most striking difference is the connection with kin. Most studies of single mothers show that such mothers receive help from grandmothers or other women in the extended family. All the studies of single fathers (De Frain & Eirick, 1979; Gasser & Taylor, 1976; Mendes, 1976) report a preference for day-care centers and nurseries for preschool children, as opposed to in-home care, whether by housekeepers or relatives.

The single fathers studied tended to have more money than did single mothers, a finding that agrees with income differences and alimony-payment information mentioned earlier. They are also, therefore, more likely to stay in their previous homes, while single mothers are more likely to move to apartments in new communities. Although the fathers as well as mothers mention problems with dating and friendship, men's problems in this area may have a different quality. Men are more in demand even if they have children to take care of. In fact, because men have greater options for remarriage, those who have not yet remarried may represent a skewed sample.

Summary

There have been periodic fluctuations in age of parents at birth of first child. A secular trend for earlier mothering and fathering was reversed in the last decade, along with the trend toward decreasing number of child-free couples and never-married people.

In spite of a new ideology of parenting shared by the mother and father, research still shows that this shared interest ends after pregnancy and birth, with mothers taking over thereafter.

First-time parenting is different from later parenting, particularly for most present-day parents who had little experience in their earlier life in taking care of children. Men who become parents at an older age tend to be happier with parenting than are those who become parents in adolescence or early adulthood. Trying to combine parenting and a job is strenuous.

Parents see both positive and negative consequences of having children. Undoubtedly, their expectations for what their children should be, combined with the match in temperament between them and their children, lead to variations in the pleasure of parenting. Three general styles of parenting have been noted: authoritarian, authoritative, and permissive. As children develop, the amount of parental control decreases, although less so for daughters than for sons.

Parental love remains constant, however, probably throughout life. In general, the parent/child bond remains strong, its weakest period probably being at the time the children are late adolescents and young adults, before they themselves get married. Most parents say they have not lost children in the "empty-nest" process but gained friends. Older parents live within a half hour of at least one of their children and visit them on the average twice a week. If they live geographically distant, they phone, write, and visit—less often but for longer duration. Help is exchanged whenever needed. The feeling tone of contact is better when the parents' health and income are sufficient to minimize burdens on children. Some adult children pay attention to old parents more out of obligation than affection. Mothers are closer to their daughters throughout life, although perhaps they are fonder of sons. Sons are more likely to interact with their parents out of affection; daughters, more often out of duty.

With increased divorces, there are more single parents. The vast majority are mothers, who must support and raise their children. When men are single fathers, they are as concerned with their children as are single mothers, and they are generally better off economically.

22

The Rest of the Family

Dyads (the primary focus of Chapters 18 through 21) are not isolated from the rest of the family but are interconnected in complex ways. Dyads have been set off conceptually from general family relationships by a number of family theorists: dyads versus dependency relationships (Gewirtz, 1972); intimate connections versus group solidarity (Bengtson & Black, 1973b); and dyads versus multiple networks (Lowenthal & Robinson, 1976). These distinctions revolve around the nature of the bonds between people and assume that two-person bonds are closest.

This chapter shifts to a more general consideration of the extended family—the network of people whom we distinguish from those who are not kin. A major problem is the lack of differentiation among various categories of kin. Kin are contrasted with friends, business associates, social workers, neighbors, and so forth. Husbands, wives, siblings, parents, and children are in the same category as are second cousins and great-aunts. Figure 17.1 (p. 276) shows that, as far as size of social network is concerned, kin represent the largest proportion of the network for both men and women and at all ages. But *kin* does not necessarily refer to parents and children.

Twenty years ago, in a book called *Family Worlds*, Hess and Handel (1959) pictured the family as a bounded universe whose members "inhabit a world of their own making, a community of feeling and fantasy, action and precept" (p. 1). Within families, there is "congruence of images which result from commonality of experience." There is a *family theme*, de-

fined as a "pattern of feelings, motives, fantasies, and conventionalized understandings grouped about some locus of concern that has a particular form in the personalities of the individual members."

The family system, according to this model, has two major dimensions: a family theme and family integration. The more pervasive the family theme among family members, the more integrated that family should be. As noted earlier, family members not only tend to share values with each other more than with unrelated members of their own generation, but they also marry people who share their values. In families where the boundary fence is low, no clear distinction is made between family members and people outside the family, such as friends. In other families, the boundary fence is high. Family "secrets" must be kept from "outsiders." In low-fence families, celebrations and rituals can include as many nonkin as kin. In high-fence families, rituals are private. (Ask the people you know whom they would invite to the wedding if they were getting married; the variation should be fascinating.)

This chapter deals with three elements of the extended-family network: grandparents, siblings, and "other relatives."

Grandparents

The word *grandparent* suggests an old person. Yet many grandparents are not old, and the important information about old people is not usually that they are grandparents. Some sociologists consider grandparenting an almost-empty role: no clear set of rights and duties is attached to grandparenting (Hess & Waring, 1978). It is ambiguous. Grandparents are not differentiated from great-grandparents, nor grandmothers from grandfathers. It is true that the inequities of longevity and of age at birth of oldest child result in the fact that there are more grandmothers than grandfathers. This imbalance is so marked that some writers feel that the attributes of grandparenting are "feminine." Some even say that grandfathers must become maternal at least in their behavior toward their grandchildren, because mothers welcome help more than do fathers.

AVAILABILITY

Grandparenting has become a phenomenon of middle age rather than of old age. Earlier marriage, earlier childbirth, and longer life expectancy over several cohorts have produced a generation of grandparents as young as their 40s. These grandparents, because their children tended to be closely spaced, are truly grandparents in identity. They are not, at the same time, parents of young children. The increase of families that have three and four and five generations has made many grandparents the second or third generation in the family, rather than the first. That is, they are not the oldest living generation. Furthermore, grandmothers as well as grandfathers now tend to be employed. The rocking-chair image is obsolete, and its disappearance may have far-reaching consequences for child and adult socialization as well as family interaction. A woman of 50 or 60 can be caring for an elderly mother of 70 or 80 and can simultaneously be involved with her children and grandchildren. She is bound to be divided in her loyalties toward the various generations in her family.

About three-fourths of people over 65 in the United States have living grandchildren. And three-fourths of these grandparents see their grandchildren at least every week or two; nearly half see their grandchildren every day or so (Harris & Associates, 1975). Few grandparents live in the same households as do grandchildren, however. Only about 5% of the households headed by older people contain grandchildren (Atchley, 1977). Typical grandparents are likely to live near grandchildren and to see them often, but not to live with them. Today, when people become grandparents, they still feel youthful and are likely to be working. These patterns affect intergenerational relationships. Many grandparents, in fact, may not become heavily involved with grandparenting until they are great-grandparents, when they are more likely to be retired and in the position of the old-fashioned "granny."

TYPES

Neugarten and Weinstein (1964) found five different styles of grandparenting:

1. *Formal grandparent.* In this style, there are clear demarcations between parents' and grandparents' roles. Grandparents only provide special treats and occasional minor services.
2. *Fun seeker.* Grandparenting is a leisure activity or a self-indulgence.
3. *Surrogate parent.* This pattern is mostly followed by grandmothers when the mothers work or are incapacitated.
4. *Reservoir of family wisdom.* This style is mostly followed by grandfathers who are dispensers of special skills.
5. *Distant figure.* The grandparent is a benevolent but infrequent visitor who emerges from the shadows on holidays and ritual occasions.

Young grandparents are diverse: some are fun seekers, and some are distant figures. Older grandparents tend to be formal or distant. Cross-cultural data (Apple, 1956) show that when grandparents are removed from family authority they have egalitarian, indulgent, or warm relationships with their grandchildren. When they retain economic power and prestige, their relationships are more authoritarian and formal.

Relationships with grandparents in fragmented and reconstituted families have so far received little research attention. If divorce rates continue to rise, the surrogate-parent role may loom larger in the future, particularly among grandparents on the maternal side. Divorced and widowed mothers and sometimes fathers turn to their own mothers for help. In our own country, lower-class Black grandmothers and those in other ethnic groups have a much more central role than in middle-class White families. Widowed grandmothers run households and care for children while the other adults work.

GRANDPARENTING PROBLEMS AND FOSTER GRANDPARENTS

Dominant grandparents may compete with their children for the grandchildren's love and attention. At least, their children may perceive them as competitors. They may conflict over child-rearing practices. Remember that there was more generational change in child-rearing values and practices between the grandparents and middle-aged parents in Hill and his associates' (1970) three-generation study than in any other area. In ethnic groups undergoing rapid acculturation, this area can be in the forefront of generational differences and conflicts. It is less likely to be a problem in stable cultures.

An opposite kind of problem occurs in families in which grandparents want to be free of child rearing and thus resent their children's assumption that they—the grandparents—would love to be baby-sitters on short notice (Lopata, 1973). Hess and Waring (1978) suggest that arrangements in which a group of grandparents provide cooperative care to a group of grandchildren would minimize this kind of problem.

Foster grandparenting is a successful example of this kind of group arrangement, although it has been used primarily in the care of deprived or retarded children (Saltz, 1970). The employment of poverty-level retirees, both men and women, as surrogate grandparents to emotionally deprived children alleviates some symptoms such children traditionally display, such as depression, lowered intellectual functioning, and social immaturity. It is even more beneficial to the foster grandparents, who become attached to their "grandchildren" and hate to lose a day at work, defying blizzards, poor bus connections, unsafe streets, and their own ailments in pursuit of such contact. An analogous program that employed adolescent "dropouts" as foster grandchildren to institutionalized older people both improved the morale of the old and "straightened out" the young. An extension of this program to "normal" children could be good.

Recently, the New York State Court ruled that grandparents are entitled to visit their grandchildren following the parents' divorce.

The local newspaper's headline was "Rights of Grandparents Recognized." We have no idea how many grandparents grieve the loss of their grandchildren in this divorce-ridden era. Fathers' rights are still at issue in many courts; grandparents' rights have just begun to be considered.

The recent trend toward delayed marriage and childbirth has resulted in many middle-aged parents who complain that their children don't seem to be going to make them grandparents. This delay is most characteristic of the "forerunner" cohort of youth, and many of these middle-aged parents are involved with their spouses and their jobs. Therefore, they are probably not referring to a feeling of being deprived of the joys of playing with or caring for grandchildren. Instead, they are voicing dismay at the nonnormative behavior of their children, which in turn reflects on their own adequacy as parents.

Grandparenting, says Robertson (1977a), has both a *function* and a *person* dimension. It is a contingent personal relationship because the importance of a particular grandparent and grandchild to each other depends in large part on their linkage through the middle generation. The mediating generation determines how often the other generations see each other, what they are told about each other, and, implicitly, how they should feel about each other.

Neugarten and Weinstein (1964) said grandparenting was an earned, not an ascribed, status. Grandparents' functions can include establishing a feeling of roots and extending the family lineage. If no living grandparents are present at family ritual occasions such as births, weddings, holiday celebrations, and funerals, another member of the grandparents' generation is often invited to fill that gap. These functions are remarkably peripheral, however. Both Hagestad (1979) and Robertson (1977a) feel that the grandparent role must be *created* in each family. The particular characteristics of the family system and the personalities of its members are important factors—perhaps more important than in parenting, where norms are much clearer.

Grandparents as individuals are important role models. Young people who know their grandparents and great-grandparents tend to have less "age prejudice" than those who do not know their grandparents. Not only do they make the age spectrum wider, but they also present a larger canvas of interpersonal relations. Grandparents treat children differently from parents, and great-grandparents differently again. Furthermore, the relationships among multiple parent/child and grandparent/grandchild combinations enhance the complexity of models for future—and also present—interactions with others in the world.

Younger grandchildren—up to about age 10—are usually closer to their grandparents than are older grandchildren and adults, and this feeling is reciprocal. Older people enjoy their youngest grandchildren because these grandchildren are likely to be the most responsive. Older grandchildren are less patient and more involved in their own activities.

Grandchildren's preference for grandparental behavior varies with the age of the grandchild (Kahana & Kahana, 1970). Four- and five-year-olds value their grandparents most if they are indulgent; and eight- and nine-year-olds value

their grandparents most if the grandparents share in fun. The eleven- and twelve-year-olds appear more distant from their grandparents. Perhaps Neugarten and Weinstein's formal or distant grandparent would suit these grandchildren best. Table 22.1 shows rankings of favorite grandparent; Table 22.2 shows the reasons grandchildren give for their rankings. Mother's mother is the consistent favorite, across all ages. This preference seems to hold true around the world (Dykers, 1974). Furthermore, grandparents' best road to favor is through indulgence.

INFLUENCE

Attachment to grandparents does not end when the grandchildren reach adulthood. Nearly three-fourths of a sample of single young adults said that grandparents were very influential in their lives (Robertson, 1977b). Hagestad (1977) obtained information from both grandpar-

TABLE 22.1 Favorite grandparent

Favorite grandparent	Ages 4–5 N = 19	Ages 8–9 N = 33	Ages 11–12 N = 33	χ^2
Mother's mother	42.1	36.4	21.2	15.40[a]
Mother's father	15.8	15.2	6.0	
Father's mother	15.8	3.0	6.0	
Father's father	5.3	6.0	6.0	
No preference	15.8	18.2	48.5	
No information	5.3	21.2	12.1	
Total	100.1	100.0	99.8	

[a]$p<.05$.

Note: All values are percentages except χ^2 (chi square).

Source: Kahana and Kahana, 1970.

TABLE 22.2 Grandchildren's favorite styles of grandparenting

Styles of grandparenting	Ages 4–5 N = 19	Ages 8–9 N = 33	Ages 11–12 N = 33	χ^2
Indulgent	42.1	18.2	33.3	45.75[a]
Intimate/affective	5.3	3.0	6.1	
Fun sharing	5.3	30.3	9.1	
Instructive	0.0	3.0	0.0	
Familiar	10.6	3.0	12.1	
Global nonspecific	10.6	0.0	21.2	
No information or preference	26.3	42.4	18.2	
Total	100.2	99.9	100.0	

[a]$p<.001$.

Note: All values are percentages except χ^2 (chi square).

Source: Kahana and Kahana, 1970.

ents and their grandchildren that not only replicates Robertson's findings but also shows that cross-generational ties are much stronger than previously found. Both generations admitted trying to influence the other, and both admitted being influenced by the other.

Among the 80 dyads Hagestad studied, one-half saw each other at least several times a month and the other twice monthly or less, but at least several times a year. The majority of grandparents said that their bonds to grandchildren were strong and positive. Grandmothers rated the amount of "warmth" as high more frequently than did grandfathers: 42% of grandmothers as compared with 22% of grandfathers. Maternal grandparents were closer than paternal grandparents; this finding agrees with other findings. Thus, the sex of both grandparents and grandchildren is important. Grandsons receive equal influencing attempts from both grandfathers and grandmothers; granddaughters receive more than twice as many attempts from grandmothers. In fact, nearly half of the grandfathers said they made no attempt to influence granddaughters. From the grandchildren's perspective, though, sex is not significant: they see equal influencing attempts by both grandfather and grandmother. In line with almost all sex differences found, grandmothers and granddaughters are more accurate in assessing each others' influencing than are the men. Grandfathers underreported their influencing attempts and also differentiated more between grandsons and granddaughters.

Grandmothers cover a wide range of topics in their influencing attempts: lifestyle, work and education, and interpersonal issues. Grandfathers mostly confine themselves to work and education. A minority confine themselves to lifestyle and primarily direct their efforts to their grandsons. One grandfather's comment illustrates this: "These [the topics suggested in the interview] aren't logical subjects. Grandfathers and grandsons don't talk about people" (p. 10). Hagestad also comments that the grandchildren tended to idealize their grandparents; she quotes a grandson, "He knows everything: I can't explain it—He knows river boat schedules in Europe!" (p. 10).

Hagestad's investigation was of three-generation Chicago families (a grandparent, both parents, and a grandchild). She did not look at other relatives. Adams's (1968) North Carolina respondents reported that they interacted with aunts and uncles more frequently than with grandparents and cousins. Only 10% interacted with grandparents more than with other secondary kin (such as cousins and aunts). Adams, however, did not control for availability, such as how many of the adults he studied still had grandparents living. The North Carolina adults may have had as close relationships with their grandparents as the Chicago young adults, but they had even closer ones with aunts and uncles. The Chicago grandchildren may have had even closer relations with aunts and uncles than with grandparents. In other words, the two studies, which focus on different issues, are more in agreement than not.

Hill's (Hill et al., 1970) major study of three-generation families of adults in Minneapolis was more like Hagestad's than like Adams's in that it did not ask about collateral relatives. It found that interaction among all three generations was significant and continuous, with middle-generation women serving as a lineage bridge. Hill and his associates comment "To function in three generation depth the modified extended family network would seem to require an active 'kin-keeping' middle generation" (p. 62). The intergenerational visiting patterns found in the Minneapolis study are shown in Table 22.3. Half of the grandchildren visited their grandparents at least monthly, with the women of both generations showing a slight edge, but not a large one (56% versus 50%). The fact that the members of these families all resided in the same area is relevant, of course. Also, these young couples visited less with their grandparents than with their parents.

Just as parent/child relationships are affected by the respective "generational stakes" hypothesized by Bengtson and Kuypers (1971), so may be grandparent/grandchild relationships. The future presumably being even more foreshortened for grandparents than for the middle generation, grandparents' wish for continuity through their descendants may be even greater than that of middle-aged parents. Their reports may thus tend to exaggerate the closeness of their ties to their grandchildren. Similarly, the desire for uniqueness of identity and autonomy may make the grandchildren minimize the importance of their relations with older family generations.

Robertson (1976) studied 86 young-adult grandchildren, ages 18 to 26. Nearly all had positive attitudes toward their grandparents but

TABLE 22.3 Intergenerational visiting according to gender

	Parent/Grandparents		Child/Parents		Child/Grandparents	
	Male	Female	Male	Female	Male	Female
Number of cases	33	46	31	48	31	48
Daily	6%	15%	32%	21%	6%	6%
Weekly	30	39	42	48	26	35
Monthly	52	39	23	25	16	15
Quarter-yearly	9	6	—	6	36	33
Yearly	3	—	3	—	16	10

Note: Percentage totals do not always add to 100, because of rounding. Dashes indicate no data.

Source: Hill, Foote, Aldous, Carlson, and Macdonald, 1970.

expected little from them except emotional gratification. More than half said they enjoyed being with them and felt they would help them if necessary. Robertson's subjects, unlike Hagestad's, did not seek out their grandparents as companions, advice givers, role models, financial resources, or liaisons between themselves and their parents, however. Recreation was notably within the same generation.

Gilford and Black (1972) found that geographic separation, which is not an important variable in the adult relationship between parents and children who had once lived together, is important in grandparent/grandchild relationships. The effect of separation is not simple, however. Grandparents' feelings toward their grandchildren have a direct effect on the feelings of the grandchildren who live nearby. But if they live apart, their relationship is contingent on the intervening parent/child dyadic bonds. In other words, grandparents who have close ties with their children, regardless of geographic separation, are likely to be important to their grandchildren even if they do not see each other often.

Hays and Mindel (1973) compared Black and White young-adult parents on kin contact. They found greater contact with grandparents, siblings, cousins, aunts, and uncles among the Black respondents than among the White. Thus, Black extended-kin networks may be stronger than White networks. Unfortunately, as noted earlier, most studies on Black/White differences do not control for social class.

SIGNIFICANCE FOR LIFE SATISFACTION

In spite of visiting and interacting, however, grandparenting is of peripheral importance for many older people. It is not a central source of their identity or life satisfaction. Variation is large in every aspect of grandparental functioning, as shown by the Neugarten and Weinstein data in Table 22.4.

Although a clear majority of the grandparents expressed comfort and pleasure in the role, nearly a third were uncomfortable enough to mention this discomfort to the interviewer. The sources of discomfort or disappointment includ-

TABLE 22.4 Ease of role performance, significance of role, and style of grandparenting in 70 pairs of grandparents

	Grand-mothers (N = 70)	Grand-fathers (N = 70)
Ease of role performance		
Comfortable/pleasant	59%	61%
Difficulty/discomfort	36	29
Insufficient data	5	10
Significance of the grandparent role		
Biological renewal and/or continuity	42[a]	23[a]
Emotional self-fulfillment	19	27
Serving as resource person to child	4	11
Vicarious achievement through child	4	4
Remote: little effect on the self	27	29
Insufficient data	4	6
Style of grandparenting		
Formal grandparent	31	33
Fun-seeker	29	24
Parent surrogate	14[a]	0[a]
Reservoir of family wisdom	1	6
Distant figure	19	29
Insufficient data	6	8

[a]The difference between grandmothers and grandfathers in this category is reliable at or beyond the .05 level (frequencies were tested for differences of proportions, using the Yates correction for continuity).

Source: Neugarten and Weinstein, 1964.

ed the strain associated with thinking of oneself as a grandparent, conflict with parents over the rearing of grandchildren, and self-chastisement about indifference toward taking care of or assuming responsibility for a grandchild.

Grandparenthood usually has multiple significance for grandparents (Neugarten & Weinstein, 1964). Table 22.4 shows four kinds of significance: biological renewal or continuity, emotional self-fulfillment, serving as a resource person to grandchildren, and vicarious achievement through grandchildren. This list is not unlike the list of satisfactions that parents say they receive (listed in Chapter 21). The prime significance of grandparenthood seems to be biological renewal and/or continuity: seeing oneself extended into the future. Men may be more inclined to trace biological continuity through sons than through daughters, but we have no information on this question. It would also be interesting to hold sex of offspring constant and to examine variation in attitude toward different grandchildren. For some people, grandparenthood offers an opportunity to succeed in a new emotional role—to be better as grandparents than they were as parents.

People who felt relatively remote from their grandchildren and for whom grandparenthood had relatively little meaning felt that their feelings were unusual. A few of these expected that the relationship might develop more fully as their grandchildren grew older.

As for style of grandparenting, Neugarten and Weinstein found that few of their respondents served primarily as reservoirs of family wisdom. Considering the rapidly changing nature of knowledge, this finding should not be surprising.

The old people in Kansas City studied by Cumming and Henry (1961) did not feel close to their grandchildren. They were "glad to see them come and glad to see them go." Clark (1969), in San Francisco, found that grandparents liked small children more as they (the grandparents) got older because older grandchildren don't want to bother with grandparents. Boyd (1969) found age, sex, and class differences in the evaluation of the grandparent role in her study of 45 upper- and middle-class and 25 working-class four-generation families. As Gilford and Black (1972) found later, Boyd (1969) reported a stronger grandparent/grandchild bond when the families lived nearby, particularly for the upper and middle classes. Geographic distance does not affect people who

once lived together and got to know each other intimately, but it does prevent close personal ties from forming. Nearness appears to be a necessary, although not sufficient, antecedent for intimacy.

RELATIONSHIPS WITH GRANDCHILDREN

Atchley (1977) has suggested that grandmothers appear to have a somewhat better chance of developing a relationship with their granddaughters than grandfathers have in developing a relationship with their grandsons. He attributes this advantage to the relative stability, over generations, of the housewife role in comparison with the occupational roles of men. Thus, grandmothers have more to offer their granddaughters that is pertinent to the lives the granddaughters will lead: for example, sewing, cooking, and child-rearing skills. In contrast, grandfathers very often find their skills unwanted, not only by industry but by their grandsons as well. This finding may be even more true of middle-class grandfathers, unless their skills involve home, gardening, or sports—with which their grandsons can identify. If women's roles in society change substantially, there is a good chance that traditional grandmothers' knowledge will also become less pertinent to the aspirations of their granddaughters. For instance, Updegraff (1968) found several areas of change in the grandmother's role when she compared three cohorts of grandmothers. Countering Atchley's hypothesis, Wood and Robertson (1976) found that less than half of the grandparents in their study had told grandchildren about family history or customs or had taught them special skills such as cooking, sewing, fishing, or crafts. A breakdown by sex of the grandparents was not provided, however; so Atchley's hypothesis remains untested.

An interesting but unanswered question is whether grandparenting is more important or satisfying to widowed than to married people. Only one study has compared older married with older widowed parents, and that study is not longitudinal. Adams (1968) found that widows were more likely to share mutual assistance with their daughters. We don't know about widowers, partly because there are fewer and because they are more likely to remarry. Old women belong to parent/child families; old men belong to husband/wife families.

Wood and Robertson (1976) developed a typology of the meanings of the grandparent role based on the two aspects of grandparenting mentioned earlier: personal and functional. The frequencies of these four types among respondents, who included 125 grandmothers and 132 grandfathers from a stable working-class area in Madison, Wisconsin, are shown in Table 22.5. The *apportional* type of grandparents derive a great deal of meaning both from fulfilling social norms and from the personal experience involved in the relationship. The *remote* grandparents do not derive much meaning from either source. The *symbolic* grandparents derive little meaning from personal experience and conceive the role almost completely in normative terms. The *individualized* grandparents are high on the personal dimension and low on the social dimension.

Grandparents in the apportioned and individualized groups, to whom the personal relationship is important, were significantly older than those who were less involved personally. They engaged in more activities with their grandchildren. I noted earlier that today's employed grandmothers are likely to be less like the "Granny image" than are retired great-grandparents—or older grandparents. Remember that older parents are more personal parents (Nydegger, 1973), too. Here again, the generalization that disengagement is *into*, not *from*, the family seems to be supported.

Among the younger grandparents who scored low on the personal dimension, those classified as remote engaged in significantly fewer activities with grandchildren than did those classified as symbolic. This finding holds true despite the fact that on the average the latter had more grandchildren. Not surprisingly, there was a sig-

nificant association between the number of activities with grandchildren and the emphasis on personal significance of parenthood: The higher the number of shared activities, the higher the score on the personal dimension, and also the smaller the number of grandchildren.

In an ongoing study of three generations, I have found that the age of the grandparents is related to the affect they show when they talk about their grandchildren. Those who are in their 50s, 60s, or 70s talk with warmth about their young-adult grandchildren, but those in their 40s and 80s are comparatively neutral. The neutral tone of the oldest may reflect their own physical weakness, which makes their interest in others weaker. Or it may reflect the fact that many have turned to grandchildren for hopes for the future after their own children have disappointed them, and now the grandchildren also have disappointed them.

As far as the relative coolness of the youngest grandparents is concerned, we may be dealing with an age-normative issue. To become grandparents at the age of 40 requires early childbearing by the children—too early, for most. Therefore, the grandchildren are witness to their own failures as parents. These generalizations are more appropriate for middle-class families, of course, than for working-class people, Blacks, or other ethnic groups, whose age norms tend to be lower across the board (see Chapter 3). The relative importance of grandchildren to grandparents, compared to the lesser importance of grandparents to grandchildren, is also suggested by these data. Of the grandparents, 27% brought up the subject of their grandchildren, usually when talking about high points in their life, the kinds of things they enjoy doing, or their ideal living arrangements. But only 10% of either of the other two generations—10% of the grandchildren and 10% of the children—referred spontaneously to their grandparents.

The most important finding of Wood and Robertson's research may be that grandparenting activity was not related to life satisfaction, which was tied instead to friendship and organizational activities. Wood and Robertson note "This supports Blau's contention (1973) that an older person who has a single good friend is more able to cope with old age than one who has a dozen grandchildren but no peer-group friends" (1976, p. 299).

Data that highlight the problems of generaliz-

TABLE 22.5 Types of role meaning for grandparents

	Meaning from personal sources	
	High	Low
High	*Apportioned* Grandfathers 41 Grandmothers 36	*Symbolic* Grandfathers 34 Grandmothers 33
Low	*Individualized* Grandfathers 22 Grandmothers 21	*Remote* Grandfathers 35 Grandmothers 35

Source: Wood and Robertson, 1976.

ing from self-reports come from a direct-observation study by Scott (1962). She brought together three generations—grandmothers, both parents, and a teenage grandchild—in an experimental situation where the amounts and kinds of family interpersonal interaction could be observed. The grandmothers proved to be singularly unimportant in the interpersonal interactions of the parents and their child. Perhaps grandparent/grandchild interaction is higher with younger grandchildren or is a secondary kind of interaction that takes on vigor only when the intervening generation is passive or not present.

Most research has focused on the grandmother role. We know selectively little about grandfathers, although we could ask many questions. Do men who were highly involved as fathers, rather than just as providers, become more highly involved as grandfathers and great-grandfathers? Do grandfathers increase their involvement with grandchildren after they retire? What effect does widowhood have? Robertson (1977a) found that grandmothers were primarily involved in baby-sitting, home recreation, and drop-in visits. Is this also true for grandfathers?

Because grandparenting is commonly a contingent, peripheral relationship to both grandparents and grandchildren, its greater significance may lie in its clue to the strength of general family unity than in its specific interpersonal aspects. Is parent/child unity, in both generations of parent/child dyads, greater where grandparents and grandchildren are closer? Can we say the same about more-distant relationships? Are siblings closer in all generations when grandparents are close to grandchildren? As I have repeatedly suggested, family systems are an important subject for future research.

A final note of caution concerns the possible uniqueness of the cohort from which most of our grandparenting data are derived. Just as this cohort of grandparents differs from past cohorts in the numbers of older people and family generations, so may it differ from future cohorts in the same ways. To cite only one relevant predictor: age of marriage and birth of first child have recently been shifting upward again. The generation born to mothers in their 30s will again have older grandparents, who will in turn have fewer grandchildren. Considering divorce statistics, also, there will be more stepgrandparents and stepgrandchildren. What effect will these differences have?

Siblings

Most American families over the past century that had children had more than one child. Therefore, 80% of all Americans have at least one brother or sister. Adams (1968) found that 87% of his Greensboro, North Carolina, respondents had siblings, and about 80% of older Americans have at least one living sibling. A 1975 study involving a national sample of people over age 65 indicated that 81% had children, 79% had siblings, 75% had grandchildren, and 4% had living parents (Harris & Associates, 1975). Thus, older people have as many siblings as they have children, and younger adults have more siblings than they have children. Shanas and her associates (1968) point out that over half of all women over 65 have husbands alive but six in seven have siblings alive. In San Francisco, people over 65 have more sibs alive than they have any other relatives—38% have spouses, 61% children, and 93% sibs (Clark & Anderson, 1967).

Developmental psychologists have been interested in the effect of siblings on children's cognitive and social development, but few have pursued this question into adulthood. Yet, as Cicirelli (1980b) points out, relationships between siblings can last longer than any other human relationship.

The sibling relationship changes structurally over the years. In childhood, it is one of daily contact and the sharing of most experiences. This closeness thins during the school years and adolescence, as siblings begin to have different school and friendship experiences. But they still share home experiences. Separation is most extreme during early adulthood, as each sibling forms his or her own home. However, many may follow parallel paths and find communication easy and meaningful when they do get together.

The obligations of caring for aging parents can bring brothers and sisters closer again. But, with the death of their parents, further interactions are determined by the siblings' personal preferences, rather than by family ritual or need. It is significant, therefore, that most studies of old people find that decreasing frequency of contact with siblings rarely means total absence of interest. Almost all older people know where their siblings are and how they are faring.

CONTACT

Studies of geographic proximity and frequency of contact between siblings generally show declines over the later years. Rosenberg and Anspach (1973) found that 75% of blue-collar workers in Philadelphia between the ages of 45 and 54 had at least one sibling in the metropolitan area. Of those between 55 and 65, 64% did, but only 49% of those over 65 did. Cicirelli (1980b) asked an Indiana sample of older people where the sibling with whom they had the most contact lived. He found that 26% lived in the same city and 56% within 100 miles.

Adams (1968) found a relation between distance and frequency of contact. Of siblings who lived within 100 miles of each other, 65% visited monthly or oftener, and 69% of those in the same city saw each other at least weekly. Rosenberg and Anspach had similar results. Of those who had siblings in the greater Philadelphia area, 68% in the 45–54 age range saw each other in the week preceding the interview, 58% in the 55–64 age range, and 47% of those over 65. Furthermore, Cicirelli found that siblings who neither visited nor telephoned each other did keep in touch by writing letters. Only a few of his 300 respondents had actually lost touch with siblings. Parron (1979) reported similar findings for the golden-wedding couples she studied. However, only 2% of Cicirelli's subjects actually lived with siblings. This percentage may be greater in other parts of the country, such as California (Clark & Anderson, 1967).

Shanas and her associates (1968) saw siblings as part of the reservoir of collateral relatives from which substitutes for more-direct kin—that is, those in the ascendant/descendant line—could be drawn. A different point of view was given by Cumming and Henry (1961), unfortunately on the basis of very sparse data. They saw sibling solidarity as a special case of generational solidarity and believed that sibling solidarity takes on new importance in middle age. Friends take the place of lost siblings more than of lost children. They concluded that the parent/child bond is dependent in nature, but the sib bond is between equals and thus more like friendship.

If for no other reason, sibs' availability could make them an important source of family interaction in later life. Parron (1979) found that her sample of golden-wedding couples seemed to have almost as much contact with siblings as with children. Some of the women were "on the phone" with siblings almost every day.

FEELINGS

What we know about relationships between sibs in childhood points to two contradictory attributes: solidarity and rivalry. Perhaps all solidarity among people has a rivalry component, and all rivalry a solidarity component. And perhaps nowhere is the contradiction so intense as among siblings. Two- and three-year-olds go about planning the destruction of a newborn sib with remarkable ingenuity. And 20- and 30-year-olds may be impelled to succeed in the world not so much because of parents' expectations as because of a desire to outdo siblings. Even 80-year-old siblings continue to debate their respective merits and the favoritism of their parents. There may be some basis for these childhood resentments, as shown by data on differential treatment in childhood according to birth order. Mothers show more affection and approval toward firstborn children and show more restrictiveness and severity to later-borns. Firstborn children, however, are treated as if they were older than their chronological age; they are expected to be more mature and to reach higher goals. Mothers try to accelerate their development. Sutton-Smith and Rosenberg (1970) found definite coalitions among siblings to oppose their parents' discrimination. In large families (Bossard & Boll, 1956), older children made very effective disciplinarians for younger children, seeming to know better than their mother or father what would work. College students who were oldest children admitted to being bossy. And those who were younger children said they tended to appeal, for help against their older siblings, to parents and other older siblings. During adolescence, older same-sex sibs can serve as models, and older opposite-sex sibs can socialize younger sibs in how to get along with members of the opposite sex.

A large-scale study of 7th- to 12th-graders (Elder, 1962) found that 65% felt close to their siblings. However, this affection lessens toward the end of high school, as the boys and girls look outside the family for intimacy. Freud used the term *Oedipus complex* to describe the psychological attachment of preschool boys to their mothers. According to Freudian theory, boys must move away from this attachment and toward closeness to others. A similar process may be at work among late adolescents who find that their ties to their siblings—particularly their opposite-sex siblings—are interfering with their efforts to form ties with nonfamily lovers. Incest is a strong taboo.

In their study of 64 adult sibs, Bossard and Boll (1956) felt that rivalry and conflict were minimal and that loyalty to each other was more important. They remembered that they were more fair to each other when they were children than their parents had been to them. In the large families that constituted their sample, the emphasis was more on sacrifice, on the group rather than on the self. A general conclusion from most studies is that the family structure provides the most important variables: (1) ages of all the siblings, as well as the number of years between them; (2) sex; (3) number of children in the family; and (4) strength of the parental dyadic bond (Schvanaveldt & Ihinger, 1979). Research on adult-sibling relationships has focused primarily on sex differences. One study that looked at the variable of ages and spacing (Troll, 1967) found that it was not significant in contributing to value and personality similarities between young adults and their parents.

Cicirelli (1980b) concludes that, when adults first leave their parents' home, they retain earlier feelings toward siblings. His study of college women (Cicirelli, 1980a) showed strong positive feelings for at least one sibling. Their feelings about their "closest" siblings were as strong as about their mothers, and they were closer to their closest siblings than to their fathers. Later-born women felt closer to their siblings than did earlier-born women. "Closest" siblings were likely to be those nearer to them in age.

In another study, Cicirelli (1979) found that 65% of older people felt "close" or "extremely close" to the siblings with whom they had the most contact. Only 5% said they did not feel close to any sibling. A different study of older people (Allan, 1977) found that, even when contact was limited, involvement with siblings continued. They kept in touch with each other's location, activities, and circumstances, even if information was gained indirectly through the family network in some cases. When negative feelings toward siblings' spouses kept them from closer interaction, they usually managed to maintain some kind of relationship. Frequent close companionship was more common among working-class families than among middle-class families. The general rule that working-class families live closer to each other and have fewer outside social contacts may apply here.

The death of parents can mark the breakup of sibling ties. Old rivalries can come to the fore as siblings settle parents' financial affairs. Common concerns are removed, too. Using age as a measure with a working-class sample, Rosenberg and Anspach (1973) report that two-thirds of people under 55 stay in touch with siblings in the area but only half of those over 55 do. Older sisters sometimes take over the kin-keeping functions of their mothers and keep the family together by communicating with all brothers and sisters and maintaining ritual family get-togethers.

As people get older, they may try to renew old family loyalties and old relationships. Many visit siblings, even at great distances, after they retire. The narrower their social worlds, the more likely they are to mention siblings spontaneously as sources of aid in times of trouble or need. Next to adult children, siblings are the best prospects for providing older people with permanent homes, except where there are long-term family feuds. Shanas and her associates (1968) report that siblings are particularly important in the lives of never-married older people. The death of a sibling, particularly when the relationship was a close one, may shock a person more than the death of any other kin. Because a sibling is of the same family and generation, his or her death brings home one's own mortality with great immediacy.

As in other family interactions, the female linkage is prominent among siblings. Most studies find the closest bonds between sisters, next between brothers and sisters, and least between brothers. Apparently this pattern starts in childhood. Lott and Lott (1970) found that brothers fight most with each other, although younger brothers also fight with sisters. There was less fighting among sisters. Adolescent girls are more likely to have favorable feelings toward siblings than are adolescent boys (Bowerman & Dobash, 1974) and are more favorable toward sisters than toward brothers. On the average, they like older sibs better than they do younger sibs. Older adolescents do not favor sibs as much as younger sibs do. There are closer sib bonds in two-child families than in larger families.

Adams's North Carolina respondents said they felt even closer to siblings in adulthood than they had in childhood. Adult-sibling solidarity seems to be enhanced by similarity of interests, residential proximity, common obligations to aging parents, and the absence of invidious comparisons (Aldous, 1978). Apparently living near each other is a necessary though not sufficient requirement for sibling closeness, as in grandparent/grandchild relations. The geographic requirement held least for sisters, who tended to keep in touch by letter even when they did not live near each other. Of Adams's respondents, 70% said they kept in touch with their brothers and sisters because they enjoyed the contact. Family ritual occasions such as holidays, birthdays, weddings, and so on help to maintain sibling contact. The fact that one sibling may "make good," and another may not, does not irrevocably cut their ties. The successful one enjoys his or her success more through comparison with a less successful brother or sister; the less successful ones may bolster their pride by "name dropping."

Lowenthal and her associates (1975) found that older respondents said they liked their cross-sex siblings more than did the younger ones. Even though sisters were close, they also were most rivalrous, at least among San Franciscans. Closeness and rivalry are not mutually exclusive. There can be frequent quarrels about the care of aged parents. Remember the communications spiral in couple relationships discussed in Chapter 20? Relationships can remain stable over many years of minimal communication but can change when interaction becomes vigorous again, as often occurs when siblings must cooperate to deal with aging parents.

In psychotherapy with married couples, Walter Toman (1976) observed that the closer a spouse matches one's siblings in birth and sex order, the more harmonious the marriage. For example, an older brother of younger sisters would be happiest married to a younger sister who had an older brother. This hypothesis, unfortunately, has not been verified in empirical research.

There is a good deal of mutual assistance among siblings (Adams, 1968), although nowhere near as much as between parents and children: 20% as compared with 80%. Lopata (1973) describes the intermittent and temporary nature of sibling assistance in the case of widowhood. A brother may come to help with funeral and financial arrangements. A sister may come to console and help with housework and child care. But both return to their own homes as soon as they can.

"Old people who have never married tend to maintain much closer relationships with their brothers and sisters than those who marry and have children. Persons without children tend to resume closer associations with siblings upon the death of a spouse, but interestingly, not as close as single persons" (Shanas et al., 1968). In Rosenberg and Anspach's (1973) data, the 360 people who were divorced, separated, or widowed visited their siblings in the area much more than did the 500 married couples. Aldous (1978) notes that unmarried siblings may move near each other or may even continue to share the family home after their parents die. Their married siblings, particularly sisters, often try to help them. As Shanas and her associates found, those who have never had children are more likely to give than to get. They are the generous bachelor uncles or aunts who contribute gifts, educational funds, and so forth.

In Black families, kinship systems are organized around siblings and other relatives more than around the parent/child relationship, at least according to Hays and Mindel (1973). At the present early stage of research on Black family relationships, this finding is hard to interpret. How much it derives from remnants of the extended-family cultures of Africa, how much from the large percentage of teenage unwed mothers and consequent child rearing by grandparents and aunts, and how much from as yet unknown causes we are in no position to judge (Staples & Mirandé, 1980).

Other kin

The same principles that operate with respect to siblings apply to other collateral kin such as cousins, aunts, uncles, nieces, and nephews. First, these relatives serve as a reservoir from which replacement and substitutions for missing or lost closer kin can be obtained. Second, ties are based on individual characteristics more than on degree of kinship. The scattered bits of research about such kin seldom ask about "favorite cousin" or "favorite uncle or niece." Instead, they ask about "best-known cousin" (Adams, 1968); or a male cousin, or mother's oldest brother, or father's oldest brother (Klatsky, 1972); or "extended family" (Brown, 1974), to cite a few examples.

In general, extended kin have served an important function in the migration history of our country. Most migrants, whether from across the oceans or out on the farm, moved toward areas where other relatives had already settled (Hareven, 1976).

For most people, extended kin become temporarily important at family ritual occasions such as weddings, funerals, reunions, and some holidays. The symbolic significance of such events can override interpersonal feelings, which are likely to depend on personal characteristics and history. Positional symbolic representation can be in terms of a particular family line ("one of the Smiths") or generation ("my grandmother's cousin"). Relatives may be invited to a wedding to represent the bridegroom's paternal family or the oldest living generation. When grandparents die, great-aunts or great-uncles are invited to give the family a more rounded presence, even if they have not been included for many years.

Involvement with extended kin can sometimes be overwhelming. For example, Cohler (1974) found that Polish-American and Italian-American women, particularly those who are middle-aged and older, have such heavy involvement and such close contact with many relatives that they are "at risk." It is easy for them to become overwhelmed by demands for their care and attention. Hess and Waring (1978) say that too much involvement with family is as bad as too little.

Lineal kin (parents and children) maintain contact in spite of distance; more-distant relatives are probably more easily estranged by geographic distance. First cousins, however, may see each other frequently when they visit their own parents, if their parents (who are siblings) live in the same community. And other distant kin can become close if they move nearby.

There are several data sources on extended families from the perspective of young-adult populations, but few from the perspective of older people. Thus, Robins and Tomanec (1962) found that young adults—both males and females—were closer to their maternal than to their paternal relatives, and were closer to female than to male relatives. After parents and siblings, these respondents were closest to (1) grandparents, (2) aunts and uncles, and (3) cousins. Adams's (1968) North Carolina sample, whose median age was about 33, showed the same ordering of importance.

Nearly 70% of the people over 55 in Brown's (1974) sample said they had experienced no change in contact with extended-family members during the previous decade. Brown found that, although older people do not disengage from children when relationships are not satisfactory, they do disengage from extended-family interactions when satisfaction is low. Only 13% said that their extended-kin relationships were less than ideal, however.

In a study of inner-city elderly, 15% reported that relatives were a source of income (Walters & Mitchell, 1974). Most people believe that their relatives—as compared with neighbors or friends—would help in emergency situations lasting one day, two weeks, or three months (Litwak & Szelenyi, 1969). Unfortunately, the generic term *relatives*, used in much gerontological research, does not distinguish among children, siblings, and other kin.

Middle-class people visit their distant relatives (in kinship terms) more than working-class people do, if geographic distance is controlled. Middle-class kin also tend to be more dispersed geographically than are working-class kin. Thus, middle-class families maintain contact in spite of greater distances. Among working-class older people, rate of interaction with both genealogically close and distant kin is largely a function of geographic proximity (Rosenberg, 1970).

Restricted contact with kin in later life is partially related to a history of income deprivation and consequent restricted mobility. In the Institute for Social Research time-sequential study mentioned earlier (Antonucci & Bornstein, 1978), respondents in 1976 were sharing worries more with "kin" than they were in 1957. Again, the term *kin* here includes spouse and children, so we cannot tell whether there has been any increase in extended-family closeness.

Gibson (1972), surveying a sample of disabled middle-aged and older people—those who had applied for OASDI (Old Age and Survivors Disability Insurance)—used a somewhat different form of reporting contact frequency. Of 5.7 non-household relatives available and not living with respondent, 0.5 were seen daily, 1.2 weekly, 1.1 monthly, and 2.9 less than monthly. Thus, half were seen monthly, a somewhat larger proportion than found by Reiss (1962) for middle-class Bostonians. The need for help among these people may be related to increased contact. Even so, 58% received no services from kin.

Gibson also found that the proportion of available kin seen at least monthly does not vary with age and is higher for unmarried than for married people. (In a study of teachers and clerical workers, however, Atchley and his associates [1975] found that married clerical workers had the highest interaction rate with extended kin.) Of the available or existing kin in Gibson's study, 38% lived in the same community. Of the total, 51% were seen at least monthly, but only 17% provided significant help. It is noteworthy that the proportion of helpful relatives mentioned did not decline with age but, as with interaction frequency, was much lower for those still married.

Because I have limited my discussion to kin in this chapter, I have not said much about such quasi-kin groups as communal households, communes, or kibbutzim. Many such groups should be considered more like extended families than like marital arrangements. Quasi-extended family arrangements are not at all new historically. Hareven (1979) reminds us that in the 19th century one-fourth to one-third of city dwellers boarded with families or took in boarders. Such arrangements helped young migrants to master the transition to adulthood and helped the older heads of households in many ways, including financial ones.

In-laws

Limited attention has been devoted to the in-law relationship in the later part of the family life cycle. Most writers refer only to the in-law problems of young married couples; few note the adjustment problems of middle-aged parents and even grandparents to the new families introduced into kin networks by each new marriage in the family. One study of in-law relationships (Duvall, 1954) found that wives reported that they had the most problems with mothers-in-law and the second-most problems with sisters-in-law.

Adams (1968) found that middle-class wives write to both sets of parents, while working-class wives concentrate on their own kin. As noted earlier, Turner (Troll & Turner, 1979) found that her women college students were writing to their lovers' parents and had taken over the female kin-keeping functions far in advance of marriage, even when eventual marriage was doubtful. Urban working-class people in the last half of the life cycle tend to reduce or lose contacts with brothers- and sisters-in-law when their marriages are disrupted either by widowhood or divorce.

At the end of the family life cycle, both aging mother and mother-in-law may require help. How does a lifelong habit of mother-in-law avoidance affect the need to assist in old age? Shanas and her associates (1968) report that women often do take over the responsibilities of care for needy older parents-in-law when no daughters are available. How does their relationship affect the quality of attentions or the feelings of the people involved, particularly if both sets of parents need care? I have already mentioned the Cassandra syndrome of the middle-aged woman who is beset with worries about her relatives of all ages; these relatives include her in-laws.

Summary

The most prominent relatives, aside from parents and children, are grandparents and siblings. Ties with such relatives are based more on personal characteristics and personal experiences than on normative considerations, as they are with parents and children.

Grandparents of today are younger and more involved in nonfamily activities than was the traditional "Granny." They are thus likely to be clearly distinguished from parents and are more formal in their relationships. The more indulgent they are, the more their grandchildren prefer them. There are sex differences in grandparental influences on grandchildren. Grandmothers are more generic (considering a wider ariety of issues their appropriate domain for influence), and grandfathers are more specific. Grandchildren do not differentiate grandparental relations by sex, though.

Siblings tend to maintain their feelings for each other—whatever those feelings have been—throughout their lives. These feelings usually are a combination of rivalry and solidarty. Events of later life, such as loss of spouse or children or parents, can change the nature of sibling relationships. Such events often bring siblings closer together, and, if they do so, may change their interactions to some extent.

More-distant kin are important more for personal reasons than are grandparents and sibs. They can substitute for missing closer kin, on occasion.

23

Wrapping It Up

The preceding 22 chapters have been organized around such obvious topics as physiology, intelligence, and personality. Underlying this surface organization are issues like the ten noted in Chapter 1. It is to these issues that I now return.

Issue 1. What is the relative contribution of heredity and environment to the way people change during the adult years? Present evidence, it seems to me, points to the impossibility of separating the genetic blueprint from the context in which it is worked out. The inverse is equally true. Biological and social conditions and life experiences cannot be separated from each other or from genetically determined inclinations that mold these conditions and experiences in unique ways.

In the beginning embryo, once the two genetically identical cells resulting from the first mitosis are separated, they are necessarily in different positions and thus surrounded by different environments. This initial minute difference enlarges step by step, through successive cell divisions, becoming vastly different body parts with unique specialized functions. The cells deriving from the original right-hand cell, let us say, can end up as skin and glands. The cells deriving from the original left-hand cell can end up as heart and muscles. Results are affected by not only initial difference in position, of course, but also by a continually increasing difference in context as each cell selects different components from its surroundings.

Identical twins, who do not typically reside together during their adult years, maintain curiously similar personalities as well as predispositions to disease and even ages of death (Kallmann & Jarvik, 1959). In fact, identical twins reared apart can be even more alike than those reared together. Apparently genetic programming plays a part in the selection of environmental input throughout life. Twins choose from different environments the same features, the same information (in Piagetian terms) to assimilate. And, having the same kind of information, they then accommodate in similar ways. If they are reared together, within the close boundaries of a family system, there are social pressures for them to take on different family roles.

Another line of evidence for heredity/environment interaction is sex difference, which initially may have had infinitesimally small genetic determinants. Gender is a powerful source of variance in all aspects of adult development and aging, as has been noted throughout this book. Finally, diet contributes differentially to longevity and health for different groups of people. But when climatic conditions change—following migration, for example—the same diet no longer has the same effect.

The preceding discussion has used the terms *heredity* and *environment*. It is equally impossible to separate the effects of biological and social causation in adult development. Attribution of biological causation seems, curiously, to go together with social discrimination. Biology is not given as the reason for behavior of middle-class White men in our society, for whom such phrases as "job burnout" are invented. But women are believed to be notorious pawns of their physiological processes, as are other social groups generally discriminated against: Blacks and old people.

The menstrual cycle and the menopause are typically believed to sway women's lives, but no comparable biological cause is attributed to men until "old age," when men are as prone to be labeled "senile" as are women. Such attributions ignore the fact that few women are disabled either by menstruation or menopause, and few old people are senile. In fact, those who do suffer from such symptoms should not be neglected "because their condition is normal," but should be given serious attention, because their condition is abnormal.

Changing lifestyles, diet, and exercise can alter menstrual and menopausal behavior and can even reverse many symptoms attributed to organic brain damage. Stress can increase problems, and counseling to reduce stress can decrease them. At the same time, people with certain genetic predispositions may be more susceptible to menstrual and menopausal difficulties or to deteriorated cognitive functioning in old age. Genetic programming is worked out in context at all points of life. It is as unwise to overlook social causation for women, Blacks, and old people as it is to overlook biological causation for middle-class White men. Neither one nor the other operates alone.

Issue 2. How much can individuals control their development? Counseling psychologists have turned enthusiastically to helping people prepare for and cope with potentially stressful life events. There are groups for preparing for retirement, for widowhood, for the "empty nest." There are self-help and peer groups for couples in the process of divorce, for adults contemplating or experiencing a return to school, and for those seeking new kinds of jobs or careers. Counselors and clients alike assume that people can influence such processes, affect future development, and even use the experiences to enhance future development.

There is clearly a continuum of viewpoint from total helplessness in the face of uncontrollable external forces to total power over one's destiny. Neither extreme is usually true.

We all must die. Before death, if we live long enough, we face the death of others and our own aging. If we have children, they grow up, and relationships must change. Many kinds of options are drastically limited during economic depressions. Probably, the more affluent the society and the individual, the more power resides in that individual.

We do generally have a choice as to whether to marry or to have children, whom to select as marriage partners, and how to rear our children. There is some choice as to where and how to live and what kind of jobs to seek, whom to select as friends and what kind of activities to pursue—from housekeeping to recreation.

We can try to assess the degree of option in situations. Development is organized partly by forces outside the individual, but to a considerable extent it is also amenable to individual control. It is true that we all must die, but we can hasten or delay the time of death by the way we live, by what we eat, and the amount of physical exercise we get. Even our perceptions of situations, our self-definitions, or self-esteem can affect life changes.

Losing a loved one is painful, but we have some control over our mourning; the pain need not destroy us. Certainly our attitudes toward our children growing up can affect our feelings about their leaving and our future relationships with them. Instead of mourning over the "empty nest," many mothers—who now have options their mothers probably did not have—can move on to other rewarding and fulfilling activities. Relationships with children that have been congenial before adulthood are likely to remain congenial—or return to congeniality—after they themselves are adults. Parents' behavior toward adult offspring influences feelings in both generations.

There is even some individual control during times of economic hardship. One avenue is social action, although this option is outside the topic of this book. Training for job flexibility can help make one more employable in times of job scarcity. And an active orientation toward oneself and the world can help the person assume control when options are available. This active orientation is Neugarten and Gutmann's "active-mastery" style, as opposed to a passive- or magical-mastery style. And we know that age is irrelevant. An old dog can learn new tricks if necessary. Beginning new careers, returning to college, even beginning basic education are all possible for old people as well as for young people.

It is foolish to ignore the amount of individual control there may be in life, but it is also foolish to ignore the fact that much is not controllable. Several years ago, I used the Tantalus metaphor to describe one dilemma facing middle-aged women today. The mythical Tantalus, remember, was tethered to the mountainside by the gods and tortured by having grapes, water, or whatever else he reached for yanked away just as his hands touched them. The historical expansion of options and the women's movement have led many women to believe that they could achieve their dreams—love, money, status, power, creativity—by going back to school and out into the job market. Most of these dreams came true for some women, and some dreams came true for many women. Yet many others found that, just as they reached for what they wanted, it moved just beyond their grasp. Women are not the only ones vulnerable to this problem, of course. Men also can be deluded by myths and know the frustrations of almost but not quite reaching their dreams.

Issue 3. Do people become less open to new information and experience as they get older? Most longitudinal investigations show increasing commitment and consolidation during the years past adolescence—increasing commitment to the definition of self, to family and job, and to values and interests. Adolescence is notoriously a time of extreme openness, and adulthood, in comparison, is a time of closing in. The extreme openness and change of adolescence, in fact, may have such negative side effects that, once adulthood is attained, it feels good to close the doors and windows to invitations for more change.

Does the evidence for progressive closing in, as shown by increasing commitment, represent loss of ability to change or increasing resistance to change? Recent theoretical interest in turning points and the impact of major life events has arisen partly in the context of this question. Significant transitions and changes, if observable in the adult years, would suggest that resistance rather than rigidity is the cause of closing in. We can say that adults try hard not to change but that sometimes they must give in to the demands of externally imposed disruptions of stabilized patterns. "Empty-nest" mothers,

widows, and divorcees are all examples of people shaken loose from old commitments, as are retirees and those who have lost jobs. Another force for openness is reciprocal socialization, the influence of offspring on parents and grandparents.

In times of societal stability, the balance is probably tipped toward forces for less input and less change. In times of rapid change, the balance tips the other way, pushing open the windows to new information and more change. Evidence of disengagement and rigidity—shutting the windows—is offset by evidence for new learning when that learning has functional relevance. In other words, relevance and function, and outside forces for change, determine openness more than does the development or aging of the individual.

Issue 4. Is qualitative change possible past age 20? When an egg changes into a tadpole and a tadpole into a frog, metamorphosis—qualitative change—has occurred. When a chameleon changes color, however, only surface change has occurred, and such change is often transitory. In between, there may be quantitative change: the tadpole that only changed quantitatively would get bigger and bigger but would stay a tadpole and would never transform into a frog. Many developmental psychologists, primarily those involved with cognitive development, believe that qualitative change—change in the nature of thinking—ends in adolescence. The same might be suggested for physical development and personality. Life-span developmental theorists do not agree at all on this issue.

One line of developmental theory follows the chameleon metaphor. Changes in adulthood are seen as surface adaptations only, responses to changing demands of the environment, such as changing age norms and expectations. Improvement in cognitive performance, in this view, could represent the lifting of environmental ceilings that previously limited expression of underlying "true" competence. Deterioration of cognitive performance could represent lowered limits. A woman might change from relational thinking to "analytic" thinking when she no longer saw analysis as "unfeminine." Similarly, old people could change from analytic thinking to relational thinking when people around them showed that they did not expect analytic thinking from older people. An enormous improvement in deductive reasoning by people who go to college in their middle years could just be the "bringing out" of previously unused abilities. Or the improvement could be caused by applying deductive reasoning, previously applied only to nonintellectual problems, to intellectual problems. Assertiveness on the part of middle-aged women who had previously been passive and dependent could be the uncovering of assertive characteristics that had been repressed in adolescence. Or the assertiveness could be caused by shifting assertive behavior against children as the target to colleagues or to problems on the job as the target.

Another line of theory follows the quantitative-change argument. In this view, adults become more and more skilled—in interpersonal manipulating, in object manipulating, or in problem solving. But the tadpole is really just getting bigger; it is too late to develop into a frog. Adults' cognitive performances improve, but the improvements are still in the same styles and still follow the same process. Improvements in deductive reasoning only occur in people who begin reasoning deductively before they become adults. Adults who have hitherto not developed beyond concrete operations cannot achieve formal operations. They have lost their chance. Middle-aged women who had been passive, nonassertive little girls and young women cannot become assertive for the first time in their 50s.

The third line of theory believes that qualitative change *is* possible. Even if the young adult is still a tadpole, it can become a frog—at any age. Adults who had never developed beyond concrete operations can, at any age, achieve formal operations. Going to college at age 40 can bring about deductive reasoning in people who never thought that way before. It is possible, with skilled counseling and individual effort, to change one's mode of behavior—to become appropriately assertive in later life, for example, even when one has never been so earlier.

I like the third line of theory best. Maybe not many people are able to truly develop, but most of us can do so if we judge it necessary or desirable. Certainly, learning and development do not stop at adolescence. Whether such learning and development are fundamentally different from what takes place earlier, we cannot yet be sure.

Issue 5. Is negative change development? To most of us, development means change in a positive direction: more skill, more ability, greater complexity. Yet this kind of straight-line change is not even true for all the changes of early childhood. Some structures, like the lens of the eye, start deteriorating at birth. Some skills acquired in infancy disappear or deteriorate before infancy is over as new skills replace them. We tend, however, to ignore negative change in early life and to believe that all childhood changes are straight-line "development." Similarly, the stereotype for adulthood is that deterioration and loss are typical. Positive or fluctuating changes are ignored, and "development" is not believed possible.

In considering negative changes at any time of life, it is necessary to separate three processes: retrogression, deterioration, and adaptation. The term *retrogression* implies a return to earlier states—as in "second childhood," for example. The term *deterioration* implies destruction or loss of structure or function. The term *adaptation* implies the adjustment of structure or function to prevailing conditions and environmental demands, which sometimes requires less rather than more complexity or skill. When spatial ability in older subjects looks more like that of young children than like that of younger adults, *retrogression* might be the appropriate term. When problem solving is not as good as it once was, we could speak of either retrogression or deterioration, although Labouvie-Vief (1980) even considers the possibility that this kind of decrement might be adaptation. Decline in girls' cognitive abilities during adolescence and "learned helplessness" are examples of this kind of adaptation involving negative change. When one's speed in running a mile decreases, that might be deterioration. Decreased involvement in society might, again, be either retrogression, deterioration, or adaptation.

The separation of these three processes is one of the current challenges to life-span developmental research: to determine when a negative change is retrogression, when it is deterioration, and when it is adaptation. But there is a larger challenge to life-span developmental theory, involving the definition of development itself. Developmental patterns don't have to be linear or unidirectional, at any time of life. Nor do they have to be irreversible—nor, for that matter, desirable. To a tadpole, becoming a frog might be an unwelcome future. To honeymooners, the contentment of midlife marriage might seem equally undesirable.

Reversibility is part of this issue. It is generally assumed that neither retrogressive nor deteriorative changes are reversible. Yet there is some evidence that old people whose behavior is so helpless that they are said to be in their "second childhood" can be brought back to a previous level of functioning by environmental manipulation. Problem solving can be improved by training. Women's cognitive abilities and achievement aspirations, which may have gone "into reverse" in adolescence, have been seen to "go back to high" when their children are older. Involvement in society can increase in older people who get more older neighbors. Even speed of running can be increased by exercise regimens.

Issue 6. Does development take place in quantum leaps? Strength builds up slowly and gradually over the early years of life and then ebbs slowly and gradually over the later years. Most people are not aware of such slow changes in development. They recognize such changes "in a leap," usually when something taken for granted is no longer true. One's father is ("suddenly") no longer tall, one's mother cannot lift a heavy load, one can no longer mow the lawn effortlessly in an hour or work around the clock in an emergency without needing more than a few hours' sleep to recuperate. The actual changes are gradual, even though the realization may not be.

Other changes are more precipitous. One day a child cannot walk; the next, she toddles around the room. One day a person goes about his business with full competence. The next day he has a stroke and has lost almost all powers: speech, locomotion, and memory. One day a woman is involved in her customary round of family activity. The next, she is a widow, and all future family interactions are different. One day, a man moves about his job with habitual aplomb. The next day he is fired, outside the scene.

Between these two extremes of gradual and precipitous change lie most changes of adult life. Most are signaled by intermittent markers. Bit by bit, appearance alters. Bit by bit, the quality of interpersonal relations shifts. Job development is a series of minor events—taking on new responsibilities, exhibiting improved skills, seeing a wider picture, letting go of old responsibilities, exhibiting poorer skills, seeing a more limited picture. Each bit by itself is only marginally notable, but they add up to a different orientation toward the world and the self.

Theorists who focus on the first kind of changes—the slow, gradual, almost imperceptible ones—are often tempted to think that adulthood is one long period of stability. Theorists who focus on the second kind of change are tempted to see stage sequences of one sort or another. I prefer the middle road. I look at evidence for different kinds of changes and ask what brings them about, and what processes are involved. There may be abrupt changes in events, but there may not be abrupt changes in responses to those events—or vice versa. For example, becoming a widow may be sudden, but changes in self-definition and in ways of behaving that are more appropriate to altered circumstances are not sudden. To describe periods of life as separate states or stages without delineating the processes of getting from one to the next seems artificial.

Issue 7. Are there turning points in life? Times when new ideas arise are messy. Changes in circumstances that demand new thinking lead to chaotic and conflicting concepts or to concepts given different definitions by different thinkers. One such change in circumstances has been the extension of the adult years consequent on the increase in life expectancy over the past century. Large numbers of older people not only survive but they also survive in relatively better health than do previous cohorts of older people. This background change, plus the unrest of present-cohort middle-aged men who grew up in the Depression and World War II, has led the attention of practitioners and theorists alike to dramatic changes in the otherwise plateaulike adult years. Terms such as *turning points, crises, major life events,* and *transitions* occupy center stage.

Starting with the observations of clinicians that they were getting many middle-aged clients with disquieting changes that might be labeled *crises,* life-span developmental theorists and researchers have become interested in exploring such "major life events" or "turning points." Stage theories, such as those of Levinson and his associates (1977) and Gould (1972), explicitly build on presumptions of universality and sequentiality of externally organized turning points. They are examples of a mechanistic world view. Their models state that everybody, at given times of life, goes through stage-specific changes. Some models, such as Levinson's, set these times by chronological ages. Other models do not see chronological age as the relevant clock but do insist on universal sequences. Social-learning theorists prefer to see less universality and sequentiality, although they also turn to life events as pivotal causes for change in adult life.

Major life events can be more or less common. Some are close to universal in our society: marriage, birth of first child, menopause, widowhood, and retirement. Others are common, but not universal: divorce, loss of job, and moving. Some are sex-related: the menopause and the empty nest. Increases in life expectancy over the past century have meant that more people experience events that happened later in life than the age to which their parents survived; for example, the empty nest and retirement.

As events become more common, they get to be expected. They become normative. People are supposed to get married and have children, to get a job, to have children grow up, to go through menopause, to lose parents, and to retire. Such events, even though not necessarily desirable or pleasant, are anticipated and rehearsed well in advance. In consequence, they rarely cause more than a ripple in the tide of life.

According to theorists such as Neugarten and Datan (1973), nonnormative, unanticipated, and rarer events are upsetting; for example, a job loss, a divorce, or the death of a spouse or child. Or it is the timing of an event that is upsetting: widowhood under 50 or major illness in early adulthood. A multiple dose of events can also be overwhelming.

Earlier, I proposed that upsetting events can be met with four possible reactions: denial or resistance to change; extreme effort to change, resulting in fragmentation of self; the minimal change necessary to return to equilibrium; and development or controlled change. Presumably, the impact of unanticipated events overcomes

the resistance to change that is inherent in the adult's posture toward experience. Whether externally or internally organized, anticipated or unanticipated, however, turning points indicate to those experiencing them the inappropriateness of previous behavior. Turning points thus lead to searches for new behavior, sometimes accompanied by stress, shock, grief, or crisis. Many middle-aged people of today, who are members of a cohort accustomed to seek counseling in times of distress, have been turning to counselors for help during these so-called transitions. Such events are considered normal rather than abnormal; no stigma is attached to them. Becoming upset when a spouse dies or when there is a move away from accustomed territory and close family and friends has no pejorative connotations. There may be more stigma to divorce or menopause or retirement, but the new labels of "turning points" help make these events normal, too.

Issue 8. How does "life time" match "social time"? From a phenomenological point of view—the perspective of the experiencer—"life time" is the important dimension. How much longer one expects to live and how one maps out the time one has left are partly determined by parental and grandparental longevity and partly by the age of people currently living.

Forty-year-olds can vary widely in how they perceive themselves, depending on these time indicators. People whose grandparents are still living and who live and work among many people over age 60 are bound to consider themselves young and to expect at least 50 more years of life ahead. They are "caught short" by, and even disbelieve, a diagnosis of major illness. They may just have started thinking about becoming parents, particularly if they are men. They may be more likely to consider divorce if they are unhappy and believe they have 40 more years of unhappiness ahead of them. They might plan new careers or turn to recreational adventures when their responsibility for children decreases.

Forty-year-olds whose parents are dead, however, or who are the oldest in their jobs and social groups, have a very different perspective. They may accept major illness; "What else can I expect at my age?" They may be more likely to think about winding down instead of starting anything new: planning their retirement, settling into auxiliary roles in job and family life.

Many eighty-year-olds today have been "caught short" by their own long life. Their parents are likely to have died at much younger ages. They are alive beyond their calculated time and don't know what to do with themselves, beyond waiting for death. When present 40-year-olds become 80, however, they may be more likely to "die with their boots on" than are present 80-year-olds.

Chronological age has only a derived meaning, depending on what that age means in social terms. If being 40 means being old, people become personally and socially old at 40. Thirty years ago, a book titled *Life Begins at 40* was a best-seller because it challenged everybody's way of thinking about becoming 40. Today, it is largely taken for granted that life can begin at 40. A profound redefinition of the meaning of chronological age can take place in one generation. Life time depends on social time and historical time.

Issue 9. How much does structure adapt to functional needs? The structuralism/functionalism dichotomy could be used as a prime example of pendulum swings in psychology. Right now, the pendulum seems to be swinging away from structuralism and back toward functionalism. Piagetian theory, which dominated structuralist thinking over the past 20 years, is not necessarily being discarded, but it is being reinterpreted by recent theorists to fit functionalist purposes. Writers such as Baltes and Willis (1977) and Labouvie-Vief (1980) demonstrate this new trend by suggesting that adult cognitive development is best seen against a background of context.

The current popularity of the term *adaptation* is in line with this trend toward functionalism. Adults exhibit more- or less-complex cognitions depending on the needs of their life situations. Changes in behavior follow life events that change situations and demand new behavior. One conclusion about such adaptation is that humans are capable of much greater variety of behavior than we used to believe. In fact, we probably do not know what humans are capable of, because at no time in history have circumstances and opportunities encouraged maximum potential.

Implicit in many references to "adaptation" is the assumption that it represents a hierarchic ordering of behavior. Vaillant (1977), for one, specifically calls more-adaptive behavior more mature. And he looks for—and finds in some cases—progression from less mature to more mature during the adult years. If we assume that any adaptive change is superior in some way to lack of adaptation, we can assume that it could be desirable to retrogress or deteriorate. There is no doubt that, from an evolutionary point of view, adaptation is necessary for survival. But does that mean that adaptation is the peak of development? The oldest men in the San Francisco study (Lowenthal et al., 1975) who were most complex were also lower in morale than those the same age who were less complex. Does this finding mean it is wrong to remain complex in old age? In a way, this perspective is reminiscent of disengagement theory. On the one hand, a high level of competence and performance is valued. On the other hand, once that level has been reached, a lower level is recommended. How can this paradox be resolved, particularly when research on disengagement shows that those who do not disengage have the highest morale?

Issue 10. How universal are the changes associated with adult development? It is easy, in a book such as this, which tries to describe general and comprehensive patterns, to sound as if everybody followed the same road. We need to emphasize, over and over again, that this generalization is just not true. For every general statement, there are many exceptions. For every pattern described, there are innumerable variant patterns. At the early stage in the game in which life-span development now is, central tendencies (averages) are focused on more than deviation from the average. It is possible to get an average of 10 for a group in which everybody who is counted is between 8 and 12. But it is equally possible to get an average of 10 for a group in which people fall between 1 and 20. Unless we look for the deviation, we do not see it.

Human variation—on almost any measure—probably is great. Therefore, any given human probably can develop in his or her unique way. There is more leeway than has been recognized until now. And therefore, there is more hope. Development is not predetermined. When economic circumstances improve for an ethnic group that has lagged in development, that group ceases to lag. When old people are discriminated against, they wilt, just as do members of other groups against which society discriminates. When old people have more options, they flourish. It is up to society to create optimal circumstances for development. It is up to us to remove obstacles.

References

Abbott, M., Murphy, E., Bolling, D., & Abbey, H. The familial component in longevity: A study of offspring of nonagenarians. II. Preliminary analysis of the completed study. *Johns Hopkins Medical Journal*, 1974, *134*, 1–16.

Acock, A. C., & Bengtson, V. L. On the relative influence of mothers or fathers: A covariance analysis of political and religious socialization. *Journal of Marriage and the Family*, 1978, *40*(3), 519–530.

Adams, B. *Kinship in an urban setting*. Chicago: Markham, 1968.

Adams, B. Mate selection in the United States: A theoretical summarization. In W. Burr, R. Hill, I. Nye, & R. Reiss (Eds.), *Contemporary theories about the family. Vol. 1: Research-based theories.* New York: Free Press, 1979.

Adams, C. E. Aging and reproduction in the female mammal with particular reference to the rabbit. *Journal of Reproductive Fertility Supplement*, 1970, *12*, 1–16.

Adams, G. R., & Huston, T. L. Social perception of middle-aged persons varying in physical attractiveness. *Developmental Psychology*, 1977, *11*(5), 657–658.

Ahammer, I. Social learning theory as a framework for the study of adult personality development. In P. B. Baltes & K. W. Schaie (Eds.), *Life-span developmental psychology: Personality and socialization.* New York: Academic Press, 1973.

Ahammer, I., & Baltes, P. B. Objective vs. perceived age differences in personality: How do adolescents, adults and older people view themselves and each other? *Journal of Gerontology*, 1972, *27*(1), 46–51.

Ainsworth, M. D. Object relations, dependency and attachment: A theoretical review of the infant-mother relationship. *Child Development*, 1969, *40*, 969–1025.

Albrecht, R. The role of older people in family rituals. In C. Tibbetts & W. Donahue (Eds.), *Social and psychological aspects of aging: Aging around the world.* New York: Columbia University Press, 1962.

Aldous, J. The consequences of intergenerational continuity. *Journal of Marriage and the Family*, 1965, *27*(4), 462–468.

Aldous, J. *Family careers: Developmental change in families.* New York: Wiley, 1978.

Aldrich, D. Familism and the prestige of the aged in two societies. Paper presented at the meeting of the Gerontological Society, Portland, Ore., October 1974.

Alexander, I., & Adlerstein, A. Death and religion. In H. Feifel (Ed.), *The meaning of death.* New York: McGraw-Hill, 1959.

Allan, G. Sibling solidarity. *Journal of Marriage and the Family*, 1977, *39*(1), 177–184.

Aller, F. A. Role of the self-concept in student marital adjustment. *Family Life Coordinator*, 1962, *11*(3), 43–45.

Allport, G. *Personality: A psychological interpretation.* New York: Holt, Rinehart & Winston, 1937.

Alpaugh, P. K. Variables affecting creativity in adulthood: A descriptive study. Unpublished master's thesis, University of Southern California, 1975.

Alston, J. P., & Dudley, C. J. Age, occupation, and life satisfaction. *Gerontologist*, 1973, *13*, 58–61.

Altman, L. K. Study disputes data on girls' puberty. *New York Times*, March 26, 1976, p. 19.

Alvarez, A. *The savage god.* New York: Random House, 1972.

Anderson, A., & Dvorak, B. Differences between college students and their elders in standards of conduct. *Journal of Abnormal and Social Psychology*, 1928, *23*(3), 286–292.

Anderson, B. J., & Standley, K. A. Methodology for observation of the childbirth environment. Paper presented at the meeting of the American Psychological Association, Washington, D. C., September 1976.

Anderson, J. E. Dynamics of development: Systems in process. In D. Harris (Ed.), *The concept of development: An issue in the study of human behavior.* Minneapolis: University of Minnesota Press, 1957.

Anderson, J. E. The use of time and energy. In J. E. Birren (Ed.), *Handbook of aging and the individual: Psychological and biological aspects.* Chicago: University of Chicago Press, 1959.

Angres, S. Intergenerational relations and value congruence between young adults and their mothers. Unpublished doctoral dissertation, University of Chicago, 1975.

Antonucci, T. On the relationship between values and adjustment in old men. *International Journal of Aging and Human Development,* 1974, *5,* 57–69.

Antonucci, T., & Bornstein, J. Changes in informal social support networks. Paper presented at the meeting of the American Psychological Association, Toronto, August 1978.

Apple, D. The social structure of grandparenthood. *American Anthropologist,* 1956, *58,* 656–663.

Aranoff, C. Old age in prime time. *Journal of Communication,* 1974, *24*(4), 86–87.

Arbeit, S. A. A study of women during their first pregnancy. Unpublished doctoral dissertation, Yale University, 1975.

Arbeiter, S. Mid-life career change. *AAHE Bulletin* (American Association for Higher Education), 1979, *32*(2), 1, 11–12.

Arenberg, D. Anticipation interval and age differences in verbal learning. *Journal of Abnormal Psychology,* 1965, *70*(6), 419–425.

Arenberg, D. A longitudinal study of problem solving in adults. *Journal of Gerontology,* 1974, *29,* 650–658.

Arenberg, D. The Baltimore longitudinal study. Paper presented at the meeting of the American Psychological Association, New York, September 1979.

Arenberg, D., & Robertson-Tchabo, E. Learning and aging. In J. E. Birren & K. W. Schaie (Eds.), *Handbook of the psychology of aging.* New York: Van Nostrand Reinhold, 1977.

Aries, P. *Centuries of childhood: A social history of family life* (R. Bladick, trans.). New York: Knopf, 1962.

Arling, G. The elderly widow and her family, neighbors and friends. *Journal of Marriage and the Family,* 1976, *38*(3), 757–768.

Astin, H. S. Continuing education and the development of adult women. *Counseling Psychologist,* 1976, *6*(1), 55–60.

Atchley, R. C. Retirement and work orientation. *Gerontologist,* 1971, *11*(1, Pt. 1), 29–32.

Atchley, R. C. Adjustment to loss of job at retirement. *International Journal of Aging and Human Development,* 1975, *6*(1), 17–27. (a)

Atchley, R. C. *The sociology of retirement.* Cambridge, Mass.: Schenkman, 1975. (b)

Atchley, R. C. The life course, age grading, and age-linked demands for decision making. In N. Datan & L. H. Ginsberg (Eds.), *Life-span developmental psychology: Normative life crises.* New York: Academic Press, 1975. (c)

Atchley, R. C. Selected social and psychological differences between men and women in later life. *Journal of Gerontology,* 1976, *31*(2), 204–211.

Atchley, R. C. *The social forces in later life* (2nd ed.). Belmont, Calif.: Wadsworth, 1977.

Atchley, R. C., & George, L. Symptomatic measurement of age. *Gerontologist,* 1973, *13,* 136–141.

Atchley, R. C., & Miller, S. J. Housing of the rural aged. In R. C. Atchley (Ed.), *Environments and the rural aged.* Washington, D. C.: Gerontological Society, 1975.

Atchley, R. C., Pignatiello, L., & Shaw, E. *The effect of marital status on social interaction patterns of older women.* Oxford, Ohio: Scripps Foundation, 1975.

Axelrod, S., & Cohen, L. D. Senescence and embedded figure performance in vision and touch. *Perceptual and Motor Skills,* 1961, *12,* 283.

Axelson, L. Personal adjustments in the postparental period. *Marriage and Family Living,* 1960, *22*(1), 66–70.

Ayllon, T., & Azrin, N. H. The measurement and reinforcement of behavior of psychotics. *Journal of Experimental Analysis of Behavior,* 1965, *8*(6), 357–383.

Babchuk, N. Primary ties of aged men. Paper presented at the meeting of the Gerontological Society, Washington, D.C., November 1979.

Babchuk, N., & Bates, A. P. The primary relations of middle-class couples: A study in male dominance. *American Sociological Review,* 1963, *8*(3), 377–384.

Back, K. W. Metaphors as test of personal philosophy of aging. *Sociological Focus,* 1971, *5,* 1–8. (a)

Back, K. W. Transition to aging and the self-image. *Aging and Human Development,* 1971, *2,* 296–304. (b)

Back, K. W., & Guptill, C. S. Retirement and self-ratings. In I. H. Simpson & J. McKinney (Eds.), *Social aspects of aging.* Durham, N.C.: Duke University Press, 1966.

Bahr, S. Effects of power and division of labor in the family. In L. Hoffman & G. Nye (Eds.), *Working mothers.* San Francisco: Jossey-Bass, 1973.

Bahrick, H. P., Bahrick, P. O., & Wittlinger, R. Fifty years of memory for names and faces: A cross-sectional approach. *Journal of Experimental Psychology: General,* 1975, *104*(1), 54–75.

Bailey, R. C., Finney, P., & Heim, B. Self-concept support and friendship duration. *Journal of Social Psychology,* 1975, *96*(2), 237–243.

Balinsky, B. An analysis of the mental factors of various age groups from nine to sixty. *Genetic Psychology Monographs,* 1941, *23,* 191–234.

Ballweg, J. A. Resolution of conjugal role adjustment after retirement. *Journal of Marriage and the Family,* 1967, *29*(2), 277–281.

Baltes, P. B. Prototypical paradigms and questions in life-span research on development and aging. *Gerontologist,* 1973, *13,* 458–467.

Baltes, P. B. Life-span developmental psychology: Some converging observations on history and theory. In P. B. Baltes & O. G. Brim (Eds.), *Life-span development and behavior* (Vol. 2). New York: Academic Press, 1979.

Baltes, P. B., & Baltes, M. Plasticity and variability in psychological aging: Methodological and theoretical issues. In C. Guerski (Ed.), *Aging and the CNS*. Berlin: Schering, 1980.

Baltes, P. B., Cornelius, S., & Nesselroade, J. R. Cohort effects in behavioral development: Theoretical and methodological perspectives. In W. A. Collins (Ed.), *Minnesota Symposium on Child Psychology* (Vol. 11). New York: Thomas Y. Crowell, 1978.

Baltes, P. B., & Labouvie, G. V. Adult development of intellectual performance: Description, explanation, and modification. In C. Eisdorfer & M. P. Lawton (Eds.), *The psychology of adult development and aging*. Washington, D.C.: American Psychological Association, 1973.

Baltes, P. B., Reese, H. W., & Nesselroade, J. R. *Life-span developmental psychology: Introduction to research methods*. Monterey, Calif.: Brooks/Cole, 1977.

Baltes, P. B., & Schaie, K. W. Epilogue: On life-span developmental research paradigms: Retrospects and prospects. In P. B. Baltes & K. W. Schaie (Eds.), *Life-span developmental psychology: Personality and socialization*. New York: Academic Press, 1973.

Baltes, P. B., & Willis, S. L. Toward psychological theories of aging and development. In J. E. Birren & K. W. Schaie (Eds.), *Handbook of the psychology of aging*. New York: Van Nostrand Reinhold, 1977.

Baltes, P. B., & Willis, S. The critical importance of appropriate methodology in the study of aging: The case of psychometric intelligence. Paper presented at Bayer-Symposium VII, Grosse Ledder, West Germany, October 1978.

Bandura, A. Social-learning theory of identificatory processes. In D. A. Goslin (Ed.), *Handbook of socialization theory and research*. Chicago: Rand McNally, 1969.

Bandura, A. *Psychological modeling: Conflicting theories*. Chicago: Aldine-Atherton, 1971.

Barber, C. E. Gender differences in experiencing the transition to the empty nest: Reports of middle-aged women and men. Paper presented at the meeting of the Gerontological Society, Dallas, November 1978.

Barczon, P. Grief and death. Unpublished paper, Psychology Department, Wayne State University, 1973.

Bardwick, J. *The psychology of women: A study of bio-cultural conflicts*. New York: Harper & Row, 1971.

Barfield, R., & Morgan, J. Trends in planned early retirement. *Gerontologist*, 1978, *18*, 13–18.

Barron, F. *Creativity and psychological health*.

Princeton, N.J.: D. Van Nostrand, 1963.

Bart, P. B. Why women's status changes in middle age: The turns of the social Ferris wheel. *Sociological Symposium*, 1969, *3*, 1–18.

Bart, P. B. Depression in middle-aged women. In V. Gornick & B. K. Moran (Eds.), *Woman in a sexist society: Studies in power and powerlessness*. New York: Basic Books, 1971.

Bart, P. B. Mother Portnoy's complaints. *Trans-Action*, 1978, *8*(1–2), 69–74.

Bartell, G. *Group sex*. New York: Wyden, 1971.

Baruch, R. The interruption and resumption of women's careers. *Harvard Studies in Career Development*, 1966, *50* (Whole Issue).

Baruch, R. The achievement motive in women: Implications for career development. *Journal of Personality and Social Psychology*, 1967, *5*(3), 260–267.

Basowitz, H., & Korchin, S. J. Age differences in the perception of closure. *Journal of Abnormal and Social Psychology*, 1957, *54*(1), 93–117.

Bastida, E. Family integration in later life among Hispanic Americans. Paper presented at the meeting of the Gerontological Society, Dallas, November 1978.

Baumrind, D. The development of instrumental competence through socialization: Focus on girls. In A. Pick (Ed.), *Minnesota Symposium on Child Psychology VII*. Minneapolis: University of Minnesota Press, 1972.

Bayley, N. Consistency of maternal and child behaviors in the Berkeley Growth Study. *Vita Humana*, 1964, *7*, 73–95.

Bayley, N. Behavioral correlates of mental growth: Birth to 36 years. *American Psychologist*, 1968, *23*(1), 1–10.

Bayley, N., & Oden, M. The maintenance of intellectual ability in gifted adults. *Journal of Gerontology*, 1955, *10*(1), 91–107.

Beard, B. B. Social and psychological correlates of residual memory in centenarians. *Gerontologist*, 1967, *7*(2, Pt. 1), 120–124.

Becker, H. S. The professional dance musician and his audience. *American Journal of Sociology*, 1951, *58*(2), 136–144.

Becker, H. S., Geer, B., Hughes, E., & Strauss, A. *Boys in white: Student culture in medical school*. Chicago: University of Chicago Press, 1961.

Becker, H. S., & Strauss, A. L. Careers, personality and adult socialization. *American Journal of Sociology*, 1956, *62*(3), 253–263.

Becker, W. C. Consequences of differential kinds of parental discipline. In M. L. Hoffman (Ed.), *Review of child development research* (Vol 1). New York: Russell Sage Foundation, 1964.

Belbin, E., & Belbin, R. M. New careers in middle age. In B. L. Neugarten (Ed.), *Middle Age and aging*. Chicago: University of Chicago Press, 1968.

Belbin, R. M. Retirement strategy in an evolving

society. In F. M. Carp (Ed.), *Retirement*. New York: Behavioral Publications, 1972.

Bell, R. R. The lower class Negro mother's aspirations for her children. *Social Forces*, 1965, *43*(4), 493–500.

Bell, R. R. Sexuality and sex roles. Ford Foundation Conference, Merrill-Palmer, Detroit, November 1975.

Bender, I. E. Changes in religious interest. A retest of 15 years. *Journal of Abnormal and Social Psychology*, 1958, *57*(1), 41–46.

Benedek, T. Sexual functions in women and their disturbance. In S. Arieti (Ed.), *American handbook of psychiatry*. New York: Basic Books, 1959.

Bengtson, V. L. The generation gap: A review and typology of social-psychological perspectives. *Youth and Society*, 1970, *2*(1), 7–32.

Bengtson, V. L. Inter-age perceptions and the generation gap. *Gerontologist*, 1971, *11*, (4, Pt. 2), 85–89.

Bengtson, V. L. Generation and family effects in value socialization. *American Sociological Review*, 1975, *40*(3), 358–371.

Bengtson, V. L., & Black, D. Intergenerational relations and continuities in socialization. In P. B. Baltes & K. W. Schaie (Eds.), *Life-span developmental psychology: Personality and socialization*. New York: Academic Press, 1973. (a)

Bengtson, V. L., & Black, K. D. Solidarity between parents and children. Paper presented at the annual meeting of the National Council on Family Relations, Toronto, October 1973. (b)

Bengtson, V. L., & Cutler, N. Generations and intergenerational relations: Perspectives on age groups and social change. In R. H. Binstock & E. Shanas (Eds.), *Handbook of aging and the social sciences*. New York: Van Nostrand Reinhold, 1976.

Bengtson, V. L., Kasschau, P., & Ragan, P. K. The impact of social structure on aging individuals. In J. E. Birren & K. W. Schaie (Eds.), *Handbook of the psychology of aging*. New York: Van Nostrand Reinhold, 1977.

Bengtson, V. L., & Kuypers, J. A. Generational difference and the developmental stake. *Aging and Human Development*, 1971, *2*, 249–260.

Bengtson, V. L. & Starr, J. M. Contrasts and consensus: A generational analysis of youth in the 1970s. In R. Havighurst (Ed.), *Youth: The 74th Yearbook of the National Society for the Study of Education*. Pt. 1. Chicago: University of Chicago Press, 1975.

Bengtson, V. L., & Troll, L. E. Youth and their parents: Feedback and intergenerational influence in socialization. In R. Lerner & G. Spanier (Eds.), *Child influences on marital and family interaction*. New York: Academic Press, 1978.

Benson, R. C. *Handbook of obstetrics and gynecology* (6th ed.) Los Altos, Calif.: Lange Medical Publications, 1977.

Berg, B., & Simms, H. Nutrition and longevity in the rat. II. Longevity and onset of disease with different levels of feed intake. *Journal of Nutrition*, 1960, *71*(3), 255–263.

Berg, B., & Simms, H. Nutrition and longevity in the rat. III. Food restriction beyond 800 days. *Journal of Nutrition*, 1961, *74*(1), 23–32.

Bergman, M., Blumenfeld, V. G., Cascardo, D., Dash, B., Levitt, H., & Margulies, M. K. Age-related decrement in hearing for speech: Sampling and longitudinal studies. *Journal of Gerontology*, 1976, *31*(5), 533–538.

Berkowitz, B., & Green, R. Changes in intellect with age. V. Differential changes as functions of time interval and original score. *Journal of Genetic Psychology*, 1965, *107*, 179–192.

Bernard, J. *The future of marriage*. New York: Bantam Books, 1973.

Bernard, J. Note on changing life styles, 1970–1974. *Journal of Marriage and the Family*, 1975, *37*(3), 582–593.

Berscheid, E., & Walster, E. H. *Interpersonal attraction*. Reading, Mass.: Addison-Wesley, 1978.

Bickel, H. F. An analysis of the work values of women: Implications for counseling. *Dissertation Abstracts*, 1968, *29*, 3761A.

Bigelow, B. J. Children's friendships expectations: A cognitive-developmental study. *Child Development*, 1977, *48*(1), 246–253.

Bigelow, B. J., & la Gaipa, J. Children's written descriptions of friendship: A multidimensional analysis. *Developmental Psychology*, 1975, *11*(6), 857–858.

Biggar, J. Who moved among the elderly, 1965 to 1970. *Research on Aging*, 1980, *2*(1), 73–91.

Birkhill, W., & Schaie, K. W. The effect of differential reinforcement of cautiousness in intellectual performance among the elderly. *Journal of Gerontology*, 1975, *30*(5), 578–583.

Birren, J. E. Age differences in learning a two-choice water maze by rats. *Journal of Gerontology*, 1962, *17*(2), 207.

Birren, J. E. Psychophysiological relations. In J. E. Birren, R. N. Butler, S. W. Greenhouse, L. Sokoloff, & M. E. Yarrow (Eds.), *Human aging: A biological and behavioral study*. Washington, D.C.: U.S. Government Printing Office, 1963.

Birren, J. E. Age and decision strategies. In A. T. Welford & J. E. Birren (Eds.), *Interdisciplinary topics in gerontology* (Vol. 4). Basel: Karger, 1969.

Birren, J. E., Butler, R., Greenhouse, S., Sokoloff, L., & Yarrow, M. *Human aging I: A biological and behavioral study*. Rockville, Md.: Section on Mental Health of the Aging, National Institute of Mental Health, 1971.

Birren, J. E., & Renner, V. Research on the psychology of aging: Principles and experimentation. In J. E. Birren & K. W. Schaie (Eds.), *Handbook of the psychology of aging*. New York:

Van Nostrand Reinhold, 1977.

Birren, J. E., Riegel, K., & Morrison, D. F. Age differences in response speed as a function of controlled variations of stimulus conditions. *Gerontologia*, 1962, *6*, 1–18.

Birren, J. E., & Schaie, K. W. (Eds.). *Handbook of the psychology of aging.* New York: Van Nostrand Reinhold, 1977.

Bischof, L. J. *Adult psychology.* New York: Harper & Row, 1969.

Blaha, G. C. Reproductive senescence in the female golden hamster. *Anatomical Record*, 1964, *150*, 405–412.

Blau, Z. S. Structural constraints on friendship in old age. *American Sociological Review*, 1961, *26*(3), 429–439.

Blau, Z. S. *Old age in a changing society.* New York: Franklin Watts, 1973.

Blenkner, M. Social work and family relationships in later life with some thoughts on filial maturity. In E. Shanas & G. Streib (Eds.), *Social structure and the family.* Englewood Cliffs, N.J.: Prentice-Hall, 1965.

Block, E. Quantitative morphological investigations of the follicular system in women: Variations at different ages. *Acta Anatomica*, 1952, *14*, 108–123.

Block, E. A quantitative morphological investigation of the follicular system in newborn female infants. *Acta Anatomica*, 1953, *17*, 201–206.

Blood, R. O., Jr., & Wolfe, D. M. *Husbands and wives: The dynamics of married living.* New York: Free Press, 1960.

Bloom, K. Age and self-concept. *American Journal of Psychiatry*, 1961, *118*(6), 534–538.

Blum, J., Fosshage, J. L., & Jarvik, L. F. Intellectual changes and sex differences in octogenarians: A twenty-year longitudinal study of aging. *Developmental Psychology*, 1972, *7*(2), 178–187.

Booth, A. Sex and social participation. *American Sociological Review*, 1972, *37*(2), 183–192.

Booth, A., & Hess, E. Cross-sex friendship. *Journal of Marriage and the Family*, 1974, *36*(1), 38–47.

Borland, D. An investigation of the empty nest syndrome among parents of different marital status categories: Evidence from national surveys. Paper presented at the meeting of the Gerontological Society, Washington, D.C., November 1979.

Bornstein, P., Clayton, P., Halikas, J., Maurice, W., & Robins, E. The depression of widowhood after thirteen months. *British Journal of Psychiatry*, 1973, *122*(5), 561–566.

Bortner, R., & Hultsch, D. Subjective deprivation: Characteristics of groups demonstrating different patterns of subjective deprivation. Unpublished manuscript, College of Human Development, Pennsylvania State University, 1976.

Bossard, J., & Boll, E. *The large family.* Philadelphia: University of Pennsylvania Press, 1956.

Bott, E. *Family and social network: Roles, norms, and external relationships in ordinary urban families.* New York: Free Press, 1971. (Originally published, 1957.)

Botwinick, J. Theories of antecedent conditions of speed of response. In A. T. Welford & J. E. Birren (Eds.), *Behavior, aging, and the nervous system.* Springfield, Ill.: Charles C Thomas, 1965.

Botwinick, J. Cautiousness in advanced age. *Journal of Gerontology*, 1966, *21*(3), 347.

Botwinick, J. *Cognitive processes in maturity and old age.* New York: Springer, 1967.

Botwinick, J. Disinclination to venture response versus cautiousness in responding: Age differences. *Journal of Genetic Psychology*, 1969, *115*(1), 55–62.

Botwinick, J. Learning in children and older adults. In L. R. Goulet & P. B. Baltes (Eds.), *Life-span developmental psychology: Research and theory.* New York: Academic Press, 1970.

Botwinick, J. Intellectual abilities. In J. E. Birren & K. W. Schaie (Eds.), *Handbook of the psychology of aging.* New York: Van Nostrand Reinhold, 1977.

Botwinick, J., Brinley, J. F., & Robbin, J. S. Learning a position discrimination and position reversals by Sprague-Dawley rats of different ages. *Journal of Gerontology*, 1962, *17*(2), 315.

Botwinick, J., Brinley, J. F., & Robbin, J. S. Learning and reversing a four-choice multiple Y-maze by rats of three ages. *Journal of Gerontology*, 1963, *18*(3), 279.

Botwinick, J., & Storandt, M. *Memory: Related functions and age.* Springfield, Ill.: Charles C Thomas, 1974.

Botwinick, J., & Thompson, L. Age differences in reaction time: An artifact. *Gerontologist*, 1968, *8*(1), 25–28.

Botwinick, J., West, R., & Storandt, M. Predicting death from behavioral test performances. *Journal of Gerontology*, 1978, *33*(5), 755–762.

Bourestom, N., & Pastalan, L. *Final report on forced relocation: Setting, staff, and patient effects.* Ann Arbor: Institute of Gerontology at the University of Michigan, 1975.

Bowerman, C., & Dobash, R. M. Structural variations in inter-sibling affect. *Journal of Marriage and the Family*, 1974, *36*, 48–54.

Bowerman, C., & Elder, G. H. Variations in adolescent perceptions of family power structure. *American Sociological Review*, 1964, *29*, 551–567.

Bowlby, J. *Attachment.* New York: Basic Books, 1969.

Boyd, R. Emerging roles of the four-generation family. In R. Boyd & C. Oakes (Eds.), *Foundations of practical gerontology.* Columbia: University of South Carolina Press, 1969.

Bracey, H. E. *In retirement: Pensioners in Great Britain and the United States.* Baton Rouge: Louisiana State University Press, 1966.

Bradburn, N., and Caplovitz, D. *Reports on*

happiness. Chicago: Aldine-Atherton, 1965.

Bradley, R. H., & Webb, R. Age-related differences in locus of control orientation in three behavioral domains. *Human Development,* 1976, *19*(1), 49–55.

Bradway, K. P., Thompson, C. W., & Cravens, R. B. Preschool I.Q.'s after twenty-five years. *Journal of Educational Psychology,* 1958, *49*(5), 278–281.

Bram, S. To have or have not: A comparison of parents, parents-to-be, and childless couples. Unpublished doctoral dissertation, University of Michigan, 1974.

Braun, H. W., & Geiselhart, R. Age differences in the acquisition and extinction of the conditioned eyelid response. *Journal of Experimental Psychology,* 1959, *57*(6), 386–388.

Bray, D. Personal communication, 1978.

Bray, D., Campbell, R., & Grant, D. *Formative years in business: A long-term study of managerial lives.* New York: Wiley, 1974.

Bray, D., & Howard, A. Career success and life satisfactions of middle-aged managers. Paper presented at the Fourth Vermont Conference on the Primary Prevention of Psychopathology, June 1978.

Breytspaak, L. Achievement and the self-concept in middle age. In E. Palmore (Ed.), *Normal aging II.* Durham, N.C.: Duke University Press, 1974.

Brim, O. G. Theories of the male mid-life crisis. In N. K. Schlossberg & A. D. Entine (Eds.), *Counseling adults.* Monterey, Calif.: Brooks/Cole, 1977.

Britton, J. H., & Britton, J. O. The middle-aged and older rural person and his family. In G. E. Youmans (Ed.), *Older rural Americans.* Lexington: University of Kentucky, 1967.

Britton, J. O., & Britton, J. H. Discrimination of age by preschool children. *Journal of Gerontology,* 1969, *24*(4), 457–460. (a)

Britton, J. O., & Britton, J. H. Discrimination and perception of age and aging by elementary school children. *Proceedings of the 77th Annual Convention of the American Psychological Association,* 1969, *4*(Pt. 2), 715–716. (b)

Britton, J. O., & Britton, J. H. *Personality changes in aging: A longitudinal study of community residents.* New York: Springer, 1972.

Broadbent, D. E., & Heron, A. Effects of a subsidiary task on performance involving immediate memory by younger and older men. *British Journal of Psychology,* 1962, *53,* 189–198.

Broderick, C. B., & Rowe, G. A. A scale of pre-adolescent heterosexual development. *Journal of Marriage and the Family,* 1968, *30,* 97–101.

Brody, E. M. Health and its social implications. In M. Marvis (Ed.), *Le vieillisement: Un defi à la science et à la politique sociale.* Paris: Institute de la Vie, 1977.

Bromley, D. B. Some effects of age on short-term learning and memory. *Journal of Gerontology,* 1958, *13*(4), 398–406.

Bromley, D. B. Age and sex differences in the serial production of creative conceptual responses. *Journal of Gerontology,* 1967, *22*(1), 32–42.

Brooks, J., & Lewis, M. Infant social perception: Responses to pictures of parents and strangers. *Developmental Psychology,* in press.

Brotman, H. *Facts and figures on older Americans, No. 5. An overview.* Washington, D.C.: U.S. Department of Health, Education, and Welfare, Administration on Aging, 1971.

Brown, A. S. Satisfying relationships for the elderly and their patterns of disengagement. *Gerontologist,* 1974, *14*(3), 258–262.

Büchi, E. C. Anderung der Körperform beim erwachsenen Menschen, eine Untersuchung nach der Individual-Methode. *Anthropologische Forschungen* (vol. 1). Wien: Anthropologische Gesellschaft, 1950.

Buhler, C. Theoretical observations about life's basic tendencies. *American Journal of Psychotherapy,* 1959, *13*(3), 561–581.

Buhler, C. The developmental structure of goal setting in group and individual studies. In C. Buhler & F. Massarik (Eds.), *The course of human life.* New York: Springer, 1968.

Bullock, J. Personal communication, 1978.

Bultena, G. L., & Wood, V. The American retirement community: Bane or blessing? *Journal of Gerontology,* 1969, *24*(2), 209–217.

Burgess, E. W., & Wallin, P. *Engagement and marriage.* Philadelphia: Lippincott, 1953.

Burkitt, D. Diverticular disease of the colon, epidemiologic evidence relating it to fiber-depleted diets. *Transactions of Medical Society of London,* 1973, *89,* 81–84.

Burnet, M. *Intrinsic mutagenesis: A genetic approach to aging.* New York: Wiley, 1974.

Burns, T. The reference of conduct in small groups: Cliques and cabals in occupational milieux. *Human Relations,* 1955, *8*(4), 476.

Burr, W. R. Satisfaction with various aspects of marriage over the life cycle: A random middle-class sample. *Journal of Marriage and the Family,* 1970, *32*(1), 29–37.

Butler, R. N. The life review: An interpretation of reminiscence in the aged. *Psychiatry,* 1963, *26*(1), 65–76.

Butler, R. N. Creativity in later life. In S. Levin & R. J. Kahana (Eds.), *Psychodynamic studies on aging: Creativity, reminiscing, and dying.* New York: International Universities Press, 1967.

Butler, R. N. Age-ism: Another form of bigotry. *Gerontologist,* 1969, *9*(2), 243.

Butler, R. N., & Lewis, M. *Sex after sixty: A guide for men and women for their later years.* New York: Harper & Row, 1976.

Byrne, D. *An introduction to personality.* Englewood Cliffs, N.J.: Prentice-Hall, 1966.

Byrne, J. D. Mobility rate of employed persons into

new occupations. Bureau of Labor Statistics, Manpower and Employment, Special Labor Force Reports. *Monthly Labor Review,* February 1975, pp. 53-59.

Cain, L. D., Jr. *Age status and generational phenomena: The new old people in contemporary America,* 1967, *7,* 83-92.

Campbell, A., Converse, P. E., & Rodgers, W. L. *The quality of American life: Perceptions, evaluation, and satisfaction.* New York: Russell Sage Foundation, 1976.

Campbell, M. E. Study of the attitudes of nursing personnel toward the geriatric patients. *Nursing Research,* 1971, *20,* 147-251.

Candy, S. A comparative analysis of friendship functions in six age groups of men and women. Unpublished doctoral dissertation, Wayne State University, 1977.

Canestrari, R. E., Jr. Paced and self-paced learning in young and elderly adults. *Journal of Gerontology,* 1963, *18*(2), 165-168.

Cantor, M. The extent and intensity of the informal support system among New York's inner city elderly—Is ethnicity a factor? Paper presented at a conference entitled "The Family's Role in Caring for the Aged: How Can We Help?" Hunter College School of Social Work, May 1977.

Cantril, H. *The pattern of human concerns.* New Brunswick, N.J.: Rutgers University Press, 1965.

Carp, F. M. Differences among older workers, volunteers and persons who are neither. *Journal of Gerontology,* 1968, *23*(2), 497-501.

Carter, H., & Glick, P. C. *Marriage and divorce: A social and economic study.* Cambridge, Mass.: Harvard University Press, 1970.

Cartwright, A., Hockey, L., & Anderson, J. S. *Life before death.* London: Routledge & Kegan Paul, 1973.

Cattell, R. B. Theory of fluid and crystallized intelligence: A critical experiment. *Journal of Educational Psychology,* 1963, *54*(1), 1-22.

Charness, N. Search in chess: Age and skill differences. *Journal of Experimental Psychology, Human Perception and Performance,* in press.

Child, C. M. *Senescence and rejuvenescence.* Chicago: University of Chicago Press, 1915.

Childers, P., & Wimmer, M. The concept of death in early childhood. *Child Development,* 1971, *42*(4), 705-715.

Chiriboga, D. Conceptualizing adult transitions: A new look at an old subject. *Generations,* 1979, *4*(1), 4-5. (a)

Chiriboga, D. Marital separation in early and late life: A comparison. Paper presented at the meeting of the Gerontological Society, Dallas, November 1979. (b)

Chown, S. M. Age and the rigidities. *Journal of Gerontology,* 1961, *16*(4), 353-362.

Christenson, C. V., & Gagnon, J. H. Sexual behavior in a group of older women. *Journal of Gerontology,* 1965, *20,* 351-356.

Cicirelli, V. Social services for elderly in relation to the kin network. Report to the National Retired Teachers Association/American Association of Retired Persons, Andrus Foundation, Washington, D.C., 1979.

Cicirelli, V. A comparison of college women's feelings toward their siblings and parents. *Journal of Marriage and the Family,* 1980, *42*(1), 111-120. (a)

Cicirelli, V. Sibling relationships in adulthood: A life span perspective. In L. Poon (Ed.), *Aging in the 1980s.* Washington, D.C.: American Psychological Association, 1980. (b)

Clague, E. The age problem in research workers: A sociological viewpoint. *Science Monthly,* 1951, *72,* 359-363.

Clark, A. L., & Wallin, P. Women's sexual responsiveness and the duration and quality of their marriages. *American Journal of Sociology,* 1965, *71*(2), 187-196.

Clark, L., & Knowles, J. B. Age differences in dichotic listening performance. *Journal of Gerontology,* 1973, *28*(2), 173-178.

Clark, M. The anthropology of aging: A new area for studies of culture and personality. *Gerontologist,* 1967, *7,* 55-64.

Clark, M. Cultural values and dependency in later life. In R. A. Kalish (Ed.), *The dependencies of old people.* Ann Arbor: Institute of Gerontology, University of Michigan, 1969.

Clark, M. An anthropological view of retirement. In F. M. Carp (Ed.), *Retirement.* New York: Behavioral Publications, 1972.

Clark, M., & Anderson, B. *Culture and aging.* Springfield, Ill.: Charles C Thomas, 1967.

Clausen, J. A. The life course of individuals. In M. W. Riley, M. Johnson, & A. Foner (Eds.), *The sociology of age stratification.* New York: Russell Sage Foundation, 1972.

Clayton, V. The meaning of wisdom to young and old in contemporary society. Paper presented at the meeting of the Gerontological Society, Louisville, Ky., October 1975.

Clement, F. J. Longitudinal and cross-sectional assessments of age changes in physical strength as related to sex, social class, and mental ability. *Journal of Gerontology,* 1974, *29*(4), 423-429.

Cleveland, W. P., & Gianturco, D. T. Remarriage probability after widowhood: A retrospective method. *Journal of Gerontology,* 1976, *31*(1), 99-103.

Coe, R. Professional perspectives on the aged. *Gerontologist,* 1967, *7*(2), 114-119.

Cohler, B. Close-knit ethnic ties can heighten stress in older women. *Behavior Today,* 1974, *7,* 3-4.

Cokinda, R. M. An identification of differences between participating and non-participating automobile workers in a pre-retirement education program. Unpublished doctoral dissertation, School of Education, Wayne State University, 1972.

Colette-Pratt, C. Attitudinal predictors of devaluation of old age in a multigenerational sample. Unpublished doctoral dissertation, University of Oregon, 1975.

Collins, G. R. Changes in optimal level of complexity as a function of age. *Dissertation Abstracts*, 1964, *24*(5538).

Comalli, P. E., Jr. Differential effects of context on perception in young and aged groups. Paper presented at the meeting of the Gerontological Society, Miami Beach, Fla., October 1962.

Comalli, P. E., Jr. Perceptual closure in middle and old age. Paper presented at the meeting of the Gerontological Society, Boston, October 1963.

Comalli, P. E., Jr. Cognitive functioning in a group of 80- to 90-year-old men. *Journal of Gerontology*, 1965, *20*(1), 14–17.

Comalli, P. E., Jr. Life-span changes in visual perception. In L. R. Goulet & P. B. Baltes (Eds.), *Life-span developmental psychology: Research and theory*. New York: Academic Press, 1970.

Comalli, P. E., Jr., Wapner, S., & Werner, H. Perception of verticality in middle and old age. *Journal of Psychology*, 1959, *47*(2), 259–266.

Comalli, P. E., Jr., Wapner, S., & Werner, H. Interference effects of the Stroop color word test in childhood, adulthood, and aging. *Journal of Genetic Psychology*, 1962, *100*(1), 47–53.

Comfort, A. *The process of aging*. New York: Signet Science Library, New American Library, 1964.

Constantine, L. L., & Constantine, J. M. *Group marriage*. New York: Collier Books, 1973.

Coombs, R. H., & Kenkel, W. F. Sex differences in dating aspirations and satisfactions with computer-selected partners. *Journal of Marriage and the Family*, 1966, *28*(1), 62–66.

Costa, P., & McCrae, R. Age differences in personality structure: A cluster analytic approach. *Journal of Gerontology*, 1976, *31*(5), 564–570.

Cottle, T. J. *Time's children: Impressions of youth*. Boston: Little, Brown, 1967.

Cottrell, W. F. *Technological change and labor in the railroad industry*. Lexington, Mass.: Heath, 1970.

Cottrell, W. F., & Atchley, R. C. *Women in retirement: A preliminary report*. Oxford, Ohio: Scripps Foundation, 1969.

Coyne, A. C., Whitbourne, S. K., & Glenwick, D. S. Adult age differences in reflection-impulsivity. *Journal of Gerontology*, 1978, *33*(3), 402–407.

Coyne, J., & Lazarus, R. The ipsative-normative framework for the longitudinal study of stress. Paper presented at the meeting of the American Psychological Association, San Francisco, August 1979.

Cozby, P. C., & Rosenblatt, P. C. Privacy, love, and in-law avoidance. *Proceedings of the 79th Annual Convention of the American Psychological Association*, 1971, *6*(Pt. 1), 277–278.

Craig, T. J. Epidemiological comparison of breast cancer patients with early and late onsets of malignancy and general population controls. *Journal of the National Cancer Institute*, 1974, *53*(6), 1577–1581.

Craik, F. I. M. The nature of the age decrement in performance on dichotic listening. *Journal of Gerontology*, 1965, *17*, 227–240.

Craik, F. I. M. Age differences in human memory. In J. E. Birren & K. W. Schaie (Eds.), *Handbook of the psychology of aging*. New York: Van Nostrand Reinhold, 1977.

Craik, F. I. M., & Masani, P. Age and intelligence differences in coding and retrieval of word lists. *British Journal of Psychology*, 1969, *60*(3), 315–319.

Crandall, V., & Battle, E. The antecedents and adult correlates of academic and intellectual achievement effort. In P. J. Hill (Ed.), *Minnesota Symposia on Child Psychology* (Vol. 4). Minneapolis: University of Minnesota Press, 1970.

Crites, J. *Vocational psychology*. New York: McGraw-Hill, 1969.

Cropley, A. J. Creativity, intelligence and intellectual style. *Australian Journal of Education*, 1969, *13*(1), 3–7.

Crowley, J. E., Levitin, T. E., & Quinn, R. P. Seven deadly half-truths about women. *Psychology Today*, 1973, *6*(10), 94–96.

Csikszentmihalyi, M., Graef, R., & Larson, R. Age differences in the quality of subjective experience. Paper presented at the meeting of the American Psychological Association, San Francisco, August 1979.

Cuber, J. F., & Harroff, P. B. The more total view: Relationships among men and women of the upper middle class. *Marriage and Family Living*, 1963, *25*, 140–145.

Cumming, E., & Henry, W. *Growing old: The process of disengagement*. New York: Basic Books, 1961.

Cunningham, W. R. Age changes in the factor structure of intellectual abilities in adulthood and old age. Unpublished doctoral dissertation, University of Southern California, 1974.

Cunningham, W. R., Clayton, V., & Overton, W. Fluid and crystallized intelligence in young adulthood and old age. *Journal of Gerontology*, 1975, *30*(1), 53–55.

Cutler, B. R., & Dyer, W. A. Initial adjustment processes in young married couples. *Social Forces*, 1965, *44*(2), 195–201.

Cutler, N. E. Demographic, social psychological and political factors in the politics of age: A call for research and political gerontology. *American Political Science Review*, 1977, *71*(3), 1011–1025.

Cutler, N. E., & Harootyan, R. Demography of the aged. In D. Woodruff & J. E. Birren (Eds.), *Aging:*

Scientific perspectives and social issues. New York: Van Nostrand Reinhold, 1975.

Cutler, S. J. Perceived prestige loss and political attitudes among the aged. *Gerontologist*, 1973, *13*, 69–74.

Darling, J. An interactional interpretation of bachelorhood and late marriage: The process of entering into, remaining in, and leaving careers of singleness. Unpublished doctoral dissertation, University of Connecticut, 1976.

Datan, N., Antonovsky, A., & Maoz, B. *A time to reap.* Baltimore, Md.: Johns Hopkins University Press, 1981.

Datan, N., & Rodeheaver, D. The sensuous grand-mother. Paper presented at the meeting of the American Psychological Association, San Francisco, August 1977.

Davies, A., & Laytham, G. Perception of verticality in adult life. *British Journal of Psychology*, 1964, *55*(3), 315–320.

Dawson, M. *Graduate and married.* Sidney, Australia: Department of Adult Education, University of Sidney, 1965.

De Beauvoir, S. *The second sex.* New York: Knopf, 1953.

De Carlo, T. Recreation participation patterns and successful aging. *Journal of Gerontology*, 1974, *29*(4), 416–422.

De Frain, J., & Eirick, R. Coping as divorced single parents: A comparative study of fathers and mothers. Paper presented at the meeting of the American Psychological Association, San Francisco, August 1979.

De Lissovoy, V. High school marriages: A longitudinal study. *Journal of Marriage and the Family*, 1973, *35*(2), 245–255.

DeLora, J., & Moses, D. V. Specialty preferences and characteristics of nursing students in baccalaureate programs. *Nursing Research*, 1969, *18*, 137–144.

Denney, N., & Lennon, M. Classification: A comparison of middle and old age. *Developmental Psychology*, 1972, *7*, 210–213.

Denney, N., & List, J. Adult age differences in performance on the Matching Familiar Figures Test. *Human Development*, 1979, *22*(1), 137–144.

Dennis, W. Age and creative productivity. *Journal of Gerontology*, 1966, *21*(1), 1–8.

Deutscher, I. The quality of postparental life: Definitions of the situation. *Journal of Marriage and the Family*, 1964, *26*(1), 52–59.

Diggory, J., & Rothman, D. Values destroyed by death. *Journal of Abnormal and Social Psychology*, 1961, *63*(1), 205–210.

Dingle, J. *The ills of man: Life and death and medicine* (a Scientific American Book). San Francisco: W. H. Freeman, 1973.

Dobrof, R., & Litwak, E. *Maintenance of family ties of long-term care patients: Theory and guide to practice.* Washington, D.C.: U.S. Government Printing Office, 1977.

Doering, C. The endocrine system. In O. G. Brim & J. Kagen (Eds.), *Constancy and change in human development.* Cambridge, Mass.: Harvard University Press, 1980.

Dolen, L. Interpersonal activity and social cognitive ability in the elderly. Unpublished doctoral dissertation, City University of New York (CUNY) Graduate Center, 1980.

Doll, R. Cancer and aging: The epidemiological evidence. In *Tenth International Cancer Congress*, pp. 133–160. Chicago: Year Book Medical Publishers, 1970.

Donelson, E., & Gullahorn, J. *Women: A psychological perspective.* New York: Wiley, 1977.

Dortzbach, J. Moral judgment in adults: Effects of education. Paper presented at the meeting of the American Psychological Association, San Francisco, August 1979.

Douglass, E., Cleveland, W., & Maddox, G. Political attitudes, age, and aging: A cohort analysis of archival data. *Journal of Gerontology*, 1974, *29*(6), 666–675.

Douvan, E. Differing views on marriage 1957 to 1976. *Newsletter, Center for Continuing Education of Women* (University of Michigan), 1979, *12*(1), 1–2.

Douvan, E., & Adelson, J. *The adolescent experience.* New York: Wiley, 1966.

Dowd, J., & Bengtson, V. Social participation, age, and ethnicity: An examination of the "double jeopardy" hypothesis. Paper presented at the meeting of the Gerontological Society, Louisville, Ky., October 1975.

Dressel, P., & Avant, W. Neogamy and older persons: An examination of alternatives for intimacy in the later years. *Alternative Lifestyles*, 1978, *1*(1), 13–36.

Dubin, R. Industrial workers' worlds: A study of the "central life interests" of industrial workers. *Social Problems*, 1956, *3*(3), 131–142.

Dublin, L. *Factbook on man.* New York: Macmillan, 1965.

Duck, S. W. Similarity and perceived similarity of personal constructs as influences on friendship choice. *British Journal of Social and Clinical Psychology*, 1973, *12*(1), 1–6.

Duck, S. W., & Spencer, C. Personal constructs and friendship formation. *Journal of Personality and Social Psychology*, 1972, *23*(1), 40–45.

Duke, M., Shaheen, J., & Nowicki, S. The determination of locus of control in a geriatric population and a subsequent test of the social learning model for interpersonal distances. *Journal of Psychology*, 1974, *86*(2), 277–285.

Duncan, O. D., Schuman, H., & Duncan, B. *Social change in a metropolitan community.* New York: Russell Sage Foundation, 1973.

Duvall, E. M. *In-laws pro and con.* New York: Associates Press, 1954.

Duvall, E. M. *Family development* (4th ed.). Philadelphia: Lippincott, 1971.

Dyer, L. Career implications of job displacement in middle-age: Experiences of managers and engineers. Paper presented at the meeting of the Gerontological Society, San Juan, Puerto Rico, November 1972.

Dykers, M. Differences between students from Western and non-Western societies in dyadic relationships with relatives and friends. Unpublished paper, Departments of Psychology and Sociology, Wayne State University, 1974.

Eckensberger, L. H., Lonner, W. J., & Poortingas, Y. H. (Eds.). *Cross-cultural contributions to psychology: Selected papers from the 4th International Conference of the International Association for Cross-Cultural Psychology, held at Berwyn, Pennsylvania.* Lisse: Swets & Zeitlinger, 1979.

Eichorn, D. The Institute of Human Development Studies, Berkeley and Oakland. In L. F. Jarvik, C. Eisdorfer, & J. Blum (Eds.), *Intellectual functioning in adults.* New York: Springer, 1973.

Eisdorfer, C. Arousal and performance: Experiments in verbal learning and a tentative theory. In G. A. Talland (Ed.), *Human aging and behavior.* New York: Academic Press, 1968.

Eisdorfer, C. Adaptation to loss of work. In F. M. Carp (Ed.), *Retirement.* New York: Academic Press, 1972.

Eisdorfer, C., Axelrod, S., & Wilkie, F. Stimulus exposure time as a factor in serial learning in an aged sample. *Journal of Abnormal and Social Psychology,* 1963, *67*(6), 594–600.

Eisdorfer, C., Nowlin, J., & Wilkie, F. Improvement of learning in the aged by modification of autonomic nervous system activity. *Science,* 1970, *170*(3964), 1327–1329.

Eisdorfer, C., & Stotsky, B. Intervention, treatment, and rehabilitation of psychiatric disorders. In J. E. Birren & K. W. Schaie (Eds.), *Handbook of the psychology of aging.* New York: Van Nostrand Reinhold, 1977.

Eisdorfer, C., & Wilkie, F. Intellectual changes with advancing age. In F. L. Jarvik, C. Eisdorfer, & J. Blum (Eds.), *Intellectual functioning in adults.* New York: Springer, 1973.

Eisner, D., & Schaie, K. W. Age changes in response to visual illusions from middle to old age. *Journal of Gerontology,* 1971, *26*(2), 146.

Ekman, P., & Friesen, W. Constants across cultures in the face and emotion. *Journal of Personality and Social Psychology,* 1971, *17*(2), 124–129.

Elder, G. Structural variations in the child rearing relationship. *Sociometry,* 1962, *25*(3), 241–262.

Elder, G. *Children of the Great Depression.* Chicago: University of Chicago Press, 1974.

Elias, M., & Elias, P. Motivation and activity. In J. E. Birren & K. W. Schaie (Eds.), *Handbook of the psychology of aging.* New York: Van Nostrand Reinhold, 1977.

Elias, M., Elias, P., & Elias, J. *Basic processes in adult developmental psychology.* St. Louis: C. V. Mosby, 1977.

Elias, M., & Kinsbourne, M. Age and sex differences in the processing of verbal and non-verbal stimuli. *Journal of Gerontology,* 1974, *29*(2), 162.

Elkind, D. *Children and adolescents.* New York: Oxford University Press, 1970.

Elo, A. Age changes in master chess performance. *Journal of Gerontology,* 1965, *20*(3), 289–299.

Ennis, P. The definition and measurement of leisure. In E. Sheldon & W. Moore (Eds.), *Indicators of social change.* New York: Russell Sage Foundation, 1968.

Erikson, E. *Childhood and society.* New York: Norton, 1950.

Erikson, E. Identity and the life cycle: Selected papers. *Psychological Issues,* *1*(Whole Issue), 1959.

Erikson, E. *Identity, youth and crisis.* New York: Norton, 1968.

Everett, A. The hypothalamic-pituitary control of aging and age-related pathology. *Experimental Gerontology,* 1973, *8*(5), 265–277.

Eyde, L. Work motivation of women college graduates: Five-year follow-up. *Journal of Counseling Psychology,* 1968, *15*(2), 199–202.

Eysenck, M. W. Age differences in incidental learning. *Developmental Psychology,* 1974, *10*(6), 936–941.

Farrimond, T. Retention and recall: Incidental learning of visual and auditory material. *Journal of Genetic Psychology,* 1968, *113*(2), 155–165.

Feifel, H., & Branscomb, A. Who's afraid of death? *Journal of Abnormal Psychology,* 1973, *81*(3), 282–288.

Feifel, H., Jones, R., & Edwards, L. Death attitudes in older persons related to nearness to death. Paper presented at the meeting of the American Psychological Association, San Francisco, August 1968.

Feldman, H. *Development of the husband-wife relationship.* Research report presented to the Department of Child Development and Family Relationships, New York State College of Home Economics, Cornell University, Ithaca, N.Y., August 1964.

Feldman, H. The effects of children on the family. In A. Michel (Ed.), *Family issues of employed women in Europe and America.* Leiden: Brill, 1971.

Feldman, S., & Nash, S. Interest in babies during young adulthood. *Child Development,* 1978, *49*(3), 617–622.

Feldman, S., & Nash, S. Sex differences in responsiveness to babies among mature adults. *Developmental Psychology,* 1979, *15*(4), 430–436.

Felton, B., & Kahana, E. Adjustment and situationally

bound locus of control among institutionalized aged. *Journal of Gerontology*, 1974, *29*(3), 295–301.

Fengler, A. P. Attitudinal orientation of wives toward their husbands' retirement. *International Journal of Aging and Human Development*, 1975, *6*(2), 149–152.

Finch, C. *Cellular pacemakers of aging in mammals.* First European Congress on Cell Differentiation, Nice, 1971.

Fischer, A., Beasley, J., & Harter, C. The occurrence of the extended family the origin of the family of procreation: A developmental approach to Negro family structure. *Journal of Marriage and the Family*, 1968, *30*(2), 290–300.

Fischer, J. S., Carlton-Ford, S. L., & Briles, B. J. Life-cycle career patterns: A typological approach to female status attainment. Technical Bulletin No. 8. Center for the Study of Aging, University of Alabama, 1979.

Flacks, R. The liberated generation: An exploration of the roots of student protest. *Journal of Social Issues*, 1967, *23*(4), 52–75.

Flavell, J. Cognitive changes in adulthood. In L. R. Goulet & P. B. Baltes (Eds.), *Life-span developmental psychology* (Vol. 1). New York: Academic Press, 1970.

Fogarty, M. P., Rapoport, R., & Rapoport, R. N. *Sex, career, and family.* Beverly Hills, Calif.: Sage Publications, 1971.

Foner, A., & Schwab, K. *Retirement and aging.* Monterey, Calif.: Brooks/Cole, 1981.

Fox, G. L. Before marriage: An assessment of organization and change in the premarital period. Paper presented at the Merrill-Palmer Conference on Changing Sex Roles and the Family, Detroit, November 1975. (a)

Fox, G. L. Sex role attitudes as predictors of con-traceptive use. Paper presented at the meeting of the National Council on Family Relations, Salt Lake City, August 1975. (b)

Fox, J. H. Effects of retirement and former work life on women's adaptation in old age. *Journal of Gerontology*, 1977, *32*(2), 196–202.

Fozard, J., Nuttall, R., & Waugh, N. Age-related differences in mental performance. *Aging and Human Development*, 1972, *3*(1), 19–43.

Fozard, J., Wolf, E., Bell, B., McFarland, R., & Podolsky, S. Visual perception and communication. In J. E. Birren & K. W. Schaie (Eds.), *Handbook of the psychology of aging.* New York: Van Nostrand Reinhold, 1977.

Framo, J. Family psychology and intimate contexts: Neglected areas in social psychology. Paper presented at the meeting of the American Psychological Association, New York, September 1979.

Francis, W. J. A. Reproduction at menarche and menopause in women. *Journal of Reproduction and Fertility*, 1970, *90* (Suppl. 12), 89–98.

Freedman, D. An ethological approach to the genetic study of human behavior. In S. G. Vandenberg (Ed.), *Methods and goals in human behavior genetics.* New York: Academic Press, 1965.

Freilich, M. The natural trends in kinship and complex systems. *American Sociological Review*, 1964, *29*, 529–540.

Freud, A. *Ego and the mechanisms of defense.* New York: International Universities Press, 1946.

Freud, S. *The ego and the id.* London: Hogarth Press, 1927.

Freud, S. *Three contributions to a theory of sex* (J. Strachey, trans.). New York: Nervous and Mental Disease Publishing, 1930. (Originally published, 1905.)

Friedan, B. *The feminine mystique.* New York: Norton, 1963.

Friedmann, E. A., & Havighurst, R. *The meaning of work and retirement.* Chicago: University of Chicago Press, 1954.

Friedmann, E. A., & Orbach, H. L. Adjustment to retirement. In *American handbook of psychiatry* (Vol. 1). New York: Basic Books, 1974.

Froehling, S. Effects of propranolol on behavioral and physiological measures of elderly males. Unpublished doctoral dissertation, Duke University, 1974.

Gajo, F. Adult age differences in the perception of visual illusion. Unpublished doctoral dissertation, University of Michigan, 1966.

Gans, H. J. *The urban villagers: Group and class life of Italian-Americans.* New York: Free Press, 1962.

Garfield, C. Psychothanatological concomitants of altered state experience: An investigation of the relationship between consciousness alteration and fear of death. Unpublished doctoral dissertation, Department of Psychology, University of California, Berkeley, 1974.

Gasser, R., & Taylor, C. Role adjustment of single parent fathers with dependent children. *Family Coordinator*, 1976, *25*(4), 397–401.

Gaylord, S., & Marsh, G. Age differences in the speed of a spatial cognitive process. *Journal of Gerontology*, 1975, *30*(6), 674–678.

Geer, J. The development of a scale to measure fear. *Behavior research and therapy*, 1965, *3*(1), 45–53.

George, L. *Role transitions in later life.* Monterey, Calif.: Brooks/Cole, 1980.

George, L., & Maddox, G. Subjective adaptation to loss of the work role: A longitudinal study. *Journal of Gerontology*, 1977, *32*(4), 456–462.

Gewirtz, J. *Attachment and dependency.* Washington, D.C.: V. H. Winston, 1972.

Ghiselli, E. E. The relationship between intelligence and age among superior adults. *Journal of Genetic Psychology*, 1957, *90*(2), 131–142.

Giambra, L. Daydreaming in males from seventeen to

seventy-seven: A preliminary report. Paper presented at the meeting of the American Psychological Association, Montreal, August 1973.

Gibbs, J. The social world of the older widow in the non-metropolitan community. Unpublished doctoral dissertation, Kansas State University, 1979.

Gibson, G. Kin family network: Overheralded structure in past conceptualizations of family functioning. *Journal of Marriage and the Family*, 1972, *34*(1), 13–23.

Gilbert, J. Thirty-five year follow-up study of intellectual functioning. *Journal of Gerontology*, 1973, *28*(1), 68–72.

Gilford, R., & Bengtson, V. L. Measuring marital satisfaction in three generations: Positive and negative dimensions. *Journal of Marriage and the Family*, 1979, *41*(2), 15–50.

Gilford, R., & Black, D. The grandchild-grandparent dyad: Ritual or relationship? Paper presented at the meeting of the Gerontological Society, San Juan, Puerto Rico, December 1972.

Gilligan, C. Stages in the moral development of women and men. *Newsletter, Center for Continuing Education of Women* (University of Michigan), 1980, *13*(1), 1.

Ginzberg, E., Ginsberg, S., Axelrod, W., & Herna, J. *Occupational choice: An approach to a general theory*. New York: Columbia University Press, 1951.

Gladis, M., & Braun, H. Age differences in transfer and retroaction as a function of intertask response similarity. *Journal of Experimental Psychology*, 1958, *55*(1), 25–30.

Glamser, F. The importance of age to conservative opinions: A multivariate analysis. *Journal of Gerontology*, 1974, *29*, 549–554.

Glamser, F. Determinants of a positive attitude toward retirement. *Journal of Gerontology*, 1976, *31*(1), 104–107.

Glamser, F., & De Jong, G. The efficacy of pre-retirement preparative programs for industrial workers. *Journal of Gerontology*, 1975, *30*(5), 595–600.

Glaser, B., & Strauss, A. *Awareness of dying*. Chicago: Aldine-Atherton, 1965.

Glenn, N. Psychological well-being in the post-parental stage: Some evidence from national surveys. *Journal of Marriage and the Family*, 1975, *37*(1), 105–110.

Glenn, N., & Weaver, C. The marital happiness of remarried divorced persons. *Journal of Marriage and the Family*, 1977, *39*(2), 331–337.

Glick, I., Weiss, R., & Parkes, C. *The first year of bereavement*. New York: Wiley, 1974.

Glick, P. C. Living arrangements of children and young adults. Paper presented at Population Association of America, Seattle, April 1975.

Glick, P. C. Updating the life cycle of the family.

Journal of Marriage and the Family, 1977, *39*(1), 5–13.

Glick, P. C. Future American families. *Washington Cofo Memo*, 1979, *11*(3), 2–5.

Glick, P. C., Heer, D., & Beresford, J. Social change and family structure: Trends and prospects. Paper presented at the meeting of the American Association for the Advancement of Science, Chicago, February 1959.

Glick, P. C., & Norton, A. J. Recent trends and variations in marriage and the family. Cited in J. Lipman-Blumen, Demographic trends and issues in women's health. Paper presented at the U.S. Department of Health, Education and Welfare Conference, Women and Their Health: Research Implications for a New Era, November 1975.

Gold, S. Cross-cultural comparisons of role change with aging. *Student Journal of Human Development* (Committee on Human Development, University of Chicago), 1960, *1*, 11–15.

Goldstein, A., & Chance, J. Effects of practice on sex-stated differences in performance on embedded figures. *Psychonomic Science*, 1965, *3*, 361–362.

Goode, W. *The Family*. Englewood Cliffs, N.J.: Prentice-Hall, 1964.

Goodman, C. Growing old in a garment factory: The effects of occupational segregation and runaway shops on working-class women. Unpublished master's thesis, Rutgers University, 1978.

Goodman, E. Stress is the problem of secretaries. *Home News*, March 1979.

Goodman, M. Reactions at different ages to the stress of heart attack. Paper presented at the meeting of the American Psychological Association, Honolulu, September 1972.

Goodrick, C. L. Learning, retention, and extinction of a complex maze habit for mature-young and senescent Wistar albino rats. *Journal of Gerontology*, 1968, *23*(3), 298.

Goodrick, C. L. Maze learning of mature young and aged rats as a function of distribution of practice. *Journal of Experimental Psychology*, 1973, *98*(2), 344–349.

Gordon, C., Gaitz, C., & Scott, J., Jr. Leisure and lives: Personal expressivity across the life span. In R. H. Binstock & E. Shanas (Eds.), *Handbook of aging and the social sciences*. New York: Van Nostrand Reinhold, 1976.

Gorer, G. *Death, grief and mourning*. New York: Doubleday, 1965.

Gorney, J. Experiencing and age: Patterns of reminiscence among the elderly. Unpublished doctoral dissertation, University of Chicago, 1968.

Gottfredson, G. Career stability and redirection in adulthood. *Journal of Applied Psychology*, 1977, *62*(1), 436–445.

Gottschalk, L. P., Kaplan, S., Gleser, G. G., & Winget, C. M. Variations in magnitude of emotion: A method applied to anxiety and hostility during phases of the menstrual cycle. *Psychosomatic Medicine*, 1962, *24*(3), 300–311.

Goudy, W., & Barb, K. Changes in attitudes toward work and retirement: A longitudinal study. Paper presented at the meeting of the Gerontological Society, Louisville, Ky., October 1975.

Gould, R. The phases of adult life: A study in developmental psychology. *American Journal of Psychiatry*, 1972, *129*(5), 521–531.

Gove, W., & Geerken, M. Response bias in surveys of mental health: An empirical investigation. *American Journal of Sociology*, 1977, *82*(6), 1289–1317.

Gozali, J. The relationship between age and attitude toward disabled persons. Paper presented at the meeting of the Gerontological Society, Toronto, October 1970.

Granick, S., & Friedmann, A. Uneven decline in mental functions with age. *Geriatric Focus*, 1967, *6*(2), 3.

Grant, C. Age differences in self-concept from early adulthood through old age. *Proceedings of the 77th Annual Convention of the American Psychological Association*, 1969, *4*, 717.

Gray, R. M., & Smith, T. C. Effect of employment on sex differences in attitudes toward the parental family. *Marriage and Family Living*, 1960, *22*(1), 36–38.

Greenberg, M., & Morris, M. Engrossment: The newborn's impact upon the father. *American Journal of Orthopsychiatry*, 1974, *44*(4), 520–531.

Grotevant, H. D. Family similarities in interests and orientation. *Merrill-Palmer Quarterly*, 1976, *22*(1), 61–72.

Gruen, W. Adult personality: An empirical study of Erikson's theory of ego development. In B. L. Neugarten & Associates, *Personality in middle and late life: Empirical studies.* New York: Atherton, 1964.

Gsell, O. R. Longitudinal gerontological research over ten years. (Basel Studies, 1955–1965.) *Gerontological Clinic*, 1967, *9*(27), 67–80.

Gubrium, J. F. Being single in old age. *International Journal of Aging and Human Development*, 1975, *6*(1), 29–41.

Gubrium, J. F. *Time, roles and self in old age.* New York: Human Sciences Press, 1976.

Guilford, J. P. *The nature of human intelligence.* New York: McGraw-Hill, 1967.

Gunter, L. M., & Estes, C. A. *Education for gerontic nursing.* New York: Springer, 1979.

Gunther, J. *Death be not proud.* New York: Modern Library, 1953.

Gurin, G., Veroff, J., & Feld, S. *Americans view their mental health.* New York: Basic Books, 1960.

Gurland, B. A broad clinical assessment of psychopathology in the aged. In C. Eisdorfer & P.

Lawton (Eds.), *Psychology of adult development and aging.* Washington, D.C.: American Psychological Association, 1973.

Gutmann, D. L. An exploration of ego configurations in middle and later life. In B. L. Neugarten & Associates, *Personality in middle and late life: Empirical studies.* New York: Atherton, 1964.

Gutmann, D. L. Female ego styles and generational conflict. In J. Bardwick, E. Douvan, M. Horner, & D. Gutmann (Eds.), *Feminine personality and conflict.* Monterey, Calif.: Brooks/Cole, 1970.

Gutmann, D. L. Ego-psychological and developmental approaches to the "retirement crises" in men. In F. M. Karp (Ed.), *Retirement.* New York: Behavioral Publications, 1972.

Gutmann, D. L. Parenthood: Key to the comparative psychology of the life cycle? In N. Datan & L. Ginsberg (Eds.), *Life-span developmental psychology: Normative life crises.* New York: Academic Press, 1975.

Gutmann, D. L. Individual adaptation in the middle years: Developmental issues in the masculine mid-life crisis. *Journal of Geriatric Psychiatry*, 1976, *9*(1), 41–59.

Gutmann, D. L. The cross-cultural perspective: Notes toward a comparative psychology of aging. In J. E. Birren & K. W. Schaie (Eds.), *Handbook of the psychology of aging.* New York: Van Nostrand Reinhold, 1977.

Guttmann, D. Leisure-time activity interests of Jewish aged. *Gerontologist*, 1973, *13*(2), 219–223.

Haan, N. Proposed model of ego functioning: Coping and defense mechanisms in relationship to I.Q. change. *Psychological Monographs*, 1963, *77*, 1–23.

Haan, N. Personality development from adolescence to adulthood in the Oakland Growth and Guidance Studies. *Seminars in Psychiatry*, 1972, *4*, 399–414.

Haan, N. Personality organizations of well-functioning younger people and older adults. *International Journal of Aging and Human Development*, 1976, *7*(2), 117–127.

Haan, N., & Day, D. A longitudinal study of change and sameness in personality development, adolescence to later adulthood. *Aging and Human Development*, 1974, *5*(1), 11–39.

Haan, N., Smith, M. B., & Block, J. Moral reasoning of young adults: Political social behavior, family background, and personality correlates. *Journal of Personality and Social Psychology*, 1968, *10*, 183–201.

Hagestad, G. O. Role change in adulthood: The transition to the empty nest. Unpublished manuscript, Committee on Human Development, University of Chicago, 1977.

Hagestad, G. O. Patterns of communication and influence between grandparents and grandchildren in a changing society. Paper presented at the World Congress of Sociology, Uppsala, Sweden, August 1978

Hagestad, G. O. Problems and promises in the social psychology of intergenerational relations. In R. Fogel, E. Hatfield, S. Kiesler, & T. March (Eds.), *Stability and change in the family.* Annapolis, Md.: National Research Council, 1979.

Hagestad, G. O., & Snow, R. Young adult offspring as interpersonal resources in middle age. Paper presented at the meeting of the Gerontological Society, San Francisco, November 1977.

Haghe, H. *Characteristics of workers, March 1977* (Labor Force Report No. 216). Washington, D.C.: U.S. Department of Labor, Bureau of Labor Statistics, 1977.

Haley, J. Family experiments: A new type of experimentation. *Family Process,* 1962, *1,* 265–293.

Haller, M., & Rosenmayr, L. The pluridimensionality of work commitment: A study of young married women in different social contexts of occupational and family life. *Human Relations,* 1971, *24*(6), 501–518.

Hamilton, J., Hamilton, R., & Mestler, G. Duration of life and causes of death in domestic cats: Influence of sex, gonadectomy, and inbreeding. *Journal of Gerontology,* 1969, *24*(4), 427–437.

Hareven, T. The last stage: Historical adulthood and old age. *Daedalus,* 1976, *105*(4), 13–28.

Hareven, T. Family time and historical time. *Daedalus,* 1977, *106*(2), 57–70.

Hareven, T. Historical changes in the life course and the family: Policy implications. In M. Yinger & S. Cutler (Eds.), *Major social issues: A multidisciplinary view.* New York: Free Press, 1979.

Harkins, E. Effects of empty-nest transition on self-report of psychological and physical well-being. *Journal of Marriage and the Family,* 1978, *40*(3), 459–556.

Harmon, L. Anatomy of career commitment in women. *Journal of Counseling Psychology,* 1970, *17*(1), 77–80.

Harris, L. Pleasant retirement expected. *Washington Post,* November 29, 1965.

Harris, L., & Associates. *The myth and reality of aging in America.* Washington, D.C.: National Council on Aging, 1975.

Hartup, W. W., & Lempers, J. A problem in life-span development: The interactional analysis of family attachments. In P. B. Baltes & K. W. Schaie (Eds.), *Life-span developmental psychology: Personality and socialization.* New York: Academic Press, 1973.

Harvey, C., & Bahr, H. Widowhood, morale, and affiliation. *Journal of Marriage and the Family,* 1974, *36*(1), 97–106.

Harwood, E., & Naylor, G. Recall and recognition in elderly and young subjects. *Australian Journal of Psychology,* 1969, *21*(3), 251–257.

Havighurst, R. J. *Developmental tasks and education.* New York: David McKay, 1952. (a)

Havighurst, R. J. Roles and status of older people. In

A. I. Lansing (Ed.), *Cowdry's problems of aging* (3rd ed.). Baltimore: Williams & Wilkins, 1952. (b)

Havighurst, R. J. The leisure activities of the middle-aged. *American Journal of Sociology,* 1957, *63* (2), 152–162.

Havighurst, R. J. The sociologic meaning of aging. *Geriatrics,* 1958, *13*(1), 43–50.

Havighurst, R. J. The nature and values of meaningful free-time activity. In R. Kleemeier (Ed.), *Aging and leisure.* New York: Oxford Press, 1961.

Havighurst, R. J., McDonald, W. J., Maewen, L., & Mogel, J. Male social scientists: Lives after sixty. *Gerontologist,* 1979, *19*(1), 55–60.

Havighurst, R. J., Munnichs, K., Neugarten, B. L., & Thomas, H. *Adjustment to retirement: A cross-national study.* New York: Humanities Press, 1969.

Havighurst, R. J., Neugarten, B. L., & Tobin, S. Disengagement and patterns of aging. In B. L. Neugarten (Ed.), *Middle age and aging.* Chicago: University of Chicago Press, 1968.

Haviland, J. Right and left hemisphere differential processing of facial expression. Unpublished paper, Department of Psychology, Rutgers State University of New Jersey, 1978.

Haviland, J., & Myers, J. Attribution of affect to faces of different ages. Unpublished manuscript, Department of Psychology, Rutgers State University of New Jersey, 1979.

Hayflick, L. The cellular basis for biological aging. In C. Finch & L. Hayflick (Eds.), *Handbook of the biology of aging.* New York: Van Nostrand Reinhold, 1977.

Hays, W., & Mindel, C. Extended kinship relations in black and white families. *Journal of Marriage and the Family,* 1973, *35*(1), 51–57.

Heath, D. What meaning and effects does fatherhood have for the maturing of professional men? *Merrill-Palmer Quarterly,* 1978, *24*(4), 265–278.

Helson, R. The changing image of the career woman. *Journal of Social Issues,* 1972, *28*(2), 33–46.

Hendy, V. Displaced homemaker finds herself ignored by society. *Home News,* 1978, *103,* B18.

Henning, M. Career development of women executives. Unpublished doctoral dissertation, Harvard Business School, 1970.

Henry, J. *Culture against man.* New York: Knopf, 1963.

Henry, W., Sims, J., & Spray, L. *The fifth profession: Becoming a psychotherapist.* San Francisco: Jossey-Bass, 1971.

Herzberg, F., Mausner, B., & Snyderman, B. *The motivation to work.* New York: Wiley, 1959.

Hess, A. Positiveness of self-concept and ideal self as a function of age. *Journal of Genetic Psychology,* 1970, *117*(1), 57–67.

Hess, B. Friendship. In M. W. Riley, M. Johnson, & A. Foner (Eds.), *Aging and society.* Vol. 3: *A sociology of age stratification*. New York: Russell Sage Foundation, 1972.

Hess, B., & Markson, E. W. *Aging and old age: An introduction to social gerontology*. New York: Macmillan, 1980.

Hess, B., & Waring, J. Parent and child in later life: Rethinking the relationship. In R. Lerner & G. Spanier (Eds.), *Child influences on marital and family interaction*. New York: Academic Press, 1978.

Hess, R., & Handel, G. *Family worlds*. Chicago: University of Chicago Press, 1959.

Hetherington, E. M., Cox, M., & Cox, R. Divorced fathers. *Family Coordinator*, 1976, 25(4), 417–428.

Heyman, D. K., & Gianturco, D. Long-term adaptation by the elderly to bereavement. *Journal of Gerontology*, 1973, 28(3), 359–362.

Heyman, D. K., & Jeffers, F. C. Wives and retirement: A pilot study. *Journal of Gerontology*, 1968, 23, 488–496.

Hickey, T. *Health and aging*. Monterey, Calif.: Brooks/Cole, 1980.

Hickey, T., Hickey, L., & Kalish, R. A. Children's perceptions of the elderly. *Journal of Genetic Psychology*, 1968, 112(2), 227–235.

Hickey, T., & Kalish, R. Young people's perceptions of adults. *Journal of Gerontology*, 1968, 23(2), 215–219.

Hicks, L., & Birren, J. E. Aging, brain damage and psychomotor slowing. *Psychological Bulletin*, 1970, 74(6), 377.

Hill, R., Foote, N., Aldous, J., Carlson, R., & Macdonald, R. *Family development in three generations*. Cambridge, Mass.: Schenkman, 1970.

Hirsch, B. Psychological dimensions of social networks: A multimethod analysis. *American Journal of Community Psychology*, 1979, 7(3), 263–277.

Hirsch, B. Natural support systems and coping with major life crises. *American Journal of Community Psychology*, 1980, 8(2), 153–166.

Hite, S. *The Hite report*. New York: Macmillan, 1976.

Hochschild, A. *The unexpected community*. Englewood Cliffs, N.J.: Prentice-Hall, 1973.

Hoffman, L. W. The decision to work. In F. I. Nye & L. Hoffman (Eds.), *The employed mother in America*. Chicago: Rand McNally, 1963.

Hoffman, L. W. Effects on child. In L. Hoffman & G. Nye (Eds.), *Working mothers*. San Francisco: Jossey-Bass, 1974.

Hoffman, L. W., & Hoffman, M. L. The value of children to parents. In J. T. Fawcett (Ed.), *Psychological perspectives on population*. New York: Basic Books, 1973.

Hoffman, L. W., & Manis, J. Influences of children on marital interaction and parental satisfaction and dissatisfactions. In R. Lerner & G. Spanier (Eds.), *Child influences on marital and family interaction*. New York: Academic Press, 1978.

Holland, J. *Making vocational choices: A theory of careers*. Englewood Cliffs, N.J.: Prentice-Hall, 1973.

Holmes, T., & Rahe, R. The social readjustment rating scale. *Journal of Psychosomatic Research*, 1967, 11(3), 213–218.

Homall, G. The motivation to be promoted among non-exempt employees: An expectancy theory approach. Unpublished master's thesis, Cornell University, 1974.

Honzik, M. Personality consistency and change: Some comments on papers by Bayley, Macfarlane, Moss and Kagan, & Murphy. *Vita Humana*, 1964, 7(2), 139–142.

Honzik, M., & Macfarlane, J. Personality development and intellectual functioning. In L. F. Jarvik, C. Eisdorfer, & J. Blum (Eds.), *Intellectual functioning in adults*. New York: Springer, 1973.

Hooper, F. H., & Storck, P. A. A life-span analysis of fluid vs. crystallized intelligence. Paper presented at 25th annual meeting of the Gerontological Society, San Juan, Puerto Rico, December 1972.

Horn, J. Organization of data on life-span development of human abilities. In L. R. Goulet & P. B. Baltes (Eds.), *Life-span developmental psychology: Research and theory*. New York: Academic Press, 1970.

Horner, M. Femininity and successful achievement: A basic inconsistency. In J. Bardwick, E. Douvan, M. Horner, & D. Gutmann (Eds.), *Feminine personality and conflict*. Monterey, Calif.: Brooks/Cole, 1970.

Horner, M. Toward an understanding of achievement-related conflicts in women. *Journal of Social Issues*, 1972, 28(2), 157–176.

Howard, A. The assessment center for mid-career and middle life individual techniques: Paper presented at the meeting of the American Psychological Association, Toronto, August 1978.

Howell, S. Familiarity and complexity in perceptual recognition. *Journal of Gerontology*, 1972, 27(3), 364–371.

Hoyer, W. J., Labouvie, G. V., & Baltes, P. B. Modification of response speed and intellectual performance in the elderly. *Human Development*, 1973, 16, 233–242.

Hulicka, I. Age and health effects on learning. *Journal of the American Geriatrics Society*, 1967, 15, 285–294.

Hulicka, I., & Grossman, J. Age-group comparisons for the use of mediators in paired-associate learning. *Journal of Gerontology*, 1967, 22(1), 46–51.

Hultsch, D. Adult age differences in retrieval: Trace-dependent and cue-dependent forgetting. *Developmental Psychology*, 1975, 11(2), 197.

Hultsch, D., & Hickey, T. External validity in the study of human development: Theoretical and methodological issues. *Human Development*, 1978, 21, 76–91.

Hultsch, D., & Plemons, J. Life events and life-span development. In P. B. Baltes & O. G. Brim, Jr. (Eds.), *Life-span development and behavior* (Vol. 2). New York: Academic Press, 1979.

Huston-Stein, A., & Higgins-Trenk, A. Development of females from childhood through adulthood: Career and feminine role orientations. In P. B. Baltes (Ed.), *Life-span development and behavior* (Vol. 1). New York: Academic Press, 1978.

Hutchison, I. The significance of marital status for morale and life satisfaction among lower-income elderly. *Journal of Marriage and the Family*, 1975, *37*(2), 287–293.

Huyck, M. Age norms and career lines in the careers of Army officers. Unpublished doctoral dissertation, University of Chicago, 1970.

Huyck, M. Sex and the older woman. In L. E. Troll, J. Israel, & K. Israel (Eds.), *Looking ahead: A woman's guide to the problems and joys of growing older*. Englewood Cliffs, N.J.: Prentice-Hall, 1977.

Illich, I. *Medical nemesis: The expropriation of health*. Toronto: McClelland & Stewart, 1976.

Ingraham, M. *My purpose holds: Reactions and experiences in retirement of TIAA-CREF annuitants*. New York: Educational Research Division, Teachers Insurance and Annuity Association College Retirement Equities Fund, 1974.

Inhelder, B., & Piaget, J. *The early growth of logic in the child*. New York: Harper & Row, 1964.

Institute of Gerontology, Environmental Studies. *Death and survival* (Relocation Report No. 2). Ann Arbor: University of Michigan, 1975.

Ivey, M., & Bardwick, J. Patterns of affective fluctuation in the menstrual cycle. *Psychosomatic Medicine*, 1968, *30*(3), 336–345.

Izard, C. Personality similarity and friendship: A follow-up study. *Journal of Abnormal and Social Psychology*, 1963, *66*(6), 598–600.

Izard, C. *The face of emotion*. New York: Appleton-Century-Crofts, 1971.

Jackson, D. The question of family homeostasis. *Psychiatric Quarterly Supplement*, 1957, *31*(1), 79–90.

Jackson, J. J. Aged Negroes: Their cultural departures from statistical stereotypes and rural-urban differences. *Gerontologist*, 1970, *10*(2), 140–145.

Jackson, J. J. Sex and social class variations in Negro older parent-adult child relationships. *Aging and Human Development*, 1971, *2*(2), 96–107.

Jackson, J. J. Older black women. In L. Troll, J. Israel, & K. Israel (Eds.), *Looking ahead: A woman's guide to the problems and joys of growing older*. Englewood Cliffs, N.J.: Prentice-Hall, 1977.

Jackson, M. A. Effect of social versus objective reward upon verbal learning in a disengaged and an engaged population. *Proceedings of the 77th Annual Convention of the American Psychological Association*, 1969, *4*(2), 747–748.

Jacobsohn, D. Willingness to retire in relation to job strain and type of work. *Journal of Industrial Gerontology*, 1972, *13*, 65–74.

Jacobson, P. H. The changing role of mortality in American family life. *Lex et Scientia*, 1966, *3*(2), 121.

Jakobson, R. Why "Mama" and "Papa." In *Selected writings of Roman Jakobson*. The Hague: Mouton, 1962.

Jarvik, L. F., & Falek, A. Intellectual stability and survival in the aged. *Journal of Gerontology*, 1963, *18*, 173–176.

Jarvik, L. F., Kallmann, F., & Falek, A. Intellectual changes in aged twins. *Journal of Gerontology*, 1962, *17*(3), 289–294.

Jaslow, P. Employment, retirement, and morale among older women. *Journal of Gerontology*, 1976, *31*(2), 212–218.

Jerome, E. A. Decay of heuristic processes in the aged. In C. Tibbitts & W. Donahue (Eds.), *Social and psychological aspects of aging*. New York: Columbia University Press, 1962.

Johnson, E., & Bursk, B. Relationships between the elderly and their adult children. *Gerontologist*, 1977, *17*(1), 90–96.

Johnson, J. A comparative study of the cognitive styles of adult chess players and non-chess players. Unpublished term paper, Wayne State University, 1971. (Contact author at Department of Educational Psychology, University of Wisconsin, Madison.)

Jones, D. Sex differences in the friendship patterns of young adults. Unpublished paper, 1974. (Contact author at Department of Psychology, University of Michigan, Dearborn.)

Jones, E. *Freud*. New York: Basic Books, 1953.

Jones, H. E., & Conrad, H. S. The growth and decline of intelligence: A study of a homogeneous group between the ages of ten and sixty. *Genetic Psychology Monographs*, 1933, *13*, 223–298.

Jourard, S., & Lasakow, P. Some factors in self-disclosure. *Journal of Abnormal and Social Psychology*, 1958, *56*(1), 91–98.

Jung, C. The stages of life (R. F. C. Hill, trans.). In J. Campbell (Ed.), *The portable Jung*. New York: Viking, 1971. (Originally published, 1930.)

Kaats, G. R., & Davis, K. E. The dynamics of sexual behavior of college students. *Journal of Marriage and the Family*, 1970, *32*, 390–399.

Kagan, J., & Moss, H. *Birth to maturity: A study in psychological development*. New York: Wiley, 1962.

Kagan, J., Moss, H., & Sigel, I. Psychological significance of styles of conceptualization. In J. Wright & J. Kagan (Eds.), Basic cognitive processes in children. *Monographs of the Society for Research in Child Development*, 1963, *28* (Whole No. 2, Serial No. 86).

Kahana, B., & Kahana, E. Grandparenthood from the perspective of the developing grandchild. *Developmental Psychology*, 1970, *3*(1), 98–105.

Kalish, R. A. Of children and grandfathers: A speculative essay on dependency. *Gerontologist*, 1967, *7*(1), 65–69.

Kalish, R. A. *Late adulthood: Perspectives on human development*. Monterey, Calif.: Brooks/Cole, 1975.

Kalish, R. A. Death and dying in a social context. In R. Binstock & E. Shanas (Eds.), *Handbook of aging and the social sciences*. New York: Van Nostrand Reinhold, 1976.

Kalish, R. A., & Johnson, A. Value similarities and differences in three generations of women. *Journal of Marriage and the Family*, 1972, *34*(1), 49–54.

Kalish, R. A., & Reynolds, D. *Death and ethnicity: A psychocultural study*. Los Angeles: University of Southern California Press, 1976.

Kallmann, F., & Jarvik, L. F. Individual differences in constitution and genetic background. In J. E. Birren (Ed.), *Handbook of aging and the individual: Psychological and biological aspects*. Chicago: University of Chicago Press, 1959.

Kandel, D., & Lesser, G. *Youth in two worlds*. San Francisco: Jossey-Bass, 1972.

Kangas, J., & Bradway, K. Intelligence at middle age: A thirty-eight year follow-up. *Developmental Psychology*, 1971, *5*(2), 333–337.

Kanter, R. M. *Men and women of the corporation*. New York: Basic Books, 1977.

Kastenbaum, R. Cognitive and personal futurity in later life. *Journal of Individual Psychology*, 1963, *19*(2), 216–222.

Kastenbaum, R. The realm of death: An emerging area in psychological research. *Journal of Human Relations*, 1965, *13*(4), 538–552.

Kastenbaum, R. Multiple perspectives on a geriatric "Death Valley." *Community Mental Health Journal*, 1967, *3*(1), 21–29.

Kastenbaum, R. Death and bereavement in later life. In A. H. Kutscher (Ed.), *Death and bereavement*. Springfield, Ill.: Charles C Thomas, 1969.

Kastenbaum, R. Childhood: The kingdom where creatures die. *Journal of Clinical Child Psychology*, 1974, *3*, 11–13.

Kastenbaum, R. *Death, society, and human experience*. St. Louis: C. V. Mosby, 1977.

Kastenbaum, R., & Aisenberg, R. *The psychology of death*. New York: Springer, 1972.

Kastenbaum, R., & Candy, S. The 4% fallacy: A methodological and empirical critique of extended care facility population statistics. *International Journal of Aging and Human Development*, 1973, *4*(1), 15–21.

Kastenbaum, R., Derbin, V., Sabatini, P., & Artt, S. The ages of me: Toward personal and interpersonal definitions of functional aging. *Aging and Human Development*, 1972, *3*(2), 197–211.

Kastenbaum, R., & Symonds, D. Those endearing young charms: Fifty years later. In L. Troll, J. Israel, & K. Israel (Eds.), *Looking ahead: A woman's guide to the problems and joys of growing older*. Englewood Cliffs, N.J.: Prentice-Hall, 1977.

Kastenbaum, R., & Weisman, A. The psychological autopsy method in gerontology. In D. Kent, R. Kastenbaum, & S. Sherwood (Eds.), *Research, planning, and action for the elderly*. New York: Behavioral Publications, 1972.

Katona, G. *Private pensions and individual saving*. Ann Arbor: University of Michigan Survey Research Center, 1965.

Kelley, L., Ohlson, M., & Harper, L. Food selection and well-being in aging women. *Journal of American Dietetic Association*, 1957, *33*(5), 466.

Kelly, E. Consistency of the adult personality. *American Psychologist*, 1955, *10*, 659–681.

Kent, S. How do we age? *Geriatrics*, 1976, March, pp. 128–134.

Kerckhoff, A. C. Husband-wife expectations and reactions to retirement. *Journal of Gerontology*, 1964, *19*(4), 510–516.

Kerckhoff, A. C. Norm value clusters and the strain toward consistency among older married couples. In I. A. Simpson & J. C. McKinney (Eds.), *Social aspects of aging*. Durham, N.C.: Duke University Press, 1966.

Kerckhoff, A. C., & Davis, K. Value consensus and need complementarity in mate selection. *American Sociological Review*, 1962, *27*(3), 295–303.

Kerckhoff, A. C., & Huff, P. Parental influence on educational goals. *Sociometry*, 1974, *37*(3), 307–327.

Kimble, G., & Pennypacker, H. Eyelid conditioning in young and aged subjects. *Journal of Genetic Psychology*, 1963, *103*(2), 283–289.

Kimmel, D. *Adulthood and aging* (2nd ed.). New York: Wiley, 1980.

Kimmel, D., & Stein, M. Variations in self-rated personality needs as a function of sex, age, and socioeconomic status from adolescence to old age. Paper presented at the meeting of the American Psychological Association, Montreal, August 1973.

Kimura, D. The asymmetry of the human brain. *Scientific American*, 1973, *3*, 70.

Kinsey, A. C., Pomeroy, W. B., & Martin, C. E. *Sexual behavior in the human male*. Philadelphia: Saunders, 1948.

Kinsey, A. C., Pomeroy, W. B., Martin, C. E., & Gebhard, P. H. *Sexual behavior in the human female*. Philadelphia: Saunders, 1953.

Kissen, D. Psychosocial factors, personality, and lung cancer in men aged 55–64. *British Journal of Medical Psychology*, 1967, *40*(1), 29–43.

Klatsky, S. Patterns of contact with relatives. (Arnold and Caroline Rose Monograph Series in Sociology.) Washington, D.C.: American Sociological Association, 1972.

Kleemeier, R. (Ed.). *Aging and leisure: A research perspective into the meaningful use of time*. New York: Oxford University Press, 1961.

Kleemeier, R. Intellectual changes in the senium. *Proceedings of the Social Statistics Section of the*

American Statistical Association, 1962, *1*, 290–295.

Klein, D. C., & Ross, A. Kindergarten entry: A study of role transition. In M. Krugman (Ed.), *Orthopsychiatry and the school*. New York: American Orthopsychiatric Association, 1958.

Klein, R. Age, sex, and task difficulty as predictors of social conformity. *Journal of Gerontology*, 1972, *27* (2), 229–236.

Klein, R., & Birren, J. E. Age, perceived self-competence and conformity. *Proceedings of the 81st Annual Convention of the American Psychological Association*, 1973, 779–780.

Kleinman, J. M., & Brodzinsky, D. M. Haptic exploration in young, middle-aged, and elderly adults. *Journal of Gerontology*, 1978, *33*(4), 521–527.

Koch, K. *I never told anybody: Teaching poetry writing in a nursing home*. New York: Random House, 1978.

Kogan, N. Creativity and cognitive style: A life-span perspective. In P. B. Baltes & K. W. Schaie (Eds.), *Life-span developmental psychology: Personality and socialization*. New York: Academic Press, 1973.

Kogan, N. Categorizing and conceptualizing styles in younger and older adults. *Human Development*, 1974, *17*(3), 218–230.

Kogan, N. Beliefs, attitudes, and stereotypes about old people: A new look at some old issues. *Research on Aging*, 1979, *1*(1), 11–36.

Kogan, N., & Wallach, M. Age changes in values and attitudes. *Journal of Gerontology*, 1961, *16*(3), 272–280.

Kohlberg, L. Continuities in childhood and adult moral development revisited. In P. B. Baltes & K. W. Schaie (Eds.), *Life-span developmental psychology: Personality and socialization*. New York: Academic Press, 1973.

Kohn, M. *Class and conformity*. Homewood, Ill.: Dorsey Press, 1969.

Kohn, M. L., & Schooler, C. Occupational experience and psychological functioning: An assessment of reciprocal effects. *American Sociological Review*, 1973, *38*(1), 97–118.

Kohn, R. R. *Aging*. Kalamazoo, Mich.: Upjohn, 1973.

Kohn, R. R. Heart and cardiovascular system. In C. Finch & L. Hayflick (Eds.), *Handbook of the physiology of aging*. New York: Van Nostrand Reinhold, 1977.

Komarovsky, M. *Blue-collar marriage*. New York: Random House, 1964.

Kramer, M., Taube, C., & Redick, R. Patterns of use of psychiatric facilities by the aged: Past, present, and future. In C. Eisdorfer & P. Lawton (Eds.), *The psychology of adult development and aging*. Washington, D.C.: American Psychological Association, 1973.

Kreiss, R. Bittersweet farewell of a grown-up child. *New York Times*, March 22, 1979, p. C7.

Krohn, A., & Gutmann, D. Changes in mastery style

with age: A study of Navajo dreams. *Psychiatry*, 1971, *34*, 289–300.

Kübler-Ross, E. *On death and dying*. New York: Macmillan, 1969.

Kuhlen, R. *Personality change*. New York: Wiley, 1964.

Kuhlen, R., & Johnson, G. Changes in goal with increasing adult age. *Journal of Consulting Psychology*, 1952, *16*(1), 1–4.

Kulys, R., & Tobin, S. The older person's responsible other: Child vs. non-child. Paper presented at the meeting of the Gerontological Society, Dallas, November 1978.

Kuypers, J. Internal-external locus of control, ego functioning, and personality characteristics in old age. *Gerontologist*, 1972, *12*(2, Pt. 1), 168–173.

Labouvie, E. Identity versus equivalence of psychological measures and constructs. In L. Poon (Ed.), *Aging in the 1980s*. Washington, D.C.: American Psychological Association, 1980.

Labouvie-Vief, G. Continuities and discontinuities between childhood and adulthood: Piaget revisited. Paper presented at the meeting of the Society for Research in Child Development, San Francisco, March 1979.

Labouvie-Vief, G. Adaptive dimensions of adult cognition. In N. Datan & N. Lohmann (Eds.), *Transitions of aging*. New York: Academic Press, 1980.

Labouvie-Vief, G., & Gonda, J. Cognitive strategy training and intellectual performance in the elderly. *Journal of Gerontology*, 1976, *31*(3), 327–332.

Lake, A. Divorcees: The new poor. *McCall's*, September 1976, pp. 103, 120, 122, 124, 152.

Lakin, M., & Eisdorfer, C. Affective expression among the aged. *Journal of Projective Techniques*, 1960, *24*(4), 403–408.

Lamb, M. Influence of the child on marital quality and family interaction during the prenatal, perinatal, and infancy periods. In R. Lerner & G. Spanier (Eds.), *Child influences on marital and family interaction: A life-span perspective*. New York: Academic Press, 1978.

Lamb, M., & Lamb, J. The nature and importance of the father-infant relationship. *Family Coordinator*, 1976, *25*(4), 379–388.

Landis, J. A comparison of children from divorced and nondivorced unhappy marriages. *Family Life Coordinator*, 1962, *11*(1), 61–65.

Lansing, A. A nongenic factor in the longevity of rotifers. *Annals of the New York Academy of Science*, 1954, *57*(5), 455–464.

Lass, N., & Golden, S. The use of isolated vowels as auditory stimulus in eliciting the verbal transformation effect. *Canadian Journal of Psychology*, 1971, *25*(4), 349.

Laurie, W. F. Health status of people over 65. *Center*

Reports on Advances in Research (Duke University Center for the Study of Aging and Human Development), 1977, *1*(2), B1.

Laws, J. L. Female sexuality through the life span. In P. B. Baltes & O. G. Brim (Eds.), *Life-span development and behavior* (Vol. 3). New York: Academic Press, 1980.

Layton, B. Perceptual noise and aging. *Psychological Bulletin*, 1975, *82*, 575–583.

Lee, A. S. Return migration in the United States. *International Migration Review*, 1974, *8*, 283–300.

LeFevre, C. The mature woman as graduate student: A study of changing self-conception. Paper presented at the meeting of the Illinois Sociological Association, 1970.

Lehman, H. *Age and achievement.* Princeton, N.J.: Princeton University Press, 1953.

Lehr, U. Attitudes towards the future in old age. *Human Development*, 1967, *10*(3–4), 230–238.

Leichter, H., & Mitchell, W. *Kinship and casework.* New York: Russell Sage Foundation, 1967.

LeMasters, E. Parenthood as crisis. *Marriage and Family Living*, 1957, *19*, 352–355.

Lemon, B. W., Bengtson, V. L., & Peterson, J. A. An exploration of the activity theory of aging: Activity types and life satisfaction among in-movers to a retirement community. *Journal of Gerontology*, 1972, *27*(4), 511–523.

LeShan, L. Mobilizing the life forces. *Annals of the New York Academy of Science*, 1969, *164*, 847–861.

Levin, S., & Kahana, R. J. (Eds.). Boston Society for Gerontologic Psychiatry. *Psychodynamic studies in aging: Creativity, reminiscing, and dying.* New York: International Universities Press, 1967.

Levine, S. V., Carr, R. P., & Horenblas, B. S. The urban commune: Fact or fad, promise or pipedream. *American Journal of Orthopsychiatry*, 1973, *43*(1), 149–163.

Levinson, D. J., Darrow, C. N., Klein, E. B., Levinson, M. H., & McKee, B. Periods in the adult development of men: Ages 18 to 45. In N. Schlossberg & A. Entine (Eds.), *Counseling adults.* Monterey, Calif.: Brooks/Cole, 1977. (Originally published in D. F. Ricks, A. Thomas, & M. Roff (Eds.), *Life history research in psychopathology* (Vol. 3). Minneapolis: University of Minnesota Press, 1974.)

Levitin, T., Quinn, R., & Staines, G. Sex discrimination against the American working woman. In L. Fidell & J. Delamater (Eds.), *Women in the professions: What's all the fuss about?* Beverly Hills, Calif.: Sage Publications, 1971.

Lewis, M. State as an infant-environment interaction: An analysis of mother-infant interaction as a function of sex. *Merrill-Palmer Quarterly*, 1972, *18*, 95–121.

Lewis, M., & Brooks, J. Infants' social perception: A constructional view. In L. Cohen & B. Salapatek (Eds.), *Infant perception.* New York: Academic Press, 1975.

Lewis, M., & Feiring, C. The child's social world. In R. Lerner & G. Spanier (Eds.), *Child influences on marital and family interaction.* New York: Academic Press, 1978.

Lewis, M., & Freedle, R. Mother-infant dyad: The cradle of meaning. In P. Pliner, L. Kramer, & T. Alloway (Eds.), *Communication and affect: Language and thought.* New York: Academic Press, 1973.

Lewis, R. A longitudinal test of a developmental framework for premarital dyadic formation. *Journal of Marriage and the Family*, 1973, *34*(1), 16–25. (a)

Lewis, R. Social reaction and the formation of dyads: An interactionist approach to mate selection. *Sociometry*, 1973, *36*(3), 409–418. (b)

Lewis, R., & Spanier, G. Theorizing about the quality and stability of marriage. In W. Burr, R. Hill, G. Nye, & I. Reiss (Eds.), *Contemporary theories about the family* (Vol. 1). New York: Free Press, 1979.

Libow, L. Interaction of medical, biologic, and behavioral factors on aging, adaptation, and survival: An 11-year longitudinal study. *Geriatrics*, 1974, *29*(11), 75–88.

Lieberman, L. Life satisfaction of the young and the old. *Psychology Reports*, 1970, *27*, 75–79.

Lieberman, M. A. Relationship of mortality rates to entrance to a home for the aged. *Geriatrics*, 1961, *16*, 515–519.

Lieberman, M. A. Psychological correlates of impending death. *Journal of Gerontology*, 1965, *20*(2), 181–190.

Lieberman, M. A. Adaptive processes in late life. In N. Datan & L. Ginsberg (Eds.), *Life-span developmental psychology: Normative life crises.* New York: Academic Press, 1975.

Lieberman, M. A., Prock, V., & Tobin, S. Psychological effects of institutionalization. *Journal of Gerontology*, 1970, *23*(3), 343–353.

Lieberman, M. A., Yalom, I., & Miles, M. *Encounter groups: First facts.* New York: Basic Books, 1973.

Liemohn, W. Strength and aging: An exploratory study. *International Journal of Human Development*, 1975, *6*(4), 347–357.

Lindemann, E. Symptomatology and management of acute grief. *American Journal of Psychiatry*, 1944, *101*(1), 141–148.

Linden, L. L., & Breed, W. The demographic epidemiology of suicide. In E. S. Shneidman (Ed.), *Suicidology: Contemporary developments.* New York: Grune & Stratton, 1976.

Lipman, A. Role conceptions and morale of couples in retirement. *Journal of Gerontology*, 1961, *16*, 267–271.

Lipman, A. Role conceptions of couples in retirement. In C. Tibbitts & W. Donahue (Eds.), *Social and psychological aspects of aging.* New York: Columbia University Press, 1962.

Lipman-Blumen, J. How ideology shapes women's lives. *Scientific American,* 1972, *226,* 34–42.

Lipman-Blumen, J. *Demographic trends and issues in women's health.* Washington, D.C.: National Health Services Research, Health Services Administration, 1975.

Lipman-Blumen, J., Stivers, P., Tickmayer, A., & Brainard, S. Participation of women in the educational research community. Paper presented at the annual meeting of the American Educational Research Association, Washington, D.C., April 1975.

Lipman-Blumen, J., & Tickmayer, A. Sex roles in transition: A ten-year perspective. *Annual Review of Sociology,* 1975, *1,* 297–337.

Litwak, E. Geographic mobility and extended family cohesion. *American Sociological Review,* 1960, *25*(6), 385–394.

Litwak, E., & Szelenyi, I. Primary group structures and their functions: Kin, neighbors, and friends. *American Sociological Review,* 1969, *34*(4), 465–481.

Livson, F. Patterns of personality development in middle-aged women: A longitudinal study. *International Journal of Aging and Human Development,* 1976, *7*(2), 107–115.

Livson, F. Coming out of the closet: Marriage and other crises of middle age. In L. Troll, J. Israel, & K. Israel (Eds.), *Looking ahead: A woman's guide to the problems and joys of growing older.* Englewood Cliffs, N.J.: Prentice-Hall, 1977. (a)

Livson, F. Coming together in the middle years: A longitudinal study of sex role convergence. Paper presented at the meeting of the American Psychological Association, 1977. (b)

Loesch, J., & Greenberg, N. Some specific areas of conflict observed during pregnancy: A comparative study of married and nonmarried pregnant women. *American Journal of Orthopsychiatry,* 1962, *32*(4), 624–636.

Loevinger, J. *Ego development: Conceptions and theories.* San Francisco: Jossey-Bass, 1976.

Looft, W. Socialization and personality throughout the life-span: An examination of contemporary psychological approaches. In P. B. Baltes & K. W. Schaie (Eds.), *Life-span developmental psychology: Personality and socialization.* New York: Academic Press, 1973.

Looft, W., & Charles, D. Egocentrism and social interaction in young and old adults. *Aging and Human Development,* 1971, *2*(1), 21–28.

Lopata, H. *Occupation: Housewife.* London: Oxford University Press, 1971.

Lopata, H. *Widowhood in an American city.* Cambridge, Mass.: Schenkman, 1973.

Lopata, H. The meaning of friendship in widowhood. In L. Troll, J. Israel, & K. Israel (Eds.), *Looking*

ahead: A woman's guide to the problems and joys of growing older. Englewood Cliffs, N.J.: Prentice-Hall, 1977.

Lorge, I. The influence of the test upon the nature of mental decline as a function of old age. *Journal of Educational Psychology,* 1936, *27,* 100–110.

Lott, A. J., & Lott, B. E. Some indirect measures of interpersonal attraction among children. *Journal of Educational Psychology,* 1970, *61*(2), 124–135.

Lowenthal, M. *Lives in distress.* New York: Basic Books, 1964.

Lowenthal, M. Some potentialities of a life-cycle approach to the study of retirement. In F. M. Carp (Ed.), *Retirement.* New York: Behavioral Publications, 1972.

Lowenthal, M. Toward a sociological theory of change in adulthood and old age. In J. E. Birren & K. W. Schaie (Eds.), *Handbook of the psychology of aging.* New York: Van Nostrand Reinhold, 1977.

Lowenthal, M., & Chiriboga, D. Transition to the empty nest. *Archives of General Psychiatry,* 1972, *26*(1), 8–14.

Lowenthal, M., & Haven, C. Interaction and adaptation: Intimacy as a critical variable. *American Sociological Review,* 1968, *33*(1), 20–30.

Lowenthal, M., & Robinson, B. Social networks and isolation. In R. Binstock & E. Shanas (Eds.), *Handbook of aging and the social sciences.* New York: Van Nostrand Reinhold, 1976.

Lowenthal, M., Thurnher, M., & Chiriboga, D. *Four stages of life.* San Francisco: Jossey-Bass, 1975.

Lozier, J., & Althouse, R. Special enforcement of behavior toward elders in an Appalachian mountain settlement. *Gerontologist,* 1974, *14*(1), 69–80.

Luck, P., & Heiss, J. Social determinants of self-esteem in adult males. *Sociology and Social Research,* 1972, *57*(1), 69–84.

Luckey, E. Marital satisfaction and congruent self-spouse concepts. *Social Forces,* 1960, *39*(2), 153–157.

Luckey, E. Perceptual congruence of self and family concepts as related to marital interaction. *Sociometry,* 1961, *24*(3), 234–250.

Ludwig, E. The process of disillusionment: The effect of aging upon the values of central Indiana farmers. Unpublished doctoral dissertation, Purdue University, 1965.

Lundberg, G. A., Komarovsky, M., & McInerny, M. A. *Leisure: A suburban study.* New York: Columbia University Press, 1934.

Lurie, E. Role scope and social participation. Unpublished Paper No. 10A, 11. San Francisco: Human Development Program, University of California, 1972.

Lurie, E. Sex and stage differences in perceptions of marital and family relationships. *Journal of Marriage and the Family,* 1974, *36*(2), 260–269.

Maas, H., & Kuypers, J. *From thirty to seventy*. San Francisco: Jossey-Bass, 1974.

Maccoby, E. E., & Jacklin, C. N. *The psychology of sex differences*. Stanford, Calif.: Stanford University Press, 1974.

MacKinnon, D. W. The personality correlates of creativity: A study of American architects. In G. S. Nielson (Ed.), *Proceedings of the 14th International Congress of Applied Psychology* (Vol. 2). Copenhagen: Munksgaard, 1962.

Maddison, D., & Viola, A. The health of widows in the year following bereavement. *Journal of Psychosomatic Research*, 1968, *12*(4), 297–306.

Maddox, G. L., & Douglass, E. B. Self-assessment of health: A longitudinal study of elderly subjects. *Journal of Health and Social Behavior*, 1973, *14*, 87–93.

Magni, K. The fear of death. In A. Godin (Ed.), *Death and presence*. Brussels: Lumen Vitae Press, 1972.

Malatesta, C. Affective development over the life span: Involution or growth. Unpublished paper, 1980. (Contact author at Department of Psychology, Rutgers State University of New Jersey.)

Mallan, L. B. Women's worklives and future Social Security benefits. *Social Security Bulletin*, 1976, *39*(4), 3–13.

Mandle, J. Undergraduate activists in the woman's movement and their public: Attitudes towards marriage and the family. *Sociological Focus*, 1975, *8*(3), 257–269.

Mannheim, K. The problem of generations. In K. Mannheim (Ed.), *Essays in the sociology of knowledge*. London: Routledge & Kegan Paul, 1952.

Markus, E., & Nielsen, M. Embedded figures test scores among five samples of aged persons. *Perceptual and Motor Skills*, 1973, *36*, 455–459.

Marotz-Baden, R., & Tallman, I. Parental aspirations and expectations for daughters and sons: A comparative analysis. *Adolescence*, 1978, *13*(50), 251–268.

Marshall, V. Age and awareness of finitude in developmental gerontology. *Omega*, 1975, *6*(2), 113–127.

Marshall, V. *Last chapters: A sociology of aging and dying*. Monterey, Calif.: Brooks/Cole, 1980.

Martel, M. Age-sex roles in American magazine fiction (1890–1955). In B. L. Neugarten (Ed.), *Middle age and aging*. Chicago: University of Chicago Press, 1968.

Martin, C. Sexual activity in the aging male. In J. Money & H. Musaph (Eds.), *Handbook of sexology*. Amsterdam: Elsevier/North Holland Biomedical Press, 1977.

Maslow, A. Deficiency motivation and growth motivation. In M. Jones (Ed.), *Nebraska Symposium on Motivation* (Vol. 3). Lincoln: University of Nebraska Press, 1955.

Mason, E. Some correlates of self-judgments of the aged. *Journal of Gerontology*, 1954, *9*(3), 324–337.

Masters, W., & Johnson, V. *Human sexual response*. Boston: Little, Brown, 1966.

Masters, W., & Johnson, V. Human sexual response: The aging female and male. In B. L. Neugarten (Ed.), *Middle age and aging*. Chicago: University of Chicago Press, 1968.

Masters, W., & Johnson, V. Emotional poverty: A marriage crisis of the middle years. In *Proceedings of the second national congress on the quality of life: The middle years*. Acton, Mass.: Publishing Sciences Group, 1974.

Maurer, A. Maturation of concepts of life. *Journal of Genetic Psychology*, 1970, *116*(1), 101–111.

Maurer, R. R., & Foote, R. H. Maternal aging and embryonic mortality in the rabbit. I. Repeated superovulation, embryo culture and transfer. *Journal of Reproductive Fertility*, 1971, *25*, 329–341.

May, W. Attitudes toward the newly dead. *Hastings Center Studies*, 1973, *1*(1), 3–13.

McCammon, R. *Human growth and development*. Springfield, Ill.: Charles C Thomas, 1970.

McCay, C., Crowell, M., & Maynard, L. The effect of retarded growth upon the length of life span and upon the ultimate body size. *Journal of Nutrition*, 1935, *10*(1), 63–79.

McCay, C., Maynard, L., Sperling, G., & Barnes, L. Retarded growth, life span, ultimate body size, and age changes in the albino rat after feeding diets restricted in calories. *Journal of Nutrition*, 1939, *18*(1), 1–13.

McClintock, M. Menstrual synchrony and suppression. *Nature*, 1971, *37*, 571–605.

McCormick, K. An exploration of the functions of friends and best friends. Unpublished doctoral dissertation, Rutgers University of New Jersey, 1982.

McFarland, R. A. The sensory and perceptual responses in aging. In K. W. Schaie (Ed.), *Theory and methods of research on aging*. Morgantown: West Virginia University, 1968.

McKain, W. *Retirement marriage*. Storrs: Agriculture Experiment Station, University of Connecticut, 1969.

McKinnon, D. A new look at estrogen and menopause. Unpublished term paper, Department of Psychology, Rutgers State University of New Jersey, 1981.

McPherson, B., & Guppy, N. Pre-retirement life-style and the degree of planning for retirement. *Journal of Gerontology*, 1979, *34*(2), 254–263.

Mead, G. H. *Mind, self and society*. Chicago: University of Chicago Press, 1934.

Means, M. Fears of one thousand college women. *Journal of Abnormal and Social Psychology*, 1936, *31*(3), 291–311.

Meddin, J. Generations and aging: A longitudinal study. *International Journal of Aging and Human Development*, 1975, *6*(2), 85–101.

Mendes, H. Single fathers. *Family Coordinator*, 1976, *25*, 439–444.

Menninger, K. *Man against himself*. New York: Harcourt Brace Jovanovich, 1938.

Metzelaar, L. *A collection of cartoons: A way of examining practices in a treatment setting*. Ann Arbor: Institute of Gerontology at the University of Michigan, 1975.

Meyerowitz, J., & Feldman, H. Transitions to parenthood. In I. Cohen (Ed.), *Family structure, dynamics, and therapy*. New York: American Psychiatric Association, 1967.

Miall, W. E., Ashcroft, M., Lovell, H. G., & Moore, F. A longitudinal study of the decline of adult height with age in two Welsh communities. *Human Biology*, 1967, *39*, 445–454.

Miall, W. E., & Lovell, H. G. Relation between change of blood pressure and age. *British Medical Journal*, 1967, *2*, 660–664.

Miller, S. J. The social dilemma of the aging leisure participant. In A. M. Rose & W. A. Peterson (Eds.), *Older people and their social world*. Philadelphia: Davis, 1965.

Miller, S. J. Widowhood and the older woman. Paper presented at the annual meeting of the Gerontological Society, New York, November 1977.

Mischel, W. *Personality and assessment*. New York: Wiley, 1968.

Mischel, W. Continuity and change in personality. *American Psychologist*, 1969, *24*(11), 1012–1018.

Mischel, W. Looking for personality. Paper presented at the meeting of the American Psychological Association, New York, September 1979.

Mitchell, G. Paternalistic behavior in primates. *Psychological Bulletin*, 1969, *71*, 399–417.

Moberg, D. O. *Spiritual well-being*. White House Conference on Aging, background papers. Washington, D.C.: U.S. Government Printing Office, 1971.

Moberg, D. O. Religion and the aged family. *Family Coordinator*, 1972, *21*(1), 47–60.

Moment, G. The Ponce de Leon trail today. *Bioscience*, 1975, *25*(10), 623–628.

Monahan, T. When married couples part: Statistical trends and relationships in the divorced. *American Sociological Review*, 1962, *27*(5), 625–633.

Monge, R. Structure of the self-concept from adolescence through old age. *Experimental Aging Research*, 1975, *1*(2), 281–291.

Monge, R., & Gardner, E. A program of research in adult differences in cognitive performance and learning: Backgrounds for adult education and vocational retraining. (Final Report, Project No. 6-1963, Grant No. OEG1-706193-0149.) Department of Psychology, Syracuse University, 1972.

Monge, R., & Hultsch, D. Paired-associate learning as a function of adult age and the length of the anticipation and inspection intervals. *Journal of Gerontology*, 1971, *26*(2), 157–162.

Moos, R. The development of a menstrual distress questionnaire. *Psychosomatic Medicine*, 1968, *30*(6), 853–867.

More executives refusing to relocate. *New York Times*, November 7, 1975.

Morgan, J. The retirement process in the United States. Paper presented at the Ninth International Congress of Gerontology, Kiev, July 1972.

Morgan, L. A re-examination of widowhood and morale. *Journal of Gerontology*, 1976, *31*(6), 687–695.

Morison, R. Dying. *Life and death and medicine* (a Scientific American Book). San Francisco: W. H. Freeman, 1973.

Moss, H. Sex, age, and state as determinants of mother-infant interaction. *Merrill-Palmer Quarterly*, 1967, *13*(1), 19–36.

Moss, J. J., Apolonio, F., & Jensen, M. The premarital dyad during the sixties. *Journal of Marriage and the Family*, 1971, *33*(1), 50–69.

Muhlbock, O. Factors influencing life span of inbred mice. *Gerontologia*, 1959, *3*(3), 177–183.

Mullener, N., & Laird, J. Some developmental changes in the organization of self-evaluations. *Developmental Psychology*, 1971, *5*(2), 233–236.

Muller, H., Grad, B., & Engelsmann, F. Biological and psychological predictors of survival in a psychogeriatric population. *Journal of Gerontology*, 1975, *30*(1), 47.

Munnichs, J. *Old age and finitude*. New York: Karger, 1966.

Murdock, B., Jr. Recent developments in short-term memory. *British Journal of Psychology*, 1967, *58*(3, 4), 421–433.

Murray, J. Family structure in the pre-retirement years. In *Almost 65: Baseline data from the Retirement History Study*. Washington, D.C.: U.S. Department of Health, Education and Welfare, 1976.

Murstein, B. Empirical tests of role complementary needs, and homogamy theories of mate selection. *Journal of Marriage and the Family*, 1967, *29*(4), 689–696.

Murstein, B. Person perception and courtship progress among premarital couples. *Journal of Marriage and the Family*, 1972, *34*(4), 621–626.

Mussen, P., & Jones, M. Self-conceptions, motivations, and inter-personal attitudes of late and early maturing boys. *Child Development*, 1957, *28*(2), 243–256.

Nagy, M. The child's theories concerning death. *Journal of Genetic Psychology*, 1948, *73*(1), 3–27.

Nardi, A. Apperception and heteroperception of personality traits in adolescents, adults, and the aged. Unpublished doctoral dissertation, West Virginia University, 1971.

National Center for Health Statistics. *Monthly Vital Statistics Report.* Washington, D.C.: National Center for Health Statistics. June 27, 1973.

National Institute of Mental Health. *Changes over time in rate of first admissions to state and county mental hospitals by age (1962, 1969, 1972)* (Statistical Note No. 97). Washington, D.C.: Survey and Reports Section, National Institute of Mental Health, 1973.

National Urban League. *Double jeopardy: The older Negro in America today.* New York: National Urban League, 1964.

Natterson, J., & Knudson, A. Observations concerning fear of death in fatally ill children and their mothers. *Psychosomatic Medicine,* 1960, *22*(6), 456–466.

Nehrke, M. Age, sex, and educational difference in logical judgments. Paper presented at the meeting of the Gerontological Society, Houston, October 1971.

Nehrke, M. Actual and perceived attitudes toward death and self-concept in three-generational families. Paper presented at the meeting of the Gerontological Society, Portland, October 1974.

Nehrke, M., & Reimanis, G. Locus of control among institutionalized males and community-dwelling males and females. Paper presented at the meeting of the Gerontological Society, Dallas, November 1978.

Nelson, E. N. P. Patterns of religious attitude shifts from college to fourteen years later. *Psychological Monographs,* 1956, *70*(Whole no. 17).

Nesselroade, J., & Harkins, S. Introduction to Section 9: Methodological issues. In L. Poon (Ed.), *Aging in the 1980s.* Washington, D.C.: American Psychological Association, 1980.

Neugarten, B. L., & Associates. *Personality in middle and late life: Empirical studies.* New York: Atherton, 1964.

Neugarten, B. L. (Ed.). *Middle age and aging.* Chicago: University of Chicago Press, 1968.

Neugarten, B. L. Adaptation and the life cycle. *Journal of Geriatric Psychiatry,* 1970, *4*(1), 71–87.

Neugarten, B. L. Personality change in late life: A developmental perspective. In C. Eisdorfer & M. P. Lawton (Eds.), *The psychology of adult development and aging.* Washington, D.C.: American Psychological Association, 1973.

Neugarten, B. L. Age groups in American society and the rise of the young-old. *Annals of the American Academy,* 1974 (September), 187–198.

Neugarten, B. L. The future and the young-old. *Gerontologist,* 1975, *15*(1, Pt. 2), 4–9.

Neugarten, B. L. Personality and aging. In J. E. Birren & K. W. Schaie (Eds.), *Handbook of the psychology of aging.* New York: Van Nostrand Reinhold, 1977.

Neugarten, B. L., Crotty, W., & Tobin, S. Personality types in an aged population. In B. L. Neugarten & Associates, *Personality in middle and late life: Empirical studies.* New York: Atherton, 1964.

Neugarten, B. L., & Datan, N. Sociological perspectives on the life cycle. In P. B. Baltes & K. W. Schaie (Eds.), *Life-span developmental psychology: Personality and socialization.* New York: Academic Press, 1973.

Neugarten, B. L., & Datan, N. The middle years. In S. Arieti (Ed.), *American handbook of psychiatry.* New York: Basic Books, 1974.

Neugarten, B. L., & Gutmann, D. L. Age-sex roles and personality in middle age: A thematic apperception study. In B. L. Neugarten & Associates, *Personality in middle and late life: Empirical studies.* New York: Atherton, 1964.

Neugarten, B. L., & Gutmann, D. L. Age-sex roles and personality in middle age. In B. L. Neugarten (Ed.), *Middle age and aging.* Chicago: University of Chicago Press, 1968.

Neugarten, B. L., & Hagestad, G. Age and the life course. In R. Binstock & E. Shanas (Eds.), *Handbook of aging and the social sciences.* New York: Van Nostrand Reinhold, 1976.

Neugarten, B. L., Havighurst, R. J., & Tobin, S. Personality and patterns of aging. In B. L. Neugarten (Ed.), *Middle age and aging.* Chicago: University of Chicago Press, 1968.

Neugarten, B. L., & Moore, J. The changing age-status system. In B. L. Neugarten (Ed.), *Middle age and aging.* Chicago: University of Chicago Press, 1968.

Neugarten, B. L., Moore, J., & Lowe, J. Age norms, age constraints, and adult socialization. *American Journal of Sociology,* 1965, *70*(6), 710–717.

Neugarten, B. L., & Peterson, W. A study of the American age-grade system. *Proceedings of the Fourth Congress of the International Association of Gerontology,* 1957, *3*, 144.

Neugarten, B. L., & Weinstein, K. The changing American grandparent. *Journal of Marriage and the Family,* 1964, *26*(2), 199–204.

Neugarten, B. L., Wood, V., Kraines, R., & Loomis, B. Women's attitudes towards the menopause. *Vita Humana,* 1963, *6*, 140–151.

Neulinger, J. *The psychology of leisure.* Springfield, Ill.: Charles C Thomas, 1974.

Neulinger, J. Leisure counseling: Process or content? Paper presented at the Dane County Recreation Coordinating Council Conference on Leisure Counseling, Madison, Wis., September 27, 1978.

Newman, S. *Housing adjustments of older people: A report of findings from the second phase.* Ann Arbor: Institute for Social Research, University of Michigan, 1976.

Noberini, M., & Neugarten, B. L. A follow-up study of adaptation in middle-aged women. Paper presented at the meeting of the Gerontological Society, Louisville, Ky., October 1975.

Norton, A. J., & Glick, P. C. Mental instability: Past, present, and future. *Journal of Social Issues*, 1976, *32*(1), 6–7.

Novak, E. Ovulation after fifty. *Obstetrical Gynecology*, 1970, *36*, 903–910.

Novak, L. Aging, total body potassium, fat-free mass, and cell mass in males and females between ages 18 and 85 years. *Journal of Gerontology*, 1972, *27* (4), 438–443.

Nowak, C. The appearance signal in adult development. Unpublished doctoral dissertation, Psychology Department, Wayne State University, 1975.

Nowak, C. Youthfulness, attractiveness and the midlife woman: An analysis of the appearance signal in adult development. Paper presented at the meeting of the Midwestern Psychological Association, Chicago, March 1976.

Nydegger, C. Late and early fathers. Paper presented at the meeting of the Gerontological Society, Miami Beach, November 1973.

Nydegger, C., & Mitteness, L. Transitions in fatherhood. *Generations*, 1979, *4*(1), 14–15.

Nye, F. I. Husband-wife relationships. In L. W. Hoffman, F. I. Nye, & Associates (Eds.), *Working mothers: An evaluative review of consequences for wife, husband, and child*. San Francisco: Jossey-Bass, 1974.

Oakley, A. *The sociology of housework*. New York: Pantheon Books, 1974.

Obrist, W., Henry, C., & Justiss, W. A longitudinal study of EEG in old age. *Excerpta medica* (International Congress Series), 1961, *37*, 180–181.

O'Connell, A. Life style: Personality, role concept, attitudes, influences, and choices. Paper presented at the meeting of the American Psychological Association, New York, September 1979.

Okun, M. Adult age and cautiousness in decision. *Human Development*, 1976, *19*(4), 220–233.

O'Leary, V. *Toward understanding women*. Monterey, Calif.: Brooks/Cole, 1977.

Oliver, D. Career and leisure patterns: Middle-aged metropolitan outmigrants. *Gerontologist*, 1971, *11*(4, Pt. 2), 13–20.

Orbach, H. L. Social values and the institutionalization of retirement. In R. H. Williams, C. Tibbitts, & W. Donahue (Eds.), *Processes of aging* (Vol. 2). New York: Atherton, 1963.

Osipow, S. Career development through the adult years. Paper presented at the Conference on Adult Development and Guidance, Wayne State University, Detroit, February 1972.

Osofsky, J. D. Neonatal characteristics and directional effects in mother-infant interaction. Paper presented at the meeting of the Society for Research in Child Development, 1975.

Osofsky, J. D., & Danzger, B. Relationships between neonatal characteristics and mother-infant interaction. *Developmental Psychology*, 1974, *10*, 124–130.

Owen, J. Work weeks and leisure: An analysis of trends, 1948–1975. *Monthly Labor Review*, 1976, *99*, 3–8.

Owens, W., Jr. Age and mental abilities: A longitudinal study. *Genetic Psychology Monographs*, 1953, *48*(1), 3–54.

Owens, W., Jr. Is age kinder to the initially more able? *Journal of Gerontology*, 1959, *14*(3), 334–337.

Palmer, R. Psychological factors in visual acuity. *Proceedings of the 97th Annual Convention of the American Psychological Association*, 1968, *10*, 539–560.

Palmore, E. Employment and retirement. In L. Epstein (Ed.), *The aged population of the United States*. Washington, D.C.: U.S. Government Printing Office, 1967.

Palmore, E. Age changes in activities and attitudes. *Gerontologist*, 1968, *8*(4), 259–263.

Palmore, E. Physical, mental, and social factors in predicting longevity. *Gerontologist*, 1969, *9*(2), 103–108.

Palmore, E. Attitudes toward aging as shown by humor. *Gerontologist*, 1971, *12*, 343–348.

Palmore, E., & Cleveland, W. Aging, terminal decline, and terminal drop. *Journal of Gerontology*, 1975, *31*(1), 76–81.

Palmore, E., & Luikart, C. Health and social factors related to life satisfaction. *Journal of Health and Social Behavior*, 1972, *13*, 68–80.

Palmore, E., & Manton, K. Ageism compared to racism and sexism. *Journal of Gerontology*, 1973, *38*(3), 353–369.

Parent, M. The nature of stress in middle age. Paper presented at the meeting of the Gerontological Society, Dallas, November 1978.

Paris, B., & Luckey, E. A longitudinal study in marital satisfaction. *Sociological and Social Research*, 1966, *50*(2), 212–222.

Parke, R. D., & O'Leary, S. Father-mother-infant interaction in the newborn period: Some findings, some observations, and some unresolved issues. In K. F. Riegel & J. Meacham (Eds.), *The developing individual in a changing world*. Vol. 2: *Social and environmental issues*. The Hague: Mouton, 1975.

Parke, R. D., & Sawin, D. B. Infant characteristics and behavior as elicitors of maternal and paternal responsivity. Paper presented at the biennial meeting of the Society for Research in Child Development, Denver, April 1975.

Parker, S. R. Work and nonwork in three occupations. *Sociological Review*, 1965, *13*, 65–75.

Parkes, C. Effects of bereavement on physical and mental health: A study of the medical records of widows. *British Medical Journal*, 1964, *2*, 274–279.

Parkes, C. *Bereavement*. New York: International Universities Press, 1972.

Parnes, H. A., Adams, A. V., Andresani, P., et al. *The pre-retirement years: Five years in the work lives of middle-aged men* (Manpower Research Monograph No. 15). Washington, D.C.: U.S. Department of Labor, 1975.

Parnes, H. A., Nestel, G., & Andresani, P. *The pre-retirement years: A longitudinal study of the labor market experience of men* (Vol. 3). Columbus: Center for Human Resource Research, Ohio State University, 1972.

Parnes, H. A., Nestel, G., & Andresani, P. *The pre-retirement years: Five years in the work lives of middle-aged men.* Columbus: Center for Human Resource Research, Ohio State University, 1974.

Parnes, H., Shea, J. R., Spitz, R. S., Zeller, F., & Associates. *Dual careers: A longitudinal study of labor market experience of women* (Vol. 1). Columbus: Center for Human Resource Research, Ohio State University, 1970. (Also published as Manpower Research Monograph No. 21. Washington, D.C.: U.S. Government Printing Office, 1970.)

Parron, E. An exploratory study of intimacy in golden wedding couples. Unpublished master's thesis, Rutgers University, 1978.

Parron, E. Relationships of Black and White golden wedding couples. Unpublished doctoral dissertation, Rutgers State University of New Jersey, 1979.

Parron, E., & Troll, L. Golden wedding couples: Effects of retirement on intimacy. *Alternate Life Styles,* 1978, *1*(4), 447–464.

Parsons, T. The organization of personality as a system of action. In T. Parsons & R. Bales, *Family: Socialization and interaction process.* New York: Free Press, 1955.

Parten, M. Social participation among pre-school children. *Journal of Abnormal and Social Psychology,* 1932, *27*(3), 243–269.

Pearl, R., & Pearl, R. De W. *The ancestry of the long-lived.* Baltimore, Md.: Johns Hopkins University Press, 1934.

Peck, R. Psychological developments in the second half of life. In B. L. Neugarten (Ed.), *Middle age and aging.* Chicago: University of Chicago Press, 1968.

Peck, R., & Berkowitz, H. Personality and adjustment in middle age. In B. L. Neugarten & Associates, *Personality in middle and late life: Empirical studies.* New York: Atherton, 1964.

Pederson, D., & Higbee, K. Self-disclosure and relationship to the target person. *Merrill-Palmer Quarterly,* 1969, *15*(2), 213–220.

Peppers, L. Patterns of leisure and adjustment to retirement. *Gerontologist,* 1976, *16*(5), 441–446.

Perlin, S., & Butler, R. Psychiatric aspects of adaptation to the aging experience. In J. E. Birren (Ed.), *Human aging* (DHEW Publication No. [ADM] 74–122). Washington, D.C.: U.S. Government Printing Office, 1971.

Peters, G. Self-conceptions of the aged, age identification, and aging. *Gerontologist,* 1971, *2*(4, Pt. 2), 69–73.

Peterson, D., & Whittington, F. Drug use among the elderly: A review. *Journal of Psychedelic Drugs,* 1977, *9*(1), 25–37.

Peterson, J. Marital and family therapy involving the aged. *Gerontologist,* 1973, *13*(1), 27–31.

Petrowsky, M. Marital status, sex, and the social networks of the elderly. *Journal of Marriage and the Family,* 1976, *38*(3), 749–756.

Pfeiffer, E. Psychopathology and social pathology. In J. E. Birren & K. W. Schaie (Eds.), *Handbook of the psychology of aging.* New York: Van Nostrand Reinhold, 1977.

Pfeiffer, E., & Davis, G. Use of leisure time in middle life. *Gerontologist,* 1971, *11*, 187–195.

Pfeiffer, E., & Davis, G. Determinants of sexual behavior in middle and old age. *Journal of the American Geriatric Society,* 1972, *20*, 151–158.

Phillips, D., & Feldman, K. A dip in deaths before ceremonial occasions: Some new relationships between social integration and mortality. *American Sociological Review,* 1973, *38*, 678–696.

Piaget, J. *The child's conception of the world.* Paterson, N.J.: Littlefield, Adams, 1960.

Piaget, J. Piaget's theory (G. Gellerier & J. Langer, trans.). In P. Mussen (Ed.), *Carmichaels' manual of child psychology* (Vol. 1). New York: Wiley, 1970.

Pihlblad, C., & Adams, D. Widowhood, social participation and life satisfaction. Paper presented at the meeting of the Gerontological Society, Houston, October 1971.

Pincus, A., Wood, V., & Kondrat, R. Perceptions of age-appropriate activities and roles. Paper presented at the meeting of the Gerontological Society, Portland, October 1974.

Pineo, P. Disenchantment in the later years of marriage. *Marriage and Family Living,* 1961, *23*, 1–12.

Pleck, J. Men's roles in the family: A new look. Paper presented at Ford Foundation Conference on Changing Sex Roles and the Family, Detroit, October 1975.

Pleck, J. The work-family role system. *Social Problems,* 1977, *24*, 417–427.

Pleck, J., Staines, G., & Lang, L. Conflicts between work and family life. *Monthly Labor Review,* 1980, March, pp. 29–32.

Plemons, J. K., Willis, S. L., & Baltes, P. B. Challenging the theory of fluid intelligence: A training approach. Paper presented at the 28th annual meeting of the Gerontological Society, Louisville, Ky., October 1975.

Plemons, J. K., Willis, S., & Baltes, P. B. Modifiability of fluid intelligence in aging: A short-term longitudinal training approach. *Journal of Gerontology*, 1978, *33*(2), 224–231.

Pokorny, A. Myths about suicide. In H. Resnick (Ed.), *Suicidal behaviors*. Boston: Little, Brown, 1968.

Pollis, C. Dating involvement and patterns of idealization: A test of Waller's hypothesis. *Journal of Marriage and the Family*, 1969, *31*(4), 765–771.

Porter, S. Women still have hard time when it comes to pensions. *Home News*, April 24, 1980, p. 40.

Powell, D. A., Buchanan, S., & Milligan, W. Relationships between learning, performance, and arousal in aged versus younger VA patients. Paper presented at the meeting of the Gerontological Society, Louisville, Ky., October 1975.

Powell, D. A., Tkacik, M. F., Buchanan, S. L., & Milligan, W. L. Cardiovascular responses elicited by electrical brain stimulation in the rabbit. *Physiology & Behavior*, 1976, *16*(2), 227–230.

Powers, E., & Bultena, G. Sex differences in intimate friendships of old age. *Journal of Marriage and the Family*, 1976, *38*(4), 739–747.

Prock, V. Effects of institutionalization: A comparison of community, waiting list, and institutionalized aged persons. Unpublished doctoral dissertation, Committee on Human Development, University of Chicago, 1965.

Quinn, R. P., & Staines, G. L. *The 1977 Quality of Employment Survey*. Ann Arbor: Survey Research Center, Institute for Social Research, University of Michigan, 1979.

Quinn, R. P., Staines, G. L., & McCullough, M. *Job satisfaction: Is there a trend?* (U.S. Department of Labor, Manpower Research Monograph No. 30). Washington, D.C.: U.S. Government Printing Office, 1974.

Rabbitt, P. M. A. Age and time for choice between stimuli and between responses. *Journal of Gerontology*, 1964, *19*(3), 307–312.

Rabbitt, P. M. A. An age decrement in the ability to ignore irrelevant information. *Journal of Gerontology*, 1965, *20*, 233–238.

Rabbitt, P. M. A. Changes in problem solving ability in old age. In J. E. Birren & K. W. Schaie (Eds.), *Handbook of the psychology of aging*. New York: Van Nostrand Reinhold, 1977.

Ragan, P. Socialization for the retirement role: "Cooling the mark out." Paper presented at the meeting of the American Psychological Association, San Francisco, August 1977.

Ragan, P., & Bengtson, V. *Black, brown, white, old: Styles of aging* (Social Organization and Behavior Laboratory Research Report). Los Angeles: Andrus Gerontology Center, University of Southern California, 1976.

Rapoport, R., & Rapoport, R. The dual-career family: A variant pattern and social change. *Human Relations*, 1969, *22*(1), 3–30.

Raush, H., Barry, W., Hertel, R., & Swain, M. *Communication, conflict, and marriage*. San Francisco: Jossey-Bass, 1974.

Raush, H., Greif, A., & Nugent, J. Communication in couples and families. In W. Burr, R. Hill, G. Nye, & I. Reiss (Eds.), *Contemporary theories about the family* (Vol. 1). New York: Free Press, 1979.

Reedy, M. Age and sex differences in personal needs and the nature of love: A study of happily married young, middle-aged, and older adult couples. Unpublished doctoral dissertation, University of Southern California, 1977.

Reedy, M., & Birren, J. E. How do lovers grow older together? Types of lovers and age. Paper presented at the meeting of the Gerontological Society, Dallas, November 1978.

Rees, W., & Lutkins, S. Mortality of bereavement. *British Medical Journal*, 1967, *4*(1), 13–16.

Reichard, S., Livson, F., & Peterson, P. *Aging and personality*. New York: Wiley, 1962.

Reiss, P. Extended kinship system: Correlates of and attitudes on frequency of interaction. *Marriage and Family Living*, 1962, *24*(4), 333–339.

Rheingold, H., & Eckerman, C. D. The infant separates himself from the mother. *Science*, 1970, *168*(1), 78–83.

Rhudick, P., & Gordon, C. The Age Center of New England study. In L. F. Jarvik, C. Eisdorfer, & J. Blum (Eds.), *Intellectual functioning in adults*. New York: Springer, 1973.

Riegel, K. The prediction of death and longevity in longitudinal research. In E. Palmore & F. Jeffers (Eds.), *Prediction of life span*. Lexington, Mass.: Heath, 1971.

Riegel, K. Adult life crises: A dialectical interpretation of development. In N. Datan & L. Ginsberg (Eds.), *Life-span developmental psychology: Normative life crises*. New York: Academic Press, 1975.

Riegel, K., & Riegel, R. Development, drop, and death. *Developmental Psychology*, 1972, *6*(2), 306–319.

Riegel, K., Riegel, R., & Meyer, G. Sociopsychological factors of aging: A cohort-sequential analysis. *Human Development*, 1967, *10*(1), 27–56.

Riley, M. W., & Foner, A. *Aging and society*. Vol. 1: *An inventory of research findings*. New York: Russell Sage Foundation, 1968.

Robertson, J. Significance of grandparents: Perceptions of young adult grandchildren. *Gerontologist*, 1976, *16*(2), 137–140.

Robertson, J. Grandmotherhood: A study of role conceptions. *Journal of Marriage and the Family*, 1977, *39*(1), 165–174. (a)

Robertson, J. Socialization into grandmotherhood. Paper presented at the meeting of the American Psychological Association, San Francisco, August 1977. (b)

Robertson, O. Survival of precociously mature king

salmon male parr (*Oncorhynchus tsohawytscha* Juv.) after spawning. *California Fish and Game,* 1957, *43,* 119–130.

Robertson, O. Prolongation of the life span of Kokanee salmon (*Onchorhynchus nerka kennerlyi*) by castration before beginning of gonadal development. *Proceedings of the National Academy of Science,* 1961, *47*(4), 609–621.

Robin, E. The almost aged. Paper presented at the meeting of the Gerontological Society, Houston, October 1971.

Robin, E. The aged in elementary school textbooks. Paper presented at the meeting of the Gerontological Society, Miami, November 1973.

Robins, L., & Tomanec, M. Closeness to blood relatives outside the immediate family. *Marriage and Family Living,* 1962, *24*(4), 340–346.

Robinson, J. How people feel about how they use their time. Paper presented at the meeting of the American Psychological Association, New York, September 1979.

Robson, K., & Moss, H. Patterns and determinants of maternal attachment. *Journal of Pediatrics,* 1970, *77*(6), 976–985.

Rockstein, M., Chesky, J., & Sussman, M. Comparative biology and evolution of aging. In C. Finch & L. Hayflick (Eds.), *Handbook of the biology of aging.* New York: Van Nostrand Reinhold, 1977.

Rockstein, M., & Miquel, J. Aging in insects. In M. Rockstein (Ed.), *The physiology of insecta* (Vol. 1). New York: Academic Press, 1973.

Roe, A. The psychology of the scientist. *Science,* 1961, *134,* 456–459.

Rollins, B., & Feldman, H. Marital satisfaction over the family life cycle. *Journal of Marriage and the Family,* 1970, *32*(1), 20–28.

Rose, A. The subculture of aging: A framework for research in social gerontology. In A. Rose & W. Peterson (Eds.), *Older people and their social world.* Philadelphia: Davis, 1965.

Rosen, B. Family structure and value transmission. *Merrill-Palmer Quarterly,* 1964, *10*(1), 59–76.

Rosen, J., & Bibring, G. Psychological reactions of hospitalized male patients to a heart attack: Age and social class differences. *Psychosomatic Medicine,* 1966, *28*(6), 62–67.

Rosen, J., & Neugarten, B. L. Ego functions in the middle and later years: A thematic apperception study of normal adults. *Journal of Gerontology,* 1960, *15*(1), 62–67.

Rosenberg, G. *The worker grows old.* San Francisco: Jossey-Bass, 1970.

Rosenberg, G., & Anspach, D. Sibling solidarity in the working class. *Journal of Marriage and the Family,* 1973, *35*(1), 108–113.

Rosow, I. *Social integration of the aged.* New York: Free Press, 1967.

Ross, D. The story of the top one percent of the women at Michigan State University. Unpublished paper, Department of Sociology, Michigan State University. Cited in J. Bernard, *The Future of Marriage* (New York: Bantam Books, 1973).

Ross, M. Protein, calories, and life expectancy. *Federation Processes,* 1959, *18*(4), 1190–1207.

Ross, M. Length of life and nutrition in the rat. *Journal of Nutrition,* 1961, *75*(2), 197–210.

Rossi, A. Equality between the sexes: An immodest proposal. *Daedalus,* 1964, *93*(2), 607–652.

Rossi, A. Personal communication, 1966.

Rossman, I. Anatomic and body composition changes with aging. In C. Finch & L. Hayflick (Eds.), *Handbook of the biology of aging.* New York: Van Nostrand Reinhold, 1977.

Rothbart, M., & Maccoby, E. Parents' differential reactions to sons and daughters. *Journal of Personality and Social Psychology,* 1966, *4*(3), 237–243.

Rotter, J. Generalized expectancies for internal versus external control of reinforcement. *Psychological Monographs,* 1966, *80*(1, Whole No. 609).

Rougemont, D. *Love in the Western world* (M. Belgian, trans.; rev. ed.). New York: Pantheon, 1956.

Rovee, C. K., Cohen, R. Y., & Shlapek, W. Life-span stability in olfactory sensitivity. *Developmental Psychology,* 1975, *11*(3), 311–318.

Rubin, K., Attewell, P., Tierney, M., & Tumolo, P. The development of spatial egocentrism and conservation across the life span. *Developmental Psychology,* 1973, *9*(3), 432.

Rubin, K., & Brown, D. Life-span look at person perception and its relationship to communicative interaction. *Journal of Gerontology,* 1975, *30*(4), 461–468.

Rubin, L. *Worlds of pain.* New York: Basic Books, 1976.

Rubin, L. Sex and sexuality: Women at midlife. Paper presented at the meeting of the American Sociological Association, San Francisco, September 1978.

Rupp, R. Understanding the problems of presbycusis: An overview of hearing loss associated with aging. *Geriatrics,* 1970, *25*(1), 100.

Russell, C. Transition to parenthood: Problems and gratifications. *Journal of Marriage and the Family,* 1974, *36*(2), 244–303.

Ryder, R. Husband-wife dyads versus married strangers. *Family Process,* 1968, *7*(2), 232–238.

Ryder, R., & Goodrich, D. Married couples' responses to disagreement. *Family Process,* 1966, *5*(1), 30–42.

Ryff, C., & Baltes, P. B. Value transition and adult development in women: The instrumentality-terminality sequence hypothesis. *Developmental Psychology,* 1978, *12*(6), 567–568.

Sabatini, P. The effect of inducing thoughts of death on college students' death anxiety. Unpublished master's thesis, Wayne State University, 1975.

Sabatini, P., & Nowak, C. Bias for the ages: Perceptions of age-appropriate behavior in adolescent, midlife, and late adult samples. Paper presented at the meeting of the Gerontological Society, Louisville, Ky., October 1975.

Sacher, G. Molecular versus systemic theories on the genesis of aging. *Experimental Gerontology*, 1968, *3*(3), 265–271.

Safier, G. A study in relationships between the life and death concepts in children. *Journal of Genetic Psychology*, 1964, *105*(2), 283–294.

Salek, S., & Otis, J. Age and level of job satisfaction. *Personnel Psychology*, 1964, *17*(4), 425–430.

Saltz, R. Evaluation of a foster-grandparent program. In A. Kalushin (Ed.), *Child welfare services: A sourcebook*. New York: Macmillan, 1970.

Sanford, A., & Maule, A. Age and the distribution of observing responses. *Psychonomic Science*, 1971, *23*(6), 419–420.

Sanford, N. *Issues in personality theory*. San Francisco: Jossey-Bass, 1970.

Scarf, M. Husbands in crisis. *McCall's*, 1972, *99*, 76–77.

Schaie, K. W. Rigidity-flexibility and intelligence: A cross-sectional study of the adult life span from 20 to 70 years. *Psychological Monographs*, 1958, *72*, 1.

Schaie, K. W. A general model for the study of developmental problems. *Psychological Bulletin*, 1965, *64*(2), 92–107.

Schaie, K. W. A reinterpretation of age-related changes in cognitive structure and functioning. In L. R. Goulet & P. B. Baltes (Eds.), *Life-span developmental psychology: Research and theory*. New York: Academic Press, 1970.

Schaie, K. W. Methodological problems in descriptive developmental research on adulthood and aging. In J. R. Nesselroade & H. W. Reese (Eds.), *Life-span developmental psychology: Methodological issues*. New York: Academic Press, 1973.

Schaie, K. W., Labouvie, G. V., & Buech, B. Generational and cohort-specific differences in adult cognitive functioning: A fourteen-year study of independent samples. *Developmental Psychology*, 1973, *9*(2), 18.

Schaie, K. W., & Parham, I. Stability of adult personality traits: Fact or fable? *Journal of Personality and Social Psychology*, 1976, *34*(1), 146–158.

Schonfield, D. Theoretical nuances and practical old questions: The psychology of aging. *Canadian Psychologist*, 1972, *13*(3), 252–266.

Schonfield, D., & Robertson, B. Memory storage and aging. *Canadian Journal of Psychology*, 1966, *20*(2), 228–236.

Schonfield, D., & Smith, G. Searching for multiple targets and age. *Educational Gerontology*, 1976, *1*(2), 119–129.

Schonfield, D., Trueman, V., & Kline, D. Recognition tests of dichotic listening and the age variable. *Journal of Gerontology*, 1972, *27*(4), 487–493.

Schorr, A. Filial responsibility in the modern American family. Washington, D.C.: Social Security Administration, 1960.

Schrödinger, E. *What is life?* Cambridge, England: Cambridge University Press, 1962.

Schultz, N., & Hoyer, W. Feedback effects on spatial egocentrism in old age. *Journal of Gerontology*, 1976, *31*(1), 72–75.

Schulz, J. H. The economics of mandatory retirement. *Industrial Gerontology*, 1974, *1*(1), 1–11.

Schulz, J. H. *The economics of aging*. Belmont, Calif.: Wadsworth, 1976.

Schulz, R. The effects of control and predictability on the physical and psychological well-being of the aged. Unpublished doctoral dissertation, Department of Psychology, Duke University, 1974.

Schvanaveldt, J., & Ihinger, M. Sibling relationships in the family. In W. Burr, R. Hill, G. Nye, & I. Reiss (Eds.), *Contemporary theories about the family* (Vol. 1). New York: Free Press, 1979.

Schwab, J., Chalmers, J., Conroy, S., Farris, P., & Markush, R. Studies in grief: A preliminary report. In B. Schoenberg, I. Gerber, A. Weiner, A. Kutscher, D. Peretz, & A. Carr (Eds.), *Psychosocial aspects of bereavement*. New York: Columbia University Press, 1975.

Schwartz, D., & Karp, S. Field dependence in a geriatric population. *Perceptual and Motor Skills*, 1967, *24*(2), 495–504.

Schwartz, E., & Elonen, A. I.Q. and the myth of stability: A 16-year longitudinal study of variations in intelligence test performance. *Journal of Clinical Psychology*, 1975, *31*(4), 687–694.

Schwartz, M. Career strategies of the never married. Paper presented at the meeting of the American Sociological Association, New York, August 1976.

Scott, F. Family group structure and patterns of social interaction. *American Journal of Sociology*, 1962(2), *68*, 214–228.

Scrimshaw, N. S. Nutrition and stress. In G. E. W. Wolstenholme & M. O'Connor (Eds.), *Ciba Foundation Study Group No. 17: Diet and bodily constitution*. Boston: Little, Brown, 1964.

Sears, P. S., & Sears, R. R. From childhood to middle age to later maturity: Longitudinal study. Paper presented at 86th annual meeting of the American Psychological Association, Toronto, August 1978.

Sedney, M. A., & Turner, B. F. A test of causal sequences in two models for development of career-orientation in women. *Journal of Vocational Behavior*, 1975, *6*, 281–291.

Segerberg, O., Jr. *The immortality factor*. New York: Dutton, 1974.

Seltzer, M., & Atchley, R. C. The concept of old: Changing attitudes and stereotypes. *Gerontologist*, 1971, *11*(3, Pt. 1), 226–230. (a)

Seltzer, M., & Atchley, R. C. The impact of structural

integration into the profession on work commitment, potential for disengagement, and leisure preferences among social workers. *Sociological Focus*, 1971, *5*(1), 9–17. (b)

Selye, N. Stress and aging. *Journal of the American Geriatrics Society*, 1970, *18*(9), 669–680.

Shanas, E., & Maddox, G. L. Aging, health, and the organization of health resources. In R. H. Binstock & E. Shanas (Eds.), *Handbook of aging and the social sciences*. New York: Van Nostrand Reinhold, 1976.

Shanas, E., Townsend, P., Wedderburn, D., Friis, H., Milhoj, P., & Stehouwer, J. *Older people in three industrial societies*. New York: Atherton, 1968.

Shapiro, E. Transition to parenthood in adult and family development. Paper presented at the meeting of the American Psychological Association, Toronto, August 1978.

Sheehy, G. *Passages: Predictable crises in adult life.* New York: Dutton, 1976.

Sheppard, H. *New perspectives on older workers.* Washington, D.C.: W. E. Upjohn Institute for Employment Research, 1971.

Sheppard, H. Work and retirement. In R. Binstock & E. Shanas (Eds.), *Handbook of aging and the social sciences*. New York: Van Nostrand Reinhold, 1976.

Sheppard, H., & Belitsky, A. *The job hunt*. Baltimore: Johns Hopkins Press, 1966.

Shmavonian, B., & Busse, E. The utilization of psychophysiological techniques in the study of the aged. In R. Williams, C. Tibbetts, & W. Donahue (Eds.), *Process of aging: Social and psychological perspectives*. New York: Atherton, 1963.

Shneidman, E. Orientations towards death: A vital aspect of the study of lives. In R. White (Ed.), *The study of lives*. New York: Prentice-Hall, 1963.

Shneidman, E. Current overview of suicide. In E. Shneidman (Ed.), *Suicidology: Contemporary developments*. New York: Grune & Stratton, 1976.

Shneidman, E., & Farberow, N. *Clues to suicide.* New York: McGraw-Hill, 1957.

Shock, N. W. Biological theories of aging. In J. E. Birren & K. W. Schaie (Eds.), *Handbook of the psychology of aging*. New York: Van Nostrand Reinhold, 1977. (a)

Shock, N. W. System integration. In C. Finch & L. Hayflick (Eds.), *Handbook of the physiology of aging*. New York: Van Nostrand Reinhold, 1977. (b)

Shope, D., & Broderick, C. Level of sexual experience and predicted adjustment in marriage. *Journal of Marriage and the Family*, 1967, *29*(3), 424–427.

Siegelman, E., Block, J., Block, J., & Von der Lippe, A. Antecedents of optimal psychological adjustment. *Journal of Consulting and Clinical Psychology*, 1970, *35*(3), 283–289.

Sigel, I. The distancing hypothesis: A causal hypothesis for the acquisition of representational thought. In M. Jones (Ed.), *Miami Symposium on the Prediction of Behavior 1968: Effect of early*

experiences. Coral Gables, Fla.: University of Miami Press, 1970.

Sigel, I., & Cocking, R. *Cognitive development from childhood to adolescence: A constructivist perspective*. New York: Holt, Rinehart & Winston, 1977.

Sigusch, V., Schmidt, G., Reinfeld, A., & Wiederman, S. Psychosexual stimulation: Sex differences. *Journal of Sex Research*, 1970, *6*(1), 10–24.

Simmons, L. *The role of the aged in primitive society*. New Haven, Conn.: Yale University Press, 1945.

Simon, A., Lowenthal, M., & Epstein, L. *Crisis and intervention*. San Francisco: Jossey-Bass, 1970.

Simon, W., Gagnon, J., & Berger, A. Beyond anxiety and fantasy: The coital experiences of college youth. *Journal of Youth and Adolescence*, 1972, *1*(3), 203–222.

Simpson, I. H., Back, K. W., & McKinney, J. C. Continuity of work and retirement activities, and self-evaluation. In I. H. Simpson & J. C. McKinney (Eds.), *Social aspects of aging*. Durham, N.C.: Duke University Press, 1966.

Singer, J., & McCraven, V. Some characteristics of adult daydreaming. *Journal of Psychology*, 1961, *51*(1), 151–164.

Skolnick, A. Motivational imagery and behavior over 20 years. *Journal of Consulting Psychology*, 1966, *30*(6), 463–478. (a)

Skolnick, A. Stability and interrelations of thematic test imagery over 20 years. *Child Development*, 1966, *37*(2), 389–396. (b)

Slater, P. E., & Scarr, H. A. Personality in old age. *Genetic Psychology Monographs*, 1964, *70*, 229–269.

Smith, R. The impact of mass layoffs. In *Proceedings of the 18th Annual Meeting of the Industrial Relations Research Association, New York 1965*. Madison, Wis.: Industrial Relations Research Association, 1966.

Sobol, M. Commitment to work. In F. Nye & L. Hoffman (Eds.), *The employed mother in America*. Chicago: Rand McNally, 1963.

Solyom, L., & Barik, H. Conditioning in senescence and senility. *Journal of Gerontology*, 1965, *20*(4), 483–488.

Sontag, L. W., Baker, C. T., & Nelson, V. L. Mental growth and personality development: A longitudinal study. *Monographs of the Society for Research in Child Development*, 1958, *23*(68).

Sontag, S. The double standard of aging. *Saturday Review of the Society*, 1972, *55*(39), 29–38.

Soule, A. The pregnant couple. Paper presented at the meeting of the American Psychological Association, New Orleans, August 1974.

Spanier, G., Lewis, R., & Coles, C. Marital adjustment over the family life cycle: The issue of curvilinearity. *Journal of Marriage and the Family*, 1975, *37*(2), 263–275.

Spence, D. The role of futurity in aging adaptation. *Gerontologist*, 1968, *8*(3), 180–183.

Spence, D., & Lonner, T. The "empty nest": A transition within motherhood. *Family Coordinator,* 1971, *20*(4), 369–375.

Spence, D., & Lonner, T. Career set: A resource through transitions and crises. Unpublished manuscript, Department of Psychology, University of Rhode Island, 1972.

Spirduso, W. Reaction and movement time as a function of age and physical activity level. *Journal of Gerontology,* 1975, *30,* 435–550.

Srole, L., & Fischer, A. The midtown Manhattan study: Longitudinal focus on aging genders and life transitions. Paper presented at the meeting of the Gerontological Society, Dallas, November 1978.

Staats, S. Internal versus external locus of control for three age groups. *International Journal of Aging and Human Development,* 1974, *5,* 7–10.

Stagner, R. Boredom on the assembly line: Age and personality variables. *Industrial Gerontology,* 1975, *2*(1), 1–44.

Staines, G. Spillover versus compensation: A review of the literature on the relationship between work and nonwork. *Human Relations,* 1980, *33*(2), 111–129.

Staples, R. Single and Black in America. Unpublished manuscript, Program in Human Development, University of California, San Francisco, 1977.

Staples, R., & Mirandé, A. Racial and cultural variations among American families: A decennial review of the literature on minority families. *Journal of Marriage and the Family,* 1980, *42*(4), 887–903.

Stark, A. At 100, what is life really like? *Sunday News Magazine,* November 19, 1972, pp. 18–19, 22, 24, 27–30.

Stein, A., & Bailey, M. The socialization of achievement orientation in females. *Psychological Bulletin,* 1973, *80*(5), 345–366.

Stein, P. On same-sex and cross-sex friendships. Paper presented at the meeting of the National Council of Family Relations, New York, November 1976.

Stein, P. The lifestyle, and life chances of the never-married. *Marriage and Family Review,* 1978, *1*(4), 1–11.

Stein, R., & Travis, J. Labor force and employment in 1960. *Monthly Labor Review,* 1961, *84,* 344–354.

Stein, R. B., Polk, B. B., & Polk, L. Communal life style: The Detroit case. Paper presented at the 50th annual meeting of the American Orthopsychiatric Association, New York, May 1973.

Stern, D. The goal and structure of mother-infant play. *Journal of the American Academy of Child Psychiatry,* 1974, *13*(3), 402–421.

Stinnett, C., Carter, L., & Montgomery, J. E. Older persons' perceptions of their marriages. *Journal of Marriage and the Family,* 1972, *34*(4), 655–670.

Stinnett, N., Collins, J., & Montgomery, J. E. Marital need satisfaction of older husbands and wives. *Journal of Marriage and the Family,* 1970, *32*(3), 428–434.

Stoudt, H., Damon, A., McFarland, R., & Roberts, J. *Weight, height, and selected body measurements of adults, United States, 1960–1962* (U.S. Public Health Service Publication No. 1000, Series 11, No. 8). Washington, D.C.: U.S. Government Printing Office, 1965.

Strehler, B., & Mildvan, A. General theory of mortality and aging. *Science,* 1960, *132*(1), 14–21.

Streib, G. F. Intergenerational relations: Perspectives of the two generations on the older parent. *Journal of Marriage and the Family,* 1965, *27*(4), 469–476.

Streib, G. F. Are the aged a minority group? In B. L. Neugarten (Ed.), *Middle age and aging.* Chicago: University of Chicago Press, 1968.

Streib, G. F., & Schneider, C. *Retirement in American society.* Ithaca, N.Y.: Cornell University Press, 1971.

Strong, E., Jr. *Change of interests with age.* Stanford, Calif.: Stanford University Press, 1959.

Stuckert, R. Role perception and marital satisfaction—A configurational approach. *Marriage and Family Living,* 1963, *25,* 415–419.

Stueve, A., & Fischer, C. Social networks and older women. Paper presented at the Workshop on Older Women, Washington, D.C., September 1978.

Super, D. *The psychology of careers.* New York: Harper & Row, 1957.

Surwillo, W. The relation of response time variability to age and the influence of brain wave frequency. *Electroencephalography and Clinical Neurophysiology,* 1963, *15*(6), 1029–1032.

Sussman, M. B. *Social and economic supports and family environments for the elderly* (final report to AOA). Grant 90-A-316, January 1979.

Sutton-Smith, B. *Child psychology.* New York: Appleton-Century-Crofts, 1973.

Sutton-Smith, B., & Rosenberg, B. *The sibling.* New York: Holt, Rinehart & Winston, 1970.

Swanson, G. E. *The birth of the gods: The origin of primitive beliefs.* Ann Arbor: University of Michigan Press, 1966.

Switzer, A. Achievement motivation in women: A three-generational study. Unpublished master's thesis, Wayne State University, 1975.

Symonds, P. *From adolescent to adult.* New York: Columbia University Press, 1961.

Szalai, A. (Ed.). *The use of time: Daily activities of urban and suburban populations in twelve countries.* The Hague: Mouton, 1972.

Szilard, L. On the nature of the aging process. *Proceedings of the National Academy of Science, U.S.A.,* 1959, *45,* 30–45.

Szinovacz, M. E. Satisfaction with work, marriage and household activities in women blue-collar and white-collar workers. Paper presented at the meeting of the International Society for the Study of Behavioral Development, University of Michigan, Ann Arbor, August 1973.

Szinovacz, M. E. Female retirement: Effects on spousal roles and marital adjustment. Unpublished paper, Department of Human Development and Family Economics, Pennsylvania State University, 1978.

Talbert, G. B. Aging of the reproductive system. In C. Finch & L. Hayflick (Eds.), *Handbook of the biology of aging*. New York: Van Nostrand Reinhold, 1977.

Talbert, G. B., & Krohn, P. L. Effect of maternal age on viability of ova and uterine support of pregnancy in mice. *Journal of Reproductive Fertility*, 1966, *11*, 399–406.

Tangri, S. Determinants of occupational role innovation among college women. *Journal of Social Issues*, 1972, *28*(2), 177–199.

Tanner, J. *Growth at adolescence* (2nd ed.). Springfield, Ill.: Charles C Thomas, 1962.

Taube, C. O. *Outpatient psychiatric services, 1967* (Pub. No. 1982). Washington, D.C.: Survey and Reports Section, Biometry Branch, Office of Program Planning and Evaluation, National Institute of Mental Health, 1969.

Taylor, C. Age and achievement of noted pianists. *Proceedings of the 77th Annual Convention of the American Psychological Association*, 1969, 745–746.

Teahan, J., & Kastenbaum, R. Future time perspective and subjective life expectancy in "hard-core unemployed" men. *Omega*, 1970, *1*, 189–200.

Templer, D., Ruff, C., & Franks, C. Death anxiety: Age, sex, and parental resemblance in diverse populations. *Developmental Psychology*, 1971, *4*(1), 108.

Terkel, S. *Working*. New York: Random House, 1972.

Terman, L. M., & Oden, M. H. *The gifted group at midlife: Thirty-five years follow-up of the superior child, genetic studies of genius*. Stanford, Calif.: Stanford University Press, 1959.

Thackrey, D. (Ed.) in cooperation with L. Pastalan of the Institute of Gerontology. *Research News*, Division of Research and Development, University of Michigan, 1975, *27*(5–6), 5.

Thomas, E., & Yamamoto, K. Attitudes toward age: An exploration in school-age children. *International Journal of Aging and Human Development*, 1975, *6*(2), 117–129.

Thomas, L., & Stankiewicz, J. Correspondence between related generations on a range of attitudes and values: An attempt to map the domain. Paper presented at the meeting of the American Psychological Association, Montreal, August 1973.

Thompson, G. Work versus leisure roles: An investigation of morale among employed and retired men. *Journal of Gerontology*, 1973, *28*(3), 339–344.

Thompson, L. W., & Marsh, G. Psychological studies

of aging. In C. Eisdorfer and M. P. Lawton (Eds.), *The psychology of adult development and aging*. Washington, D.C.: American Psychological Association, 1973.

Thompson, L. W., & Nowlin, J. B. Relation of increased attention to central and autonomic nervous system states. In L. F. Jarvik, C. Eisdorfer, & J. E. Blum (Eds.), *Intellectual functioning in adults*. New York: Springer, 1973.

Thompson, W. E., & Streib, G. F. Meaningful activity in a family context. In R. Kleemeier (Ed.), *Aging and leisure: A research perspective into the meaningful use of time*. New York: Oxford University Press, 1961.

Thorson, J., Hancock, K., & Whatley, L. Attitudes towards the aged as a function of age and education. *Gerontologist*, 1974, *14*(4), 316–318.

Thurnher, M. Becoming old: Perspectives on women and marriage. Paper presented at the meeting of the American Psychological Association, San Francisco, August 1977.

Thurstone, L. L. *The vectors of the mind*. Chicago: University of Chicago Press, 1935.

Tickton, S. The magnitude of American higher education in 1980. In A. Eurich (Ed.), *Campus, 1980*. New York: Delacorte, 1968.

Timiras, P. *Developmental physiology and aging*. New York: Macmillan, 1972.

Tobin, S., & Kulys, R. The family and services. In C. Eisdorfer (Ed.), *Annual review of gerontology and geriatrics*. New York: Springer, 1979.

Toffler, A. *Future shock*. New York: Random House, 1970.

Traxler, A. Intergenerational differences in attitudes toward old people. Paper presented at the meeting of the Gerontological Society, Miami Beach, November 1973.

Treas, J., & Van Hilst, A. Marriage and remarriage rates among older Americans. *Gerontologist*, 1976, *16*(2), 132–136.

Treybig, D. Language, children, and attitudes toward the aged: A longitudinal study. Paper presented at the meeting of the Gerontological Society, Portland, October 1974.

Troll, L. E. Personality similarities between college students and their parents. Unpublished doctoral dissertation, Committee on Human Development, University of Chicago, 1967.

Troll, L. E. The family of later life: A decade review. *Journal of Marriage and the Family*, 1971, *33*, 263–290.

Troll, L. E. Is parent-child conflict what we mean by the generation gap? *Family Coordinator*, 1972, *21*, 347–349. (a)

Troll, L. E. The salience of members of three-generation families for each other. Paper presented at the meeting of the American Psychological Association, Honolulu, September 1972. (b)

Troll, L. E. *Early and middle adulthood.* Monterey, Calif.: Brooks/Cole, 1975.

Troll, L. E., & Bengtson, V. Generations in the family. In W. Burr, R. Hill, F. Nye, & I. Reiss (Eds.), *Contemporary theories about the family.* New York: Free Press, 1979.

Troll, L. E., Miller, S., & Atchley, R. C. *Families of later life.* Belmont, Calif.: Wadsworth, 1979.

Troll, L. E., Neugarten, B. L., & Kraines, R. Similarities in values and other personality characteristics in college students and their parents. *Merrill-Palmer Quarterly,* 1969, *15,* 323–337.

Troll, L. E., & Nowak, C. "How old are you?"—The question of age bias in the counseling of adults. *Counseling Psychologist,* 1976, *6*(1), 41–44.

Troll, L. E., Saltz, R., & Dunin-Markiewicz, A. A seven-year follow-up of intelligence test scores of foster grandparents. *Journal of Gerontology,* 1976, *31*(5), 583–585.

Troll, L. E., & Schlossberg, N. Explorations in age bias: A preliminary investigation of age bias in the helping professions. Paper presented at the meeting of the Gerontological Society, Toronto, October 1970.

Troll, L., & Schlossberg, N. How age-biased are college counselors? *Industrial Gerontology,* 1971, *10*(1), 14–20.

Troll, L., & Smith, J. Three-generation lineage changes in cognitive style and value traits. Paper presented at the meeting of the Gerontological Society, San Juan, Puerto Rico, December 1972.

Troll, L. E., & Smith, J. Attachment through the life span: Some questions about dyadic bonds among adults. *Human Development,* 1976, *19*(3), 156–170.

Troll, L., & Turner, B. Sex differences in problems of aging. In E. Gomberg & V. Franks (Eds.), *Gender and disordered behavior.* New York: Brunner/Mazel, 1979.

Troll, L., & Turner, J. Overcoming age-sex discrimination. In U.S. Congress, House, Select Committee on Aging, 95th Cong., *Women in Midlife—Security and fulfillment* (Pt. 1). Washington, D.C.: U.S. Government Printing Office, 1978.

Tuckman, J., & Lorge, I. Attitudes toward old people. *Journal of Social Psychology,* 1953, *37,* 249–260.

Tuckman, J., Lorge, I., & Zeman, F. The self-image in aging. *Journal of Genetic Psychology,* 1961, *99*(2), 317–321.

Tuddenham, R., Blumenkrantz, J., & Wilkin, W. Age changes on AGCT: A longitudinal study of average adults. *Journal of Consulting and Clinical Psychology,* 1968, *32*(6), 659–663.

Tulving, E., & Thomson, D. Encoding specificity and retrieval processes in episodic memory. *Psychological Review,* 1973, *80*(5), 352–373.

Turner, B. Socialization and career orientation among black and white college women. Paper presented at the meeting of the American Psychological Association, 1972.

Turner, B. F., & McCaffrey, J. H. Socialization and career orientation among black and white college women. *Journal of Vocational Behavior,* 1974, *5,* 307–319.

Turner, R. Some aspects of women's ambition. *American Journal of Sociology,* 1964, *70*(3), 271–285.

Tyler, L. Personal views of possibilities in three cultures. Paper presented at the meeting of the American Psychological Association, San Francisco, August 1968.

U.N. Department of Economic and Social Affairs. Percentage of the elderly in the population of selected nations. *Demographic Yearbook, 1971.* Statistical Office of the United Nations, 1972.

Unseem, R. Functions of neighboring for the middle-class male. *Human Organizations,* 1969, *19*(2), 68–76.

Updegraff, S. G. Changing role of the grandmother. *Journal of Home Economics,* 1968, *60,* 177–180.

U.S. Commission on Civil Rights. *The age discrimination study.* Washington, D.C.: U.S. Government Printing Office, 1977.

U.S. Department of Commerce, Bureau of the Census. *Census of the population: Characteristics of the population.* Washington, D.C.: U.S. Government Printing Office, 1940.

U.S. Department of Commerce, Bureau of the Census. *Census of the population: Characteristics of the population.* Washington, D.C.: U.S. Government Printing Office, 1970.

U.S. Department of Commerce, Bureau of the Census. *Subject report: Marital status: Percentage separated or divorced, by age.* PC(2)-4C. Washington, D.C.: U.S. Government Printing Office, 1972.

U.S. Department of Commerce, Bureau of the Census. *Current population reports: Some demographic aspects of aging in the United States.* Series P-23, No. 43. Washington, D.C.: U.S. Government Printing Office, 1973.

U.S. Department of Commerce, Bureau of the Census. *Current population reports: Characteristics of the population.* Series P-20, No. 297. Washington, D.C.: U.S. Government Printing Office, 1976.

U.S. Department of Commerce, Bureau of the Census. *Current population reports: Marital status and living arrangements, March 1976.* Series P-20, No. 306. Washington, D.C.: U.S. Government Printing Office, 1977.

U.S. Department of Health, Education, and Welfare, National Center for Education Statistics. *Digest of educational statistics, 1980.* Washington, D.C.: Author, 1980.

U.S. Department of Health, Education, and Welfare, National Center for Health Statistics. Disability and use of health resources (1970): Health in the later years of life. (Adapted by N. Shock, October 1971.) Paper presented at annual meeting of the American Psychological Association, Montreal, August 1973.

U.S. Department of Health, Education, and Welfare, National Center for Health Statistics. *Vital statistics of the United States, 1970. Vol. 2: Mortality* (Pt. A). Washington, D.C.: Public Health Service, 1974. (a)

U.S. Department of Health, Education, and Welfare, National Center for Health Statistics. *Vital statistics of the United States, 1970. Vol. 3: Marriage and divorce.* Washington, D.C.: Public Health Service, 1974. (b)

U.S. Department of Health, Education, and Welfare, National Center for Health Statistics. *Vital statistics of the United States, 1976.* Washington, D.C.: Public Health Service, 1977.

U.S. Department of Health, Education, and Welfare, National Center for Health Statistics. *Current estimates from the Health Interview Survey: United States, 1977.* Vital and Health Statistics, No. 126. Washington, D.C.: Public Health Service, 1978.

U.S. Department of Health and Human Services, Public Health Service, Office of Health Research, Statistics, and Technology. *Vital statistics of the United States, 1976. Vol. 3: Marriage and divorce.* D.H.H.S. Pub. No. (PHS) 81-1103. Hyattsville, Md.: Author, 1980.

U.S. Department of Labor, Bureau of Labor Statistics. *Manpower report of the President.* Washington, D.C.: Author, 1970.

U.S. Department of Labor, Bureau of Labor Statistics. *Monthly labor review, April 1974.* Special Labor Force Rep. No. 173. Washington, D.C.: Author, 1974.

U.S. Department of Labor, Bureau of Labor Statistics. *Employment and training report of the President.* Washington, D.C.: Author, 1979.

U.S. Department of Labor, Women's Bureau. *1969 handbook on women workers.* Washington, D.C.: U.S. Government Printing Office, 1969. (a)

U.S. Department of Labor, Women's Bureau. *Fact sheet on women's professional and technical positions.* Washington, D.C.: U.S. Government Printing Office, 1969. (b)

U.S. Department of Labor, Women's Bureau. *1975 handbook on women workers.* Washington, D.C.: U.S. Government Printing Office, 1975.

Vaillant, G. E. *Adaptation to life.* Boston: Little, Brown, 1977.

Veroff, J., & Depner, C. Changes in perceived well-being. Paper presented at the meeting of the Gerontological Society, Dallas, November 1978.

Veroff, J., & Feld, S. *Marriage and work in America: A study of motives and roles.* New York: Van Nostrand Reinhold, 1970.

Verwoerdt, A., Pfeiffer, E., & Wang, H. Sexual behavior in senescence. II. Patterns of sexual activity and interest. *Geriatrics,* 1969, *24*(2), 137–154.

Vietze, P., Strain, B., & Falsey, S. Contingent responsiveness between mother and infant: Who's reinforcing whom? Paper presented at the meeting of the Southeastern Psychological Association, Nashville, Tenn., March 1975.

Voydanoff, P. An analysis of sources of job satisfaction by age. In National Institute of Mental Health, *Research on the mental health of the aging 1960–1976.* Washington, D.C.: U.S. Government Printing Office, 1977. (R03 MH 27080)

Wachtel, H. Hard-core unemployment in Detroit: Causes and remedies. *Proceedings of the 18th Annual Meeting of the Industrial Relations Research Association, New York, 1965.* Madison, Wisc.: Industrial Relations Research Association, 1966.

Wake, F. Attitudes of parents towards the premarital sex behavior of their children and themselves. *Journal of Sex Research,* 1969, *5,* 170–171.

Walker, K. Time spent by husbands in household work. *Family Economics Review,* June 1970, pp. 8–11. Washington, D.C.: U.S. Department of Agriculture.

Walker, L., & Wright, P. Self-disclosure in friendship. *Perceptual and Motor Skills,* 1976, *42*(3), 735–742.

Wallace, J. Some studies of perception in relation to age. *British Journal of Psychology,* 1956, *47*(4), 283–297.

Walsh, D. Age differences in learning and memory. In D. Woodruff & J. E. Birren (Eds.), *Aging: Scientific perspectives and social issues.* New York: Van Nostrand, 1975.

Walsh, D. Age differences in central perceptual processing: A dichoptic backward masking investigation. *Journal of Gerontology,* 1976, *31*(2), 178–185.

Walters, E., & Mitchell, D. Selected aspects of urban living among the transition area aged in comparative perspective. In *Characteristics and needs of the population living near the Greensboro business district* (Technical Report 13). Greensboro: Home Economics Center for Research, University of North Carolina, 1974.

Walters, J., & Stinnett, N. Parent-child relationships: A decade review of research. In C. Broderick (Ed.), *A decade of family research and action.* Minneapolis: National Council on Family Relations, 1971.

Wang, H., & Busse, E. EEG of healthy older persons— A longitudinal study: Dominant background activity and occipital rhythm. *Journal of Gerontology,* 1969, *24*(4), 419–426.

Wapner, S., & Werner, H. *Perceptual development.* Worcester, Mass.: Clark University Press, 1957.

Wapner, S., Werner, H., & Comalli, P., Jr. Perception of part-whole relationships in middle and old age. *Journal of Gerontology,* 1960, *15*(4), 412–415.

Ward, R. The impact of subjective age and stigma on older persons. *Journal of Gerontology*, 1977, *32*(2), 227–232.

Waring, J. Conflict between the middle-aged and old: Why not? Paper presented at the meeting of the American Sociological Association, 1975.

Warren, R. Illusory changes in repeated words: Differences between young adults and the aged. *American Journal of Psychology*, 1961, *74*(4), 506.

Warrington, E., & Sanders, H. The fate of old memories. *Quarterly Journal of Experimental Psychology*, 1971, *23*(4), 432–442.

Warrington, E., & Silberstein, M. A questionnaire technique for investigating very long-term memory. *Quarterly Journal of Experimental Psychology*, 1970, *22*(3), 508–512.

Waugh, N., & Norman, D. Primary memory. *Psychological Review*, 1965, *72*(1), 89–104.

Weg, R. More than wrinkles. In L. Troll, J. Israel, & K. Israel (Eds.), *Looking ahead: A woman's guide to the problems and joys of growing older*. Englewood Cliffs, N.J.: Prentice-Hall, 1977.

Weinberg, J. Personal and social adjustment. In J. E. Anderson (Ed.), *Psychological aspects of aging*. Washington, D.C.: American Psychological Association, 1956.

Weingarten, K., & Daniels, P. Family/career transitions in women's lives: Report on research in progress. Paper presented at the meeting of the American Psychological Association, Toronto, August 1978.

Weir, A. Value judgments and personality in old age. *Acta Psychologica*, 1961, *19*, 148–149.

Weisman, A. On death and dying: Does old age make sense? Decisions and destiny in growing older. *Journal of Geriatric Psychiatry*, 1974, *7*(1), 84–93.

Weisman, A., & Kastenbaum, R. The psychological autopsy: A study of the terminal phase of life (Monograph No. 4 of *Community Mental Health Journal*). New York: Behavioral Publications, 1968.

Weismann, A. The duration of life. In E. B. Poulton (Ed.), *Collected essays upon heredity and kindred biological problems*. Oxford, England: Clarendon Press, 1889.

Weiss, A. Auditory perception in relation to age. In J. E. Birren, R. Butler, S. Greenhouse, L. Sokoloff, & M. Yarrow (Eds.), *Human aging I: A biological and behavioral study*. Rockville, Md.: National Institute of Mental Health, 1971.

Weiss, L., & Lowenthal, M. Life course perspectives on friendship. In M. Lowenthal, M. Thurnher, & D. Chiriboga (Eds.), *Four stages of life*. San Francisco: Jossey-Bass, 1975.

Weiss, R. The provisions of social relationships. In Z. Rubin (Ed.), *Doing unto others*. Englewood Cliffs, N.J.: Prentice-Hall, 1975.

Weiss, R. The emotional impact of marital separation. *Journal of Social Issues*, 1976, *32*(1), 135–145. (a)

Weiss, R. Transition states and other stressful situations: Their nature and programs for their management. In G. Caplan & M. Killian (Eds.), *Support systems and mutual help: Multidisciplinary explorations*. New York: Grune & Stratton, 1976. (b)

Weissman, M. M., & Klerman, G. L. Sex differences and the epidemiology of depression. In E. S. Gomberg & V. Franks (Eds.), *Gender and disordered behavior: Sex differences in psychopathology*. New York: Brunner/Mazel, 1979.

Welford, A. T. *Aging and human skill*. Oxford, England: Oxford University Press, 1958.

Welford, A. T. Motor performance. In J. E. Birren & K. W. Schaie (Eds.), *Handbook of the psychology of aging*. New York: Van Nostrand Reinhold, 1977.

Werner, H. *Comparative psychology of mental development*. New York: International Universities Press, 1948.

Westley, W., & Epstein, N. Family structure and emotional health: A case study approach. *Marriage and Family Living*, 1960, *22*(1), 25–27.

Wetherick, N. A comparison of the problem-solving ability of young, middle-aged and old subjects. *Gerontologia*, 1964, *9*(2–3), 164–178.

Wetherick, N. The psychology of aging. *Occupational Therapy*, 1969, *32*(1), 15–17.

Wexley, K., McLaughlin, J., & Sterns, H. A study of perceived need fulfillment and life satisfaction before and after retirement. *Journal of Vocational Behavior*, 1975, *7*, 81–87.

Whittington, S., Wilkie, F., & Eisdorfer, C. Attitudes of young adults and older people toward concepts related to old age. Paper presented at the meeting of the Gerontological Society, San Juan, Puerto Rico, December 1972.

Wilcock, R., & Franke, W. *Unwanted workers*. New York: Free Press, 1963.

Wilder, C. S. Chronic conditions and limitations of activity and mobility: United States, July 1965 to June 1967. *U.S. Vital and Health Statistics*, 1971, *10*(6).

Wilder, M. H. Home care for persons 55 and over: United States, July 1966 to June 1968. *U.S. Vital and Health Statistics*, 1972, *10*(73).

Wilensky, H. Orderly careers and social participation: The impact of work history on social integration in the middle mass. *American Sociological Review*, 1961, *26*(4), 521–539.

Wilkie, F. L., & Eisdorfer, C. Intelligence and blood pressure in the aged. *Science*, 1971, *172* (3986), 959–962.

Wilkie, F. L., & Eisdorfer, C. Terminal changes in intelligence. In E. Palmore (Ed.), *Normal aging II*. Durham, N.C.: Duke University Press, 1974.

Willmott, P., & Young, M. *Family and class in a London suburb*. London: Routledge & Kegan Paul, 1960.

Wilson, W. The distribution of selected sexual

attitudes and behaviors among the adult population of the United States. *Journal of Sex Research*, 1975, *11*(1), 46–64.

Winter, W., Ferreira, A., & Bowers, N. Decision-making in married and unrelated couples. *Family Process*, 1973, *12*(1), 83–94.

Witkin, H., Lewis, H., Hartman, M., Machover, K., Meisser, P., & Wapner, S. *Personality through perception*. New York: Harper & Row, 1954.

Wood, V. Age-appropriate behavior for older people. *Gerontologist*, 1971, *11* (4, Pt. 2), 74–78.

Wood, V., & O'Brien, J. Normative expectations for age roles: The views of three age groups. Unpublished paper, School of Social Work, University of Wisconsin. Cited in V. Wood. Age-appropriate behavior for older people. *Gerontologist*, 1971, *11* (4, Pt. 2), 74–78.

Wood, V., & Robertson, J. The significance of grandparenthood. In J. Gubrium (Ed.), *Time, roles and self in old age*. New York: Human Sciences Press, 1976.

Woodford, J. N. Why Negro suicides are increasing. *Ebony*, 1965, *20*, 89–90.

Woodruff, D. Relationships between EEG alpha frequency, reaction time, and age: A biofeedback study. *Psychophysiology*, 1975, *12*(6), 673–681.

Woodruff, D. Brain activity and development. In P. B. Baltes (Ed.), *Life-span development and behavior* (Vol. 1). New York: Academic Press, 1978.

Woodruff, D., & Birren, J. E. Age changes and cohort differences in personality. *Developmental Psychology*, 1972, *6*(2), 252–259.

Wyly, M., & Hulicka, I. Problems and compensations of widowhood: A comparison of age groups. Paper presented at the meeting of the American Psychological Association, Chicago, August 1975.

Yankelovich, D. *Generations apart: A study of the generation gap*. A survey conducted for CBS News, 1970.

Yankelovich, D. The new psychological contracts at work. *Psychology Today*, 1978, *11*, 46–50.

Yarrow, M., Waxler, C., & Scott, P. Child effects on adult behavior. *Developmental Psychology*, 1971, *5*(2), 300–311.

Youmans, E. G. Aging patterns in a rural and urban area of Kentucky. Lexington: Agricultural Experiment Station, University of Kentucky, 1963.

Youmans, E. G. Generations and perceptions of old age: An urban-rural comparison. *Gerontologist*, 1971, *11*(4, Pt. 1), 284–288.

Youmans, E. G., & Yarrow, M. Aging and social adaptation: A longitudinal study of healthy old men. In J. E. Birren (Ed.), *Human aging. II: An eleven-year followup biomedical and behavioral study* (DHEW Pub. No. [ADM] 74–123). Washington, D.C.: U.S. Department of Health, Education and Welfare, 1971.

Zajonc, R., & Markus, G. Birth order and intellectual development. *Psychological Review*, 1975, *82*(1), 74–88.

Zelnick, M., & Kantner, J. Sexual and contraceptive experience of young married women in the United States, 1976 and 1971. *Family Planning Perspectives*, 1977, *9*(1), 55–71.

Zimmerman, M. A. The process of sex-role socialization and its effects on female and male responses to aging. Paper presented at the 27th annual meeting of the Gerontological Society, Portland, October 1974.

Zimmerman, R. An exploratory study of platonic love. Student paper, Psychology Department, Rutgers University, 1978.

Name Index

Subject Index